arihant

SUCCESS AND NOTHING LESS

AF814180

All in One®

COMPLETE STUDY | COMPLETE PRACTICE | COMPLETE ASSESSMENT

Science

Based on Latest NCERT

Class 7

Authors

Rahul Kumar *(Physics)*
Er. Abhishek Kumar Gupta *(Chemistry)*
Himanshi Gambhir *(Biology)*

Allinone
COMPLETE STUDY | COMPLETE PRACTICE | COMPLETE ASSESSMENT

arihant
SUCCESS AND NOTHING LESS

ARIHANT PRAKASHAN
(School Division Series)

卐 ADMINISTRATIVE & PRODUCTION OFFICES
Regd. Office
'Ramchhaya' 4577/15, Agarwal Road, Darya Ganj, New Delhi -110002
Tele: 011- 47630600, 43518550; Fax: 011- 23280316

卐 **Head Office**
Kalindi, TP Nagar, Meerut (UP) - 250002, Tel: 0121-7156203, 7156204

卐 SALES & SUPPORT OFFICES
Agra, Ahmedabad, Bengaluru, Bareilly, Chennai, Delhi, Guwahati, Hyderabad, Jaipur, Jhansi, Kolkata, Lucknow, Nagpur & Pune.

PO No : TXT-XX-XXXXXXX-X-XX

Published By Arihant Publications (India) Ltd.

For further information about the books published by Arihant, log on to www.arihantbooks.com or e-mail at info@arihantbooks.com

Follow us on

卐 PRICE ₹**290.00**

PRODUCTION TEAM

Publishing Managers
Mahendra Singh Rawat &
Keshav Mohan

Project Head
Ashwani

Cover Designer
Bilal Hashmi

Inner Designer
Ankit Tyagi

Page Layouting
Mayank Saini

Proof Readers
Mukul Kaushik
Manish Kumar

Inside the Book

Key Features

Science Class 7

Chapter Intro

A quick information about the coverage of the chapter to explain students about what they are going to study.

CHAPTER 02

Nutrition in Animals

All organisms including humans require food for growth, repair and functioning of the body. Plants can prepare their own food by the process of photosynthesis, but animals including humans cannot. They get their food from plants, either directly by eating plants and their products or indirectly by eating animals that eat plants. Some animals eat both plants and other animals. The process of taking food by an animal is called **animal nutrition.** It includes **nutrient requirement, mode of intake of food** and **its utilisation in the body.**

Science Insight

Additional but informational matter related to given concept. It helps & motivate students to explore more beyond their books.

The carbohydrates get broken down into simple sugar called **glucose**, while fats in fatty acid and **glycerol** and proteins get broken down into **amino acids**. These simpler compounds are now easily absorbed by the walls of small intestine into the blood.

SCIENCE INSIGHT Fats in goat's milk are much simpler than those in cow's milk. Therefore, the goat's milk is much easier to digest than the cow's milk.

Boxed Matter

Information given in the boxes is related to the explanation of daily life phenomena related to the concept given.

What happens when we eat food in hurry?

The windpipe (that carries air from nostril to our lungs) and foodpipe runs adjacent to each other. Air and food share a common passage in the throat.

When we swallow food, a flap-like valve closes the passage of the windpipe and guides the food into the foodpipe. But if we in hurry, laugh or talk while eating, the windpipe remains open and food particle enters into the windpipe and we experience **hiccups, cough** or **choking sensation**.

Try These

A set of 3-5 Questions given in between the text, helps students to remain connected with the text while studying. They can instantly assess themselves for their understanding.

(v) **Egestion** The process by which the undigested food material is removed from the body is called egestion.

Try These 2.1

1. **Give two example of animals, along with the kind of food they eat, whose mode of feeding is sucking.**
2. **Which animal captures and swallows the prey as a whole?**
3. **What happens to the food after its absorption by the cells of the body?**

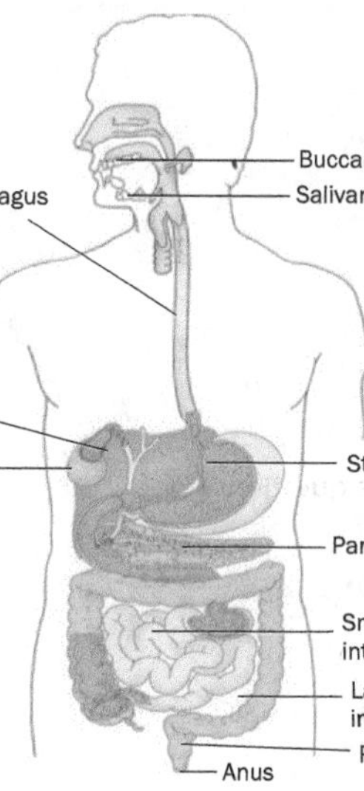

Human digestive system

Illustrative Figures

To make the concepts completely visible, illustrative diagrams have been given at various place.

Science Glossary

Absorption The uptake of simple substances produced during digestion.

Amino acid During the process of digestion, proteins are broken down into amino acids.

Amoeba It is a microscopic single-celled organism found in pond water.

Assimilation In this the absorbed simple substances are used to build complex substances required by the body.

Bile It is a juice secreted by liver that helps in the digestion of fats.

Buccal cavity It consists of salivary glands, teeth and tongue.

Canines These are present on the sides of incisors. They have sharp pointed edges for tearing the food.

Cellulose It is a type of carbohydrate, which cannot be digested by humans.

Science Glossary

List of important scientific terms used in the chapter with their definitions.

Let's Investigate

To connect the theory to related practical aspects, this section contains scientific activity with complete procedural details.

Mind Map

A quick revision visual tool for the complete chapter.

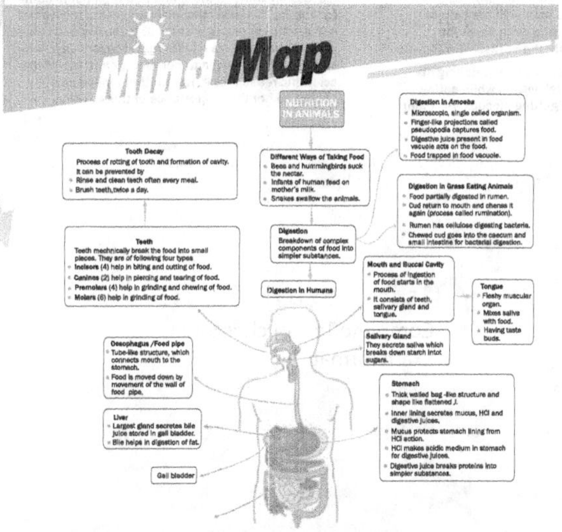

Let's Investigate

ACTIVITY 1 (Page 13)

Aim To show the presence of different types of teeth and their arrangement in buccal cavity.

Materials Required Mirror, apple/bread.

Procedure

1. Wash your hands properly.
2. Look into the mirror and count your teeth.
3. Use your index finger to feel the shape of each teeth.
4. Take a piece of apple or bread and eat it.
5. Observe, which teeth we use for biting and cutting and which one for piercing and tearing.

NCERT Folder

Complete explanations of all the questions of NCERT Exercises.

NCERT FOLDER

Complete Explanations of all NCERT's Questions

Intext Questions

Q.1 You have studied in previous class that food consists of many components. Try to recall and list them. Page 11

Ans. 1. Carbohydrates, 2. Proteins, 3. Fat, 4. Vitamins, 5. Minerals, 6. Roughage

Q.2 What happens to the food inside the body?

Ans. Refer to text on page no. 18. Page 12

Q.3 How many kinds of teeth can you find in your mouth?

Ans. We can find four types of teeth in our mouth. Page 13

Q.4 Which type of teeth do you use for biting and cutting and which one for piercing and tearing? Page 13

Ans. For biting and cutting, we use incisors and for piercing and tearing we use canines.

(b) The largest gland in the human body is ....

(c) The stomach releases hydrochloric acid and .... juices, which act on food.

(d) The inner wall of the small intestine has many finger-like outgrowths called ....

(e) *Amoeba* digests its food in the ....

Ans. (a) ingestion, digestion, absorption, assimilation and egestion.

(b) liver (c) digestive

(d) villi (e) food vacuole

Q.2 Mark 'T' if the statement is True and 'F' if it is False.

(a) Digestion of starch starts in the stomach

(b) The tongue helps in mixing food with saliva

(c) The gall bladder temporarily stores bile

(d) The ruminants bring back swallowed grass into their mouth and chew it for some time

REVIEW EXERCISE

Including Competency Based Questions

Part I

Multiple Choice Questions

1. Where does digestion of food start in the human digestive system? Competency Based Que.
   (a) Mouth (b) Oesophagus
   (c) Stomach (d) Small intestine
2. Which of the following pair of teeth differ in structure, but are similar in function? NCERT Exemplar
   (a) Canines and incisors
   (b) Molars and premolars
   (c) Incisors and molars
   (d) Premolars and canines
8. The acid present in the stomach
   (a) kills the harmful bacteria that may enter along with the food
   (b) protects the stomach lining from harmful substances
   (c) digests starch into simple sugars
   (d) makes the medium alkaline
9. What are proteins broken down into? Competency Based Que.
   (a) Glucose (b) Glycerol
   (c) Fatty acids (d) Amino acids
10. Read the following statements with reference to the villi of small intestine.

Review Exercise

Chapter exercise having all types of questions; MCQs, Assertion-Reason, True-False, Fillers, Matching, Case based, VSA, SA, LA.

NEP 2020 Based Exercise

Questions based on elements/skills given in NEP 2020; Thinking Skills, Experimental Skills, Enquiry Skills etc.

Skill Based Questions as per NEP 2020

1. A person met with an accident while driving. After examination, the doctor told him that since he got a fracture in the wrist operation would be required. After the operation, the patient was put on a glucose drip and was not given food for a few hours.
   (i) Why was the patient not given food directly?
   (ii) How does the glucose help the patient recover? Thinking skill
2. Take a chart paper and divide it into two sections longitudinally. In one section explain the process of digestion in humans and in other the process of digestion in cows. Compare both with the help of diagram and/or flow chart, and write down the differences you found in both the cases. Thinking skill
3. Little Rishi (a student of class VI) was watching his favourite cartoon serial on television, while eating lunch. Suddenly he started getting hiccups. His elder He asked his father. His father smiled and explained him that it is only a myth. He also explained him the proper scientific reason behind it.
   (i) What is hiccups?
   (ii) Why do we get hiccup? Experimental skill
4. Jaya returned from school and found that her grandmother was scolding their maid Rani, as she did not come the day before. The maid told that her son was passing watery stools frequently that's why she did not come. Jaya's mother who was listening the discussion came to them and told Rani not to come for coming 3-4 days. She also suggested to give her son a solution of sugar and salt in (boiled and cooled) water, many times a day for fast recovery. Jaya was surprised. She rushed to her mother and asked the scientific reason for it. Her mother smiled and explained her the importance of this solution.

ASSESSMENT EXERCISE

Part I

Multiple Choice Questions

1. Digestion of starch starts in
   (a) stomach (b) mouth
   (c) small intestine (d) large intestine
2. The long muscular tube that starts from buccal cavity to the stomach is called
   (a) oesophagus (b) small intestine
   (c) large intestine (d) rectum
3. Which of the following organ does not secrete digestive juice?
   (a) Liver (b) Pancreas (c) Stomach (d) Oesophagus
4. Which organ stores bile juice?
   (a) Gall bladder (b) Liver
   (c) Stomach (d) Pancreas
5. The finger-like projections present on the inner lining of small intestine are known as
   (a) villi (b) stomach (c) rumen (d) diarrhoea

Assertion-Reason

The following questions consist of two statements **Assertion (A)** and **Reason (R)**. Answer these questions selecting the appropriate option given below.

(a) Both A and R are true and R is the correct explanation of A

(b) Both A and R are true, but R is not the correct explanation of A

(c) A is true, but R is false

(d) A is false, but R is true

13. **Assertion** (A) Ingestion of food is difficult without teeth.
    Reason (R) Teeth help in breaking down the food into small pieces.
14. **Assertion** (A) Herbivorous animals like cows, that eat grass are called ruminants.
    Reason (R) The partially digested food called cud is brought back into the mouth of the cow.

Assessment Exercise

Complete Test of chapter in Exam format.

CHAPTER 01

Nutrition in Plants

All the living organisms require food to survive. The food gives energy to the organisms for growth and maintenance of their body functions. Carbohydrates, proteins, fats, vitamins and minerals are the components of food. These components are necessary for our body and are called **nutrients**.

Nutrition is the process of taking food by an organism and its utilisation by the body. Green plants can prepare their own food while humans and animals are directly or indirectly dependent on plants for their food.

1.1 Modes of Nutrition

On the basis of different modes of nutrition, organisms can be placed into two major types, i.e. autotrophic and heterotrophic.

(i) **Autotrophic Nutrition** In this mode of nutrition, organisms make their own food from simple substances. The organisms that exhibit this mode of nutrition are known as **autotrophs** (*auto*-self; *trophos* = nourishment), e.g. all green plants.

(ii) **Heterotrophic Nutrition** In this mode of nutrition, organisms cannot prepare their own food instead they depend directly or indirectly on green plants for their nutrition. Such organisms that exhibit this mode of nutrition are known as **heterotrophs** (*heteros* = other; *trophos* = nourishment), e.g. all animals, non-green plants, insectivorous plants and fungi.

Cells

All living organisms are made from small building units called cells. The cells are the structural and functional units of the body of all living organisms. They can only be seen under microscope. The cell has a thin outer boundary called **cell membrane,** a distinct, centrally located spherical structure called **nucleus** and jelly-like substance surrounding the nucleus called **cytoplasm.**

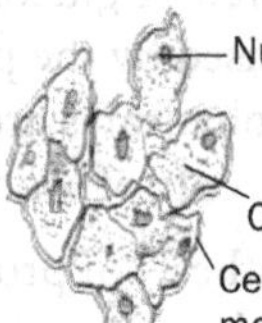

Cell

1.2 Photosynthesis: Food Making Process in Plants

The process by which autotrophic green plants make their own food by using carbon dioxide, water and minerals in the presence of sunlight and chlorophyll is known as photosynthesis.

Reactions Involved in Photosynthesis

The whole process of photosynthesis can be represented by the following equation

$$\underset{\text{(from air)}}{\text{Carbon dioxide}} + \underset{\text{(from soil)}}{\text{Water}} \xrightarrow[\text{Chlorophyll}]{\text{Sunlight}} \underset{\text{(Carbohydrate) (food)}}{\text{Glucose}} + \underset{\text{(released in air)}}{\text{Oxygen}}$$

Site of Photosynthesis

The process of photosynthesis takes place in green leaves, therefore leaves are referred to as the food factories of plants. The leaves have green pigment called **chlorophyll** which helps the leaves to capture the energy of sunlight.

The photosynthetic process also occurs in other green parts of plant like stem, but it is not enough for meeting all the needs of plant.

The cactus or desert plants modify their leaves into spines to reduce water loss from them by transpiration. In these plants photosynthesis occurs through their green stem.

Process of Photosynthesis

The process of photosynthesis can be explained in the following steps

- The inorganic raw material, i.e. CO_2 is taken from air through the tiny pores present on the surface of leaves called **stomata**. These pores are surrounded by 'guard cells'.
- The water and minerals present in the soil are absorbed by the roots.
- These are transported to leaves by vessels which act like pipes. Vessels form a continuous path or passage from roots to leaves for the movement of nutrients and water.

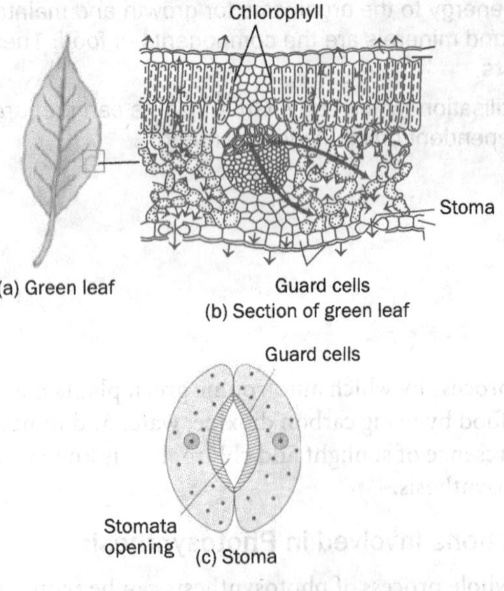

A section of green leaf showing chlorophyll and stomatal opening

- The energy of sunlight captured by the chlorophyll is used to prepare food (carbohydrates).
- During this process, oxygen is also released.

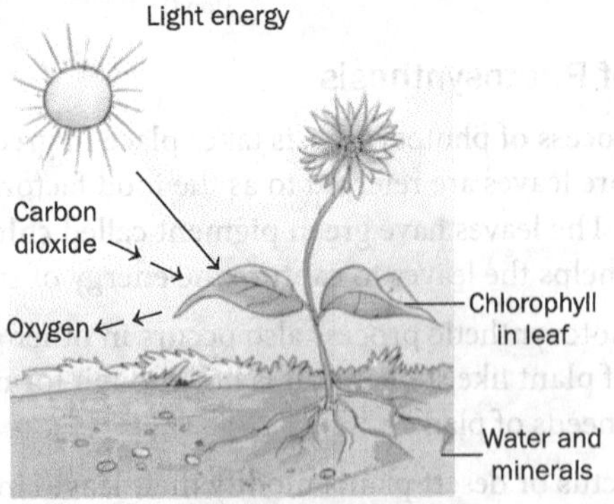

A green plant showing process of photosynthesis

- Photosynthesis is a unique process in which solar energy is captured by the leaves and stored in the plants in the form of food. Thus, **'Sun is the ultimate source of energy for all the living organisms.'**

Products of Photosynthesis

Carbohydrates (glucose) and oxygen are the products of photosynthesis. Glucose is produced as main food material. This later gets converted into starch. The presence of starch in leaves indicates the occurrence of photosynthesis.

Importance of Photosynthesis

- If the plants do not perform photosynthesis, there would be no food on Earth.
- Photosynthesis is necessary for the production of oxygen gas in atmosphere which is necessary for survival of all organisms.

Therefore, it can be said that no life is possible in the absence of photosynthesis.

Photosynthesis in Leaves of Various Colours

In green plants, chlorophyll absorbs light-energy from the Sun to perform photosynthesis. Besides green colour, some plants have leaves that have red, brown and violet coloured pigments. These pigments are present in large amounts and mask the green colour of chlorophyll in leaves. Thus, these leaves also perform photosynthesis and synthesise starch in them.

Photosynthesis by Green Algae

The green algae are slimy, green patches that float in pond or stagnant water bodies. Algae contain chlorophyll which gives them the green colour. Due to the presence of chlorophyll, they can also prepare their own food by photosynthesis.

1.3 Synthesis of Plant Food other than Carbohydrates

The starch or glucose is the simplest form of carbohydrate synthesised by the plants. Sometimes these simplest forms of carbohydrates are utilised to synthesise other components of food like fats (oils), proteins, etc.

For synthesis of proteins, plants also need nitrogen along with carbon dioxide (CO_2) and water. Plants absorb nitrogen in the soluble form from the soil. Although nitrogen is present in abundance in the atmosphere, but plants cannot absorb nitrogen in gaseous form. Soil has certain bacteria that convert gaseous nitrogen into usable form and release it into the soil.

In this way, the plants fulfill their requirements of nitrogen along with the other constituents. Plants can then synthesise proteins and vitamins.

Try These 1.1

1. **Non-green plants cannot prepare their own food. Instead, they depend upon the green plants directly or indirectly. Name the mode of nutrition they exhibit.**
2. **A green coloured pigment present in the leaves of plant aids in synthesis of food. Name that pigment.**
3. **Radha observed slimy green patches floating on the surface of the pond, what are these organisms?**
4. **Name the additional element that is required for synthesis of proteins.**

1.4 Other Modes of Nutrition in Plants

There are some plants which do not contain chlorophyll in them and thus, cannot prepare their own food.
These plants obtain their food from other plants or animals, i.e. they are heterotrophic in nature. These are of following types

Parasitic Plants

A parasitic plant is one that derives its nutrition from another plant. The non-green plant which obtain its food from other plants is called **parasite** and the plant from which the parasite absorbs food is called **host**, e.g. amarbel or *Cuscuta*. It is a yellow wiry branched structure twining around the stem and branches of other plants. *Cuscuta* takes readymade food from the plant on which it is climbing.

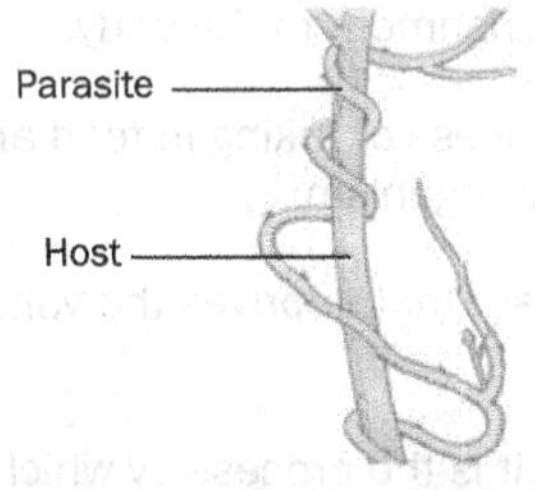

***Cuscuta* (Amarbel) on host plant**

SCIENCE INSIGHT Parasitic plants take food from host through special type of roots called sucking roots, which penetrate into host plant's stem and absorb food material from the host, e.g. *Cuscuta*.

Insectivorous Plants

There are some plants which can trap insects and digest them for their nutrition. These plants may or may not be green in colour, but lack nitrogen elements as they are generally found in nitrogen deficient soil. To overcome this problem, these plants eat insects. Hence, they are called insectivorous plant or **carnivorous plants.**

In some insectivorous plants, leaf is modified to form **pitcher-like** or **jug-like structure**. The apex of leaf forms a lid that can open and close the mouth of pitcher. There are hair inside the pitcher which are directed downwards and used to entangle the insects.

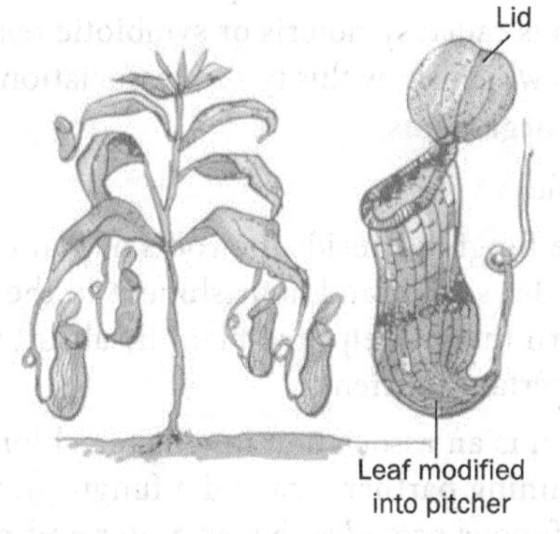

Pitcher plant showing lid and pitcher

When insect comes in contact with the plant lid its gets closed. The insect trapped inside the pitcher is digested by digestive juices secreted by the pitcher to obtain nitrogen compounds from them, e.g. pitcher plant and Venus flytrap.
Since, these can synthesise their own food, but fulfill their nitrogen deficiency by eating insects, these are called as **partial heterotrophs.**

1.5 Saprotrophs

The mode of nutrition in which organisms take their nutrients from dead and decaying matter is called **saprotrophic nutrition.**
Organisms which use saprotrophic mode of nutrition are called **saprotrophs**, e.g. fungi like mushrooms, bread mould and yeast are non-green organisms that grow on dead and decaying matter for their food.
Fungi can be seen as fluffy umbrella-like patches growing in moist soil or on rotting wood during the rainy season. It can also grow on pickles, leather, clothes and other articles that are left in hot and humid weather for long time. Fungi reproduce by fungal spores. These spores are generally present in the air. When they land on wet and warm things they germinate and grow.

Note Many fungi like yeast and mushrooms are useful, but some fungi cause diseases in plants, animals and humans. Some fungi are also used as medicine.

SCIENCE INSIGHT *Amantia phalloides* is the world's most poisonous mushroom. It is commonly known as the death cap mushroom and is responsible for 90% of the world's mushroom related fatalities.

1.6 Symbiosis

Sometimes, two organisms of different species live together and help each other in obtaining food and shelter. This association is called symbiosis or symbiotic relationship. Organisms which show this type of association is called **symbiotic organisms**.

For example,

(i) Some fungi live inside the roots of plants. The plant provides shelter and nourishment to the fungus and in turn fungus helps the plant by absorbing water and certain nutrients.

(ii) Lichen is an association in which a chlorophyll containing partner alga and a fungus live together. The fungus provides shelter, water and minerals to the alga and in return, the alga provides food which it prepares by photosynthesis.

1.7 Replenishment of Nutrients in Soil

The plants absorb mineral and nutrients from the soil. The key nutrients that are required by the plants are **nitrogen**, **phosphorus** and **potassium**. Overtime, the soil's nutrient levels diminish. To ensure a healthy crop, it is essential to **replenish soil with nutrients**.

The plant nutrients or minerals are replenished in the soil in the following ways

- Usually crops absorb a lot of nitrogen. After the harvest, the soil becomes deficient in nitrogen. They need nitrogen in a soluble form.
- Action of certain bacteria like *Rhizobium* can convert the atmospherics nitrogen into soluble form that can be readily used by plants.
- These bacteria live in the root nodules of **leguminous plants** such as gram, peas, moong, beans, etc.
- They take nitrogen gas from the atmosphere and convert it into water soluble nitrogen compounds, making it available to the leguminous plants for their growth.
- In return, leguminous plants provide food and shelter to the bacterium as it cannot prepare its own food. Thus, they have a symbiotic relationship.
- This association is very important for the farmers, as they do not need to add nitrogen fertilisers to the soil in which leguminous plants are grown. Most of the pulses (dals) are obtained from leguminous plants.

Try These 1.2

1. **Radha noticed a yellow, wiry, branched plant twining around the stem of a tree. Name this structure.**
2. **The pitcher plant obtain its nutrition from digesting the insect which gets trapped inside them. Name the part of the plant that gets modified into pitcher.**
3. **Sam observed fluffy umbrella-like patches growing in moist soil during rainy season in his garden. Name this structure.**
4. **Bacteria like *Rhizobium* can live in the root nodules of certain plants. Name any two such plants.**

Science Glossary

Autotrophic It is the mode of nutrition in which organisms prepare their own food.

Chlorophyll It is a photosynthetic pigment found in all green plants.

Heterotrophs Organisms that cannot manufacture their own food.

Host The living organism from which parasite takes its food.

Insectivorous Plants which feed on insects to get nutrition.

Nutrients The fundamental components of the food, that provide nourishment to the body.

Nutrition The process of taking in food and its utilisation by the organism.

Parasite Organism that deprives the valuable nutrients from the host.

Photosynthesis It is the process by which green plants prepare their own food from carbon dioxide and water in the presence of sunlight and chlorophyll.

Saprotrophic It is the mode of nutrition in which organisms feed on dead and decaying matter.

Saprotrophs Organisms that show saprotrophic mode of nutrition.

Stomata Tiny pores present on the surface of leaves that are used for gaseous exchange.

Let's Investigate

ACTIVITY 1 (Page 3, 4)

Aim To test that sunlight is necessary for the process of photosynthesis.

Materials Required Two potted plants (same kind), alcohol, beakers, test tube, burner, iodine solution, match stick.

Procedure

1. Take two plants of same kind in different pots.
2. Label them as 'Pot A' and 'Pot B'.
3. Keep the 'Pot A' in dark and 'Pot B' in light for 3 days.
4. After 3 days pick one leaf from both the plants and perform iodine test as follows
   (i) Boil the leaves in alcohol over a water bath to remove green colour.
   (ii) Wash the decolourised leaf with water and place them in separate petridishes.
   (iii) Pour few drops of iodine on these decolourised leaves.

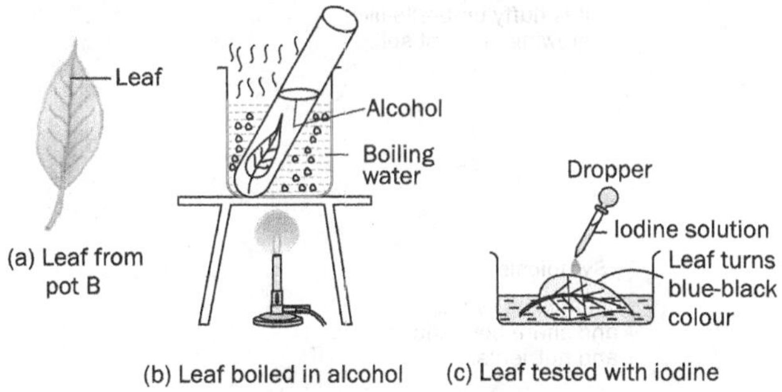

Starch is present in the leaf kept in sunlight

Observation We observe that the leaf which was kept in sunlight turns blue-black in colour, indicating the presence of starch. The leaf kept in dark does not show any change in colour.

Conclusion This activity shows that sunlight is necessary for photosynthesis.

Viva Questions

1. Why did we boil the leaves in alcohol?
2. Why did the leaf kept in dark not show positive iodine test?

ACTIVITY 2 (Page 6)

Aim To observe saprophytic fungus.

Materials Required Stale bread, water.

Procedure

1. Take a piece of stale bread and moisten it with water.
2. Leave the bread in a moist, warm and dark place for 2-3 days.

Observation We will see the fluffy patches of white, green or brown colour on bread slice. These patches are of fungus growing on the moist bread.

Conclusion We conclude that fungus has saprotrophic mode of nutrition. They feed on dead and decaying matter.

Viva Questions

1. Why do we moisten the stale bread?
2. If we refrigerate a bread slice, will it develop fluffy spots of brown, green or white colour?

Mind Map

NUTRITION IN PLANTS

Nutrition
Process of taking food by an organisms.

Heterotropic nutrition
Depends directly or indirectly on green plants for their nutrition, e.g. all animals, fungi, etc.

Autotrophic nutrition
Organisms make their own food through photosynthesis, e.g. all green plants.

Photosynthesis
Process of synthesis of food in green plants.

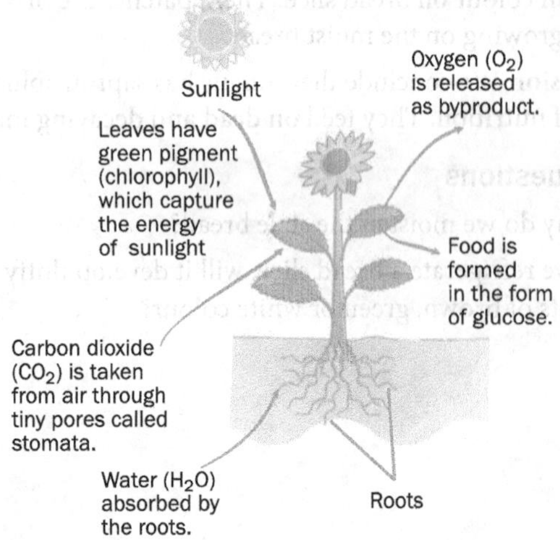

Replenishment of nutrients in soil
Rhizobium bacteria lives in the root nodules of leguminous plants, e.g. gram, peas, etc. fixes atmospheric N_2 into soluble nitrogen compounds.

Other modes of nutrition in plants

Parasitic plants
- Derives nutrition from other plant.
- Chlorophyll less plants, e.g. *Cuscuta* takes food from host plant.

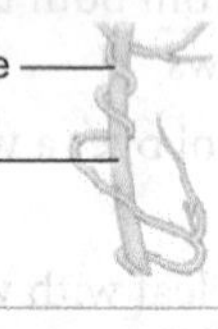

Insectivorous plants
- Traps insect and digest them for nutrition, e.g. pitcher plant.
- The leaves form pitcher like structure which trap and digest insect.

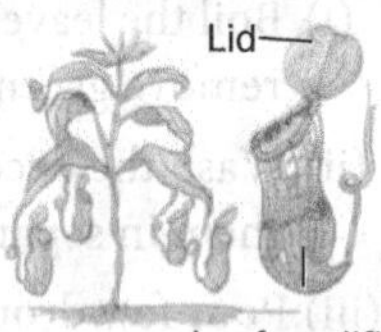

Saprotrophs
- Obtain their nutrients from dead and decaying matter, e.g. fungi.
- It is fluffy umbrella-like growing in moist soil.

Symbiosis
Organisms live together and share both shelter and nutrients.

Examples

- Lichen is an association of algae and fungi.
- The fungus provides shelter, water and minerals to the alga and in return algae provide food.

- Certain fungi live inside the roots of plants.
- Plant provides shelter and food and fungi helps plants to absorb water and nutrients.

NCERT FOLDER

Complete Explanations of all NCERT's Questions

Intext Questions

Q.1 Boojho wants to know how plants prepare their own food? Page 1

Ans. Plants prepare their own food by the process known as photosynthesis.

Q.2 Paheli wants to know why our body cannot make food from carbon dioxide, water and minerals like plants do? Page 1

Ans. Our body cannot make food from carbon dioxide, water and minerals because we do not have chlorophyll in our body as plants do.

Q.3 Boojho wants to know how water and minerals absorbed by roots reach the leaves? Page 2

Ans. Refer to text on page no. 2.

Q.4 Paheli wants to know what is so special about the leaves that they can synthesise food but other parts of the plant cannot? Page 2

Ans. Leaves can synthesise their own food as they posses a green pigment known as chlorophyll.

Q.5 Boojho has observed some plants with deep red, violet or brown leaves. He want to know whether these leaves also carry out photosynthesis. Page 3

Ans. Refer to text on page no. 2.

Q.6 Paheli wants to know whether mosquitoes, bed bugs, lice and leeches that suck our blood are also parasites. Page 5

Ans. Yes, mosquitoes, bed bugs, lice and leeches are parasites because they suck our blood and get nutrition without providing any benefit to us.

Q.7 Boojho is confused. If the pitcher plant is green and carries out photosynthesis, then why does it feed on insects? Page 5

Ans. Pitcher plant feeds on insects to fulfill its nitrogen deficiency. It grows in a soil that lacks in nitrogen content.

Q.8 Boojho wants to know how these organisms acquire nutrients? They do not have mouths like animals do. They are not like green plants as they lack chlorophyll and cannot make food by photosynthesis. Page 6

Ans. These organisms acquire nutrients from dead and decaying matter.

Q.9 Paheli is keen to know whether her beautiful shoes, which she wore on special occasions, were spoiled by fungi during the rainy season. She wants to know how fungi appear suddenly during the rainy season? Page 6

Ans. Fungal spores are usually present in the air. As they land on wet and warm things, they germinate and grow. During rainy season, there is moisture in air. So, fungi spoils more things in rainy season.

Q.10 Boojho says once his grandfather told him that his wheat fields were spoiled by a fungus. He wants to know if fungi cause diseases also. Page 7

Ans. Yes, fungi cause many diseases in plants and animals.

Exercise

Q.1 Why do organisms take food?

Ans. The organisms take food to build their bodies, to grow, to repair damaged part of their bodies and to obtain the energy to carry out life processes. Food provide energy to fight against diseases and protection from different infections.

Q.2 Distinguish between a parasite and a saprotroph.

Ans. Differences between parasites and saprotrophs are as follows

Parasites	Saprotrophs
These organisms obtain nutrients from a living host organism.	These are the organisms that feed on dead and decaying organic matter.
They harm the body of the host, e.g. *Cuscuta*	They do not require any host, e.g. Fungi

Q.3 How would you test the presence of starch in leaves?

Ans. The presence of starch, a carbohydrate in leaves can be tested by iodine test. Iodine turns starch solution into blue-black colour.

Pour few drops of dilute iodine solution on a boiled and decolourised leaf. The leaf becomes blue-black in colour which proves the presence of starch in it.

Q.4 Give a brief description of the process of synthesis of food in green plants.

Ans. Refer to text on page no. 2 and 3.

Q.5 Show with the help of a sketch that plants are the ultimate source of food.

Ans. The following sketch shows that the plants are the ultimate source of food.

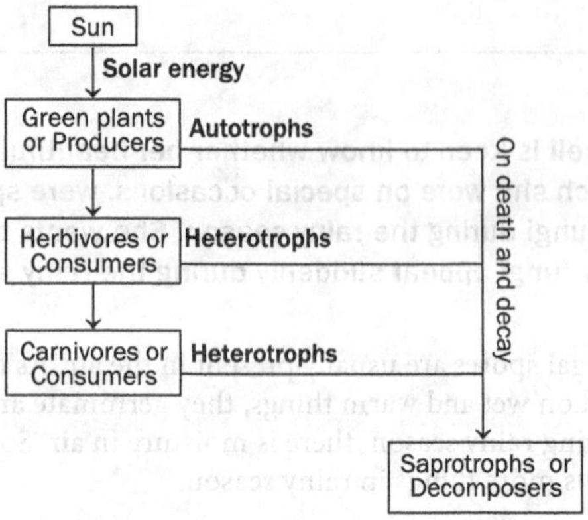

Q.6 Fill in the blanks.

(a) Green plants are called .... since they synthesise their own food.

(b) The food synthesised by plants is stored as ....

(c) In photosynthesis solar energy is captured by the pigment called ....

(d) During photosynthesis, plants take in .... and release .... gas.

Ans. (a) autotrophs

(b) starch

(c) chlorophyll

(d) carbon dioxide, oxygen

Q.7 Name the following

(a) A parasitic plant with yellow, slender and branched stem.

(b) A plant that is partially autotrophic.

(c) The pores through which leaves exchange gases.

Ans. (a) *Cuscuta* (amarbel)

(b) Pitcher plant (insectivorous plant)

(c) Stomata

Q.8 Tick the correct answer.

(i) *Cuscuta* is an example of

(a) autotroph (b) parasite

(c) saprotroph (d) host

(ii) The plant which traps and feeds on insects is

(a) *Cuscuta*

(b) China rose

(c) pitcher plant

(d) rose

Ans. (i) (b) *Cuscuta* is an example of parasite.

(ii) (c) The plant which traps and feeds on insects is pitcher plant.

Q.9 Match the items given in Column I with those in Column II.

Column I		Column II	
A.	Chlorophyll	1.	*Rhizobium*
B.	Nitrogen	2.	Heterotrophs
C.	*Cuscuta*	3.	Pitcher plant
D.	Animals	4.	Leaf
E.	Insects	5.	Parasite

Ans. A–4, B–1, C–5, D–2, E–3

Q.10 Mark 'T' if the statement is True and 'F' if it is False.

(a) Carbon dioxide is released during photosynthesis.

(b) Plants which synthesise their food are called saprotrophs.

(c) The product of photosynthesis is not a protein.

(d) Solar energy is converted into chemical energy during photosynthesis.

Ans. (a) False, oxygen is released during photosynthesis.

(b) False, plants which synthesise their own food are called autotrophs.

(c) True, the product of photosynthesis is carbohydrates.

(d) True

Q.11 Choose the correct option from the following :

(a) Which part of the plant takes in carbon dioxide from the air for photosynthesis?

(i) Root hair (ii) Stomata (iii) Leaf veins (iv) Petals

Ans. (ii) Stomata, takes in carbon dioxide from the air for photosynthesis.

Q.12 Choose the correct option from the following.

(b) Plants take carbon dioxide from the atmosphere mainly through their

(i) roots (ii) stem (iii) flowers (iv) leaves

Ans. (iv) Plants take carbon dioxide from the atmosphere mainly through their leaves.

Q.13 Why do farmers grow many fruits and vegetable crops inside large greenhouses? What are the advantages to the farmers?

Ans. Farmers utilise large greenhouses to create optimal conditions for cultivating fruits and vegetable plants. As greenhouse is constructed from materials such as plastic or glass, through which sunlight can pass. This provides continuous solar energy for photosynthesis to plants.

Farmers get many advantages for growing fruits and vegetable inside large greenhouses, which are as follows

(i) A diverse range of plants can be grown.

(ii) It provides protection to the plants against pest and rodents.

(iii) It provides optimal temperature for the growth of plants.

REVIEW EXERCISE

Including Competency Based Questions

Part I

Multiple Choice Questions

1. Which of the following option has all the components of food? NCERT Exemplar

(a) Carbohydrate, fats, vitamins, protein and mineral
(b) Carbohydrate, oxygen, vitamins, protein and mineral
(c) Fats, water, carbon dioxide, protein and mineral
(d) Oxygen, water, fat, protein and mineral

2. A teacher instructs the student to outline the reasons about the importance of nutrition in living organisms. The table exhibits the list prepared by the students. Competency Based Que.

A.	It supports the normal growth and development.
B.	It allows each organism to prepare its own food.
C.	It promotes overall health of the organism.
D.	It allows organism to reduce its body weight.

Based on the table, which statements are correct?

(a) A and C (b) B and D (c) A and B (d) C and D

3. Organisms which prepare food by themselves using simple naturally available raw materials are referred to as NCERT Exemplar

(a) heterotrophs (b) autotrophs
(c) parasites (d) saprophytes

4. Which of the following raw material is available in the air for photosynthesis? NCERT Exemplar

(a) Oxygen (b) Carbon dioxide
(c) Nitrogen (d) Hydrogen

5. Which equation accurately represents the process of photosynthesis ?

(a) Oxygen + Water $\xrightarrow[\text{Chlorophyll}]{\text{Sunlight}}$ Carbohydrate + Water
(b) Carbon dioxide + Water $\xrightarrow[\text{Chlorophyll}]{\text{Sunlight}}$ Carbohydrate + Water
(c) Carbon dioxide + Oxygen $\xrightarrow[\text{Chlorophyll}]{\text{Sunlight}}$ Carbohydrate + Water
(d) Carbodydrate + Water $\xrightarrow[\text{Chlorophyll}]{\text{Sunlight}}$ Carbodydrate + Oxygen

6. In the absence of which of the following will photosynthesis not occur in leaves? NCERT Exemplar

(a) Guard cells (b) Chlorophyll
(c) Vacuole (d) Space between cells

7. When we observe the lower surface of a leaf through a magnifying lens, we see numerous small openings. Which of the following is the term given to such openings? NCERT Exemplar

(a) Stomata (b) Lamina
(c) Midrib (d) Veins

8. In the process of photosynthesis, plants

(a) take O_2 and release CO_2
(b) take CO_2 and release O_2
(c) take water vapour and release O_2
(d) take O_2 and release water

9. Which of the following statements is/are correct?

(i) All green plants can prepare their own food.
(ii) Most animals are autotrophs.
(iii) Carbon dioxide is not required for photosynthesis.
(iv) Oxygen is liberated during photosynthesis.

Choose the correct answer from the options given below. NCERT Exemplar

(a) (i) and (iv) (b) Only (ii)
(c) (ii) and (iii) (d) (i) and (ii)

10. Which of the following energy conversions occur during the process of photosynthesis?

(a) Solar energy is changed into chemical energy
(b) Solar energy is changed into mechanical energy
(c) Bioenergy is converted into chemical energy
(d) Chemical energy is changed into light energy

11. If iodine is dropped on the boiled decolourised leaf it gives blue-black colour due to the presence of

(a) starch (b) protein
(c) fat (d) vitamin

12. Which option accurately lists the nutrients found in plants, excluding carbohydrates ? CBSE Question Bank

(a) Water, fibres, minerals
(b) Fat, proteins, vitamins
(c) Fibres, vitamins, water
(d) Flavouring agents, water, vitamins

13. Insectivorous plant among the following is

(a) lichen
(b) *Cuscuta*
(c) pitcher plant
(d) bread mould

14. **The table provides information on the traits of an insectivorous plant.** **Competency Based Que.**

A. It is green in colour.

B. The body of the plant consists of a lid and pitcher.

C. It traps the insects and digests them by secreting digestive juices.

Based on these characteristics, what could be the probable mode of nutrition of this plant ?

(a) Autotrophic
(b) Autotrophic and heterotrophic
(c) Both autotrophic and saprotrophic
(d) Both heterotrophic and saprotrophic

15. **Pitcher plant traps insects because it** **NCERT Exemplar**

(a) is a heterotroph
(b) grows in soils which lack in nitrogen
(c) does not have chlorophyll
(d) has a digestive system like human beings

16. **The term that is used for the mode of nutrition in yeast, mushroom and bread mould is**

(a) autotrophic
(b) insectivorous
(c) saprophytic
(d) parasitic

17. **Two organisms are good friends and live together. One provides shelter, water and nutrients, while the other prepares and provides food. Such an association of organisms is termed as** **NCERT Exemplar**

(a) saprophyte
(b) parasite
(c) autotroph
(d) symbiosis

18. **Listed below are some of the traits exhibited by saprophytes and symbionts.** **Competency Based Que.**

A. They absorb nutrients from dead and decay.

B. They depend on plants and animals for nutrition.

C. They live together with other organisms to share space and food.

Which option correctly classifies these characteristics?

	A	B	C
(a)	Symbionts	Both saprophytes and symbionts	Saprophytes
(b)	Saprophytes	Both saprophytes and symbionts	Symbionts
(c)	Both saprophytes and symbionts	Saprophytes	Symbionts
(d)	Symbionts	Saprophytes	Both saprophytes and symbionts

19. **The symbiotic association is seen in which of the following?**

(a) Lichens (b) Algae
(c) Fungi (d) Bacteria

20. **Farmers use manure and fertilisers to**

(a) replenish plant with minerals
(b) replenish soil with nutrieints
(c) replenish air with nitrogen
(d) replenish fungi

21. **What additional nutrients is likely to be produced by plants, when the soil contains abundant nitrogen-fixing bacteria during photosynthesis ?**

(a) Minerals (b) Proteins **NCERT Exemplar**
(c) Vitamins (d) Water

Answers

1. (a)	2. (a)	3. (b)	4. (b)	5. (b)
6. (b)	7. (a)	8. (b)	9. (a)	10. (a)
11. (a)	12. (b)	13. (c)	14. (b)	15. (b)
16. (c)	17. (d)	18. (b)	19. (a)	20. (b)
21. (b)				

Fill in the Blanks

1. **Leaves are called the .... of plants.**

2. **The openings present on the surface of leaves are surrounded by cells called.................. .**

3. ***Cuscuta* plant does not contain ....**

4. **.............. organisms derive their nutrient from dead and decaying animals or plants.**

Answers

1. food factory 2. guard cells
3. chlorophyll 4. Saprotrophic

2. **Fill in the blanks of the paragraph given below with the words provided in the box.**

Chlorophyll, Energy, Food, Carbon dioxide, Water, Photosynthesis

(Note : A word can be used more than once) **NCERT Exemplar**

Leaves have a green pigment called ......(a)......which captures ....(b).........from sunlight. This ....(c)......... is used in the process of ....(d)......... and along with other raw materials like ....(e) .... and ....(f).........to synthesises ....(g)......... .

Answers

(a) chlorophyll (b) energy
(c) energy (d) photosynthesis
(e) carbon dioxide (f) water
(g) food

3. Can you give me a name ?

Solve each of the following riddles by writing the name of the organism and its mode of nutrition. One riddle is solved to help you. **NCERT Exemplar**

(a) I am tall, but I cannot move. I am green and can prepare my own food. ...., ...

(b) I live in water; people keep me in an aquarium and feed me. .... , ...

(c) I am small and I can fly. I disturb your sleep, bite you and suck your blood which is my food .... , ...

(d) I am white and soft. I grow well in the rainy season. Children pluck me from the ground and admire me. I absorb nutrients from decomposed dead parts of plants and animals in the soil, ... ,............ .

Answers

(a) tree, autotroph

(b) fish, heterotroph

(c) mosquito, parasite

(d) mushroom, saprophyte

True/False

1. **Food is necessary for plants only.**
2. **Animals are heterotrophs.**
3. **Chlorophyll is present in an animal cell.**
4. **Pitcher plant eats insects.**
5. **Lichen is a saprophytic plant.**

Answers

1. False, food is necessary for all the living organisms as all of them grow and require maintenance of body functions from time to time.
2. True
3. False, chlorophyll is present in leaf of plants not in animals cells.
4. True
5. False, lichen is a symbiotic association between an alga and a fungi. It is not a saprophytic organism.

Match the Columns

1. Match the Column I with Column II.

	Column I		Column II
A.	Saprotroph	1.	Pitcher plant
B.	Chlorophyll	2.	Parasite
C.	*Rhizobium*	3.	Green leaf
D.	*Cuscuta*	4.	Fungi
E.	Insects	5.	N_2-fixing bacteria

2. Match the Column I with Column II.

	Column I		Column II
A.	Vessels	1.	Food factory of plant
B.	Leaf	2.	Stomata
C.	Tiny pores present on leaf	3.	Raw material
D.	CO_2 and water	4.	Saprophyte
E.	Mushroom	5.	Water and mineral

Answers

1. A–4, B–3, C–5, D–2, E–1
2. A–5, B–1, C–2, D–3, E–4

Assertion-Reason Questions

The following questions consist of two statements Assertion (A) and Reason (R). Answer these questions by selecting the appropriate option given below.

(a) Both A and R are true and R is the correct explanation of A

(b) Both A and R are true, but R is not the correct explanation of A

(c) A is true, but R is false

(d) A is false, but R is true

1. **Assertion** (A) Green plants can make their own food.
   Reason (R) They have chlorophyll pigment stored in chloroplast.
2. **Assertion** (A) The green pigment present in the leaves is called stomata.
   Reason (R) It plays an important role in the process of photosynthesis in plants.
3. **Assertion** (A) The leaves of cactus plant are reduced to spines.
   Reason (R) It is an adaptation in cactus plant to increase the rate of photosynthesis.
4. **Assertion** (A) Pitcher plant is an insectivorous plant.
   Reason (R) It derives its nutrition from another plant.

Answers

1. (a) Both A and R are true and R is the correct explanation of A.
2. (d) A is false, but R is true. A can be corrected as The green pigment present in the leaves is called chlorophyll.
3. (c) A is true, but R is false. R can be corrected as The leaves of *Cactus* plant are reduced to spine to decrease the rate of transpiration in the desert plants.
4. (c) A is true, but R is false. R can be corrected as Insectivorous plants like pitcher plant derives their nutrition by eating insects. On the another hand parasitic plants like *Cuscuta* derive their nutrition from another plants.

Case Based Questions

1. The picture below shows the process through which green plants make their food. *X*, *Y* and *Z* are three different components of this process.
The direction of arrows show what is absorbed and what is released by the plant. For example, sunlight is absorbed by the plants.

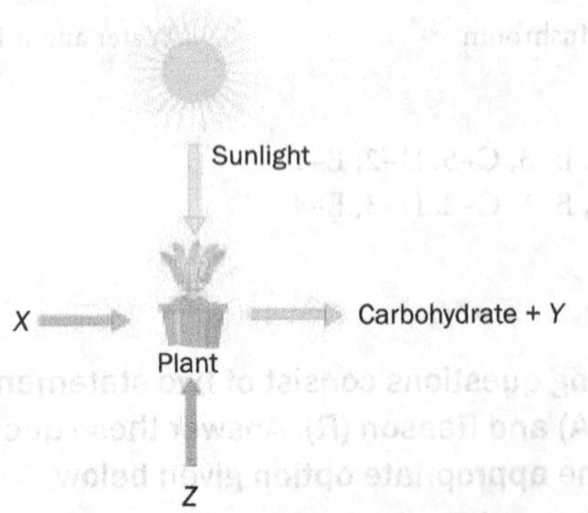

The equation below shows how green plants make their own food?

$$\text{Carbon dioxide} + \text{Water} \xrightarrow[\text{chlorophyll}]{\text{sunlight}} \text{Carbohydrate} + \text{Oxygen}$$

What does *X*, *Y* and *Z* stand for in the picture above ? **Competency Based Que.**

	X	*Y*	*Z*
(a)	Carbon dioxide	Water	Oxygen
(b)	Water	Oxygen	Carbon dioxide
(c)	Oxygen	Water	Carbon dioxide
(d)	Carbon dioxide	Oxygen	Water

2. We often find green slimy layers on the surface of ponds. The layers are formed by tiny organisms that make their own food. Which of these is/are true about the organisms ? **CBSE Question Bank**
Circle 'Yes' or 'No' in each row.

	Is the statement about the organisms true?	Yes/No
(a)	They contain chlorophyll.	Yes/No
(b)	They release oxygen.	Yes/No
(c)	They require sunlight for making food.	Yes/No

Answers

1. (d) *X*- Carbon dioxide, *Y*- Oxygen and *Z*- Water
2. (a) Yes (b) Yes (c) Yes

Part II

Very Short Answer Type Questions

1. What do you understand by nutrition?

Ans. The process of utilising nutrients like carbohydrates, proteins, fats, etc. to generate energy is called nutrition.

2. Which parts of the plants are called food factories of the plant?

Ans. Leaves are referred to as food factories of plants, because leaves synthesise food by the process of photosynthesis.

3. The tiny openings present on the leaf surface help in gaseous exchange. What are they called?

Ans. Stomata are the tiny openings present on the surface of leaves through which gaseous exchange takes place in plants.

4. Except plants, why cannot other living organisms prepare their food using CO_2, water and minerals?

Ans. Other living organisms do not contain chlorophyll for absorbing solar energy which is necessary for preparing food using carbon dioxide and water.

5. Potato and ginger are both underground parts that store food. Where is the food prepared in these plants? **NCERT Exemplar**

Ans. In both the plants, shoot system and leaves are above the ground. They prepare food through photosynthesis and transport it to the underground part for storage.

6. A goat eats away all the leaves of a small plant (balsam). However, in a few days, new leaves could be seen sprouting in the plant again. How did the plant survive without leaves? **Competency Based Que.**

Ans. The plant of balsam survived on the food stored in the stem and roots.

7. Some, plants have red, brown and violet pigment. Do these leaves carry out photosynthesis?

Ans. The leaves other than green also have chlorophyll. The large amount of red and brown pigments mask the green colour. Photosynthesis takes place in these leaves also.

8. Algae are green in colour. Why?

Ans. Algae contain chlorophyll which imparts green colour to them.

9. A carbohydrate is produced by plants as food source. It is constituted from which molecules?

Ans. Carbohydrates are composed of carbon, hydrogen and oxygen.

10. Why is *Cuscuta*, categorised as a parasite?

Ans. *Cuscuta* is categorised as a parasite because it deprives its host of all valuable nutrients and absorbs them itself. Hence, it is called a parasitic plant.

11. Insectivorous plants have one or the other specialised organs to trap their prey. What is that organ?

Ans. Leaves of insectivorous plants are modified to trap the prey.

12. Why are insectivorous plants called partial heterotrophs?

Ans. Insectivorous plants can synthesise their own food, but fulfill their nitrogen deficiency by eating insects, therefore these are called as partial heterotrophs.

13. What do you understand by saprotrophic mode of nutrition?

Ans. The mode of nutrition in which organisms take their nutrients from dead and decaying matter is called saprotrophic mode of nutrition.

14. Farmers spread manure and fertilisers in the field or in gardens, etc. Why are these added to the soil?

Ans. Plants absorb mineral nutrients from soil thus, declining their concentration in soil. By adding fertilisers and manures farmers enhance or add these essential nutrients back in soil.

15. Name the bacteria that can fix atmospheric nitrogen.

Ans. *Rhizobium* is the bacterium which can fix atmospheric nitrogen.

Short Answer Type Questions

1. Autotrophs and heterotrophs are two different organisms with distinct modes of nutrition state. How are they different from each other?

Ans. Differences between autotrophs and heterotrophs are as follows

Autotrophs	Heterotrophs
They can prepare their own food.	They cannot prepare their own food.
Autotrophs take simple inorganic substances like CO_2 and H_2O and change them into food, e.g. green plants.	They take in complex food and break it down into simple compounds, e.g. all animals, fungi and non-green plants.

2. Based on the image given below, what is the mode of nutrition in grasshopper?

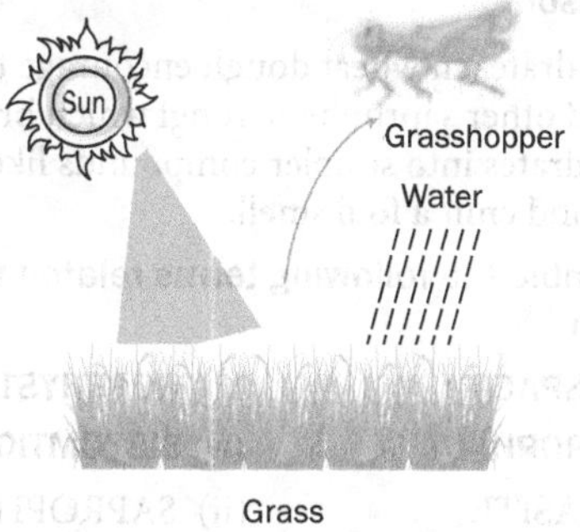

Ans. Heterotrophic, as the grasshopper takes food prepared by the grass.

3. Sunlight, chlorophyll, carbon dioxide, water and minerals are raw materials essential for photosynthesis.

Do you know where they are available? Fill in the blanks with the appropriate raw materials.

(a) Available in the plant : ....

(b) Available in the soil : ....

(c) Available in the air : ....

(d) Available during day : .... **NCERT Exemplar**

Ans. (a) Available in the plant : chlorophyll

(b) Available in the soil : water, minerals

(c) Available in the air : carbon dioxide

(d) Available during day : sunlight

4. Plants are considered an essential part of Earth as they keep a check on lot of process occurring all over. What would happen if all the green plants are wiped from Earth? **Competency Based Que.**

Ans. Green plants are the source of energy for all the living organisms, so that they can perform their normal functions. If all green plants and trees disappear, all the organism depending on them for food and shelter will also die.

The lack of gaseous exchange will lead to increase in the amount of CO_2, causing death in humans and other animals also. The cycle of life will gradually disappear.

5. In what unique manner does a pitcher plant derive its nutrition?

Ans. Pitcher plant modifies its leaf axis into a long tubular pitcher or Jug-like structure. The apex of the leaf forms a lid which can open and close the mouth of pitcher. Inside the pitcher there are hairs which are directed downwards. When any insect comes in contact with the leaf, the lid present on it is closed and the insect is trapped. Then the insect is digested by digestive juices secreted in the pitcher and its nutrients get absorbed by the plant.

6. Wheat dough if left in the open, after a few days, starts to emit a foul smell and becomes unfit for use. Give reason. **NCERT Exemplar**

Ans. Carbohydrates in wheat dough encourage the growth of yeast and other saprophytic fungi which breakdown carbohydrates into simpler compounds like CO_2 and alcohol and emit a foul smell.

7. Unscramble the following terms related to modes of nutrition

(i) RASPAEIT (ii) ROPEHYSTAP

(iii) TOROPHAUT (iv) SIBYOMTIC

Ans. (i) PARASITE (ii) SAPROPHYTE

(iii) AUTOTROPH (iv) SYMBIOTIC

8. Nitrogen is an essential nutrient for plants growth. But farmers who cultivate pulses as crops like green gram, bengal gram, black gram, etc., do not apply nitrogenous fertilisers during cultivation. Why? **NCERT Exemplar**

Ans. Roots of pulses (leguminous plants) have a symbiotic association with a bacterium called *Rhizobium*. This bacteria converts gaseous nitrogen of air into water soluble nitrogen compounds and give them to the leguminous plants for their growth. Hence, farmers need not use nitrogenous fertilisers.

Long Answer Type Questions

1. Describe the process by which plants prepare their food using different raw materials.

Ans. The process by which green plants can prepare their own food is called photosynthesis. Green plants possess chlorophyll in their leaf and utilises carbon dioxide (from air) water, minerals (from soil, through root) as raw material and sunlight as source of energy and convert light energy into chemical energy. The food thus synthesised is in the form of carbohydrate.

The overall reaction for photosynthesis can be given as follows

$$\underset{\text{(from air)}}{\text{Carbon dioxide}} + \underset{\text{(from soil)}}{\text{Water}} \xrightarrow[\text{Chlorophyll}]{\text{Sunlight}} \underset{\text{(carbohydrate)}}{\text{Glucose}} + \underset{\text{(released in air)}}{\text{Oxygen}\uparrow}$$

2. Wild animals like tiger, wolf, lion and leopard do not eat plants. Does this mean that they can survive without plants? Can you provide a suitable explanation?

Ans. Animals like tiger, wolf, lion and leopard are carnivores and do not eat plants. They hunt and eat herbivorous animals like deer, gaur, bison, zebra, giraffe, etc. which are dependent on plants for food.

If there are no plants, herbivorous animals will not survive and ultimately animals like tiger, wolf, lion and leopard will have nothing to eat.

3. What is symbiosis ? Explain with an example.

Ans. Refer to text on page no. 4.

4. Describe the method for replenishing the soil with minerals and other essential constituents used by plants growing in those soil by farmers.

Ans. Refer to text on page no. 4.

Case Based Questions

1. Australian sundew is a type of plant that has green stems and green leaves. It traps insects with its sticky tentacles. The plant sucks the nutrients from the body of its prey.

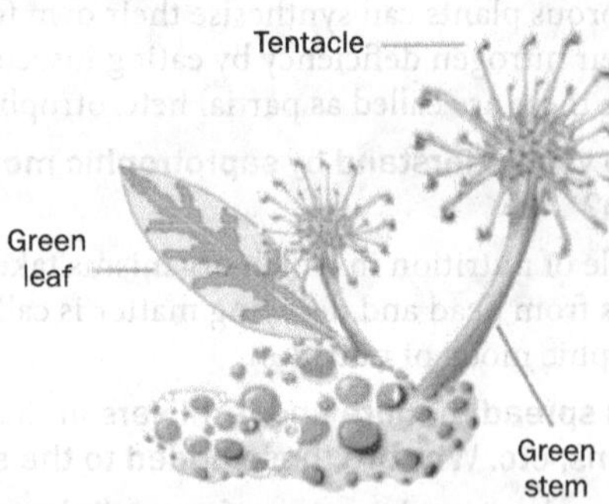

Australian sundew is a part autotroph and part heterotroph.
Write two features of the plant that support this. **Competency Based Que.**

2. Jessy wanted to find out the conditions that best support the rotting of bread. The growth of coloured fluffy patches on the surface of bread confirms rotting. She kept four bread slices in different conditions for five days. The table below shows Jessy's findings after five days.

Bread slice	Where the slice is placed	Number of coloured fluffy patches after five days
Slice 1	On wet cotton at 5°C	Two patches
Slice 2	On a dry plate at 30°C	Six patches
Slice 3	On wet cotton at 30°C	Ten patches
Slice 4	On a dry plate at 5°C	No patch

Competency Based Que.

(i) Which microorganism forms the coloured fluffy patches on the bread ?

(ii) Which condition can best prevent rotting for a long time ?

(a) Cold and humid (b) Warm and dry

(c) Warm and humid (d) Cold and dry

3. **The picture below shows thread-like fungi that live near some plants. The fungi wrap around and pierce the plant's roots. It helps the plant to get minerals and water from the soil. The plant provides carbohydrates to the fungi.** Competency Based Que.

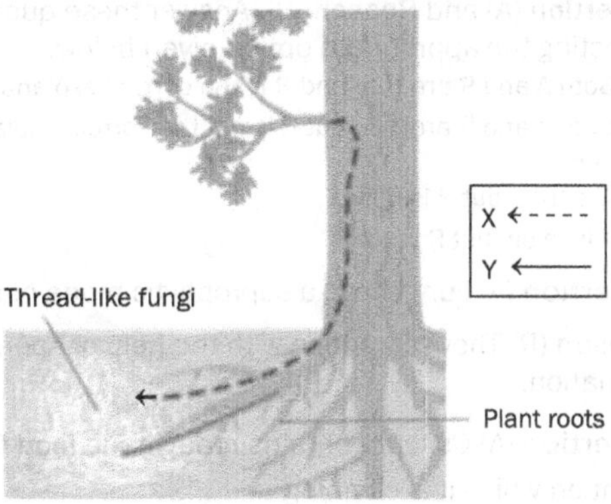

(i) *X* and *Y* show the direction of flow of substances from one source to another. Which substances move in

- *X* direction
- *Y* direction

(ii) Parasite is an organism that lives in or on the body of another organism. It receives energy and nutrients from the host organism. Parasite does not give anything in return to its host. Is the group of fungi shown in the picture a type of parasite ? Explain your answer.

Ans. 1. Australian sundew is a part autotroph as it has green stem and green leaves. It is a part heterotroph as it sucks nutrients from the body of its prey.

2. (i) Fungi forms the coloured fluffy patches on the bread.

(ii) (d) Cold and dry.

3. (i) In the given picture, the direction of movement of carbohydrate, water and minerals is as follows

X- shows the movement of carbohydrate.

Y- shows the movement of water and minerals.

(ii) The group of fungi shown in the picture is not a type of parasite. As parasites receives energy and nutrients from the host organism and does not give anything in return. But in this picture fungi is helping the plant to get nutrients and water from the soil, in return of carbohydrates.

This is the example of symbiotic relationship.

Skill Based Questions as per NEP 2020

1. **Radha on her trip to the hills of Meghalaya saw a plant whose leaf was modified into a jug-like structure and trapped the insects that landed on it. She found it startling. Can you name this plant, why does this plants need to feed on insects?** Thinking skill

2. **Take three potted plants, name them *A*, *B* and *C*.**

Keep the pot *A* in sunlight but do not water it keep the pot B in the dark room but water it regularly and keep the pot *C* in the sunlight cover it with black polythene bag and water it regularly.

Repeat this for 3-4 days. Which among these will give positive iodine test? Experimental skill

3. **Asha went to visit her grandfather in his village. He was having a serious discussion with his fellow members regarding the productivity level of crops for present year.**

They all were worried about how to increase the productivity of crop. Asha listened to this and then suggested to the group that the reason may be the decreased level of minerals in soil. She told her grandfather to plant crops like pulses, gram, beans, etc., for a year then follow with regular crops. This will increase the crop productivity.

(i) Why is there decrease in crop productivity?

(ii) What are the noted benefits of growing leguminous plants? Will the results be as what Asha expressed? Thinking skill

4. **Visit a greenhouse if there is one near your place. Observe how they grow plants. Find out how they regulate the amount of light, water and carbon dioxide to grow the plants.** Observation skill

5. **Try growing a sweet potato just in water. Describe your experiment and observations.** Experimental skill

ASSESSMENT EXERCISE

Part I

Multiple Choice Questions

1. How do the farmers increase the fertility of soil?
(a) By adding nutrient to soil
(b) By adding oxygen to soil
(c) By removing microbes from soil
(d) By removing excess moisture from soil

2. Which of the following plant traps and feed on insects?
(a) Rose (b) China rose
(c) Pitcher plant (d) *Cuscuta*

3. What is the product of photosynthesis?
(a) Starch (b) Fats
(c) Protein (d) Vitamins

4. Lichen is an example of
(a) parasites
(b) insectivorous
(c) heterotrophs
(d) symbiosis

5. Which of the following element is needed along with carbon, hydrogen and oxygen to make proteins?
(a) Calcium (b) Nitrogen
(c) Potassium (d) Iron

Fill in the Blanks

6. .... (gas) is released during photosynthesis.

7. .... energy is converted into chemical energy during photosynthesis.

True/False

8. Plants obtain nitrogen from the air.

9. Autotrophs can synthesise their own food.

10. Fungus grows quickly on moist matter due to the presence of fungal spores in the air.

Match the Columns

11. Match the Column I with Column II.

Column I	Column II
A. Lichen	1. Guard cells
B. Pitcher plant	2. Heterotrophs
C. Animals	3. Saprophyte
D. Stomata	4. Symbiotic relationship
E. Fungi	5. Insectivorous plant

Assertion-Reason Questions

The following questions consist of two statements Assertion (A) and **Reason** (R). Answer these questions by selecting the appropriate option given below.
(a) Both A and R are true and R is the correct explanation of A
(b) Both A and R are true but R is not the correct explanation of A
(c) A is true, but R is false
(d) A is false, but R is true

12. Assertion (A) Fungi have a saprophytic mode of nutrition.
Reason (R) They reproduce with the help of spore formation.

13. Assertion (A) *Cuscuta* obtains readymade food from the plant on which it is climbing.
Reason (R) It shows autotrophic mode of nutrition.

Part II

Very Short Answer Type Questions

14. The iodine on starch produces which type of colour?

15. What is the colour of chlorophyll present in leaf?

16. What is the function of guard cells of stomata?

Short Answer Type Questions

17. Parasite and saprophyte are two different modes of nutrition. How are the two different from one another?

18. The relationship between soil bacteria and certain crop plant is beneficial to farmers. Explain how.

19. Plants synthesise other components besides carbohydrates, what are those substances?

Long Answer Type Question

20. An association between two organisms benefitting both partners has been observed. What is this association? Name one plant which shows this type of association.

Answers

1. (a) 2. (c) 3. (a) 4. (d) 5. (b)
6. Oxygen 7. Solar 8. False 9. True 10. True
11. A-4, B-5, C-2, D-1, E-3
12. (b) 13. (c)

CHAPTER 02

Nutrition in Animals

All organisms including humans requires food for growth, repair and functioning of the body. Plants can prepare their own food by the process of photosynthesis, but animals including humans cannot. They get their food from plants, either directly by eating plants and their products or indirectly by eating animals that eat plants. Some animals eat both plants and other animals. The process of taking food by an animal is called **animal nutrition**. It includes **nutrient requirement, mode of intake of food** and **its utilisation in the body**.

The food that we eat is in the form of complex substances such as carbohydrate cannot be utilised directly by the body. So, they are broken down into simpler substances. These can be absorbed by the cells of the body. This process of breakdown of complex components of food into simpler substances is called **digestion**.

2.1 Different Ways of Taking Food

Different types of animals show different modes of nutrition. Some aquatic animals filter tiny food particles and feed upon them. Bees and humming birds **suck the nectar** of flowers, infants of many animals including humans, **feed on mother's milk.**

The type of food and mode of nutrition in different animals depend on the special structure or organ used for taking food inside the body.

Some of these are listed in the table given below.

Various modes of feeding in different animals

Name of the animals	Kinds of food	Modes of feeding
Snail	Grass	Chewing
Ant	Plant material and other animals	Biting and chewing
Eagle	Flesh of prey	Tearing
Humming bird	Nectar from flower	Sucking
Lice	Blood from skin of scalp	Sucking
Mosquito	Blood from animals	Sucking
Butterfly	Nectar from flower	Siphoning
Housefly	Filth and refuses	Sucking
Amoeba	Tiny aquatic animals	Capturing and swallowing
Snake (python)	Animal as a whole	Swallowing

Feeding Mechanism in Starfish

Starfish is a marine animal, which feeds on animals covered by hard shells of **calcium carbonate**. It has a unique mode of nutrition. After opening the shell, starfish pops out its stomach through its mouth to eat the soft animal inside the shell. After eating its prey, it brings back its stomach inside its body. This food is then digested slowly by starfish.

2.2 Different Processes Involved in Nutrition

The various processes that are involved in the nutrition are as follows

(i) **Ingestion** The process by which food is taken into the body of an organism is called ingestion.

(ii) **Digestion** The process by which the food containing large insoluble substances is broken down into small water soluble substances is called digestion. There are two methods of digesting food, i.e., **physical** method (including chewing and grinding of food in mouth) and **chemical method** (addition of digestive juices to the food by the body itself).

(iii) **Absorption** The process by which the digested food passes through the intestinal wall into blood stream is called absorption.

(iv) **Assimilation** The process by which the absorbed food is taken in by body cells and used for energy, growth and repair is called assimilation.

(v) **Egestion** The process by which the undigested food material is removed from the body is called egestion.

Try These 2.1

1. **Give two example of animals, whose mode of feeding is sucking.**
2. **Which animal captures and swallows the prey as a whole?**
3. **What happens to the food after its absorption by the cells of the body?**

2.3 Digestion in Humans

Humans take in food through the mouth, digest and utilise it. The unused part of the food is removed from the body.

The food inside our body passes through a continuous canal called **alimentary canal** or **digestive tract**. It starts from mouth and ends at anus of human beings.

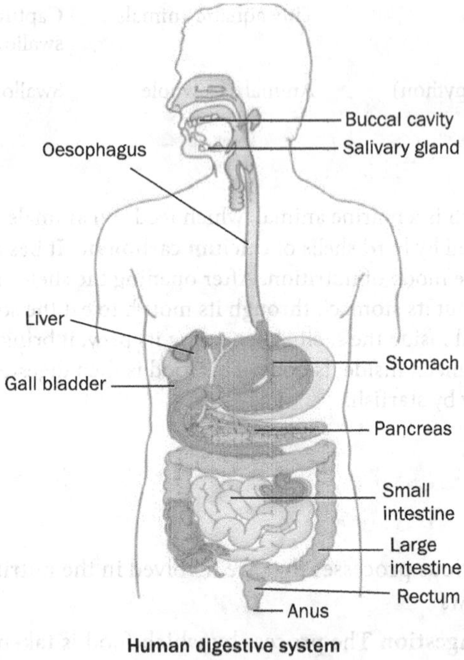

Human digestive system

The alimentary canal can be divided into various compartments

(i) The buccal cavity
(ii) Food pipe or oesophagus
(iii) Stomach
(iv) Small intestine
(v) Large intestine ending in the rectum
(vi) The anus

After the intake, the food gradually gets digested as it travels through these various compartments. There are various glands that are associated with the canal, e.g. **salivary glands, liver** and **pancreas.** These glands along with the inner wall of the stomach and small intestine secrete digestive juices. These juices convert complex substances of food into simpler substances.

The system that consists of digestive tract along with the associated glands is called **digestive system.** Now, we will learn what happens to the food in different parts of digestive tract.

1. Mouth and Buccal Cavity

The process of ingestion starts in the mouth or buccal cavity. It consists of teeth, salivary glands and tongue.

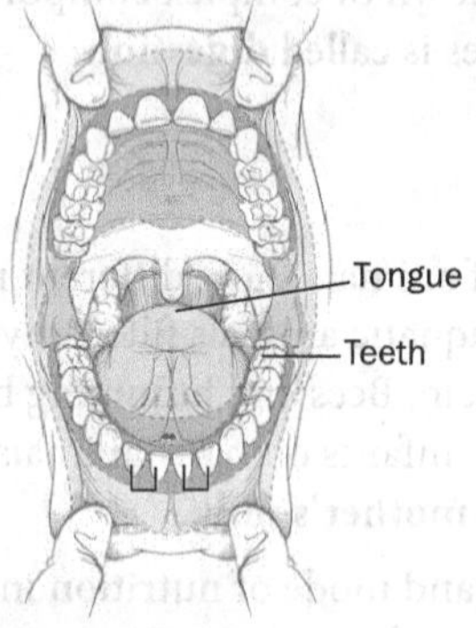

Mouth and buccal cavity

Teeth

The food is chewed by the teeth inside the mouth. Teeth mechanically break the food into small pieces. Each tooth is rooted in a separate socket in the gums.

Teeth vary in appearance and perform different functions. Accordingly, teeth, in each jaw, are divided into four types

(i) **Incisors** (4) They help in biting and cutting the food.

(ii) **Canines** (2) They help in piercing and tearing the food.

(iii) **Premolars** (4) These help in grinding and chewing of food.

(iv) **Molars** (6) These teeth are used for grinding of food.

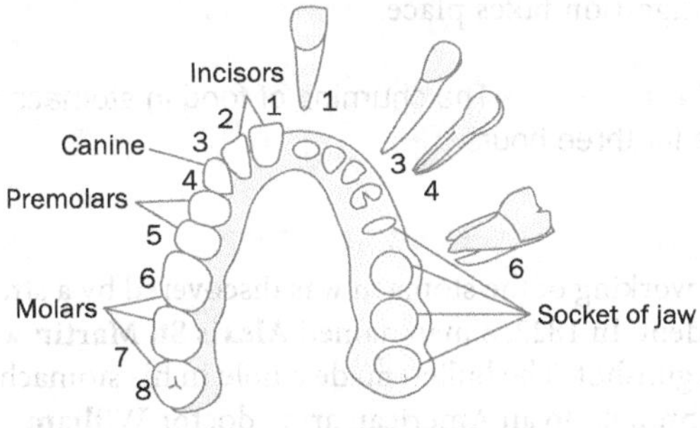

Types and arrangement of teeth

Milk Teeth and Permanent Teeth

In human beings, teeth grows twice. The sets of teeth that grow during infancy (when one is a small baby), are called **milk teeth**. These are also called as **temporary teeth**. These teeth loosen up and fall off at the age of 6-8 years. When milk teeth fall off, new set of teeth grows in their place. This second set of teeth is called **permanent teeth** because these remain throughout life or fall off during old age or due to some dental disease. If these teeth fall down, no new teeth arise on their place.

Sweets and Tooth Decay

Generally bacteria are present in our mouth, but they are not harmful to us. However, if we do not clean our teeth and mouth after eating, many harmful bacteria also begin to live and grow in it.

These bacteria breakdown the sugars present from the leftover food and release acids. The acids gradually damage the teeth. This is called **tooth decay.**

Therefore, tooth decay is defined as the process of rotting of tooth and formation of cavity or holes in it. If these cavities are not treated on time it causes severe toothache and may result in tooth loss.

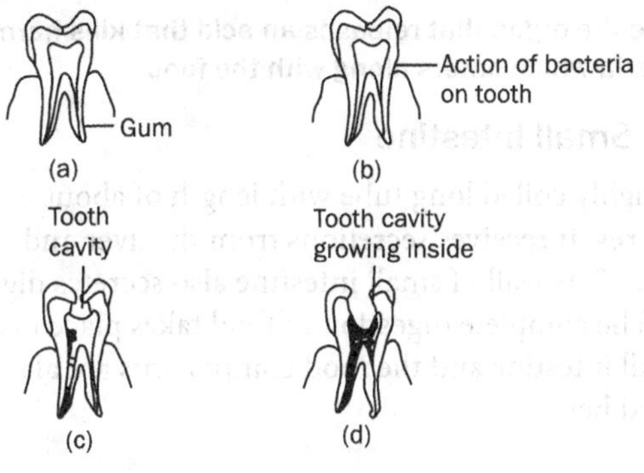

Gradual decaying of human tooth

Tooth decay can be prevented by adapting following measures

(i) We should rinse and clean our teeth thoroughly after every meal.

(ii) We should clean our teeth with the help of datun or brush and toothpaste, twice a day.

(iii) We should use dental floss, which is a special strong thread. It is moved between two teeth to take out trapped food particles.

(iv) Dirty fingers or unwashed objects should not be put in the mouth.

(v) We should avoid the use of sweets, chocolates, toffees, ice-cream, etc. Too much intake of cold drink should also be avoided.

Salivary Glands

When we eat food the salivary glands secrete a watery liquid called **saliva**. This saliva contains digestive enzymes which help in partial digestion of food. It breaks down the starch into sugars.

Tongue

It is a fleshy muscular organ attached at the back to the floor of the buccal cavity. It is free at the front and can be moved in all direction.

It helps in talking and tasting the food with the help of taste buds present on it. These buds can detect different tastes of food, e.g. sweet, sour, salt and bitter.

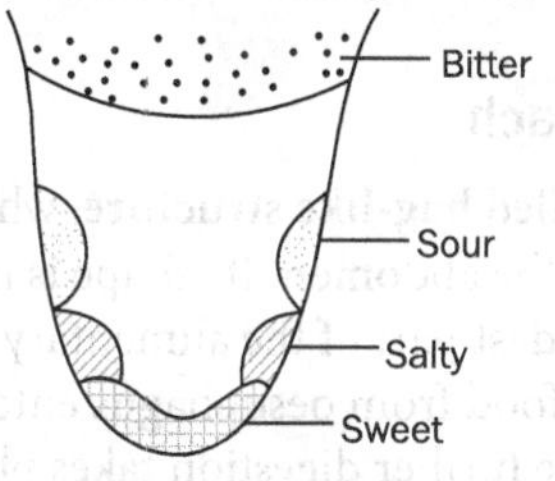

A tongue showing different regions for taste buds

It also helps in mixing the saliva with the food and swallowing the food. This food is then passed down to oesophagus or food pipe.

2. The Foodpipe or Oesophagus

It is a tube-like structure, which connects the mouth to the stomach and runs along the neck and chest. It carries slightly digested food from the mouth to the stomach. Food is pushed downward by a wave-like movement of the wall of foodpipe as a result of alternate contraction and relaxation. This movement takes place throughout the alimentary canal and pushes the food downwards.

Sometimes, food is not accepted by our stomach and is **vomited out** during which the food moves in the opposite direction, i.e. from stomach to mouth.

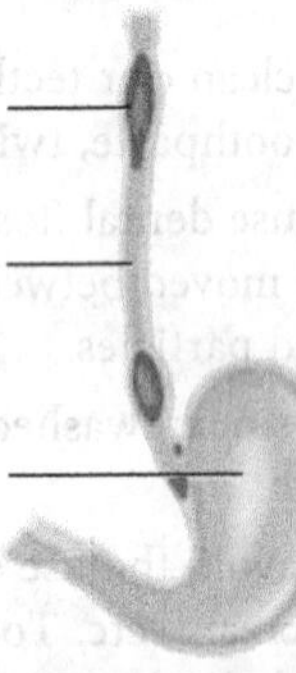

Movement of food in oesophagus

What happens when we eat food in hurry?

The windpipe (that carries air from nostril to our lungs) and foodpipe runs adjacent to each other. Air and food share a common passage in the throat.

When we swallow food, a flap-like valve closes the passage of the windpipe and guides the food into the foodpipe. But if we eat in hurry, laugh or talk while eating, the windpipe remains open and food particle enters into the windpipe and we experience **hiccups, cough** or **choking sensation**.

SCIENCE INSIGHT A wave-like movement takes place throughout the alimentary canal. This movement pushes the food downwards. This movement is called peristalsis.

3. The Stomach

It is a thick walled **bag-like structure**, which is present on the left side of the abdomen. Its shape is like flattened **'J'** and it is the widest part of the alimentary canal. The semi-digested food from oesophagus enters into the stomach, where further digestion takes place.

The food is broken down into smaller pieces and forms semi-solid paste. The inner lining of stomach secretes **mucus, hydrochloric acid** and **digestive enzymes** or **juices.**

These juices perform the following functions

(i) The function of **mucus** is to protect the lining of stomach from the action of hydrochloric acid.

(ii) The secretion of hydrochloric acid makes the medium acidic inside the stomach and helps the digestive juices to act. These digestive juices breakdown **proteins** into **simpler substances.**

(iii) Hydrochloric acid also kills the harmful bacteria that enter along with the food.

Stomach opens into small intestine where further digestion takes place.

SCIENCE INSIGHT The churning of food in stomach takes place for three hours.

Discovery of Digestion in Stomach

The working of the stomach was discovered by a strange accident. In 1822, a man named **Alexis St. Martin** was hit by a gunshot. The bullet made a hole in his stomach. He was brought to an American army doctor **William Beaumont**. The doctor saved the patient, but was unable to close the hole properly and left it bandaged. He saw the inside of the stomach through the hole and found that stomach was churning food. Its wall secreted a fluid, which could digest the food. He also observed that the end of the stomach opens into the intestine only after the digestion of the food inside the stomach is completed.

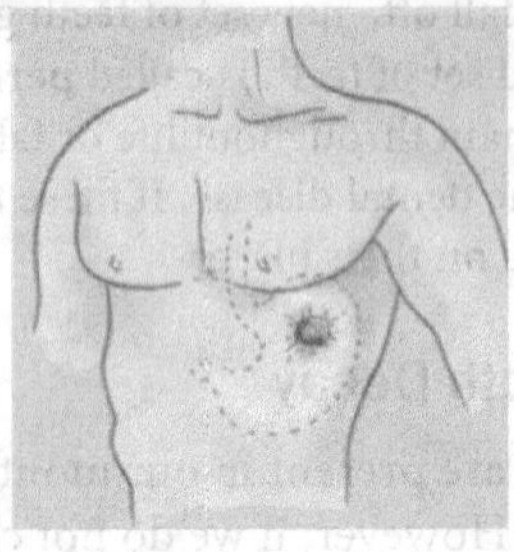
Alexis St. Martin's shotgun wound

Try These 2.2

1. **Which glands secrete juices that convert complex food substances into simpler ones?**
2. **Name the type of teeth used by organisms for tearing the food.**
3. **Name the compartments of a canal through which food is passed down once ingested.**
4. **Name the organ that releases an acid that kills harmful bacteria which enters along with the food.**

4. The Small Intestine

It is a highly coiled long tube with length of about **7.5 metres**. It receives secretions from the liver and pancreas. The wall of small intestine also secretes digestive juices. The complete digestion of food takes place inside the small intestine and the food components are also absorbed here.

Liver

The largest gland of the body, i.e. liver is the reddish-brown coloured gland, situated in the upper part of the abdomen on the right side. It secretes bile juices, which is stored in a sac-like structure called as **gall bladder**. The bile helps in the **digestion of fats**. It breaks the fat molecules into tiny droplets, so its its further breakdown into simpler compounds, becomes easy.

Pancreas

The pancreas is a large cream coloured gland, which is located just below the stomach. It secretes pancreatic juices, which acts on carbohydrates, fat and proteins and changes them into simpler forms. The partly digested food now reaches the lower part of the small intestine. Here, the intestinal juices completes the digestion of all components of the food.

The carbohydrates get broken down into simple sugar called **glucose**, while fats into fatty acid and **glycerol** and proteins get broken down into **amino acids**. These simpler compounds are now easily absorbed by the walls of small intestine into the blood.

> SCIENCE INSIGHT Fats in goat's milk are much simpler than those in cow's milk. Therefore, the goat's milk is much easier to digest than the cow's milk.

Absorption in the Small Intestine

The blood vessels in the walls of the intestine absorb the digested food to produce energy for growth and development of animals. The inner walls of small intestine have thousands of finger-like outgrowths called **villi** (singular villus).

These villi help in increasing the surface area of small intestine for the absorption of digested food. Each villus possesses a network of thin and small blood vessels close to its surface.

Assimilation of Food

The digested food material is absorbed by the surface of the villi which is then transported through blood to different parts of the body. These absorbed substances are used to build complex substances required by the body, e.g. proteins. This is called **assimilation**.

Inside the cell, the glucose breaks down into carbon dioxide and water and releases huge amounts of energy with the help of oxygen.

The undigested food material that is not absorbed by the small intestine passes to the large intestine.

5. Large Intestine

It is about **1.5 meter** long tube. It is wider and shorter than small intestine. The undigested semi-solid food is passed from small intestine to large intestine. The large intestine absorbs water and salt from the undigested food.

The remaining waste material then passes to the rectum and remains there for some time in the form of semi-solid faeces. This waste faecal matter is then removed through the anus from the body by the process called **egestion**.

> **Diarrhoea**
>
> It is a disease that is caused by an infection, food poisoning or indigestion. It is very common in India and usually occurs in children. In this condition, there is a loss of water and salts from the body of a person through frequent watery stools. It may be fatal under severe conditions. In order to prevent dehydration, the person suffering from diarrhoea should be given plenty of boiled and cooled water with a pinch of salt and sugar dissolved in it.
>
> This solution is called **Oral Rehydration Solution** (ORS). In the mean time, the doctors should be called for medicines for the cure of diarrhoea.

Try These 2.3

1. **The intestinal juices from small intestine helps in the complete digestion of which components of food?**
2. **Name the finger-like projections present in the small intestinal wall.**
3. **Which process is involved in the formation of complex substances from absorbed food materials?**
4. **Name the solution being used for the cure of diarrhoea.**

2.4 Digestion in Grass-Eating Animals

The herbivorous animals such as cow, buffaloes, etc. that eat grass chew continuously even when they are not eating.

These animals quickly swallow the grass and store it in a part of the stomach called **rumen**. Here the food is partially digested and is called **cud**.

This cud is brought back into the mouth of the cow from the rumen in small lumps and the animal chews it again. This process is called **rumination** and these animals are called **ruminants**.

The grass is rich in **cellulose**, i.e. a type of carbohydrate. In ruminants like cattle, deer, etc. bacteria present in the rumen helps in the digestion of cellulose.

When this cud is thoroughly chewed in the mouth of the cow, it is swallowed again. This time the chewed cud does not go back to rumen.

Cows have a large sac-like structure called **caecum** between the food pipe (oesophagus) and the small intestine. The cellulose of the food is digested here by the action of certain bacteria.

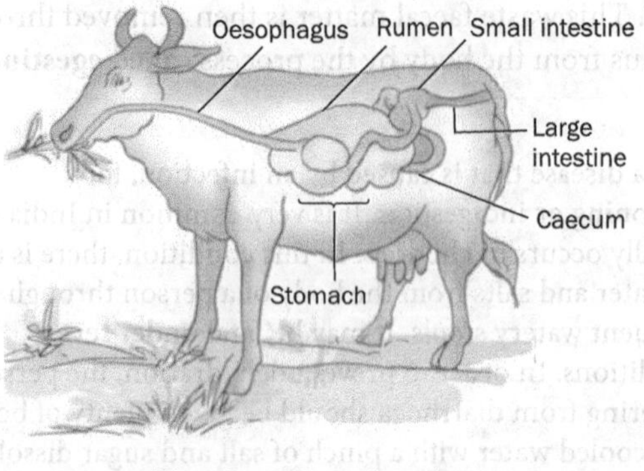

Digestive system of ruminant

This is also seen in some animals like horses, rabbits, etc. The cellulose digesting bacteria are not present in the body of human being, therefore human beings and other carnivores cannot digest cellulose present in plant food items.

SCIENCE INSIGHT Ruminants have a four-chambered stomach consisting of rumen, reticulum, omasum and abomasum designed for digesting cellulose.

2.5 Feeding and Digestion in *Amoeba*

The *Amoeba* is a microscopic single-celled organism, which is found in pond water. It has a cell membrane, a rounded dense nucleus and many small bubble-like vacuoles in its cytoplasm.

Its shape is not fixed, i.e. it constantly changes its shape and position. The body of *Amoeba* has finger-like projections called **pseudopodia** or **false feet.** It captures food and helps in locomotion of *Amoeba.*

Amoeba feeds on microscopic organisms present in pond water. When *Amoeba* senses its food, it pushes out pseudopodia around the food particle and engulfs it.

The two pseudopodia join around the food particle and trap the food particle forming a vacuole around food, called as **food vacuole.**

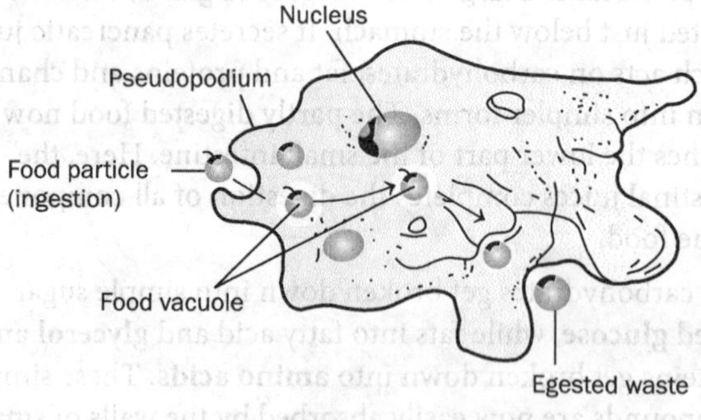

Amoeba

Digestive juices present inside the vacuole, acts on the food and break it into simpler substances.

This digested food is then absorbed and is used for growth, maintenance and multiplication of *Amoeba.* The undigested food residue is expelled outside by the vacuole. The basic process of digestion of food and release of energy is same in all animals.

Try These 2.4

1. **What cannot be digested by humans and other carnivores?**
2. **Which types of vacuoles are present in *Amoeba*?**
3. **Name a pond organism that uses false feet for capturing food.**

Science Glossary

Absorption The uptake of simple substances produced during digestion.

Amino acid The building blocks of proteins.

Amoeba It is a microscopic single-celled organism found in pond water.

Assimilation In this the absorbed simple substances are used to build complex substances required by the body.

Bile It is a juice secreted by liver that helps in the digestion of fats.

Buccal cavity It consists of salivary glands, teeth and tongue.

Canines These are present on the sides of incisors. They have sharp pointed edges for tearing the food.

Cellulose It is a type of carbohydrate, which cannot be digested by humans.

Digestion In this process, complex substances are broken down into smaller, simpler substances.

Egestion Removal of faecal matter through the anus.

Fatty acid During complete digestion of food, fats are broken down into fatty acids and glycerol.

Food vacuole It is a membrane-bound sac that digests food particles taken in by a cell, e.g. *Amoeba*.

Gall bladder It is a sac-like structure, which stores bile juice secreted by the liver.

Glycerol Fats are broken into fatty acids and glycerol during digestion.

Incisors These are the front teeth present in the centre. They have flat and sharp edges, for cutting and biting food.

Ingestion It is the process of taking food into the body.

Liver It is the largest gland in the body. It is of reddish brown colour and situated in the upper part of the abdomen on the right side.

Milk teeth These are the first set of teeth that grows during infancy and fall off at the age between 6 to 8 years.

Molar These are present behind the premolars. They have larger, flat surfaces for chewing the food.

Oesophagus It is a tube-like structure, which connects the mouth to the stomach.

Permanent teeth These are the second set of teeth that replace milk teeth.

Pancreas It is a large cream coloured gland located just below the stomach. It secretes pancreatic juice, which helps in digestion.

Premolar These are present at the back of the mouth and have large, flat surfaces for chewing the food.

Pseudopodia These are finger-like projections in *Amoeba* which help in movement and capturing of food. They are also known as false feet.

Rumen It is a part of stomach in animals like cows that eat grass. Food is partially digested here and is called cud. It contains cellulose digesting enzymes.

Ruminants These are herbivorous animals that eat grass.

Rumination It is the process of chewing cud that occurs in the mouth of ruminants.

Saliva It is secreted by salivary glands. It breaks down the starch into sugars.

Salivary glands These glands secrete saliva, which aids in digestion of food.

Villi These are the finger-like outgrowths present on the inner walls of small intestine. They increase the surface area for absorption of food.

Let's Investigate

ACTIVITY 1 (Page 13)

Aim To show the presence of different types of teeth and their arrangement in buccal cavity.

Materials Required Mirror, apple/bread.

Procedure

1. Wash your hands properly.
2. Look into the mirror and count your teeth.
3. Use your index finger to feel the shape of each teeth.
4. Take a piece of apple or bread and eat it.
5. Observe, which teeth you use for biting and cutting and which one for piercing and tearing.

Observation We observe four different types of teeth present in the buccal cavity.

The front four teeth of each jaw are blunt, these are called **incisors**. Next to it, one sharp teeth is present at each side of each jaw. These are called **canines**.

Just behind the canines there are two teeth on each side of both the jaws (8 teeth) called **premolars**, these have large flat surface.

Behind these, very large teeth are present at the back of our mouth called **molars**. These are three in numbers at each side of both the jaws, i.e. 6 in both the jaws.

The observations of different types of teeth for an adult are as follows

Types of teeth	Number of teeth		Total teeth
	Lower jaw	Upper jaw	
Cutting and biting teeth	4 Incisors	4 Incisors	8
Piercing and tearing teeth	2 Canines	2 Canines	4
Chewing and grinding teeth	4 + 6 (Premolars + Molars)	4 + 6 (Premolars + Molars)	20
		Total	32 teeth

Conclusion From this activity it can be concluded that there are four different kinds of teeth and each type performs different functions, while chewing the food.

Viva Questions

1. Name the types of teeth present in humans.
2. How many incisor teeth are present in lower jaw?

ACTIVITY 2 (Page 14)

Aim To observe the action of saliva on food.

Materials Required Two test tubes, boiled rice, dropper, iodine solution, water.

Procedure

1. Take two test tubes. Label them '*A*' and '*B*'.
2. Put some boiled rice in test tube '*A*'.
3. Chew one teaspoonful of boiled rice for 3-5 minutes. Put these chewed rice in test tube '*B*'.
4. Add 3-4 mL of water in both the test tubes.
5. Now pour 2-3 drops of iodine solution in each test tube and observe.

Observation We will observe a change in colour in the test tube '*A*', but not in test tube '*B*'.

The solution in test tube '*A*' turns into blue-black colour due to the presence of starch in boiled rice.

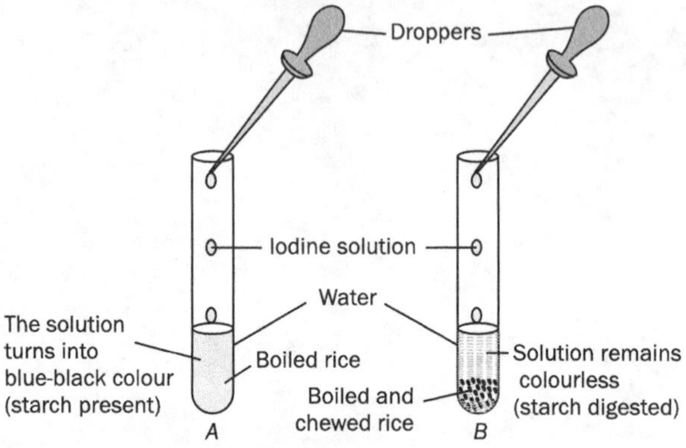

Effect of saliva on starch

The test tube 'B' contains saliva, which breaks down starch into simple sugars. Therefore, it does not show any change in colour.

Conclusion From this activity it can be concluded that the digestive enzymes present in saliva helps in the digestion of starch present in food.

Viva Questions

1. Why does the test tube '*B*' not show any change in colour?
2. Do we get the same observations if we take bread instead of boiled rice?

ACTIVITY 3 (Page 15)

Aim To observe different regions of taste buds on tongue.

Materials Required, Sugar, salt, lemon, crushed neem leaf/bittergourd, toothpicks, water.

Procedure

1. Prepare a separate sample each of
   (i) Sugar solution
   (ii) Common salt solution
   (iii) Lemon juice
   (iv) Juice of crushed neem leaf or bittergourd.
2. Blindfold your friend and ask him/her to take out the tongue and keep it in straight and flat position.
3. Now clean a toothpick and put these solutions/samples one by one on different areas of the tongue. Use a new toothpick for each sample.
4. Ask your friend, which areas of the tongue could detect the sweet, salty, sour and bitter substances.

Observation It is observed that front end of the tongue, i.e. tip of the tongue detects sweet taste. Behind it, he/she detects salty solution.
The side portions of the tongue have taste buds for sour solution and back of the tongue detects bitter taste.

Conclusion This activity shows that different parts of the tongue are sensitive to different tastes. Each part is not sensitive to all of the four different types of taste.

Viva Questions

1. Which region of the tongue detects sweet taste?
2. Which part of the tongue detects bitter taste?

Mind Map

NUTRITION IN ANIMALS

Different Ways of Taking Food
- Bees and hummingbirds suck the nectar.
- Infants of human feed on mother's milk.
- Snakes swallow the animals.

Digestion in *Amoeba*
- Microscopic, single celled organism.
- Finger-like projections called pseudopodia captures food.
- Food trapped in food vacuole.
- Digestive juice present in food vacuole acts on the food.

Digestion in Grass Eating Animals
- Food partially digested in rumen.
- Cud return to mouth and chewed it again (process called rumination).
- Rumen has cellulose digesting bacteria.
- Chewed cud goes into the caecum and small intestine for bacterial digestion.

Digestion
Breakdown of complex components of food into simpler substances.

Digestion in Humans

Teeth
Teeth mechnically break the food into small pieces. Following four types of teeth are found in each jaw
- **Incisors** (4) help in biting and cutting of food.
- **Canines** (2) help in piercing and tearing of food.
- **Premolars** (4) help in grinding and chewing of food.
- **Molars** (6) help in grinding of food.

Tooth Decay
Process of rotting of tooth and formation of cavity.
It can be prevented by
- Rinse and clean teeth often after every meal.
- Brush teeth, twice a day.

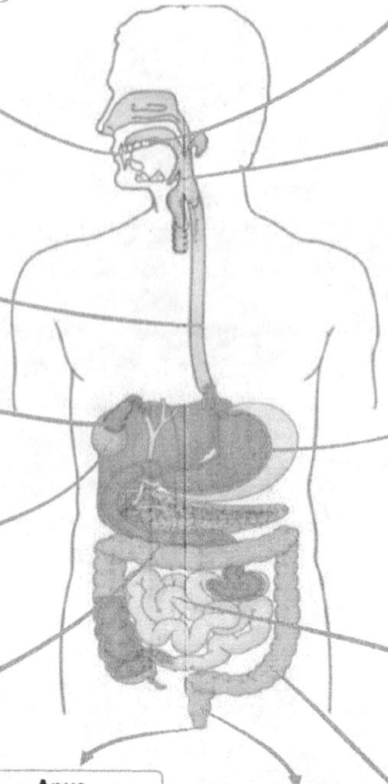

Mouth and Buccal Cavity
- Process of ingestion of food takes place in the mouth.
- It consists of teeth, salivary gland and tongue.

Tongue
- Fleshy muscular organ.
- Mixes saliva with food.
- Has taste buds.

Salivary Gland
They secrete saliva which breaks down starch into sugars.

Oesophagus /Food pipe
- Tube-like structure, which connects mouth to the stomach.
- Food is moved down by movement of the wall of food pipe.

Stomach
- Thick walled bag -like structure and shape like flattened J.
- Inner lining secretes mucus, HCl and digestive juices.
- Mucus protects stomach lining from HCl action.
- HCl kills bacteria entering with food and makes acidic medium in stomach for digestive juices.
- Digestive juice breaks proteins into simpler substances.

Liver
- Largest gland secretes bile juice which is stored in gall bladder.
- Bile helps in the digestion of fat.

Gall bladder

Pancreas
- Large and cream colour gland.
- Pancreatic juice acts on carbohydrate, fats and proteins and change them into simpler forms.

Small intestine
- Highly coiled, 7.5 meter long.
- Receives secretions from liver and pancreas.
- Complete digestion of food takes place here.
- Finger-like villi in the inner wall helps in absorption.

Anus
Waste from digestion leaves the body through it.

Rectum
Collect waste and hold until its time to release it.

Large intestine
- 1.5 meter in length.
- Absorbs water and salts.
- Recurring waste passes into rectum then anus for egestion.

NCERT FOLDER

Complete Explanations of all NCERT's Questions

Intext Questions

Q.1 You have studied in previous class that food consists of many components. Try to recall and list them. Page 11

Ans. 1. Carbohydrates, 2. Proteins, 3. Fat, 4. Vitamins, 5. Minerals, 6. Roughage

Q.2 What happens to the food inside the body?

Ans. Refer to text on page no. 18. Page 12

Q.3 How many kinds of teeth can you find in your mouth?

Ans. We can find four types of teeth in our mouth. Page 13

Q.4 Which type of teeth do you use for biting and cutting and which one for piercing and tearing? Page 13

Ans. For biting and cutting, we use incisors and for piercing and tearing we use canines.

Q.5 Which type of teeth are used for chewing and grinding? Page 13

Ans. For chewing and grinding we use premolars and molars.

Q.6 Do you know the action of saliva on food?

Ans. Refer to text on page no. 19. Page 14

Q.7 Paheli wants to know how food moves in the opposite direction during vomiting? Page 15

Ans. The intense pressure is formed in the stomach when the food is not accepted by the stomach. The content in the stomach is then pushed back. This returned content is expelled out from the mouth in the form of vomiting.

Q.8 What is the role of villi in the intestine? Page 17

Ans. Refer to text on page no. 21.

Q.9 Paheli wants to know why ruminants cannot chew food properly at the time they take it in? Page 18

Ans. Refer to text on page no. 22.

Q.10 Boojho wants to know why we cannot digest cellulose like the cattle do?

Ans. Refer to text on page no. 22. Page 18

Exercise

Q.1 Fill in the blanks.

(a) The main steps of nutrition in humans are ...., ..., ..., ... and ....

(b) The largest gland in the human body is ....

(c) The stomach releases hydrochloric acid and .... juices, which act on food.

(d) The inner wall of the small intestine has many finger-like outgrowths called ....

(e) *Amoeba* digests its food in the ....

Ans. (a) ingestion, digestion, absorption, assimilation and egestion.

(b) liver (c) digestive

(d) villi (e) food vacuole

Q.2 Mark 'T' if the statement is True and 'F' if it is False.

(a) Digestion of starch starts in the stomach.

(b) The tongue helps in mixing food with saliva.

(c) The gall bladder temporarily stores bile.

(d) The ruminants bring back swallowed grass into their mouth and chew it for some time.

Ans. (a) F, digestion of starch starts in the mouth.

(b) T (c) T (d) T

Q.3 Tick (✓) mark the correct answer in each of the following.

(a) Fat is completely digested in the

(i) stomach (ii) mouth

(iii) small intestine (iv) large intestine

(b) Water from the undigested food is absorbed mainly in the

(i) stomach (ii) foodpipe

(iii) small intestine (iv) large intestine

Ans. (a) (iii) **Small intestine** is the site for complete digestion of fats by the action of bile juice.

(b) (iv) **Large intestine** absorbs the water from undigested food.

Q.4 Match the items of Column I with those given in Column II.

Column I (Food components)	Column II (Products of digestion)
A. Carbohydrates	1. Fatty acid and glycerol
B. Proteins	2. Sugar
C. Fats	3. Amino acids

Ans. A–2, B–3, C–1.

Q.5 What are villi? What is their location and function?

Ans. Villi are the finger-like projections in the inner walls of the small intestine. They increase the surface area for absorption of digested food.

Q.6 Where is the bile produced? Which component of the food does it help to digest?

Ans. Bile juice is produced by the liver and stored in gall bladder. It helps in digestion of fats present in food.

Q.7 Name the type of carbohydrate that can be digested by ruminants, but not by humans. Give the reason also.

Ans. Refer to text on page no. 21 and 22.

Q.8 Why do we get instant energy from glucose?

Ans. Glucose is a simple sugar or carbohydrate, which is easily absorbed by the blood. It is then broken down in the presence of oxygen into CO_2 and H_2O and releases instant energy.

Q.9 Which part of the digestive canal is involved in

(a) absorption of food ....
(b) chewing of food ....
(c) killing of bacteria ....
(d) complete digestion of food ....
(e) formation of faeces ....

Ans. Parts of digestive canal that are involved in the following processes are

(a) small intestine
(b) buccal cavity
(c) stomach
(d) small intestine
(e) large intestine

Q.10 Write one similarity and one difference between nutrition in *Amoeba* and human beings.

Ans. Both *Amoeba* and humans require energy for the growth and maintenance of their bodies. This energy is derived from the food they eat. The food is in a complex form and is therefore broken down into simple forms by the process of digestion. Both these organisms are heterotrophs, i.e. they derive their food from other plants or animals.

Difference between nutrition in *Amoeba* and human beings are as follows

Digestion in *Amoeba*	Digestion in human
Mouth and digestive system are absent in *Amoeba*.	Humans have a mouth and a complex digestive system.
Digestive juices are secreted in the food vacuole.	Digestive juices are secreted in the buccal cavity, stomach and small intestine.
All the food components are digested in the food vacuole.	Digestion of carbohydrates, proteins and fats occur in separate regions.

Q.11 Match the items of Column I with suitable items in Column II.

	Column I		Column II
A.	Salivary gland	1.	Bile juice secretion
B.	Stomach	2.	Storage of undigested food
C.	Liver	3.	Saliva secretion
D.	Rectum	4.	Acid release
E.	Small intestine	5.	Digestion is completed
F.	Large intestine	6.	Absorption of water
		7.	Release of faeces

Ans. A–3, B–4, C–1, D–2, E–5, F–6

Q.12 Label the given figure of the digestive system.

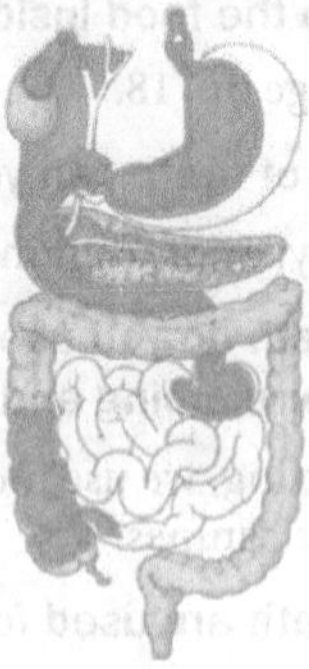

Ans. The digestive system is composed of following parts

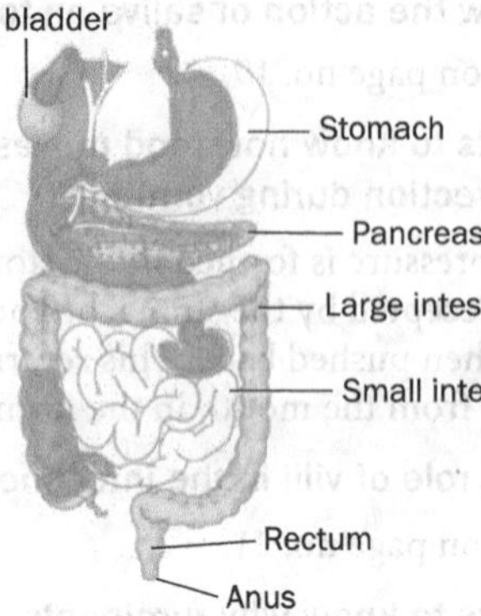

Q.13 Can we survive only on raw, leafy vegetables/grass? Discuss.

Ans. No, we cannot survive only on raw, leafy vegetables/grass. This is due to the absence of cellulose degrading/digesting enzymes. Raw, leafy vegetables and grasses, etc. contain cellulose, which is digested in ruminants by the action of microorganism, but humans do not possess these microorganisms. Therefore, we will not be able to digest cellulose and meet our energy requirements.

REVIEW EXERCISE

Including Competency Based Questions

Part I

Multiple Choice Questions

1. Where does digestion of food start in the human digestive system? **Competency Based Que.**

(a) Mouth (b) Oesophagus
(c) Stomach (d) Small intestine

2. Which of the following pair of teeth differ in structure, but are similar in function? **NCERT Exemplar**

(a) Canines and incisors
(b) Molars and premolars
(c) Incisors and molars
(d) Premolars and canines

3. The enzymes present in the saliva convert

(a) fats into fatty acids and glycerol
(b) starch into simple sugars
(c) proteins into amino acids
(d) complex sugars into simple sugars

4. The tip or front of tongue taste

(a) sour (b) bitter (c) sweet (d) All of these

5. If, by chance food particles enter the windpipe, we feel **NCERT Exemplar**

(a) hiccups and cough
(b) yawning
(c) sleep
(d) None of the above

6. The swallowed food moves downwards in the alimentary canal because of

(a) force provided by the muscular tongue
(b) the flow of water taken with the food
(c) gravitational pull
(d) the contraction of muscles in the wall of foodpipe

7. The acid present in the stomach

(a) kills the harmful bacteria that may enter along with the food
(b) protects the stomach lining from harmful substances
(c) digests starch into simple sugars
(d) makes the medium alkaline

8. What are proteins broken down into? **Competency Based Que.**

(a) Glucose (b) Glycerol
(c) Fatty acids (d) Amino acids

9. Read the following statements with reference to the villi of small intestine.

(i) They have very thin walls.
(ii) They have a network of thin and small blood vessels close to the surface.
(iii) They have small pores through which food can easily pass.
(iv) They are finger-like projections.

Identify those statements which enable the villi to absorb digested food.

(a) (i), (ii) and (iv) (b) (ii), (iii) and (iv)
(c) (iii) and (iv) (d) (i) and (iv)

10. The greatest amount of digestion of food takes place in **CBSE Question Bank**

(a) large intestine (b) small intestine
(c) mouth (d) stomach

11. Read carefully the terms given below. Which of the following set is the correct combination of organs that do not carry out any digestive functions? **NCERT Exemplar**

(a) Oesophagus, Large intestine, Rectum
(b) Buccal cavity, Oesophagus, Rectum
(c) Buccal cavity, Oesophagus, Large intestine
(d) Small intestine, Large intestine, Rectum

12. A baby passed watery stool for two days. The doctor suggested oral rehydration solution (ORS) for the baby. How would the ORS help the baby ? **Competency Based Que.**

(a) It would help in digesting food
(b) It would kill the bacteria that caused the infection
(c) It would prevent water from moving out of the body
(d) It would replace the fluids and minerals lost from the body

13. Cud is the name given to the food of ruminants which is

(a) swallowed and undigested
(b) swallowed and partially digested
(c) properly chewed and partially digested
(d) properly chewed and completely digested

14. Choose the correct order of terms that describes the process of nutrition in ruminants **NCERT Exemplar**

(a) Swallowing → Partial digestion → Chewing of cud → Complete digestion
(b) Chewing of cud → Swallowing → Partial digestion → Complete digestion

(c) Chewing of cud → Swallowing → Mixing with digestive juices → Digestion
(d) Swallowing → Chewing and mixing → Partial digestion → Complete digestion

15. Cellulose rich food substances are good sources of roughage in human beings because
(a) human beings do not have cellulose digesting enzymes
(b) cellulose gets absorbed in the human blood and converts into fibres
(c) the cellulose digesting bacteria convert cellulose into fibres
(d) cellulose breaks down into smaller components which are egested as roughage

16. The finger-like outgrowths of *Amoeba* helps to ingest food. However, the finger-like outgrowths of human intestine helps to NCERT Exemplar
(a) digest the fatty food substances
(b) make the food soluble
(c) absorb the digested food
(d) absorb the undigested food

17. The false feet of *Amoeba* are used for
(a) movement only
(b) capture of food only
(c) capture of food and movement
(d) exchange of gases only

18. An *Amoeba* ingests a food particle.
Which of these shows the correct sequence of nutrition in the *Amoeba*? Competency Based Que.
(a) Egestion → Digestion → Assimilation → Absorption
(b) Digestion → Absorption → Assimilation → Egestion
(c) Digestion → Assimilation → Absorption → Egestion
(d) Egestion → Digestion → Assimilation → Absorption

19. Given below from (i) to (iv) are some food items. Competency Based Que.
(i) Boiled and mashed potato
(ii) Glucose solution
(iii) A slice of bread
(iv) Mustard oil
Which of the above will give blue-black colour when tested with iodine ?
(a) (i) and (ii) (b) (i) and (iii)
(c) (ii) and (iii) (d) (iii) and (iv)

Answers

1. (a)	2. (b)	3. (b)	4. (c)	5. (a)
6. (d)	7. (a)	8. (d)	9. (a)	10. (b)
11. (a)	12. (d)	13. (b)	14. (a)	15. (a)
16. (c)	17. (c)	18. (b)	19. (b)	

Fill in the Blanks

1. The alimentary canal stretches from ...... to ....
2. Digestion of food starts in .... and gets completed in ....
3. .... is the process of taking food inside the body.
4. Four kinds of teeth present in human are .... , ... ,........... and ....

Answers

1. mouth, anus
2. buccal cavity, small intestine
3. Ingestion
4. incisors, canines, premolar, molar

True/False

1. All heterotrophs have a similar basic process of nutrition. NCERT Exemplar
2. Tongue is attached to the root of the mouth cavity at the back.
3. Mucus protects the stomach lining from damage.
4. The large intestine is longer and wider than the small intestine of the human alimentary canal.
5. Ruminant can digest cellulose (carbohydrate).

Answers

1. True
2. False, tongue is attached to the floor of the mouth cavity at the back.
3. True
4. False, the large intestine is shorter and wider than the small intestine of the human alimentary canal.
5. True

Match the Columns

1. Match the Column I with Column II.

Column I	Column II
A. Rectum	1. Mucus
B. Gall bladder	2. Villi
C. Stomach	3. Taste buds
D. Tongue	4. Faeces
E. Small intestine	5. Bile juice

2. Match the Column I with Column II.

Column I (Animals)	Column II (Mode of feeding)
A. Butterfly	1. Bitting and chewing
B. Ant	2. Swallowing
C. Mosquito	3. Siphoning
D. Snake	4. Sucking

Answers

1. A-4, B-5, C-1, D-3, E-2
2. A-3, B-1, C-4, D-2

Assertion-Reason Questions

The following questions consist of two statements. Assertion (A) and Reason (R). Answer the following questions by selecting the appropriate option given below.

(a) Both A and R are true and R is the correct explanation of A
(b) Both A and R are true, but R is not the correct explanation of A
(c) A is true, but R is false
(d) A is false, but R is true

1. Assertion (A) Bread taste sour when chewed for some time.
Reason (R) Bread contains starch.

2. Assertion (A) The inner lining of stomach is protected from the effect of hydrochloric acid.
Reason (R) The inner lining of the stomach secrete mucus.

3. Assertion (A) Pancreas secrete bile juice.
Reason (R) Liver is the largest gland in our body.

4. Assertion (A) Human beings cannot digest cellulose.
Reason (R) Humans do not have cellulose digesting bacteria.

5. Assertion (A) Boiled and chewed rice does not give blue-black colour with iodine solution.
Reason (R) Boiled and chewed rice contains starch.

Answers

1. (d) A is false, but R is true. A can be corrected as Bread tastes sweet when chewed for some time.
2. (a) Both A and R are true and R is the correct explanation of A.
3. (d) A is false, but R is true. A can be corrected as Liver secretes bile juice.
4. (a) Both A and R are true and R is the correct explanation of A.
5. (c) A is true, but R is false. R can be corrected as Boiled and chewed rice does not give blue-black colour with iodine solution because they do not contain starch. Saliva converts starch into glucose after chewing boiled rice for some time.

Case Based Questions

1. The picture shows arrangement of teeth in the upper jaw of an animal. **Competency Based Que.**

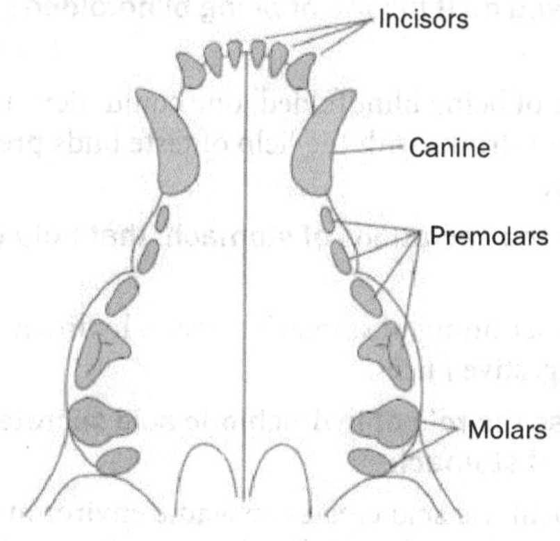

(i) Which animal has a similar teeth arrangement ?
(a) Deer (b) Dog
(c) Rabbit (d) Buffalo

(ii) Which set of teeth is used for biting into food ?
(a) Incisors (b) Canines
(c) Premolars (d) Molars

2. Which of these is part of the digestive system? Circle 'Yes' or 'No' for each raw.

	Is this a part of the digestive system?	Yes or No
(i)	Teeth	Yes/No
(ii)	Liver	Yes/No
(iii)	Rectum	Yes/No

Competency Based Que.

Answers

1. (i) (b) Dog, (ii) (a) Incisors
2. (i) Yes, (ii) Yes, (iii) Yes

Part II

Very Short Answer Type Questions

1. Define digestion.

Ans. It is defined as the process of breakdown of complex substances of food into simpler ones.

2. Describe alimentary canal briefly.

Ans. Alimentary canal is the tube running from mouth to anus in animals including humans. Here, digestion and absorption of food take place.

3. You were blindfolded and asked to identify the drinks provided in two different glasses. You could identify drink *A* as lime juice and *B* as bitter gourd juice. How could you do it inspite of being blindfolded? NCERT Exemplar

Ans. Inspite of being blindfolded, one could identify two different drinks with the help of taste buds present in the tongue.

4. Name the secretions of stomach, that help to digest food.

Ans. The inner lining of stomach secretes hydrochloric acid and digestive juices.

5. Discuss the role of hydrochloric acid secreted by inner lining of stomach.

Ans. Hydrochloric acid creates an acidic environment, which facilitates the action of the digestive enzymes in the stomach. It also kills many bacteria that enter along with the food.

6. Name the simple forms of carbohydrates, fats and proteins.

Ans. The simple forms of carbohydrates are sugars, of fats are fatty acids and glycerol, and of proteins are amino acids.

7. What is assimilation ?

Ans. The process by which absorbed food is taken by body cells and is used for energy, growth and repair is called assimilation.

8. Choose the odd one out from each group and given reasons. NCERT Exemplar

(i) Liver, salivary gland, starch, gall bladder
(ii) Stomach, liver, pancreas, salivary gland
(iii) Tongue, absorption, taste, swallow
(iv) Oesophagus, small intestine, large intestine, rectum

Ans. (i) Starch, as others are glands.
(ii) Stomach, as others are digestive glands.
(iii) Absorption, as others are parts and functions of the mouth.
(iv) Small intestine, as no juices are released by other parts/no digestion occurs in other parts.

9. Name the parts of the alimentary canal where NCERT Exemplar

(a) water gets absorbed from undigested food
(b) digested food gets absorbed
(c) taste of the food is perceived
(d) bile juice is produced

Ans. (a) large intestine (b) small intestine
(c) tongue (d) liver

10. What is rumination?

Ans. It is the process occurring in ruminants, e.g. cows and buffaloes. In this the animals bring back the food, which was already consumed, into the mouth and chew it again.

Short Answer Type Questions

1. Mention the different steps of nutrition in animals.

Ans. Refer to text on page no. 17 and 18.

2. Following statements describe the five steps in animal nutrition. Read each statement and give one word for each statement. Write the terms that describe each process.

(i) Transportation of absorbed food to different parts of body and their utilisation.
(ii) Breaking of complex food substances into simpler and soluble substances.
(iii) Removal of undigested and unabsorbed solid residues of food from the body.
(iv) Taking food into the body.
(v) Transport of digested and soluble food from the intestine to blood vessels. Competency Based Que.

Ans. (i) Assimilation (ii) Digestion (iii) Egestion
(iv) Ingestion (v) Absorption

3. Write the difference between milk teeth and permanent teeth.

Ans. The difference between milk teeth and permanent teeth are as follows

Milk teeth	Permanent teeth
They grow during infancy, i.e. when one is small baby.	They grow at the age of 6-8 years.
They are also called as temporary teeth because these are lost at the age of 6-8 years.	They do not fall until old age or due to some dental disease.
They can be replaced by permanent teeth.	If these teeth fall down, no new teeth arise on their place.

4. List the preventive measures that one should adopt for avoiding tooth decay.

Ans. Refer to text on page no. 19.

5. Draw the labelled diagram of tongue showing different regions for taste buds.

Ans. Refer to figure on page no. 19.

6. The swallowed food moves downwards in the alimentary canal. Explain.

Ans. The swallowed food moves downwards in the alimentary canal because of the alternate relaxation one contraction movement of muscles in the walls of the foodpipe.

7. Boojho and Paheli were eating their food hurriedly so that they could go out and play during the recess. Suddenly, Boojho started coughing violently. Think of the reasons, why he was coughing and discuss with your friends? **NCERT Exemplar**

Ans. Sometimes, when we eat hurriedly, talk or laugh, while eating, the flap-like valve (called epiglottis) which closes the passage of windpipe remains open. Therefore, the food may enter into the windpipe. Coughing helps to clear the passage and returns the food particle back to the foodpipe.

8. '*A*' got her gall bladder removed surgically as she was diagnosed with stones in her gall bladder. After the surgery, she faced problems in digestion of certain food items, when consumed in bulk. Can you tell which kind of food items would they be and why?

Ans. After surgical removal of gall bladder, '*A*' would face problems in digestion of fat and fatty substances when consumed in bulk. This is because the bile juice stored in the gall bladder helps in the digestion of fats.

9. Ruminants such as cows and buffaloes swallow their food hurriedly and then sit restfully and chew their food. Give reason.

Ans. Ruminants such as cows and buffaloes swallow their food hurriedly and store it in a part of the stomach called rumen. The cellulose of the food is digested here by the action of certain bacteria, which are not present in humans. Later their partially digested food is returned to the buccal cavity of the animals in small lumps and animals chew it to complete the process of digestion. This process is called rumination.

10. Boojho took some grains of boiled rice in test tube '*A*' and Paheli took boiled and chewed rice in test tube '*B*. Both of them poured 1-2 drops of iodine solution into the test tube and observed the colour change. What colour change would they have observed? Give reasons for your answer. **NCERT Exemplar**

Ans. In test tube *A*, blue-black colour appeared because of presence of starch.

In test tube *B*, colour will not change because of digestion of starch into sugars by the action of saliva in our mouth.

Long Answer Type Questions

1. Label the given figure as directed below in *A* to *D* and give the name of each type of teeth. **NCERT Exemplar**

(a) The cutting and biting teeth as *A*

(b) The piercing and tearing teeth as *B*

(c) The grinding and chewing teeth as *C*

(d) The grinding teeth present only in adult as *D*

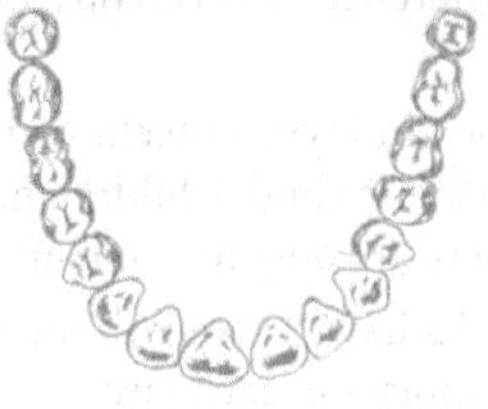

Ans.

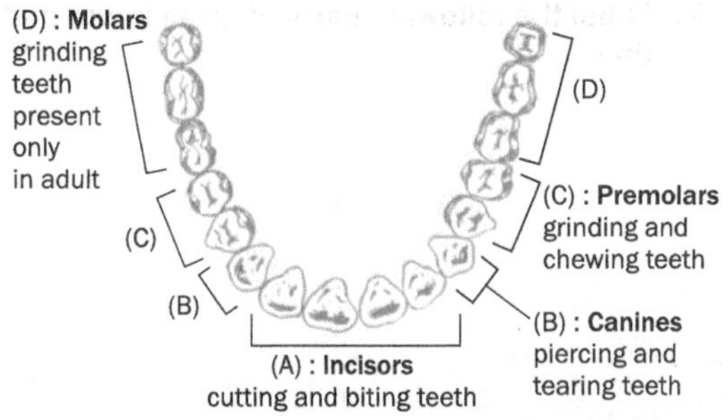

5. Open your mouth, look into a mirror and try to count the different types of teeth in your mouth. Compare them with figure 2.3 on page 13 of your NCERT textbook. Record your observations in the table below **NCERT Exemplar**

	Types of teeth	Numbers of teeth
	In my mouth	In the figure
Incisors		
Canines		
Premolars		
Molars		

(i) Did you observe any difference in the number of teeth? If yes, could you identify which type of teeth showed the difference?

(ii) Compare the number and type of teeth in an adult (say your parents or cousins who have reached the age of 25-30 or more). Note your observation.

Ans.

Types of teeth	Numbers of teeth	
	In my mouth	In the figure
Incisors	4	4
Canines	2	2
Premolars	4	4
Molars	4	6

(i) Yes, the difference has been observed in the number of molars.

(ii) The number and type of teeth varies in an adult as compared to the child. Children have 28 teeth in their mouth.There are only four molars in each jaw.

While, adults have 32 teeth in their mouth, which means six molars in each jaw.

2. Label the following parts of given figure and name them.

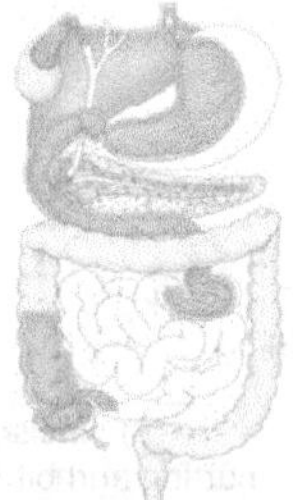

(a) The largest gland in our body.
(b) The organ where protein digestion starts.
(c) The organ that releases digestive juice into the small intestine.
(d) The organ where bile juice gets stored. **NCERT Exemplar**

Ans.

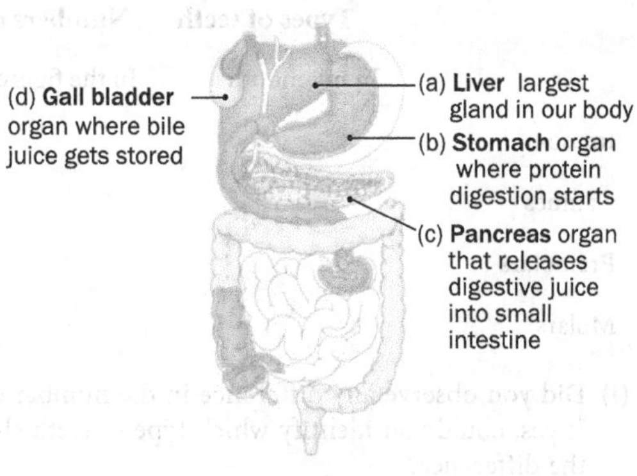

3. Define oral rehydration solution and when is it given to the patient? How can you prepare ORS at home?

Ans. Oral rehydration solution is the solution of sugar and salt in a particular ratio in the clean water. When a person passes out watery stools frequently, the disease is called **diarrhoea**. In this condition there is a loss of water and salt from the body of a person.

This is called **dehydration**, which may be fatal if not cured at proper time. In order to prevent dehydration, the person or patient should be given ORS. It makes up the loss of water and salts in the body and sugar provides energy which helps in the recovery of disease. It should be given to a patient suffering from diarrhoea at a regular interval.

At home the ORS can be prepared by dissolving a teaspoonful of sugar and pinch of salt in a glass of clean water. The water used for preparing ORS should be first boiled and then cooled so that all the microorganisms or harmful bacteria may be killed.

4. Explain how the digestion of cellulose occurs in grass eating animals?

Ans. Refer to text on page no. 21 and 22.

Case Based Questions

1. All bacteria present in the digestive system are not harmful. Explain how bacteria present in the digestive system of cows help in the digestion of food?

2. *Amoeba* uses finger-like projections to capture food particles. **Competency Based Que.**

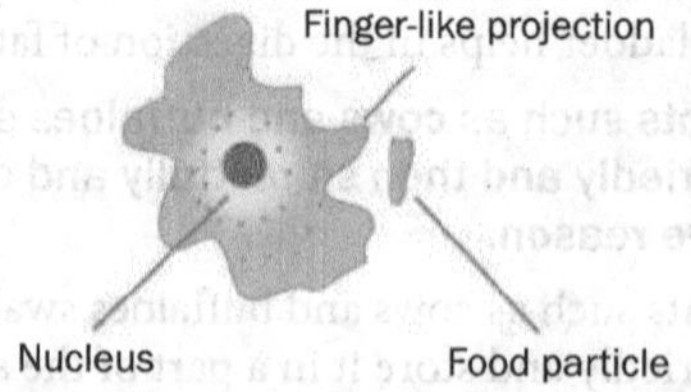

(i) Which of these is the next step of capturing food ?

(a)  (b) 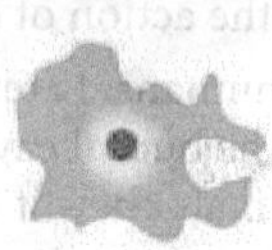

(c)  (d) 

(ii) What are the finger-like projections called ?

3. Read the following passage carefully and answer the questions that follow it.

Bile juice is stored in a sac called, gall bladder, located near its organ of secretion, liver. The gall bladder releases the bile juice into the small intestine, whenever food reaches there.

Though bile juice is devoid of any digestive enzymes, it is required for the digestion of fats. The fats cannot be digested easily because they are insoluble in water and are present as large globules.

Bile juice breaks down big fat droplets into smaller droplets. These are then easily digested by the enzymes released from the pancreas.

(i) Which organ secretes the bile juice?

(ii) Why is digestion of fats difficult as compared to that of other nutrients?

(iii) How does bile juice helps in the digestion of fat?

(iv) Where is the digestion of fat completed?

(v) Does bile juice digest fat completely?

NCERT Exemplar

Ans. 1. Bacteria present in the digestive system of cows (grass-eating animals) helps in the digestion of cellulose.

2. (i) (c)

(ii) The finger-like projections are called pseudopodia.

3. (i) Bile juice is secreted by liver.

(ii) Digestion of fats is difficult as compared to that of other nutrients because of insolubility of fat in water.

(iii) Bile juice helps in digestion of fat by breaking down big fat droplets into smaller droplet.

(iv) Digestion of fat is completed in small intestine.

(v) No, fat is not completely digested by bile juice.

Skill Based Questions as per NEP 2020

1. A person met with an accident while driving. After examination, the doctor told him that since he got a fracture in the wrist, operation would be required. After the operation, the patient was put on a glucose drip and was not given food for a few hours.

(i) Why was the patient not given food directly?

(ii) How does the glucose help the patient recover?

Thinking skill

2. Take a chart paper and divide it into two sections longitudinally. In one section explain the process of digestion in humans and in other the process of digestion in cows. Compare both with the help of diagram and/or flowchart, and write down the differences you found in both the cases. **Thinking skill**

3. Little Rishi (a student of class VI) was watching his favourite cartoon serial on television, while eating lunch. Suddenly he started getting hiccups. His elder brother Shubham, who was sitting near by him, gave him a glass of water and suggested not to eat too fast in a hurry. Little Rishi got confused as he had heard that 'hichki' comes when someone remembers. He asked his father. His father smiled and explained him that it is only a myth. He also explained him the proper scientific reason behind it.

(i) What is hiccup?

(ii) Why do we get hiccup? **Experimental skill**

4. Jaya returned from school and found that her grandmother was scolding their maid Rani, as she did not come the day before. The maid told that her son was passing watery stools frequently that's why she did not come. Jaya's mother who was listening the discussion came to them and told Rani not to come for coming 3-4 days. She also suggested to give her son a solution of sugar and salt in (boiled and cooled) water, many times a day for fast recovery. Jaya was surprised. She rushed to her mother and asked the scientific reason for it. Her mother smiled and explained her the importance of this solution.

(i) Name the term used to describe the condition in which a person passes out watery stools.

(ii) Name the solution of sugar and salt in water. Why is it given to a person suffering from this condition?

Experimental skill

ASSESSMENT EXERCISE

Part I

Multiple Choice Questions

1. Digestion of starch starts in
(a) stomach (b) mouth
(c) small intestine (d) large intestine

2. The long muscular tube that starts from buccal cavity to the stomach is called
(a) oesophagus (b) small intestine
(c) large intestine (d) rectum

3. Which of the following organ does not secrete digestive juice?
(a) Liver (b) Pancreas (c) Stomach (d) Oesophagus

4. Which organ stores bile juice?
(a) Gall bladder (b) Liver
(c) Stomach (d) Pancreas

5. The finger-like projections present on the inner lining of small intestine are known as
(a) villi (b) stomach (c) rumen (d) diarrhoea

Fill in the Blanks

6. .... teeth replaces the milk teeth.

7. .... is the long tube-like structure, which constitutes digestive organs and associated glands.

8. Liver secretes .... into the small intestine.

True/False

9. Diarrhoea can be treated by only giving water to the patient.

10. Source of energy for living being is food.

11. The digestion of starch only takes place in the stomach.

Match the Columns

12. Match the Column I with Column II.

	Column I		Column II
A.	*Amoeba*	1.	Release of faeces
B.	Incisors	2.	Cud chewing animals
C.	Ruminant	3.	Pseudopodia
D.	Anus	4.	Cutting and biting

Assertion-Reason Questions

The following questions consist of two statements **Assertion** (A) and **Reason** (R). Answer these questions by selecting the appropriate option given below.
(a) Both A and R are true and R is the correct explanation of A
(b) Both A and R are true, but R is not the correct explanation of A
(c) A is true, but R is false
(d) A is false, but R is true

13. Assertion (A) Ingestion of food is difficult without teeth.

Reason (R) Teeth helps in breaking down the food into small pieces.

14. Assertion (A) Herbivorous animals like cows, that eat grass are called ruminants.

Reason (R) The partially digested food called cud is brought back into the mouth of the cow.

Part II

Very Short Answer Type Questions

15. State the role of premolars in our mouth.

16. Name the different types of teeth found in mouth.

17. Name a muscular organ, which helps in speaking.

Short Answer Type Questions

18. Write the name of the mode of nutrition in the following organisms.
(i) Butterfly (ii) Snail
(iii) Frogs (iv) Snake
(v) Ant

19. Briefly describe the role of pancreas in a digestive system.

20. Write two functions of the tongue.

Long Answer Type Question

21 Explain digestion. Draw a well-labelled diagram of a human digestive system and its associated gland. Also mention the role of every organs shown in the diagram.

Answers

1. (b) 2. (a) 3. (d) 4. (a) 5. (a)
6. Permanent teeth 7. Alimentary canal
8. bile
9. False,
10. True 11. False
12. A-3, B-4, C-2, D-1
13. (a) 14. (b)

CHAPTER 03

Heat

Heat is a form of energy which gives us the sensation of hotness and the coldness. Heat cannot be seen, but we can feel it. In winter, it is common that we feel cold inside the house and if we come out in front of the sun rays, then we feel warm. On the other hand in summer, we feel hot even inside the house. So, we can say that things become hot or cold depends on the heat present in them.

3.1 Hot and Cold

In our daily routine, we come across a number of objects, out of which some are hot while other objects are cold. e.g.

- A frying pan kept on a burning gas stove becomes hot but the handle of pan is cold.
- When we touch a cup of freshly made tea, it feels hot but when we touch boiling water, it feels hotter.

Hence, the **hotness and coldness of an object are relative.** The most reliable way to know how hot or cold an object is to **measure its temperature.** A hot object will have a higher temperature than a cold object.

3.2 Temperature and its Measurements

The degree of hotness or coldness of the object is known as **temperature**. The most common unit for measuring temperature is **degree celsius** (°C).

The instrument which is used to measure the temperature is called **thermometer.**

The two most common types of thermometers are

(i) **Clinical** thermometer

(ii) **Laboratory** thermometer

Both the clinical thermometer and laboratory thermometer are mercury thermometers.

So, when a particular amount of heat is supplied to the thermometer bulb consisting of mercury (by the hot body whose temperature is to be measured), then the mercury expands and get rises in the glass tube of thermometer. This fact is used in measuring the temperature.

SCIENCE INSIGHT A German physicist Daniel Gabriel Fahrenheit invented the first mercury thermometer in 1714. It is also known as the **modern** and practical thermometer.

Clinical Thermometer

The thermometer which is used for measuring the temperature of human body is called **clinical thermometer**. The smallest reading in this thermometer is 0.2°C.

Construction and Features

- It consists of a long narrow and thin glass tube with a glass bulb at one end that contains mercury.
- It has a kink in the thin glass tube to prevent back flow of mercury. Due to this, we can read the correct body temperature of the patient even after removing the thermometer bulb from his mouth.

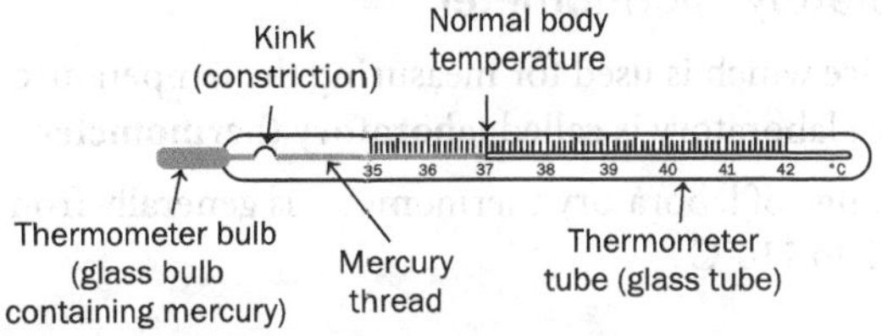

A clinical thermometer

- It has two temperature scales marked on its glass tube
  (i) Celsius scale (from 35°C to 42°C)
  (ii) Fahrenheit scale (from 94°F to 108°F)
- This thermometer has the range of 35°C to 42°C because the temperature of human body normally does not go below 35°C or above 42°C. So, normal body temperature is considered 37°C (98.6°F).

Reading a Clinical Thermometer

There are following steps to read the temperature on a clinical thermometer

1. Firstly, wash the thermometer with an antiseptic solution and if in case, the antiseptic solution is not available, then wash it with a clean water.
2. Gently, hold the thermometer tube in your hand and give it a jerk in such a way that the mercury thread in the thermometer tube falls below the reading of 35°C.
3. Now, put the bulb of the thermometer under the tongue of the patient for about one minute. Then, take out the thermometer from patient's mouth.
4. In order to read the temperature, hold the thermometer horizontally in your hand and rotate it slowly.
5. Now, read the temperature on thermometer tube in level with the top of the mercury thread.

Precautions while Using a Clinical Thermometer

A clinical thermometer should not be used for any object other than the human body because it may break.

There are some precautions which are to be observed while reading a clinical thermometer.

- Wash the clinical thermometer before and after using preferably with an antiseptic solution.
- Be ensure that, the mercury level before using the clinical thermometer should be below 35°C.
- The clinical thermometer should be read by keeping the level of mercury along the line of sight.
- While reading the clinical thermometer, it should never be held by the bulb.
- The clinical thermometer should be carefully handled.

Laboratory Thermometer

A device which is used for measuring the temperature in a science laboratory is called **laboratory thermometer**.

The range of laboratory thermometer is generally from –10°C to 110°C.

The smallest reading for laboratory thermometer is 1°C. It does not have kink in the mercury column.

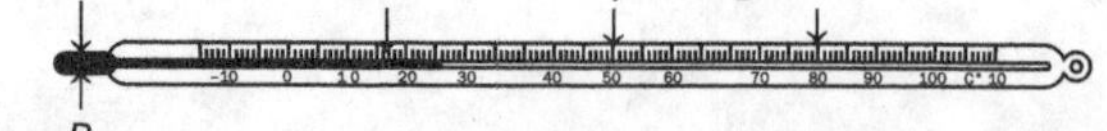

A laboratory thermometer

Note These are the special thermometers which automatically record the maximum and minimum temperatures of the day. The maximum and minimum temperature of the last day reported in weather reports in TV and newspapers are measured by the **maximum-minimum thermometers.**

Reading a Laboratory Thermometer

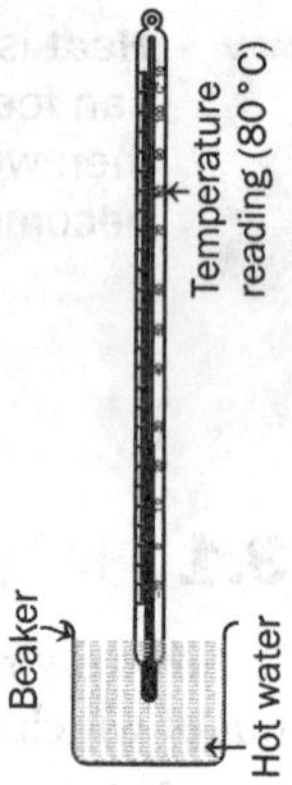

1. First of all, take some hot water in a beaker.
2. Now, try to hold the laboratory thermometer from its glass tube and immerse the bulb of the thermometer in hot water taken in the beaker. The bulb of the thermometer should not touch the sides or the bottom of the beaker.
3. Here, we will observe the shining thread of mercury moving up in the thermometer tube. After sometime, the mercury will stop rising and stand at one place.

   Now, read the temperature on thermometer tube which corresponds to the top of mercury thread. This will give us the temperature of hot water taken in the beaker.

Precautions while Using a Laboratory Thermometer

- The laboratory thermometer should be held vertically.
- The thermometer bulb should be surrounded from all sides by the substance whose temperature is to be measured.
- The thermometer should not be held by the bulb.
- Temperature reading should be noted down by keeping the thermometer bulb immersed in hot water because if the thermometer bulb is taken out of hot water, then its mercury thread will start falling and give a wrong reading.

  This is the only reason that we cannot use a laboratory thermometer to measure the human body temperature.

Note Mercury is a toxic substance (poisonous substance) and thus, it is very difficult to dispose it safely, if a thermometer breaks. So, there is a lot of concern over the use of mercury in thermometers. During these days, digital thermometers are available which do not use mercury.

A digital thermometer

Try These 3.1

1. **What is the smallest reading for laboratory thermometer ?**
2. **A student wants to measure his body temperature. Which type of thermometer should he use?**
3. **Rajat is measuring the temperature of hot water with a clinical thermometer. Will he be able to get accurate reading?**

3.3 Transfer of Heat

Heat flows from a hot object to a cold object or **heat flows from an object at higher temperature to another object which is at lower temperature**. This flow of heat is known as **transfer of heat**.

e.g. If you dip a steel spoon into a cup of hot tea, then we will find that the temperature of spoon rises and it becomes hot. In this case, some of the heat contained in hot tea has been transferred to spoon which is placed inside it.

When the two objects attain the same temperature, then the flow of heat stops. This means that **no heat will be transferred from one object to another, if the temperature of the two objects is the same.**

There are three ways through which heat can be transferred from a hot object to a cold object

1. By conduction (**in solid**, heat is transferred by conduction)
2. By convection (**in liquid and gases**, heat is transferred by convection)
3. By radiation (**in free space or vacuum**, heat is transferred by radiation)

Let us discuss all the three ways of heat transfer.

Conduction

The process by which heat is transferred from the hotter end to the colder end without the actual movement of an object or by direct contact with each other is known as **conduction**. e.g. Hotness of iron pin.

It takes place only in solids.

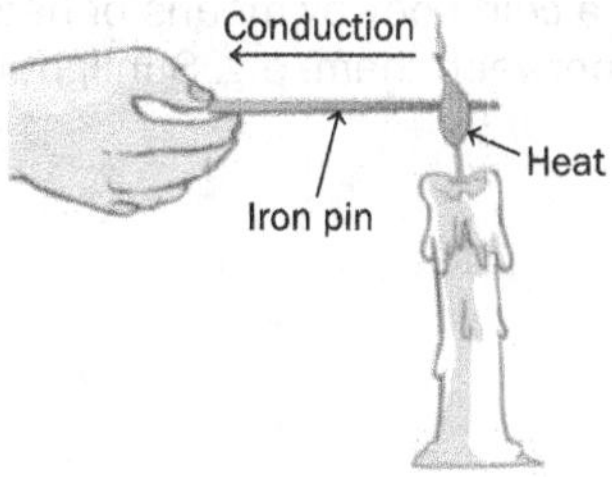

Flow of heat through an iron pin

The rate of heat transfer by conduction is directly proportional to the temperature difference between the substances that are in contact.

Conductors and Insulators of Heat

- The materials which allow heat to pass through them easily are the **conductors** of heat. e.g. Iron, copper, silver, etc.
- The materials which do not allow heat to pass through them easily are the **poor conductors** of heat. These are known as **insulators**. e.g. Glass, plastic, wood, water, air etc.

Convection

The mode of transfer of heat from the hotter part of a fluid (liquid or gas) to its colder parts by the movement of the liquid or gas itself is known as **convection.**

e.g. Boiling of water, breeze.

The transfer of heat by convection can take place only in liquids and gases. It is due to the reason that the particles in liquids and gases can move about freely.

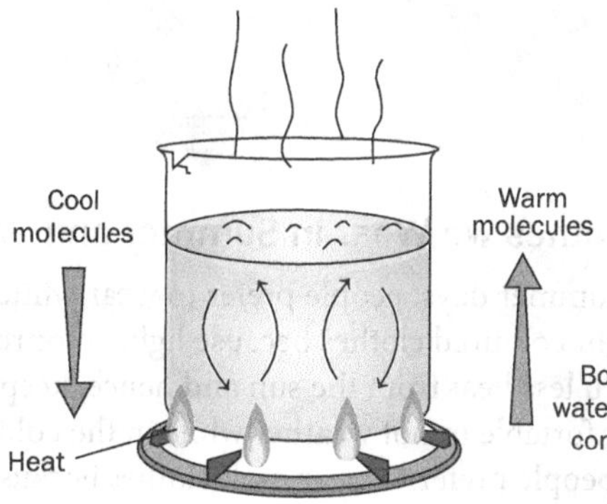

Image of convection

Sea and Land Breezes

The blowing of sea breeze and land breeze in coastal areas is generally due to the convection of heat in air.

During the day, land heats up more than water. Due to this, the air over the land becomes hotter and lighter and rises up. So, the air from the sea which is cooler and heavier, rushes to take the place created by hot rising air. Therefore, a sea breeze blows during the day.

During the night, land loses heat faster than water and becomes cooler and the air over the sea is now warmer. Due to which, it rises up and the cooler air over the land rushes to take its place. Therefore, we observe a land breeze at night.

Sea breeze and land breeze

Radiation

The process of flow of heat energy from a hot body to a cold body by means of heat rays without any medium between them is known as radiation.

e.g. Sun rays reaches to earth from space (vacuum), the heating of a room by an open-hearth fireplace.

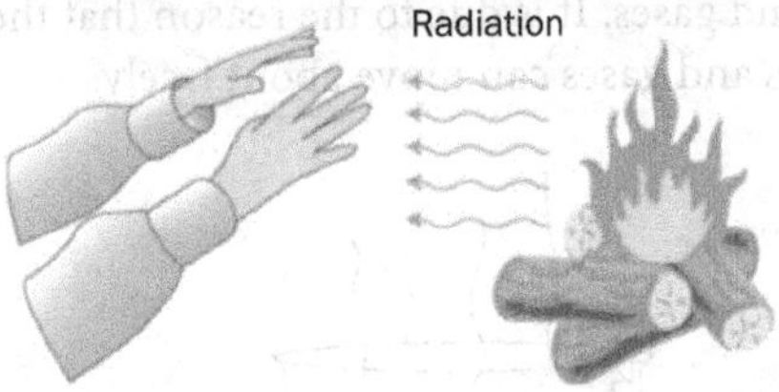

Radiation

Kinds of Clothes we Wear in Summer and Winter

During hot summer days, people prefer to wear white clothes or light coloured clothes because light coloured clothes absorb less heat from the sun and hence, keep us cool and comfortable in hot weather while in the cold winter days people prefer to wear dark clothes because the dark coloured clothes absorb more heat rays from the sun and keep us warm in winter season.

Thus , we can say that **dark coloured objects absorb heat better and also emit heat better than light coloured objects.**

In the winters, we use woollen clothes. **Wool is a poor conductor of heat.** Moreover, there is air trapped in between the wool fibres. This air prevents the flow of heat from our body to the cold surroundings. So, we feel warm.

Try These 3.2

1. **A metal spoon becomes hot when placed in a hot cup of tea. Which process is responsible here for transfer of heat from a hot cup tea to metal spoon?**
2. **The handle of the pan is made of plastic because plastic is .... conductor of heat.**
3. **The moment we stand next to a burning fire, we can feel the heat on our face. Name the process which transfers the heat from fire.**
4. **While constructing a house in a coastal area, in which direction should the windows preferably face?**

Science Glossary

Temperature The degree of hotness or coldness of the body is known as temperature.

Clinical thermometer is used for measuring the temperature of human body.

Laboratory thermometer is used for measuring the temperature in a science laboratory.

Conduction is the process by which heat is transferred from hotter end to the colder end without the actual movement of an object. e.g. Hotness of iron rod.

Conductor The material which allow heat to pass through them easily is called conductor. e.g. silver, copper.

Insulator The material which do not allow heat to pass through them easily is called insulator. e.g. Plastic, glass.

Convection is the process of flow of heat through a fluid from places of higher temperature to the places of lower temperature is called insulation. e.g. Boiling of water.

Radiation is the process of the flow of heat energy from a hot body to a cold body by means of heat rays without any medium between them. e.g. Sunlight reaches to the earth.

Let's Investigate

ACTIVITY 1 (Page 24-25)

Aim To show that the sense of touching is not reliable.

Material Required Three mugs contain cold water, hot water and lukewarm water.

Procedure

1. Choose the three mugs *A*, *B* and *C* and put cold water in mug *A*, hot water in mug *B* and lukewarm water in mug *C* as shown in figure .
2. Firstly, dip your left hand in cold water (mug *A*) and right hand in hot water (mug *B*) for about 2-3 min.
3. Now, take out the hands from mugs *A* and *B* and dip both hand swiftly in lukewarm water in mug *C*.
   We will notice that the water in mug *C* does not feel equally warm to both the hands.

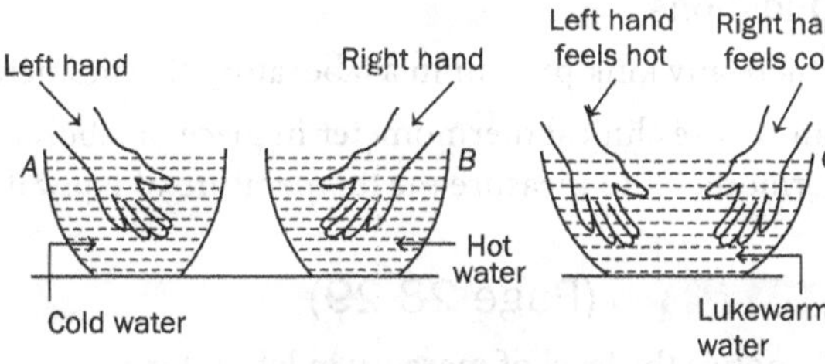

Feeling water in three mugs

Conclusion We have concluded that we cannot depend on our sense of touch, for estimating the hotness or coldness of an object.

Viva Questions

1. What is the direction of flow of heat?
2. Can we always identify object is hot or cold by touching?
3. We feel hot in container *A* and cold in container *B*, is it true?

ACTIVITY 2 (Page 25-26)

Aim To find out the normal body temperature by clinical thermometer.

Material Required A clinical thermometer, an antiseptic solution.

Procedure

1. Firstly, determine the least count of the clinical thermometer.
2. Wash the thermometer with clean water or antiseptic solution.
3. Gently, hold the thermometer and give it a jerk in such a way that the mercury thread falls below 35°C.
4. Now, place the bulb of the thermometer under your tongue.
5. After one mintue, take out the thermometer and note the reading.

Correct method of reading a clinical thermometer

Conclusion We have concluded that the normal temperature of a human body is 37°C.

Viva Questions

1. What is the temperature of a normal body in fahrenheit?
2. What is the range of temperature scale in clinical thermometer?
3. What is the temperature difference indicated between the two bigger marks?

ACTIVITY 3 (Page 26-27)

Aim To determine the average body temperature of humans is 37°C.

Material Required A clinical thermometer

Procedure

1. Firstly, take a clinical thermometer and make it ready for use.

2. Start measuring the body temperature of your friends (at least 10). After each observation, wash the clinical thermometer with antiseptic solution.

A student is measuring body temperature

3. Observe the body temperature in temperature scale of thermometer and prepare a table.

Name	Body Temperature
Sunil	37.2°C
Manoj Singh	38.6°C
Anil Chauhan	36.2°C
Deepak Kumar	37°C
Kunal Bhardwaj	36.8°C
Atul Phogat	37.4°C
Rohit vats	38°C
Himanshu Gulia	38.4°C
Kulveer Phogat	36.8°C
Suresh	37°C

Conclusion We have concluded from our observation that the average normal body temperature of humans is approx 37°C .

Viva Questions

1. Which liquid is filled in the glass bulb of a thermometer?
2. What is the average body temperature of a normal human beings?

ACTIVITY 4 (Page 27-28)

Aim To measure and compare the temperature of tap water in a beaker by laboratory thermometer.

Material Required Tap water, a laboratory thermometer, a beaker

Procedure

1. Firstly, take some tap water in a beaker.
2. Now, dip the thermometer in water, so that the bulb immersed in water but does not touch the bottom or sides of the beaker as shown in figure.
3. Hold the thermometer vertically till the mercury thread becomes steady.
4. Note the reading, on the thermometer scale, while it is still immersed in tap water.
5. Now, compare the temperature of water recorded by other students in the class.

Measuring the temperature of tap water with a laboratory thermometer

Conclusion We have concluded after comparison of readings that there is small variation in the readings of each student.

Viva Questions

1. Is there any kink present in a laboratory thermometer?
2. Can we use clinical thermometer in place of laboratory thermometer to measure the temperature of tap water?

ACTIVITY 5 (Page 28-29)

Aim To notice the level of mercury in laboratory thermometer when you take it out from hot water.

Material Required A laboratory thermometer, hot water.

Procedure

1. Firstly, take a laboratory thermometer and immerse its glass bulb completely in hot water.
2. Hold the thermometer vertically and ensure that, the bulb does not touch the side or the bottom of the beaker that contains hot water.

Observing the mercury level of laboratory thermometer after taking it out from hot water

3. Now, wait till the mercury thread become steady and note the reading on the thermometer.
4. Take out the thermometer from hot water and observe the temperature scale in thermometer, you will find that the level of mercury falls.

Conclusion We have concluded that the level of mercury rise or falls when the laboratory thermometer is taken out from the water.

Viva Questions

1. What is the range of temperature scale in laboratory thermometer?
2. What will happen to mercury level, when the laboratory thermometer is taken out from the hot water?

ACTIVITY 6 (Page 29-30)

Aim To understand the conduction of heat.
Material Required A stand or bricks, a iron rod, few small pieces of wax.
Procedure

1. Firstly, take an iron rod and try to clamp one end of the rod between bricks as shown in figure.
2. Now, fix few small pieces of wax at nearly equal distance from each other on the iron rod.
3. Now, with the help of candle, heat the other end of rod. You will find that pieces of wax start melting one-by-one.

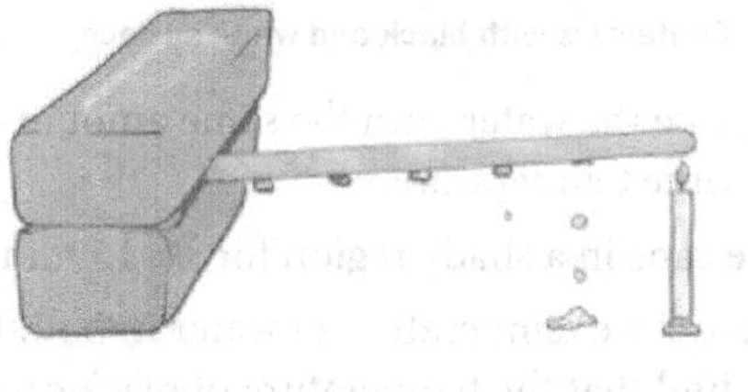

Flow of heat through a metal strip

Conclusion We have concluded that heat can be transferred from one end to another end of a metal rod by the conduction process.

Viva Questions

1. Which process is responsible for transfer of heat in solids?
2. Which metal can be used in place of iron rod?

ACTIVITY 7 (Page 30)

Aim To show that some materials are good conductors of heat and some are bad conductors.

Material Required Some articles like steel spoon, plastic scale, pencil, divider, etc.

Procedure

1. Firstly, heat some water in a small beaker.
2. Collect some articles and dip one end of each of these articles in hot water.
3. Now, wait for 5 - 8 min and touch the other end of articles. You will find that some articles are hot and some are not hot at other end.

Conduction of heat by different materials

Observation Table

Article	Material from which the article is made of	Does the other end get hot Yes/ No
Plastic scale	Plastic	No
Steel spoon	Steel	Yes
Pencil	Wood	No
Divider	Iron	Yes

Conclusion We have concluded that the materials which allow to pass heat through them are called **good conductors** like iron, steel. The materials which do not allow to pass heat through them are called **bad conductors** or **insulator** like wood, plastic.

Viva Questions

1. Is air a good or bad conductor of heat?
2. What do you call a material which do not allow heat to pass through it?

ACTIVITY 8 (Page 30-31)

Aim To show the transfer of heat by convection in water.

Material Required Few crystals of potassium permanganate, a beaker, a tripod stand, a candle.

Procedure

1. Firstly, take a beaker and fill its $\frac{2}{3}$rd part with water.
2. Now, place it on a tripod stand in such a way that you can heat it by placing a candle below it as shown in figure.
3. Drop few crystals of potassium permangante into water and heat the beaker on a slow flame.

Convection of heat in water

4. Wait for few minutes and start observing the crystals of potassium permanganate. You will find that the coloured water rises from the place where the heat is supplied.

Conclusion We have concluded that the cold water being heavier comes down from the sides and it gets heated up and rises again.

Viva Questions

1. Which colour do you observe in water after dropping the crystals of potassium permanganate?
2. Which process is responsible for boiling of water?

ACTIVITY 9 (Page 31)

Aim To show the transfer of heat in air by convection.

Material Required A candle.

Procedure

1. Gently, fix a lighted candle on a table.
2. Now, keep one hand above the flame and another hand on the side of flame as shown in figure.

Transfer of heat by convection in air

3. Now, feel the changes between both the hands. You will feel that the hand kept above the candle flame appears to be quite hot and the hand kept on the side of the flame does not seem to be so hot.

Conclusion We have concluded that the air just above the candle flame gets heated first and rises upwards carrying the heat along with it. The cold air from above sinks downwards to take the place of hot rising air.

Hence, we can say that, transfer of heat in air is due to convection process.

Viva Questions

1. Do you feel your hands equally hot?
2. How does the heat travels in air?

ACTIVITY 10 (Page 32-33)

Aim To show that black bodies are good absorber and radiator of heat than white bodies.

Material Required Two identical tin cans, a laboratory thermometer.

Procedure

1. Firstly, take two identical tin cans filled with equal amount of water.
2. Now, paint one can with black colour and other with white colour.
3. Leave them in the mid-day sun for about an hour.
4. Now, measure the temperature of water in both the cans with laboratory thermometer. You will find that, the black colour tin has higher temperature as compared to white colour tin.

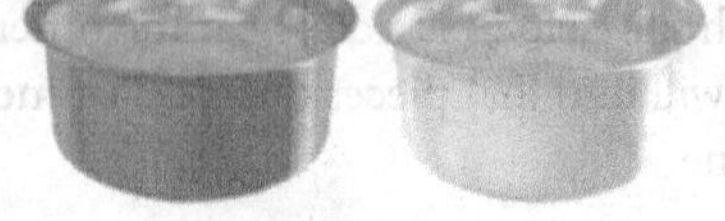
Containers with black and white surface

5. Now, replace the water with the same amount of hot water at same temperature.
6. Leave the cans in a shady region for 10-15 min.
7. Now, record the temperature of water in both the cans. You will find that the temperature of black can is less as compared to white can.

Conclusion We have concluded that the black bodies are better absorber and radiator of heat as compared to white bodies.

Viva Questions

1. Which tin do you find more warmer?
2. Which type of thermometer will you use for this activity?
3. Which of these two containers radiates more heat?

Mind Map

HEAT

Meaning

Form of energy which gives us the sensation of hotness or coldness.

Conductor

Material which allow heat to pass through it easily are called conductor.
e.g. Iron, copper, etc.

Sliver spoon   Copper wire

Insulator

Material which do not allow heat to pass through it, are called insulator.
e.g. Glass, wood, etc.

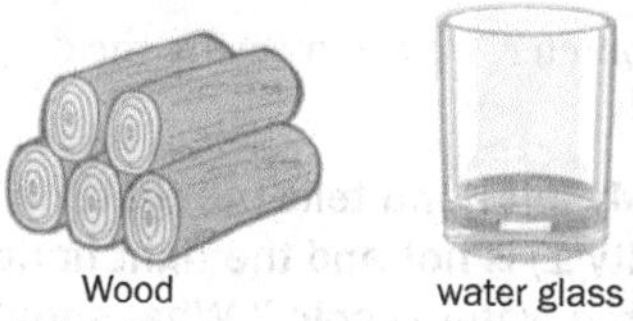

Wood   water glass

Temperature

- Degrees of hotness or coldness of an object.
- Hotness or coldness of object are relative.
- Normal body temperature is 37 °C.

Measurement

Temperature is measured by Thermometer

Clinical Thermometer

- → Used to measure body temperature.
- → Smallest reading is 0.2 °C.
- → Celsius scale (35 °C to 42 °C) (Because body temperature does not go below 35 °C or above 42 °C).
- → Fahrenheit scale (94 °F to 108 °F).
- → Has a kink in thin glass tube.

Laboratory Thermometer

- → Used for experimental purpose.
- → Smallest reading is 1 °C.
- → Celsius scale (−10 °C to 110 °C).
- → Do not have kink in thin glass tube.

Transfer of Heat

The flow of heat from an object at higher temperature to another object at lower temperature.

Conduction

Process by which heat is transferred from the hotter end to colder end without actual movement.
e.g. Iron, copper.

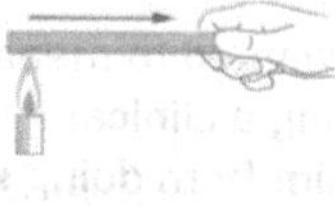

Convection

Process of flow of heat through a fluid from places of higher temperature to the places of lower temperature.
e.g. Boiling of water.

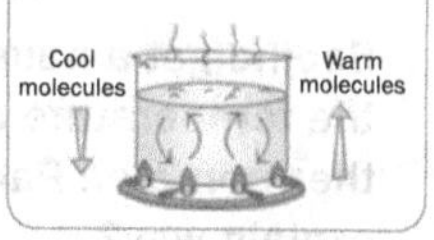

Radiation

Process of flow of heat energy from a hot body to a cold body by mean of heat rays.
e.g. Sunlight reaches to earth.

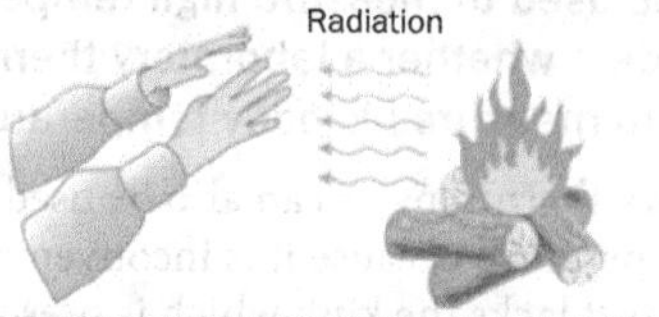

NCERT FOLDER

Complete Explanations of all NCERT's Questions

Intext Questions

Q.1 How do we find out how hot an object really is? **Page 25**

Ans. By using thermometer, we can measure the degree of hotness of a body.

Q.2 Boojho says, "My left hand tells me that the water in mug *C* (in Activity 1) is hot and the right hand tells me that the same water is cold." What should we conclude? **Page 25**

Ans. Both the conclusions are correct relative to each hand but this shows that we cannot arrive at conclusions just based on our sense of touch.

Q.3 Boojho wondered which of the two scales shown in figure should he read. **Page 25**

Ans. India has adopted the celsius scale, so he should read that scale. The other scale with the range 94-108 degrees is the fahrenheit scale (°F) which was used earlier.

Q.4 Paheli measured her body temperature. She got worried as it was not exactly 37 °C, explain why? **Page 26**

Ans. The temperature of every person may not be 37°C. It could be slightly higher or lower. So, we consider the average body temperature for human i.e. 37°C.

Q.5 Boojho got a naughty idea. He wanted to measure the temperature of hot milk using a clinical thermometer. Paheli stopped him from doing so, explain why? **Page 27**

Ans. The clinical thermometer has the range 35°C to 42°C and it is designed to measure the temperature of human body. That's why, paheli stopped him from doing so.

Q.6 Boojho now understands why clinical thermometer cannot be used to measure high temperatures. But still wonders whether a laboratory thermometer can be used to measure his body temperature. **Page 27**

Ans. Laboratory thermometer can also be used for measuring body temperature because it is inconvenient for this purpose as it lacks the kink which is present in clinical thermometer.

Q.7 Boojho wonders, why the level of mercury should change at all when the bulb of the thermometer is brought in contact with another object? **Page 28**

Ans. The level of the mercury changes when the bulb of the thermometer is brought in contact with another object because the temperature of other object may not be the same as that of the bulb of the thermometer.

Q.8 Paheli asks, "Does it mean that heat will not be transferred, if the temperature of two objects is the same"? **Page 29**

Ans. The net energy transfer does not take place when the temperature of two objects is same.

Q.9 What is the use of the kink? **Page 29**

Ans. The clinical thermometer consists of kink which prevents the mercury level from falling on its own.

Q.10 The mercury does not fall or rise in a clinical thermometer when taken out of the mouth. Explain why? **Page 29**

Ans. Because of the kink present in the thermometer, the mercury does not fall or rise.

Q.11 How does the heat transfer take place in water and air? **Page 30**

Ans. In water, mode of heat transfer is convection and in air, mode of heat transfer is radiation.

Q.12 How does the heat from the sun reach us? **Page 31**

Ans. By radiation.

Q.13 Why are you advised to use an umbrella when you go out in the sun? **Page 32**

Ans. An umbrella prevent us from the harmful radiation coming from the sun.

Q.14 Why do we prefer light coloured clothes in summer and dark coloured clothes in winter? **Page 32**

Ans. We prefer light coloured clothes in summer because light colour reflect sunlight as well as heat, so we feel comfortable during summer. But in winter, we wear dark coloured clothes because dark colour absorb sunlight as well as heat. So, our body remains warm.

Q.15 It is preferred to use two thin blankets rather than one thick blanket. Explain the reason. **Page 33**

Ans. In case of two thin blankets, there is an air gap which does not allow heat to pass out from the body and it is not as such in case of one thick blanket.

Exercise

Q.1 State similarities and differences between the laboratory thermometer and the clinical thermometer.

Ans. **Similarities** Both thermometers are used to measure temperature and both of them use mercury.

Differences Clinical thermometer is used to measure human body temperature whereas, laboratory thermometer is used to measure temperature of other object which has higher temperature than human body temperature.

Q.2 Give two examples each of conductors and insulators of heat.

Ans. Examples of conductors are metal and steel and examples of insulators are wood and plastic.

Q.3 Fill in the blanks.

(a) The hotness of a body is determined by its ....

(b) Temperature of boiling water cannot be measured by a .... thermometer.

(c) Temperature is measured in degree ....

(d) No medium is required for transfer of heat by the process of ....

(e) A cold steel spoon is dipped in a cup of hot milk. It transfers heat to its other end by the process of ....

(f) Clothes of .... colours absorb heat better than clothes of light colours.

Ans. (a) temperature (b) clinical
(c) celsius (d) radiation
(e) conduction (f) black or dark

Q.4 Match the columns.

Column I	Column II
(a) Land breeze blows during	(i) Summer
(b) Sea breeze blows during	(ii) Winter
(c) Dark coloured clothes are preferred during	(iii) Day
(d) Light coloured clothes are preferred during	(iv) Night

Ans. (a)–(iv), (b)–(iii), (c)–(ii), (d)–(i)

Q.5 Discuss why wearing more layers of clothing during winter keeps us warmer than wearing just one thick piece of clothing.

Ans. Wearing more number of clothes makes air gap which does not allow heat to pass out but in case of one thick cloth it is not as such, so we should wear more layers of clothing during winter to keep us warmer.

Q.6 Look at the figure, mark where the heat is being transferred by conduction, by convection and by radiation.

Ans. (i) Heat is being transferred in the steel vessel by conduction.

(ii) Heat is being transferred from vessel to water by convection.

(iii) Heat is being transferred from vessel to surroundings by radiation.

Q.7 In places of hot climate, it is advised that the outer walls of houses be painted white. Explain.

Ans. In places of hot climate, it is advised that the outer walls of houses be painted white because white colour does not absorb any heat radiation from the sun which keep inside cool even if there is hot climate outside the house.

Q.8 One litre of water at 30 °C is mixed with one litre of water at 50 °C. The temperature of the mixture will be

(a) 80 °C (b) more than 50 °C but less than 80 °C
(c) 20 °C (d) between 30 °C and 50 °C

Ans. (d) Temperature of mixture is in between 30°C to 50°C because water at 50°C losses some heat and water at 30°C gains some heat.

Q.9 An iron ball at 40 °C is dropped in a mug containing water at 40 °C. The heat will

(a) flow from iron ball to water

(b) not flow from iron ball to water or from water to iron ball

(c) flow from water to iron ball

(d) increase the temperature of both

Ans. (b) As heat can only flow from higher temperature to lower temperature. Thus, the heat will not flow from iron ball to water or *vice-versa.*

Q.10 A wooden spoon is dipped in a cup of icecream, then its other end

(a) becomes cold by the process of conduction

(b) becomes cold by the process of convection

(c) becomes cold by the process of radiation

(d) does not become cold

Ans. (d) It does not become cold because it is an insulator.

Q.11 Stainless steel pans are usually provided with copper bottoms. The reason for this could be that

(a) copper bottom makes the pan more durable

(b) such pans appear colourful

(c) copper is a better conductor of heat than the stainless steel

(d) copper is easier to clean than the stainless steel

Ans. (c) As copper is a better conductor of heat than the stainless steel, so stainless steel pans are usually provided with copper bottoms.

REVIEW EXERCISE

Including Competency Based Questions

Part I

Multiple Choice Questions

1. Heat always flows

(a) from a colder object to a hotter object
(b) from a hotter object to a colder object
(c) in both the directions
(d) None of the above

2. Paheli and Boojho measured their body temperature. Paheli found her to be 98.6 °F and Boojho recorded 37 °C. Which of the following statements is true? **NCERT Exemplar**

(a) Paheli has a higher body temperature than Boojho.
(b) Paheli has a lower body temperature than Boojho.
(c) Both have normal body temperature.
(d) Both are suffering from fever.

3. Figure (a, b, c, d) shows the reading of four different thermometers. Indicate which of the reading shows the normal human body temperature? **Competency Based Que.**

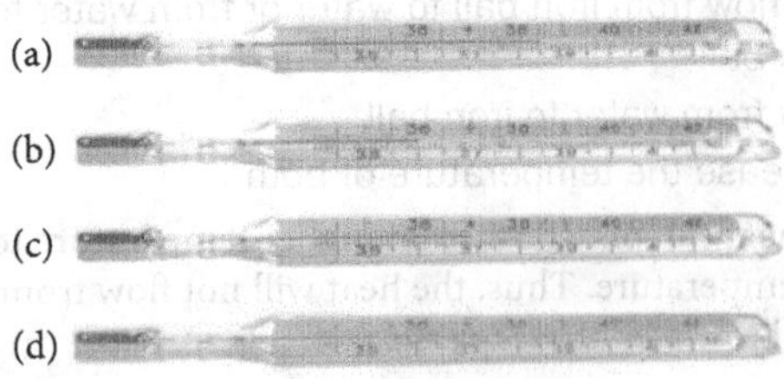

4. Figure (a, b, c, d) shows a student reading a doctor's thermometer. Which of the figure indicates the correct method of reading temperature?

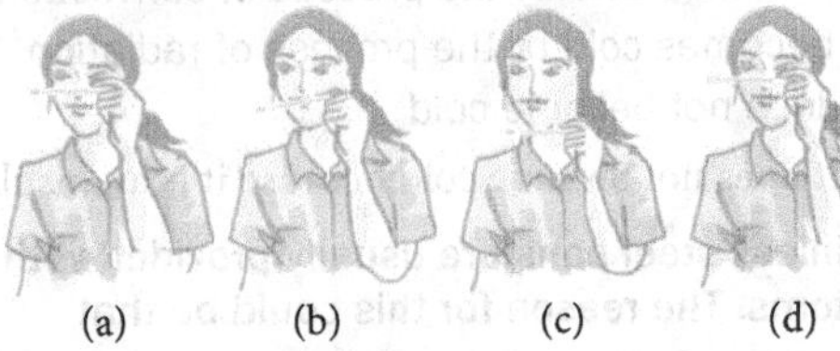

5. Which of the following instrument should be used to measure the boiling point of water? **CBSE Question Bank**

(a) Clinical thermometer
(b) Laboratory thermometer
(c) Both (a) and (b)
(d) None of the above

6. Boojho has three thermometers as shown in figure. He wants to measure the temperature of his body and that of boiling water. Which thermometer(s) should he choose? **NCERT Exemplar**

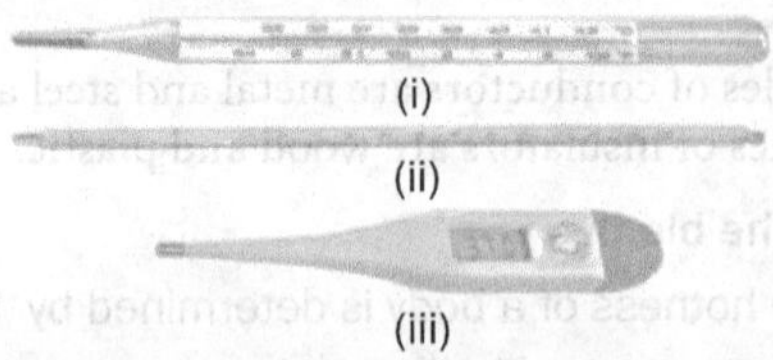

(a) Thermometers (i) and (iii) for measuring body temperature and (ii) for measuring the temperature of boiling water.
(b) Thermometer (i) for measuring both of the temperature.
(c) Thermometer (ii) for measuring both of the temperature.
(d) Thermometer (iii) for measuring both of the temperature.

7. Four arrangements to measure temperature of ice in beaker with laboratory thermometer are shown in figure (a, b, c, d). Which one of them shows the correct arrangement for accurate measurement of temperature? **NCERT Exemplar**

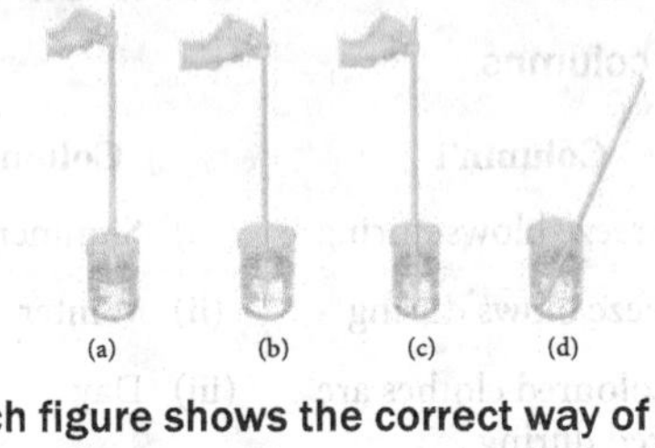

8. Which figure shows the correct way of reading the temperature on a thermometer ?

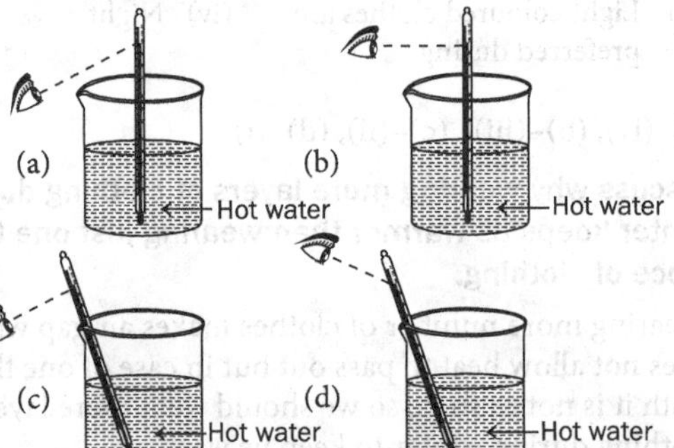

9. **A maximum-minimum thermometer has two stems which record the highest and lowest temperature during a period of time. A small metallic piece in each stem indicates the temperature.** **CBSE Diksha**

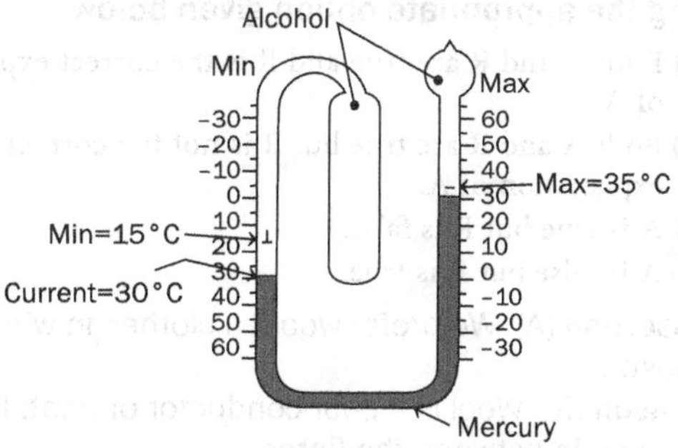

What are the maximum, minimum and current (Fig. 1) Temperatures shown in this thermometer (Fig. 2)

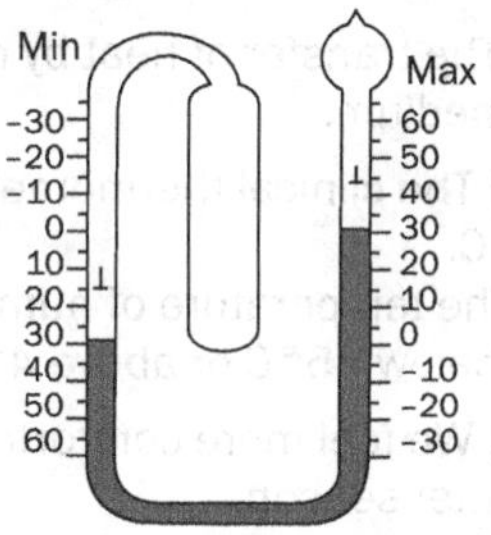

(a) 55°C, 35°C, 45°C (b) 45°C, 25°C, 35°C
(c) 55°C, 25°C, 35°C (d) 45°C, 25°C, 30°C

10. **Mercury and alcohol are two common liquids used in thermometers. The boiling point of mercury is 357 °C, while its freezing point is – 39 °C. For alcohol, the boiling point is 78 °C and the freezing point is – 80 °C. It is required in a laboratory to make measurements which are in the region of – 60 °C. Which type of thermometer would be more suitable?** **CBSE Diksha**

(a) A mercury thermometer since the freezing point of mercury is higher than – 60°C.
(b) A mercury thermometer since the boiling point of mercury is as high as 357°C.
(c) An alcohol thermometer since the boiling point of alcohol is lower at 78°C.
(d) An alcohol thermometer since the freezing point of alcohol is lower than – 60° C.

11. **Which process causes the air above the hot tea to get heated?** **Competency Based Que.**

(a) Conduction (b) Evaporation
(c) Convection (d) Radiation

12. **A beggar wrapped himself with a few layers of newspaper on a cold winter night. This helped him to keep himself warm because** **NCERT Exemplar**

(a) friction between the layers of newspaper produces heat
(b) air trapped between the layers of newspaper is a bad conductor of heat
(c) newspaper is a conductor of heat
(d) newspaper is at a higher temperature than the temperature of the surroundings

13. **A marble tile would feel cold as compared to a wooden tile on a winter morning because the marble tile**

(a) is a better conductor of heat than the wooden tile
(b) is polished while wooden tile is not polished
(c) reflects more heat than wooden tile
(d) is a poor conductor of heat than the wooden tile

14. **What kind of material can be used for the handle (labelled *A*)?**

(a) Copper (b) Wood (c) Iron (d) Stone

15. **What acts as an indication of the weather outside being very cold, with temperature in the range of – 2° C to 8 °C?** **CBSE Question Bank**

(a) Mild sunlight
(b) Fogged window panes
(c) Leaves rustling in the wind
(d) Heavy clouds and grey skies

16. **In a tropical country, during summers, which of the following materials is likely to absorb the least heat?** **CBSE Question Bank**

(a) Yellow rayon cloth (b) White cotton cloth
(c) Blue denim cloth (d) Maroon silk cloth

17. **A student observes that when a folded sweater is pressed down and released, it easily gets pressed and then, instantly bounces back in shape. The student concludes that thick woollen fibres can trap a lot of air within their strands. Which option explains how woollen sweaters protect us from cold weather?** **CBSE Question Bank**

(a) Convection provided by the wool fibres and insulation by air
(b) Insulation provided by the wool and conduction of body heat
(c) Insulation provided by the wool fibres and air trapped in them
(d) Convection of heat by the human body and reflection by wool

Answers

1. (b)	**2.** (c)	**3.** (c)	**4.** (a)	**5.** (b)
6. (a)	**7.** (a)	**8.** (b)	**9.** (b)	**10.** (d)
11. (d)	**12.** (b)	**13.** (a)	**14.** (b)	**15.** (b)
16. (b)	**17.** (c)			

Fill in the Blanks

1. Temperature is the measure of ....of an object.
2. All hot bodies radiate .... energy.
3. A ....near the bulb of a clinical thermometer prevents mercury level from falling of its own.
4. In .... generally, the heat is transferred by the process of conduction.
5. Wool is a .... conductor of heat.
6. In coastal areas, cold air flows in the day from sea to land. It is called ....

Answers

1. hotness 2. heat 3. kink
4. solids 5. poor 6. sea breeze

True/False

1. Our sense of touch about hotness or coldness is not always reliable.
2. In all cases, heat flows from a hotter object to a colder object.
3. Normal temperature of human body is 98.6 °C.
4. Shining thread in thermometer is the column of mercury.
5. Marking on clinical thermometer is from 0 °C to 100 °C.
6. The materials which allow heat to pass through them easily are called conductors.
7. Water and air are good conductors of heat.

Answers

1. True 2. True 3. False
4. True 5. False 6. True
7. False

Match the Columns

1. Match the Column I with Column II.

Column I	Column II
(a) Conduction	(i) Wood, plastic, wool, air, water
(b) Convection	(ii) Requires no medium
(c) Radiation	(iii) Solids
(d) Conductors	(iv) Metals
(e) Insulators	(v) Liquids

Answer

1. (a)–(iii), (b)–(v), (c)–(ii), (d)–(iv), (e)–(i)

Assertion-Reason Questions

The following question consist of two statement Assertion (A) and Reason (R). Answer these questions by selecting the appropriate option given below

(a) Both A and R are true and R is the correct explanation of A.
(b) Both A and R are true but R is not the correct explanation of A.
(c) A is true but R is false.
(d) A is false but R is true.

1. **Assertion** (A) We prefer woollen clothes in winter season.
 Reason (R) Wool is a poor conductor of heat. It has air trapped in between the fibres.
2. **Assertion** (A) Sunlight reaches to the earth by radiation process.
 Reason (R) The transfer of heat by radiation does not require any medium.
3. **Assertion** (A) The clinical thermometer has the range of 35 °C to 42 °C.
 Reason (R) The temperature of human body normally does not go below 35 °C or above 42 °C.
4. **Assertion** (A) We feel more comfortable in dark coloured clothes in winter season.
 Reason (R) Dark coloured clothes reflect most of the heat that falls on them.

Answers

1. (a) Wool is poor conductor of heat. The air gets trapped in between the wool fibres. This air prevents the flow of heat from our body to the cold surroundings.
2. (a) The process of transfer of heat energy from a hot body to a cold body by means of heat rays without any medium between them is known as radiation. So, sunlight does not require any medium to reach earth from space.
3. (a) The temperature of human body does not go below 35°C or above 42°C that's why the temperature scale of a clinical thermometer is in between 35°C to 42°C.
4. (c) Dark coloured clothes absorb most of the heat that falls on them that's why we feel more comfortable in dark coloured clothes in winter season.

Case Based Question

1. **Fatima keeps four boxes containing equal sized butter cubes under the sun. The boxes are of the same shape and size but made of different materials. Fatima notes how long the butter cubes in each box take to melt.**

Competency Based Que.

Box	Time the butter cubes take to melt
Box 1	12 min
Box 2	16 min
Box 3	7 min
Box 4	8 min

(i) Which box is the best conductor of heat ?

(a) Box 1

(b) Box 2

(c) Box 3

(d) Box 4

(ii) What can Fatima do to confirm the results of her activity ?

(a) Repeat the activity with boxes of different size

(b) Repeat the activity keeping all conditions the same

(c) Repeat the activity with boxes made of same material

(d) Repeat the activity with boxes containing different sized butter cubes

(iii) Fatima repeated the activity with each box wrapped in a thick layer of newspaper. Which of the following is likely to have happened ?

(a) The butter cubes in the boxes would not have melted

(b) The butter cubes in the boxes would have melted faster

(c) The readings in the table would have remained the same

(d) The butter cubes in each box would have taken longer to melt

Answer

1. (i) (c), (ii) (c), (iii) (c)

Part II

Very Short Answer Type Questions

1. How can we measure the temperature of other object rather than human body?

Ans. Temperature of other object is measured with laboratory thermometer because clinical thermometer is not suitable for higher temperature.

2. You may have noticed that a few sharp jerks are given to clinical thermometer before using it. Why is it done so?

Ans. Jerks are given to clinical thermometer before using it to settle down the mercury level below normal temperature, so that the measurement taken of a body be accurate.

3. Why is it advised not to hold the thermometer by its bulb while reading it? **NCERT Exemplar**

Ans. It is advised not to hold the thermometer bulb while reading it as the level of mercury increases from the actual reading by our body temperature.

4. In a mercury thermometer, the level of mercury rises when its bulb comes in contact with a hot object. What is the reason for this rise in the level of mercury? **NCERT Exemplar**

Ans. As the temperature increases, then expansion in mercury takes place which leads to the rise in the level of mercury in thermometer.

5. Is the body temperature of every person 37°C?

Ans. No, the body temperature of every person is not 37°C. It is an average temperature. It could be slightly higher or slightly lower.

6. A laboratory thermometer *A* is kept 7 cm away on the side of the flame while a similar thermometer *B* is kept 7 cm above the flame of a candle as shown in figure. Which of the thermometers *A* or *B* will show a greater rise in temperature? Give reason for your answer. **NCERT Exemplar**

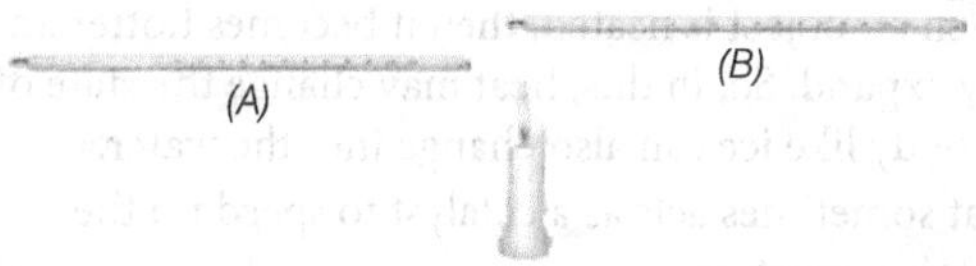

Ans. Thermometer *B* will show a greater rise in temperature because heated air above the candle rises immediately and increases the temperature of bulb of thermometer *B* quite greater than *A*.

7. A circular metal loop is heated at point *O* as shown in figure. **Competency Based Que.**

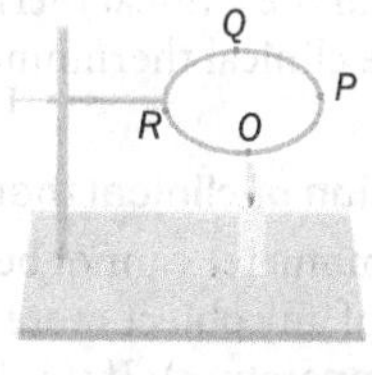

(i) In which direction, would heat flow in the loop?

(ii) In which order, the pins at points *P*, *Q* and *R* fixed with the help of wax fall if points *O*, *P*, *Q* and *R* are equidistant from each other?

Ans. (i) Heat will flow in both the directions from *O* to *P* and from *O* to *R*.

(ii) First of all pin at *P* and *R* will fall simultaneously after that pin at *Q* will fall.

8. While constructing a house in a coastal area, in which direction should the windows preferably face and why?

Ans. Window should preferably face towards the sea beach, so that the sea breeze coming from sea keeps the house cool during the day time.

9. To keep her soup warm, Paheli wrapped the container in which it was kept with a woollen clothes. Can she apply the same method to keep a glass of cold drink cool? Give reason for your answer. **NCERT Exemplar**

Ans. Yes, she can apply the same method to keep a glass of cold drink cool because wool is a thermal insulator and it cannot allow to heat pass through it.

10. Shopkeepers selling ice blocks usually cover them with jute sacks. Explain why? **NCERT Exemplar**

Ans. As we know that jute sack is thermal insulator, it helps ice not to be melt immediately. So, shopkeepers used to cover ice blocks with jute sacks.

11. Name the mode of transfer of heat in which medium is not required.

Ans. Radiation is the mode of transfer of heat in which medium is not required.

Short Answer Type Questions

1. Describe the effects of heat.

Ans. The effects of heat are

(i) When an object is heated, then it becomes hotter and may expand. So, in this, heat may change the state of the body like ice can also change into the water.

(ii) Heat sometimes acts as a catalyst to speed up the chemical reaction.

(iii) Heat can even kill the bacteria as well.

2. The clinical thermometer is not used to measure high temperature. Why?

Ans. Clinical thermometer has the range 35°C to 42°C. If we use it to measure high temperature, it may break and mercury present in the clinical thermometer is harmful. So, we cannot use clinical thermometer to measure high temperature.

3. State the limitation of clinical thermometer.

Ans. The clinical thermometer cannot be used for measuring the temperature of any object more than 42°C (i.e. more than the body temperature). If it is kept in the sun or near a flame, then this clinical thermometer can be break.

4. Instead of water explain the reason, why is the mercury used in the thermometer?

Ans. Due to following reasons, mercury is used in the thermometers instead of water

(i) When the thermometer breaks, the mercury can be easily collected.

(ii) Mercury can expand more than the water.

(iii) Also, mercury do not stick on the walls of thermometer like water.

5. Briefly explain the maximum and minimum thermometers.

Ans. Maximum and minimum thermometers are the special thermometers which automatically record the maximum and minimum temperature of the day.

The maximum and minimum temperature of the last day reported in weather reports in TV and newspapers are measured by the maximum and minimum thermometers.

6. The handle of a pressure cooker is covered with the thick plastic. Explain why?

Ans. As we know that plastic is a bad conductor of heat due to which the heat from the cooker does not flow to its handle and we can hold it easily.

So, that's why, the handle of a pressure cooker is covered with the thick plastic.

7. For setting curd, a small amount of curd is added to warm milk. The microbes present in the curd help in setting if the temperature of the mixture remains approximately between 35°C to 40°C. At places where room temperature remains much below the range, setting of curd becomes difficult. Suggest a way to set curd in such a situation. **NCERT Exemplar**

Ans. For the setting of curd where temperature is below room temperature, the container in which curd is to be made must be kept in a thermally insulated cover or it can be wrapped with wool or jute sacks, so that temperature is maintained for the setting of curd.

8. In the arrangements *A* and *B* as shown in figure, pins *P* and *Q* are fixed to a metal loop and an iron rod with the help of wax. In which case, both the pins are likely to fall at different times? Explain. **Competency Based Que.**

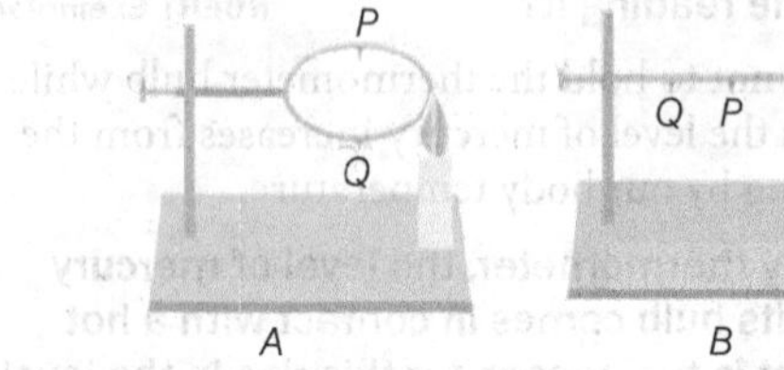

Ans. In case of *A*, points *P* and *Q* being equidistant get equal heat. That is why, pins at *P* and *Q* are likely to fall simultaneously. But in case of *B*, pin at point *P* falls earlier than pin at *Q* because heat received at *P* is greater than that received at *Q* in the same time.

9. Why does our hand burn on touching a hot pan, but not on touching its bakelite handle? **CBSE Question Bank**

Ans. Since, bakelite is an insulator. It does not conduct heat energy. That's why, on touching the bakelite handle of a hot pan, our hand does not burn.

10. The length of wire *PQ* in case of *A* is equal to the diameter of the semi-circle formed by the wire *CDE*. In case *B*, one pin is attached to each wire with the help of wax as shown in figure. Which pin will fall first? Explain. NCERT Exemplar

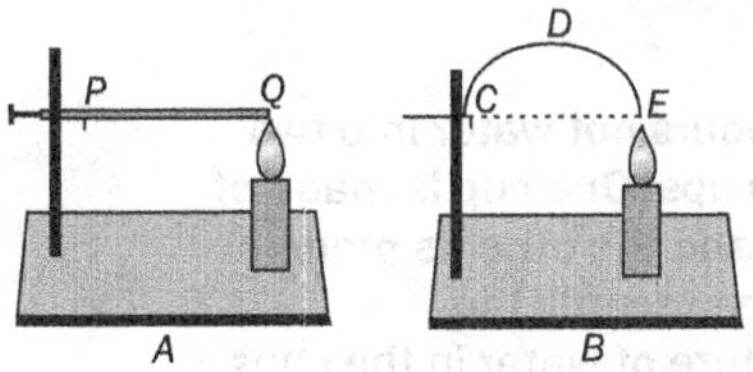

Ans. The pin on the wire in case *A* will fall first as heat will reach to it before it reaches the pin in case *B* because the diameter is smaller than the circumference of semi-circle.

11. Explain the reason for serving of tea in China clay cup and plates.

Ans. Tea is generally served in China clay cup and plates because China clay is a bad conductor of heat which does not allow the heat to pass through it and hence keeps the tea hot.

12. The freezer is located at the top of the refrigerator. Explain why?

Ans. The freezer is located at the top of the refrigerator. It is because the air inside and around the compartments of freezer gets cool and moves downwards and on the other side, the lesser cool air moves upward to get cooled.

So, as a result of this, convections of heat are set up in the air and the lower section of the refrigerator also gets cooled faster.

13. Differentiate between two modes of transfer of heat, i.e. convection and conduction.

Ans. Difference between convection and conduction

Convection	Conduction
The mode of transfer of heat from the hotter part of a fluid to its colder parts by the movement of liquid itself. So, this phenomenon is known as convection.	The mode of transfer of heat from the hotter part of a material to its colder part or from a hot material to a cold material in contact with it without the movement of material as a whole. So, this phenomenon is known as conduction.
In all the liquids and gases, heat is transferred by the process of convection	In all the solids, heat is transferred by the process of conduction.

14. Observe the given figure, water is being boiled in a pan of wide base. NCERT Exemplar

(i) Which position *P* or *T* will feel warmer?

(ii) Fill up the boxes *P* and *T* to indicate the mode of flow of heat to the hand.

Ans. (i) As in the given diagram, position *P* will feel warmer because of heat, air becomes warmer and rises up.

(ii) The flow of heat to *P* is a convection process and flow of heat to *T* is radiation.

15. Briefly explain, why do the kites and eagles fly without flapping their wings?

Ans. As it is a fact that the hot air during the day-time surrounds the land gradually and rises up, due to which a convection air of heat develops.

So, kites and eagles start moving along this rising current of heat without flapping the wings to fly high up in the sky.

16. Explain the reason for the shiny reflectors of room heaters.

Ans. The shiny surface absorbs very little heat due to which the reflectors reflect all the heat which makes the room heaters more effective. So, due to this reason, room heaters have shiny reflectors.

17. At a camp site, there are tents of two shades. One made with black fabric and the other with white fabric. Which one will you prefer for resting on a hot summer afternoon? Give reason for your choice. Would you like to prefer the same tent during winter? NCERT Exemplar

Ans. We will prefer white fabric tent in case of summer because it reflects all the radiations from the sun and keeps us cool inside the tent.

But in case of winter, we should not use white fabric tent, we should use black fabric tent as it absorbs all colours of light from the sun and keeps us warm inside the tent.

Long Answer Type Questions

1. Explain the differences between heat and temperature.

Ans. The differences between heat and temperature are given below

Heat	Temperature
It is a form of energy which flows from one body to another when there is a difference in temperature between the objects.	It is the thermal condition of a body that indicates whether heat is present or not and in which direction, heat will flow from one body to the other.
It is equal to the sum of internal energies of the molecules of a body.	It is proportional to average kinetic energy of the molecules of the body.

Heat	Temperature
As a heat exchange between two bodies, total amount of heat of two bodies remains unchanged.	As a conclusion of exchange of heat between two bodies, sum of their temperatures before and after exchange is not same.
SI unit of heat is joule (J).	SI unit of temperature is kelvin (K).

2. On last Monday, Pankaj was dealing with immense cough and cold. Besides this, he was suffering from a headache. So, he decided to take a leave on that day so that he could take some rest at his home. After one hour he thought to check his fever through a clinical thermometer, so before using it, he washed it and started shaking it very fastly in his hand, so that the mercury level of thermometer gets reduced. At the same time, his elder brother Vishwas scold him and suggested him to shake the thermometer slowly.

(i) State some precautionary measures while checking the fever through a clinical thermometer.

(ii) Mention the values showed by the elder brother of Pankaj (i.e. Vishwas). **Competency Based Que.**

Ans. (i) The following precautionary measures while checking the fever through a clinical thermometer are

(a) While reading the clinical thermometer, it should never be held by the bulb.

(b) The clinical thermometer should be washed properly (before and after use).

(ii) The values showed by the elder brother of Pankaj, Vishwas are concern towards the way of using the clinical thermometer and the importance of money as well.

3. Last Sunday, Pooja on her week off entered in her kitchen to cook rice for her family in lunch time. The moment she put fry pan on the gas stove and lighted it through the matchstick, all of sudden her 5 years small daughter entered into the kitchen and tends to touch the hot fry pan. At the same time, Pooja saw her and pushed her away from the hot fry pan. In this way, she saved her child.

(i) Explain why are the fry pan provided with the plastic handles?

(ii) Mention the values represented by Pooja here towards her 5 years small daughter.

Ans. (i) As we know that plastic is a bad conductor of heat which does not allow the heat to pass through itself. So, heat from the fry pan does not flow to the handle due to which we can hold it easily. That's why, the fry pans are provided with the plastic handles.

(ii) The value showed by Pooja here is great concern and care towards her 5 years old small daughter.

Case Based Questions

1. Reema pours hot water into two types of cups. One cup is made of ceramic and the other is made of paper. She records the temperature of water in the cups after 5 min. **CBSE Diksha; Competency Based Que.**

	Temperature of the hot water	Temperature of water in the cup after 5 min
Ceramic cup	90°C	75°C
Paper cup	90°C	60°C

(i) What is Reema testing ?

(a) Is paper a bad conductor of heat ?

(b) Does the shape of a cup prevent loss of heat ?

(c) Does the colour of a cup prevent loss of heat ?

(d) Is paper a better conductor of heat than ceramic ?

(ii) Would there be a change in the temperature readings if both the cups were covered with a lid ? Explain.

2. The thermometer shows the indoor temperature of a house. **Competency Based Que.**

(i) What is the indoor temperature of the house in degree celsius ?

(ii) What should be the colour of the roof surface to keep the house warm ?

(a) Silver (b) Yellow

(c) Sky blue (d) Dark brown

Ans.

1. (i) (d)

(ii) If both the cups were covered with a lid, the readings for temperature would be higher as lids would not allow the heat to escape.

2. (i) 20°C (ii) (d)

Skill Based Questions as per NEP 2020

1. The question assesses the student's ability to identify and explain heat transfer process in real life situations. Thinking Skill

(i) By what method of heat transfer does heat energy from the sun reach the earth?

(ii) Select the process of heat transfer which causes a breeze (wind) over land and sea.

(a) Conduction (b) Convection

(c) Radiation

(iii) Explain in term of heat transfer, why houses at coastal area often have their windows facing the sea?

(iv) Suggest two domestic insulation techniques that the houses build at coastal areas could have to maintain constant temperatures.

2. A student took hot milk and poured it into four containers at same level as shown below. Which container will cause temperature of hot milk to drop at the slowest rate? Knowledge Based Que.

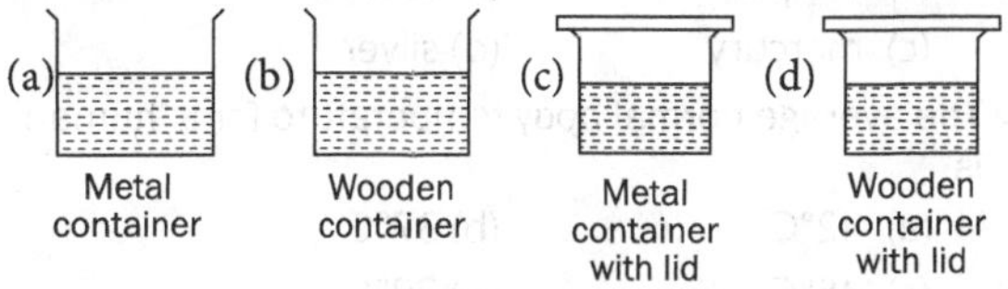

3. Govind is a student. He set up an experiment as shown here. Experimental Skill

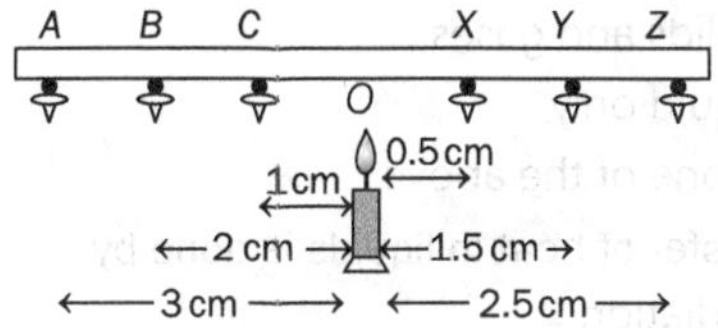

He placed the lighted candle below the iron rod at position O He used the same amount of wax to hold all the drawing pin at positions *A*, *B*, *C*, *X*, *Y* and *Z* on the rod. Arrange the drawing pin according to the time, they take to drop from the rod, from the last to the first.

ASSESSMENT EXERCISE

Part I

Multiple Choice Questions

1. The liquid metal used in thermometer is
(a) copper (b) zinc
(c) mercury (d) silver

2. The average normal body temperature for a human is
(a) 42°C (b) 37°C
(c) 48°C (d) 29°C

3. Conduction occurs in
(a) solids only
(b) solids and gases
(c) liquid only
(d) None of the above

4. The transfer of heat in liquids is done by
(a) radiation
(b) convection
(c) conduction
(d) None of the above

5. Which of the following do not require any medium for heat transfer?
(a) Radiation (b) Conduction
(c) Convection (d) All of these

Fill in the Blanks

6. Kink prevents the mercury from falling in a .... thermometer.

7. The range of laboratory thermometer is from ..... °C to .... °C.

8. Sea breeze blows during the .... and land breeze blows during the ....

True/False

9. Temperature of boiling water can be measured by clinical thermometer.

10. Dark coloured surfaces are better absorbers of heat than light coloured surfaces.

11. During day-time, air blows from the land to the sea.

Assertion-Reason Questions

The following questions consist of two statements **Assertion** (A) and **Reason** (R). Answer these questions by selecting the appropriate option given below.

(a) Both A and R are true and R is the correct explanation of A.
(b) Both A and R are true but R is not the correct explanation of A.
(c) A is true but R is false.
(d) A is false but R are true.

12. Assertion (A) A clinical thermometer has a scale in the range of – 10 °C to 110 °C.
Reason (R) The normal body temperature of a human is 37 °C.

13. Assertion (A) We feel more comfortable in light coloured clothes in the summer.
Reason (R) Light coloured clothes absorb less heat from the sun.

Part II

Very Short Answer Type Questions

14. How do you define heat flow?

15. What is the range of laboratory thermometer?

16. Why convection not possible in solids? Briefly explain.

17. Describe in brief about the term radiation.

18. Name the process through which the heat of sun reaches us.

Short Answer Type Questions

19. Write differences between clinical thermometer and laboratory thermometer.

20. The method of transfer of heat, i.e. convection is only possible in fluids. Explain why?

21. Explain why does a shiny tea pot stay hotter than a dull brown pot?

Long Answer Type Questions

22. A laboratory thermometer is not suitable for measuring human body temperature. Explain why?

23. Describe in detail that how land breeze and sea breeze take place?

Answers

1. (c)	**2.** (b)	**3.** (a)	**4.** (b)	**8.** day, night		**9.** False	**10.** True
5. (a)	**6.** clinical		**7.** – 10 , 110	**11.** False		**12.** (d)	**13.** (a)

CHAPTER 04

Acids, Bases and Salts

In our daily life, we consume a large number of edible substances such as lemon, baking soda, tamarind, common salt, sugar, curd and vinegar. Some of these substances taste sour, some taste bitter, some taste sweet and some taste salty.

Classification of Edible Substance

Some edible substances and their tastes are listed in the table shown below

Edible Substances and their Taste

Substances	Taste	Substances	Taste
Lemon juice	Sour	Sugar	Sweet
Orange juice	Sour	Common salt	Salty
Vinegar	Sour	Amla	Sour
Curd	Sour	Baking soda	Bitter
Tamarind (imli)	Sour	Grapes	Sweet/Sour

Based on their taste, substances can be classified into three important groups of chemical substance, i.e. acids, bases and salts.

4.1 Acids

The word acid has been derived from a Latin word '**acere**' which means 'sour'. Thus, those substances that taste sour are called acids, e.g. lemon juice, orange juice, unripe mango, curd, etc. These contain natural acids in them. The chemical nature of such substances is **acidic**.

Acids and their Sources

Name of acids	Sources
Acetic acid	Vinegar
Formic acid	Ant's sting
Citric acid	Citrus fruits such as oranges, lemons, etc.
Lactic acid	Curd
Oxalic acid	Spinach
Ascorbic acid (vitamin-C)	Amla, citrus fruits
Tartaric acid	Tamarind, grapes, unripe mangoes, etc.

SCIENCE INSIGHT Acids are either strong or weak. Strong acids like sulphuric acid can even melt metals. These should be handled with care.

4.2 Bases

Those substances which taste bitter and feel slippery to touch are known as bases, e.g. baking soda, soap, etc. The chemical nature of such substances is said to be **basic**.

Bases and their Sources

Name of bases	Sources
Calcium hydroxide	Lime water
Ammonium hydroxide	Window cleaner
Sodium hydroxide/Potassium hydroxide	Soap
Magnesium hydroxide	Milk of magnesia

4.3 Natural Indicators Around Us

There are some special substances that are used to identify acidic or basic nature of a substance are known as **indicators.**

Some naturally occurring indicators are litmus, turmeric, China rose petals (gudhal) and red cabbage juice. They are used to test whether a substance is acidic or basic in nature.

Litmus-A Natural dye

Litmus is naturally obtained from **lichens.** Usually, it is available in the form of a solution or as **red** and **blue litmus paper**.

Litmus have mauve (purple) colour in distilled water. In an acidic solution, it turns **red**. When it is added to basic solution, it turns **blue**. The solutions, which do not change the colour of either red or blue litmus paper are called **neutral solution**.

Turmeric

It is a bright yellow powder obtained from a plant. It is called '**Haldi**' in hindi. Turmeric contains a yellow dye that turns red in basic solution.

For example, turmeric stain on clothes turn red when it is washed with soap. It is because the soap solution is basic in nature.

It is used as indicator in the form of turmeric paper.

China Rose

It is also known as '**Gudhal**' in hindi. When the petals of this flower are added to water, a light pink solution is formed. This light pink solution is used as an indicator, when added to another solution.

If the colour of the solution changes to **deep pink** (magenta), the solution is **acidic**.

If the colour of the solution changes to **green**, the solution is **basic**.

Acid Rain

Several oxides such as **carbon dioxide, sulphur dioxide, nitrogen dioxide** are released into air as pollutants. When these oxides mix with water, acids like nitric acid, sulphuric acid are formed. These acids then fall on Earth as acid rain. Acids are corrosive in nature. Hence, acid rain cause damage to buildings, historical monuments, plants and animals.

Try These 4.1

1. **Which substance is responsible for sour taste of grapes?**
2. **What gives detergents a slippery feel to touch?**
3. **What colour of the litmus solution extracted from the lichen plant?**
4. **Name an indicator which gives red or pink colour on adding a basic solution.**
5. **When a basic solution is added to an indicator, a green colour is produced. Write the name of this indicator.**

4.4 Neutralisation

The reaction in which an acid reacts with a base to form salt and water is called neutralisation. Acids and bases are chemically opposite substances. So, when an acid is mixed with a base, they neutralise (or cancel) the effect of each other. In this process, both the acidic nature of acid and basic nature of base are destroyed.

The solution formed is neutral, but salt produced during the reaction can be acidic, basic or neutral.

Some heat is always evolved, during the reaction, which raises the temperature of the mixture.

The general reaction takes place is given as

Acid + Base $\longrightarrow$ Salt + Water (Heat is evolved)

This can be understand by following example

Hydrochloric acid (HCl) + Sodium hydroxide (NaOH)
(Acid) (Base)

$\longrightarrow$ Sodium chloride (NaCl) + Water (H_2O)
(Salt)

Phenolphthalein as an indicator

To know about the nature of the solution during neutralisation process, we use **phenolphthalein** as an indicator. It is a **synthetic** (non-natural) **indicator**.

When the solution is basic, it gives a pink colour, but if solution is acidic, phenolphthalein remains colourless.

4.5 Neutralisation in Everyday Life

The neutralisation reactions play a very important role in our everyday life.

Some of the examples that involves neutralisation reaction are as follows

Indigestion

Our stomach produces **Hydrochloric Acid** (HCl) which helps in digesting the food present in it. Sometimes, excess of hydrochloric acid causes indigestion. It can lead to pain and irritation in the stomach.

To relieve indigestion, we take an **antacid** which contains bases, e.g. milk of magnesia has magnesium hydroxide. It neutralises the excess acid present in the stomach and cures indigestion.

Ant Bite

When an ant bites, it injects an acidic liquid into the skin of the person which causes **burning sensation**. The sting of an ant contains an acid called **formic acid**.

The effect of the acid can be neutralised by rubbing a mild base, e.g. **baking soda solution** (sodium hydrogen carbonate) or **calamine solution** which contains zinc carbonate.

Thus, being a base, baking soda solution or calamine solution neutralises the acidic liquid injected by the ant and cancel its effect.

SCIENCE INSIGHT A bee sting is treated by rubbing pickle on the site. It is because bee sting contains a base called 'Melittin'. It reacts with the acetic acid (vinegar) in pickles and gets neutralised.

Soil Treatment

The soil may be acidic or basic naturally. The plants do not grow well, if the soil at a place is too **acidic** or too **basic**.

Excessive use of chemical fertilisers makes the soil acidic. When the soil is too acidic, it is treated with bases like **quicklime** (calcium oxide) or **slaked lime** (calcium hydroxide). These bases neutralise the excess acid present in the soil and reduce its acidic nature.

If the soil is basic, organic matter called **manure** or **compost** is added to it. The organic matter releases acids which neutralises the basic nature of the soil.

Factory Wastes

The waste substances discharged by many factories contain acids. If these factory wastes are allowed to flow into the water bodies (like rivers, ponds, lakes, etc.) then the acid present in them will kill fish and other organisms. The factory wastes are therefore neutralised by adding basic substances before discharging them into the water bodies.

Try These 4.2

1. **An acid and a base are mixed in a beaker, placed on a ice cube which starts to melt during the reaction. Give reason.**
2. **Name one substance other than milk of magnesia which cures indigestion.**
3. **Which property does compost have when added to a basic soil?**
4. **Using which type of substance can factory waste be neutralised?**

Science Glossary

Acid The substances which have sour taste are called acids, e.g. lemon juice, orange, etc. The chemical nature of such substances is acidic.

Base The substances which have bitter taste and are soapy to touch are called base, e.g. quicklime, etc. The chemical nature of such substances is basic.

Indicators These are special substances used to test whether the taken substance is acidic or basic in nature.

Neutralisation The reaction in which an acid reacts with a base in suitable amount to form salt and water is called neutralisation reaction.

Neutral substance Those substances which do not bring any colour change with litmus paper are called neutral substances.

Salt It is a compound which is formed by the neutralisation of an acid with a base.

Synthetic indicators These indicators which are made by human beings, e.g. phenolphthalein.

Let's Investigate

ACTIVITY 1 (Page 40)

Aim To show the effect of acidic and basic solutions on red and blue litmus paper.

Materials Required Lemon juice and some common solutions, water, test tube/tumbler, red litmus paper, dropper, blue litmus paper, etc.

Procedure

1. Take the solution of lemon juice and water in a test tube/tumbler.
2. Now, put a drop of this solution on the strip of the red litmus paper with a dropper.
3. Note the colour change of the litmus paper.
4. Repeat the same exercise with blue litmus paper.
5. Again note the colour change.
6. Perform the same activity with tap water, detergent solution, aerated drink, soap solution, shampoo, common salt solution, sugar solution, vinegar, baking soda solution, milk of magnesia, washing soda and lime water.
7. Record your observations in tabular form.

Observation

Test solution	Effect on red litmus paper	Effect on blue litmus paper	Inference
Lemon juice	No change	Turns red	Acidic
Tap water	No change	No change	Neutral
Detergent solution	Turns blue	No change	Basic
Aerated drink	No change	Turns red	Acidic
Soap solution	Turns blue	No change	Basic
Shampoo	Turns blue	No change	Basic
Common salt solution	No change	No change	Neutral
Sugar solution	No change	No change	Neutral
Vinegar	No change	Turns red	Acidic
Baking soda solution	Turns blue	No change	Basic
Milk of magnesia	Turns blue	No change	Basic
Washing soda	Turns blue	No change	Basic
Lime water	Turns blue	No change	Basic

Conclusion We conclude that when red litmus paper is dipped into basic solution, it turns blue.

Similarly, when blue litmus paper is dipped in acidic solution, it turns red. Neutral solutions do not show any colour change.

Viva Questions

1. What is a litmus paper?
2. What will be the effect of soap water on red litmus paper and blue litmus paper?

ACTIVITY 2 (Page 40)

Aim To prepare a turmeric paper and show the effect of acidic or basic solution on it.

Materials Required Teaspoon, turmeric powder, water, blotting paper (filter paper), scissors, dropper, soap solution and some common solutions, etc.

Procedure

1. Take a teaspoonful of turmeric powder, add a little water and make a paste.
2. Deposit the turmeric paste on blotting paper and dry it.
3. The yellow paper thus obtained is turmeric paper.
4. Cut thin strips of turmeric paper.
5. Use these strips of turmeric paper as indicator.
6. Now, put a drop of soap solution on one strip and note colour change of strip.
7. Perform the same activity with lemon juice, orange juice, vinegar, milk of magnesia, baking soda, lime water, sugar and common salt.
8. Record your observation in tabular form.

Observation

Test solution	Effect on turmeric paper	Remarks
Soap solution	Turns red	Basic
Lemon juice	Remains yellow	Acidic
Orange juice	Remains yellow	Acidic
Vinegar	Remains yellow	Acidic
Milk of magnesia	Turns red	Basic
Baking soda	Turns red	Basic
Lime water	Turns red	Basic
Sugar	No change	Neutral
Common salt	No change	Neutral

Conclusion We conclude that yellow colour of turmeric paper turns red when put in a basic solution and remains yellow in acidic solution.

Viva Questions

1. How does turmeric behave with neutral solution?
2. How is the effect of acidic solution with turmeric paper is different from acidic solution with litmus paper?

ACTIVITY 3 (Page 41)

Aim To prepare China rose indicator and show the effect of some acidic or basic solutions on it.

Materials Required China rose petals, beakers, water, funnel, filter paper, etc.

Procedure

1. Collect some China rose petals and place them in a beaker.
2. Add some warm water. Keep the China rose petals immersed in water till the water turns light pink in colour.
3. Remove the petals by filtration.
4. The light pink solution thus obtained is the China rose indicator.
5. Observe the effect of China rose indicator on different test solution like shampoo (dilute shampoo), lemon juice, soda water, sodium hydrogen carbonate solution, sugar solution, vinegar and common salt solution.
6. Note the initial and final colour of test solution and record your observation in tabular form.

Observation

Test solution	Initial colour	Final colour	Remaks
Shampoo (dilute shampoo)	White	Green	Basic
Lemon juice	Colourless	Deep pink (magenta)	Acidic
Soda water	Colourless	Pink	Acidic
Sodium hydrogen carbonate solution	Colourless	Green	Basic
Sugar solution	Colourless	No change	Neutral
Vinegar	Colourless	Deep pink (magenta)	Acidic
Common salt solution	Colourless	No change	Neutral

Conclusion We conclude that China rose indicator turns acidic solution to dark pink (magenta) and basic solution to green in colour. Neutral solutions remain colourless.

Viva Questions

1. In neutral solution what is the colour of China rose indicatror?
2. What colour will appear when lime water is added to China rose solution?

ACTIVITY 4 (Page 42)

Aim To demonstrate the effect of some common solutions on litmus paper, turmeric paper and China rose solution.

Materials Required Litmus paper, turmeric paper, China rose solution, dilute hydrochloric acid, sulphuric acid, nitric acid, acetic acid, sodium hydroxide, ammonium hydroxide, calcium hydroxide (lime water), etc.

Procedure

1. Take the solutions and test its nature with litmus paper, turmeric paper and China rose solution.
2. Observe the effect of different solutions and note your observation in tabular form.

Observation

Name of acid/base	Effect on litmus paper	Effect on turmeric paper	Effect on China rose solution
Dilute hydrochloric acid	Blue to red	Yellow	Dark pink
Sulphuric acid	Blue to red	Yellow	Dark pink
Nitric acid	Blue to red	Yellow	Dark pink
Acetic acid	Blue to red	Yellow	Dark pink
Sodium hydroxide	Red to blue	Red	Green
Ammonium hydroxide	Red to blue	Red	Green
Calcium hydroxide (lime water)	Red to blue	Red	Green

Conclusion We conclude that all the three indicators give different effects with acids, bases and neutral solutions.

Viva Questions

1. Name one substance which gives yellow colour with turmeric, light pink colour with China rose and blue colour with blue litmus paper.
2. Which colours will common salt give with all three indicator?

ACTIVITY 5 (Page 43)

Aim To show the effect of a synthetic indicator phenolphthalein in an acidic and basic solution.

Materials Required Hydrochloric acid (5 mL), test tube, phenolphthalein indicator, dropper, sodium hydroxide.

Procedure

1. We take small amount of hydrochloric acid (5mL) in a test tube. Note down its colour.
2. Note down the colour of phenolphthalein. Add 2-3 drops of phenolphthalein indicator to the acid in a test tube.
3. Shake the test tube gently. Observe any change in colour of the acid.
4. Now take sodium hydroxide solution in a dropper.
5. Add this to hydrochloric acid in test tube dropwise. Stir the tube gently. Observe the change in colour.

Observation

1. Hydrochloric acid and phenolphthalein are colourless.
2. After adding the phenolphthalein drops to the test tube containing hydrochloric acid, the solution remains colourless.
3. If we continue to add sodium hydroxide solution dropwise (while stirring), a light pink colour just appears.
4. At this stage, all the hydrochloric acid in a test tube has been completely neutralised by sodium hydroxide solution.
5. If we add one more drop of dilute hydrochloric acid, the solution again becomes colourless.
6. We observed that the process of neutralisation has taken place.

Conclusion We conclude that when solution is basic, phenolphthalein gives pink colour on the other hand, when the solution is acidic, it remains colourless.

Viva Questions

1. What changes occur during neutralisation?
2. Which salt is formed in the above neutralisation reaction?

Mind Map

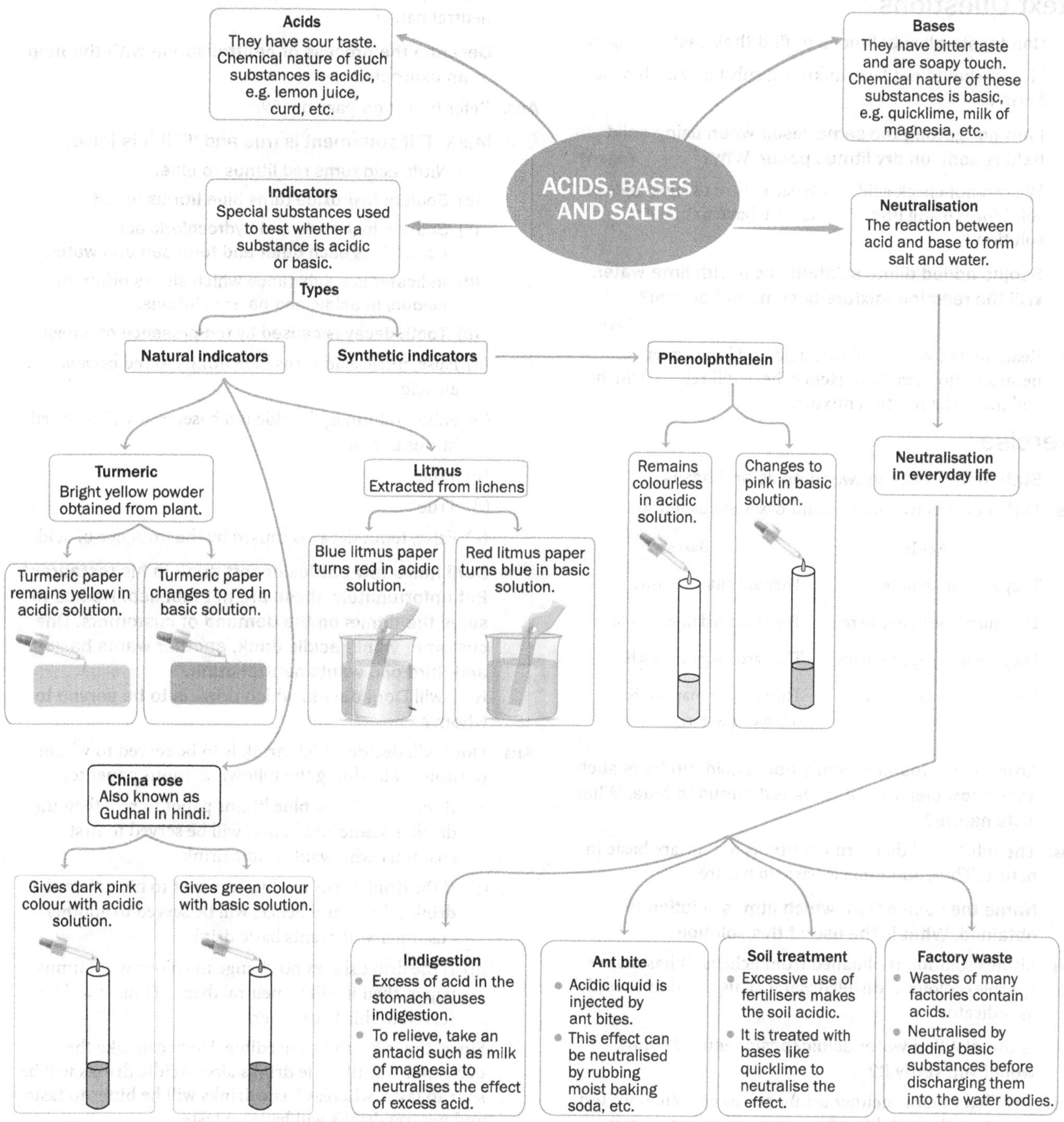

ACIDS, BASES AND SALTS
Acids
They have sour taste. Chemical nature of such substances is acidic, e.g. lemon juice, curd, etc.
Bases
They have bitter taste and are soapy touch. Chemical nature of these substances is basic, e.g. quicklime, milk of magnesia, etc.
Indicators
Special substances used to test whether a substance is acidic or basic.
Neutralisation
The reaction between acid and base to form salt and water.
Types
Natural indicators
Synthetic indicators
Phenolphthalein
Remains colourless in acidic solution.
Changes to pink in basic solution.
Neutralisation in everyday life
Turmeric
Bright yellow powder obtained from plant.
Turmeric paper remains yellow in acidic solution.
Turmeric paper changes to red in basic solution.
Litmus
Extracted from lichens
Blue litmus paper turns red in acidic solution.
Red litmus paper turns blue in basic solution.
China rose
Also known as Gudhal in hindi.
Gives dark pink colour with acidic solution.
Gives green colour with basic solution.
Indigestion
Excess of acid in the stomach causes indigestion.
To relieve, take an antacid such as milk of magnesia to neutralises the effect of excess acid.
Ant bite
Acidic liquid is injected by ant bites.
This effect can be neutralised by rubbing moist baking soda, etc.
Soil treatment
Excessive use of fertilisers makes the soil acidic.
It is treated with bases like quicklime to neutralise the effect.
Factory waste
Wastes of many factories contain acids.
Neutralised by adding basic substances before discharging them into the water bodies.

NCERT FOLDER

Complete Explanations of all NCERT's Questions

Intext Questions

Q.1 Can I taste all substances to find their taste? Page 39

Ans. No, we should not taste unknown substances. They can harm us.

Q.2 I am not getting the same result when using solid baking soda on dry litmus paper. Why? Page 42

Ans. We can not check acidic or basic nature of substance in solid form using litmus paper. We have to make it solution.

Q.3 Boojho added dilute sulphuric acid with lime water. Will the reaction mixture become hot or cool? Page 44

Ans. Reaction between sulphuric acid and lime water is neutralisation reaction. Hence, heat will release which will make the reaction mixture hot.

Exercise

Q.1 State differences between acids and bases.

Ans. Differences between acids and bases are as follows

Acids	Bases
They are sour in taste.	They are bitter in taste.
They turn blue litmus to red.	They turn red litmus to blue.
They are not soapy to touch.	They are soapy to touch.
They are soluble in water.	They may or may not be soluble in water.

Q.2 Ammonia is found in many household products such as window cleaners. It turns red litmus to blue. What is its nature?

Ans. The substances that turn red litmus to blue are basic in nature. Thus, ammonia is basic in nature.

Q.3 Name the source from which litmus solution is obtained. What is the use of this solution?

Ans. Litmus solution is obtained from lichens. It has mauve (purple) colour in distilled water. This solution is used as indicator.

Q.4 Is the distilled water acidic/basic/neutral? How would you verify it?

Ans. Distilled water is neither acidic nor basic. When we test its nature through litmus paper strips, we have found neither red nor blue changes in colour which verifies its neutral nature.

Q.5 Describe the process of neutralisation with the help of an example.

Ans. Refer to text on page no. 59.

Q.6 Mark 'T' if statement is true and 'F' if it is false.

(a) Nitric acid turns red litmus to blue.

(b) Sodium hydroxide turns blue litmus to red.

(c) Sodium hydroxide and hydrochloric acid neutralises each other and form salt and water.

(d) Indicator is a substance which shows different colours in acidic and basic solutions.

(e) Tooth decay is caused by the presence of a base.

Ans. (a) False, nitric acid turns blue litmus to red because it is an acid.

(b) False, sodium hydroxide is a base, so it will turn red litmus to blue.

(c) True

(d) True

(e) False, tooth decay is caused by the presence of acid.

Q.7 Dorji has a few bottles of soft drink in his restaurant. But unfortunately, these are not labelled. He has to serve the drinks on the demand of customers. One customer wants acidic drink, another wants basic and third one wants neutral drink. How will Dorji decide which drink is to be served to whom?

Ans. Dorji will decide which drink is to be served to whom (customer) by doing the following litmus paper tests.

(i) If the drink turns blue litmus paper to red, then the drink is acidic and hence, will be served to first customer who wants acidic drink.

(ii) If the drink turns red litmus paper to blue, then the drink is basic and hence, will be served to another customer who wants basic drink.

(iii) If the drink shows no change in colour with litmus paper, then it will be neutral drink. Thus, it will be served to third customer.

Since, the soft drinks are edible. Dorji can take the decision by tasting the drinks also. Acidic drinks will be sour to taste, whereas basic drinks will be bitter to taste and neutral drinks will have no taste.

Q.8 Explain why

(a) an antacid tablet is taken when you suffer from acidity?

(b) calamine solution is applied on the skin, when an ant bites?

(c) factory waste is neutralised before disposing it into the water bodies?

Ans. (a) We take an antacid tablet such as milk of magnesia to neutralise the excessive acid released in stomach during acidity.

(b) When an ant bites, it injects the formic acid into the skin. The effect of acid can be neutralised by applying calamine solution that contains zinc carbonate which is a base.

(c) The factory wastes contain acids if they are allowed to flow into the water bodies without neutralising it, the acid can kill fishes and other organisms. The factory wastes are thus neutralised by adding basic substances.

Q.9 Three liquids are given to you. One is hydrochloric acid, another is sodium hydroxide and third is a sugar solution. How will you identify them? You have only turmeric indicator.

Ans. We will put a drop each of hydrochloric acid, sodium hydroxide and sugar solution on the turmeric indicator one by one. The liquid which changes the colour of turmeric indicator to red is basic in nature that is sodium hydroxide.

Now, this red turmeric paper may be used to identify which one of the remaining two liquids is hydrochloric acid. Put one drop of each of these remaining liquid on the red turmeric paper. The liquid whose drop will turn this red paper to yellow is hydrochloric acid. This is because hydrochloric acid neutralised the effect of sodium hydroxide on turmeric paper. There is no effect on turmeric solution by sugar solution as it is a neutral solution.

Q.10 What could be the nature of the solution if there is no change observed when a blue litmus paper is dipped in a solution?

Ans. The nature of the solution could be basic or neutral, as if it is acidic it would change its colour to red, but instead it remains same.

Q.11 Consider the following statements

(i) Both acids and bases change colour of all indicators.

(ii) If an indicator gives a colour change with an acid, it does not give a change with a base.

(iii) If an indicator changes colour with a base, it does not change colour with an acid.

(iv) Change of colour with an acid and a base depends on the type of the indicator.

Which of the above statements is/are correct?

(a) Only (iv)

(b) (i) and (iv)

(c) (ii) (iii) and (iv)

(d) All of the above

Ans. (a) All indicators do not change colour with acids as well as bases, e.g. turmeric changes its colour to pink with base, but it remains yellow with acid. Therefore, statement (i) is incorrect.

There are some indicators which changes colour with both acid and base, e.g. methyl orange, litmus, thus statement (ii) and (iii) are also incorrect. Change of colour with an acid and a base depends on the type of the indicator used. Hence, only statement (iv) is correct.

REVIEW EXERCISE

Including Competency Based Questions

Part I

Multiple Choice Questions

1. Which of the following sets of substances contains acids only? NCERT Exemplar

(a) Grapes, lime water (b) Vinegar, soap
(c) Curd, milk of magnesia (d) Curd, vinegar

2. The correct way of making a solution of acid in water is to

(a) add water to acid
(b) add acid to water
(c) mix acid and water simultaneously
(d) add water to acid in a shallow container

3. Which of the following substances is basic in nature? CBSE Question Bank

(a) Baking soda (b) Curd
(c) Lemon (d) Orange

4. 'Litmus', a natural dye is an extract of which of the following?

(a) China rose (gudhal) (b) Beetroot
(c) Lichen (d) Blue berries (jamun)

5. A student understands that litmus solution has purple colour in distilled water. What colour is likely to be observed when it is placed in an acidic solution? CBSE Question Bank

(a) Blue (b) Green
(c) Purple (d) Red

6. A student has four solutions among which one is acidic in nature. She wants to identify the acidic solution using a litmus paper. Which of these observations would help to identify the acidic solution? CBSE Question Bank

(a) Place blue litmus in the solution and see if it turns white
(b) Place red litmus in the solution and see if it turns white
(c) Place blue litmus in the solution and see if it turns red
(d) Place red litmus in the solution and see if it turns blue

7. Turmeric is a natural indicator. On adding its paste to acid and base separately, which colours would be observed?

(a) Yellow in both acid and base
(b) Yellow in acid and red in base
(c) Pink in acid and yellow in base
(d) Red in acid and blue in base

8. Which of the following is an acid-base indicator?

(a) Vinegar (b) Lime water NCERT Exemplar
(c) Turmeric (d) Baking soda

9. A solution changes the colour of turmeric indicator from yellow to red. The solution is

(a) basic (b) acidic
(c) neutral (d) either neutral or acidic

10. Which of the following mixtures represents a neutralisation reaction? CBSE Question Bank

(a) Acid + Acid (b) Acid + Base
(c) Acid + Water (d) Base + Water

11. Products of a neutralisation reaction are always

(a) an acid and a base (b) an acid and a salt
(c) a salt and water (d) a salt and a base

12. Neutralisation reaction is a

(a) physical and reversible change
(b) physical change that cannot be reversed
(c) chemical and reversible change
(d) chemical change that cannot be reversed

13. Phenolphthalein is a synthetic indicator and its colours in acidic and basic solutions respectively are NCERT Exemplar

(a) red and blue (b) blue and red
(c) pink and colourless (d) colourless and pink

14. A student took a half-filled test tube with dilute hydrochloric acid and a few drops of phenolphthalein in the solution. As he put a few drops of sodium hydroxide into the solution, it turns to light pink. Further, he put a few extra drops of acid and observe that the colour disappears. What caused the colour to disappear from the solution? CBSE Question Bank

(a) The volume of the solution increased
(b) Turning of the mixture into a neutral solution
(c) Decrease in the amount of acid in the solution
(d) An increase in the amount of base in the solution

15. On adding phenolphthalein indicator to a colourless solution no change is observed. What is the nature of this solution?

(a) Basic
(b) Either acidic or basic
(c) Either acidic or neutral
(d) Either basic or neutral

16. **Anu re-visited a historical monument after 10 years. She noticed that the white monument had turned yellowish.**

Which event is most likely to have caused the change in colour of the monument? **Competency Based Que.**

(a) Flood (b) Drought
(c) Acid rain (d) Thunderstorm

17. **Which of these activities represents a neutralisation reaction in everyday life?** **CBSE Question Bank**

(a) Meditation before going to bed
(b) Drinking of water after consumption of food
(c) Exercise in the morning with an empty stomach
(d) Consumption of milk of magnesia during indigestion

18. **A student is sting by an ant while playing. An elderly person suggests rubbing moist baking soda in the region to get quick relief. What does moist soda do to the sting of an ant?** **CBSE Question Bank**

(a) Increases the strength of the acid
(b) Neutralises the acid for a longer time
(c) Preserves the acid for a longer time
(d) Condenses the acid, so that it does not spread

19. **When the soil is too basic, plants do not grow well in it. To improve its quality, what must be added to the soil?**

(a) Organic matter (b) Quicklime
(c) Slaked lime (d) Calamine solution

20. **A scientist tests a soil sample from a uncultivated field and concludes that the soil is highly basic in nature. She suggests that adding organic matter in the soil could improve the quality of the soil. How does organic matter improve the quality of the soil?** **CBSE Question Bank**

(a) It releases acids which neutralises the soil
(b) It traps water vapour and increases the moisture content
(c) It makes the soil lighter so that it can be easily transported
(d) It acts as food for the organisms already present in the soil

Answers

1. (d)	2. (b)	3. (a)	4. (c)	5. (d)
6. (c)	7. (b)	8. (c)	9. (a)	10. (b)
11. (c)	12. (d)	13. (d)	14. (b)	15. (c)
16. (c)	17. (d)	18. (b)	19. (a)	20. (a)

Fill in the Blanks

1. **Lemon juice and vinegar taste .... because they contain ....** **NCERT Exemplar**

2. **The substances which show different colours in acidic, basic and neutral solutions are called........**

3. **Turmeric and litmus are .... acid-base indicators.** **NCERT Exemplar**

4. **When an acidic solution is mixed with a basic solution, they .... each other forming .... and water.**

5. **Complete the following chemical reaction.**
Acid + Base $\rightarrow X + Y$ **Competency Based Que.**
What does X and Y stand for?

X =.............. Y =...............

6. **Phenolphthalein gives .... colour with lime water.**

Answers

1. sour, acids
2. indicators
3. natural
4. neutralise, salt
5. X = Salt, Y = Water
6. pink

True/False

1. **All substances are either acidic or basic.** **NCERT Exemplar**

2. **Lemon water is basic in nature.**

3. **Lime water turns red litmus to blue litmus.** **NCERT Exemplar**

4. **Common salt dissolved in water turns blue litmus to red litmus.**

5. **Phenolphthalein is a natural indicator.**

Answers

1. False, substances can be neutral as well.
2. False, lemon water is acidic in nature.
3. True
4. False, salt water solution is a neutral solution, hence, it cannot change the colour of litmus.
5. False, phenolphthalein is a man-made indicator.

Match the Columns

1. **Match the Column I with Column II.**

Column I	Column II
A. Tartaric acid	1. Soap
B. Calcium hydroxide	2. Curd
C. Formic acid	3. Unripe mangoes
D. Sodium hydroxide	4. Ant's sting
E. Lactic acid	5. Lime water

2. **Match the Column I with Column II.** **NCERT Exemplar**

Column I	Column II
A. Vinegar	1. is used as indicator
B. Sodium chloride	2. is sour to taste
C. Milk of magnesia	3. major salt of sea
D. Turmeric	4. changes red litmus blue

Answers

1. A-3, B-5, C-4, D-1, E-2, 2. A-2, B-3, C-4, D-1

Assertion-Reason Questions

The following questions consist of two statements- Assertion (A) and Reason (R). Answer these questions by selecting the appropriate option given below.

(a) Both A and R are true and R is the correct explanation of A
(b) Both A and R are true, but R is not the correct explanation of A
(c) A is true, but R is false
(d) A is false, but R is true

1. Assertion (A) Sugar solution do not change the colour of blue or red litmus paper.
Reason (R) Neutral solution do not change the colour of either red or blue litmus paper.

2. Assertion (A) Turmeric stain on clothes turn red when it is washed with soap.
Reason (R) The soap solution is basic in nature.

3. Assertion (A) When an acid is mixed with a base in any amount, the reaction is termed as neutralisation reaction.
Reason (R) The salt formed during neutralisation reaction can be acidic, basic or neutral.

Answers

1. (a) Both A and R are true and R is the correct explanation of A.
2. (a) Both A and R are true and R is the correct explanation of A.
3. (d) A is false, but R is true. A can be corrected as During neutralisation reaction, an acid and a base is mixed in suitable amounts.

Case Based Questions

1. Pema wants to do an acitivity with hydrochloric acid and lime water (base).

Most acids and bases can damage human skin.

(i) Which step must she follow during the activity to ensure safety

(a) Unite her hair
(b) Wear gloves
(c) Remove her shoes
(d) Wear a shirt with short sleeves

(ii) Lime water is a base.

Which of the following statements is true for lime water?

Circle 'Yes' or 'No' to marks your response.

	It the statement true for lime water	Yes/No
(a)	Lime water is sour in taste.	Yes/No
(b)	Lime water is slippery to touch.	Yes/No
(c)	Lime water turns red litmus paper blue	Yes/No

Competency Based Que.

2. The picture shows how acid rain occurs and what its effects are **Competency Based Que.**

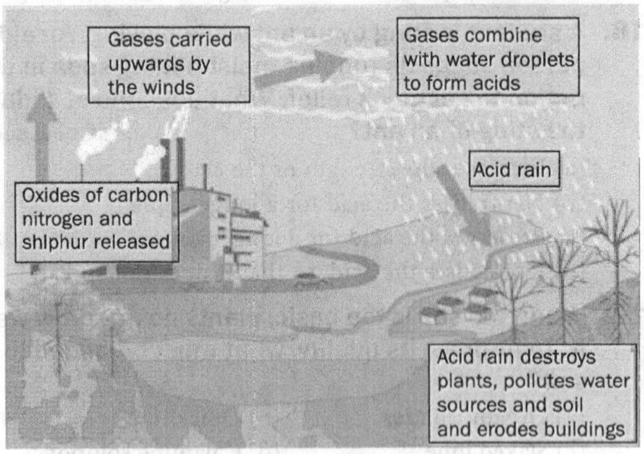

(i) Which of the following contributes to acid rain ? Circle 'Yes' or 'No' to mark your response.

	Does this contribute to acid rain?	Yes/No
(a)	Emission by vehicles	Yes/No
(b)	Emission by factories	Yes/No
(c)	Photosynthesis by plants	Yes/No

(ii) Which of the following is correct about the effects of acid rain ? Select the correct row.

	Acid rain damages some crops	Acid rain kills some aquatic animals
(a)	No	No
(b)	No	Yes
(c)	Yes	No
(d)	Yes	Yes

Answers

1. (i) (b) Wear gloves, (ii) (a) No, (b) Yes, (c) Yes
2. (i) (a) Yes, (b) Yes, (c) No, (ii) (d)

Part II

Very Short Answer Type Questions

1. What is the effect of acids and bases on blue and red litmus paper?

Ans. Acids turn blue litmus paper red, while bases turn red litmus paper blue.

2. What name is given to those substances which do not change the colour of either red or blue litmus paper?

Ans. The solutions or substances which do not change the colour of either red or blue litmus paper are neutral.

3. Write the name of two indicators which occur naturally.

Ans. (i) Turmeric (ii) China rose

4. Name the acid present in lemon juice and tomato.

Ans. Citric acid is present in lemon juice and oxalic acid is present in tomato.

5. Is lime water an acidic or basic solution?

Ans. Lime water (calcium hydroxide) is a basic solution.

6. Name the reaction which occurs when an acid is mixed with base.

Ans. Neutralisation reaction.

7. Which acid is injected into our body by an ant sting that causes pain?

Ans. The acid is formic acid which is injected into the skin of a person when an ant bites.

8. Write two basic substances which we use in our daily life.

Ans. (i) Baking soda (ii) Soap or detergent

9. (i) Name one indicator which turns red on adding an acid.

(ii) Name one indicator which turns red on adding a base.

Ans. (i) Litmus (blue litmus paper)

(ii) Turmeric

10. Form a sentence using the following words : baking soda, ant bite, moist, effect, neutralised, rubbing. NCERT Exemplar

Ans. The effect of an ant bite can be neutralised by rubbing moist baking soda.

Short Answer Type Questions

1. Write the characteristics of acids by which we can identify them.

Ans. Characteristics of acids are

(i) They are sour in taste.

(ii) They turn blue litmus paper/solution to red.

(iii) They react with bases to form salt and water.

2. Look at the figure which shows solutions taken in test tubes *A*, *B*, *C* and *D*. What colour is expected, when a piece of red litmus paper is dropped in each test tube? Nature of the solutions is given in the table for your help.

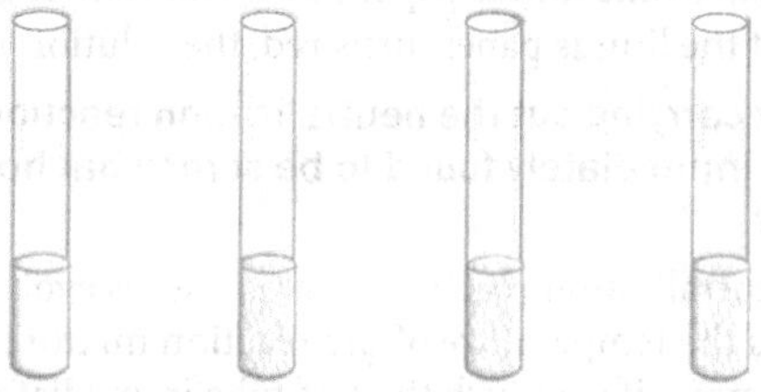

A Milk in water | *B* Baking powder in water | *C* Vinegar in water | *D* Glucose in water

Test tube	Nature of solution	Change in colour of red litmus
A	Neutral	
B	Basic	
C	Acidic	
D	Neutral	

NCERT Exemplar

Ans. Nature of solution is given below

Test tubes	Nature of solution	Changes in colour of red litmus
A	Neutral	No change
B	Basic	Turn blue
C	Acidic	No change
D	Neutral	No change

3. While playing in a park, a child was sting by a wasp. Some elders suggested applying paste of baking soda and others lemon juice as remedy. Which remedy do you think is appropriate and why? NCERT Exemplar

Ans. Wasp sting inject a liquid in the skin which is acidic in nature. Hence, baking soda is the appropriate remedy as it is basic in nature and neutralises the acid.

4. A small amount of hydrochloric acid is always produced in the stomach. Is it useful or harmful for us? If excess of acid is produced in the stomach, what should we do? Competency Based Que.

Ans. A small amount of hydrochloric acid produced in the stomach is useful as it can kill the harmful bacteria that may enter into the stomach along with the food. However, if excess of acid is produced, there is a burning sensation in the stomach. We should take milk of magnesia as an antacid medicine to neutralise the excess acid.

5. To test the presence of an acid in any substance, what methods can be used?

Ans. Acid can be tested in any substance by the following methods

(i) Take a drop of the dilute solution of the substance on the tips of your tongue. If tastes sour, it is acidic.

(ii) Dip a blue litmus paper in the solution. If the colour of the litmus paper turns red, the solution is acidic.

6. After carrying out the neutralisation reaction, the test tube immediately found to be somewhat hot. Explain why?

Ans. In neutralisation reaction, heat is always evolved which raises the temperature of the reaction mixture. Therefore, if we touch the test tube immediately after the neutralisation reaction, it is found to be hot.

Acid + Base $\longrightarrow$ Salt + Water (heat is evolved)

7. Paheli is suffering from indigestion due to acidity. Is it advisable to give her orange juice in this situation and why? **NCERT Exemplar**

Ans. No, because orange juice is acidic in nature. Excess of acid in her stomach can increase indigestion. She should take an antacid such as milk of magnesia which contains magnesium hydroxide to neutralise the excess acid.

8. Explain two neutralisation reactions related to daily life situation.

Ans. Refer to text on page no. 59.

9. Paheli observed that most of the fish in the pond of her village were gradually dying. She also observed that the wastes of a factory in their village are flowing into the pond which probably caused the fish to die.

(i) Explain why the fish were dying?

(ii) If the factory waste is acidic in nature, how can it be neutralised? **NCERT Exemplar**

Ans. (i) If the wastes of a factory flow into waterbodies, it can cause a threat to the lives of sea creatures. Thus, fish were dying because factory waste may contain acids or bases or other toxic materials.

(ii) If the factory waste is acidic in nature, it can be neutralised by adding basic substances.

10. Look at the given reaction.

Hydrochloric acid + Sodium hydroxide (base)

$\longrightarrow$ Sodium chloride (salt) + Water

Sodium chloride formed in this reaction remains in solution form. Can we get solid sodium chloride from this solution? Suggest a method (if any). **NCERT Exemplar**

Ans. We can get solid sodium chloride by evaporation method. It is the process by which water changes from a liquid to a gas or vapour by heating the solution.

Rate of evaporation increases with temperature.

Long Answer Type Questions

1. A farmer was unhappy because of his low crop yield. He discussed the problem with an agricultural scientist and realised that the soil of his field was either too acidic or too basic. What remedy would you suggest the farmer to neutralise the soil?

Ans. The reason for low crop yield in farmer's field was that the soil at a place is either too acidic or too basic. The soil may be acidic or basic naturally. The excessive use of fertilisers in the fields also makes the soil too acidic. In this case, it is treated with base such as quicklime (calcium oxide) or slaked lime (calcium hydroxide) which neutralises the excess acid present in the soil and reduces its acidic nature.

If the soil is too basic, then decaying organic matter (called manure or compost) is added to it. The decaying organic matter releases acid which neutralises the excess bases present in the soil and reduces its basic nature.

2. You are provided with three test tubes *A*, *B* and *C* as shown in figure with different liquids.

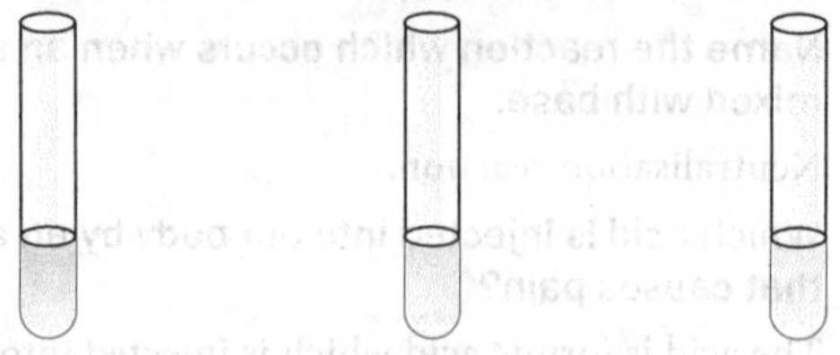

A Solution of tartaric acid　*B* Soap solution　*C* Pure water

What will you observe when you put

(i) a piece of blue litmus paper in each test tube?

(ii) a piece of red litmus paper in each test tube?

(iii) a few drops of phenolphthalein solution to each test tube? **NCERT Exemplar**

Ans.

Test tubes	Effect on blue litmus paper	Effect on red litmus paper	Effect on phenolphthale in solution
A	Turns red	Remains red	Colourless
B	Remains blue	Turns blue	Pink colour
C	Remains blue	Remains red	Colourless

3. Boojho, Paheli and their friend Golu were provided with a test, each containing China rose solution which was pink in colour. Boojho added 2 drops of solution '*A*' in his test tube and got dark pink colour. Paheli added 2 drops of solution '*B*' to her test tube and got green colour. Golu added 2 drops of solution '*C*, but could not get any change in colour. Suggest the possible cause for the variation in their results. **NCERT Exemplar**

Ans. China rose (gudhal) is an acid-base indicator which shows the following changes in different mediums.

China rose + acid → Give dark pink colour

China rose + base → Give green colour

China rose + neutral → No change in colour

They got variation in their results because solution 'A' was acidic, solution 'B' was basic and solution 'C' was neutral which gave different results with China rose indicator.

4. Explain neutralisation reaction with the help of an example, which indicator is used in this process.

Ans. Refer to text on page no. 58.

5. Write any three applications of neutralisation reaction.

Ans. Refer to text on page no. 59.

Case Based Questions

1. China rose is a natural indicator use for the detection of acids and bases.

The flower's petals are put in warm water for an hour.

The water, after one hour can be used as an indicator.

It is light pink in neutral conditions.

It turns green in basic conditions and dark pink in acidic conditions.

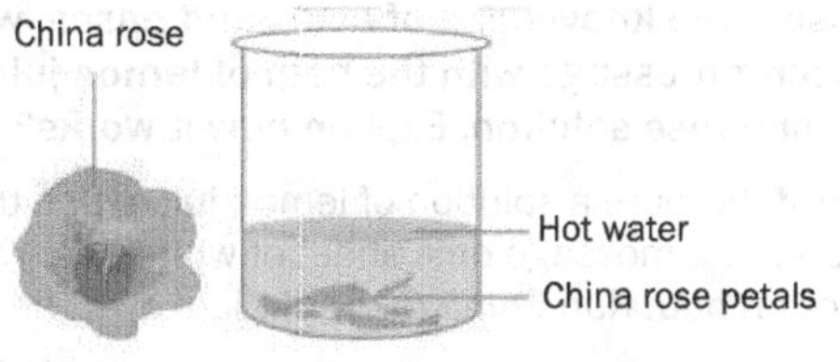

Zeenat takes 10 mL of three colourless liquids in separate test tubes.

She add 5 drops of China rose indicator to each test tube.

The pictures show the colour of the liquid in each test tube after the addition of indicator.

Competency Based Que.

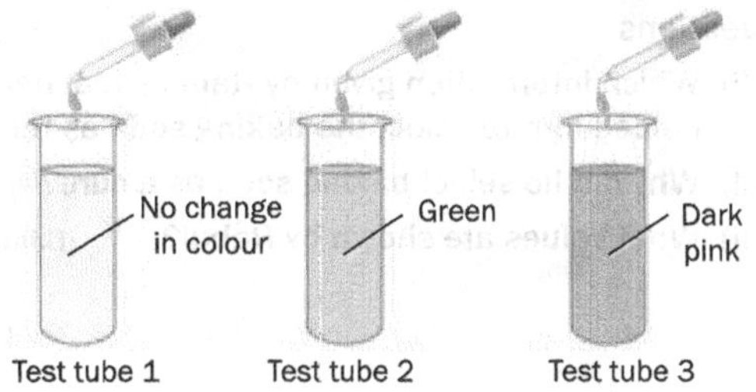

(i) Which test tube contains liquid soap?

(ii) Why are China rose petals put in warm water to make the indicator?

(a) To darken the colour of the petals

(b) To keep the petals fresh for a long time

(c) To destory the germs present on the petals

(d) To make the chemicals in the petals dissolve faster.

(iii) Why did Zeenat add the same amount of indicator to the three test tubes ?

2. Priya a class 7 student tested the nature of some common substances with the help of acid-base indicators and noted down her observations in the given table. **Diksha**

Substance	Phenolphthalein indicator	China rose indicator
X	Colourless	Dark pink
Y	Pink	Green
Z	Colourless	Pink
O	Colourless	Dark pink

(i) Substances *X, Y, Z* and *O* could be respectively.

(a) Tamarind juice, window cleaner, soap solution and lime water

(b) Soap solution, spinach juice, sugar solution and lemon juice

(c) Spinach juice, soap soluiton, sugar solution and lemon juice

(d) Window cleaner, tamarind juice, sugar solution and soap solution

(ii) What will be the colour of substance Y when reacted with turmeric indicator?

(iii) Give one difference between the China rose indicator and phenolphthalein indicator.

3. Study the image carefully and answer the following question.

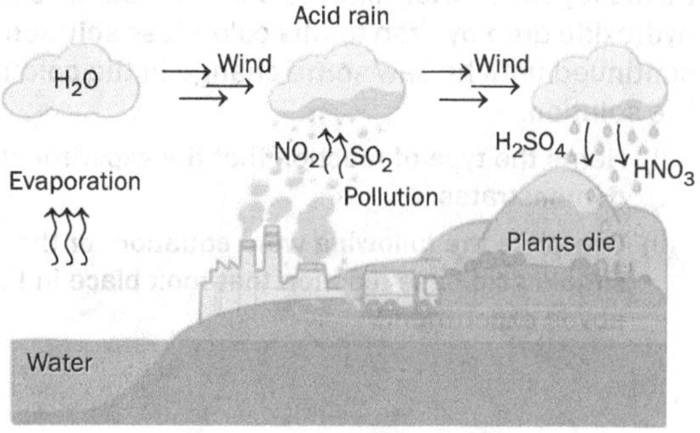

(i) Name one gas responsible for acid rain.

(ii) Write two harms caused to soil due to acid rain.

CBSE Question Bank

Ans. 1. (i) The test tube 2 contains liquid soap as it turned green due to basic nature of soap.

(ii) (d) To make the chemicals in the petals dissolve faster.

(iii) Zeenat added the same amount of indicator to the three test tube, so that we can compare the results effectively.

2. (i) (c) From the colour changes shown with different indicators, it can be conclude that the substance X is acidic, i.e. spinach juice, Y is basic, i.e. soap solution, Z is neutral, i.e. sugar solution and O is again acidic, i.e. lemeon juice.

(ii) Substance 'Y' is basic hence, it will give red colour with turmeric indicator.

(iii) Difference between China rose indicator and phenolpthalein indicator is

China rose indicator give dark pink colour with acidic substance, while phenolphnalein indicatior with acidic subsatnce remains colourless.

3. (i) SO_2 gas is responsible for acid rain.

(ii) The harms caused by acid rain to soil are as follows

(a) Soil becomes highly acidic and releases toxic substances into the soil thereby affecting the plant growth.

(b) The acidic water dissolves the helpful nutrients present in the soil and washes them away before plants use them.

Skill Based Questions as per NEP 2020

1. Three test tubes *A*, *B* and *C* are taken as shown in figure below. Red litmus paper was dipped in all three test tubes to test which solution is basic in nature. Identify in which test tube the red litmus paper will change its colour to blue? **Experimental skill**

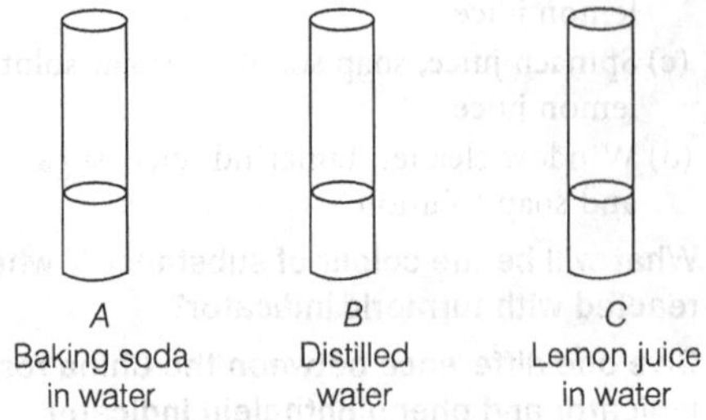

2. A student took some dilute hydrochloric acid in a flask, added a few drops of phenolphthalein and mixed it gently. After that the student added sodium hydroxide drop by drop to this colourless solution and continued until he saw some change in the colour of the solution.

(i) Name the type of reaction that the experiment demonstrates.

(ii) Complete the following word equation for the simple acid-base reaction that took place in the abvoe experiment.

Sodium hydroxide + Hydrochloric acid → ....

(iii) Describe and explain the colour of the solution when sodium hydroxide was added. **Analytical skill**

3. Using the knowledge of acids and bases, write a secret message with the help of lemon juice and China rose soluiton. Explain how it works?

Hint Prepare a solution of lemon juice. Use this solution to write a message on a sheet of white paper with a cotton bud. Rub China rose solution over the message.

Experimental skill

4. One day Rahul's mother after taking meal felt pain and irritation in her stomach at that time his father was out of station. Rahul remembered his teacher's statement and gave his mother some baking soda solution which gave her a relief from pain and irritation in stomach.

Read the above passage and answer the following questions

(i) Which information given by Rahul's teacher, that helped him to select the baking soda as remedy?

(ii) Why did he select baking soda as a cure?

(iii) What values are shown by Rahul? **Thinking skill**

ASSESSMENT EXERCISE

Part I

Multiple Choice Questions

1. Calcium hydroxide is also known as ....
(a) soap (b) vinegar
(c) lime water (d) milk of magnesia

2. Turmeric indicator in acidic solution gives
(a) red (b) colourless
(c) yellow (d) pink

3. Tartaric acid is found in ....
(a) tamarind (b) soap (c) curd (d) orange

4. The solutions which do not change the colour of the litmus paper are called as ....
(a) acidic solution (b) neutral solution
(c) basic solution (d) acid rain

5. Phenolphthalein is used as an indicator
(a) in neutralisation process
(b) to indicate the presence of an acid
(c) to indicate the presence of a base
(d) to indicate presence of both acid and base

Fill in the Blanks

6. Phenolphthalein indicator remains colourless in .... solution.

7. Complete the following :

Acid + Base ⟶ .... + ...

True/False

8. China rose indicator turns acidic solution to dark pink and basic solution to green.

9. Tartaric acid is present in amla fruit.

10. Magnesium hydroxide is called as milk of magnesia.

Match the Columns

11. Match the Column I with Column II.

	Column I		Column II
A.	Lactic acid	1.	Harmful for crops, buildings
B.	Acid rain	2.	Acidic
C.	Aerated drink	3.	Indicator
D.	Phenolphthalein	4.	Curd
E.	Sodium chloride	5.	Salt

Assertion-Reason Questions

The following questions consist of two statements **Assertion** (A) and **Reason** (R). Answer these questions by selecting the appropriate option given below.

(a) Both A and R are true and R is the correct explanation of A
(b) Both A and R are true but R is not the correct explanation of A
(c) A is true, but R is false
(d) A is false, but R is true

12. Assertion (A) Plants grow well when the soil is acidic.
Reason (R) Compost is added to the basic soil.

13. Assertion (A) During neutralisation reaction, the reaction mixture becomes hot.
Reason (R) Dilute sulphuric acid when added to lime water (which is a base), releases heat energy.

Part II

Very Short Answer Type Questions

14. If a liquid turns blue litmus red, is it an acid, base or salt?

15. What is the colour of phenolphthalein indicator in a basic solution?

16. Why are organic matters added to the soil?

Short Answer Type Questions

17. Why does a yellow curry stain on a white shirt turn red when it is washed with soap?

18. Which acid is used in the making of paneer at home?

19. What is the effect of ant bite? Explain its cure.

Long Answer Type Questions

20. If someone is suffering from the problem of acidity after over eating, which of the following would you suggest as remedy?
Lemon juice, vinegar, baking soda solution.
Give reason for your choice.

21. The wastes of many factories contain acids. Why is it considered necessary to neutralise them before allowing the wastes to flow into waterbodies?

Answers

1. (c) **2.** (c) **3.** (a) **4.** (b) **5.** (d) **9.** False **10.** True **11.** A-4, B-1, C-2, D-3, E-5
6. acidic **7.** Salt + water **8.** True **12.** (d) **13.** (a)

Physical and Chemical Changes

CHAPTER 05

Everyday we come across many changes taking place all around us. These changes may involve one or more substances. For example, Souring of milk is a change, making a sugar solution is a change, similarly setting curd from milk is a change. Other common changes that we have noticed around us are making of ice cream, melting of wax, stretching a rubber band, evaporation of water, cutting of paper, breaking of glass pane, bending of glass tube by heating, etc. Broadly, these changes are of two types, i.e.

(i) Physical change (ii) Chemical change

5.1 Physical Change

Properties of substance which are related to shape, size, colour and state of the substance are called its **physical properties.**

The changes in which no new substances are formed, but changes occurs only in its physical properties are called **physical changes**. e.g. melting of ice, freezing of water, breaking of glass, boiling of water, folding of paper, mixing sand with water, etc.

Characteristics of Physical Changes

The important characteristics of physical changes are as follows

(i) No new substance is formed in this change.

(ii) It is a temporary change and can be easily reversed to its original form. For example, temporary change in colour, shape, size, etc.

(iii) Very little energy (heat, etc.) is either absorbed or evolved.

We shall perform some activities (1-5) on page no. 77-78 to show the physical changes that are taking place all around us.

5.2 Chemical Change

A chemical change occurs, when two substances react chemically to form a new substance with different chemical properties.

All new substances, which we use in various fields of our life, are produced as a result of chemical changes. These are also called **chemical reactions**, e.g. rusting of iron, cooking of food, etc.

Characteristics of Chemical Changes

The important characteristics of chemical changes are as follows

(i) New substance(s) is/are formed in this change.

(ii) Heat, light or any other radiation (e.g. ultraviolet) may be released or absorbed.

(iii) Sound may be produced.

(iv) A change in smell or a new smell may be given off.

(v) A change in colour can take place.

(vi) A gas may be formed.

(vii) It is a permanent change and cannot be reversed.

We will perform some activities (6-8) on page no. 78-80 to show the chemical changes where new substances are formed.

Examples of Chemical Changes

Some examples of chemical changes are as follows

(i) Burning of any substance is a chemical change, e.g. burning of coal, wood or leaves.

(ii) Explosion of a firework (or crackers) is also a chemical change, which produces **heat, light, sound** and **unpleasant gases** that pollute the atmosphere.

(iii) When food gets spoiled, it produces a **foul smell**. Which shows that new substances have been formed in it. So, the spoilage of food is a chemical change.

(iv) If we cut an apple into slices and keep in the open for some time, we will find that the cut surface of apple acquires a brown colour. This **change in colour** is due to the formation of new substance by the action of oxygen (or air). So, this change in colour is a chemical change.

(v) When an acid reacts with a base, then a **neutralisation reaction** takes place in which two new substances, salt and water are formed. So, neutralisation reaction is a chemical change.

(vi) During **photosynthesis**, plants take in carbon dioxide and water in the presence of chlorophyll and sunlight to form new substances, i.e. glucose (food) and oxygen. So, photosynthesis is a chemical change.

(vii) In the **process of digestion**, the various food materials breakdown to form new substances, which can be absorbed by the body. So the process of digestion is a chemical change.

(viii) **Ripening of fruits** and **fermentation of grapes** are also common examples of chemical change.

Importance of Chemical Changes

Chemical changes are very important in our lives. In fact, every new material is discovered by studying chemical changes, e.g.

- If a metal such as iron is to be extracted from its impure form, we need to carry out a series of chemical changes.
- A medicine is the end product of a chain of chemical reactions.
- Important and useful new materials such as plastics and detergents are produced by chemical reactions.

A Protective Shield

There is a layer of ozone gas high up in the atmosphere. It protects us from the harmful ultraviolet radiations, which come from the Sun. Ozone absorbs this radiation and breaks down to oxygen. In this way, ozone layer prevents radiations from reaching to the Earth.

The breaking down of ozone into oxygen is a chemical change. If ultraviolet radiations were not absorbed by ozone layer, they would reach the Earth's surface and cause harm to us and other living things.

Try These 5.1

1. **Is a stretched spring reversible change or irreversible change?**
2. **CO_2 gas is dissolved in cold drinks. Is this a physical change or chemical change?**
3. **Is photosynthesis a chemical change or physical change?**
4. **How do you tell if a chemical change occurred in food?**
5. **What are the new substances formed during the chemical change in photosynthesis?**

5.3 Rusting of Iron

When an iron object is left exposed to moist air, it chemically reacts with oxygen and water in the air to form a red brown flaky substance called **rust**. The process of formation of this flaky substance on the iron objects is called rusting.

Chemical Changes During Rusting

The process of rusting can be represented by the following equation

$$\text{Iron (Fe)} + \text{Oxygen}(O_2)\ \text{(From the air)} + \text{Water}(H_2O) \longrightarrow \text{Rust (Iron oxide } Fe_2O_3)$$

The more humid the air, faster the rusting occurs. The rust slowly eats away or corrodes the iron, leading to considerable loss.

Prevention of Rusting

Rusting can be prevented by not allowing iron to come in contact with moisture and air.

Some methods of prevention of rusting are given below

(i) The simple method is to **coat the iron** with **oil, grease** or **paint**. These coats should be applied regularly to prevent rusting.

(ii) A more efficient method is to coat the iron with another metal such as **zinc** or **chromium**. The process of depositing a layer of zinc on iron is called **galvanisation**. The iron pipes used in our homes to carry water are galvanised to prevent rusting.

(iii) It can also be prevented by making alloys, e.g. stainless steel. Stainless steel is made by mixing iron with carbon and metals like chromium, nickel and manganese. It does not rust.

The Rust-Free Iron Pillar

Near the Qutub Minar in Delhi, an iron pillar stands which is more than 7 metres high. It weighs about 6000 kg. It was built in the Gupta period, about 1600 years ago. Even after such a long period, it has not rusted.

For it's unique rust-resistance, it has been examined by scientists from all over the world. This monument is a reflection of advances, India had made in metal technology so long ago.

5.4 Crystallisation

The process of cooling a hot concentrated solution of a substance to obtain crystals is called crystallisation. The process of crystallisation is used to obtain crystals of a pure solid substance from the impure solid substance.

For example

(i) Sea water contains dissolved salts, which makes it salty. Salt can be obtained from sea water by the process of **evaporation**. The salt obtained in this process is not pure and its crystals are small. The shape of the crystals cannot be seen clearly. Large crystals of pure substances can however, be obtained from their solutions by the process of crystallisation. It is an example of a physical change.

(ii) Impure copper sulphate powder can be purified by the process of crystallisation to obtain large crystals of pure copper sulphate.

For better understanding of crystallisation see activity 9 on page no. 80.

Try These 5.2

1. **What is the effect of moistures on iron?**
2. **How is rust different from iron?**
3. **Iron gets rusted. Is this a reversible process?**
4. **Among Fe_2O_3, FeO and Fe_3O_4, What is the formula of rust?**
5. **Name one substance which can be obtained from it's solution by crystallisation.**

Science Glossary

Chemical change A change in which two or more substances react to form new substances.

Chemical reaction A reaction in which one or more new substances are formed.

Crystallisation A process by which crystals of pure substances can be formed from their solutions.

Galvanisation A process of depositing a layer of zinc to protect from rusting.

Physical change A change in which a substance undergoes a change in its physical properties such as colour, shape and size.

Rusting It is the formation of rust, i.e. iron oxide due to the reaciton of air and moisture on iron.

Let's Investigate

ACTIVITY 1 (Page 47)

Aim To show that cutting of paper (or tearing of paper) is a physical change.

Materials Required Sheet of paper and a scissors.

Procedure

1. Take the sheet of paper.
2. Cut it into a number of pieces.
3. Try to join the pieces back to make the original sheet.

Observation You cannot join the pieces together to make original sheet of paper, but the piece of paper is still paper. It has not turned into new substance.

Conclusion During the cutting of paper into pieces only the size and shape of paper has changed, but no new substance has been formed. So, cutting of paper is a physical change.

Viva Questions

1. The change observed in the activity is reversible or irreversible?
2. Is burning of paper also a physical change?

ACTIVITY 2 (Page 47)

Aim To show that the conversion of chalk stick into chalk dust is a physical change.

Materials Required Chalk dust, water and chalk stick.

Procedure

1. Collect the chalk dust lying on the floor near the blackboard in classroom. If is not available, crush a chalk into fine powder.
2. Now, take the chalk dust and add a little water to it.
3. Make a thick paste of chalk dust.
4. Mould the thick paste into a chalk stick.
5. Let it dry.

Observation After making thick paste of chalk powder, it can be moulded back into chalk sticks. Hence, crushing of chalk stick is a physical change. It was easily reversed by converting chalk dust into chalk stick.

Conclusion Since, we can get back the original chalk stick from chalk dust, it is a physical change.

Viva Questions

1. Is this change reversible?
2. Did you recover chalk from chalk dust?

ACTIVITY 3 (Page 47)

Aim To show that melting of ice and freezing of water is a physical change.

Materials Required Ice and a glass tumbler.

Procedure

1. Take some ice in the glass tumbler.
2. Melt the small portion of ice by placing the tumbler in the Sun. Note the observation.
3. Now, keep the tumbler containing ice and water in the freezing mixture (ice + common salt). Note the observation.

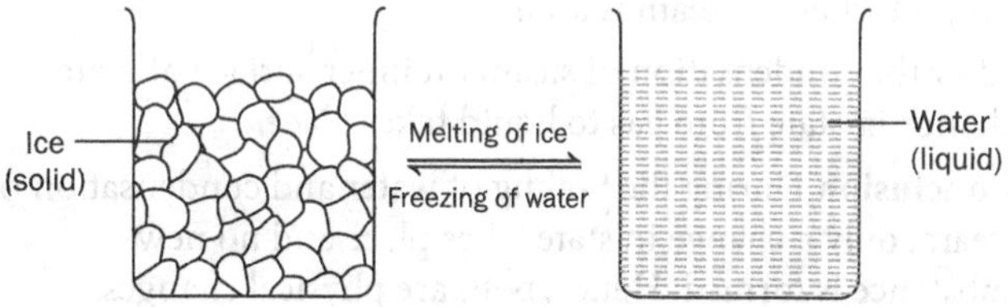

Reversible change of ice into water

Observation After placing the glass tumbler containing ice in the Sun, we notice that the ice has started melting.

Melted water freezes into ice after the tumbler is placed in the freezing mixture.

Conclusion No new substance is formed. Only a change in state (from solid to liquid) on melting of ice and (from liquid to solid) on freezing of water takes place. Hence, both are a physical changes.

Viva Questions

1. Are water and ice of same physical state?
2. What type of change occurs in this activity?

ACTIVITY 4 (Page 48)

Aim To show that the boiling of water and condensation of steam is a physical change.

Materials Required Water, hard glass beaker, burner and a plate.

Procedure

1. Take some water in the beaker.
2. Heat it using the burner until it starts boiling.
3. Notice the steam rising from the surface of hot water.
4. Now, hold an inverted plate over the rising steam.
5. Let the steam condense on the inner surface of plate.
6. Note the observation.

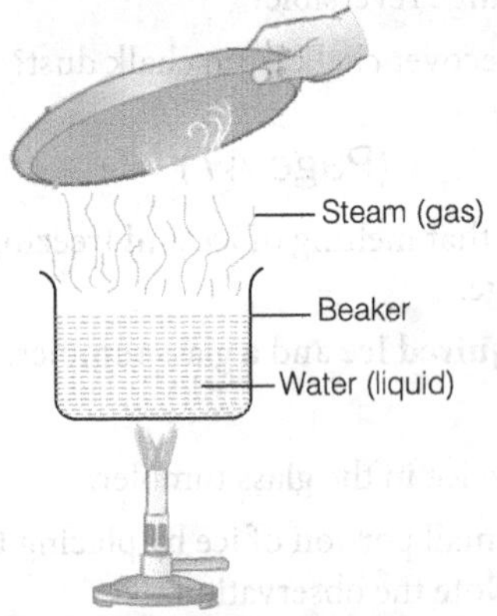

The boiling of water (to form steam) is a physical change

Observation When water starts boiling, steam rises. Water is a liquid whereas steam is a gas.

After the condensation of steam on inner surface of plate, change in state from gas to liquid takes place.

Conclusion During the boiling of water and condensation of steam, only a change in state takes place and no new substance is formed. Hence, both are physical changes.

Viva Questions

1. What is the physical state of steam?
2. Will steam condense when the plate is hot or when it is cold?

ACTIVITY 5 (Page 48)

Aim To show that the heating of hecksaw blade to the red hot stage is a physical change.

Materials Required A hecksaw blade, pair of tongs and a burner or stove.

Procedure

1. Take the hecksaw blade. Hold it's one end using pair of tongs.
2. Keep the other end of the blade on the burner flame.
3. Heat it until the tip of the blade turns red in colour.
4. Remove the blade from flame and allow it to cool.
5. Observe the change in colour of the tip of the blade on cooling.

Observation On cooling, tip of the blade gets back to it's original grey black colour.

Conclusion On heating the hecksaw blade, only a temporary change in colour takes place. No new substance is formed. Hence, it is a physical change.

Viva Questions

1. Suggest another material that can be used instead of hecksaw blade in the above experiment? Give reason.
2. Why do you need pair of tongs?

ACTIVITY 6 (Page 49)

Aim To prepare magnesium hydroxide in the laboratory.

Materials Required A thin strip of magnesium ribbon, sand paper, pair of tongs, burner, glass rod, watch glass and litmus paper.

Procedure

1. Clean the surface of magnesium ribbon using sand paper.
2. Hold one end of the ribbon using pair of tongs.
3. Bring the other end over the flame of the burner.
4. Keep it there until it starts burning with brilliant white light.
5. Collect the white powdery ash of magnesium oxide in the watch glass.
6. Mix the ash with small amount of water.
7. Stir the mixture with glass rod slowly to make aqueous solution of magnesium oxide.

8. Test the solution with litmus paper and note your observations.

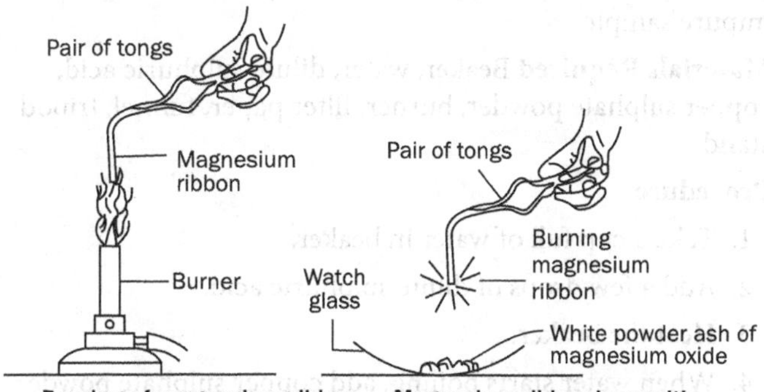

Burning of magnesium ribbon **Magnesium ribbon burn with white light and produce ash of magnesium oxide**

Observation

When magnesium ribbon is burnt, following change occurs

$$\underset{\text{Magnesium}}{2Mg} + \underset{\text{Oxygen}}{O_2} \longrightarrow \underset{\text{Magnesium oxide}}{2MgO}$$

When it is dissolved in water, following change happens

$$\underset{\text{Magnesium oxide}}{2MgO} + \underset{\text{Water}}{2H_2O} \longrightarrow \underset{\text{Magnesium hydroxide}}{2Mg(OH)_2}$$

When tested with red litmus paper, it turns the paper blue. It shows no change with blue litmus paper which indicates that the solution is basic in nature.

Conclusion Burning of magnesium ribbon is a chemical change as new substance is formed, i.e. MgO. The dissolving of magnesium oxide is also a chemical change as new substance $Mg(OH)_2$ is formed.

Viva Questions

1. Does the ash look like the magnesium ribbon?
2. Can we get Mg back from MgO in the above acitivity?

ACTIVITY 7 (Page 50)

Aim To study the reaction between copper sulphate (neela thotha) and iron.

Materials Required Copper sulphate salt, glass beaker, dilute sulphuric acid, test tube, an iron nail or used shaving blade.

Procedure

1. Dissolve about a teaspoonful of copper sulphate in about half a cup of water in glass beaker.
2. Add few drops of dilute sulphuric acid to obtain a clear blue solution of copper sulphate.
3. Keep a part of this solution in a test tube.
4. Drop the iron nail or shaving blade in the solution in glass beaker.
5. Keep the beaker for half an hour.
6. The colour of the solution should change.
7. Compare it with the colour of the solution saved separately.

Change in colour of the copper sulphate solution due to reaction with iron

Observation On dropping the nail or blade in the solution, we will see the colour of the solution fade gradually.

It ultimately changes to light green colour. A brown deposit is formed on the iron blade.

Conclusion These changes are due to the chemical reaction between copper sulphate and iron, which proceeds as follows

Copper sulphate solution (Blue) + Iron $\longrightarrow$ Iron sulphate solution (Green) + Copper (Brown deposit).

In this reaction, new substances iron sulphate and copper are formed. Hence, this is a chemical change.

Viva Questions

1. Which characteristic of a chemical change is shown in the activity?
2. Is this change reversible?

ACTIVITY 8 (Page 50)

Aim To study the reaction between baking soda and vinegar.

Materials Required Vinegar, test tube, teaspoon, baking soda, cork, glass delivery tube and lime water.

Procedure

1. Take a teaspoonful of vinegar in a test tube.
2. Add a pinch of baking soda to it.

3. Observe the bubbles of a gas comes out with a hissing sound.
4. Pass the released gas through a solution of lime water.

Observation When baking soda is added to vinegar, CO_2 gas is formed with a hissing sound. Bubbles of CO_2 gas rise in the test tube. Following reaction take place in the test tube.

Sodium hydrogen carbonate (Baking soda) + Acetic acid (Vinegar) $\longrightarrow$ Sodium acetate + Carbon dioxide + Water.

Lime water is a solution of calcium hydroxide. When CO_2 gas is passed through lime water, the solution turns milky. The reaction is as follows

Calcium hydroxide ($Ca(OH)_2$) + Carbon dioxide (CO_2) $\longrightarrow$ Calcium carbonate ($CaCO_3$) + Water (H_2O)

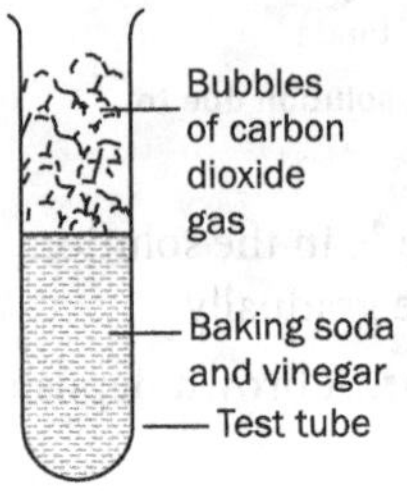

Chemical reaction between baking soda and vinegar

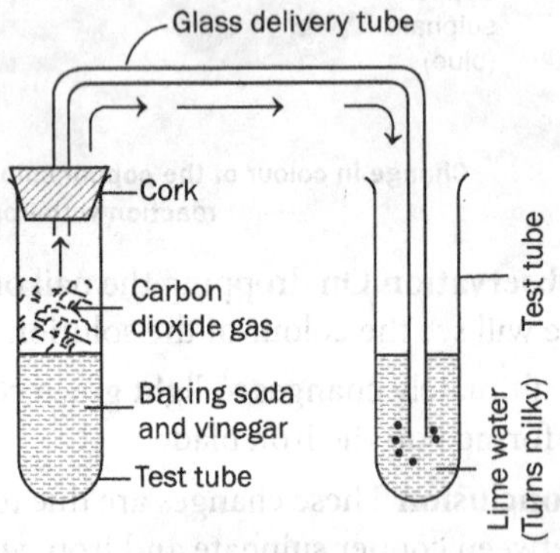

Passing carbon dioxide gas through lime water

Conclusion The reaction between lime water and CO_2 gas is a chemical change because a new substance, $CaCO_3$ is formed.

Turning of lime water into milky is a standard test of carbon dioxide.

Viva Questions

1. Which type of reaction occurs between baking soda and vinegar in the beaker?
2. How do we know when the gas is formed in the beaker?

ACTIVITY 9 (Page 53)

Aim To obtain pure copper sulphate crystals from an impure sample.

Materials Required Beaker, water, dilute sulphuric acid, copper sulphate powder, burner, filter paper, funnel, tripod stand.

Procedure

1. Take a cup full of water in beaker.
2. Add a few drops of dilute sulphuric acid.
3. Heat the beaker.
4. When water starts boiling, add copper sulphate powder slowly with continuous stirring.
5. Continue adding copper sulphate powder till no more can be dissolved with continuous stirring.
6. Filter the solution and leave it for cooling.
7. Note the observation.

Observation After the solution of copper sulphate getting cold, we can see the crystals of pure copper sulphate.

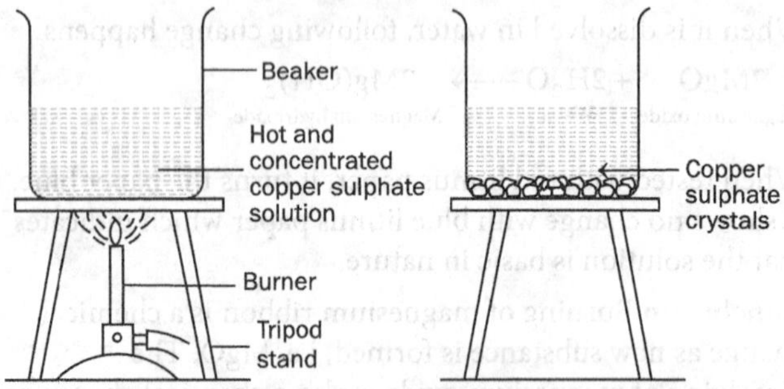

Making crystals of copper sulphate

Conclusion Pure copper sulphate can be obtained from the impure sample by the process of crystallisation.

Viva Questions

1. Why $CuSO_4$ is added in hot boiling water only?
2. Is copper sulphate obtained in its hydrated form or dehydrated form?

Mind Map

PHYSICAL AND CHEMICAL CHANGES

Physical change
A change in which a substance undergoes a change in its physical properties like, shape, size, colour, etc.

Examples

Characteristics
- No new substance is formed.
- It is a temporary change and can be reversed.
- Very little energy (heat) is evolved.

Crystallisation
It is the process by which a large crystals of pure substances can be formed from the solutions.

Example-Formation of copper sulphate crystals.

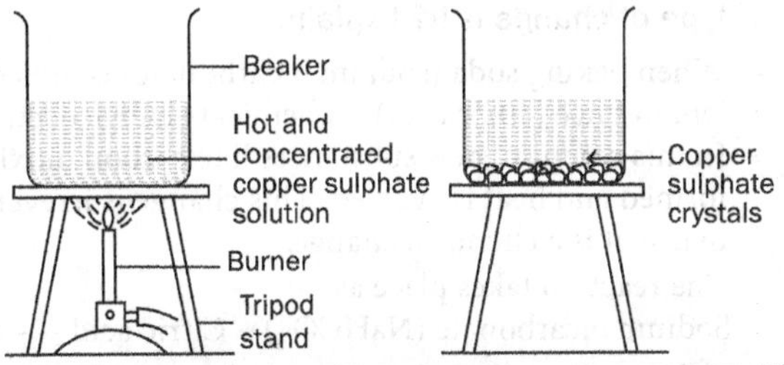

Chemical change
A change in which one or more new substances are formed.

Examples

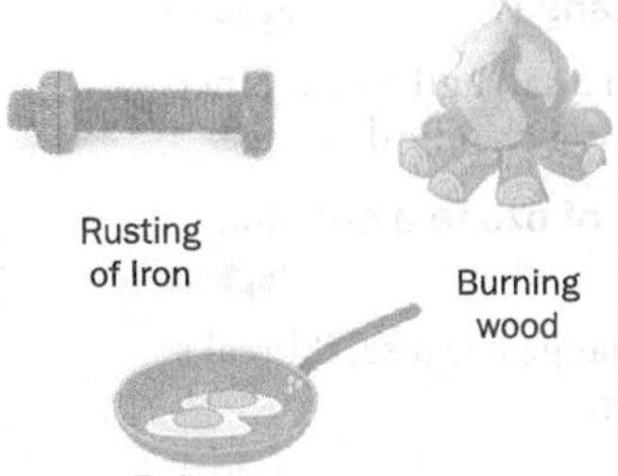

Characteristics
- New substance is formed.
- Changes are permanent and irreversible.
- Heat may be released or absorbed.
- New smell may be given off.
- Sound may be produced.

Rusting
It is the process of formation of a brown layer on iron object when it is exposed to moist air.

Process of rusting

$$O_2 + Fe + H_2O \rightarrow Fe_2O_3H_2O$$

Prevention

Galvanisation
Deposition of layer of a metal like chromium or zinc on iron to prevents rusting.
- Painting
- Alloying

NCERT FOLDER

Complete Explanations of all NCERT's Questions

Intext Questions

Q.1 Make a list of ten changes you have noticed around you. **Page 47**

Ans. Stretching of rubber band, burning of paper, burning of candle, rotting of food, steams rising from boiling water, making of curd, sublimation of camphor, breaking of a glass, bending of iron pipe, freezing of water.

Q.2 We learnt in chapter 1 that plants produce their food by a process called photosynthesis. Can we call photosynthesis a chemical change? **Page 52**

Ans. Yes, photosynthesis is a chemical change.

Q.3 Is digestion process a chemical change? **Page 52**

Ans. Yes, digestion is a chemical changes as new substances are formed in the process.

Q.4 Is neutralisation a chemical change? **Page 52**

Ans. An acid and a base reacts to form a salt and water. Since new substances are formed so, it is a chemical change.

Q.5 Can we call the breaking down of ozone a chemical change? **Page 52**

Ans. Ozone depletion is a chemical change because, it breaks down to oxygen as a new product.

Exercise

Q.1 Classify the changes involved in the following processes as physical or chemical changes.

(a) Photosynthesis **(b) Dissolving sugar in water**
(c) Burning of coal **(d) Melting of wax**
(e) Beating aluminium to make aluminium foil
(f) Digestion of food

Ans. (a) Photosynthesis – Chemical change
(b) Dissolving sugar in water – Physical change
(c) Burning of coal – Chemical change
(d) Melting of wax – Physical change
(e) Beating aluminium to make aluminium foil – Physical change
(f) Digestion of food – Chemical change

Q.2 State whether the following statements are true or false.
In case a statement is false, write the correct statement in your notebook.

(a) Cutting a log of wood into pieces is a chemical change.
(b) Formation of manure from leaves is a physical change.
(c) Iron pipes coated with zinc do not get rusted easily.
(d) Iron and rust are the same substances.
(e) Condensation of steam is not a chemical change.

Ans. (a) False, cutting a log of wood into pieces is a physical change.
(b) False, formation of manure from leaves is a chemical change,
(c) True
(d) False, iron and rust are two different substances.
(e) True

Q.3 Fill in the blanks in the following statements.

(a) When carbon dioxide is passed through lime water, it turns milky due to the formation of ....
(b) The chemical name of baking soda is ..... .
(c) Two methods by which rusting of iron can be prevented are ...... and ....
(d) Changes in which only ...... properties of a substance change are called physical changes.
(e) Changes in which new substances are formed are called ...... changes.

Ans. (a) calcium carbonate

The reaction takes place as,

$$\underset{\text{Lime water}}{Ca(OH)_2} + \underset{\text{Carbon dioxide}}{CO_2} \longrightarrow \underset{\text{Calcium carbonate}}{CaCO_3} + \underset{\text{Water}}{H_2O}$$

(b) sodium hydrogen carbonate
(c) galvanisation, painting
(d) physical
(e) chemical

Q.4 When baking soda is mixed with lemon juice, bubbles are formed with the evolution of a gas. What type of change is it? Explain.

Ans. When baking soda (sodium bicarbonate) is mixed with lemon juice (citric acid), a chemical change occurs.
In this reaction, new substances like carbon dioxide is formed and heat is evolved. This change is irreversible hence, it is a chemical change.
The reaction takes place as
Sodium bicarbonate ($NaHCO_3$) + Citric acid $\longrightarrow$
Sodium citrate + Carbon dioxide $\uparrow$ + Water + Heat

Q.5 When a candle burns, both physical and chemical changes take place. Identify these changes. Give another example of a familiar process in which both the chemical and physical changes take place.

Ans. **Physical changes in burning candle** On heating, candle's wax melts. Since, it can be turned into solid wax again on cooling. Hence, it is a physical change.

Chemical changes in burning candle The wax near to flame burns and gives new substances like carbon dioxide, carbon soot, water vapours, heat and light. Hence, it is a chemical change.

Cooking of food, boiling of eggs are examples of both physical and chemical changes. In both cases, the physical appearance of the substances change and new substances are formed together.

Q.6 How would you show that setting of curd is a chemical change?

Ans. Setting of curd is a chemical change because we cannot get the original substance (milk) back. The new substance, i.e. curd is different from the milk in taste, smell and chemical properties.

Q.7 Explain why burning of wood and cutting it into small pieces are considered as two different types of changes?

Ans. Burning of wood is a chemical change, while cutting of wood is a physical change because during burning, new substances are formed. After burning, we cannot get original substance (i.e. wood) back. Cutting of wood into small pieces is a physical change because no new substance is formed.

Q.8 Describe how crystals of copper sulphate are prepared?

Ans. Crystals of copper sulphate are prepared in the following manner.

(i) Take a cup full of water in a beaker.

(ii) Add a few drops of dilute sulphuric acid.

[**Caution** Never add water to the acid as the acid may splash on you].

(iii) Heat the water.

Copper sulphate solution (A) Beaker containing $CuSO_4$ solution (fresh solution)

Crystals of copper sulphate (B) Beaker containing crystals of $CuSO_4$

(iv) When it starts boiling, add copper sulphate powder slowly with constant stirring.

(v) Continue adding copper sulphate powder till no more powder can be dissolved.

(vi) Filter the solution.

(vii) Allow it to cool.

(viii) Do not disturb the solution, when it is cooling.

(ix) Look at the solution after some time and wait till it changes into crystals.

Q.9 Explain how painting of an iron gate prevents it from rusting?

Ans. Refer to text on page no. 76.

Q.10 Explain why rusting of iron objects is faster in coastal areas than in deserts?

Ans. We know that for rusting, the presence of both oxygen and water (water vapours) is essential. Thus, in coastal areas, the air contains high moisture, which means more humid environment so, rusting becomes faster. Whereas in deserts, moisture in air is less. Hence, rusting of iron is very slow there.

Q.11 The gas we use in the kitchen is called Liquified Petroleum Gas (LPG). In the cylinder, it exist as a liquid. When it comes out from the cylinder, it becomes a gas (change A). Then, it burns (change B).
The following statements pertain to these changes. Choose the correct one.

(a) Process A is a chemical change

(b) Process B is a chemical change

(c) Both processes A and B are chemical changes

(d) None of these processes is a chemical change

Ans. (b) Process B, i.e. burning of gas is a chemical change. Process A is a physical change. The LPG in cylinder is in liquid form because of high pressure. When it comes from cylinder, it turns into gas which is a physical change.

Q.12 Anaerobic bacteria digest animal waste and produce biogas (change A). The biogas is then burnt as fuel (change B). The following statements certain to these changes. Choose the correct one.

(a) Process A is a chemical change

(b) Process B is a chemical change

(c) Both processes A and B are chemical changes

(d) None of the above processes is a chemical change

Ans. (c) Both processes A and B are chemical changes. Bacteria acts on waste and converts it to biogas (change A). During biogas production it works as fuel(change B) and produces CO_2 and heat. Hence, A and B both are chemical changes.

REVIEW EXERCISE

Including Competency Based Questions

Part I

Multiple Choice Questions

1. Which of the following is a physical change? NCERT Exemplar

(a) Rusting of iron
(b) Combustion of magnesium ribbon
(c) Burning of candle
(d) Melting of wax

2. Which of these is a physical change? Competency Based Que.

(a) A flower turning into a fruit
(b) A lizard changing it's skin colour
(c) A plant making food
(d) A butterfly larva changing into cocoon

3. Which of these can never happen in physical change? Competency Based Que.

(a) Change in size of object
(b) Change in state of matter
(c) Change in shape of object
(d) Change in composition of matter

4. A student collects wax from a burning candle. He melts the wax and adds a new wick to it and leaves it to cool. What type of change is the cooling of wax to get back original candle?

(a) Physical change as it is a reversible change
(b) Chemical change as it is an irreversible change
(c) Chemical change as it is an reversible change
(d) Physical change as it is a irreversible change

5. Which one of the following is a chemical change?

(a) Twinkling of stars (b) Cooking of vegetables
(c) Cutting of fruits (d) Boiling of water

6. A chemical change may involve

(a) change in colour only (b) change in temperature only
(c) evolution of gas only (d) All of the above

7. Which of the following are true when milk changes into curd? NCERT Exemplar

(i) Its state is changed from liquid to semi-solid.
(ii) It changes colour.
(iii) It changes taste.
(iv) The change cannot be reversed.

Choose the correct option.

(a) (i) and (ii) (b) (ii) and (iii)
(c) (i), (iii) and (iv) (d) (i) and (iv)

8. An iron rod is heated till it becomes red hot.

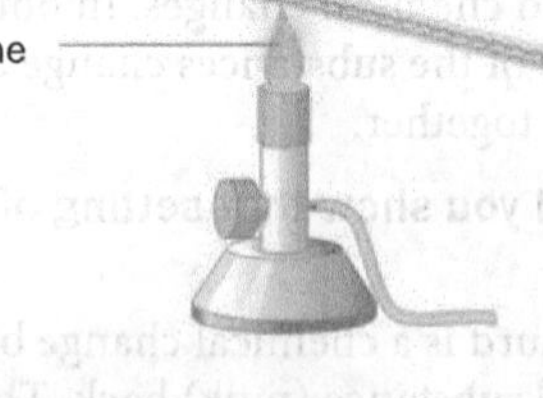

Is heating of iron rod a chemical change? Select the correct response. Competency Based Que.

(a) No, because no new substance is formed
(b) No, because the rod does not change it's state
(c) Yes, because the iron rod turns red when heated
(d) Yes, because heat is absorbed by the iron rod

9. Which of the following does not classify as a chemical change?

(a) Switching on a fan
(b) Cooking food
(c) Depletion of ozone layer
(d) Making of paneer

10. A woman wants to make tea. The steps in the process are

Step 1 : Boil water
Step 2 : Add tea and sugar to boiling water.
What type of changes to each of these steps represent?

(a) 1 : Physical change, 2 : Chemical change
(b) 1 : Physical change, 2 : Physical change
(c) 1 : Chemical change, 2 : Chemical change
(d) 1 : Chemical change, 2 : Physical change

11. When a piece of magnesium ribbon is burnt, a bright white flame glows. It, then turns into a white ash. Choose the correct statement.

(a) Magnesium ribbon heats up and disintegrates into smaller particles
(b) Pure magnesium bonds with oxygen in air to form a new substance
(c) Magnesium changes it's state from solid to gas and gas to solid
(d) Ash can be converted to magnesium by heating

12. **You brought some fruits from the market. Some days later, they rotted. What change did occur there?**
(a) Physical change as it is reversible
(b) Physical change as the colour changed
(c) Chemical change because it cannot be reversed
(d) Chemical change because shape changed

13. **Which of the following statements is incorrect for a chemical reaction?** **NCERT Exemplar**
(a) Heat may be given out, but never absorbed
(b) Sound may be produced
(c) A colour change may take place
(d) A gas may be evolved

14. **Which of these will not affect the rusting of iron?**
(a) Oxygen gas
(b) Moisture
(c) Salts
(d) Hydrogen gas

15. **It is monsoon season. It rains everyday. You left your iron pan outside. What will happen to it after one month?**
(a) It will remain same
(b) It will be clean and shiny
(c) It will form rust (Fe_2O_3)
(d) It reacts with water to form Iron hydroxide $Fe(OH)_3$.

16. **How do you prevent the rusting of iron?**
(a) By cleaning it with water
(b) By rubbing it with sand paper
(c) By painting it
(d) By keeping it in moist soil

17. **A man painted his main gate made up of iron, to** **NCERT Exemplar**

(i) prevent it from rusting.
(ii) protect it from the Sun.
(iii) make it look beautiful.
(iv) make it dust free.

Which of the above statements is/are correct?
(a) (i) and (ii)
(b) (ii) and (iii)
(c) Only (ii)
(d) (i) and (iii)

18. **Galvanisation is a process used to prevent the rusting of which of the following?**
(a) Iron (b) Zinc (c) Aluminium (d) Copper

19. **Paheli's mother made a concentrated sugar syrup by dissolving sugar in hot water. On cooling, crystals of sugar got separated.**
This indicates a **NCERT Exemplar**
(a) physical change that can be reversed
(b) chemical change that can be reversed
(c) physical change that cannot be reversed
(d) chemical change that cannot be reversed

20. **In the crystallisation process, solution is first heated and then allowed to cool. We let the solution be cold to**
(a) dissolve impurities in the solution
(b) make handling of beaker easy
(c) let the crystals form
(d) allow impurities to solidify in the solution

21. **Two drops of dilute sulphuric acid were added to 1g of copper sulphate powder and then small amount of hot water was added to dissolve it (Step I). On cooling, beautiful blue coloured crystals got separated (Step II). Step I and Step II are** **Competency Based Que.**
(a) physical and chemical changes, respectively
(b) chemical and physical changes, respectively
(c) both physical change
(d) both chemical change

22. **Which of the following cannot be obtained by crystallisation?**
(a) Sugar from sugar solution
(b) Salt from sea water
(c) Crushed coffee powder
(d) Copper sulphate

23. **Iron pillar near the Qutab Minar in Delhi is famous for the following facts. Which of these facts is responsible for its long stability?** **NCERT Exemplar**
(a) It is more than 7 m high
(b) It weighs about 6000 kg
(c) It was built more than 1600 years ago
(d) It has not rusted after such a long period

Answers

1. (d)	2. (b)	3. (d)	4. (a)	5. (b)
6. (d)	7. (c)	8. (a)	9. (a)	10. (a)
11. (a)	12. (c)	13. (a)	14. (d)	15. (c)
16. (c)	17. (d)	18. (a)	19. (a)	20. (c)
21. (c)	22. (c)	23. (d)		

Fill in the Blanks

1. **A physical change is generally ....** **NCERT Exemplar**
2. **Making sugar solution is a .... change.**
3. **Grinding of wheat grain changes its size. It is a .... change.**
4. **Iron benches kept in lawns and gardens get .... It is a .... change because a new .... is formed.** **NCERT Exemplar**
5. **Some substances can be obtained in pure state from their solution by ....**

Answers

1. reversible 2. physical 3. physical
4. rusted, chemical, substance 5. crystallisation

True/False

1. Stretching of rubber band is not a physical change. NCERT Exemplar

2. Formation of clouds is a physical change.

3. When a candle burns, both physical and chemical changes take place. NCERT Exemplar

4. Within our bodies, food is digested due to chemical reaction.

5. Cooking of rice is a physical change.

Answers

1. False, stretching of rubber band is a physical change.
2. True 3. True 4. True
5. False, cooking of rice is a chemical change.

Match the Columns

1. Match the Column I with Column II.

	Column I		Column II
A.	Large crystals	1.	Galvanisation
B	Depositing a layer of zinc on iron	2.	Chemical change
C.	Souring of milk	3.	Turn lime water milky
D.	Carbon dioxide	4.	Sugar candy (mishri)
E.	Iron oxide	5.	Physical change
F.	dissolving common salt in water	6.	Rust

2. Match the Column I with Column II.

	Column I		Column II
A.	Irreversible	1.	Physical change
B.	Galvanisation	2.	Crystallisation
C.	Melting of wax	3.	Red litmus to blue
D.	Purification of copper sulphate	4.	Rust
E.	Magnesium hydroxide	5.	Zinc
F.	Moisture and air with iron	6.	Chemical change

Answers

1. A-4, B-1, C-2, D-3, E-6, F-5
2. A-4, B-5, C-1, D-2, E-3, F-4

Assertion-Reason Questions

The following questions consist of two statements Assertion (A) and Reason (R). Answer these questions by selecting the appropriate option given below.

(a) Both A and R are true and R is the correct explanation of A
(b) Both A and R are true, but R is not the correct explanation of A
(c) A is true, but R is false
(d) A is false, but R is true

1. Assertion (A) Rusting is prevented by galvanisation.
Reason (R) Galvanisation is depositing a layer of zinc on iron.

2. Assertion (A) Rotting of fruit is a chemical change.
Reason (R) In rotting of fruit, a new substance is formed.

3. Assertion (A) Rusting is the formation of rust.
Reason (R) Heating speeds up rusting.

4. Assertion (A) Sugar can be obtained from its solution by crystallisation.
Reason (R) It is a chemical change.

Answers

1. (a) Both A and R are true and R is the correct explanation of A.
2. (a) Both A and R are true and R is the correct explanation of A.
3. (c) A is true, but R is false. R can be corrected as Heating does not speed up rusting. Moisture, air and salt in water speeds up rusting.
4. (c) A is true, but R is false. R can be corrected as Crystallisation is a physical change.

Case Based Questions

1. Ramesh describes how roti is made in his house in 5 steps. Here are the 5 steps.

(a) Wheat grains are ground to make flour.
(b) Flour mixed with water to make soft dough.
(c) Small balls of dough are flattened out with a rolling pin.
(d) The flat round dough is cooked on a pan.
(e) The crisp roti is coated with a layer of butter.

(i) In which step does a physical change take place
(a) in making a dough
(b) rolled the dough to make chapati
(c) baked the chapati on a pan
(d) dried the chapati and ground it in a grinder to make powder

(ii) Ramesh observed that cooking pan is coated with some brown substance. What is the reason for this?

(a) Cooking pan is old

(b) It is used for cooking purpose

(c) It often comes in contact with moistures and air

(d) It is not washed properly

2. During Diwali, Rajesh was helping his mother in cleaning the house. He found an old artifact that belonged to his grandmother. He kept it for himself though it was made of and was rusty. He needs to clean it and prevent it from getting rusted further. Answer the following questions.

(i) Rajesh can remove rust by

(a) washing the artifact with water

(b) washing the artifact with soap

(c) scrubbing the artifact with sandpaper

(d) scrubbing the artifact with cloth

(ii) Rajesh can prevent artifact from rusting in future by

(a) coating it with honey

(b) coating it with salt water

(c) keeping it hidden in garden

(d) coating it with oil

Answers

1. (i) (b) rolled the dough to make a chapati.

   (ii) (c) It often comes in contact with air and moistures.

2. (i) (c) scrubbing the artifact with sandpaper.

   (ii) (d) coating it with oil.

Part II

Very Short Answer Type Questions

1. What kind of change is shown by tearing of paper? **NCERT Exemplar**

Ans. Tearing of paper is a physical change as no new substance is formed.

2. Melting of wax is a change, where a solid changes to liquid state. Give one more such change, which you observe in your surroundings. **NCERT Exemplar**

Ans. Melting of ice is also a change, where solid changes into liquid state.

3. Give example of a physical change, which occurs by the action of heat.

Ans. Melting of ice to form water is a physical change, which occurs by the action of heat.

4. What colour of flame is observed when magnesium ribbon burnt in air?

Ans. When magnesium is burnt in air then a brilliant white flame is observed.

5. What is the nature of magnesium oxide solution?

Ans. Magnesium oxide solution is basic in nature because it turns red litmus solution to blue.

6. How can you say that ripening of a fruit is a chemical change?

Ans. Ripening of a fruit is a chemical change because after ripening, a new product with different properties is formed.

7. We should eat freshly cut apple. Why?

Ans. We should eat freshly cut apple because if we leave the apple after cutting, it starts turn to brownish by the action of air on it and its food value decreases.

8. Name the gas, which turns lime water milky.

Ans. Carbon dioxide gas (CO_2) turns lime water milky.

9. Complete the following reaction

$$Ca(OH)_2 + CO_2 \longrightarrow$$

Ans.
$$\underset{\text{Calcium hydroxide}}{Ca(OH)_2} + \underset{\text{Carbon dioxide}}{CO_2} \rightarrow \underset{\text{Calcium carbonate}}{CaCO_3} + \underset{\text{Water}}{H_2O}$$

10. Write the colour of copper sulphate solution obtained when iron nails are dipped in it?

Ans. When iron nails are dipped in copper sulphate solution, then the colour of the solution changes from blue to green.

11. Write word equations for two chemical reactions with the help of materials given in the box.

Air, copper sulphate, iron, vinegar, iron oxide, carbon dioxide, iron sulphate, copper, lime water, water

Ans. (i) Iron + air + water ⟶ iron oxide

(ii) Copper sulphate + iron ⟶ iron sulphate + copper

12. Suggest two methods to prevent rusting.

Ans. The two methods to prevent rusting are

(i) Painting the iron articles.

(ii) Greasing or oiling the iron articles.

13. Name the metals, which are mixed (alloyed) with iron to make stainless steel.

Ans. Metals like chromium and nickel are mixed (alloyed) with iron to make stainless steel.

Short Answer Type Questions

1. Classify the following processes into physical or chemical changes. NCERT Exemplar

(a) Beating of aluminium metal to make aluminium foil
(b) Digestion of food
(c) Cutting of a log of wood into pieces
(d) Burning of crackers

Ans. Physical changes are beating of aluminium metal to make aluminium foil and cutting of a log of wood into pieces. Chemical changes are digestion of food and burning of crackers.

2. Is cloud formation a physical change or chemical change? Explain.

Ans. Formation of clouds is a physical change. Clouds are formed by the condensation of water vapours present in the atmosphere. When rainwater goes back on the Earth, no new product is formed.

3. Write the differences between physical and chemical changes.

Ans. Differences between physical and chemical changes are as follows

Physical change	Chemical change
No new substance is formed.	New substance is formed.
It is a temporary change	It is a permanent change.
Physical change is easily reversible.	Chemical change is irreversible.
Very little energy (heat, etc.) is absorbed or given out in a physical change.	A lot of energy (in the form of heat, light, sound etc.) is absorbed or given out in a chemical change.

4. Magnesium ribbon burns in air and changes to white substance, i.e. magnesium oxide. When magnesium oxide dissolves in water, what type of change take place? Give reason in support of your answer. Express the change in the form of equation. Competency Based Que.

Ans. Mixing of ash obtained by the burning of magnesium with water is a chemical change. When magnesium is burnt in air, it forms magnesium oxide in the form of white ash.

Magnesium (Mg) + Oxygen (O_2) $\longrightarrow$
Magnesium oxide (MgO)

When magnesium oxide dissolves in water, it forms a new substance, magnesium hydroxide.

Magnesium oxide (MgO) + Water (H_2O) $\longrightarrow$
Magnesium hydroxide $Mg(OH)_2$

So, it is a chemical change.

5. Explain the following.

(i) Lime water turns milky on passing carbon dioxide gas through it.

(ii) Bubbles are produced when acetic acid is added to a solution of sodium hydrogen carbonate. NCERT Exemplar

Ans. (i) Refer to text on page no. 80.

(ii) Refer to text on page no. 80.

6. The process of digestion is a chemical change. Explain.

Ans. In the process of digestion, the various food materials breakdown to form new substances, which can be absorbed by the body. So, the process of digestion is a chemical change.

7. Which type of change takes place in the following and state whether the energy is evolved or absorbed during the change?

Burning of a candle, lightning of a bulb, preparation of food by green plants, volcanic eruption, evaporation of petrol, burning of LPG.

Ans. (i) **Burning of a candle** Chemical change as well as physical change and energy is evolved.

(ii) **Lightning of a bulb** Physical change, energy is evolved.

(iii) **Preparation of food by green plants** Chemical change, energy is absorbed.

(iv) **Volcanic eruption** Chemical change, energy is evolved.

(v) **Evaporation of petrol** Physical change as no new chemical substance is formed, energy is absorbed.

(vi) **Burning of LPG** Chemical change because LPG on burning form CO_2 and H_2O, energy is evolved.

8. In addition to the formation of new products, what changes do the chemical changes accompany?

Ans. Refer to text on page no. 74.

9. Plants prepare their food by a process called photosynthesis. Can we call photosynthesis is a chemical change? Explain.

Ans. During photosynthesis, the plants intake carbon dioxide and water in the presence of chlorophyll and sunlight to form two new substances, i.e. glucose (food) and oxygen gas.

So, photosynthesis is a chemical change.

10. Explosion of a cracker is a chemical change. Explain.

Ans. When we burn a cracker, it explods. Explosion produces heat, light, sound and unpleasant gases that pollute the atmosphere. Many new products are formed. So, it is a chemical change.

11. Why cannot a chemical change be normally reversed?

Ans. In a chemical change, the new substances formed are quite different from the original ones. Therefore, a chemical change cannot be normally reversed.

12. Give two examples for each of the following cases

(i) Physical changes, which are reversible.

(ii) Physical changes, which are not reversible.

(iii) Chemical changes **NCERT Exemplar**

Ans. (i) (a) Folding of paper (b) Melting of ice

(ii) (a) Tearing of paper (b) Breaking of glass

(iii) (a) Reaction between vinegar and baking soda.

(b) Burning of a matchstick.

13. How ozone layer acts as a protective shield?

Ans. The ozone layer protects us from the harmful ultraviolet radiations, which come from the Sun. It absorbs ultraviolet radiations coming from the Sun and breaks down to form oxygen.

In this way, ozone layer absorbs harmful ultraviolet radiations.

14. A student took a solution of copper sulphate in a beaker and put a clean iron nail into it and left it for about an hour.

(i) What changes do you expect?

(ii) Are these changes chemical in nature?

(iii) Write a word equation for the chemical change, if any. **NCERT Exemplar**

Ans. (i) (a) Colour of the solution in the beaker changes from blue to green.

(b) A brown coloured deposit is found on the surface of the iron nail.

(ii) The changes are chemical in nature as new substances, iron sulphate (green) and copper (brown) are formed.

(iii) Copper sulphate (Blue) + Iron ⟶ Iron sulphate (Green) + Copper (Brown)

15. What happens when an iron blade of a knife is dipped in a copper sulphate solution? What kind of change takes place?

Ans. When an iron blade of a knife is dipped in a copper sulphate solution, then iron blade is coated with reddish brown deposits of copper.

And the blue colour of copper sulphate solution changes to light green due to the formation of new substance iron sulphate. So, it is a chemical change.

16. What is stainless steel? How is stainless steel made? State an important property of stainless steel.

Ans. Refer to text on page no. 76.

Long Answer Type Questions

1. Give an example of a chemical reaction for each of the following situations **NCERT Exemplar**

(i) A change in colour is observed.

(ii) A gas is evolved.

(iii) Sound is produced.

Ans. (i) Chemical reaction between copper sulphate solution and iron metal. In this reaction, blue colour of copper sulphate solution changes to light green colour due to the formation of iron sulphate.

Copper sulphate (Blue) + Iron (Grey) ⟶ Iron sulphate (Light green) + Copper (Brown)

(ii) When baking soda and vinegar are mixed together then a chemical change takes place and bubbles of carbon dioxide gas are formed along with some other substances.

Baking soda (Sodium hydrogen carbonate) + Vinegar (Acetic acid) ⟶ Sodium acetate + Carbon dioxide + Water

(iii) Explosion of a firework produces heat, light, sound and unpleasant gases. Explosion of a firework is a chemical change.

2. If you leave a piece of iron in the open for a few days, it acquires a film of brownish substance, called rust.

(i) Do you think rust is different from iron?

(ii) Can you change rust back into iron by some simple method?

(iii) Do you think formation of rust on iron is a chemical change?

(iv) Give two other examples of a similar type of change.

Ans. (i) Yes, rust is iron oxide (Fe_2O_3). Thus, rust and iron are not the same substance.

(ii) No, in the process of rusting, a new substance, rust (iron oxide) is formed. It cannot be reversed by any method.

(iii) Yes, rusting of iron is a chemical change. During the rusting of iron, it combines with the oxygen in the presence of water (moisture) to form a new compound 'iron oxide'. This iron oxide is a rust.

Iron + Oxygen + Water (From damp air) ⟶ Iron oxide (Rust)

It is a permanent change which cannot be reversed back. So, rusting of iron is a chemical change.

(iv) Two other examples of chemical change are

(a) Setting of curd from milk.

(b) Burning of magnesium ribbon to form magnesium oxide.

Case Based Question

1. Sania adds a piece of magnesium ribbon to a test tube containing dilute hydrochloric acid.

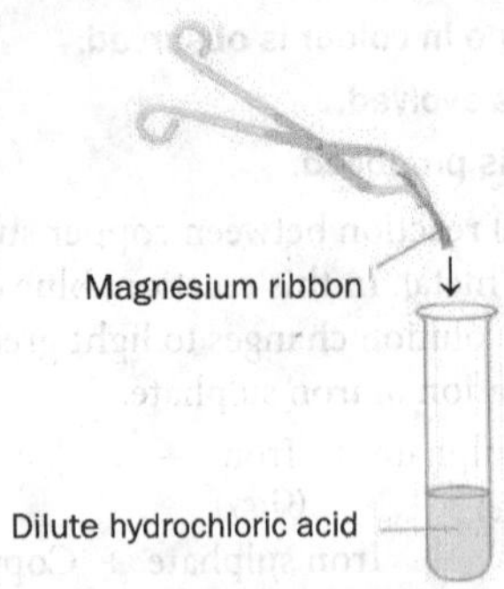

She observes the following events

I. The test tube gets hot.

II. Gas bubbles are formed.

III. The magnesium ribbon dissolves in the acid.

Competency Based Que.

(i) Which observation(s) shows that a chemical change may have taken place in the test tube?

(a) Only I (b) Only II (c) I and II (d) I, II and III

(ii) After observing the given events. Sania adds a few more magnesium ribbons to the same test tube. This time she observes tiny pieces of magnesium ribbon floating in the test tube. Sania thinks that the reaction was not completed.

What does sania need to do to complete the reaction?

(a) Heat the test tube

(b) Add more magnesium ribbons to the test tube

(c) Add more acid to the test tube

(d) Shake the test tube to mix magnesium ribbons and acid

(iii) Sania later repeats her activity using magnesium powder instead of magnesium ribbon. Will there be a change in her first three observations? Explain your answer.

Ans. 1. (i) (c)

(ii) (c)

(iii) No, because magnesium powder and magnesium ribbon are made of the some substance, i.e. magnesium. Hence, both will react in the same way and give the same observations.

Skill Based Questions as per NEP 2020

1. Amit dissolved sugar in water and observed the change. His friend Raj took a little sugar in a spatula and directly heated it on a bunsen burner on a high flame.

Answer the following questions. **Experimental skill**

(i) Which type of changes is observed by the Amit? Is it reversible or irreversible?

(ii) Who of the two will observe chemical change?

2. Abhi burned a substance *X* over the candle flame and white dazzling light is observed. Also white powdery ash left behind. He mixed the white ash formed with small amount of water. Then he dipped red and blue litmus papers into the solution one by one. **Analytical skill**

(i) Identify the substance *X*.

(ii) Which substance is formed after substance *X* gets burnt?

(iii) What is the nature of solution formed after mixing the white ash into the water acidic or basic?

3. Rahul was a student of class VII. His father purchased a new bicycle for him on his birthday. After few months, he found that the cycle chain and the handle gets rusted. His father advised him to apply a coating of paint to the cycle and not to keep it in the open in future. **Thinking skill**

Now, answer the following questions

(i) Why his cycle gets rusted?

(ii) What do you mean by rusting of iron?

4. In the summer holidays, Karan went to Rann of Kutch in Gujarat with his parents. Karan was aware that in the coastal regions of India especially in the Rann of Kutch common salt is obtained from sea water. Karan was very excited to see that place. He requested his father that he want to see the process of obtaining salt from sea. His father helped him and they went to see the place where common salt was collecting. And he also explained the whole process. Karan was very happy to see the process. **Thinking skill**

Now, answer the following questions.

(i) How the crystals of common salt obtained from sea water?

(ii) Name the process by which salt is collected from sea water?

ASSESSMENT EXERCISE

Part I

Multiple Choice Questions

1. Which property among the following will stay the same during physical and chemical changes?
(a) Density (b) Shape
(c) Mass (d) Arrangement of particles

2. Formation of a substance is
(a) temporary change
(b) physical change
(c) chemical change
(d) reversible change

3. Which of the following is the formula of ozone?
(a) Fe_2O_3 (b) O_2
(c) O_3 (d) H_2O

Fill in the Blanks

4. Stains are removed from clothes using soap. It is a .... as well as .... change.

5. Rusting is the formation of rust whose formula is ....

6. Crystallisation is the process of obtaining .... of solute from their solution.

Match the Columns

7. Match the Column I with Column II.

Column I	Column II
A. A protective shield	1. Chemical change
B. Brownish coating on iron	2. Crystallisation
C. Impure solid to pure solid	3. Rust
D. Evolution of heat	4. Ozone

True/False

8. We can retrieve milk from curd.

9. In cutting of paper, a new substance is formed.

10. We can separate salt from salt water solution using crystallisation.

Assertion-Reason Questions

The following questions consist of two statements Assertion (A) and Reason (R). Answer these questions by selecting the appropriate option given below.
(a) Both A and R are true and R is the correct explanation of A.
(b) Both A and R are true, but R is not the correct explanation of A.
(c) A is true, but R is false.
(d) A is false, but R is true.

11. Assertion (A) Burning of candle is a physical as well as a chemical change.

Reason (R) Melting of wax is a physical change, while burning of wick and evaporation of some wax is a chemical change.

12. Assertion (A) Iron can be prevented from rusting.

Reason (R) Objects made up of iron are painted to break its direct contact with air and moisture.

Part II

Very Short Answer Type Questions

13. What method will you use to get a pure liquid if it has dissolved impurities present in it?

14. For which purpose sand paper is used?

15. Which gas is given off when calcium carbonate is heated?

Short Answer Type Questions

16. What happens when magnesium is burnt in the presence of air?

17. Write the reaction that takes place when iron nails are dipped in copper sulphate solution.

18. Write two points which tell us that formation of curd from milk is a chemical change.

Long Answer Type Questions

19. What happens when magnesium oxide is dissolved in water? Write a word equation for this process. Name the type of change which takes place.

20. Explain, how rusting damages iron objects?

Answers

1. (c) 2. (c) 3. (c)
4. physical, chemical 5. Fe_2O_3
6. Pure crystals
7. The correct match is A-4, B-3, C-2, D-1
8. False
9. False
10. True
11. (a)
12. (a)

CHAPTER 06

Respiration in Organisms

All living organisms (animals and plants) performs various functions like nutrition, transport, excretion and reproduction. To perform these functions, they needs energy. We require energy even when we are eating, sleeping or reading. Our food has stored energy, which is released during respiration. Therefore, all living organisms respire to get energy from food.

6.1 Respiration

The process of breakdown of food in the cells of living beings with the release of energy is called **cellular respiration**. During respiration, we breathe in air rich in oxygen and breathe out air rich in carbon dioxide. The air rich in oxygen is transported to all parts of the body and ultimately to each cell. This oxygen is utilised by the cell for respiration.

Types of Respiration

On the basis of the presence or absence of oxygen, respiration is classified into two types.

1. Aerobic Respiration

When breakdown of food (glucose) occurs in the presence of oxygen, it is called aerobic respiration. During aerobic respiration, food (glucose) is completely broken down into carbon dioxide and water and energy is released. It can be shown by the following equation

$$\underset{\text{(Glucose)}}{\text{Food}} \xrightarrow{\text{Oxygen}} \text{Carbon dioxide} + \text{Water} + \text{Energy}$$

Aerobic respiration occurs in most of the organisms such as humans, dogs, cats, lions, elephants, cows, buffaloes, goats, snakes, earthworms, frogs, fishes, etc.

2. Anaerobic Respiration

When breakdown of food (glucose) takes place in the absence of oxygen, it is called anaerobic respiration. In this type of respiration, food (glucose) is not completely broken down into carbon dioxide and water. During this process an intermediate compound is formed with the release of less amount of energy.

Yeasts and certain bacteria carry out anaerobic respiration. The organisms that carry out respiration in the absence of oxygen are called **anaerobes**.

Anaerobic Respiration in Yeast

Yeast is a single-celled organism. In the absence of oxygen, yeast breaks down glucose into alcohol and carbon dioxide. Small amount of energy is also released during this process.

The byproduct, i.e. alcohol produced in this reaction is used in making beer and wine.

$$\underset{\text{(Glucose)}}{\text{Food}} \xrightarrow{\text{Without oxygen or air}} \text{Alcohol} + \text{Carbon dioxide} + \text{Energy}$$

Anaerobic Respiration in Muscles

In human body, when muscles are overworked, e.g. during exercise, the oxygen demand is not met through aerobic respiration. Thus, muscle cells begin to respire anaerobically in low oxygen conditions due to which glucose gets converted into lactic acid.
It can be summarised as

$$\underset{\text{(Food)}}{\text{Glucose}} \xrightarrow[\text{(Anaerobic respiration in muscles)}]{\text{No oxygen or air}} \text{Lactic acid} + \text{Energy}$$

Accumulation of excess lactic acid in the muscles causes pain and leads to muscles **fatigue** (cramp). We can get relief from muscle cramps by taking a hot water bath or massage.

This improves the circulation of blood and therefore, oxygen supply to the muscle cells of affected area increases. The increased supply of oxygen results in the complete breakdown of lactic acid into carbon dioxide and water, thereby giving relief from cramps.

Differences between aerobic and anaerobic respiration

Aerobic respiration	Anaerobic respiration
It occurs in the presence of oxygen.	It takes place in the absence of oxygen.
Complete breakdown of food takes place in aerobic respiration.	Partial breakdown of food occurs in anaerobic respiration.
End products of aerobic respiration are CO_2 and water.	End products of anaerobic respiration are alcohol and CO_2 or lactic acid.
Large amount of energy is produced during aerobic respiration. e.g. humans, dogs, etc.	Less amount of energy is produced during anaerobic respiration. e.g. yeast.

Try These 6.1

1. **Among the two types of respiration processes, name the type of respiration which produces high amount of energy.**
2. **Identify the process given in the equation below.**
   $$C_6H_{12}O_6 + 6O_2 \longrightarrow 6\,CO_2 + 6H_2O + \text{Energy}$$
3. **Are there any organisms that can survive without oxygen? If yes, what are they called?**
4. **A cell in our body can respire both aerobically as well as anaerobically. Give its name.**

6.2 Breathing

It is the process in which air rich in oxygen is taken inside the body and air rich in CO_2 is given out, with the help of respiratory organs. Thus, breathing involves following two steps which take place alternatively.

(i) **Inhalation** Taking in air rich in oxygen into our body is called inhalation.

(ii) **Exhalation** Giving out air rich in carbon dioxide from our body to the external environment is called exhalation.

Breathing is a continuous process which occurs all the time throughout the life of an organism.

Breathing Rate

The number of times a person breathes in a minute is termed as breathing rate.
Breathing rate of a person is not always constant. It changes according to the oxygen requirement of the body.

(i) During rest, an adult human being can inhale and exhale 15-18 times in a minute. It is the average breathing rate of an adult human being.

(ii) Breathing rate is somewhat faster in women than in men. In children, it is higher (20-30 times/min) than adults.

(iii) Breathing rate is slowest while sleeping (as less energy is required), while maximum during heavy exercise like running, weight lifting, etc. (since much energy is required).

(iv) During heavy exercise, the breathing rate can increase upto 25 times per minute. Because of this, food gets broken down at a faster rate thus, making us feel hungry.

(v) When we feel drowsy, sleepy or tired, we yawn (i.e., open our mouth wide to take a long and deep breathe) because our breathing rate slows down and our body does not receive sufficient oxygen.

6.3 Mechanism of Breathing

The air enters into the lungs by the following ways

(i) Normally, we take in air through our **nostrils**. When we inhale air, it passes through our nostrils into the **nasal cavity**.

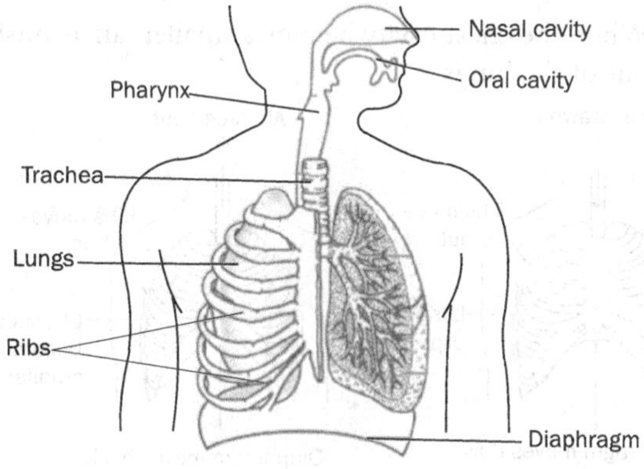

Human respiratory system

(ii) From the nasal cavity, the air reaches our **lungs** through the **windpipe or trachea.**

(iii) Lungs are present in the chest cavity. This cavity is surrounded by **ribs** on the sides.

(iv) A large, muscular sheet called **diaphragm** forms the floor of the **chest cavity**.

The mechanism of breathing involves the movement of the diaphragm and ribcage. The complete process of breathing is discussed as follows.

Breathing In or Inhalation

The term inhalation refers to the process of taking in air into the lungs. It occurs in the following steps.

(i) When we breath air in (or inhale) two processes occur together, i.e. the ribcage moves upward and outward, while the diaphragm contracts and moves downwards.

(ii) This movement of ribcage and diaphragm increases the space in the chest cavity.

(iii) As the chest cavity becomes larger, it sucks air from outside and the lungs get filled with air and expand.

Breathing Out or Exhalation

The term exhalation refers to the expulsion of the carbon dioxide rich air from the lungs to the outside. It is basically a reverse process of inhalation. It occurs in the following steps

(i) When we breath air out (or exhale), the reverse process takes place, i.e. the ribcage moves downward and inwards, while diaphragm relaxes and moves upward.

(ii) This movement of the rib cage and diaphragm decreases the space in our chest cavity.

(iii) When the chest cavity becomes smaller, air is pushed out of the lungs.

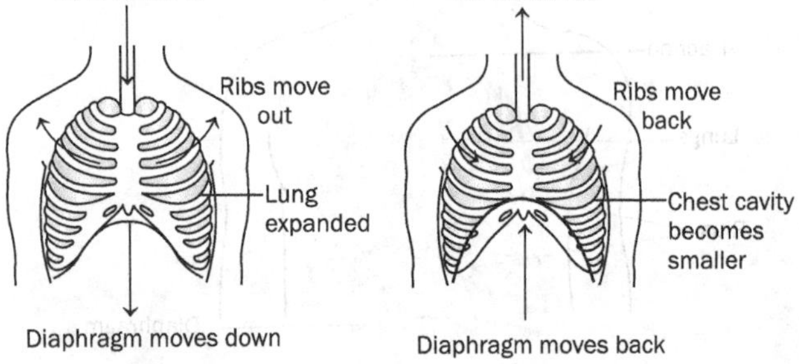

Mechanism of breathing in human beings

Smoking

Lungs are very delicate organs and essential for breathing, thus they keeps us alive. Smoking tobacco in the form of beedi, cigarette or cigar damages our lungs gradually and deteriorate our health. While smoking, the chemicals present in tobacco enter our body.
These chemicals damage the lungs in many ways, thus making breathing difficult and causing lung cancer, heart disease, etc.

Exhaled Air Contains Carbon Dioxide

The air is a mixture of gases like nitrogen, oxygen, carbon dioxide and water vapour. The difference between the composition of inhaled air and exhaled air is that the inhaled air contains more oxygen while exhaled air contains more carbon dioxide.
Besides oxygen and carbon dioxide, the air also contains water vapour. The exhaled air contains more water vapour than the inhaled air. The percentage of O_2 and CO_2 in inhaled and exhaled air is shown in the table given below.

	Percentage of O_2	Percentage of CO_2
Inhaled air	21%	0.04%
Exhaled air	16.4%	4.4%

Sneezing

The air we inhale contains various types of unwanted particles like smoke, dust, pollen, etc. These particles are called **allergens**. During inhalation, these particles get trapped in the hair present in our nasal cavity. However, sometimes these particles may get past the hair in the nasal cavity. They cause irritation in the lining of the nasal cavity, as a result of which we sneeze. Sneezing expels the foreign particles from the nasal passage and a dust-free, clean air enters into the lungs.While sneezing we should cover our nose, so that the foreign particles expelled by us during sneezing may not be inhaled by other person nearby.

Try These 6.2

1. **The inhaled air is a mixture of different gases. During breathing, which gas is used by us from all of those present in air?**
2. **During the process of breathing, our chest move in and out. This movement is caused by two organs. Identify and name them.**
3. **How does our ribcage show movement during inhalation?**
4. **The exhaled air contains a mixture of gases. Which gas is present in large amount in the exhaled air?**

6.4 Breathing in Other Animals

Different animals possess different organs for the exchange of oxygen and carbon dioxide. Animals such as elephants, lions, cows, goats, frogs, lizards, snakes, birds, etc., have lungs in their chest cavities just like humans, for respiration.

The smaller animals like cockroaches, earthworms, fishes, ants and mosquitoes do not have lungs. Therefore, respiration in these animals takes place by other means.

Cockroach

Insects like cockroaches, grasshoppers, etc., have tiny holes or openings on the sides of their bodies. These openings are called **spiracles.**

The spiracles on the body of insects are connected to a network of thin air tubes called **trachea**. These are present throughout the body of insect and helps in the exchange of gases.

Air rich in oxygen rushes through spiracles into the tracheal tubes, diffuses into the body tissues and reaches every cell of the body. Similarly, CO_2 from the cells enters into tracheal tubes and moves out through spiracles.

The **tracheal system** or spiracles are only seen in insects and not in any other group of animals.

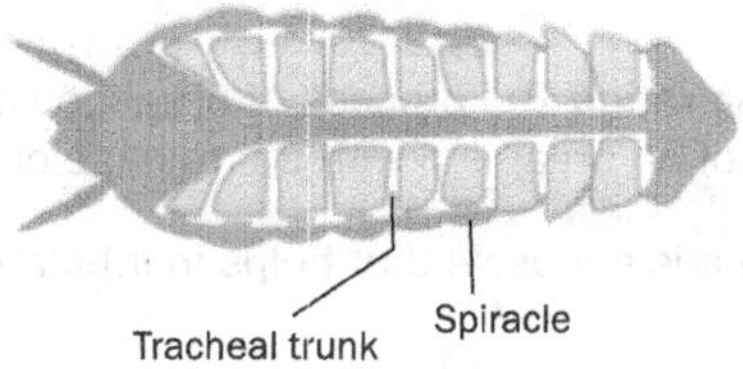

Tracheal system

Earthworm

Earthworms and leeches breathe through their **moist and slimy skin** because gases can easily pass through it. The atmospheric oxygen gets absorbed through their moist skin and transported through blood to all the cells of body.

Frog

Just like humans. Frogs possess a pair of lungs. When they are on land, they breathe through their nostrils and a pair of lungs. But when they are in water, they breathe through their moist and slippery skin.

Fish

Fishes are the aquatic animals that live in water. They have a special organ for breathing called **gills**. These are actually the projections of skin and have blood vessels for the exchange of respiratory gases.

The fish breathes by taking in water through its mouth and sending it over the gills. The oxygen dissolved in the water is extracted by the gills and is absorbed by the blood.

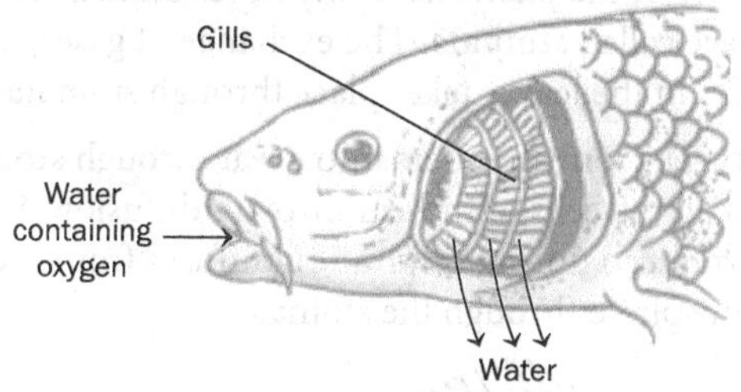

Breathing in fish

This oxygen is then carried to all the parts of the fish for respiration. The carbon dioxide produced during respiration is brought back by the blood into the gills and expelled into the surrounding water.

Dolphins and Whales

Animals like dolphins and whales live in sea water, but unlike fishes, they do not possess gills for respiration. They have nostrils which are called **blow holes**. These blow holes are located on the upper parts of their heads. These animals breathe in through their nostrils and lungs.

Dolphins and whales come to the surface of sea water at intervals to breathe in air. Sometimes whales release a fountain of water that moves upwards like a spray.

It can be seen from many miles away. Blow holes are surrounded by muscles that keep the holes closed when the animal is under water and opens them when the animal is at the surface and needs to breathe.

Try These 6.3

1. **Name two animals that have lungs for respiration?**
2. **What are the tiny holes on the sides of insects bodies called?**
3. **How do frogs breathe when they are in water?**
4. **How do dolphins breathe in air despite living in water?**

6.5 Respiration in Plants

All organisms in the world respire, whether animals or plants. The respiration in plants differs from animals because in plants, each part can independently take in oxygen from air, utilise it to obtain energy and give out CO_2.

Respiration in Leaves

The leaves of the plants have tiny pores on their surface which are called **stomata**. The exchange of gases, i.e. O_2 and CO_2 in the leaves takes place through stomata.

The oxygen from air enters into a leaf through stomata and reaches all the cells of the leaf through diffusion. Similarly, CO_2 produced during respiration diffuses from the leaf to the atmosphere through the stomata.

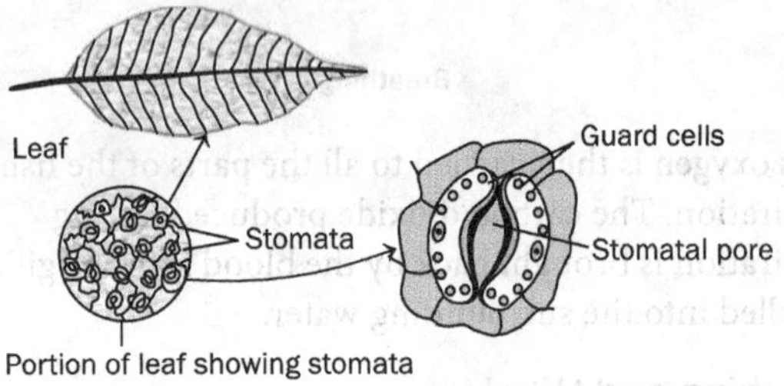

Respiration in leaves

> **SCIENCE INSIGHT** In the older portion of roots and in woody stem, exchange of gases takes place through small openings called **lenticels**. Unlike stomata, lenticels are always open.

Respiration in Roots

The root cells of the plants also need oxygen to carry out respiration and release energy for their own use. These cells get oxygen from the air present in the spaces between the soil particles.

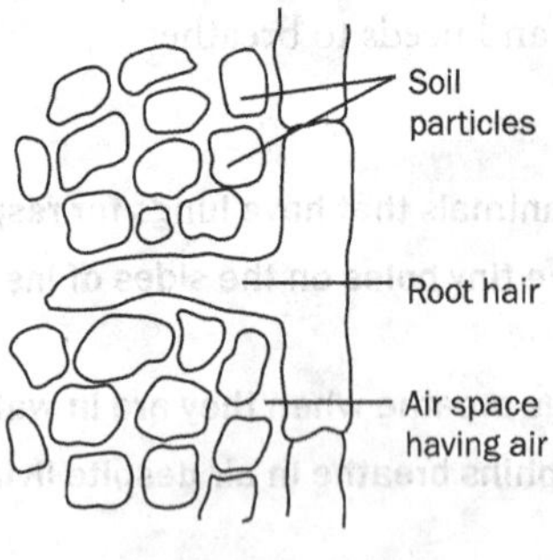

Respiration in plant roots

Plant roots have large number of tiny hairs which are called **root hairs**. Oxygen from the air present in between soil particles diffuses into root hair and reaches to all the cells of the root where it is utilised for respiration.

> **SCIENCE INSIGHT** The plants that grow in swampy areas develop specialised roots called **pneumatophores** that help in the exchange of gases.

Try These 6.4

1. **How does oxygen enter a leaf for respiration?**
2. **Through what process does oxygen reach all the cells in a leaf?**
3. **Which structure facilitate diffusion of oxygen in plant roots?**
4. **Water is very essential for plants. What will happen if a potted plant is over watered for a long time?**

Science Glossary

Aerobic respiration Breakdown of food in the presence of oxygen.

Anaerobic respiration Breakdown of food in the absence of oxygen.

Breathing rate The number of times a person breathes in a minute.

Cellular respiration The process of breakdown of food in the cells of an organism with the release of energy.

Diaphragm It is a muscle that helps in inhalation and exhalation.

Exhalation Process of breathing the air out or exhaling.

Gills These are the breathing organs present in aquatic animals, e.g. fish.

Inhalation Process of breathing the air in or inhaling.

Lungs Main organs of respiratory system in land animals.

Ribs Bony framework in the chest region.

Spiracles Small openings on the body of insects that take in and give out the air.

Tracheae Air tubes connected to the spiracles in insects.

Let's Investigate

ACTIVITY 1 (Page 58)

Aim To show that breathing is necessary for survival.

Materials Required Watch

Caution Perform this activity under the supervision of your teacher.

Procedure

1. Close your nostrils and mouth tightly and look at a watch.
2. Note down the time for which you could hold you breathe.

Observation We observed that we started feeling uneasy and cannot hold our breathe for more than one minute.

Conclusion This activity shows that breathing air is essential to keep us alive. Also, when we release the breath after holding it for a short time, we have to breathe heavily. This is done in order to supply extra oxygen to our body to make up for the oxygen, which was unavailable during the time when we held our breathe.

Therefore, breathing is a continuous process which goes on all the time and throughout the life in all the animals.

Viva Questions

1. How did you feel after some time holding your breath?
2. How long were you able to hold your breath?

ACTIVITY 2 (Page 59)

Aim To observe breathing rate under different conditions.

Materials Required Playground, watch, note book, pen.

Procedure

1. Count the number of breaths in normal condition, i.e., breathe in and out normally.
2. Do a brisk walk for 10 minutes and then count your breathing rate again.
3. Record your breathing rate after running fast for 100 m and then again, after complete rest.
4. Record your results among different individuals.

Observation The observations of the breathing rate under different conditions are tabulated below.

Changes in breathing rate under different conditions

Name of the classmates	Breathing rate			
	Normal	After a brisk walk for 10 minutes	After running fast 100 m	At rest
Parul	15	18	24	16
Himanshi	16	18	25	15
Priyamvada	15	18	24	15

Conclusion From this activity, it is concluded that whenever a person needs extra energy, he/she breathes faster. As a result, more oxygen is supplied to the cells. This speeds up the breakdown of food and more energy is released. When we take rest, our breathing rate returns to a normal level.

Viva Questions

1. How does the breathing rate vary with different activities?
2. What is the breathing rate?

ACTIVITY 3 (Page 62)

Aim To measure the size of the chest during inhalation and exhalation.

Materials Required A measuring tape, note book, pen.

Procedure

1. Take a deep breath.
2. Measure the size of the chest with measuring tape.
3. Release your breath. Now, measure the size of the chest again.
4. Record your observations among different individuals.

Observation The observations of the measurement of the size of the chest during inhalation and exhalation are tabulated below.

Name of the classmates	Size of the chest (cm)		
	During inhalation	During exhalation	Differences in size
Nitin	65	60	5
Vivek	70	66	4
Akash	68	63	5
Ankit	69	66	3

Conclusion From this activity, it is concluded that the size of the chest is greater during inhalation than exhalation. During inhalation, the ribs move upwards and outwards thus, increasing the size of the chest while during exhalation, the ribs moves downwards and inwards thus, decreasing the size of the chest.

Viva Question

1. What is the reason behind the difference in the measurement of the size of the chest?

ACTIVITY 4 (Page 62)

Aim To demonstrate the mechanism of breathing.

Materials Required A wide plastic bottle, a Y-shaped, glass/plastic tube, two balloons, a thin rubber/plastic sheet, a large rubber band.

Procedure

1. Take a wide plastic bottle.
2. Remove the bottom of bottle (it will represent the chest cavity).
3. Take the Y-shaped glass/plastic tube.
4. Make a hole in the lid so that the tube may pass through it.
5. To the forked end of the tube, fix two deflated balloons.
6. Introduce the tube into the bottle.
7. Now cap the bottle. Seal it to make it air tight.
8. To the open base of the bottle, tie a thin rubber or plastic sheet using a large rubber band. (This will represent the diaphragm).
9. To observe or understand the expansion of the lungs, pull the rubber sheet from the base downwards and watch the balloons.
10. Next, push the rubber/plastic sheet up and observe the balloon.

Observation When we pull the rubber sheet from the base downwards, we will observe that deflated balloons get inflated. This is because the air rushes in from outside through the tube into balloons. It shows that the diaphragm moves downward and the lungs get inflated during inhalation.

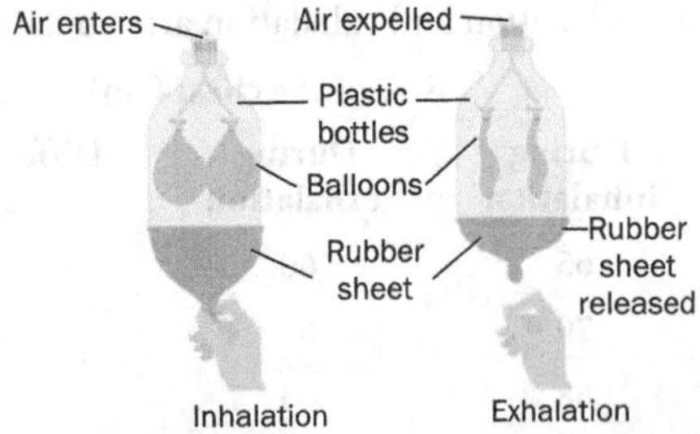

When we push the rubber sheet up or release it, we will observe that the space between the bottle and sheet has decreased. Therefore, the air from inside the balloon goes out through the tube due to which the balloons get deflated again. This shows the movement of diaphragm during exhalation.

Conclusion This activity shows the movement of diaphragm during breathing. It shows that the diaphragm moves downward during inhalation, increasing the space in our chest cavity.

Therefore, air rushes into the lungs. When the diaphragm moves upwards during exhalation, the air is forced to go out of the lungs because of the reduction in the size of the chest cavity.

Viva Question

1. What is the movement of diaphragm during exhalation?

ACTIVITY 5 (Page 63)

Aim To show that carbon dioxide is released during respiration.

Materials Required Test tube/Glass or plastic bottle, lime water, straw.

Procedure

1. Take a slender, clean test tube or a glass/plastic bottle.
2. Make a hole in its lid and fix it to the bottle.
3. Pour some freshly prepared lime water into the test tube.
4. Insert a plastic straw through the hole in the lid in such a way that it dips into lime water.
5. Now blow gently through the straw a few times.
6. Observe the change in the appearance of lime water.

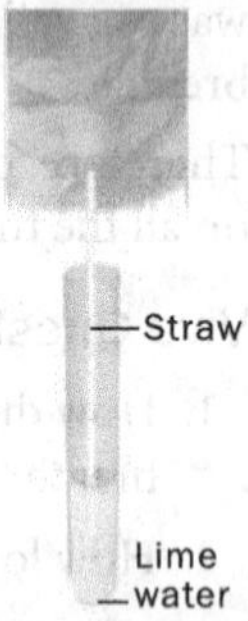

Effect of exhaled

Observation We will observe that the lime water changes its colour. The carbon dioxide makes the lime water milky.

Therefore, it is clear that the air we breath out contains carbon dioxide.

Conclusion From this activity, we conclude that carbon dioxide is released during respiration.

Viva Question

1. What is the reason for the change in the appearance of lime water?

Mind Map

RESPIRATION IN ORGANISMS

Respiration
Process of breakdown of food in the cells and release of energy.

Aerobic Respiration
- Occurs in the presence of O_2.
- More energy is released.

Anaerobic Respiration
- Occurs in the absence of O_2.
- Less energy is released.

In Yeast
Alcohol is formed.

In Muscles
Lactic acid is formed.

Respiration in Plants
- Leaves have stomata for the exchange of gases.

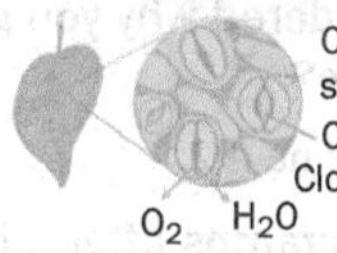

- Roots absorb oxygen from air present in between the soil particles through the root hair.

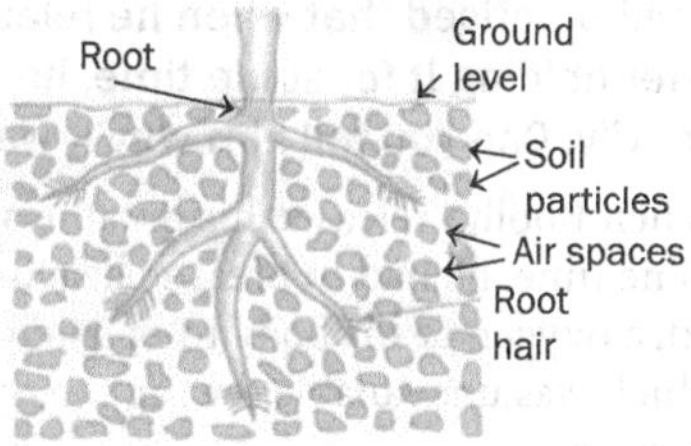

Breathing
Process of taking in O_2 rich air and expelling CO_2 rich air with the help of respiratory organs.

Breathing in Humans

Steps

Inhalation
- Taking in oxygen rich air.
- Ribcage moves upward and outward.
- Diaphragm moves downward.
- Inhaled air contain 21% O_2 and 0.04% CO_2.

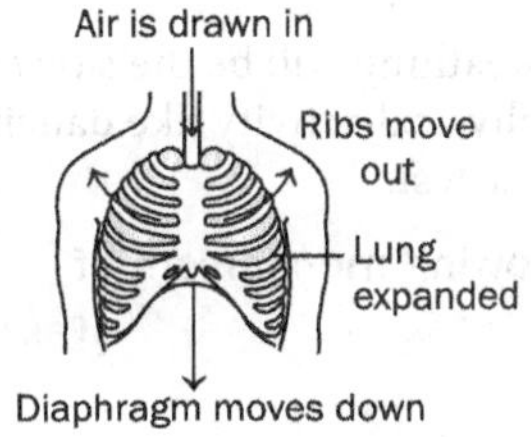

Exhalation
- Expelling CO_2 rich air.
- Ribcage move downward and inward.
- Diaphragm move upward.
- Exhaled air contain 16.4 % O_2 and 4.4% CO_2.

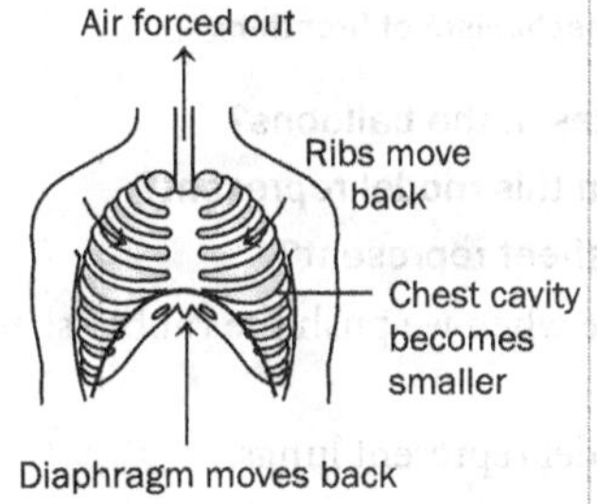

Breathing Rate
- Number of times a person breathes in a minute.
- During rest, average breathing rate in adult is 15-18 times/min.

Breathing in Other Animals

Cockroach
- Spiracle on the sides of body take in and expel air.
- Spiracles are connected to air tubes called trachea.

Earthworm
Breathes through moist and slimy skin.

Frog
- Breathes through moist and slippery skin in water.
- Breathes through lungs on land.

Fish
Breathes through gills that are projections of skin and have blood vessels.

Dolphin and Whales
- Possess nostrils called blow holes
- These animals breathe through nostrils and lungs.

NCERT FOLDER

Complete Explanations of all NCERT's Questions

Intext Questions

Q.1 Even when we are eating, sleeping or reading we require energy. But where does this energy come from? **Page 59**

Ans. Refer to text on page no. 92.

Q.2 Have you even wondered why you get muscle cramps after heavy exercise? **Page 59**

Ans. Refer to text on page no. 92.

Q.3 We get relief from cramps after a hot water bath or a massage. Can you guess why it is so? **Page 59**

Ans. Refer to text on page no. 92 and 93.

Q.4 Boojho noticed that when he released his breathe after holding it for some time, he had to breathe heavily. Can you tell him why it was so? **Page 59**

Ans. When Boojho released his breathe after holding it for some time, he had to breathe heavily in order to supply extra oxygen to his body to make up for the oxygen which was unavailable during the time when he held his breathe.

Q.5 Find out how many times you breathe in and breathe out in a minute? **Page 59**

Ans. On an average, an adult human being at rest breathes in and out 15 to 18 times in a minute.

Q.6 Did you inhale the same number of times as you exhaled? **Page 59**

Ans. Yes.

Q.7 Why do we feel hungry after a physical activity? **Page 60**

Ans. During physical activity, food gets broken down at a faster rate to supply energy. Therefore, we feel hungry.

Q.8 When you feel drowsy, does your breathing rate slow down? Does your body receive sufficient oxygen? **Page 60**

Ans. Refer to text on page no. 93.

Q.9 Paheli wants to know why we yawn when we are sleepy or drowsy? **Page 60**

Ans. We yawn when we feel sleepy or drowsy to increase oxygen intake and promote alertness. Yawning helps to bring in more oxygen and expel carbon dioxide.

Q.10 Can you say in which activity the rate of breathing will be the slowest and in which it will be the fastest? **Page 60**

Ans. While sleeping, the rate of breathing will be the slowest and while doing strenuous physical activity like dancing the rate of breathing will be fastest.

Q.11 Given below is a model showing mechanism of breathing? **Page 63**

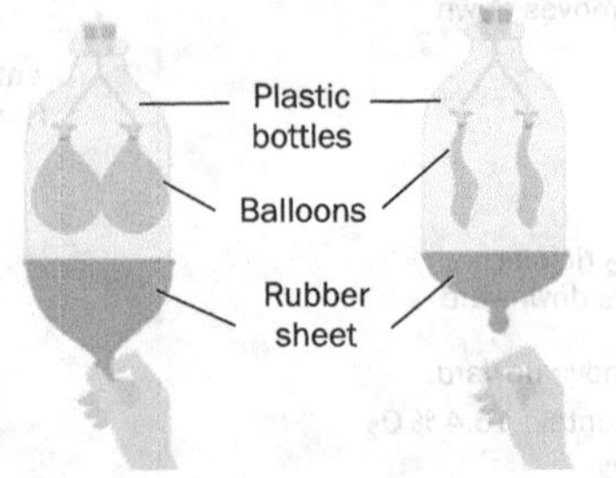

Model to show mechanism of breathing

(a) Did you see any changes in the balloons?

(b) What do the balloons in this model represent?

(c) What does the rubber sheet represent?

Ans. (a) Yes, balloons deflate when we push the rubber sheet up.

(b) Balloons in this model represent lungs.

(c) Rubber sheet represents diaphragm.

Q.12 Air we inhale or exhale is a mixture of gases. What do we exhale? Do we exhale only carbon dioxide or a mixture of gases along with it? **Page 63**

Ans. Refer to text on page no. 93.

Q.13 Boojho wants to know how much air a person can hold in the lungs? **Page 63**

Ans. A person can hold a maximum of 6 litres of air in the lungs.

Q.14 Boojho wants to know if cockroaches, snails, fish, earthworms, ants and mosquitoes also have lungs. **Page 64**

Ans. No, these animals do not have lungs.

Q.15 Boojho has seen in television programmes that whales and dolphins often come up to the water surface. They even release a fountain of water sometimes while moving upwards. Why do they do so? **Page 65**

Ans. Whales and dolphins come up to the water surface and release a fountain of water sometimes while moving upwards. This is because they tend to breathe the fresh air and eject carbon dioxide along with the water. The hole that ejects water is called a 'blow hole'. When they expell the air out of it, it appears like a fountain of water.

Q.16 Paheli wants to know whether roots, which are underground also take in oxygen. If so, how? **Page 65**

Ans. Yes, the roots which are underground also take in oxygen from the air spaces found between the soil particles.

Exercise

Q.1 Why does an athlete breathe faster and deeper than usual after finishing the race?

Ans. Our body needs energy to perform all activities. While doing heavy exercises like running, demand for energy increases. Hence, more oxygen is required to meet this requirement. Therefore, an athlete breathes faster and deeper than usual after finishing the race.

Q.2 List the similarities and differences between aerobic and anaerobic respiration.

Ans. Similarities between aerobic and anaerobic respiration are as follows

(i) Both processes involve the breakdown of glucose.

(ii) Release of energy takes place in both processes.

(iii) CO_2 is the common product in both processes.

Differences between aerobic and anaerobic respiration:

Refer to text on page no. 93.

Q.3 Why do we often sneeze when we inhale a lot of dust-laden air?

Ans. We often sneeze after inhaling dust-laden air because it helps to remove the irritating foreign particles from the nasal passage.

Q.4 Take three test tubes. Fill 3/4th of each with water. Label them *A*, *B* and *C*. Keep a snail in test tube *A*, a water-plant in test tube *B* and in *C*, keep snail and plant both. Which test tube would have the highest concentration of CO_2?

Ans.

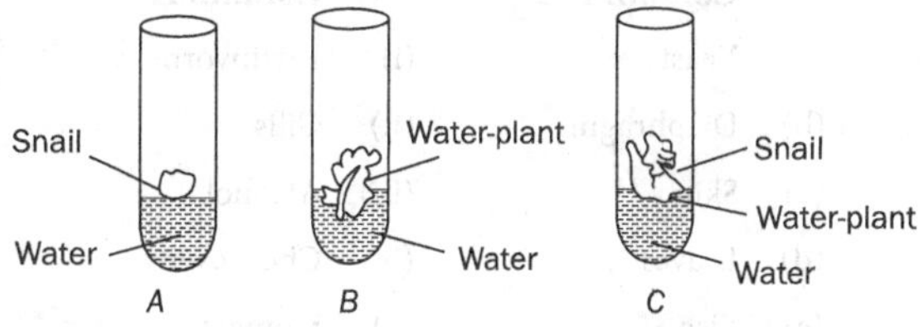

Test tube *A* will have the highest concentration of CO_2. This experiment shows the relationship between plants and animals. During breathing, snail inhales oxygen and releases CO_2.

Water-plant along with respiration performs another important function called photosynthesis. During photosynthesis, water-plant absorbs CO_2, prepares food and releases oxygen.

Therefore, test tube *B* and *C* will have less amount of CO_2 as compared to test tube *A*.

Q.5 Tick the correct answer.

(a) In cockroaches, air enters the body through

(i) lungs (ii) gills

(iii) spiracles (iv) skin

(b) During heavy exercise, we get cramps in the legs due to the accumulation of

(i) carbon dioxide (ii) lactic acid

(iii) alcohol (iv) water

(c) Normal range of breathing rate per minute in an average adult person at rest is

(i) 9-12 (ii) 15-18

(iii) 21-24 (iv) 30-33

(d) During exhalation, the ribs

(i) move outwards

(ii) move downwards

(iii) move upwards

(iv) do not move at all

Ans. (a) (iii) **Spiracles** In cockroaches, air for respiration enters through small holes present on the body called spiracles.

(b) (ii) **Lactic acid** It is produced during heavy exercise as sufficient oxygen is not available to muscles.

(c) (ii) **15-18** Normal range of breathing rate is 15-18 breathe per minute, for an average adult person at rest.

(d) (ii) **Move downwards** During exhalation the ribs moves downwards causing a decrease in area of chest cavity forcing the air out.

Q.6 Match the items in Column I with those in Column II.

Column I		Column II	
(a)	Yeast	(i)	Earthworm
(b)	Diaphragm	(ii)	Gills
(c)	Skin	(iii)	Alcohol
(d)	Leaves	(iv)	Chest cavity
(e)	Fish	(v)	Stomata
(f)	Frog	(vi)	Lungs and skin
		(vii)	Tracheae

Ans. (a)–(iii), (b)–(iv), (c)–(i), (d)–(v), (e)–(ii), (f)–(vi)

Q.7 Mark 'T' if the statement is true and 'F' if it is false.

(a) During heavy exercise the breathing rate of a person slows down.

(b) Plants carry out photosynthesis only during the day and respiration only at night.

(c) Frogs breath through their skins as well as their lungs.

(d) The fishes have lungs for respiration.

(e) The size of the chest cavity increases during inhalation.

Ans. (a) False. During heavy exercise, the breathing rate of a person increases.

(b) False. Photosynthesis occurs in the presence of sunlight, i.e. during the day. Respiration is a continuous process and it occurs all the time (day and night).

(c) True

(d) False. Fishes breathe through their gills.

(e) True

Q.8 The mountaineers carry oxygen with them because

(a) at an altitude of more than 5 km, there is no air

(b) the amount of air available to a person is less than that available on the ground

(c) the temperature of air is higher than that on the ground

(d) the pressure of air is higher than that on the ground

Ans. (b) The mountaineers carry oxygen with them because the amount of air available to a person at higher altitude is less than that available on the ground.

REVIEW EXERCISE

Including Competency Based Questions

Part I

Multiple Choice Questions

1. Cells perform various functions like digestion, excretion, reproduction and transport. This is the reason the cells require energy to perform all these activities in organism. What is the source of the energy which is utilised by the cells? **CBSE Question Bank**

(a)Stored energy in the water which releases during nutrition
(b) Stored energy in the food which releases during respiration
(c) Stored energy in the body which releases during reproduction
(d) Stored energy in the blood which releases during transportation

2. The breakdown of food particles takes place inside the cell and during this process, lots of energy releases out. Which life process helps the cell to perform this function ? **CBSE Questions Bank**

(a) Excretion (b) Reproduction
(c) Transportation (d) Cellular respiration

3. Breathing is a process that **NCERT Exemplar**

(i) provides O_2 to the body
(ii) breaks down food to release energy
(iii) help the body to get rid of CO_2
(iv) produces water in the cells

Which of the following gives the correct combination of functions of breathing ?

(a) (i) and (ii) (b) (ii) and (iii)
(c) (i) and (iii) (d) (ii) and (iv)

4. The raw material for cellular respiration is

(a) glucose (b) sucrose
(c) fructose (d) starch

5. Yeast is used in wine and beer industries because it respires

(a) aerobically to produce oxygen
(b) aerobically to produce alcohol
(c) anaerobically to produce alcohol
(d) anaerobically to produce CO_2

6. Yeasts are used in

(a) wine and beer industry (b) bakery industry
(c) Both (a) and (b) (d) None of these

7. Sometimes when we do heavy exercise, anaerobic respiration takes place in our muscle cells. What is produced during this process?

(a) Alcohol and lactic acid (b) Alcohol and CO_2
(c) Lactic acid and CO_2 (d) Lactic acid only

8. Joggers often develop cramps in calf muscles. Which of these chemicals, when produced, causes muscle cramps ? **Competency Based Questions**

(a) Glucose (b) Alcohol
(c) Lactic acid (d) Carbon dioxide

9. Naman recorded that at rest, he was breathing in and out at the rate of 18 times per minute. After playing the football for 15 minutes, his breathing rate increased up to 27 times per minute. What could be the reason for the change in breathing rate? **CBSE Question Bank**

(a) To fulfil the increased demand for water by the body
(b) To fulfil the increased demand for oxygen by the body
(c) To fulfil the increased demand for energy by the body
(d) To fulfil the increased demand for carbon dioxide by the body

10. Minimum loss of energy takes place while we are

(a) walking (b) swimming
(c) running (d) sleeping

11. Main organ of human respiratory system is

(a) lungs (b) heart (c) liver (d) stomach

12. During the process of exhalation, the ribs move

(a) down and inwards (b) up and inwards
(c) down and outwards (d) up and outwards

13. A teacher asked a student to observe inhalation. The student observed an expansion in his chest during inhalation. The teacher told the student that it is because of the movement of ribs and diaphragm. What movement is likely to be found in ribs and diaphragm of the student during inhalation ? **CBSE Question Bank**

(a) **Diaphragm** Moves up — **Ribs** Moves up and inward
(b) **Ribs** Moves up and outward — **Diaphragm** Moves down
(c) **Ribs** Moves down and inward — **Diaphragm** Moves up
(d) **Ribs** Moves up and inward — **Diaphgragm** Moves down

14. **People use different methods to get rid of nose hairs such as trimmers, waxing and many more. However, some health specialists are against the idea of removing nose hair. What likely is the concern regarding the removal of nose hairs ?** CBSE Question Bank

(a) If may affect the sensitivity of the nose for odour
(b) The amount of inhaled oxygen will be affected
(c) Germs and foreign particles will get entry inside the body easily
(d) It may lead to the production of mucous in excessive amounts inside the nose

15. **Spiracles on the body of insects are connected to a network of thin air tubes called**
(a) lungs (b) tracheae
(c) gills (d) blow holes

16. **Earthworms and frogs breathe through their skin because of which the skin of both the organisms is**
(a) moist and rough (b) dry and rough
(c) dry and slimy (d) moist and slimy

17. **Which of these animals breathes through its skin ?**
(a) Fish (b) Bird (c) Snake (d) Earthworm

18. **Choose which among the following can breathe through lungs as well as through skin?**
(a) Fish (b) Frog
(c) Earthworm (d) Dolphin

19. **Fish breathe with the help of gills which are richly supplied with blood vessels. The gills help the fish to** NCERT Exemplar
(a) take in oxygen from air
(b) take in oxygen dissolved in water
(c) absorb nutrients present in water
(d) release waste substances in water

Answers

1. (b)	2. (d)	3. (c)	4. (a)	5. (c)
6. (c)	7. (d)	8. (c)	9. (b)	10. (d)
11. (a)	12. (a)	13. (b)	14. (c)	15. (b)
16. (d)	17. (d)	18. (b)	19. (b)	

Fill in the Blanks

1. **......... is an essential phenomenon for the survival of living organisms.**

2. **During aerobic respiration, the food is broken down into .... and .... and releases a lot of ....**

3. **Taking in air rich in O_2 inside the body is called ....**

4. **Diaphragm forms the .... of the chest cavity.** NCERT Exemplar

5. **Cockroaches breathe with the help of air tubes called ....**

Answers

1. Breathing 2. carbon dioxide, water, energy
3. inhalation 4. floor 5. tracheae

True/False

1. **All living organisms respire to get energy from glucose/food.**

2. **Oxygen breaks down glucose outside the cells of organisms.** NCERT Exemplar

3. **Always breathe in air through your nose.**

4. **Exhaled air has more percentage of CO_2 than inhaled air.** NCERT Exemplar

5. **Insects have spiracles on the lower surface of their body.**

Answers

1. True
2. False, oxygen breaks down glucose inside the cells of organisms.
3. True
4. True
5. False, insects have spiracles on the sides of their body.

Match the Columns

1. **Match the Column I with Column II.**

Column I	Column II
A. Butterfly	1. Lungs
B. Earthworm	2. Gills
C. Sparrow	3. Spiracles
D. Fish	4. Skin

2. **Match the Column I with Column II.**

	Column I		Column II
A.	Plant	1.	Earthworm
B.	Glucose	2.	Stomata
C.	Frog	3.	Single-celled
D.	Lungs	4.	Lungs
E.	Skin	5.	Spiracles
F.	Yeast	6.	Oxygen
G.	Mammals	7.	Source of energy
H.	Leaves	8.	Chest cavity
I.	Inhalation	9.	Lungs and moist skin
J.	Cockroaches	10.	Stomata and roots

Answers

1. A–3, B–4, C–1, D–2
2. A–10, B–7, C–9, D–8, E–1, F–3, G–4, H–2, I–6, J–5

Assertion-Reason Questions

The following questions consist of two statements. Assertion (A) and Reason (R). Answer the following questions by selecting the appropriate option given below.

(a) Both A and R are true and R is the correct explanation of A
(b) Both A and R are true, but R is not the correct explanation of A
(c) A is true, but R is false
(d) A is false, but R is true

1. **Assertion** (A) Yeast is an anaerobes.
   Reason (R) In anaerobic respiration, glucose breaks down into carbon dioxide and water only.
2. **Assertion** (A) The breathing rate decreases during exercise.
   Reason (R) More oxygen is needed by the muscles during exercise.
3. **Assertion** (A) We exhale only carbon dioxide.
   Reason (R) Carbon dioxide turns lime water cloudy.
4. **Assertion** (A) Dolphins and whales keep coming to the water surface.
   Reason (R) Dolphins and whales come up to water surface in the search of food.

Answers

1. (c) A is true, but R is false. R can be corrected as In anaerobic respiration, glucose breaks down into ethanol, carbon dioxide and energy.
2. (d) A is false, but R is true. A can be corrected as Breathing rate increases during exercise.
3. (d) A is false, but R is true. A can be corrected as We exhale a mixture of gases containing nitrogen. water vapour together with carbon dioxide.
4. (c) A is true, but R is false. R can be corrected as Dolphins and whales keep coming up to the water surface to breathe in air.

Case Based Question

1. **In a class project about respiration, Pankaj measured the chests of various students and recorded his observation in a table.**

	Chest measurements			
	Student 1	**Student 2**	**Student 3**	**Student 4**
Inhalation	62 cm	58 cm	60 cm	65 cm
Exhalation	45 cm	54 cm	53 cm	56 cm

Competency Based Que.

(i) **Chest expansion is the difference in chest sizes during inhalation and exhalation. Which student's chest expanded the most ?**
(a) Student 1 (b) Student 2
(c) Student 3 (d) Student 4

(ii) **What should be done to confirm the chest measurement of the four students ?**
(a) Repeat the chest measurement with four new students.
(b) Repeat each student's chest measurement for inhalation only.
(c) Repeat the chest measurement using a different measuring tape.
(d) Repeat each student's chest measurement for both inhalation and exhalation.

Answer

(i) (a) Student 1
(ii) (d) Repeat each student's chest measurement for both inhalation and exhalation.

Part II

Very Short Answer Type Questions

1. Explain cellular respiration.

Ans. The process of breakdown of food in the cell with the release of energy is called cellular respiration.

2. What are the end products of aerobic respiration?

Ans. During aerobic respiration, carbon dioxide and water are released along with a large amount of energy.

$$\text{Glucose} \xrightarrow{O_2} CO_2 + \text{Water} + \text{Energy}$$

3. Name the end products of anaerobic respiration in yeast.

Ans. The end product formed during anaerobic respiration in yeast are

(i) ethyl alcohol (ii) carbon dioxide (iii) energy

4. Name the term used for organisms that respire using anaerobic mode. Give an example of any such organism.

Ans. Anaerobes respire using anaerobic mode. Yeast is an organism that respire anaerobically.

5. What happens to your breathing rate when you (i) exercise (ii) go to sleep

Ans. The breathing rate increases during exercise and decreases when we go to sleep.

6. Is the rate of breathing same for all the respiring organism?

Ans. No, different organisms respire at different rate because they all perform different activities at all times.

7. What changes are observed in diaphragm during inhalation?

Ans. During the process of inhalation, diaphragm contracts and moves downwards.

8. Which of these statement is correct for the respiratory system ?

Circle 'Yes' or 'No' for the correct response.

	Is the statement correct?	Yes or No
(i)	The ribs move in during exhalation.	Yes/No
(ii)	The lungs constrict during inhalation.	Yes/No
(iii)	The diaphragm expands during exhalation.	Yes/No

Competency Based Que.

Ans. (i) Yes

(ii) No, the lungs expand during inhalation.

(iii) No, the diaphragm moves up during exhalation.

9. Our nostrils have hair and mucous. What is the need to have them in our nasal cavity?

Ans. Our nostrils possess hairs and mucous lining. These help in preventing dirt, dust and germs from entering our respiratory system.

10. In an experiment, Ria exhale into a glass containing lime water. What changes would be observed by Ria?

Ans. When Ria exhale into lime water, its colour changes to slightly milky white because the exhaled air contains CO_2.

11. Insects have a special organ to carry out respiration. What is that organ called?

Ans. Insects possess special organ called spiracles for respiration.

12. Name respiratory organs in frogs.

Ans. Frogs respire through their moist skin in water as well as through a pair of lungs on land.

13. Sometimes we see that farmers loosen the soil. What is the reason behind it?

Ans. The farmers sometimes loosen the soil. This helps the roots to respire through the air present in the space between soil particles.

14. All organisms breathe in O_2 and breathe out CO_2. Should not there be less O_2 and excess of CO_2 in our environment. **Competency Based Que.**

Ans. All organisms breathe in O_2 and breathe out CO_2. The CO_2 released by us is used by plants during the process of photosynthesis and they release O_2. This maintains a balance between O_2 and CO_2 in the atmosphere.

15. Respiration is a continuous process. What is the need for it to be continuous rather than being like photosynthesis?

Ans. Process of respiration yields energy which is required to perform a variety of routine activities. Thus, it needs to be a continuous process.

Short Answer Type Questions

1. Which gas present in air is essential for aerobic respiration ? What is the role of this gas during respiration? **NCERT Exemplar**

Ans. Oxygen present in air is essential for aerobic respiration. It breaks down food and releases energy during respiration.

2. Respiration can occur in two different manners. Briefly explain the process of aerobic respiration. How does it differ from anaerobic respiration?

Ans. Refer to text on page no. 93 and 93.

3. Name one organism which respires anaerobically. How does this organism help in beverage and baking industry?

Ans. Refer to text on page no. 92.

4. What happens when breathe is released after holding for a few minutes? Give reason for its occurrence.

Ans. Releasing breathe after holding it for some time results in rapid breathing. It occurs to maintain a healthy balance between intake of O_2 and release of carbon dioxide.

5. After we work hard or perform physical activity, we feel hungry. Explain why?

Ans. When we work hard or perform a physical activity (like running, swimming, cycling), we need more energy. To fulfill the energy requirement, we breathe faster. Fast breathing helps in the supply of more oxygen to our cells. Due to this, rate of breakdown of food increases and more energy is released. The rapid breakdown of food makes us feel more hungry.

6. Whenever we feel drowsy or sleepy, we start yawning. Does yawning help us in anyway? **NCERT Exemplar**

Ans. Refer to text on page no. 93.

7. Observe the given diagram of human respiratory system. List the organs from *A* to *G*.

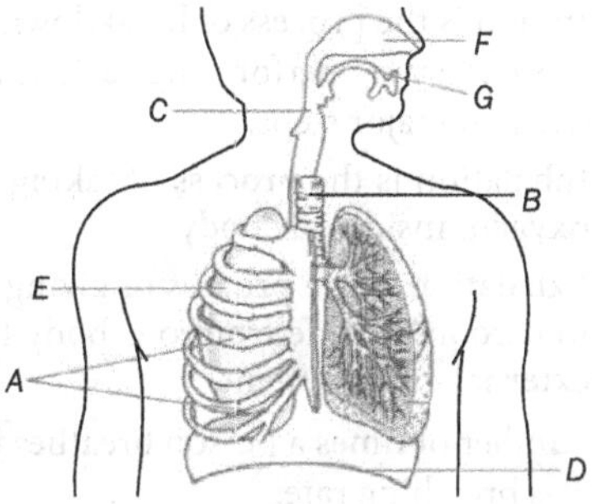

Ans. The human respiratory system has the following organs

A–Ribs	*B*–Trachea
C–Pharynx	*D*–Diaphragm
E– Lungs	*F*–Nasal passage
G–Oral cavity	

8. On a very cold morning, Boojho and Paheli were talking with each other as they walked down to their school. They observed that the air coming out of their mouth looked like smoke. They were amazed and wondered how it happened. Help them to find the answer.

Ans. On a cold day, the warm and moist air exhaled by us condenses into mist when it comes in contact with the cold air of the atmosphere. This look like white smoke.

9. Frogs are amphibians. They survive on land and water, do they have any respiratory issue? How do frogs breathe when they are in water? Do they possess lungs? Explain the role of lungs in frogs. **Competency Based Que.**

Ans. Frogs breathe by their moist skin and also through lungs. So, they do not have any respiratory issue. When frogs enters into water, the skin of frog helps in respiration. The oxygen rich air enters through the skin.

When the frog is on land, a pair of lungs helps in respiration.

The lungs take the oxygen rich air through the nostrils from where the oxygen is absorbed by the blood and carried throughout the body. The carbon dioxide from the blood diffuses back through the skin and lungs into the atmosphere.

10. Pick the odd one out from each of the groups given below on the basis of respiratory organs. Give reason for your answer. **NCERT Exemplar**

(a) Cockroach, grasshopper, snail, ant
(b) Lizard, cow, earthworm, snake
(c) Crocodile, whale, dolphin, fish
(d) Snake, tadpole, crow, goat

Ans. (a) Snail, as it does not breathe by means of trachea.
(b) Earthworm, because it breathes through its skin and it does not have lungs.
(c) Fish, as most fishes breathe through their gills and do not have lungs.
(d) Tadpole, as it breathes through gills and do not have lungs.

11. There are three animals named *A*, *B* and *C*. Among them *A* can stay on land as well as in water. When it stays at land it respires through lungs, but when it goes into water, it respires through its moist skin. Animal *B* has specific organs to respire in the water which is not found in any other water animal. While animal *C* is a water animal which respires through nostrils and lungs. Now give the names of animal *A*, *B* and *C*.

Ans. Animal *A* can live on land as well as in water and can respire through lungs as well as moist skin. The animal is frog.
Animal *B* lives in water and respires through a specific organ called gills. The animal is fish.
Animal *C* is also an aquatic animal which lives in water and respires through nostrils and lungs, but not by the gills. The animal is whale.

12. Respiration in fish is different from that in humans. Explain in brief how fish can breathe through gills?

Ans. Refer to text on page no. 95.

13. Whales and dolphins are seen many times releasing a fountain of water at the surface of water. Why do they do so?

Ans. Refer to text on page no. 95.

14. Insects and leaves of plant have pores through which they exchange gases with the atmosphere. Can you write two points of difference between these pores with respect to their position, number and extension into the body?

Ans. Pores present on the sides of insects are called spiracles while pores present on the surface of leaves are called stomata. These structures are responsible for the exchange of gases with the atmosphere.

Differences between these two are as follows

(i) Spiracles are fewer in number as compared to stomata.

(ii) Spiracles lead to an extensive network of tracheal system which is absent in the leaves.

Long Answer Type Questions

1. A food stall owner was preparing dough for making bhaturas. He added a pinch of yeast and sugar to the dough and left it in a warm place. After few hours, the dough had risen. There was a sour smell too.

(i) Why did the dough rise?

(ii) Why did the dough smell sour?

(iii) Why was sugar added to the dough?

(iv) What would have happened if the dough was kept in the refrigerator, soon after it was prepared?

Ans. (i) The dough rises due to the release of carbon dioxide during anaerobic respiration by yeast cell.

(ii) During anaerobic respiration, yeast also produces alcohol which results in the sour smell of dough.

(iii) Sugar is added into the dough, because it acts as a food for yeast. Yeast, upon incomplete breakdown of sugar or food, produces CO_2, alcohol and energy (in less amount).

(iv) If the dough was kept in the refrigerator soon after it was prepared, then dough would rise neither nor become sour. Yeast requires warm temperatures to grow, multiply and respire. At low temperature, yeast does not respire to produce the byproducts of anaerobic respiration.

2. Paheli participated in a 400 m race competition held at her school and won the race. When she came home she had mixed feelings of joy and pain as she had cramps in her leg muscles. After a massage, she was relieved of the pain. Answer the following questions related to the situation.

(i) What can be the possible reasons for the pain in her legs?

(ii) Why did she feel comfortable after a massage?

NCERT Exemplar

Ans. (i) Paheli had cramps in her leg muscles after running. She felt pain in her legs because of the accumulation of lactic acid in the leg muscles. Lactic acid is formed due to the anaerobic respiration in the muscle cells after heavy exercise, e.g. running.

During heavy exercise, we require large amount of energy.

To produce more energy, muscle cells perform anaerobic respiration for a short duration. As a result, lactic acid is formed due to partial breakdown of glucose. It gets accumulated in the muscle cells and causes pain and muscle cramps.

(ii) The massage or hot water bath gives the relief from muscle cramp or pain, because it improves the circulation of blood and lead to an increase in the supply of oxygen to the muscle cells. It helps in the complete breakdown of lactic acid into carbon dioxide and water.

3. (i) Respiratory process occurs in two phases, what are those two major steps of respiration? Describe each one of them.

(ii) Define the term breathing rate.

Ans. (i) Respiration is the process of breakdown of food to produce energy for performing various functions. It involves two major steps:

(a) Inhalation is the process of taking in air rich in oxygen, inside our body.

(b) Exhalation is the process of giving out air rich in carbon dioxide from our body to the external environment.

(ii) The number of times a person breathes in a minute is called as breathing rate.

An adult human being can inhale and exhale 15-18 times in a minute. It is the average breathing rate in an adult human being. Breathing rate is not always constant.

4. Observe the given figures labelled as *A* and *B* and answer the following questions.

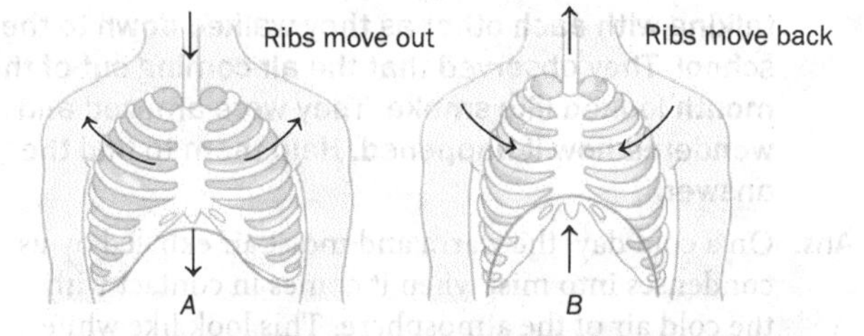

(i) Among both figures identify which *A* or *B* indicates the process of inhalation and which shows the process of exhalation?

(ii) **In the figure label the arrows and indicate the direction of**

(i) movement of air (ii) movement of diaphragm (iii) movement of ribs **NCERT Exemplar**

Ans. (i) Figure *A* indicates inhalation and figure *B* indicates exhalation.

(ii) Movement of air, diaphragm and ribs are indicated in below figure

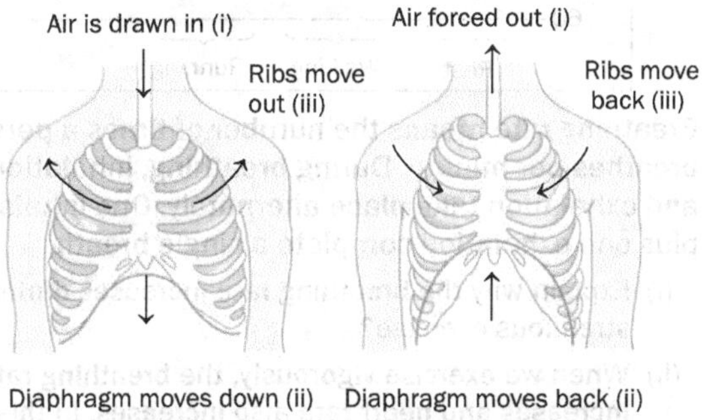

A (Inhalation) *B* (Exhalation)

5. Observe the figures carefully and answer the following questions.

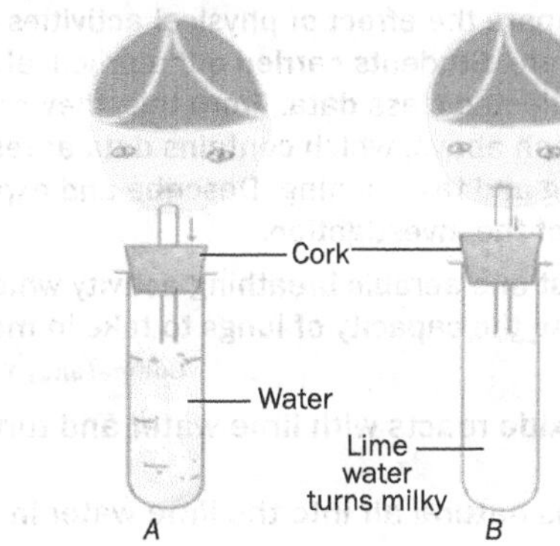

(i) Which process is being tested in the activity?

(ii) What is the result of the activity? Give reasons. **NCERT Exemplar**

Ans. (i) Exhalation process of respiration is being tested in the activity.

(ii) The lime water in test tube B turns milky but water in test tube *A* remains unchanged. This is because CO_2 is present in the exhaled air, which mixes with lime water in test tube *B* and turns it milky.

6. List some animals around you. Now group them as follows

(i) Animals that can breathe only through skin.

(ii) The animal that can breathe through skin as well as through lungs.

(iii) The animal that can breathe through lungs.

(iv) Animals that can breathe through gills.

(v) Animals that can breathe through spiracle and tracheae?

Ans. (i) Animals that can breathe only through skin are earthworm and leech.

(ii) Animals that can breathe through skin as well as through lungs are frogs.

(iii) Animals that can breathe through lungs are buffaloes, human and dolphins.

(iv) Animals that can breathe through gills are tadpole and fish.

(v) Animals that can breathe through spiracles and tracheae are grasshopper, cockroaches, ants, housefly and mosquito.

7. A person put some warm water in an aquarium having fish during winter season. He thought that fishes would be more comfortable in luke warm water, than cold water. But he observed that fishes in the aquarium died. Why did the fishes die in warm water?

Ans. The fishes have special type of organs for respiration called gills. These gills absorb oxygen dissolved in water and through blood vessels, this oxygen is passed to all the parts of the body. The amount of dissolved oxygen is comparatively less in water than the amount of oxygen in air. Therefore, the rate of breathing is also high in aquatic animals.

If we add warm water to the aquarium, the dissolved oxygen dissociates and moves into the atmosphere again thus, leaving the least percentage of oxygen in the water. Therefore, fishes will have difficulty in breathing in the absence or low amount of oxygen in water and will die.

8. It is not wise to sleep under a tree during night. Why?

Ans. During the day, plants photosynthesise in the presence of sunlight and uses CO_2 produced during respiration. During this process O_2 is released as a byproduct and a balance between O_2 and CO_2 is maintained in the atmosphere.

But in the night, plants do not photosynthesise. Moreover, during night they produce CO_2 and take O_2 during respiration. This leads to the increase in the proportion of CO_2 in the air.

So, if one sleeps under a tree at night, he will have problems in breathing as the amount of CO_2 in the air around will certainly be more than oxygen.

Therefore, it is not advisable to sleep under trees during night because the person will suffer from suffocation and will feel excess weight on chest.

Case Based Quesitons

1. The reactions below show two types of respiration.

Competency Based Que.

(a) Glucose $\xrightarrow{\text{with oxygen}}$ Carbon dioxide + Water + Energy

(b) Glucose $\xrightarrow{\text{without oxygen}}$ Carbon dioxide + Alcohol + Energy

(i) Name the types of respiration shown in reaction (a) and (b).

(ii) What causes the reactions to be different ?

(a) Release of energy

(b) Production of a gas

(c) Breakdown of glucose

(d) Presence or absence of oxygen

2.

	Breathing rate (time per minute)
Sleeping	15
Cycling	30
Jogging	45
Reading	20

(i) Complete the graph below to show the data in the table.

Shade the columns in the graph correctly.

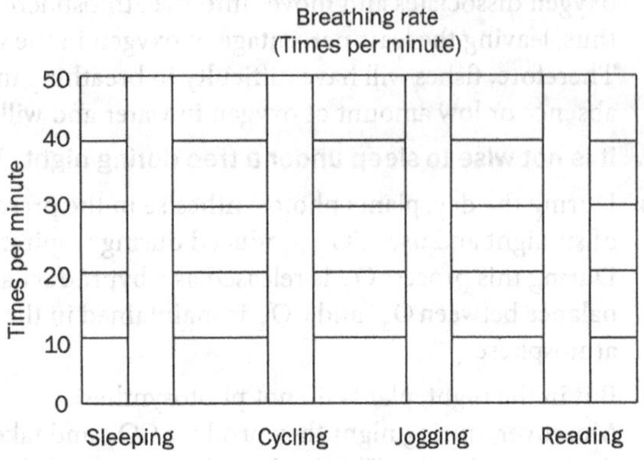

(ii) For which activity does the girl require maximum energy ?

(a) Sleeping

(b) Cycling

(c) Jogging

(d) Reading

3.

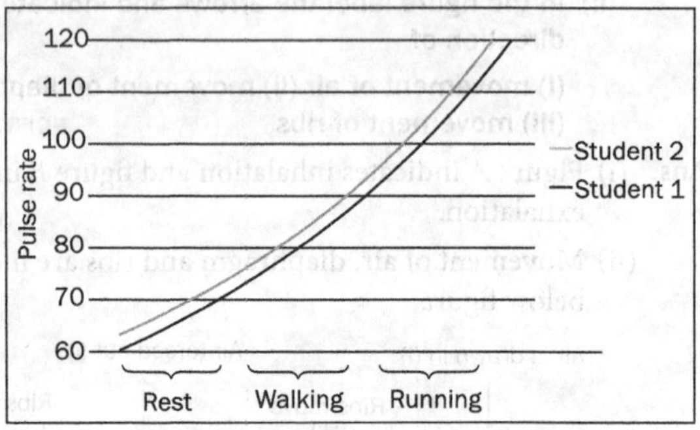

Breathing rate means the number of times a person breathes per minute. During breathing, inhalation and exhalation take place alternately. One inhalation plus one exhalation complete a single breath.

(i) Explain why the breathing rate increases during strenuous exercise?

(ii) When we exercise vigorously, the breathing rate increases and heart rate also increases. In this process, exhalation is also a very important part of exercise. Explain the importance of exhalation.

(iii) A teacher in the class assigned two students a task to compare the effect of physical activities on pulse rate. Students carried out a practical activity and collected class data. From this, they produced the graph above, which contains data at rest, brisk walking and fast running. Describe and explain the result of the investigation.

(iv) Suggest one aerobic breathing activity which can increase the capacity of lungs to take in more air.

Competency Based Que.

4. Carbon dioxide reacts with lime water and turns it milky.

Asha pumps natural air into the lime water in beaker 1.

She blows air from her mouth into the lime water in beaker 2.

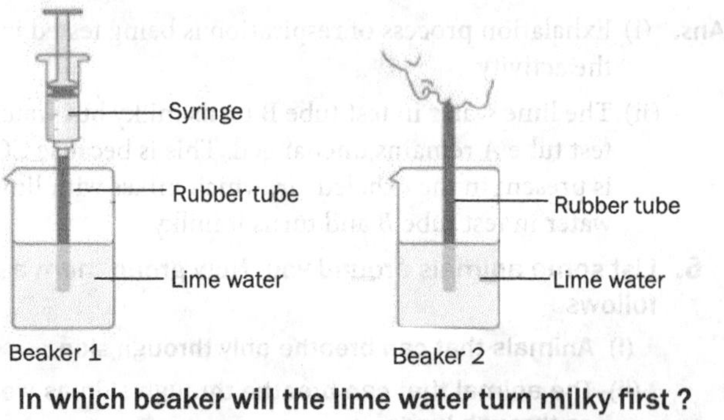

In which beaker will the lime water turn milky first ? Explain your answer.

Competency Based Que.

Ans. 1. (i) Reaction (a) shows aerobic respiration and reaction (b) shows anaerobic respiration.

(ii) (d) Presence or absence of oxygen.

2. (i)

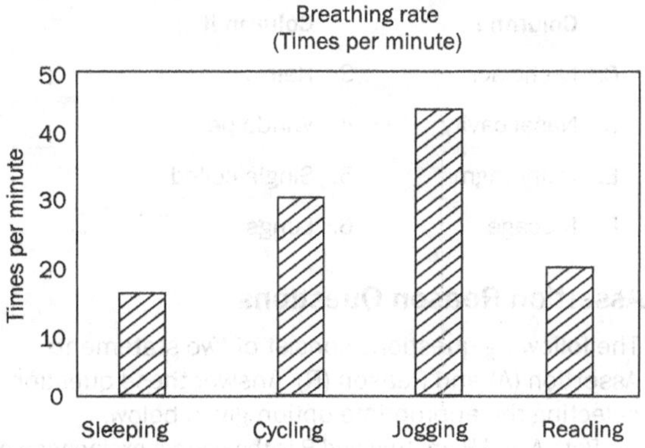

(ii) (c)

3. (i) Breathing rate increases during strenuous exercise because there is more muscle contraction which requires more oxygen to produce more energy.

(ii) When we exercise vigorously, the breathing rate increases, and heart rate also increases to meet the increased demand of energy by our muscles. In this process, exhalation is also very important part of exercise because it helps to get rid of carbon dioxide.

(iii) The graph produced shows that the two students got similar results because age of the students is similar. The graph also shows that the pulse rate increases with more vigorous exercise because of the need for more oxygen.

(iv) Running/swimming/cycling

4. The lime water in beaker 2 will turn milky first as exhaled air contains greater concentration of carbon dioxide than the normal air.

Skill Based Questions as per NEP 2020

1. Measure the breathing rate of the members of your family. Evaluate

(i) If the breathing rate of males is the same or different from that of females.

(ii) If the breathing rate changes with age.

Research skill

2. Roots of the plants get oxygen from the air present in the spaces between the soil particles. Find out how the plants living in the marshy areas respire?

Thinking skill

3. A girl was suffering from cold and was sneezing continuously. She joined her family at dinner and suddenly started sneezing without covering her nose, thus spreading particles all over the place.

On realising her mistake, said sorry and next time covered her nose. **Thinking skill**

(i) During sneezing, what are the precautionary steps to be followed?

(ii) Is sneezing a respiratory process?

4. Palak wants to be a great cyclist. She cycles daily for about 2 hours followed by some exercises. Today, she thought she will cycle for longer and managed it for 4½ hours. Now she is feeling cramped up and her breathing is disturbed. Her mother took her to hospital where the doctor examined and told her not to push herself more than necessary. Palak understood and promised herself to move slow and steadily.

Answer the following questions.

(i) Why did Palak have cramps in her legs?

(ii) Is breathing rate also affected after doing long hour of exercise? Why? **Observation skill**

5. A group of people were smoking cigarettes in a restaurant. The atmosphere was full of smoke. An old man sitting next to the group asked them to stop smoking while sitting in the premises or move out. They agreed to do so and promised not to repeat the mistake.

Answer the following questions.

(i) Write any three hazards of smoking.

(ii) Can smoking also affect the person who does not smoke? **Thinking skill**

ASSESSMENT EXERCISE

Part I

Multiple Choice Questions

1. Which of the following processes allow exchange of gases?
   (a) Excretion (b) Respiration
   (c) Digestion (d) None of these
2. Chemical used to test the presence of CO_2 in exhaled air is
   (a) water (b) lime water
   (c) orange juice (d) lemon juice
3. Unwanted particles in air are trapped in which part of the human respiratory system?
   (a) Tracheae (b) Bronchi
   (c) Larynx (d) Nasal cavity
4. Birds breathe through
   (a) lungs (b) gills
   (c) tracheae (d) skin
5. Percentage of oxygen in the exhaled air is
   (a) 21% (b) 16.4%
   (c) 18% (d) 20%

Fill in the Blanks

6. Breathing rate of a person is not .... always.
7. Unwanted particles like smoke, dust, pollen, etc. are called ....
8. Lungs are very .... organs.

True/False

9. We take deep breaths after we hold on breath for the one minute.
10. The exchange of gases in plants takes place through stomata.
11. The balance between CO_2 and O_2 is maintained by the plants.

Match the Columns

12. Match Column I with Column II.

Column I	Column II
A. Yeast	1. Muscle cramps
B. Trachea	2. Muscular sheet
C. Lactic acid	3. Hair
D. Nasal cavity	4. Windpipe
E. Diaphragm	5. Single-celled
F. Ribcage	6. Lungs

Assertion-Reason Questions

The following questions consist of two statements Assertion (A) and Reason (R). Answer these questions by selecting the appropriate option given below.

(a) Both A and R are true and R is the correct explanation of A
(b) Both A and R are true, but R is not the correct explanation of A.
(c) A is true, but R is false
(d) A is false, but R is true

13. **Assertion** (A) Hot water and massage both give relief from cramps.
    Reason (R) Hot water and massage increases blood circulation and causes breakdown of lactic acid into carbon dioxide and water.
14. **Assertion** (A) The requirement of oxygen is more in higher animals.
    Reason (R) Higher organisms need more energy.

Part II

Very Short Answer Type Questions

15. Define the term exhalation.
16. Rate of respiration is an important factor in respiratory process. Give its definition.
17. List three organs that help is cellular respiration.

Short Answer Type Questions

18. Respiration can be classified into two types. Name them and explain in brief.
19. What is the difference between breathing and respiration?

Long Answer Type Question

20. Draw a well-labelled diagram of human respiratory system.

Answers

1. (b) 2. (b) 3. (d) 4. (a) 5. (b)
6. same 7. allergens 8. elastic
9. True 10. True 11. True
12. A-5, B-4, C-1, D-3, E-2, F-6
13. (a)
14. (a)

Transportation in Animals and Plants

CHAPTER 07

Transport means **'to carry things from one place to another'.** The food, water and oxygen are transported from one part of our body to another as these are needed for our survival. Similarly waste products produced due to the various activities inside the body are transported and removed. Therefore, the term transport may be defined as a life process in which a materials are transported from one part of an organ to another part in the body. Animals and plants have different types of transport systems for transporting materials within their bodies.

7.1 Transportation in Animals

In animal body, transportation of substances is carried out by an internal transport system called **circulatory system.**

It is the main transport system in animals including human beings. It makes food, water and oxygen available to every part of the body and helps in removing waste materials (urea, CO_2, etc.) from the body.

7.2 Human Circulatory System

The circulatory system in human consists of blood, blood vessels (arteries veins and capillaries) and heart.

7.3 Blood

It is a red coloured fluid that flows through a network of tubes called **blood vessels** (arteries, veins and capillaries).

It consists of four components, i.e. Plasma, Red Blood Cells (RBCs), White Blood Cells (WBCs) and platelets. Plasma is a liquid, while RBCs, WBCs and platelets are different types of cells that are suspended in it.

1. Plasma

It is the liquid part of the blood which is pale yellow in colour. It contains dissolved substance such as digested food and waste products (like carbon dioxide and urea).

2. Red Blood Cells (RBCs)

They contain a red coloured pigment called **haemoglobin.** This pigment binds with oxygen and transports it to all the parts of the body and ultimately to all the cells. Due to the presence of haemoglobin in RBCs, the blood appear red.

3. White Blood Cells (WBCs)

They fight against infection and protect us from diseases. WBCs destroys the germs (like bacteria) that cause diseases.

4. Platelets

They are small, irregular shaped cell fragments in the blood. These are colourless and help in clotting of blood. For example, during an injury due to a cut or wound, the blood starts flowing from it. However, after some time, the bleeding stops due to the formation of a dark red clot, i.e. the cut has been plugged by the platelets. If the platelets are not present in the blood, the blood flow from the cut or wound will not stop. It will lead to an excess loss of blood which may be fatal to a person.

Functions of Blood

Various functions of blood are

(i) It transports substances like digested food from the small intestine to other parts of the body.

(ii) It carries oxygen from lungs to all the cells of the body.

(iii) It carries waste products like urea from liver to kidney for excretion in urine.

(iv) It protects the body from diseases.

Blood Donation

Hundreds of lives can be saved through blood donation. It is a painless and harmless procedure. Blood can be donated at hospitals and at other places that are authorised by the government. The donated blood is stored with special care in the blood banks for future use.

7.4 Blood Vessels

These are the network of tubes through which blood is pumped all over the body. These vessels run between the heart and the rest of the body. There are three major types of blood vessels in the body, i.e. arteries, veins and capillaries.

1. Arteries

These **carry oxygen-rich blood** from the heart to all the parts of body. These are found deep under our skin and cannot be seen easily.The throbbing movement fell on the inner side of the wrist are due to blood flow in arteries. These constitute a pulse. Arteries have **thick elastic walls** as the blood flows through them at high pressure due to the pumping action of heart.

All the arteries carry oxygenated blood from the heart, an an exception to this is **pulmonary artery** which carries deoxygenated blood from the heart to the lungs.

> **Oxygenated and Deoxygenated Blood**
>
> The blood that carries oxygen in it is called **oxygenated blood**, i.e. it is rich in oxygen. The oxygenated blood comes from the lungs, where oxygen from the fresh air gets mixed into blood and is carried towards the heart.
>
> The blood that is rich in carbon dioxide is called **deoxygenated blood.** It is transported to the lungs for the removal of carbon dioxide from the body.
> Oxygenated blood is bright red in colour while deoxygenated blood is darker in colour.

2. Veins

These are the blood vessels that carry **carbon dioxide -rich blood**, i.e. deoxygenated blood from all the parts of the body back to the heart. These can easily be seen as greenish-blue tubes or lines below the skin.

Veins have thin walls and blood flows through them at low pressure. All the veins carry deoxygenated blood, except **pulmonary vein** that carries oxygenated blood from the lungs to the heart.

3. Capillaries

Arteries are divided further into extremely thin tubes called capillaries. The capillaries join to form veins which empty into the heart. The exchange of substances like food, O_2, CO_2, etc., between the blood and the body cells take place through the capillaries.

Try These 7.1

1. **Amit noticed a reddish-pink colour under his nail when he pressed its base. What pigment causes the appearance of this colour?**
2. **Raju fell down from stairs and blood started coming out from his knees, but after a while, bleeding stopped. Name the component of blood responsible for this action.**
3. **Which type of blood vessel carries blood from the heart to the capillaries?**
4. **Which blood vessel is situated below the skin?**

7.5 Heart

The heart is a vital organ that continually beats as a pump to transport blood and other dissolved substances through blood (and using a network of blood vessels). The heart pumps blood throughout our life without stopping or relaxing.

Location of Heart

The heart is located in the chest cavity with its lower tip slightly tilted towards the left side. It lies between the two lungs, above the diaphragm. The size of our heart is roughly equal to the size of our fist.

The heart is made up of special muscles called **cardiac muscles** that do not get fatigue.

Structure of Heart

The heart has **four chambers.** The upper two chambers of heart are called **atria** (sing. atrium) and the lower two chambers of heart are called **ventricles**. On the left side of heart are the left atrium and left ventricle, while on the right side are the right atrium and right ventricle.

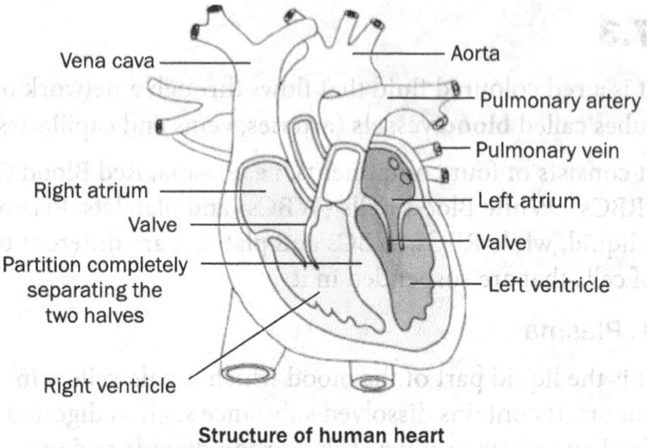

Structure of human heart

The right side of the heart carries deoxygenated blood, while the left side of the heart carries oxygenated blood.

The heart is separated by a partition called **septum** (from right side of the heart to the left side). This prevents the mixing of oxygenated and deoxygenated blood inside the heart.

Left and Right Side of the Heart

The left and right sides of the heart acts as two separate pumps. The left side of the heart pumps the oxygenated blood in the whole body, while the right side of heart pumps the deoxygenated blood to the lungs.
If the oxygenated and deoxygenated blood mix with each other, the body cells will not be able to get enough oxygen for respiration. As a result, less energy will be released in the body.

Heartbeat

The walls of the chambers of the heart are made up of muscles.

The **rhythmic contraction** and **relaxation** of heart muscles constitute a heartbeat. The average heartbeat of an adult person is 72-80 beats per minute at rest. The number of heartbeats increase during and after physical exercise or when the person is excited.

Each heartbeat generates one pulse in the arteries. The number of pulses per minute, i.e. pulse rate indicates the number of heartbeat. The heartbeats persists continuously throughout the life. If we place our hand on the left side of the chest, we can feel our heartbeat.

Stethoscope

The heartbeat can be heard by an instrument called as stethoscope. It is used by doctors to listen to the amplified sound of the heartbeat. It consists of

(i) a chest piece that carries a sensitive diaphragm.
(ii) two ear pieces.
(iii) a rubber tube joining both the parts.

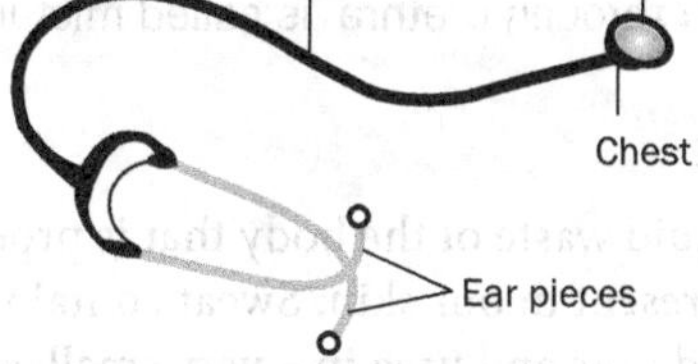

A stethoscope

Doctors assess the condition of the heart by listening to the heart's sound through a stethoscope. The heartbeat increases while running, climbing stairs or exercising as the heart needs to pump blood faster to supply more O_2 to the body cells.

Mechanism of Circulation

The blood is circulated in the human body due to the rhythmic contractions and relaxations of the heart muscles. The contraction of two atria, followed by the contraction of two ventricles ensures a continuous flow of blood in the human body. The mechanism of circulation can be summarised as follows

(i) When blood passes through the capillaries of the lungs, oxygen from air enters into the blood. This oxygenated blood is then carried from the lungs to the left atrium by pulmonary veins.
(ii) The left atrium contracts and the oxygenated blood is pumped into left ventricle.
(iii) The left ventricle pumps this oxygenated blood into arteries which distributes oxygen-rich blood to the different parts of the body, through capillaries. Body cells absorb oxygen and release carbon dioxide.
(iv) The deoxygenated or carbon dioxide rich blood from various body cells enters from the capillaries to veins and then to the right atrium.

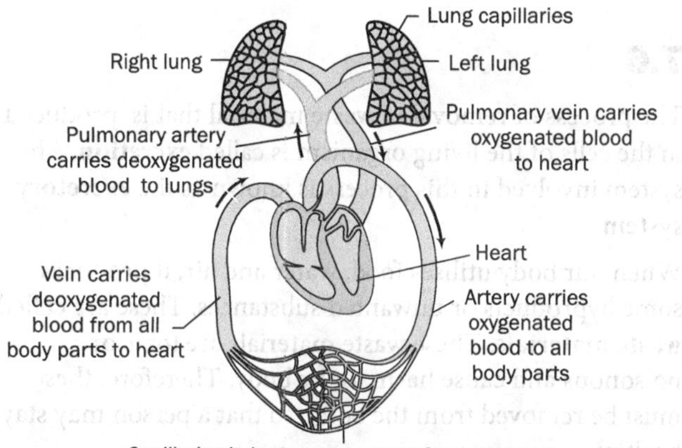

Schematic diagram of circulation

(v) The right atrium contracts and pushes the deoxygenated blood into right ventricles.
(vi) Right ventricle pumps the impure blood (deoxygenated) into pulmonary arteries that carry it to the lungs for purification.

This cycle keeps on repeating continuously day and night, even when we sleep.

> **Discovery of Blood Circulation**
>
> The English physician, **William Harvey** (A.D.1578-1657), discovered the circulation of blood. Back then, people thought that blood oscillates in the vessels of the body. Because of his idea. Harvey was ridiculed and was called **circulator**. He lost most of his patients. However, before he died, Harvey's idea about circulation was accepted as a biological fact.

Circulation in Sponges and *Hydra*

Sponges and *Hydra* are simple animals that do not possess any circulatory system. They live in water and therefore, the food and oxygen enter into their bodies along with water. The water also carry away CO_2 and other waste materials as it moves out of their bodies.

Try These 7.2

1. **Which muscle in our body does not get fatigued and work throughout our life?**
2. **Name the chamber of the heart that receives blood from the lungs.**
3. **Which type of blood is transported to the lungs from the heart?**
4. **If the heartbeat of an athlete is 90 beats per minute, what will be his pulse rate?**
5. **Name two animals that do not possess circulatory system.**

7.6 Excretion in Animals

The process of removal of waste material that is produced in the cells of the living organism is called **excretion**. The system involved in this process is known as the **excretory system.**

When our body utilises food, water and air, it produces some byproducts or unwanted substances. These are called **waste materials.** These waste materials are toxic or poisonous and cause harm to the body. Therefore, these must be removed from the body, so that a person may stay healthy.

The waste material produced in our body cells include CO_2, urea, sweat, etc. These waste materials are removed by different organs of the body such as, **lungs** (CO_2), **kidney** (urea) and **sweat glands** (sweat).

Excretory System in Humans

Urea is the major waste product formed in our body. It is a poisonous substance which must be removed immediately. The kidneys remove urea from the blood. Therefore, kidney is the main excretory organ in our body. The urea and other unwanted salts when dissolve in water, form a yellowish liquid waste called **urine.**

It consists of 2.5% urea, 2.5% other waste products and 95% water. An adult human being normally pass out 1-1.8 L of urine per day. The excretory system collects the urine and remove it. The excretory system of human beings consists of **two kidneys, two ureters, a bladder** and a **urethra.**

(i) **Kidneys** The waste that is present in the blood has to be removed from the body. This is done by the blood capillaries present in the kidneys. When the blood reaches the two kidneys, it contains both useful and harmful substances (urea and unwanted salts). The useful substances are absorbed back into the blood. The waste products get dissolved in water and are removed as **urine.**

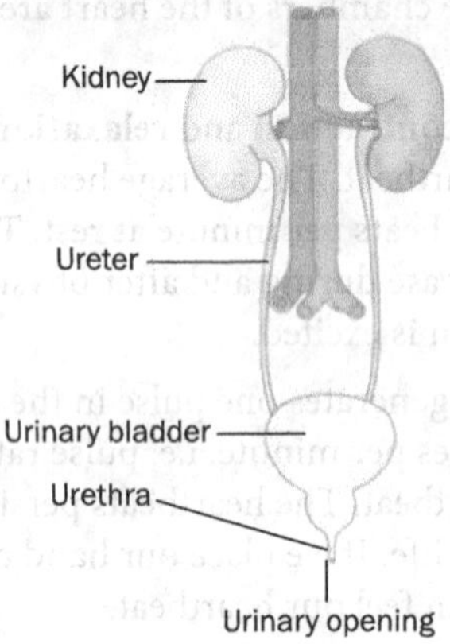

Human excretory system

(ii) **Ureter** The urine thus formed by each kidney is passed through the ureters (two tube-like structures) to the **urinary bladder.**

(iii) **Urinary bladder and Urethra** The urine is stored in the urinary bladder for some time. It is removed at regular intervals through the opening present at the end of muscular tube called urethra.

> **SCIENCE INSIGHT** The process of ejection of urine from urinary bladder through urethra is called micturition.

Sweat Glands

Sweat is the liquid waste of the body that is produced by the sweat glands present in our skin. Sweat contains water, some unwanted salts and urea in a very small amount.

During hot summers, white patches are formed on our clothes, especially in areas like underarms. These marks are left by salts present in the sweat.

The two major functions of sweat are as follows

(i) It helps to remove excess water, salt and urea from the body.

(ii) It helps to keep our body cool during hot summer days.

> **Dialysis**
>
> The normal functioning of kidney is necessary for the good health of a person, but sometimes the kidney may stop working due to an infection or injury. This condition of kidney is called **kidney failure**.
> It may lead to the accumulation of urea in the blood. Person suffering from kidney failure cannot survive unless his blood is filtered periodically through the artificial kidney machine to remove urea. The process of artificial removal of harmful substances is called **dialysis**.

Excretion in Other Animals

Like humans, animals also excrete waste products from their body. The way in which waste materials are removed from the body of the animal depends upon the availability of water.

(i) **Fishes** are the aquatic animals that **excrete ammonia** as their waste product. This ammonia is excreted in the gaseous form which directly gets dissolved in water.

(ii) The **land animals** like lizards, birds, snakes, etc. have less water availability. These animals excrete waste materials in the form of **uric acid pellets**. These are white coloured, semi-solid excretory products in several land animals.

(iii) **Urea** is the excretory product in various animals like human, cow, goat, etc. and it is eliminated as urine.

Try These 7.3

1. **Name an organ which removes urea from the body of humans.**
2. **During hot summer why do white patches appear on our clothes?**
3. **Why are the waste products excreted by the fish not visible?**

7.7 Transport of Substances in Plants

Plants absorb water and dissolved minerals from the soil through their roots and transport it to their leaves. The leaves use water and carbon dioxide for synthesising their food by the process called **photosynthesis**. The food prepared by the leaves is transported to all parts of the plants.

Transport of Water and Minerals

Water and minerals in plants are transported in the following ways

(i) The roots of the plants absorbs water and minerals from the soil.

(ii) The roots possess root hairs which increases the surface area of the roots for absorption of water and mineral nutrients that are dissolved in the water. The root hairs are in direct contact with the water present between the soil particles.

(iii) Water and minerals are moved from the roots up to the stem and leaves through the tube-like **vascular tissue** called as **xylem**. (A tissue is a group of cells that perform specialised function in an organism).

(iv) Xylem tissue forms the continuous network of channels that connect roots to the leaves through the stems and branches. It thus, transports water and minerals to the entire plant.

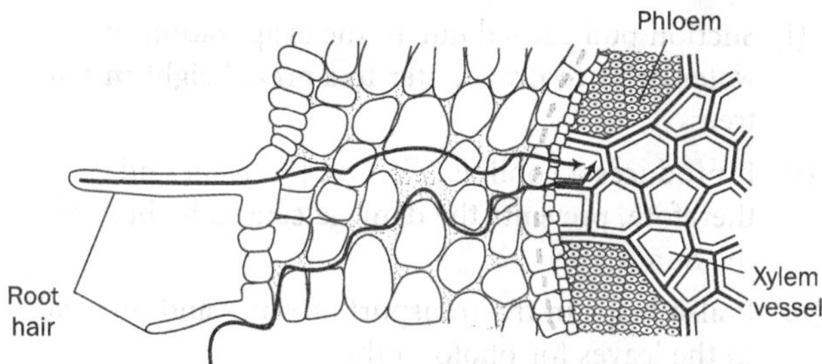

Transport of water and minerals through xylem in a section of root

Transport of Food Material

The food manufactured in the leaf is transported to different parts of plant. This transportation of food material from leaves to the other parts of plants is carried out by the vascular tissue called **phloem**.

The xylem and phloem tissues together form the **vascular bundles** or **conducting tissues**, i.e. they transport substances in the plants.

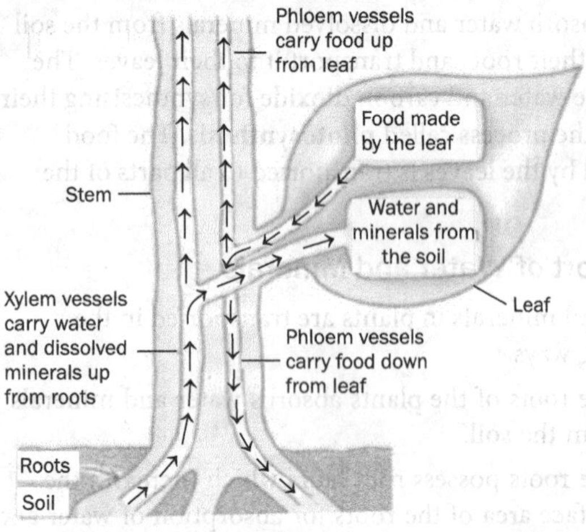

Diagram to show the transport system in plants

7.8 Transpiration

The process of evaporation of water through the stomata present on the surface of leaves is called transpiration. The continuous evaporation of water from the leaves produces an upward pull called **suction force.** This force pulls the water from the roots upward through the stem, branches and finally to the leaves. Though transpiration causes loss of water from the plants, still it is a necessary process for plants due to the following reasons

(i) Suction pull caused due to the evaporation of water helps to draw water to a great height in tall trees.

(ii) It produces a cooling effect on the plant and therefore, prevents the damage caused by heat of the Sun.

(iii) It also helps in the transport of water and minerals to the leaves for photosynthesis.

The rate of transpiration increases in a hot sunny day or in moving air. This happens because the heat from Sun or moving air causes evaporation of water at faster rate from the stomata.

Try These 7.4

1. **Plants absorb water *via* roots, but how do they transport it to different parts of the body?**
2. **Name the tissue through which the food from the kitchen of the plant is transported to all the parts of the plant.**
3. **A potted plant is kept in a dark room for 7-8 hours. What will be its effect on transpiration?**

Science Glossary

Ammonia Aquatic animals like fishes excrete ammonia as their waste product.

Artery Tube that carries oxygen - rich blood from the heart to all parts of the body.

Blood Red coloured fluid that flows in blood vessels.

Blood vessels Tubes which carry blood throughout the body.

Capillary Extremely thin blood vessel that connects arteries to the veins.

Circulatory system Heart, blood and blood vessels together constitute the circulatory system. It transports various substances from one part of the body to another.

Dialysis The process of removal of waste products from blood by artificial kidney.

Excretion The process of removal of waste products from the body.

Excretory system Parts involved in excretion forms excretory system.

Haemoglobin A red coloured protein present in RBC that binds with oxygen.

Heartbeat The rhythmic contraction and relaxation of heart muscles.

Kidneys Main excretory organs that filter blood and remove the wastes.

Phloem Vascular tissue that transports food material from leaves to other parts of the plant.

Plasma A pale yellow coloured fluid in the blood.

Platelets Type of blood cell fragments which help in the clotting of blood.

Pulse The throbbing movement due to the blood flowing in the arteries.

Red blood cell Blood cells that contain a red coloured pigment called haemoglobin, which transports oxygen in the body.

Root hair Roots possess root hair which increase the surface area of the root for absoption of water and mineral from the soil.

Stethoscope Instrument used to measure heartbeat.

Sweat Liquid waste of the body produced by sweat glands present in our skin.

Tissue A group of cells that perform a specialised function in an organism.

Urea Excretory product of animals like human, cow, goat , etc.

Ureter A pair of long tube-like structures that carry urine from kidney to urinary bladder.

Urethra An opening through which urine is excreted out from the body.

Uric acid Excretory product of animals like lizard, birds and snakes, that have less availability of water.

Urinary bladder Bag-like structure that store urine until it is excreted out.

Veins Tubes that carry carbon dioxide-rich blood from all parts of the body to heart.

White blood cell Colourless blood cells that protect the body against diseases.

Xylem Vascular tissue that transports water and minerals from roots to the entire plant.

Let's Investigate

ACTIVITY 1 (Page 71)

Aim To measure pulse rate.

Procedure

1. Place the middle and index fingers of your right hand on the inner side of your left wrist.
2. You will feel some throbbing movements.
3. Count these movements for one minute.
4. Record your own observations and those of your classmates.

Observation We observe some throbbing movement due to the blood flowing in the artery. This is called a pulse. The number of pulse beats per minute is called the pulse rate. The observations of the pulse rate are tabulated below.

Name	Pulse per minute
Parul	78
Himanshi	76
Priyanka	77
Aaditri	73
Divya	72

Conclusion From this activity we can conclude that a resting person usually has a pulse rate between 72-80 beats per minute.

Viva Questions

1. Why do we feel the throbbing movements in the artery?
2. What will be the change in pulse rate of a normal person after climbing stairs?

ACTIVITY 2 (Page 74)

Aim To construct a model of stethoscope.

Materials Required Small funnel (6 - 7 cm in diameter), a rubber tube (50 cm long), a rubber sheet / balloon, rubber band.

Procedure

1. Take a small funnel of 6 -7 cm in diameter.
2. Fix a rubber tube (50 cm long) tightly on the stem of the funnel.
3. Stretch a rubber sheet (or a balloon) on the mouth of the funnel and fix it tightly with the help of a rubber band.
4. Place the open end of the tube on one of your ears.
5. Place the mouth of the funnel on your chest near the heart.
6. Now try to listen carefully.
7. Count the number of times your heart beats in a minute.

Model of stethoscope

Observation We will hear a regular thumping sound. Which is the heartbeat. The heart beats around 70- 72 times in one minute.

Viva Questions

1. Do you hear a regular thumping sound ?
2. How many times does your heart beat in a minute?

ACTIVITY 3 (Page 78)

Aim To show that water is transported through xylem.

Materials Required A glass tumbler, water and red ink, tender herb (e.g. Balsam) and a blade.

Procedure

1. Pour water to fill one third of the tumbler.
2. Add few drops of red ink to the water.
3. Cut the base of the herb's stem and place it in the glass.
4. Observe it the next day.
5. Cut the stem across and observe carefully.

Stem placed in coloured

Observation You will observe that some parts of the stem become red. When you observe the cut part of the stem, the red colour is seen inside the stem.

Conclusion From this activity, we can conclude that water moves up the stem through xylem. Like the red ink, water and minerals are transported to the leaves and other plant parts through these narrow tubes inside the stem.

Viva Questions

1. Which tissue transports water through stem?
2. Why does the part of the herb appear red ?

Mind Map

TRANSPORTION IN ANIMALS AND PLANTS

Excretory System in Humans
Urea is the major waste product, excreted as urine. It consists of the following

Kidney
Paired structure, absorb useful products, expel harmful products as urine.

Ureter
Paired tubes carry urine from kidney to urinary bladder.

Urinary bladder
Bag-like structure that store urine.

Urethra
Muscular connecting the bladder to the outside.

Excretion in Animals
Helps in the removal of waste products.

Excretory Products
- **Ammonia** in fishes, ammonia gets dissolved in water.
- **Uric acid** in animals like lizard, birds, etc. due to less availability of water.
- **Urea** in humans, cow, etc. under sufficient water availability.

Transportation in Plants
Mainly water and food are transported.

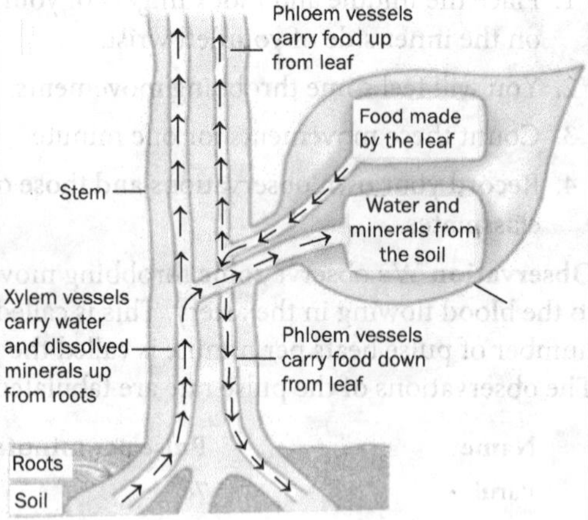

Transportation in Animals
Carried out by internal transport system.

Human Circulatory System
Consists of blood, blood vessels and heart.

Blood
Red coloured fluid flows through a net work of blood vessels.

Components of Blood

Plasma
Liquid part of blood, pale yellow, contain digested food and wastes.

RBCs
- Contain red colour pigment, haemoglobin.
- Transport O_2 and CO_2.

WBCs
Fight against diseases.

Platelets
Colourless cell fragments help in blood clotting.

Blood Vessels
Network of tubes through which blood is pumped in body.

Types

Artery
Carry oxygenated blood from heart to all body parts thick walls, blood flows under high pressure.

Veins
- Carry deoxygenated blood from all body parts to the heart, thin walls, blood flows under low-pressure possess valves.

Capillary
- Thin tubes formed by division of artery joins to form the veins.
- Exchange substances like, O_2, CO_2, etc. between blood and body cells.

Heart
Blood pumping organs in body present between two lungs, composed of cardiac muscles.

Structure
- Has two upper chambers atria and two lower chambers ventricles.
- Right side carry deoxygenated blood and left side carry oxygenated blood.
- Chambers are partitioned by septum.

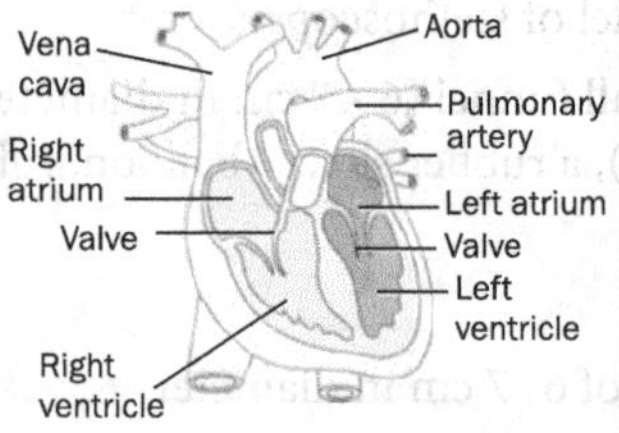

Heartbeat
- Rhythmic contraction and relaxation of heart.
- Average heartbeat is 72-80 beats per minute.
- Heard by an instrument called stethoscope.

NCERT FOLDER

Complete Explanations of all NCERT's Questions

Intext Questions

Q.1 What happens when you get a cut on your body?

Ans. Blood flows out. **Page 70**

Q.2 What is blood? **Page 70**

Ans. Blood is the fluid which flows in blood vessels. It transports substances from one part to another part of the body.

Q.3 Why is the colour of blood is red? **Page 70**

Ans. Refer to text on page no. 113.

Q.4 How does the blood carry various substances? **Page 71**

Ans. Blood is composed of a fluid called plasma which transport substances like digested food from the small intestine to other parts of the body. Red blood cells present in blood helps in the transportation of oxygen to all body cells.

Q.5 What will happen if the blood rich in oxygen and the blood rich in carbon dioxide mix with each other? **Page 73**

Ans. If the blood rich in oxgyen and the blood rich in carbon dioxide mix with each other, the body cells will not be able to get enough oxygen for respiration due to which less energy will be released in the body.

Q.6 Paheli wonders which side of the heart will have oxygen-rich blood and which side will have carbon dioxide-rich blood. **Page 73**

Ans. Left side of the heart will have oxygen- rich blood and right side of the heart will have carbon dioxide-rich blood.

Q.7 Boojho wonders if sponges and *Hydra* also have blood? **Page 75**

Ans. Refer to text on page no. 116.

Q.8 The waste which is present in the blood has to be removed from the body. How can this be done?

Ans. Refer to text on page no. 116. **Page 75**

Q.9 Does sweat serve any other function? **Page 76**

Ans. Refer to text on page no. 117.

Q.10 Paheli wants to know whether animals also urinate.

Ans. Yes, other animals also urinate. **Page 76**

Q.11 How water and nutrients absorbed by the root are transported to the leaves? **Page 77**

Ans. Refer to text on page no. 117 and 118.

Q.12 How is the food prepared by the leaves carried to the parts which cannot make food? **Page 77**

Ans. Refer to text on page no. 117-118.

Q.13 What kind of transport system is present in plants?

Ans. Refer to text on page no. 117 and 118. **Page 77**

Q.14 Boojho thinks that plants may have pipes to transport water to the entire plant like we have in our homes for the supply of water. **Page 77**

Ans. Yes, Boojho is thinking right as plants also have pipes to transport water to the entire plant like we have in our homes for the supply of water.

Q.15 Paheli says her mother puts ladyfinger and other vegetables in water if they are some what dry. She wants to know how water enters into them. **Page 78**

Ans. By soaking the vegetables in water, the skin of the vegetables become moist and water start moving from one cell to another until the vegetables are fresh again.

Q.16 Boojho wants to know why plants absorb a large quantity of water from the soil, then give it off by transpiration? **Page 78**

Ans. Plants absorb large quantity of water from the soil because they need nutrients which are dissolved in water. The excess water evaporates through the stomata present on the surface of the leaf by the process of transpiration.

Exercise

Q.1 Match structures given in Column I with functions given in Column II.

Column I	Column II
(a) Stomata	(i) Absorption of water
(b) Xylem	(ii) Transpiration
(c) Root hairs	(iii) Transport of food
(d) Phloem	(iv) Transport of water
	(v) Synthesis of carbohydrates

Ans. (a)–(ii), (b)–(iv), (c)–(i), (d)–(iii)

Q.2 Fill in the Blanks.

(a) **The blood from the heart is transported to all parts of the body by the ....**

(b) **Haemoglobin is present in ....cells.**

(c) **Arteries and veins are joined by a network of ....**

(d) **The rhythmic expansion and contraction of the heart is called ....**

(e) **The main excretory product in human beings is ....**

(f) **Sweat contains water and ....**

(g) **Kidneys eliminate the waste materials in the liquid form called ....**

(h) **Water reaches great heights in the trees because of suction pull caused by ....**

Ans. (a) arteries

(b) Red Blood Cells (RBCs)

(c) capillaries (d) heartbeats

(e) urea (f) salts

(g) urine (h) transpiration

Q.3 Choose the correct option.

(a) **In plants, water is transported through**

(i) **xylem** (ii) **phloem**

(iii) **stomata** (iv) **root hair**

(b) **Water absorption through roots can be increased by keeping the plants**

(i) **in the shade**

(ii) **in dim light**

(iii) **under the fan**

(iv) **covered with a polythene bag**

Ans. (a) (i) In plants, water is transported through xylem.

(b) (iii) Water absorption through roots can be increased by keeping the plants under the fan.

Q.4 Why is transport of materials necessary in a plant or in an animal? Explain.

Ans. All organisms (plants and animals) need food, water and oxygen for survival. They need to transport all these to various parts of their body. Further, animals need to transport wastes to the parts from where they can be removed or excreted. Thats why transportation is necessary in both plants and animals.

Q.5 What will happen if there are no platelets in the blood?

Ans. The blood clot is formed due to the presence of the cells called platelets in the blood. If there were no platelets in the blood, then bleeding caused by a cut from an injury would not stop. This would cause loss of too much blood from the body of a person leading to death.

Q.6 What are stomata? Give two functions of stomata.

Ans. The tiny pores present on the surface of leaves are called stomata.

Functions of stomata are as follows

(i) Stomata help in the exchange of gases.

(ii) The water evaporates through the stomata present on the surface of the leaves by the process of transpiration.

Q.7 Does transpiration serve any useful function in the plants? Explain.

Ans. Transpiration is the evaporation of water from the surface of plants. It is important for plants as

(i) It generates a force which pulls up water absorbed by the roots from the soil, to reach the stem and leaves.

(ii) It also helps in cooling in plants.

Q.8 What are the components of blood?

Ans. Refer to text on page no. 113.

Q.9 Why is blood needed by all the parts of a body?

Ans. Refer to text on page no. 113 and 114.

Q.10 What makes the blood look red?

Ans. The red pigment (haemoglobin) present in the red blood cells of the blood makes the blood look red. The haemoglobin carries oxygen and transports it to all the parts of the body.

Q.11 Describe the function of the heart.

Ans. The heart acts as a pump for the transport of blood. The human heart is divided into four chambers. The upper two chambers are called the atria and the lower two chambers are called the ventricles. The right side of the heart, i.e. the right atrium and ventricle receive carbon dioxide rich-blood from all parts of the body and transport it to the lungs. Its left side, i.e. the left atrium and ventricle, receive oxygen-rich blood from the lungs which is transported it to all parts of the body.

Q.12 Why is it necessary to excrete waste products?

Ans. When our cells perform their functions, certain waste products are produced. These waste products are toxic and hence, need to be removed from the body. The process of removing waste products produced in the cells of the living organisms is called **excretion**.

Q.13 Draw a diagram of the human excretory system and lable the various parts.

Ans. Refer to figure on page no. 116.

REVIEW EXERCISE

Including Competency Based Questions

Part I

Multiple Choice Questions

1. Which of the following is the main circulatory fluid in our body?

(a) Plasma (b) Lymph
(c) Blood (d) None of these

2. Which among the following contains haemoglobin?

(a) Red blood cells (b) White blood cells
(c) Both (a) and (b) (d) None of these

3. A person was facing trouble in breathing. What role does haemoglobin play in breathing?

(a) Haemoglobin helps in the transportation of oxygen to all body cells
(b) Haemoglobin prevents clot formation inside the respiratory tract
(c) Haemoglobin helps the lungs to take in more air from the surroundings
(d) Haemoglobin fights against germs that enter into the respiratory tract

4. Certain type of cells that help in the destruction of disease causing microorganisms are known as

(a) thrombocytes (b) white blood cells
(c) osteocytes (d) red blood cells

5. While playing cricket, Anant got an injury on his knee. The blood oozed out from the injured site, but after some time a dark red coloured clot formed there. Which component of the blood is responsible for the formation of clot?

(a) Plasma (b) Platelets
(c) Red blood cells (d) White blood cells

6. The list shows few characteristic features of a blood vessel.

I. Carries carbon dioxide rich blood.
II. Presence of thin walls.
III. Presence of valves.
IV. Carries blood towards the heart.

Which of the following will have all these characteristics mentioned? **Competency Based Que.**

(a) Only pulmonary vein
(b) Only pulmonary artery
(c) All veins except the pulmonary vein
(d) All arteries except the pulmonary artery

7. The absorption of nutrients and exchange of respiratory gases between blood and tissues takes place in **NCERT Exemplar**

(a) veins (b) arteries
(c) heart (d) capillaries

8. The organ which controls the blood circulation in body is

(a) liver (b) lungs (c) heart (d) kidney

9. How would you locate the heart in the circulatory system?

(a) A structure that is located in the chest cavity with its lower tip slightly tilted towards the left
(b) A structure that is located in the chest cavity with its upper tip slightly tilted towards the left
(c) A structure that is located in the abdominal cavity with its lower tip slightly tilted towards the right
(d) A structure that is located in the abdominal cavity with its upper tip slightly tilted towards the left

10. The lower chambers of heart are called

(a) atria (b) ventricles
(c) aorta (d) vena cava

11. Select the appropriate reason for the partition between the four chambers of human heart.

(a) To maintain the pressure of blood in each chamber of the heart
(b) To avoid mixing of oxygenated blood with the deoxygenated blood
(c) To increase the volume of all chambers so that more blood can be pumped
(d) To provide more volume to oxygenated blood than the deoxygenated blood

12. To prevent the mixing of oxygenated and deoxygenated blood, human beings have fours chambers in the heart. What will happen if there is no partition between these chambers? **Competency Based Que.**

(a) More carbon monoxide would be available to the body cells
(b) Lesser oxygen would be available to the body cells
(c) More amount of blood would be available to the body cells
(d) More pressure would be exerted on the circulating blood

13. **A person placed his fingers of the right hand on the inner side of his left wrist. He felt some throbbing movements. This throbbing movement is known as .... and it occurs ....**

(a) Pulse rate; due to flow of blood into veins
(b) Pulse rate; due to flow of blood into arteries
(c) Pulse rate; due to flow of blood into capillaries
(d) Pulse rate; due to flow of blood into wrist

14. **The filtration of blood is done by**

(a) heart (b) kidney (c) blood (d) urethra

15. **What happens when the blood passes through the kidney?**

(a) Harmful substances dissolve in water and are removed from the body as urine
(b) Harmful substances get accumulated in the kidney and are released out as sweat
(c) Harmful substances get absorbed by the blood and then are delivered to the lungs for filtration
(d) Harmful substances dissolve in water and then are delivered back to the kidney for filtration

16. **The muscular tube through which stored urine is passed out of the body is called** **CBSE Question Bank**

(a) kidney (b) ureter
(c) urethra (d) urinary bladder

17. **A patient complained that his urine output is very low from the past 3 months. After examination, it was diagnosed that this is due to the malfunctioning of the blood capillaries that help in the filtering of blood. Which of the following organ of the excretory system helps in filtration of blood?**

(a) Kidney (b) Ureter
(c) Urethra (d) Urinary bladder

18. **In which of the following parts of human body are sweat glands absent?** **NCERT Exemplar**

(a) Scalp (b) Armpits
(c) Lips (d) Palms

19. **Aquatic animals like fish excrete their wastes in gaseous form as**

(a) oxygen (b) hydrogen
(c) ammonia (d) nitrogen

20. **Transport of water in plants takes place through**

(a) xylem (b) vascular bundle
(c) phloem (d) None of these

21. **They are pipe-like consisting of a group of specialised cells. They transport substances and form a two-way traffic in plants. Which of the following terms qualifies for the features mentioned above?**

(a) Xylem tissue (b) Vascular tissue
(c) Root hairs (d) Phloem tissue

22. **When plants absorb water from the soil not all of the water absorbed is utilised within the plant. What happens to the excess water, and how is this helpful for the plants?** **Competency Based Que.**

(a) Water condenses on leaves and aids in dew formation
(b) Water condenses on the plant body and falls back to the soil
(c) Water evaporates through leaves and keeps the plant cool
(d) Water evaporates through the plant and causes warmer climate

23. **In a tall tree which force is responsible for pulling water and minerals from the soil?** **NCERT Exemplar**

(a) Gravitational force (b) Transportation force
(c) Suction force (d) Conduction force

24. **Various factors are responsible for the absorption of water by the plants. Among the given factors which of the following will be responsible for the decrease in the absorption of water?**

(a) A decrease in soil temperature
(b) A decrease in the rate of transpiration
(c) An increase in the number of root hairs
(d) A decrease in the amount of water in the soil

25. **The table given below shows the features of four different plants.**

Plants	Transpiration rate	Number of root hairs
A	Low	Less
B	Low	More
C	High	Less
D	High	More

Which plant will absorb water at the fastest rate?

(a) A (b) B
(c) C (d) D

Answers

1. (c)	2. (a)	3. (a)	4. (b)	5. (b)
6. (c)	7. (d)	8. (c)	9. (a)	10. (b)
11. (b)	12. (b)	13. (b)	14. (b)	15. (a)
16. (c)	17. (a)	18. (c)	19. (c)	20. (a)
21. (d)	22. (c)	23. (c)	24. (b)	25. (d)

Fill in the Blanks

1. **Blood consists of ......, ..., ... and platelets.**

2. **Human heart beats about ...... times per minute in an adult person.**

3. .... are the vessels which carry CO_2 rich blood from the body parts to the heart.

4. Fill in the blanks of the following paragraph using just two words-arteries and veins. **NCERT Exemplar**

...... (a) ...... carry oxygen-rich blood from the heart to all parts of the body and .... (b) .... carry carbon dioxide-rich blood from all parts of the body back to the heart ...(c).... have thin walls and ....(d)... have thick elastic walls. Blood flows at high pressure in ....(e)... . Valves are present in .....(f)..... which allow blood to flow only towards the heart. ....(g).... divide into smaller vessels. These vessels further divide into extremely thin tubes called capillaries. The capillaries join up to form .....(h).... .

5. Urine is stored in the .... and excreted out through the ....

Answers

1. plasma, RBCs, WBCs
2. 70-80
3. Veins
4. (a) Arteries (b) veins (c) veins (d) arteries (e) arteries (f) veins (g) arteries (h) veins
5. urinary bladder, urethra

True/False

1. Haemoglobin is the red colour pigment present in blood.
2. Platelets help in blood clotting.
3. Digested food, oxygen and CO_2 passes through the walls of the capillaries.
4. Valves are present in arteries.
5. Atria are the two upper chambers of the heart.

Answers

1. True 2. True
3. True
4. False, valves are present in veins.
5. True

Match the Columns

1. Match the Column I with Column II. **NCERT Exemplar**

Column I	Column II
A. Right ventricle	1. Pushes blood into the pulmonary artery.
B. Pulmonary veins	2. Take deoxygenated blood from the heart to lungs.
C. Left atrium	3. Receives blood from different parts of the body.
D. Pulmonary arteries	4. Bring oxygenated blood from lungs to the heart.
E. Left ventricle	5. Pushes blood into the aorta.
F. Right auricle	6. Receives oxygenated blood from the pulmonary veins.

2. Match the Column I with Column II.

Column I	Column II
A. Circulatory system	1. Thin walled
B. Most arteries	2. Heart and blood vessels
C. Veins	3. Oxygenated blood
D. Kidney	4. Circulation of blood
E. William Harvey	5. Excretion

3. Match the Column I with Column II.

Column I	Column II
A. Haemoglobin	1. Artificial kindney
B. Ventricle	2. Upper chamber
C. Sweat	3. Lower chamber
D. Dialysis	4. Red colour
E. Atrium	5. Water and salts

Answers

1. A–1, B–4, C–6, D–2, E–5, F–3
2. A–2, B–3, C–1, D–5, E–4
3. A–4, B–3, C–5, D–1, E–2

Assertion-Reason Questions

The following questions consist of two statements. Assertion (A) and Reason (R). Answer the following questions by selecting the appropriate option given below.

(a) Both A and R are true and R is the correct explanation of A
(b) Both A and R are true, but R is not the correct explanation of A
(c) A is true, but R is false
(d) A is false, but R is true

1. **Assertion** (A) Arteries carry carbon dioxide rich blood.
Reason (R) Arteries supply blood from heart to all parts of the body.

2. Assertion (A) All veins except pulmonary vein carry CO_2 rich blood.

Reason (R) Veins have thin walls.

3. Assertion (A) Aquatic animals like fishes, excrete waste as uric acid.

Reason (R) The way in which waste chemicals are removed from the body of the animal depends on the availability of water.

4. Assertion (A) Xylem transports food and minerals in the plant.

Reason (R) Xylem and phloem transport different substances in plants.

Answers

1. (d) A is false, but R is true. A can be corrected as Arteries carry oxygen rich blood.
2. (b) Both A and R are true, but R is not the correct explanation of A.
3. (d) A is false, but R is true. A can be corrected as Aquatic animals like fishes, excrete waste as ammonia which gets dissolved in water.
4. (d) A is false, but R is true. A can be corrected as Xylem transports water and minerals in the plant.

Case Based Questions

1. Which of these statements is correct? Circle 'Yes' or 'No' for the correct response.

Competency Based Que.

	Is this statement correct?	Yes or No
(i)	All arteries carry oxygen-rich blood	Yes/No
(ii)	All veins are thin walled	Yes/No
(iii)	Capillaries originate from veins	Yes/No

2. The urine colour chart help to assess how hydrated you are. It is important to drink plenty of water everyday.

Competency Based Que.

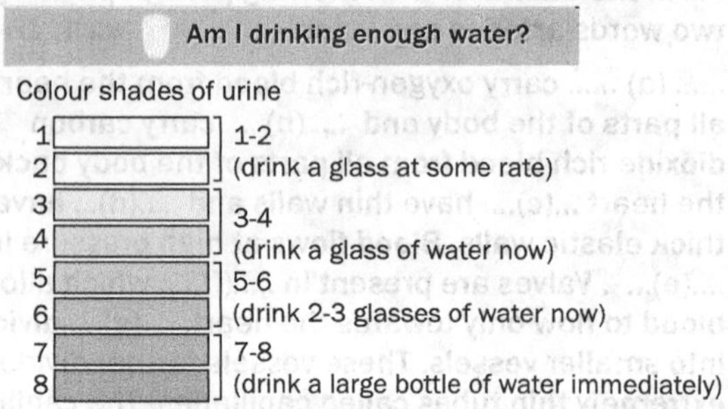

(i) Which colour shade indicates that the body is well hydrated?

(a) Shade 1
(b) Shade 4
(c) Shade 6
(d) Shade 8

(ii) Under normal conditions, human urine contains 95% water and 5% waste products. What would be the percentage of waste products in a darker shade of urine?

(a) 0% (b) Less than 5%
(c) 5% (d) More than 5%

Answers

1. (i) No, all arteries do not carry oxygen rich blood, e.g. pulmonary artery carries deoxygenated blood.
   (ii) Yes, all veins are thin walled vessels.
   (iii) No, capillaries originate from arteries.
2. (i) (a) Shade 1.
   (ii) (d) More than 5%

Part II

Very Short Answer Type Questions

1. Name some useful products or materials that are carried by blood.

Ans. Food, water and oxygen are the useful products that are carried by blood to every part of the body.

2. Circulatory system consists of three major organs. Name those organs.

Ans. The circulatory system consists of three major organs, namely blood, blood vessels and heart.

3. Give the name of blood component which is liquid and contains 90% water.

Ans. The sticky liquid part of the blood, containing 90% water is called plasma.

4. RBCs contains a red coloured pigment which carries oxygen with it. What is the pigment called?

Ans. The red coloured pigment in RBCs that carries oxygen with it is called haemoglobin.

5. Blood performs various functions including protection against infections. How?

Ans. Blood contains WBCs which forms the defense system of our body. They destroy antigens and fights against infections.

6. Arteries have a very thick and elastic walls. Why?

Ans. Arteries carry blood at a very high pressure due to the pumping action of heart. Hence, they need thicker walls to withstand the high pressure of blood.

7. Veins have valves which allow blood to flow only in one direction. Arteries do not have valves. Yet the blood flows in one direction only. Can you explain why? **NCERT Exemplar**

Ans. Veins have valves to prevent the blood from flowing backwards. The arteries pump blood at very high pressures, which naturally prevents the back flow of blood.

8. Usually veins carry deoxygenated blood, except in one case. Specify.

Ans. Pulmonary veins carry oxygenated blood from lungs to heart.

9. Exchange of gases, food and other substances occurs between arteries and veins. How does this exchange occur?

Ans. Exchange of substances between arteries and veins occurs *via* capillaries.

10. Name the organ which is located in the chest cavity with its lower tip slightly tilted towards the left. **NCERT Exemplar**

Ans. The heart is located in the chest cavity with its lower tip slightly tilted towards the left.

11. If the heartbeats of a person are more than 72-80 beats per minute, what does it signify?

Ans. The faster heartbeats signify that heart is pumping more blood to the organs as they need increased oxygen and energy supply.

12. Pulse rate can indicate the health state of an individual. How?

Ans. Pulse rate increases or decreases from the normal rate if a person is not well. Thus, it indicates the health state of an individual.

13. What is the purpose of using stethoscope by doctors?

Ans. A stethoscope helps the doctor to listen to the heartbeats as diaphragm amplifies the sounds of heartbeat when placed on specific areas.

14. Urine is called an excretory product. Why?

Ans. Urine is the mixture of urea and other unwanted salts with water. It is needed to be excreted out as its presence in blood can make a person ill.

15. Urinary bladder is the part of human excretory system. What is its role in excretion?

Ans. Bladder stores the excretory product released after the filtration of blood from kidney and excrete it out at specific times.

Short Answer Type Questions

1. (i) Name the only artery that carries carbon dioxide rich blood.

(ii) Why is it called an artery if it does not carry oxygen-rich blood? **NCERT Exemplar**

Ans. (i) The only artery that carries carbon dioxide-rich blood is pulmonary artery.

(ii) The main function of artery is to carry blood away from heart. Also, arteries have thick wall and do not contain valves in them. In arteries, the blood flows at high pressure. All these characteristics are found in pulmonary artery. It carries deoxygenated blood from heart to lungs for oxygenation.

2. The major function of the arteries is to carry the oxygenated blood throughout the body and that of veins is to carry deoxygenated blood from body parts to heart for purification. There is one artery that carries deoxygenated blood and one vein that carries oxygenated blood. Name the artery and the vein.

Ans. The artery which carries deoxygenated blood or blood rich in CO_2 is pulmonary artery, while the pulmonary vein is one which carries oxygenated blood.

The pulmonary artery carries deoxygenated blood from heart to lungs, while pulmonary vein carries oxygenated blood from lungs to heart.

3. Make a table depicting the function of all the chambers of the human heart.

Ans. The human heart is divided into four chambers, i.e. upper two atrium and lower two ventricles. The functions of these chambers is tabulated below

Chambers	Functions
Left atrium	Receives oxygenated blood from lungs through pulmonary veins and pours it into left ventricle.
Right atrium	Receives deoxygenated blood from various body parts and pours it into right ventricle.
Left ventricle	Pumps oxygenated blood to various parts of body through aorta (largest artery).
Right ventricle	Pumps deoxygenated blood into lungs through pulmonary artery.

4. Observe the given diagram of human heart and label all the parts from *A* to *H*.

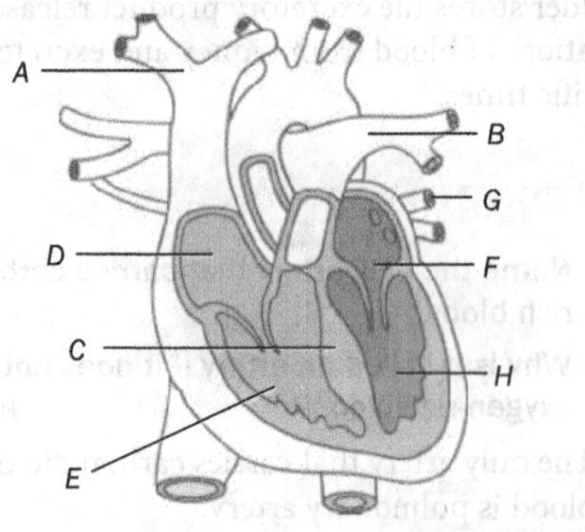

Ans. Refer to text on page no. 114.

5. What is the special feature present in a human heart which does not allow mixing of blood when oxygen-rich and carbon dioxide-rich blood reach the heart? **NCERT Exemplar**

Ans. In humans, the heart has four chambers. The two upper chambers are called the atria and the two lower chambers are called the ventricles.

The partition between the chambers helps to avoid the mixing of oxygen-rich blood with the blood rich in carbon dioxide.

6. Observe given figure and answer the given questions.

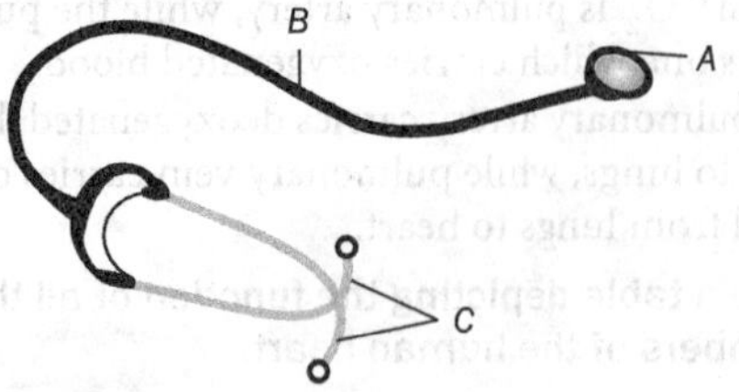

(i) Name the instrument.

(ii) Label the parts *A*, *B* and *C*. **NCERT Exemplar**

Ans. (i) The name of the given instrument is stethoscope.

(ii) Labelled diagram of stethoscope.

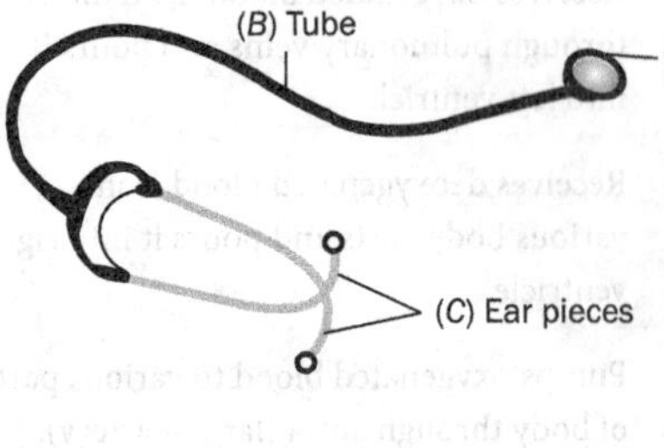

7. The given diagram is of human excretory system. Lable the marked parts of it.

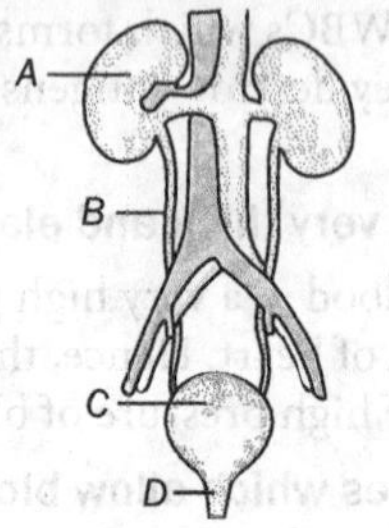

Ans. The various parts of human excretory system are as follows

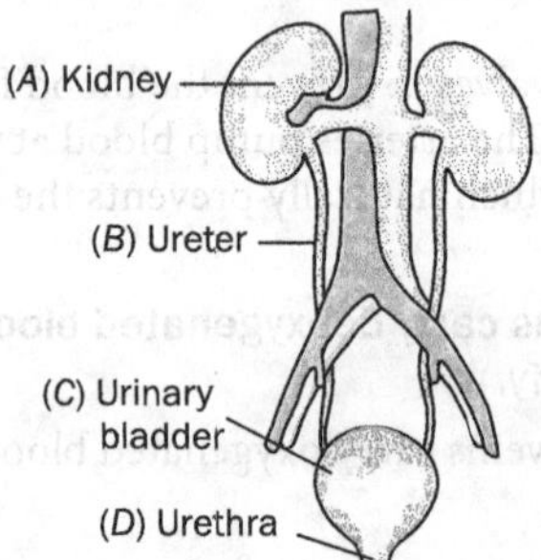

8. Arrange the following statements in the correct order in which they occur during the formation and removal of urine in human beings.

(i) Ureters carry urine to the urinary bladder.

(ii) Wastes dissolved in water are filtered out as urine in the kidneys.

(iii) Urine stored in urinary bladder is passed out through the the urethra.

(iv) Blood containing useful and harmful substances reaches the kidneys for filtration.

(v) Useful substances are absorbed back into the blood.

Ans. The correct order of the formation and removal of urine in human beings is (iv), (v), (ii), (i), (iii).

(i) Blood containing useful and harmful substances reaches the kidneys for filtration.

(ii) Urine stored in urinary bladder is passed out through the urethra.

(iii) Useful substances are absorbed back into the blood.

(iv) Ureters carry urine to the urinary bladder.

(v) Wastes dissolved in water are filtered out as urine in the kidneys.

9. Boojho's uncle was hospitalised and put on dialysis after a severe infection in both of his kidneys.

(i) What is dialysis?

(ii) When does it become necessary to take such a treatment?

Ans. Refer to text on page no. 117.

10. Humans have two major organs that perform transport of materials. Organ 'A' is bean-shaped, dark red in colour and lie just above the waist. It helps in the removal of 'Q', a waste material from blood. The organ 'S' has the opening at the end of the urinary bladder through which the waste material is eliminated.

Organ 'B' lies in the chest cavity, slightly tilted towards the left side. It pumps continuously and pours liquid 'C' into arteries and through very fine tube-like structure 'D', distributes the liquid to various parts of the body. What are the name of these organs? **Competency Based Que.**

Ans. Organ 'A' is kidney which is bean-shaped and helps in the removal of urea (Q), which is a waste material from the blood. 'S' is urethra that has urinary opening at the end of urinary bladder.

Organ 'B' is heart which acts as pump. It pumps continuously and pours blood (c) into arteries and through capillaries (D) which are fine tube-like structure, distributes the blood to various parts of the body.

11. Name the process and the organ which help in removing the following wastes from the body. **NCERT Exemplar**

(i) Carbon dioxide

(ii) Undigested food

(iii) Urine

(iv) Sweat

Ans.

	Wastes	Processes	Organs
(i)	Carbon dioxide	Exhalation	Lungs
(ii)	Undigested food	Egestion	Large intestine and anus
(iii)	Urine	Excretion	Kidneys
(iv)	Sweat	Perspiration (sweating)	Sweat glands

12. List some animals found in your locality and categorise them into following groups.

(i) Animals that excrete ammonia in gaseous forms.

(ii) Animals that excrete uric acid in the form of pellets.

(iii) Animals that excrete urea in the form urine.

Ans. Some animals that are found in our locality are fish, frog, birds, tadpole larva, snake, cow, human, rat, monkey, lizard, toad and snail.

These can be categorised as follows

(i) Animals that excrete ammonia in gaseous form, i.e. ammonotelics, fish, tadpole larva.

(ii) Animals that excrete uric acid in the form of pellets, i.e. uricotelics, bird, snake, rat, lizard, snail.

(iii) Animals that excrete urea in the form of urine, i.e. ureotelics, frog, cow, human, monkey, toad.

13. Look at figure and draw another figure of the same set up as would be observed after a few hours. **NCERT Exemplar**

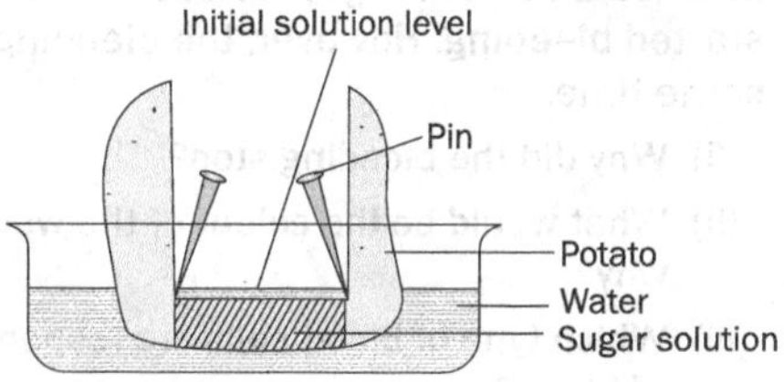

Ans. After the few hours, the setup will appear as follows

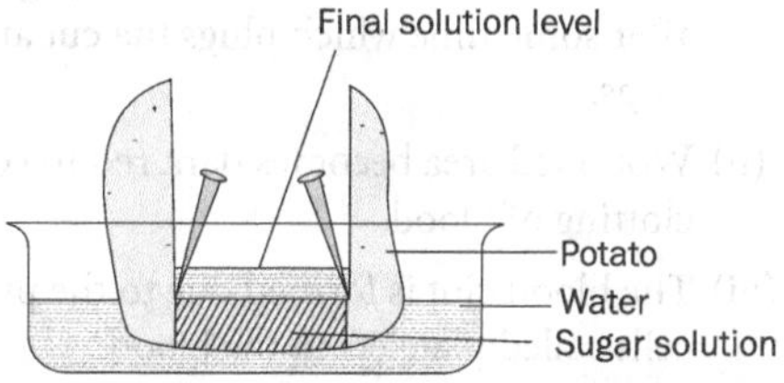

This figure shows that there will be an increase in the level of sugar solution in the potato piece. This increase in the level of sugar solution is due to water that passes through the wall of potato and goes inside it.

14. Paheli uprooted a rose plant from the soil. Most of the root tips with root hairs got left behind in the soil. She planted it in a pot with new soil and watered it regularly. Will the plant grow or die? Give reason for your answer. **NCERT Exemplar**

Ans. Possible answers are

(i) Without the root hairs, the roots will not be able to absorb water and nutrients from the soil and the plant will die.

(ii) The stem of the rose plant may grow new roots and the plant might survive.

(iii) The rose plant may not be able to survive in the different type of soil.

15. Paheli noticed water being pulled up by a motor pump to an overhead tank of a five storeyed building. She wondered how water moves up to great heights in the tall trees standing next to the building. Can you tell why? **NCERT Exemplar**

Ans. When the water is pulled up by a motor-pump to an overhead tank of a five storeyed building, it moves to a great height due to the suction pull. This pull forms the continuous column of water and water rises up to a great height. Similarly, when transpiration occurs in the plants, water is evaporated and it creates a suction pull in the plants.

Due to this suction pressure, water from the soil rises up through the roots of the plants and reaches to a great height in tall plants.

Long Answer Type Questions

1. While learning to ride a bicycle, Boojho lost his balance and fell. He got bruises on his knees and it started bleeding. However, the bleeding stopped after some time.

(i) Why did the bleeding stop?

(ii) What would be the colour of the wounded area and why?

(iii) Which type of blood cells are responsible for clotting of blood? **NCERT Exemplar**

Ans. (i) When a cut or wound starts bleeding, a clot is formed after some time which plugs the cut and bleeding stops.

(ii) Wounded area becomes dark red in colour due to, clotting of blood.

(iii) The blood clot is formed due to the presence of the cells called platelets in the blood.

2. Blood from heart is carried by certain tube-like structure. What are they? Give the structure and functions of different types of blood carrying tubes.

Ans. Refer to text on page no. 114 and 115.

3. Read the following terms given below.

root hairs	xylem	urethra
arteries	kidneys	veins
atria	capillaries	heart
ureter	phloem	urinary bladder

Group the terms on the basis of the categories given below.

(i) Circulatory system of animals.

(ii) Excretory system in human.

(iii) Transport of substances in plants. **NCERT Exemplar**

Ans. The terms on the basis of the categories can be grouped as follows

(i) **Circulatory system of human**
Arteries, atria, capillaries, veins, heart.

(ii) **Excretory system in human**
Urethra, kidneys, ureter, urinary bladder.

(iii) **Transport of substances in plants**
Root hairs, xylem, phloem.

4. Like humans and animals, transportation of water, mineral and nutrients also take place in plants. How?

Ans. Refer to text on page no. 117 and 118 .

Case Based Questions

1. Geeta measured the pulse rate of four students. The table below shows her findings. **Competency Based Que.**

	Pulse rate of the student (beats per minute)		
	1st Reading	**2nd Reading**	**3rd Reading**
Student 1	74	73	74
Student 2	80	78	79
Student 3	72	72	78
Student 4	72	71	72

(i) Which student has the highest pulse rate?

(a) Student 1 (b) Student 2

(c) Student 3 (d) Student 4

(ii) Why did Geeta measure the pulse rate of each student thrice?

(iii) Geeta made an error in one of the readings. Which one is it most likely to be?

(a) Student 1 reading 3

(b) Student 2 reading 1

(c) Student 3 reading 3

(d) Student 4 reading 2

2. The table shows the heart rate of a student before and after different types of exercise. **Competency Based Que.**

	Number of heart beats per minute	
	Before exercise	**Just after exercise**
Exercise 1	92	135
Exercise 2	88	105
Exercise 3	90	155
Exercise 4	93	115

(i) **Which exercise resulted in the maximum change in heart rate?**

(a) Exercise 1 (b) Exercise 2

(c) Exercise 3 (d) Exercise 4

(ii) **The normal heart rate for an adult human is 60-100 beats per minute. Why does the heart rate vary among individuals?**

3.

Breathing Rate	Pulse Rate	Activity level (High, Moderate, Low)
16	81	
22	95	
12	62	

(i) **What is pulse rate and how can we measure it?**

(ii) **What is a typical heart rate of a person at rest?**

(iii) **Interpret the data given in the table about changes in breathing rate and pulse rate to complete the table by filling in the activity level.**

Competency Based Que.

4. The picture shows the directions of movement of two different substances in plants. **Competency Based Que.**

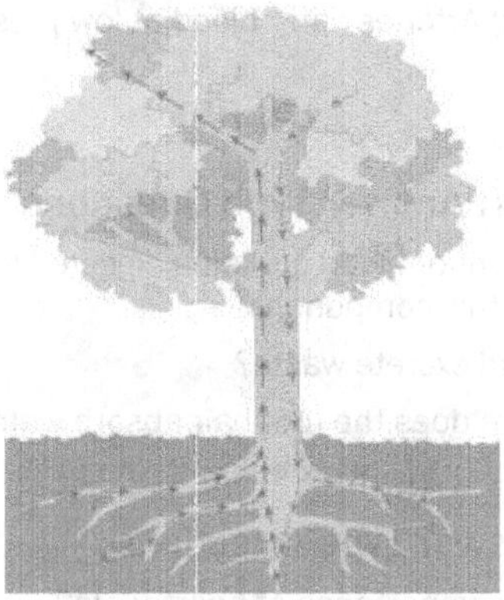

(i) **What do the two types of arrows in the picture show?**

	⟶	- - →
(a)	Movement of air	Movement of water
(b)	Movement of food	Movement of air
(c)	Movement of water	Movement of food
(d)	Movement of air	Movement of minerals

(ii) **Name the process that helps the plants to regulate their temperature.**

Ans. 1. (i) (b) Student 2

(ii) Geeta measured the pulse rate of each student thrice to confirm the results of her activity.

(iii) (c) Student 3 reading 3.

2. (i) (c) Exercise 3.

(ii) The normal heart rate for an adult human is 60 - 100 beats per minute. The heart rate vary among individuals because of the differences in the age groups.

3. (i) Pulse rate is the number of heartbeats per minute. We can measure the pulse rate by measuring the throbbing near our wrist for one minute.

(ii) The heart rate of a normal person at rest is around 72 beats per minute.

(iii)

Breathing Rate	Pulse Rate	Activity level (High, Moderate, Low)
16	81	Moderate
22	95	High
12	62	Low

4. (i) (c) Movement of water, movement of food.

(ii) Transpiration helps the plants to regulate their temperature.

Skill Based Questions as per NEP 2020

1. Why are the patients suffering from disease of the kidney advised to take less salts? **Thinking skill**

2. We excrete more yellowish urine during the summers as compared to the winters give reason. **Thinking skill**

3. Some birds pooped on Ramesh and to his amazement, the colour of the excretory product was white instead of the usual brown that humans normally have. Explain the reason behind this. **Thinking skill**

4. In dry regions, leaves of the plants are modified in such a way that transpiration is reduced to a great extent. Find out the reason behind this. **Thinking skill**

5. Skin acts as an excretory organ by removing waste in the form of sweat in human beings.
Find examples of some animals in which excretion takes place through the skin only. **Research skill**

ASSESSMENT EXERCISE

Part I

Multiple Choice Questions

1. The fluid part of the blood is called
(a) RBC (b) WBC
(c) plasma (d) blood platelets

2. Blood vessels that carry oxygen rich blood from heart to all parts of the body.
(a) Veins (b) Capillaries
(c) Arteries (d) None of these

3. Which of the following blood vessels have valves?
(a) Arteries (b) Veins
(c) Capillaries (d) All of these

4. Which artery carries deoxygenated blood?
(a) Aorta (b) Pulmonary artery
(c) Both (a) and (b) (d) None of these

5. Phloem tissue is responsible for the transportation of
(a) water (b) minerals
(c) food (d) All of these

Fill in the Blanks

6. Heart has .... chambers.

7. The parts or organs involved in excretion to form the ....

8. The function of kidney is to filter the .... to remove ....

True/False

9. Platelets fight against germs that may enter our body.

10. Insects excrete uric acid in semi solid form.

Match the Columns

11. Match the Column I with Column II.

	Column I		Column II
A.	Lizards	1.	Tube-like structure
B.	Ureters	2.	Blood clotting
C.	Root hairs	3.	Ammonia
D.	Platelets	4.	Largest artery
E.	Aorta	5.	Absorption of water and minerals
F.	Fish	6.	Uric acid

Assertion-Reason Questions

The following questions consist of two statements **Assertion** (A) and **Reason** (R). Answer these questions by selecting the appropriate option given below.
(a) Both A and R are true and R is the correct explanation of A
(b) Both A and R are true, but R is not the correct explanation of A
(c) A is true, but R is false
(d) A is false, but R is true

12. Assertion (A) It is necessary to excrete wastes from the body.
Reason (R) Waste materials are toxic and causes harm to the body.

13. Assertion (A) The walls of the arteries are thick.
Reason (R) Arteries carry blood at low pressure.

Part II

Very Short Answer Type Questions

14. A component of blood contains digested food material in it. Identify this component.

15. How do bird excrete waste?

16. From where does the root hair absorb water and minerals?

Short Answer Type Questions

17. What is the importance of heartbeats?

18. Sweating helps us to maintain our body temperature during summer. Explain how?

19. Write the differences between
(i) Xylem and Phloem. (ii) Arteries and Veins

Long Answer Type Question

20. Explain the working of human heart.

Answers

1. (c) **2.** (c) **3.** (b) **4.** (b) **5.** (c)
6. four **7.** excretory system
8. blood, urea
9. False, **10.** True
11. A-6, B-1, C-5, D-2, E-4, F-3
12. (a)
13. (c)

CHAPTER 08

Reproduction in Plants

All the living organisms including plants and animals have the capability to produce new individuals during their lifespan. This process of producing new organism from the existing organism (or the parent) of same species is called **reproduction**.

The new individuals produced, are the copies of their parents. The process of reproduction is one of the important life process and is essential for the continuity of the species.

8.1 Modes of Reproduction in Plants

Different organisms reproduce in a different way. In plants, there are two different methods of reproduction

1. Asexual reproduction
2. Sexual reproduction

8.2 Asexual Reproduction

The process in which only one parent is involved in the production of new individuals of same kind is called asexual reproduction. In plants, asexual reproduction results in the formation of offspring or new plants without production of seeds.

Asexual reproduction in plants occurs by the following methods

1. Vegetative propagation
2. Budding
3. Fragmentation
4. Spore formation

1. Vegetative Propagation

It is the method of producing new plants from **vegetative parts** of a plant like stem, root, leaf and bud.

The stems or branches of plant normally bear **buds** in the axil. The buds that are present in the axil (i.e. the point of attachment of leaf at the node) of leaves develops into shoot. These are called **vegetative buds**.

The vegetative buds can give rise to a new plant. These buds consist of a short stem around which immature overlapping leaves are present. These can produce new plant by vegetative propagation.

Vegetative reproduction may take place using various plant parts as given below

(i) Vegetative Propagation by Stem

Many plants like potato, sugarcane, rose and ginger can be grown by stem cutting.

- **Potato** has small buds called **eyes**. If potato is cut into small pieces with a bud or eye and buried in the moist soil, after some time potato bud grows into new plant.
- Similarly, **ginger** and **turmeric** can also be grown.

(ii) Vegetative Propagation by Leaves

Some plants like *Bryophyllum* (sprout leaf plant) has buds in the margins of leaves.

If a leaf of these plants falls on a moist soil, each bud can give rise to new plant that resembles the parent plant.

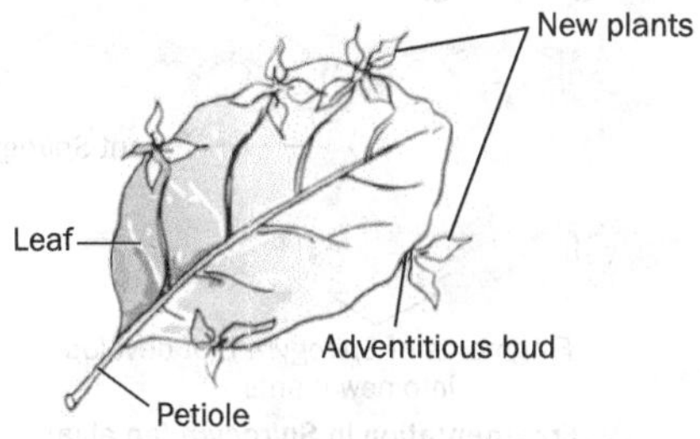

Vegetative propagation in leaf of *Bryophyllum*

(iii) Vegetative Propagation by Roots

Some plants like sweet potato and *Dahlia* have adventitious buds on roots. Each bud can grow to produce new plant.

> **Vegetative Propagation in Cacti**
> Plants like cacti produce new plants when their parts get detached from the main plant body. Each detached part can grow into a new plant.

Advantages of Vegetative Propagation

The plants produced by vegetative propagation has following advantages

(i) Plants produced vegetatively take less time to grow bear flowers and fruits earlier than those produced from seeds.

(ii) The new plants are the exact copies of parent plant because they are produced from a single parent.

2. Budding

In this process, a small bulb-like projection called bud is formed on the parent body. The bud gradually grows in size and finally detaches itself from the parent plant. In this manner, a new individual is formed.

Yeast is a **single-celled organism** reproduced by the process of budding. Sometimes in yeast, another bud arises from the bud forming a **chain of buds** producing large number of yeast cells in short period of time.

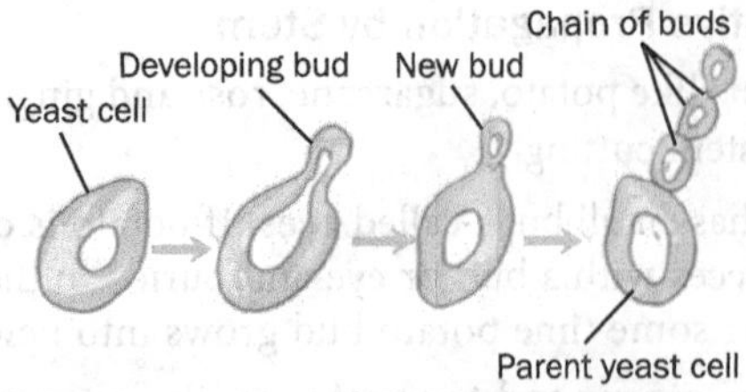

Asexual reproduction in yeast by budding

3. Fragmentation

In this method, the body of the parent breaks into small pieces called **fragments** and each fragment grows into a new plant. Fragmentation of parent body occurs when they are matured, e.g. *Spirogyra*, (an alga), etc.

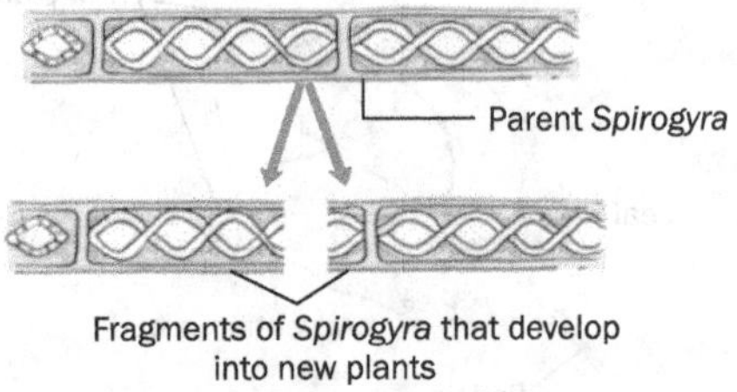

Fragmentation in *Spirogyra* (an alga)

During favourable conditions when water and nutrients are available in plenty algae grow and multiply rapidly by fragmentation. If this process continues, it will cover a large area in a short period of time.

4. Spore Formation

Spores are very light **asexually reproducing bodies**, which can be carried over a long distance by air or wind.

Each spore is covered by a hard protective coat that protects them from unfavourable conditions such as **high temperature** and **low humidity**. So they can survive for long time. When favourable conditions arrive the spores burst and germinate to develop into new individual.

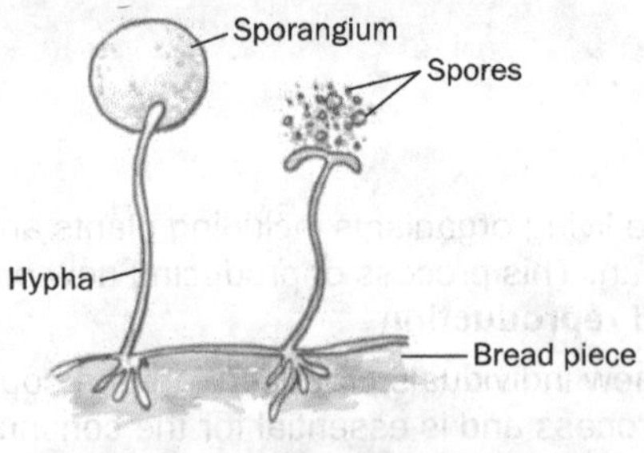

Reproduction in fungus (bread mould) by spore formation

Plants like mosses and ferns along with fungi like bread mould also reproduce by spore formation.

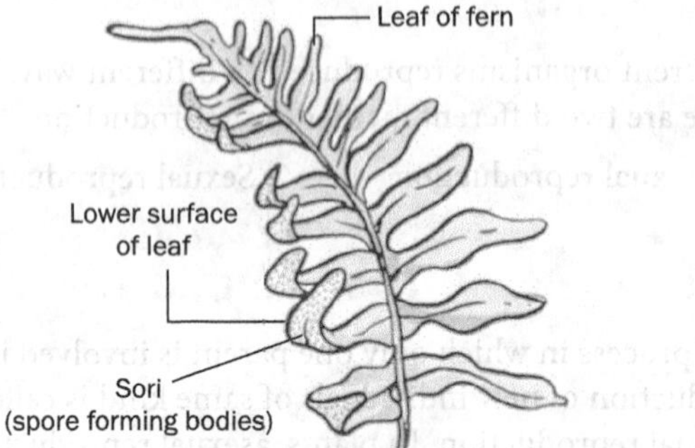

Reproduction through spore formation in fern

> **SCIENCE INSIGHT** In mosses the spores are produced in a structure called capsule while in ferns, they are produced in sori present on leaves called **sporophylls.**

Try These 8.1

1. **Which method of reproduction does not involve production of seeds?**
2. **Which plant part is used in the vegetative reproduction?**
3. **The leaf of a plant was burried in a moist soil. The margins of leaves developed into a new plant that resembled the parent. Name the plant.**
4. **We often find fungus growing on the stale bread kept in a moist environment. How does this fungus reproduce?**

8.3 Sexual Reproduction

The method of reproduction that involves the fusion of male and female gamete is called sexual reproduction. In plants, sexual reproduction results in the formation of offspring or new plant with production of seed.

Flowers are the reproductive part of plant. A flower consists of sepals, petals, stamens and pistil. Stamen and pistil constitute the reproductive part of the flower. These are described below.

(i) **Stamen** It is the **male reproductive part** of a flower. It is made up of two parts, i.e. **filament** and anther. The stalk of stamen is called filament and swollen structure at the tip of filament is called **anther.** The anther contains pollen grains, which produce male gametes.

(ii) **Pistil** It is the **female reproductive part** of a flower. It consists of **stigma, style** and **ovary**. The ovary contains one or more ovules. The female gamete or egg is formed in an ovule.

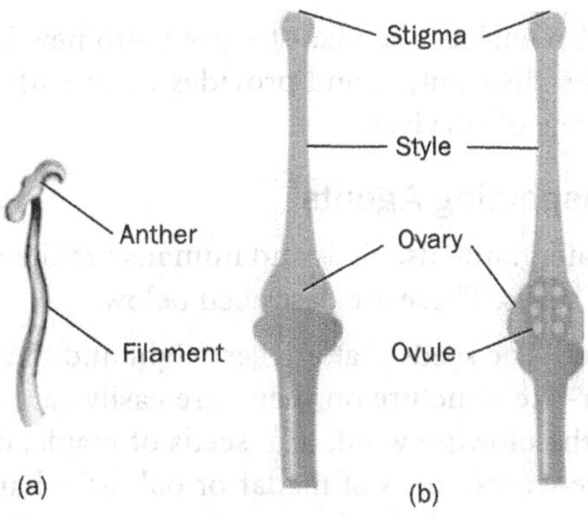

Reproductive parts of a flower
(a) Stamen and (b) Pistil

Types of Flower

On the basis of the type of reproductive organs present in a flower, the flowers are of following types

(i) **Unisexual Flower** The flower which contains only one reproductive organ (i.e. either stamen or pistil) is called unisexual flower. Such flowers are also called **incomplete flowers**, e.g. papaya, watermelon, corn, cucumber, etc. Both male and female unisexual flowers may be present in the same plant or in different plants.

(ii) **Bisexual Flower** The flower that contains both reproductive parts (i.e. stamen and pistil) in a single flower is called bisexual flower. Such flowers are also termed as **complete flower,** e.g. rose, *Petunia*, mustard, *Hibiscus*, etc.

Pollination

The transfer of pollen grains from the anther to the stigma of a flower is called pollination. It takes place in two different ways

(i) **Self-Pollination** It generally occurs in a bisexual flower. When the pollen grain from the anther of one flower reaches to the stigma of the same flower or another flower on the same plant, it is called self-pollination.

(ii) **Cross-Pollination** It can occur both in unisexual and bisexual flowers. When the pollen grains from the anther of a flower lands on the stigma of a flower of a different plant of the same kind it is called cross-pollination.

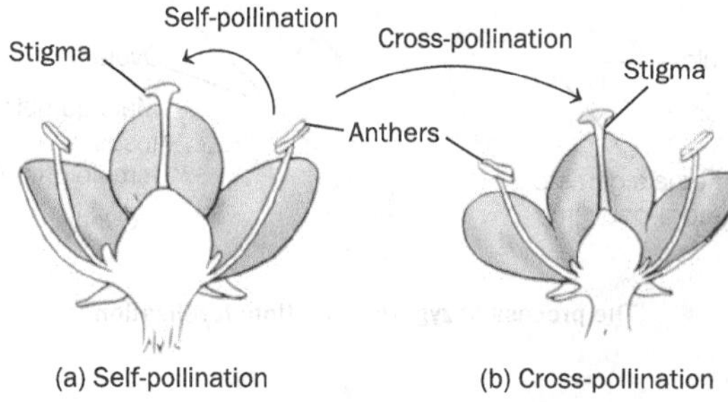

Types of pollination

Agents of Pollination

Generally, pollen grains have tough protective coat which prevents them from drying up. Due to their light weight nature they can be carried by wind or water.

Insects visit flowers and carry away pollen on their bodies. Some of these pollen grains land on the stigma of the flower of the same kind and carries out pollination.

SCIENCE INSIGHT Bats are known to pollinate over 500 plant species including mango, guava and *Agave*.

Fertilisation

The process in which the male gamete fuses with female gamete to form a new cell (i.e. zygote) is called fertilisation.

The process of fertilisation in plants is as follows

(i) When the pollen is deposited on the stigma of the pistil, it begins to germinate. After some time, a long pollen tube is developed from the pollen grain which passes through the style towards the female gametes in the ovary.

(ii) The male gametes move down the pollen tube and the tube enters the ovule present inside the ovary.

(iii) The tip of pollen tube bursts and the male gamete comes out of the pollen tube. Inside the ovary, the male gametes fuse with the female gametes present in the ovule to form a fertilised egg cell which is called **zygote**.

(iv) The zygote develops into an embryo which is a part of a seed that develops into a new plant.

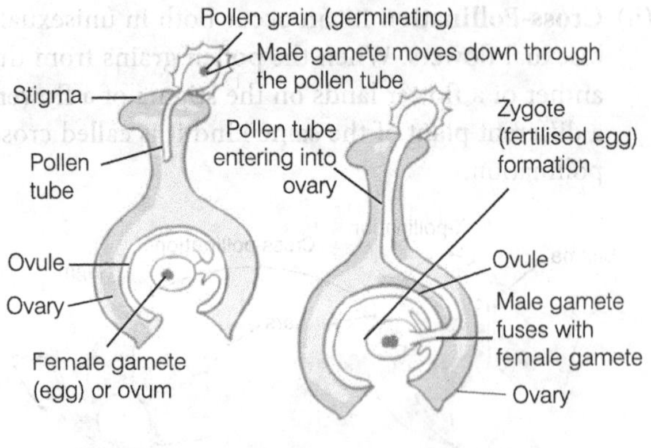

The process of zygote formation: fertilisation

Try These 8.2

1. **Name the method of reproduction that involves the fusion of gametes.**
2. **Name the part of plant which is differentiated into stigma, style and ovary.**
3. **Which type of flowers does the tree of papaya have?**
4. **Which type of pollination can occur both in unisexual and bisexual flowers?**

8.4 Fruit and Seed Formation

After fertilisation, the ovary grows into fruit and the ovule develops into seeds. The other parts of the flower, i.e. petals, sepals and stamen become dry and fall off. The seed contains an embryo enclosed in a protective seed coat.

Fruits are the ripened ovary of a flower which protect the seeds. Some fruits are fleshy and juicy, e.g. mango, apple and orange, while some are hard like almonds and walnuts.

8.5 Seed Dispersal

The process by which the seeds are scattered to different places (far and wide from their parents) is called seed dispersal. Plants produce large number of seeds. When these seeds fall down, they start growing. If large number of seeds falls on the same place, they will not get enough space for water and light, and will not develop into a healthy plant. Thus, the seeds are dispersed by some external agencies to far off places.

Benefits of Seed Dispersal

Some benefits of seed dispersal are

(i) Seed dispersal avoids overcrowding of young plants around their parent plants.

(ii) It helps in preventing competition between the plants and its own seedlings for sunlight, water and minerals.

(iii) It also enables the plant to grow into new habitats for wider distribution and provides them with better chance of survival.

Seed Dispersing Agents

Wind, water, animals, birds and humans are the dispersing agents of seeds. These are described below

(i) **Wind** The seeds that are very light and have wing or hair-like structure on them, are easily carried away by the blowing wind, e.g. seeds of maple, drumstick have wings, seeds of madar or oak have hairs on them, while seeds of grasses are very small and light. These seeds can be easily carried away by the wind and dispersed away from their natural habitat, e.g. hairy fruit sunflower.

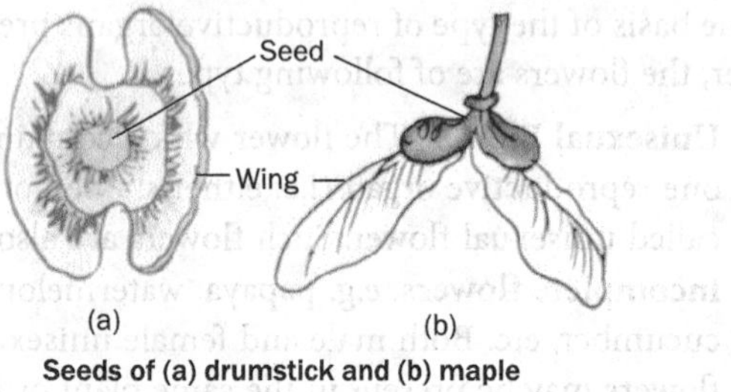

Seeds of (a) drumstick and (b) maple

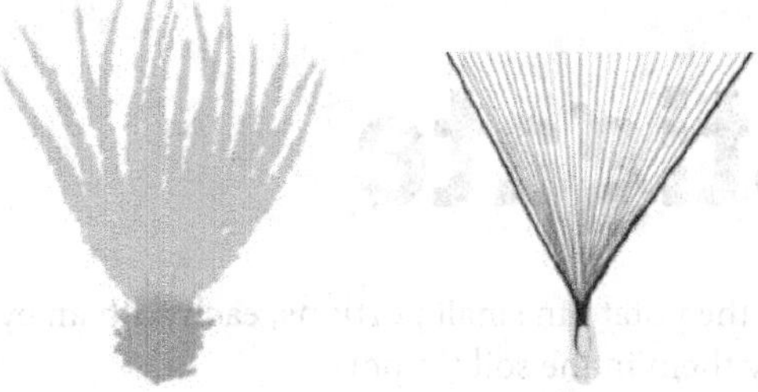

(a) (b)

(a) The hairy fruit of sunflower and (b) hairy seed of madar (oak)

(ii) **Water** The seeds of some plants that have an outer fibrous or spongy covering are dispersed through water. They have the ability to float in the water and drift along with its flow, e.g. coconut.

(iii) **Animals** Some seeds have hooks or spines which get attached to the fur or body of animals. When these animals move to a distant place the seeds get dispersed (while animal rub their body surface), e.g. *Xanthium* and *Urena* plants.

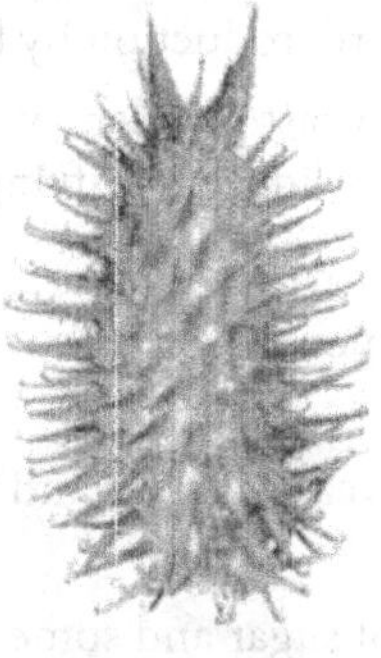

Xanthium

(iv) **Bursting of Fruits** Sometimes fruits mature and a strain is produced in their walls. This produces a sudden jerk causing fruits to break open, thus allowing the seeds to scatter far away from their parent, e.g. castor and balsam.

Try These 8.3

1. **Name the parts of flower that fall off after fertilisation.**
2. **Which part of the flower develops into the fruit?**
3. **What is the seed dispersal agent in *Urena* plant?**

Science Glossary

Asexual reproduction Plants give rise to new plants without the formation of seed.

Budding A new organism develops from a bud of an existing organism.

Embryo The zygote develops into an embryo.

Fertilisation It is the process of fusion of male and female gamete.

Fragmentation Organism breakdown into several fragments and each fragment develop into new individual.

Gametes A reproductive cell of an animal or plant.

Hypha A single filament in fungi.

Pollen grains It contains the male reproductive cell of a plant.

Pollen tube It is a hollow tube-like structure formed from pollen deposited on the stigma.

Pollination Transfer of pollen grains from anthers to the stigma of a flower.

Seed dispersal Scattering of seeds over a large area.

Sexual reproduction Formation of new plant through the fusion of male and female gamete.

Spore Small microscopic structure with thick wall to withstand unfavourable conditions.

Sporangium It contains spores and release them on maturity.

Vegetative propagation Production of new plants from vegetative part of plants like stem, roots, leaf and bud.

Zygote Formed as a result of fertilisation.

Let's Investigate

ACTIVITY 1 (Page 82)

Aim To observe the vegetative propagation in rose or champa plant.

Materials Required Rose or champa plant, moist soil, sharp knife.

Procedure

1. Using a sharp knife, cut a branch of rose or champa with a node. This piece of branch is termed as cutting. The stem cutting must have some buds on it.

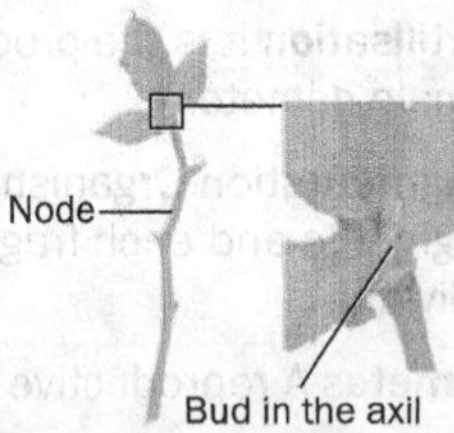

2. Bury the stem cutting in the moist soil.
3. Water, the cutting everyday and observe its growth.

Observation We will observe that after few days, this cutting develops new roots. The bud grows and produces a shoot (i.e. branches and leaves). Thus, a new plant is produced which is similar to the parent plant.

Conclusion From this activity we conclude that rose or champa plant reproduces by vegetative propagation.

Viva Questions

1. What will happen if the cutting does not have any bud on it?
2. Can we grow the money plant in a jar of water by the process of vegetative propagation?

ACTIVITY 2 (Page 83)

Aim To demonstrate vegetative reproduction in the potato tuber.

Materials Required Fresh potato, pot, soil, water, magnifying glass.

Procedure

1. Take a fresh potato and observe it with the help of magnifying glass. Certain scars, present on the potato tubers, called 'eyes' should be present.

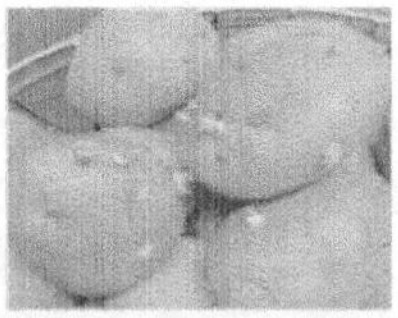

Plant potato sprouting from an 'eye'.

2. Cut the potato in small portions, each with an eye and bury them in the soil (in pot).
3. Water, these pieces regularly for few days and observe their progress.

Observation We will observe that new plants will come out from tuber of potato.

Conclusion From this activity we conclude that potato reproduces by vegetative propagation.

Viva Questions

1. What will happen if the burried portion does not have 'eye' on it?
2. Will you observe similar observation using ginger ?

ACTIVITY 3 (Page 84)

Aim To demonstrate reproduction by budding in yeast.

Materials Required Yeast powder / yeast cake, sugar, water, container, glass slide, magnifying glass.

Procedure

1. Take some yeast powder or yeast cake from bakery or chemist shop.
2. Take a pinch of yeast powder and put it into a container.
3. Add a spoonful of sugar and some water in the container.
4. Shake the container to dissolve it properly.
5. Keep the container in the warm part of a room.
6. Let it sit undisturbed for 60 minutes.
7. Now, take a drop of a liquid on a glass slide and observe it under the microscope.

Observation We will observe that, small bulb - like projections are coming out of yeast cell. These called bud .

Conclusion From this activity we conclude that yeast reproduce by budding.

Viva Questions

1. Provide the reason for adding sugar in container having yeast powder.
2. Why did we keep the yeast solution in warm environment?

Mind Map

REPRODUCTION IN PLANTS

Asexual Reproduction
Production of new plants without production of seeds.

- **Vegetative Propagation**
  - New plants produced from roots, stem and buds.
  - Root, stem and leaves have vegetative buds which can give rise to a new plant.
- **Propagation by Stem**
  - Many plants like potato, sugarcane, rose and ginger can be grown by stem cutting.

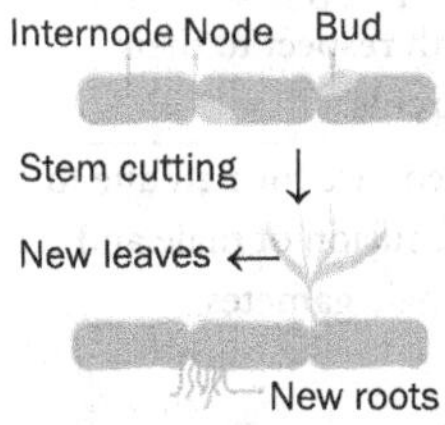

- **Propagation by Leaves**
  Bryophyllum leaves are used for reproduction.

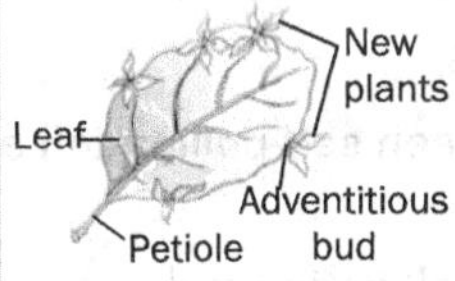

- **Propagation by Roots**
  Sweet potato and *Dahlia* have adventitious buds on roots used for reproduction.

- **Budding**
  - Small bulb-like bud formed on parent body.
  - Bud grows and detaches to form new individual, e.g. yeast.

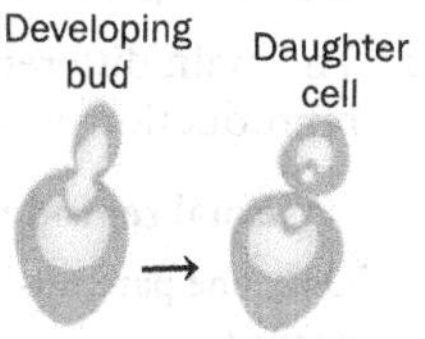

- **Spore Formation**
  - It is light weight, microscopic and covered by protective coat.
  - In favourable conditions a spore germinates and develop into new plant, e.g. Bread mould.

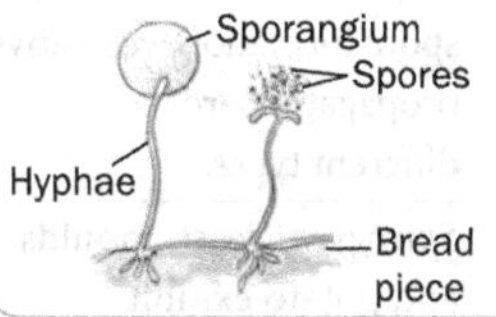

- **Fragmentation**
  - Parent body breaks into small fragments, which grows into new plants, e.g. *Spirogyra*.

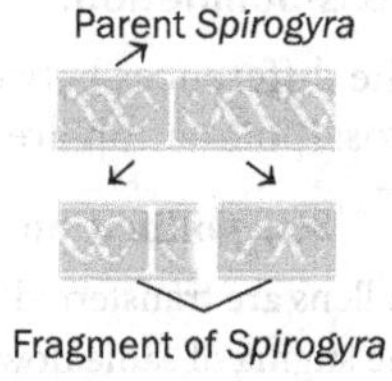

Sexual Reproduction
New plants are obtained with production of seeds.

- **Flower**
  - Reproductive part of plant.
  - **Stamens** are male reproductive part, contains male gametes.
  - **Pistil** is the female reproductive part, contains female gamete or egg.
  - **Unisexual Flower**: Contain either only pistil or only stamens, e.g. corn, papaya and cucumber.
  - **Bisexual Flower**: Contain both stamens and pistil, e.g. mustard, rose and *Petunia.*
- **Process of Sexual Reproduction**
  - **Pollination**: Transfer of pollen grains from anther to the stigma of a flower.
    - Types
    - **Self-Pollination**
      - Occurs in bisexual flower.
      - Pollen grains from one flower reaches to the stigma of same or another flower of same plant.
    - **Cross-Pollination**
      - Occur in both bisexual and unisexual flower.
      - Pollen grains from a flower lands on the stigrna of a flower of a different plant of the same kind.
  - **Fertilisation**
    - Fusion of male and female gamete.
    - Forms zygote which develops into an embryo.
  - **Fruits and Seed Formation**
    - Ovary grows into the fruit.
    - Seeds develop from ovules, contains embryo.
  - **Seed Dispersal**: Seeds are scattered to different places.
    - **Benefits**
      - Avoids overcrowding of young plants.
      - Prevents competition between the seedlings.
      - Enables plant to grow into new habitats.
    - **Bursting of Fruits**: Castor and balsam fruits burst with sudden jerks.
    - **Animal**: Some seeds have hook or spines, e.g. *Xanthium* and *Urena* which get attached to the fur body of animals.
    - **Water**: Coconut has spongy or fibrous covering which has ability to float on water.
    - **Wind**
      - Seeds of maple and drumstick have wings.
      - Seeds of madar or oak have hairs.
      - Seeds of grasses are very small and light weight.
      - These seeds are easily carried away by blowing wind.

NCERT FOLDER

Complete Explanations of all NCERT's Questions

Intext Questions

Q.1 Paheli thought that new plants always grow from seeds. But, she has never seen the seeds of sugarcane, potato and rose. She wants to know how these plants reproduce? **Page 82**

Ans. Sugarcane, potato and rose can be reproduced using stem or buds of the parent plants.

Q.2 Boojho wants to know if there is any advantage of vegetative propagation. **Page 84**

Ans. Refer to text on page no. 134.

Q.3 Boojho wants to know how the male gamete in the pollen grain reaches the female gamete present in the ovule? **Page 86**

Ans. Pollen grain lands and germinate on the stigma. A pollen tube arises from a pollen grain and it carries male gametes. This pollen tube makes its way through the style and enters the ovule. The male gamete fertilises female gametes present in the ovule to form a zygote. The zygote develops into embryo. .

Q.4 Boojho wants to know why flowers are generally so colourful and fragrant? Is it to attract insects? **Page 87**

Ans. Flowers are colourful and fragrant to attract insects which help in pollination.

Exercise

Q.1 Fill in the blanks

(a) Production of new individuals from the vegetative part of parent is called ....

(b) A flower may have either male or female reproductive parts. Such a flower is called ....

(c) The transfer of pollen grains from the anther to the stigma of the same or another flower of the same kind is known as ....

(d) The fusion of male and female gametes is termed as ....

(e) Seed dispersal takes place by means of ...., ... and ....

Ans. (a) vegetative propagation

(b) unisexual flower

(c) pollination

(d) fertilisation

(e) wind, water, animals

Q.2 Describe the different methods of asexual reproduction. Give examples.

Ans. Refer to text on page no. 133 and 134.

Q.3 Explain what do you understand by sexual reproduction?

Ans. Refer to text on page no. 135.

Q.4 State the main differences between asexual and sexual reproduction.

Ans. The main differences between asexual and sexual reproduction are as follows

Asexual reproduction	Sexual reproduction
Only one parent is needed.	Two parents, a male and a female are required.
Offspring are identical to their parents.	Offspring exhibit variation with respect to their parents.
No seed is formed. Fragmentation, budding, spore formation, vegetative propagation are its different types.	Seeds are formed due to the fusion of male and female gametes.
Spirogyra, yeast, moulds and potato exhibit asexual reproduction.	Fruit bearing plants, like mango and China rose, reproduce sexually.

Q.5 Sketch the reproductive parts of a flower.

Ans. Refer to figure on page no. 135.

Q.6 Explain the differences between self-pollination and cross-pollination.

Ans. The differences between self-pollination and cross-pollination are as follows

Self-pollination	Cross-pollination
Pollens are transferred to the stigma of same flower.	Pollens are transferred to the stigma of different flower.
Does not require pollinating agents.	Requires pollinating agents.
Occurs in papaya, corn, cucumber, etc.	Common in most of flowers like rose, China rose, etc.

Q.7 How does the process of fertilisation take place in flowers?

Ans. Refer to text on page no. 135 and 136.

Q.8 Describe the various ways by which seeds are dispersed.

Ans. Refer to text on page no. 136 and 137.

Q.9 Match the following columns.

Column I	Column II
(a) Bud	(i) Maple
(b) Eyes	(ii) *Spirogyra*
(c) Fragmentation	(iii) Yeast
(d) Wings	(iv) Bread mould
(e) Spores	(v) Potato
	(vi) Rose

Ans. (a)–(iii), (b)–(v), (c)–(ii), (d)–(i), (e)–(iv)

Q.10 Tick (✓) the correct answer.

(a) The reproductive part of a plant is the

(i) leaf (ii) stem (iii) root (iv) flower

(b) The process of fusion of the male and the female gametes is called

(i) fertilisation

(ii) pollination

(iii) reproduction

(iv) seed formation

(c) Mature ovary forms the

(i) seed (ii) stamen

(iii) pistil (iv) fruit

(d) A spore producing organism is

(i) rose

(ii) bread mould

(iii) potato

(iv) ginger

(d) *Bryophyllum* can reproduce by its

(i) stem

(ii) leaves

(iii) roots

(iv) flower

Ans. (a) (iv)The reproductive part of a plant is the flower.

(b) (i) The process of fusion of the male and female gametes is called fertilisation.

(c) (iv) Mature ovary forms the fruit.

(d) (ii) A spore producing organism is bread mould.

(e) (ii) *Bryophyllum* can reproduce by its leaves.

REVIEW EXERCISE

Including Competency Based Questions

Part I

Multiple Choice Questions

1. The 'eye' of the potato plant is what? NCERT Exemplar

(a) The root is to any plant
(b) The bud is to a flower
(c) The bud is to *Bryophyllum* leaf
(d) The anther is to stamen

2. A teacher showed ginger to students from which some sprouts were coming out. After some time, the teacher asked the students to observe a slide in which a yeast cell was reproducing. Which method of reproduction has been examined by the students in both of these organisms? Competency Based Que.

	Ginger	Yeast
(a)	Vegetative propagation	Vegetative propagation
(b)	Budding	Budding
(c)	Budding	Vegetative propagation
(d)	Vegetative propagation	Budding

3. Lila observed that a pond with clear water was covered up with a green algae within a week.

By which method of reproduction did the algae spread so rapidly? NCERT Exemplar

(a) Budding (b) Sexual reproduction
(c) Fragmentation (d) Pollination

4. Which among the following does not reproduce by vegetative reproduction?

(a) Corn (b) Sugarcane
(c) Rose (d) Jasmine

5. The ovaries of different flowers may contain NCERT Exemplar

(a) only one ovule (b) many ovules
(c) one to many ovules (d) only two ovules

6. The female gamete of a flowering plant is present in which part?

(a) Ovules (b) Buds
(c) Pollen (d) Anther

7. Pollination refers to the NCERT Exemplar

(a) transfer of pollen from anther to ovary
(b) transfer of male gametes from anther to stigma
(c) transfer of pollen from anther to stigma
(d) transfer of pollen from anther to ovule

8. The fusion of male and female gametes is called

(a) ovulation (b) population
(c) pollination (d) fertilisation

9. Which of the following statements is/are true for sexual reproduction in plants?

(i) Plants are obtained from seeds
(ii) Two plants are always essential
(iii) Fertilisation can occur only after pollination
(iv) Only insects are agents of pollination

Choose from the options given below. NCERT Exemplar

(a) (i) and (iii) (b) Only (i)
(c) (ii) and (iii) (d) (i) and (iv)

10. Which of the following parts of a plant take part in sexual reproduction? NCERT Exemplar

(i) Flower (ii) Seed
(iii) Fruit (iv) Branch

Choose the correct answer given below.

(a) (i) and (ii) (b) (i), (ii) and (iii)
(c) (iii) and (iv) (d) (ii), (iii) and (iv)

11. Plants use their different parts to produce new plants as listed below in the table.

Plants	Part used
Rose	Stem-cutting
Bryophyllum	Leaf
Fern	Spores
Cucumber	Seed

Which of the following plant uses a sexual mode of reproduction?

(a) *Bryophyllum* (b) Cucumber
(c) Fern (d) Rose

12. Seeds of drumstick and maple are carried to long distances by wind because they possess NCERT Exemplar

(a) winged seeds (b) large and hairy seeds
(c) long and ridged fruits (d) spiny seeds

Answers

1. (c) 2. (d) 3. (c) 4. (a) 5. (c)
6. (a) 7. (c) 8. (d) 9. (a) 10. (b)
11. (b) 12. (a)

Fill in the Blanks

1. Roots, stems and leaves are called .... of a plant.
2. The scars present on the potato tubers are called ....
3. The small bulb-like projection coming out from the yeast cell is called a ....
4. *Spirogyra* is an alga which may break up into two or more ....
5. The male and female gametes fuse to form a .... during the process of .... This grows into an .... which is enclosed within a seed. After fertilisation the ovules develop into .... and the ovary develops into a .... **NCERT Exemplar**

Answers

1. vegetative part 2. eye
3. bud 4. fragments
5. zygote, fertilisation, embryo, seed, fruit

True/False

1. The potato tuber reproduces from seeds.
2. Asexual reproduction in yeast takes place by budding.
3. Two individuals are needed for the sexual reproduction.
4. Pistil is the male reproductive part of a flower.
5. *Hibiscus* or China rose is a bisexual flower.

Answers

1. False, potato tuber reproduces from 'eyes' which are buds present on its body.
2. True 3. True
4. False, pistil is the female reproductive part of a flower.
5. True

Match the Columns

1. Match the Column I with Column II

Column I	Column II
A. *Bryophyllum*	1. Stem cutting
B. Cactus	2. Detached body parts
C. Rose	3. Fragmentation
D. *Spirogyra*	4. Vegetative reproduction by roots
E. Sweet potato	5. Spores
F. Bread mould	6. Leaves

Answer

1. A–6, B–2, C–1, D–3, E–4, F–5.

Assertion-Reason Questions

The following questions consist of two statements Assertion (A) and Reason (R). Answer the following questions by selecting the appropriate option given below.

(a) Both A and R are true and R is the correct explanation of A
(b) Both A and R are true, but R is not the correct explanation of A
(c) A is true, but R is false
(d) A is false, but R is true

1. **Assertion** (A) Corn and papaya produce unisexual flowers.
   Reason (R) Unisexual flowers contain both stamen and pistil.
2. **Assertion** (A) Pollen grains have a tough protective coat.
   Reason (R) It protects the male gamete from adverse conditions like high temperature and low humidity.
3. **Assertion** (A) Seeds are dispersed to different places.
   Reason (R) Drumstick and maple have winged seeds.

Answers

1. (c) A is true, but R is false. R can be corrected as
   The unisexual flowers contain either pistil or stamen. They are also known as incomplete flower.
2. (a) Both A and R are true and R is the correct explanation of A.
3. (b) Both A and R are true, but R is not the correct explanation of A. It can be corrected as
   Seeds are dispersed to different places to prevent competition between the plants and its own seedlings for sunlight, water and minerals.

Case Based Questions

1. The picture shows parts of a flower.
   P, Q, R and *S* are the four labelled parts. **Competency Based Que.**

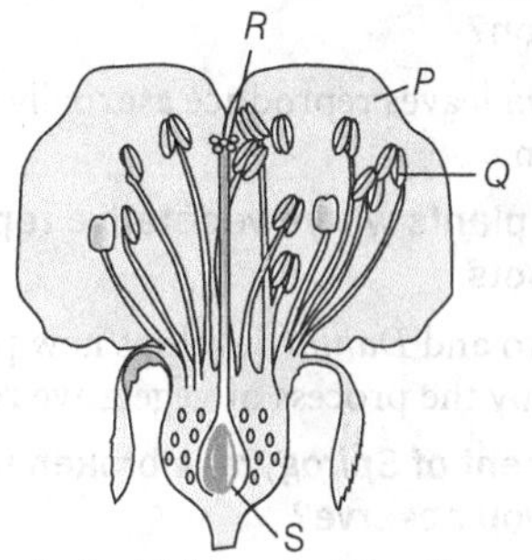

(i) Removal of which part of the flower will not stop reproduction in the plant?
(a) *P* (b) *Q* (c) *R* (d) *S*

(ii) **Why is part *P* brightly coloured in most flowers?**

(a) To repel animals
(b) To attract insects
(c) To help the plant make food
(d) To help the plant retain water

2. Observe the given table and answer the following question.

Type of seeds	Pictures	Features
Seed 1		Very light weight, has feathery hairs
Seed 2		Hard, has tiny hooks
Seed 3		Hard, has spikes
Seed 4		Light weight, hard and hollow

Competency Based Que.

Which seed is most likely to be dispersed by water?

(a) Seed 1 (b) Seed 2
(c) Seed 3 (d) Seed 4

Answers

1. (i)-(a), (ii)-(b), 2. (d)

Part II

Very Short Answer Type Questions

1. Formation of new, but similar individuals from parents is the characteristic feature of which process?

Ans. Formation of new, but similar individual is the characteristic feature of asexual reproduction.

2. Why is the process of reproduction necessary?

Ans. The process of reproduction is necessary for the perpetuation and preservation of species because it increases the number of members of species.

3. Boojho had the following parts of a rose plant–a leaf, roots, a branch, a flower, a bud and pollen grains. Which of them can be used to grow a new rose plant? **NCERT Exemplar**

Ans. Branch can be used to grow a new rose plant. As, rose reproduces by vegetative propagation. i.e. stem cutting method.

4. *Bryophyllum* leaves reproduce using which mode of reproduction?

Ans. *Bryophyllum* leaves reproduce asexually by vegetative propagation.

5. Name two plants where vegetative reproduction takes place by roots.

Ans. Sweet potato and *Dahlia* develops new plants through their roots by the process of vegetative reproduction.

6. If the filament of *Spirogyra* is broken into fragments. What will you observe?

Ans. If the filament of *Spirogyra* is broken into fragments, then each fragment will develop into a new plant.

7. Mention the mode of reproduction in the following organisms.

(i) *Spirogyra* (ii) Yeast (iii) Money plants

Ans. (i) *Spirogyra* – Fragmentation
(ii) Yeast – Budding
(iii) Money plant –Vegetative propagation (stem cutting)

8. Fungus, moss and fern reproduce by a common method of asexual reproduction. Name the method. **NCERT Exemplar**

Ans. Fungus, moss and fern reproduce by the common method of spore formation which is a type of asexual reproduction.

9. Name the spore producing bodies in fern.

Ans. Sori is a yellow-brown cluster of structure that produces spores. They are usually found on the lower surface of the leaves of ferns.

10. Pick the odd one out from the following on the basis of mode of reproduction and give reason for it, Sugarcane, Potato, Rice, Rose. **NCERT Exemplar**

Ans. The odd one out is rice.
In the above given pairs, rice reproduces by sexual reproduction but sugarcane, potato and rose reproduce vegetatively.

11. Write the male and female reproductive parts present on the flowers.

Ans. The male reproductive part is stamen and the female reproductive part is pistil.

12. Give one difference between unisexual and bisexual flower.

Ans. Unisexual flowers are those which contain either male or female reproductive part and bisexual flower has both reproductive parts (i.e. male and female) on the same flower.

13. Pollen grains are present inside anthers for long time yet they do not die. Why?

Ans. Pollen grains have a tough protective coat which prevents them from drying up.

14. Which type of pollination does the given figure indicate?

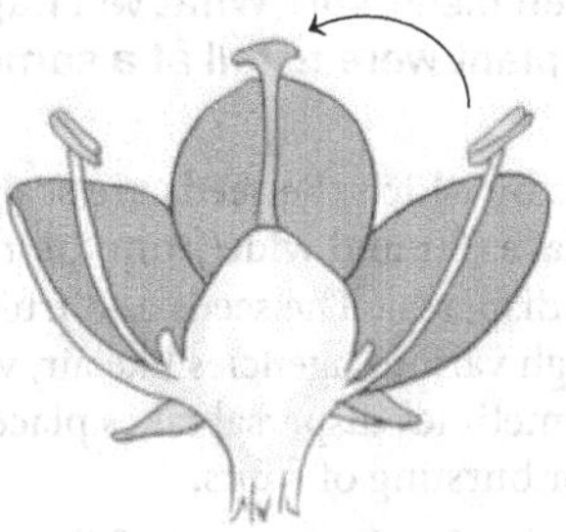

NCERT Exemplar

Ans. The given figure shows self-pollination, as the pollen grains from anther of flower are transferred to the stigma of the same flower.

15. In which part of flower does fertilisation occur?

Ans. Ovary is the part where fertilisation occur, i.e. male and female gametes fuse together.

16. Fruit is the ripened ovary of a flower. Explain.

Ans. After fertilisation, the ovary of a flower develops and becomes a fruit with seeds present inside.

17. Coconut is a large and heavy fruit. How is it adapted for dispersal by water? NCERT Exemplar

Ans. Coconut fruit has fibrous outer coat, which helps it to float in water.

Short Answer Type Questions

1. How do the plants like sugarcane, potato and rose reproduce when they cannot produce seeds?

Ans. Sugarcane and rose are propagated by stem cutting that is a method of vegetative propagation. In this, stem cutting with nodes is capable of growing into mature independent plants that are identical to their parents.

Potato is an underground modified stem having bud called eyes, which sprout and develop into a new identical plant.

Thus, the plants which cannot produce seeds, can be propagated vegetatively with the help of vegetative parts such as stem, roots, buds and leaves.

2. Observe the given figure.

(i) Which plant is this? Give another name of the plant.

(ii) What does it show?

(iii) From where the new plants are developing?

Ans. (i) The given figure is of *Bryophyllum* leaf. It is also called as sprout leaf plant.

(ii) It shows vegetative reproduction by leaves.

(iii) The leaves of *Bryophyllum* develops buds in its margin or edges which grow into new plants, when buried in the soil.

3. Why is vegetative propagation a preferred method of asexual reproduction?

Ans. The following advantages of vegetative reproduction makes it a preferred method

(i) It takes less time to grow and bear flower and fruits than those produced from seeds.

(ii) The new plants are the exact copies of parent plant because they are produced from a single parent.

4. What is a bud? Which organism reproduce by budding? Give the diagrammatic representation of budding in an individual.

Ans. Refer to text on page no. 134.

5. When you keep food items like bread and fruits outside for a long time especially during the rainy season, you will observe a cottony growth on them. NCERT Exemplar

(i) What is this growth called?

(ii) How does the growth take place?

Ans. (i) When food items like bread and fruits are kept outside for a long time especially during rainy season, a **cottony growth of bread mould**, a fungus is observed.

(ii) The growth of fungus takes place by spores present in air, which when come in contact with moisture in bread germinate and grow to produce new individual.

6. Place a piece of bread in a moist and warm place for few days. Observe it after few days. What will you see?

(i) Name the organism that grows on the bread piece?

(ii) What are the thread-like projections called?

(iii) What is the knob-like structure present on the top of thin stem called?

(iv) Which type of reproduction does this organism show?

Ans. (i) It is a bread mould, a fungus.

(ii) The thread-like projections are called hyphae or mycelium.

(iii) The knob-like structure present on the top of thin stem is called sporangia or sporangium which contains hundred of minute spores.

(iv) Bread mould shows asexual mode of reproduction.

7. A student was given a flower. He was asked to pick the different whorls of flower by the forcep. He pulled each part of the flower and laid them on the chart paper in a sequence and named them W, X, Y, Z (from outer to inner whorl). He was unable to name them.
Help the student to name the different parts of a flower. Also help him to tell which part produces male gamete and female gametes. **Competency Based Que.**

Ans. The four whorls of the flower are outermost whorl 'W' is green part which is called sepal. Inside sepal the next whorl is 'X' which is coloured and attractive part of the flower called petals. The 'Y' is the inner whorl of flower called stamen. It is the male reproductive part of a flower. It consist of two parts, i.e. anther and filament. The anther contains several pollen grain which have male gamete. The whorl 'Z' is the innermost part of the flower called pistil. It is the female reproductive part of flower. It consists of three parts, i.e. stigma, style and ovary. The ovary contains ovule which produces the female gametes or egg cell.

8. Collect some flowers of different plants like papaya, rose, mustard, *Petunia*, cucumber, corn, etc. and group them under following heads.

(i) Which of these plants have unisexual flowers?

(ii) Which of these plants have bisexual flower?

(iii) What is the other name of unisexual and bisexual flower?

Ans. (i) **Unisexual flowers** are papaya, cucumber and corn.

(ii) **Bisexual flowers** are rose, mustard and *Petunia*.

(iii) Unisexual flowers are also called as incomplete flowers while bisexual flowers are called complete flowers.

9. In the figure given below, label the part marked (i), (ii) and (iii).

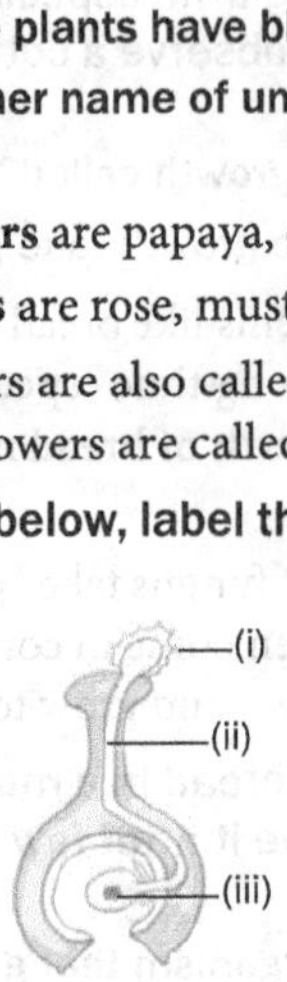

NCERT Exemplar

Ans. The parts in the given figure are labelled as follows

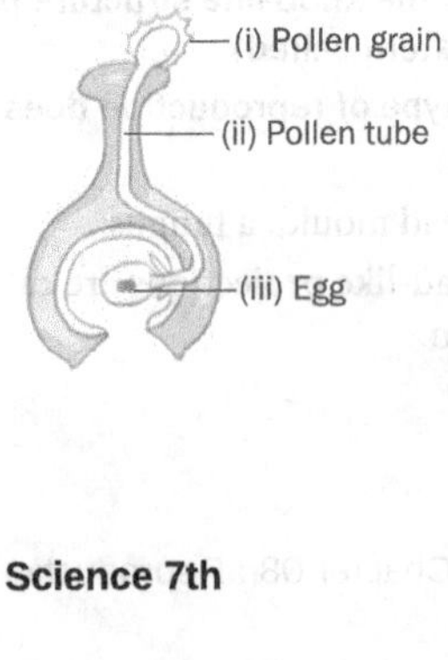

10. One morning as Paheli strolled in her garden she noticed many small plants, which were not there a week ago. She wondered, where they had come from as nobody had planted them there. Explain the reason for the growth of these plants. **NCERT Exemplar**

Ans. The small plants which were not there in the garden a weak ago have grown up due to seed dispersal. The seeds from the tree may have fallen below or have been dispersed by wind or animals on the ground, which on germination developed into new small plants.

11. What is seed dispersal? What will happen if all the seeds of a plant were to fall at a same place and grow?

Ans. The process by which the seeds are scattered to different place (far and wide from their parents) is called seed dispersal. The seeds and fruits are dispersed away through various agencies like air, water and animals. Sometimes dispersal takes place by the explosion or bursting of fruits.

If all the seeds of a plant were to fall at the same place and grow, there would be a severe competition for sunlight, water, mineral and space. As a result, the survival for the plants will be difficult and the plants who survive will not grow into healthy plants.

12. Mention the benefits of seed dispersal.

Ans. Refer to text on page no. 136.

13. Group the seeds given in figure (i) to (iii) according to their means of dispersal.

(i) Seed dispersed by wind

(ii) Seed dispersed by water

(iii) Seed dispersed by animal **NCERT Exemplar**

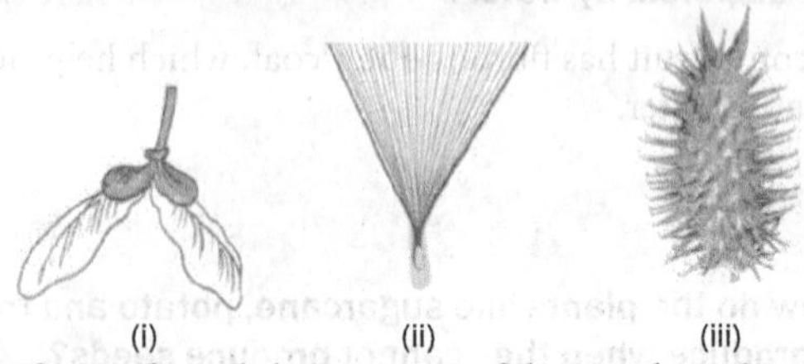

Ans. The seeds and their means of dispersal can be given as follows

(i) The seed of maple is dispersed by wind. It has winged seed which are light in weight.

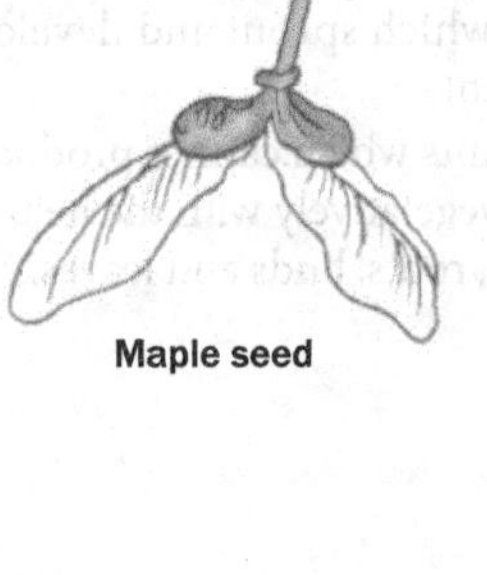

Maple seed

(ii) Seed of oak or madar has hairy outgrowth which makes it lighter and can be dispersed by wind.

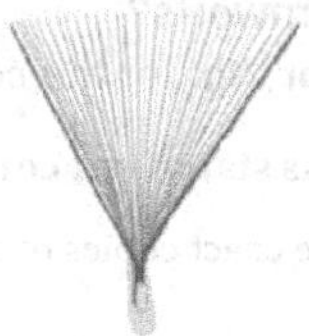

Seed of oak or madar

(iii) Seed of *Xanthium* have numerous spines on them which gets attached to the fur of animals. Hence, these are dispersed by animals.

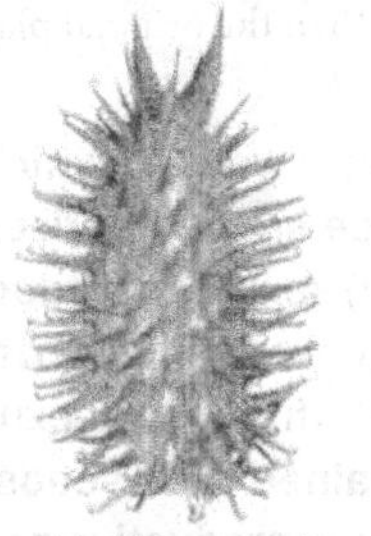

Xanthium seed

None of the seed given in the figure is dispersed by water.

14. Write how the following seeds are dispersed? **NCERT Exemplar**

(i) **Seeds with wings**
(ii) **Small and light seeds**
(iii) **Seeds with spines/hooks**

Ans. The mode of dispersal of the seeds having following properties are as follows

(i) **Seeds with wings-like** seeds of drumstick and maple are light weight and can be blown away by air. Thus, these are dispersed by wind.

(ii) **Small and light seeds like** of grasses are also dispersed through wind.

(iii) **Seeds with spines/hooks** seeds of *Xanthium*, *Urena* have spines and hooks on them, these hooks or spines are attached to the fur of the animal body. When animals move to other places and rub their body with tree, etc. These seeds fall from their body and get dispersed. Therefore, these are dispersed through animals.

Long Answer Type Questions

1. Observe the given figure and answer the following questions.

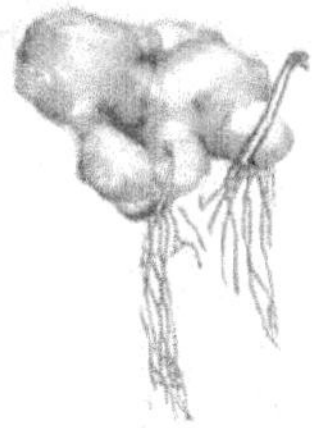

(i) **Name the plant.**
(ii) **Which type of reproduction is seen in this plant?**
(iii) **Label the parts of this plant.**

Ans. (i) The given figure is of ginger.
(ii) Asexual reproduction is seen in this plant.
(iii) Various parts of this plant can be shown as follows

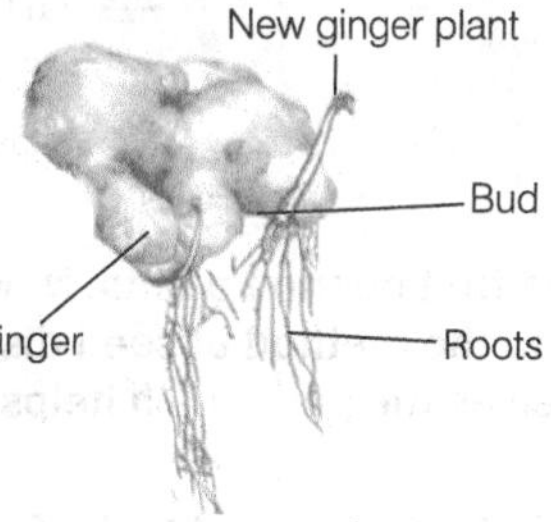

2. In the figure of a flower given below, label the parts whose functions are given below and give their names.

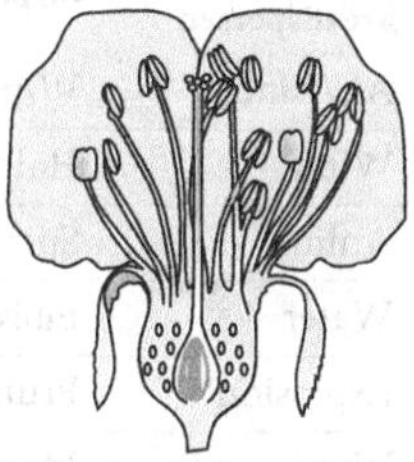

(i) **The part which contains pollen grains.**
(ii) **The part where the female gamete is formed.**
(iii) **The female reproductive part, where pollen grains germinate.**
(iv) **The colourful part of flower which attracts insects.**

Ans. The various parts of a flower whose functions are mentioned above are labelled as follows

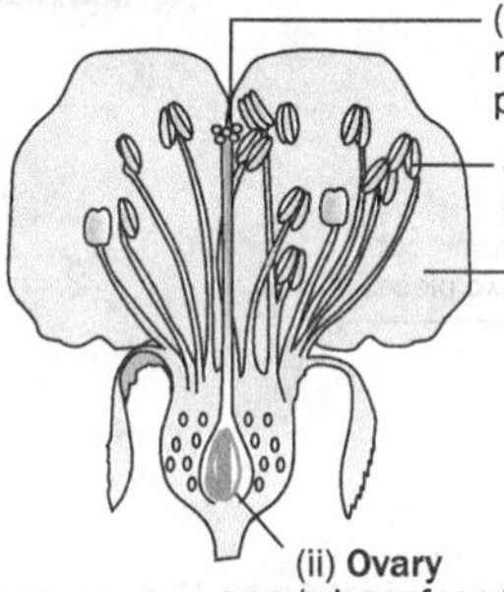

3. In the diagram of a bisexual flower given as figure, draw the missing part and label the parts marked (a), (b) and (c). Also label the missing part that you draw.

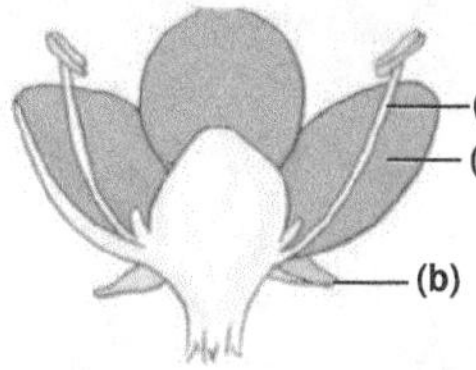

NCERT Exemplar

Ans.

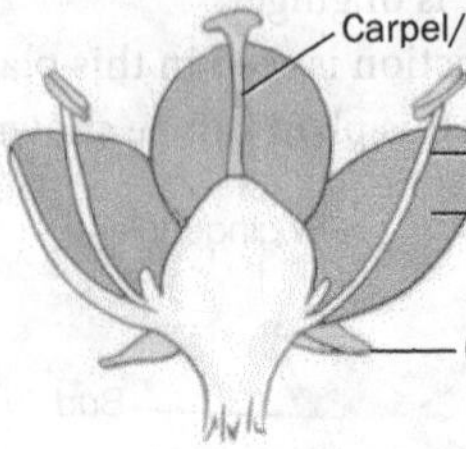

4. Name some fruit bearing plants. Now make a table and describe the method of seed dispersal in these fruits as well as the part which helps in the seed dispersal.

Ans. The method of seed dispersal in the fruits and the parts which help in the seed dispersal are as follows

Name of fruit bearing plants	Agents through which seeds are dispersed	Parts or seeds which helps in dispersal
Drumstick	Air/wind	Winged seeds
Sunflower	Wind	Hairy seeds
Xanthium	Animal	Spines and hooks
Coconut	Water	Fibrous coating
Castor	Explosion	Fruit bursts
Grass	Wind	Minute, light weight seeds

Case Based Questions

1. Shekhar cut the stem of a hornwort plant into two pieces.
He placed both the pieces under water.
After a week, Shekhar found both the pieces growing as new plants. **Competency Based Que.**

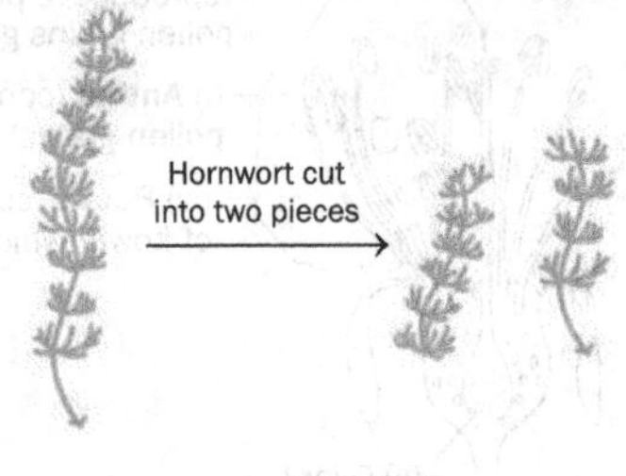

(i) What can be concluded from the activity?
(a) Hornworts can survive only under water
(b) Hornworts can absorb nutrients through leaves
(c) Hornworts bear spores that help it to reproduce
(d Hornworts can reproduce by vegetative propagation

(ii) How can Shekhar confirm the result of activity?

(iii) Which of these statements is true about the two new hornworts?
Circle 'Yes' or 'No' for the correct response.

	Is this statement correct?	Yes or No
(a)	They are exact copies of each other	Yes/No
(b)	They will grow differently than the original plant.	Yes/No
(c)	They will have a different life span than the original plant.	Yes/No

2. There are several ways by which plants produce their offspring. These are categorised into two types: (i) asexual and (ii) sexual reproduction. In asexual reproduction plants can give rise to new plants without seeds, whereas in sexual reproduction, new plants are obtained from seeds. You know that the flowers are the reproductive parts of a plant. The stamens are the male reproductive part and the pistil is the female reproductive part. Insects visit flowers and carry away pollen on their bodies. Some of the pollen lands on the stigma of a flower of the same kind. The transfer of pollen from the anther to the stigma of a flower is called pollination. If the pollen lands on the stigma of the same flower, or another flower of the same plant, it is called self-pollination. When the pollen of a flower lands on the stigma of a flower of a different plant of the same kind, it is called cross-pollination. Seeds and fruits of plants are carried away by wind, water and animals. Plants benefit from seed dispersal.

(i) A teacher visited a vegetable farm with students. The table shows the plants growing in that farm

- Pumpkin plant
- Cucumber plant
- Potato plant
- Tomato plant

The teacher pointed out a plant and said that its mode of reproduction is different from the other three plants. Which plant might have been pointed out by the teacher and why?

(ii) **State the numbers of the parts of the flower which continue to develop after fertilisation?**

The diagram shows a flower in vertical section

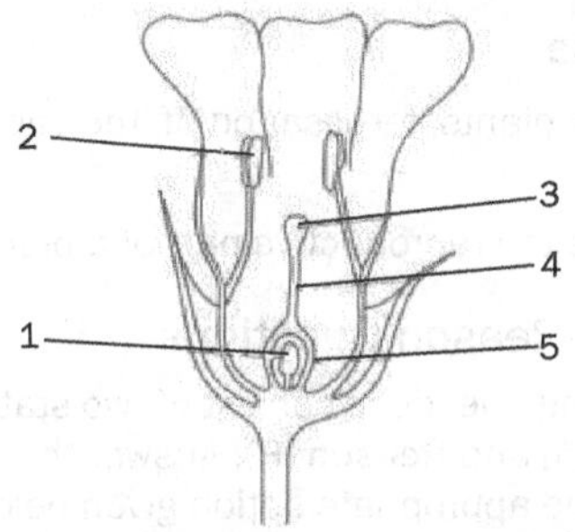

(iii) **A fruit has spongy or fibrous outer coat. What could be their mode of seed dispersal?**

Ans. 1. (i) (d) Hornworts can reproduce by vegetative propagation.

(ii) Shekhar can confirm the result of activity by repeating this activity again.

(iii) (a) Yes (b) No (c) No

2. (i) The potato plant might have been pointed out by the teacher, because among the given plants potato reproduces asexually and other three plants reproduce sexually.

(ii) In the given diagram number 1 and 5, i.e. ovule and ovary are the parts of flower that will continue to develop after fertilisation.

(iii) Their seeds are dispersed by water as they possess spongy or fibrous outer coat.

Skill Based Questions as per NEP 2020

1. **Students of class 7th went on school trip to forest. There they observed a pond covered with a green film on surface. What can be these organisms covering the pond? Does these organisms harm the living bodies inside the pond?** **Observation skill**

2. **The transfer of pollen grains from anther to stigma of flower is termed as pollnation. Find out five wind pollinated flowers and list them.** **Thinking skill**

3. **Ria went to a plant nursery with her mother. The gardener approached them and asked about their choice of plant. Ria's mother wanted a flowering plant with fragrance. Gardner showed them a plant and told them that this variety has been prepared by a method of vegetative propagation of stems. Ria grew curious and asked some questions to the gardener.**

(i) **What is vegetative propagation?**

(ii) **What is the method of producing new plants using stem?** **Thinking skill**

4. **Ravi was sitting in a garden with his family. His younger sister came running with different types of flowers and started to name their parts. She stoped as she forgot some names and Ravi noticing this, came to help her.**

His sister asked many questions related to flowers and Ravi answered her with all information he had.

(i) **What is a flower? Mention its function during reproduction.**

(ii) **Flowers help in pollination and fertilisation. Yes/No. Give reason.** **Observation skill**

ASSESSMENT EXERCISE

Part I

Multiple Choice Questions

1. Which of the following plants uses animals for seed dispersal?

(a) Coconut (b) Grass
(c) *Urena* (d) Madar

2. When the pollen grain from anther of one flower reaches the stigma of same flower or another flower in same plant is termed as

(a) cross-pollination
(b) fertilisation
(c) self-pollination
(d) wind pollination

3. Bread mould reproduces by

(a) fragmentation (b) budding
(c) spore formation (d) stem cutting

4. Ripened ovary of a plant produces

(a) fruit (b) zygote
(c) seed (d) ovule

5. Reproduction through seed occurs in

(a) bread mould (b) wheat
(c) fern (d) yeast

Fill in the Blanks

6. In .... reproduction, seeds are formed.

7. Seed dispersal takes place by ......, ... and ....

Match the Columns

8. Match the Column I with Column II.

Column I	Column II
A. Vegetative part	1. Vegetative reproduction by roots
B. *Dahlia*	2. Sori
C. Bread mould	3. Stem
D. Fern	4. Sporangium

True/False

9. In flowering plants, fertilisation of the egg occurs in stamen.

10. Flowers are the reproductive part of a plant.

Assertion-Reason Questions

The following questions consist of two statements **Assertion** (A) and **Reason** (R). Answer these questions by selecting the appropriate option given below.

(a) Both A and R are true and R is the correct explanation of A
(b) Both A and R are true, but R is not the correct explanation of A
(c) A is true, but R is false
(d) A is false, but R is true

11. **Assertion** (A) *Bryophyllum* reproduces asexually through stem cutting.

Reason (R) Plants produced by vegetative propagation are exact copies of their parent plant.

12. **Assertion** (A) The transfer of pollen from the anther to the stigma of a flower is called pollination.

Reason (R) Pollen grains have tough protective coat which prevents them from drying up.

Part II

Very Short Answer Type Questions

13. The process of fertilisation in plants occurs in which part?

14. What is the name of scars present on potato tuber?

Short Answer Type Questions

15. Differentiate between zygote and embryo.

16. Can animals pollinate flowers? Describe the process.

Long Answer Type Question

17. Distinguish between the following

(i) Unisexual flower and bisexual flower
(ii) Stamen and pistil.

Answers

1. (c) **2.** (c) **3.** (c) **4.** (a) **5.** (b)
6. sexual
7. wind, water, animals
8. A-3, B-1, C-4, D-2
9. False **10.** True
11. (d) **12.** (b)

CHAPTER 09

Motion and Time

In day-to-day life, we observe that some objects are in state of rest and some are in state of motion, e.g. birds fly, fishes swimming, planets moving around the sun, etc., are all in motion. **When an object changes its position with time, it is said to be in motion**. e.g. When the position of a car changes with time, we say that the car is moving or the car is in motion.

Types of Motion

We have learnt in previous class that motion can be circular, periodic or along a straight line (rectilinear). Let us recall them,

Rectilinear motion The motion possessed by a body moving along a straight line path is called rectilinear motion. e.g. Soldiers in a march past, bullock cart moving on a straight road.

Circular motion The motion possessed by a body when it moves along a circular path is called circular motion. e.g. Pedalling of a bicycle, motion of the earth around the sun.

Periodic motion The motion which repeats itself after regular intervals of time is called periodic motion. e.g. Motion of a swing, motion of a pendulum.

9.1 Slow or Fast Motion

The motion of an object with respect to another object can be slow or fast. **The distance covered by objects in a given set of time decides which object is faster or slower.**

An object which takes longer time with respect to another object to cover a certain distance is said to be **slow** while the other object which takes shorter time with respect to another object to cover the same distance is said to be **fast**.

e.g. If your school is at a distance of 5 km from your home and you want to go to school by bicycle, then it may take about 25 min to reach the school and if you go to school by school bus, then the same distance can be covered only in 10 min. It means that a bicycle is slower as compared to bus.

Thus, the most convenient way to determine which of the two objects is moving faster is to compare the distance covered by them in a unit time which is known as **speed**.

9.2 Speed

Speed is defined as the distance covered by an object in unit time. i.e.

$$\text{Speed} = \frac{\text{Distance travelled}}{\text{Time taken}}$$

e.g. Suppose a car travels a distance of 100 km in 2h, then the speed of car is given by

$$\text{Speed} = \frac{100\ \text{km}}{2\ \text{h}} = 50\ \text{km/h}$$

It shows that this car travels a distance of 50 km in 1 h.

Average Speed

Average speed can be defined as the total distance covered by an object divided by total time taken to cover that distance.

$$\text{Average speed} = \frac{\text{Total distance travelled}}{\text{Total time taken}}$$

SCIENCE INSIGHT The fastest possible speed in the universe is the speed of light. The speed of light is 299,792,458 m/s or roughly 3×10^8 m/s or 3×10^5 km/s. It means, light can travel 3 lakh km in one second.

Uniform or Non-Uniform Motion

- When an object moves with constant speed along a straight line, then its motion is called **uniform motion**. e.g. Motion of a rocket.
- When an object changes its speed during its motion, then its motion is called **non-uniform motion**. e.g. Motion of a car moving in traffic.

Try These 9.1

1. **Classify the following as rectilinear motion, circular motion or periodic (oscillatory) motion.**
   (a) Motion of rocking chair
   (b) Motion of a child running on circular track
   (c) Pedals of a moving bicycle
2. **A man riding a scooter travels 50 m in 20 s. What is the speed of the scooter?**
3. **Which of the following is a uniform motion ?**
   (a) A bullet shot from the gun
   (b) A bullock in a field running

9.3 Measurement of Time

A duration or moment in which things occur is known as **time**. We generally measure time with the help of clocks and watches.

In order to measure the time, ancient people used some natural events which repeated regularly after fixed time intervals. e.g.

- They found that the sun rises everyday in the morning, so the time between one sunrise and the next was known as a **day**.
- In the similar manner, the time from one full moon to the next full moon was called a **month**.
- A **year** was fixed as the time taken by the earth to complete one revolution around the sun.

Simple Pendulum

A simple pendulum is a device which is used to measure time. It was discovered by **Galileo Galilei**.

- It contains a small metal ball called **bob** which is suspended by a **long thread** from a **rigid support** such that bob is free to swing back and forth.

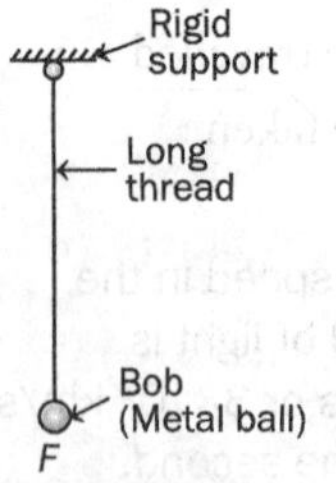

Simple pendulum

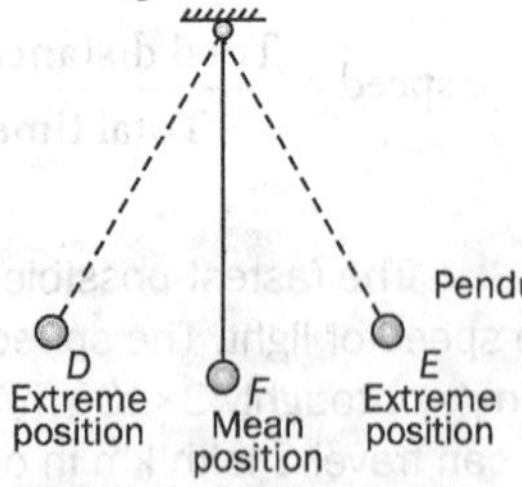

Motion of a simple pendulum

Pendulum clock

- The pendulum is said to have completed one oscillation when its bob starting from its mean position *F*, moves to *D*, to *E* and back to *F*.
- The time taken by the pendulum to complete one oscillation is called **time period**. The time period of a pendulum depends on its length.
- The **length of a pendulum** is the length of thread from the point of suspension to the centre of bob.
- The to and fro motion of the pendulum is an example of **periodic** or **oscillatory motion**.
- The pendulum clock was invented based on the principle of the oscillatory motion of the pendulum.

Before the pendulum clock, many other time measuring devices were used like **sundials, water clocks, sand clocks**, etc.

(i) **Sundial** It has a triangular blade fixed vertically on a dial marked with hours of the day. It measures time by the position of the shadow cast by the sun.

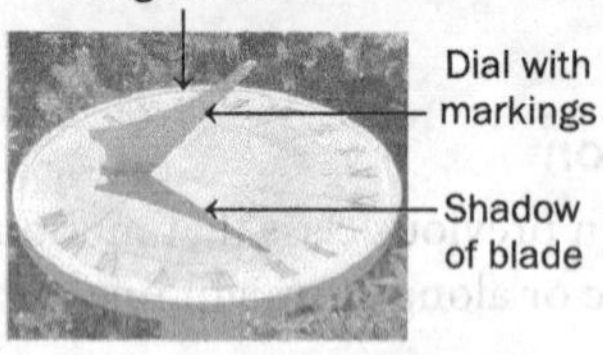

Sundial

(ii) **Sand Clock** It consists of two glass bulbs joined by a narrow neck. This device uses the flow of sand from one glass bulb to another in order to measure time.

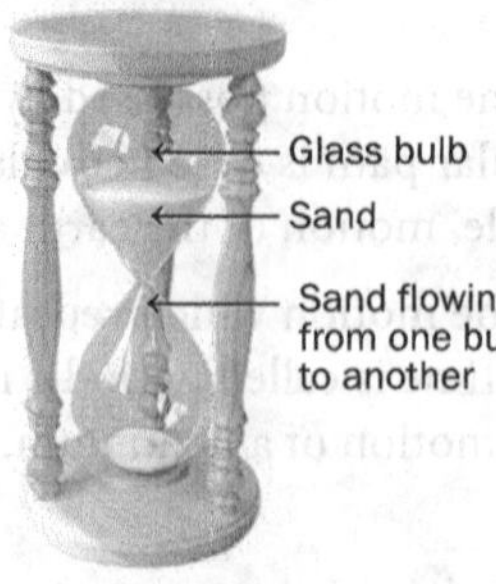

Sand clock

(iii) **Water Clock** It consists of two containers kept at different levels. This device uses the rate at which water drips from one vessel to another to measure the time intervals.

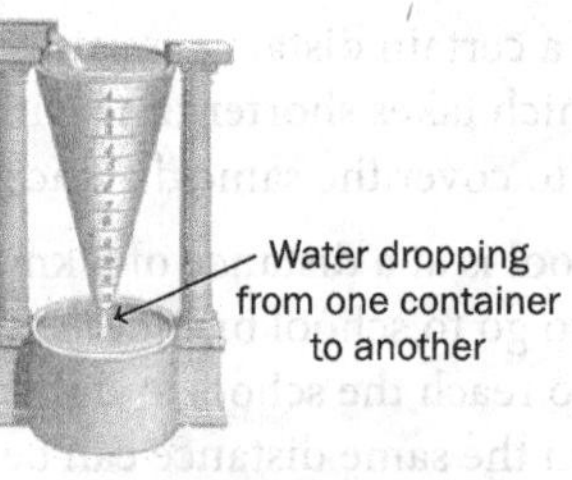

Water clock

Nowadays, most clocks or watches have an electric circuit with one or more cells. These clocks are called **quartz clocks**. The time measured by quartz clocks is much more accurate than that by the clocks available earlier.

SCIENCE INSIGHT Sundial at Jaipur is the biggest sundial in the world. It is called Samrat yantra.

Units of Time and Speed

- The standard unit of time is **second**. It is denoted by symbol 's'.
- In order to express longer time intervals we use **minutes (min)** or **hours (h)** as the unit of time.
- Since, the speed is distance divided by upon time, so the unit of speed is **m/s**. It can also be expressed in other units such as **m/min** or **km/h**.

The usage of different units depends on the need. e.g. it is convenient to express our age in years rather than in days or hours.

Note We must remember that the symbols of all units are written in singular form. e.g. we write 50 km and not 50 kms or 8 cm and not 8 cms.

9.4 Measuring Speed

A **speedometer** is a device which is used to measure the speed of a vehicle. It records the speed directly in km/h.

It is usually combined with a device which is used to measure the distance covered by vehicle, known as **odometer**.

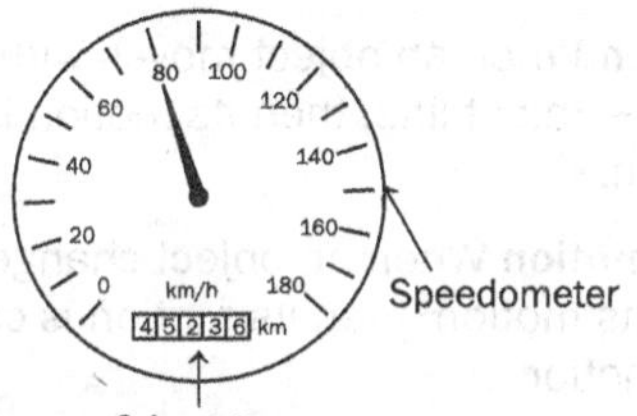

Try These 9.2

1. Name the ancient clock that measured time on the basis of the length of shadow with the change in sun's position.
2. An athlete is running with a speed of 2 km/h to cover a distance of 10 km. How much time, he will take to cover it?
3. In which units, the speed of fast moving object is commonly expressed ?

9.5 Distance - Time Graph

A plot between distance and time is known as distance-time graph. A distance-time graph shows the distance travelled by an object in a given interval of time. This type of graph is represented by line. Hence, it is known as **line-graph**.

(i) Firstly, take a sheet of graph paper and draw two lines perpendicular to each other on it as shown in the figure.

(ii) Mark the **horizontal line** as *XOX'* which is known as the **X-axis**. Similarly, mark the **vertical line** *YOY'* which is known as **Y-axis**.

The point of intersection of *XOX'* and *YOY'* is known as the **origin *O***.

(iii) The two quantities between which the graph is drawn are shown along the *X*-axis and *Y*-axis.

(iv) The positive value on the *X*-axis are shown along *OX*. Similarly, positive values on the *Y*-axis are shown along *OY*.

The shaded part of the graph shows the positive values of quantities.

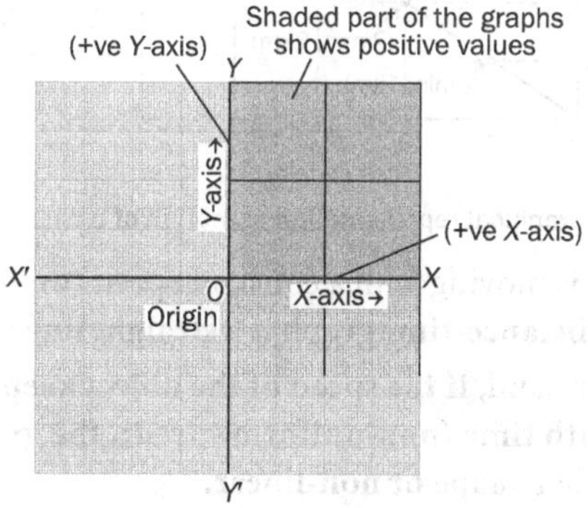

X-axis and Y-axis on a graph paper

Representation of Motion of a Car by Line Graph

For drawing the distance-time graph for a moving object, we require the readings of distance travelled by the object and the corresponding time values. The distances travelled by a car at various times are shown as below.

S. No.	Time (min)	Distance (km)
1.	0	0
2.	1	1
3.	2	2
4.	3	3
5.	4	4
6.	5	5

We can make the graph by following steps given below

(i) Firstly, draw two perpendicular lines to represent the two axes and mark them as OX and OY.

(ii) In this case, we show the time along the X-axis and the distance along the Y-axis.

(iii) Choose a scale to represent the distance and another to represent the time on graph like
For time 1 min = 1 cm, **For distance** 1 km = 1 cm

(iv) Now, mark values for the time and the distance on the respective axes according to the scale, we have chosen.

(v) We have to mark the points on the graph paper to represent each set of values for distance and time as shown in above table.

(vi) At last, join all the points on the graph as shown in figure.

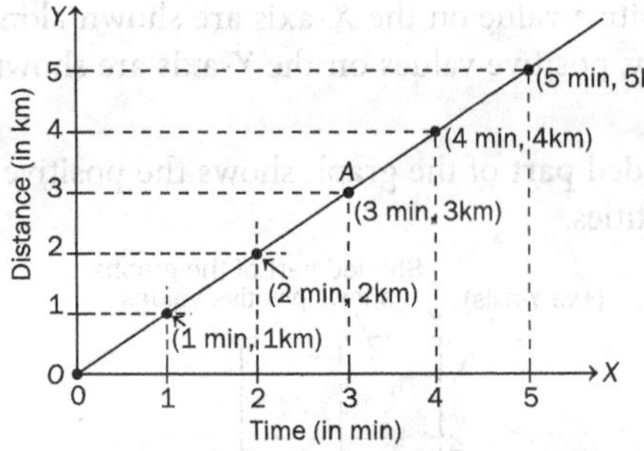

Graphical representation of motion of a car

If the object is moving with a constant speed (uniform speed), **the distance-time graph is a straight line or linear.** On the other hand, **if the speed of the object keeps changing with time (non-uniform speed), the graph can be of any other shape or non-linear.**

Things Must Keep in Mind while choosing the Scale

Suppose, the total distance covered by a body is 80 km. If we choose a scale of 1 km = 1 cm, we shall have to draw an axis of length 80 cm. This is not possible on a sheet of paper. On the other hand, if we choose a scale of 10 km = 1cm, we shall have to draw an axis of length 8 cm, which is quite convenient to show on graph sheet.

Thus, while choosing the scale, we should keep certain points in mind.

(i) The difference between the highest and the lowest values of each quantity.

(ii) The intermediate values of each quantity, so that with the scale chosen it is convenient to mark the values on the graph.

(iii) To utilise the maximum part of the paper on which the graph is to be drawn.

Other Types of Graphs

Along with line-graph, there are some other types of graphs like **bar graph** and **pie chart.**

- A diagram which shows information as thin rectangles (known as bars) of different heights is known as **bar graph** as shown in Fig. (a).

  In this graph, the position and heights of the bars represent the values of the variable quantity about which information is being given.

- A kind of graph or diagram which shows the percentage composition of something in the form of slices of a circle (the whole circle representing 100 percent), is known as a **pie chart** as shown in Fig (b).

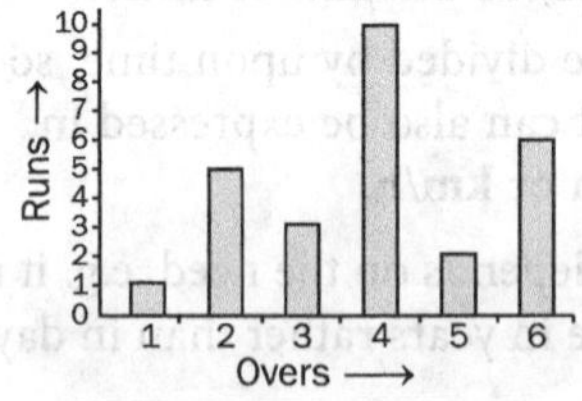

(a) A bar graph showing in the runs scored in six overs of a cricket match

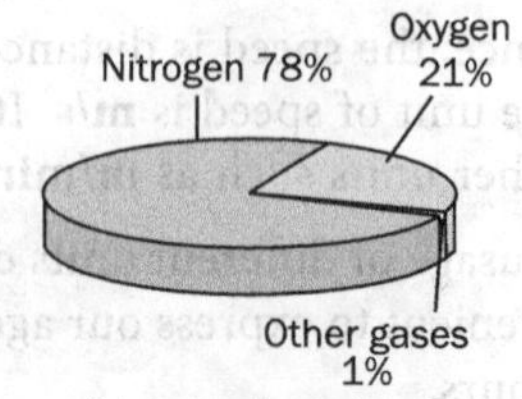

(b) A pie chart showing the composition of air

Try These 9.3

1. **Which axis is represented by horizontal line in a graph?**
2. **What is the shape of a line graph, when an object is moving with uniform speed?**
3. **Which graph shows the data in a circular form?**

Science Glossary

Speed Total distance covered by an object divided by total time taken is called speed.

Uniform motion When an object moves with constant speed along a straight line, then its motion is called uniform motion.

Non-uniform motion When an object changes its speed during its motion, then its motion is called non-uniform motion.

Simple pendulum It contains a mass hung with a thread to a rigid support. The mass can move freely to and fro.

Oscillation To and fro motion of pendulum is known as oscillation.

Time period The time taken by pendulum to complete one oscillation is called time period.

Speedometer An instrument which is used to measure the speed is called speedometer.

Odometer An instrument which is used to measure the total distance covered by a vehicle is called odometer.

Let's Investigate

ACTIVITY 1 (Page 92, 93)

Aim To observe slow and fast moving vehicles according to change in their position.

Material required Two pictures of vehicles moving on a road clicked in small time interval.

Procedure

1. Look at both the pictures very carefully.
2. Observe the position of every vehicle with respect to other vehicles.
3. Identify the slowest and fastest moving vehicle.

Vehicles moving on a road at sometime | Position of vehicles after 1s

Conclusion The car marked with circle is moving fastest and the car mark with '✓' is moving slowest.

Viva Questions

1. Can you see an object moving faster than light?
2. Out of minute hand and hour hand of a clock, which one moves faster ?

ACTIVITY 2 (Page 95, 96)

Aim To determine the time period of a simple pendulum.

Material required A string of length slightly more than 1 m, a weight like stone or 5 rupee coin and a stopwatch or wrist watch.

Procedure

1. Make a pendulum by hanging a weight like a stone or 5 rupee coin.
2. Attach the other side of the string with a rigid support such that the length of string is approximately 1m.
3. Switch OFF any fan nearby and let the pendulum come to rest at its mean position.
4. Mark the mean position on the floor.
5. Now, gently hold the pendulum and move it slightly to one side, then release it.
6. Note the time on the watch when the bob is at its mean position. Instead of the mean position, you may note time when the bob is at one of its extreme positions.
7. Measure the time of 20 oscillations and calculate the time period of pendulum.

   Time period of pendulum

   $$= \frac{\text{Total time of 20 oscillations}}{20}$$

8. Now, repeat the same procedure 3 times and record time period in the following table.

Time period of a simple pendulum

S. No.	Time taken for 20 oscillations (s)	Time period (s)
1.	45	2.25
2.	40	2
3.	38	1.9

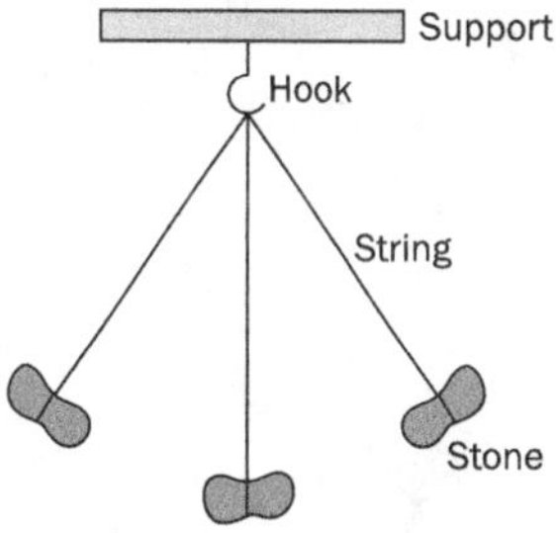

Simple pendulum

Conclusion Time period of simple pendulum in this case is approximately 2s.

Viva Questions

1. If you increase the length of the pendulum, then what will happen to the time period?
2. On changing the mass of the pendulum, how will it affect the time period?

ACTIVITY 3 (Page 97-99)

Aim To calculate the speed of a ball.

Material Required A ball, chalk powder and a stopwatch.

Procedure

1. Make four groups, each group having 2 children.
2. Draw a straight line on the ground with chalk powder and ask the other friend to stand 1 to 2 m away from it.

Measuring the speed of a ball

2. Draw a straight line on the ground with chalk powder and ask the other friend to stand 1 to 2 m away from it.

3. Now, ask your friend to roll a ball along the ground in a direction perpendicular to the line.
4. Note the time at the moment ball crosses the line and also when it comes to rest.
5. Measure the distance between the point where the ball comes to rest and the line drawn.
6. Let different groups repeat the activity and record time of all groups and calculate the speed in each case as shown in table.

Distance moved and time taken by a moving ball

Name of the group	Distance moved by the ball (m)	Time taken (s)	Speed = Distance / Time taken (m/s)
Red	4.3	10	0.43
Blue	6.8	12	0.57
White	3.4	6	0.57
Green	8.2	14	0.59

Conclusion Speed of ball is different for different groups.

Viva Questions

1. What is the formula for calculating speed?
2. For which group, speed of the ball is the highest?

Mind Map

Speed

Speed is defined as the distance covered by an object in unit time.

$$\text{Speed} = \frac{\text{Distance}}{\text{Time}}, \text{ unit} = \text{km/h or m/s}$$

$$\text{Average speed} = \frac{\text{Total distance travelled}}{\text{Total time taken}}$$

- **Measuring Device**

→ Device used to measure the speed of vehicle is **speedometer.**

→ Device used to measure the distance covered by vehicle is **odometer.**

Types of Motion on the Basis of Speed

Uniform Motion

- When an object moves with constant speed along a straight line, then its motion is called uniform motion. e.g. Motion of a rocket.

Non-uniform Motion

- When an object changes its speed during its motion, then its motion is called non-uniform motion. e.g Motion of car in traffic jam.

Slow and Fast Motion

Motion of an object with respect to another object can be slow or fast.

- **Slow motion** An object which takes longer time with respect to another object to cover a certain distance is said to be slow.
- **Fast motion** An object which takes shorter time with respect to another object to cover the same distance is said to be fast.

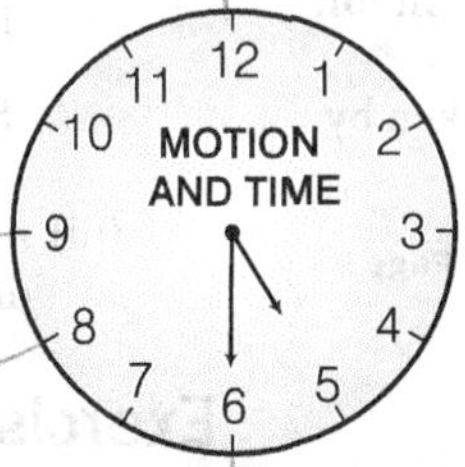

Motion

When an object change its position with time, it said to be in motion.

Types of Motion

→ **Rectilinear motion** Motion possessed by an object moving along a straight line path. e.g. Motion of bullet.

Motion of bullet

→ **Circular motion** Motion possessed by a body when it moves along a circular path. e.g. Motion of fan.

Motion of fan

→ **Periodic motion** Motion which repeates itself after regular intervals of time. e.g. Motion of pendulum.

Motion of pendulum

Time

A duration or moment in which things occurs is known as time. The unit of time is second.

- **Measurement of time**

→ **Day** Time between one sunrise to the next sunrise.

→ **Month** Time from one full moon to next full moon.

→ **Year** Time taken by the earth to complete one revolution around sun.

→ **Pendulum** Device used to measure time

→ **Sundials** Measure time by the position of the shadow cast by sun.

→ **Sand clocks** Measure time by the flow of sand from one glass bulb to another

→ **Water clock** Measure time by the rate at which water drips from one vessel to another.

Graphs

- Diagrammatical representation of any data

Types of Graph

Line Graph

→ Plot between distance and time

→ Horizontal line *X*-axis

→ Vertical line *Y*-axis

→ Graph will be linear, if motion is uniform.

→ Graph will be non-linear, if motion is non-uniform.

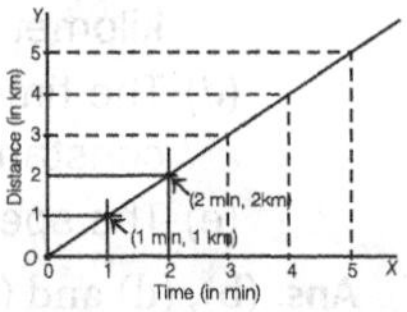

Bar Graph

→ Diagram which shows information as thin rectangles of different heights

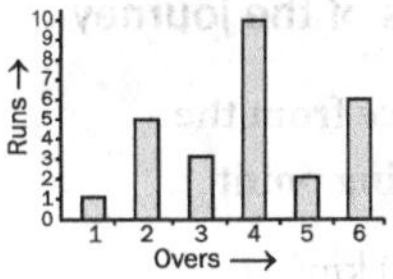

Pie Charts

→ Diagram which shows the percentage composition of something in the form of slices of circle

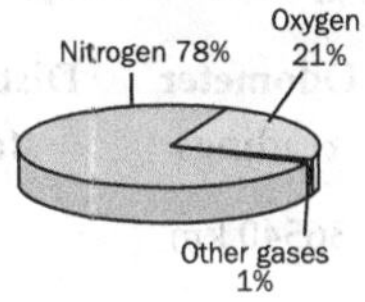

NCERT FOLDER

Complete Explanations of all NCERT's Questions

Intext Questions

Q.1 How will you decide which object is moving fast and which one is moving slow? Page 92

Ans. If an object covers more distance in equal intervals of time with respect to other, then we can say that object is moving faster with respect to the other object.

Q.2 If you did not have a clock, how would you decide what time of the day is? Page 94

Ans. We can decide time of the day without clock by seeing shadow formed by the sun, e.g. at noon, shadow formed by the sun is shorter than at evening.

Q.3 State how do we measure time interval of a month and a year? Page 94

Ans. Time interval of a month is measured by one new moon to the next.
Time interval of a year is measured as the time taken by the earth to complete one revolution of the sun.

Q.4 Determine the number of seconds in a day. Page 96

Ans. In a day, we have 24 h.
We know that 1 h = 3600 s
So, 24 h = $3600 \times 24 = 86400$s

Q.5 Estimate that how many hours are there in a year?

Ans. In a year, we have 365 days and 1 day = 24 h Page 96
So, for 365 days, we have 24×365 h = 8760 h

Q.6 Paheli wondered how time was measured when pendulum clocks were not available? Page 97

Ans. Before the discovery of pendulum clocks, sundials, water clocks and sand clocks were used.

Q.7 While going for a school picnic, Paheli decided to note the reading on the odometer of the bus after every 30 min till the end of the journey. Later on she recorded her readings in table. Page 100

Odometer reading at different times of the journey

Time (AM)	Odometer readings	Distance from the starting point
8:00	36540 km	0 km
8:30	36560 km	20 km
9:00	36580 km	40 km
9:30	36600 km	60 km
10:00	36620 km	80 km

(i) Can you tell how far was the picnic spot from the school?
(ii) Can you calculate the speed of the bus?
(iii) Looking at the table, Boojho asked Paheli whether she can tell how far they would have travelled till 9:45 AM.

Ans. (i) 80 km
(ii) Total distance = 80 km
Total time = 2 h

$$\text{Speed} = \frac{\text{Total distance}}{\text{Total time}} = \frac{80}{2} = 40 \text{ km/h}$$

(iii) As they are moving with constant velocity, so the distance travelled till 9:45 AM is 70 km.

Exercise

Q.1 Classify the following as motion along a straight line, circular or oscillatory motion.
(a) Motion of your hands while running.
(b) Motion of a horse pulling a cart on a straight road.
(c) Motion of a child in a merry-go-round.
(d) Motion of a child on a see-saw.
(e) Motion of the hammer of an electric bell.
(f) Motion of a train on a straight bridge.

Ans. (a) Oscillatory (b) Straight line
(c) Circular (d) Oscillatory
(e) Oscillatory (f) Straight line

Q.2 Which of the following are not correct?
(a) The basic unit of time is second.
(b) Every object moves with a constant speed.
(c) Distances between two cities are measured in kilometres.
(d) The time period of a given pendulum is not constant.
(e) The speed of a train is expressed in m/h.

Ans. (b), (d) and (e) are not correct.

Q.3 A simple pendulum takes 32s to complete 20 oscillations. What is the time period of the pendulum?

Ans. Time period of simple pendulum is given by

$$\frac{\text{Time taken}}{\text{Number of oscillations}} = \frac{32}{20} \text{s} = 1.6 \text{ s}$$

(i.e. the time to complete one cycle)

Q.4 The distance between two stations is 240 km. A train takes 4 h to cover this distance. Calculate the speed of the train.

Ans. As we know that, the speed of a body is given by

$$\text{Speed} = \frac{\text{Distance travelled}}{\text{Time taken}}$$

$$= \frac{240}{4} = 60 \text{ km/h}$$

Q.5 The odometer of a car reads 57321 km when the clock shows the time 08:30 AM. What is the distance moved by the car, if at 08:50 AM, the odometer reading has changed to 57336 km? Calculate the speed of the car in km/min during this time. Express the speed in km/h also.

Ans. As we know that,

$$\text{Speed} = \frac{\text{Distance covered}}{\text{Time taken}}$$

Given, distance covered

$= 57336 - 57321 = 15$ km

Time taken $= 8:50$ AM $- 8:30$ AM $= 20$ min

So, speed $= \frac{15}{20} = \frac{3}{4}$ km/min

Now, speed in km/h is given by $\frac{3}{4} \times 60$

$= 45$ km/h $\quad \left[1 \text{min} = \frac{1}{60} \text{h}\right]$

Q.6 Salma takes 15 min from her house to reach school on a bicycle. If the bicycle has a speed of 2 m/s, calculate the distance between her house and the school.

Ans. As, we know that

Distance covered by the body = Speed × Time

Given, speed = 2 m/s

Time = 15 min = 15 × 60 = 900 s

So, distance = 900 × 2 = 1800 m = 1.8 km

Q.7 Show the shape of the distance-time graph for the motion in the following cases **NCERT Exemplar**

(a) A car moving with a constant speed.

(b) A car parked on a road side.

Ans.

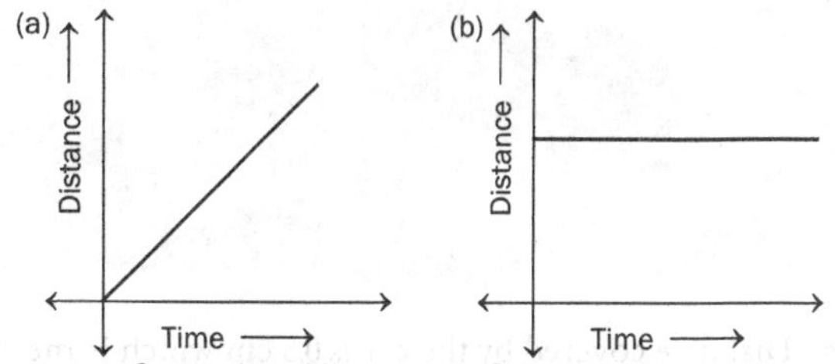

Car moving with a constant speed

Car parked on a road side

Q.8 Which of the following relations is correct?

(a) Speed = Distance × Time

(b) $\text{Speed} = \frac{\text{Distance}}{\text{Time}}$

(c) $\text{Speed} = \frac{\text{Time}}{\text{Distance}}$

(d) $\text{Speed} = \frac{1}{\text{Distance} \times \text{Time}}$

Ans. Relation (b) is correct as speed is given by total distance covered by total time taken.

Q.9 The basic unit of speed is

(a) km/min
(b) m/min
(c) km/h
(d) m/s

Ans. The basic unit of speed is metre/second or m/s, so option (d) is correct.

Q.10 A car moves with a speed of 40 km/h for 15 min and then with a speed of 60 km/h for the next 15 min. The total distance covered by the car is

(a) 100 km
(b) 25 km
(c) 15 km
(d) 10 km

Ans. Given, speed for first 15 min = 40 km/h

Speed for next 15 min = 60 km/h

As, we know that distance = Speed × Time

So, for first 15 min, distance travelled

$= 40 \times \frac{15}{60} = 10$ km $\quad \left(1 \text{ min} = \frac{1}{60} \text{ h}\right)$

For second 15 min, distance travelled

$= 60 \times \frac{15}{60} = 15$ km $\quad \left(1 \text{ min} = \frac{1}{60} \text{ h}\right)$

So, total distance = 15 + 10 = 25 km

Q.11 Suppose, the two photographs, shown in two figures had been taken at an interval of 10 s. If a distance of 100 m is shown by 1 cm in these photographs, then calculate the speed of the circled car.

Ans. Distance covered by the car is 0.5 cm which is measured by scale in this photograph.

Given, 1 cm = 100 m, then 0.5 cm = 50 m

So, distance travelled by the car = 50 m

Time interval = 10 s

$$\text{Speed} = \frac{\text{Distance}}{\text{Time}} = \frac{50}{10} = 5 \text{ m/s}$$

Q.12 Figure shows the distance-time graph for the motion of two vehicles *A* and *B*. Which one of them is moving faster?

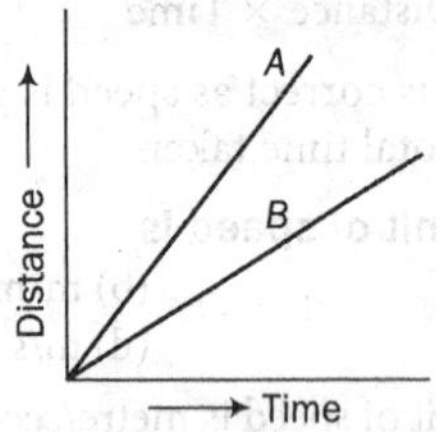

Ans. As, from the given graph, slope of *A* is greater than *B*, i.e. distance covered by *A* in same time with respect to *B* is greater. So, *A* is moving with faster speed than *B*.

Q.13 Which of the following distance-time graphs shows a truck moving with speed which is not constant?

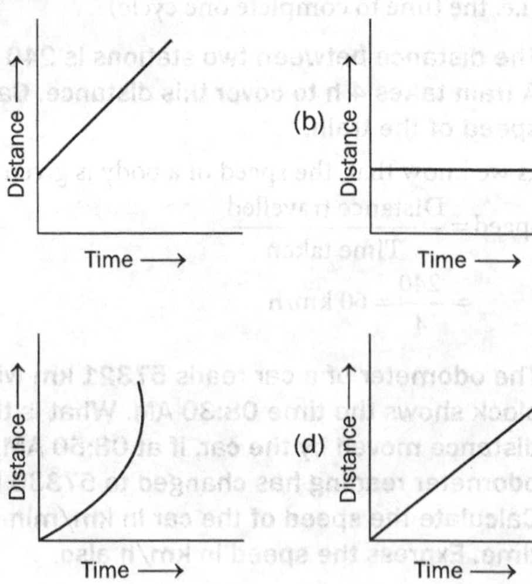

Ans. As, we know that if the distance-time graph is a straight line, the motion is said to be uniform and if the graph between distance-time graph is not straight line, then the motion is said to be non-uniform. So, option (c) is correct.

REVIEW EXERCISE

Including Competency Based Questions

Part I

Multiple Choice Questions

1. Which of these actions is an example of circular motion? **Competency Based Que.**

(a) A child riding a see-saw
(b) A child pumping air in a tyre
(c) A player bowling a cricket ball
(d) A player serving a tennis ball with racket

2. The maximum speed of a car is 180 km/h. What is the maximum speed? **Competency Based Que.**

(a) 20 m/s (b) 30 m/s
(c) 50 m/s (d) 60 m/s

3. What is the relation between distance and speed?

(a) Distance = Speed × Time
(b) Distance = Speed / Time
(c) Distance = Time/Speed
(d) None of the above

4. How will you convert the speed given in km/h to m/s?

(a) By multiplying with 5/16
(b) By multiplying with 6/5
(c) By multiplying with 18/5
(d) By multiplying with 5/18

5. If we denote speed by *S*, distance by *D* and time by *T*, then the relationship between these quantities is

(a) $S = D \times T$ (b) $T = \frac{S}{D}$
(c) $S = \frac{1}{T} \times D$ (d) $S = \frac{T}{D}$

6. The correct symbol to represent the speed of an object is **NCERT Exemplar**

(a) 5 m/s (b) 5 mp
(c) 5 m/s^{-1} (d) 5 s/m

7. Boojho walks to his school which is at a distance of 3 km from his home in 30 min. On reaching, he finds that the school is closed and comes back by a bicycle with his friend and reaches home in 20 min. His average speed in km/h is **NCERT Exemplar**

(a) 8.3 (b) 7.2
(c) 5 (d) 3.6

8. A bus travels 54 km in 90 min. The speed of the bus is

(a) 0.6 m/s (b) 10 m/s (c) 5.4 m/s (d) 3.6 m/s

9. Two clocks *A* and *B* are shown in figure. Clock *A* has an hour and a minute hand whereas clock *B* has an hour hand, minute hand as well as a second hand. Which of the following statement is correct for these clocks? **Competency Based Que.**

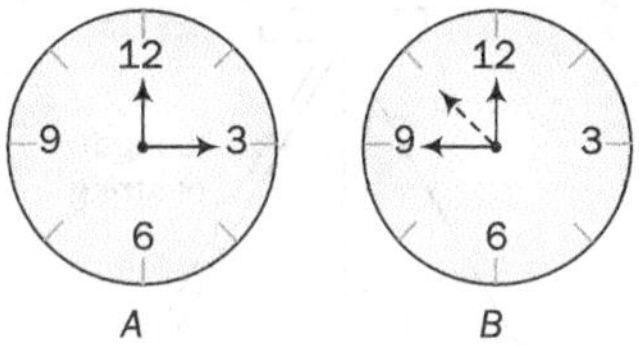

(a) A time interval of 30s can be measured by clock *A*
(b) A time interval of 30s cannot be measured by clock *B*
(c) Time interval of 5 min can be measured by both *A* and *B*
(d) Time interval of 4 min 10s can be measured by clock *A*

10. Which of the following cannot be used for the measurement of time?

(a) A leaking tap
(b) Simple pendulum
(c) Shadow of an object during the day
(d) Blinking of eyes

11. Observe the given figure.

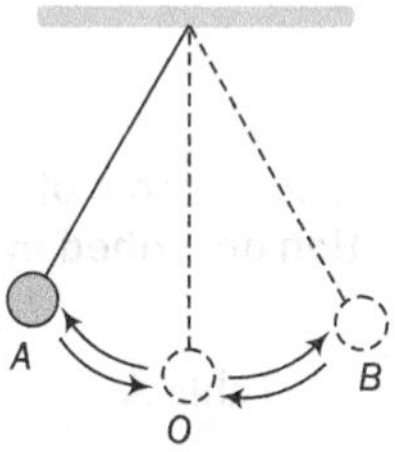

The time period of a simple pendulum is the time taken by it to travel from

(a) *A* to *B* and back to *A*
(b) *O* to *A*, *A* to *B* and *B* to *A*
(c) *B* to *A*, *A* to *B* and *B* to *O*
(d) *A* to *B*

12. Figure shows an oscillating pendulum

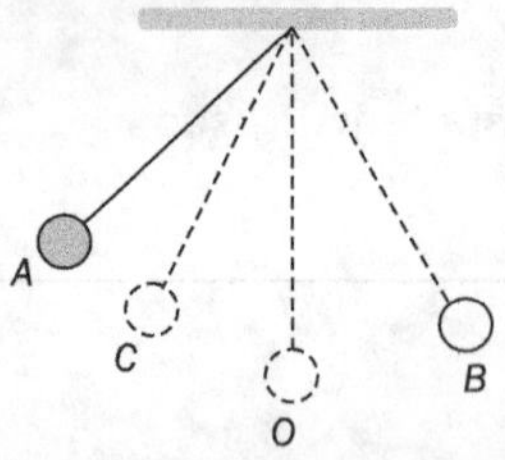

Time taken by the bob to move from *A* to *C* is t_1 and from *C* to *O* is t_2. The time period of this simple pendulum is

(a) $(t_1 + t_2)$ (b) $2(t_1 + t_2)$
(c) $3(t_1 + t_2)$ (d) $4(t_1 + t_2)$

13. The diagram shows a pendulum in periodic motion. The time period of a pendulum is the time taken by the bob to make one complete oscillation. **Competency Based Que.**

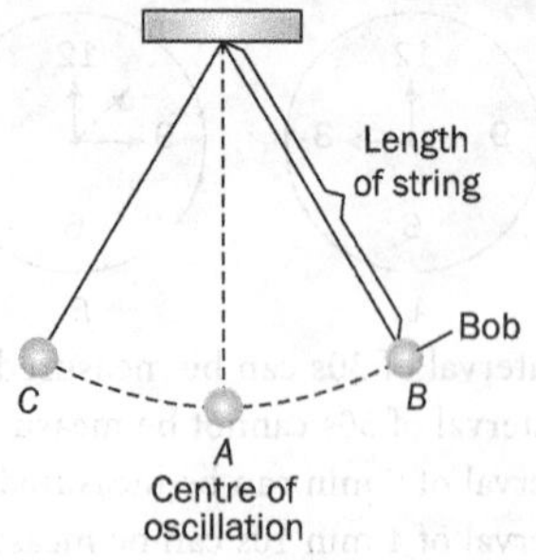

What would be the movement of the bob for one complete oscillation of the pendulum ?

(a) *C* to *B* (b) *C* to *A*
(c) *B* to *C* to *A* (d) *B* to *C* to *B*

14. Which one records the distance travelled by a vehicle?

(a) Speedometer
(b) Manometer
(c) Motometer
(d) Odometer

15. Two students were asked to plot a distance-time graph for the motion described by Table *A* and Table *B*. **NCERT Exemplar**

Table A

Distance moved (m)	0	10	20	30	40	50
Time (min)	0	2	4	6	8	10

Table B

Distance moved (m)	0	5	10	15	20	25
Time (min)	0	1	2	3	4	5

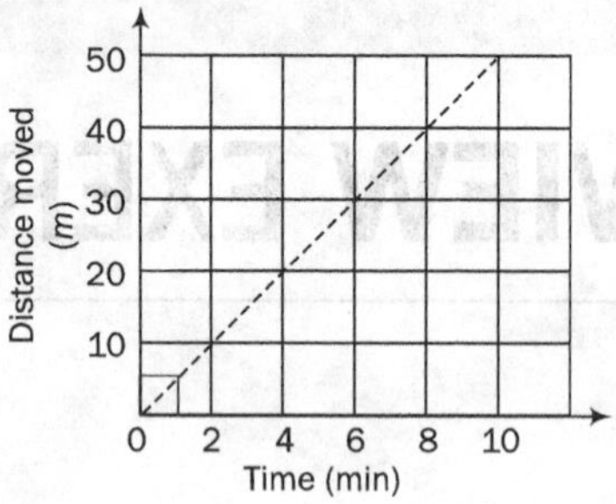

The graph given in figure is true for

(a) Both *A* and *B* (b) Only *A*
(c) Only *B* (d) Neither *A* nor *B*

16. On which axis is dependent variable represented?

(a) *X*-axis
(b) *Y*-axis
(c) On any axis
(d) Depends on the data

17. The distance-time graph for the motion of an object moving with a constant speed is

(a) a curved line leaving towards *X*-axis
(b) a curved line inclined towards *Y*-axis
(c) a straight line inclined at some angles towards *X*-axis
(d) None of the above

18. The distance-time graph for a vehicle standing on a road side will be

(a) straight line inclined by some angle to *X*-axis
(b) straight line parallel to *X*-axis
(c) straight line parallel to *Y*-axis
(d) None of the above

19. A student wants to measure the speed of a ball rolling down a ramp. He found a few instruments which are listed in the lists.

(i) Hourglass
(ii) Thermometer
(iii) Measuring tape
(iv) Stopwatch
(v) Balance scale

Which of these are required to measure the speed of the ball?

(a) Hourglass and thermometer
(b) Balance scale and stopwatch
(c) Measuring tape and stopwatch
(d) Measuring tape and thermometer

20. The table lists a few motions which relate to measuring time.

(i) Motion of pendulum.
(ii) Sand falling in an hourglass.
(iii) Change in the position of shadow.

Which of these motions can be considered as a periodic motion?

(a) Only (i) (b) Only (ii)
(c) Both (i) and (ii) (d) Both (ii) and (iii)

Answers

1. (c)	2. (c)	3. (a)	4. (d)
5. (c)	6. (a)	7. (b)	8. (b)
9. (c)	10. (d)	11. (a)	12. (d)
13. (d)	14. (d)	15. (a)	16. (b)
17. (c)	18. (b)	19. (c)	20. (c)

Fill in the Blanks

1. The distance covered by an object in a .... is called its speed.
2. The symbols of all units are written in ....
3. A .... is one billionth of a second.
4. Time period of a pendulum depends on its ....
5. In a simple pendulum, the metallic ball suspended by thread is called its ....
6. Time between one sunrise and the next sunrise was called a ....
7. Motion of objects can be represented in the pictorial form by their .... graph.
8. The distance-time graph for the motion of an object moving with a constant speed is a ....

Answers

1. unit time	2. singular
3. nanosecond	4. length
5. bob	6. day
7. distance-time	8. straight line

True/False

1. The motion of a spinning top is rotational motion.
2. Faster vehicle has a higher speed.
3. The basic unit of speed is km/h.
4. All the clocks make use of some periodic motion.
5. The time period of simple pendulum is not constant.
6. The smallest time interval that can be measured with commonly available clocks and watches is one second.
7. Periodic events are used for the measurement of time.

Answers

1. True	2. True	3. False	4. True
5. True	6. True	7. True	

Match the Columns

1. Match the Column I with Column II.

Column I	Column II
(a) Years	(i) Rotation period of the earth on its axis
(b) Hour	(ii) Time to complete 100 m race
(c) Days	(iii) Gestation period in humans
(d) Second	(iv) Age of a person
(e) Month	(v) Train reaches from one city to other

2. Match the Column I with Column II.

(a) Speed	(i) Speed × Time
(b) Wheel of cycle	(ii) Nanosecond
(c) Time	(iii) km/h
(d) Distance	(iv) Circular motion

Answers

1. (a)–(iv), (b)–(v), (c)–(i), (d)–(ii), (e)–(iii)
2. (a)–(iii), (b)–(iv), (c)–(ii), (d)–(i)

Assertion-Reason Questions

The following questions consist of two statements Assertion (A) and Reason (R). Answer these questions by selecting the appropriate option given below

(a) Both A and R are true and R is the correct explanation of A.
(b) Both A and R are true but R is not the correct explanation of A.
(c) A is true but R is false.
(d) A is false but R is true.

1. **Assertion** (A) Motion of the moon around the earth is a circular motion.
   Reason (R) When a body moves along a circular path, then it is said to be circular motion.
2. **Assertion** (A) Speed of a vehicle in traffic jam is uniform.
   Reason (R) When an object moves with constant speed, then its speed is uniform.
3. **Assertion** (A) A simple pendulum is an example of non-periodic motion.
   Reason (R) A simple pendulum does to and fro motion which is known as oscillatory motion.
4. **Assertion** (A) Speedometer is a device used to measure the speed of vehicle.
   Reason (R) Speed is the total time taken divided by total distance covered by an object.

Answers

1. (a) When the distance of an object remains constant from a fixed point during its motion, then it is said to be circular motion, e.g. motion of moon around earth.
2. (d) Speed of a vehicle in traffic jam is non-uniform because it does not move with constant speed.
3. (d) A simple pendulum is an example of periodic motion.
4. (c) Speed is the total distance covered divided by total time taken by an object and speed is measured by speedometer.

Case Based Question

1. Sunil was a business man. He lived in Pune. One day he had an official meeting in Bombay. The cab driver asked Sunil to come to the nearest pick-up point at 8:00 AM. When Sunil seated in the cab, he noticed that the odometer of a car read 14000 km. He reached to Bombay is 5 h. At the end of the trip, he checked that the odometer read 14500 km.

(i) Odometer is used to measure the

(a) total distance (b) total time
(c) total speed (d) Both (a) and (b)

(ii) A vehicle moves on a busy road is an example of

(a) periodic motion (b) circulatory motion
(c) uniform motion (d) non-uniform motion

(iii) What was the speed of cab in this journey?

(a) 100 km/h (b) 150 km/h
(c) 140 km/h (d) 50 km/h

Answer

1. (i) (a) (ii) (d)

(iii) (a) Speed $= \dfrac{\text{Total distance}}{\text{Total time}}$

$= \dfrac{500}{5} = 100 \text{ km/h}$

Part II

Very Short Answer Type Questions

1. If Boojho covers a certain distance in one hour and Paheli covers the same distance in two hours, who travels with a higher speed? NCERT Exemplar

Ans. Boojho travels with a higher speed as he has covered same distance in lesser time with respect to Paheli.

2. Paheli and Boojho have to cover different distances to reach their school but they take the same time to reach the school. What can you say about their speed?

Ans. They do not have equal speed because they cover unequal distances in equal intervals of time.

One of them has higher speed whom has to cover larger distances with respect to other.

3. Give the basic unit of speed.

Ans. Metre/second is the basic unit of speed.

4. A spaceship travels 36000 km in one hour. Express its speed in km/s. NCERT Exemplar

Ans. As, speed $= \dfrac{\text{distance}}{\text{time}} = \dfrac{36000}{1 \times 3600}$ [$\because$ 1 h = 3600 s]

$= 10$ km/s

5. Mention which is the most common thing in almost all the clocks.

Ans. The most common thing in almost all the clocks is that all of them show periodic motion.

6. Out of the two given clocks, a pendulum clock or a quartz clock. Mention which of the clock between the given ones requires an electric cell for its working?

Ans. A quartz clock requires an electric cell for its working.

7. Name the most ancient unit of time ?

Ans. Solar day is the most ancient unit of time.

8. State the factors on which the time period of a simple pendulum depends.

Ans. The factors on which the time period of a simple pendulum depends are

(i) Length of the pendulum
(ii) Acceleration due to gravity

9. State the way through which we can prepare a pendulum by our own.

Ans. By suspending a metal ball with the help of a cotton thread and the other end of the thread can be tied to some fixed support, In this way, we can prepare a pendulum by our own.

10. A simple pendulum is oscillating between two points *A* and *B* as shown in figure. Is the motion of the bob uniform or non-uniform?

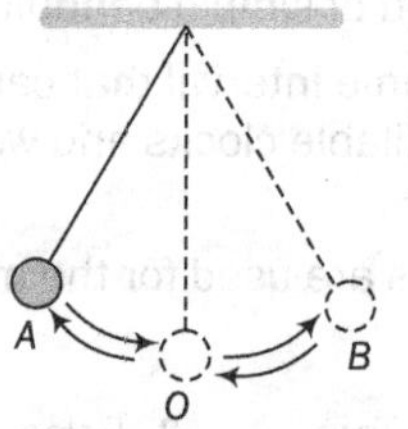

Competency Based Que.

Ans. The motion of bob is uniform as it covers equal distance in equal intervals of time.

11. State the characteristic of distance-time graph for the motion of an object moving with a constant speed.

Ans. The distance-time graph for the motion of an object moving with a constant speed is a straight line inclined on X-axis at some angles.

Short Answer Type Questions

1. Differentiate between uniform and non-uniform motion.

Ans. When a body travels equal distance in an equal interval of time, then the body is said to be in uniform motion.

When a body travels unequal distance in an equal interval of time, then the body is said to be in non-uniform motion.

2. Last Sunday, Priyanka decided to go outside with her family for the dinner in some particular restaurant. Then, she thought to go through her own car. So, while moving she increased the speed of the car from 36 km/h to 54 km/h.

All of sudden, a rickshaw came in front of her car but due to applying of brakes at the right time, both of them got safe from meeting with an accident.

Competency Based Que.

(i) Calculate the increase in the speed of the car in the terms of m/s.

(ii) Mention a positive action performed by Priyanka here.

Ans. (i) Initial speed $= 36 \text{ km/h} = \frac{5}{18} \times 36 = 10 \text{ m/s}$

Final speed $= 54 \text{ km/h} = \frac{5}{18} \times 54$

$= 15 \text{ m/s}$

$\therefore$ Increase in speed = Final speed − Initial speed

$= (15 - 10) \text{ m/s}$

$= 5 \text{ m/s}$

(ii) Priyanka applied the brakes at the right time while driving the car and prevented her family and the person on rickshaw from meeting with an accident.

3. The average age of children of class VII is 12 years and 3 months. Express his age in second.

NCERT Exemplar

Ans. Given, the average age of children 12 years and 3 months

1 year = 365 days = 365 × 24 h [1 day = 24 h]

= 365 × 24 × 3600 s [1 h = 3600 s]

12 years = 31536000 s × 12 = 378432000 s

3 months = 30 × 3 days = 30 × 3 × 24 h

= 30 × 3 × 24 × 3600s

= 7776000s

So, total age in second = 378432000 + 7776000

= 386208000 s

4. One day, a five years old boy, Chintoo was playing with his toys in his room. After few minutes, he saw a wristwatch on his study table, so after seeing it, he got crazy and so much eager to play with that watch. Then, for 2 to 3 min, he was trying to analyse it that whether its a toy or something else, then suddenly, he was just about to throw it but at the same his mother entered into the room and took the watch back immediately from his hand.

(i) State the benefits of a wristwatch.

(ii) Briefly mention the values showed by Chintoo's mother here.

Ans. (i) The wristwatch can be handled very easily to check the time in comparison to the wall clock.

(ii) The values showed by Chintoo's mother here is the concern towards her four years old child and also the concern towards that wristwatch while considering the importance of money.

5. The following distance-time graph of three objects (D, E and F) are given (see figure given below). What can you say about the motion of the objects?

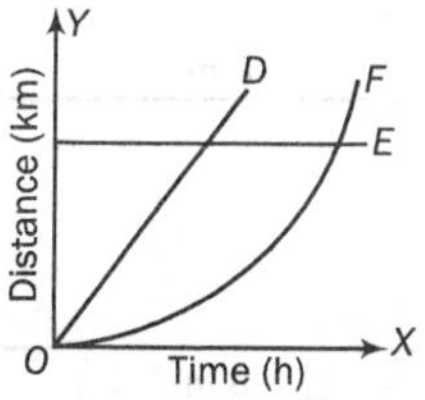

Ans. Since, the distance-time graph of an object D is a straight line therefore, its motion is uniform.

Also here, we can see that the distance-time graph of object E is parallel to X-axis (time-axis), therefore object E is at rest.

As, the distance-time graph of object F is a curved line, therefore the object C is moving with a non-uniform speed and its motion is non-uniform.

6. The following figure shows the distance-time graph for the motion of two objects D and E. Which one of them is moving slower?

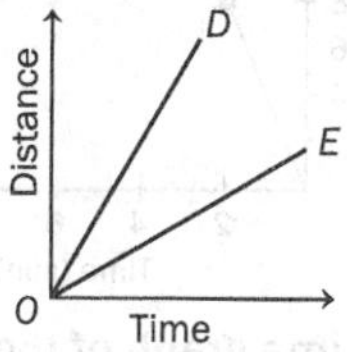

Ans. After studying the figure given above, E is moving slower as the slope of distance-time graph of E is less than that of graph D.

7. The following figure shows the distance-time graph for the motion of two vehicles (C and D). At what time and distance (from the starting point), they will cross each other?

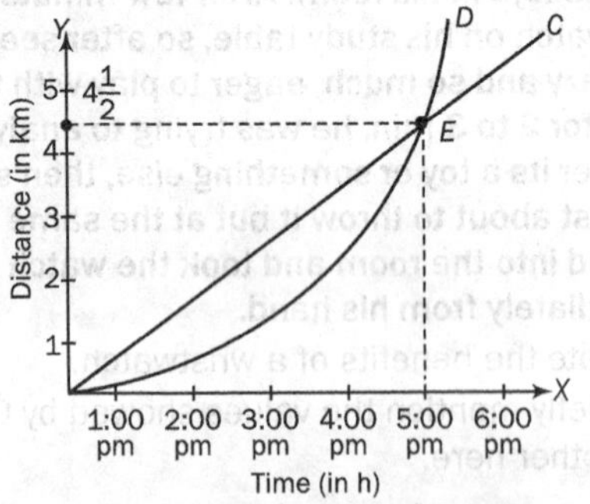

Ans. Firstly, draw perpendicular lines from point E on X-axis and Y-axis.

The two vehicles (C and D) will meet (or cross) each other at 5:00 PM after travelling a distance of $4\frac{1}{2}$ km.

8. Starting from A, Paheli moves along a rectangular path ABCD as shown in figure. She takes 2 min to travel each side. Plot a distance-time graph and explain whether the motion is uniform or non-uniform. NCERT Exemplar

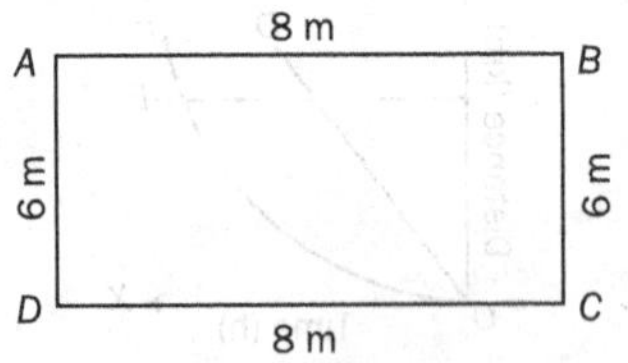

Ans. Since, the distance covered per unit time for the entire distance is not same so, the motion is a non-uniform motion.

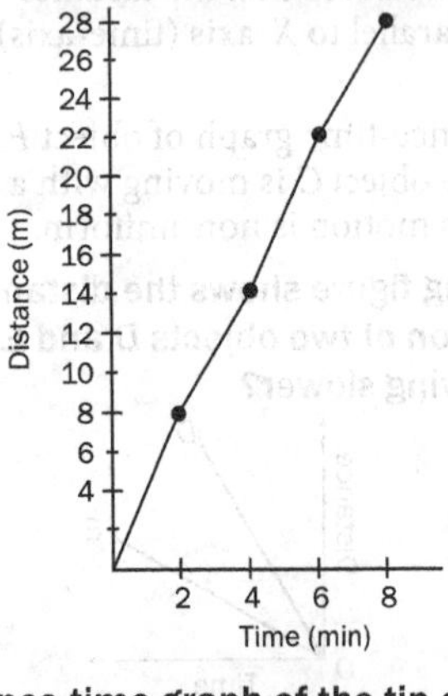

9. Plot a distance-time graph of the tip of the second hand of a clock by selecting 4 points on X-axis and Y-axis, respectively. The circumference of the circle traced by the second hand is 64 cm. NCERT Exemplar

Ans.

Time (s)	X	15	30	45	60
Distance (cm)	Y	16	32	48	64

As, equal distance is covered in equal intervals of time.

So, graph will be a straight line.

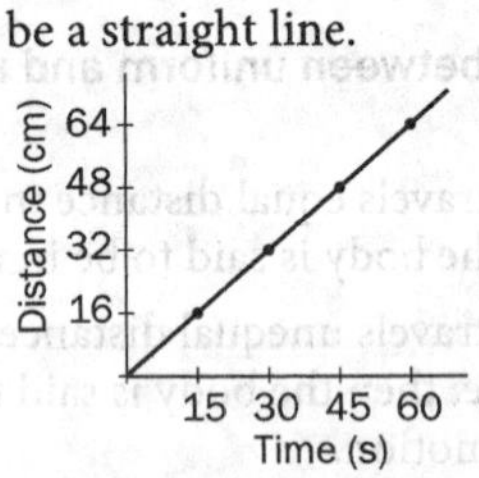

10. Complete the data of the table given below with the help of the distance-time graph given in figure.

Distance (m)	0	4	?	12	?	20
Time (s)	0	2	4	?	8	10

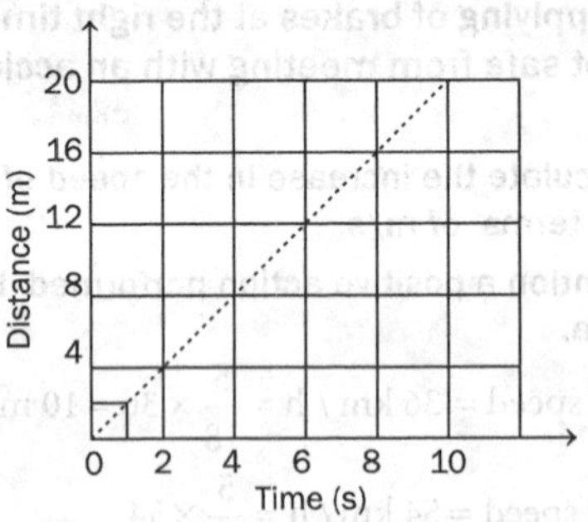

NCERT Exemplar

Ans. This distance-time graph shows that the body is moving with a constant speed. It means that, it covers equal distance in equal interval of time. So, with the help of distance-time graph, the data can be completed as

Distance (m)	0	4	8	12	16	20
Time (s)	0	2	4	6	8	10

11. Three students start running from the starting point at the same time. The picture shows the position of the students on the path after a minute.

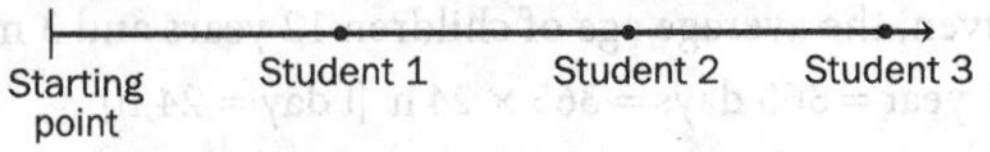

Which student ran the fastest ? Explain your answer.

Ans. Student 3 ran the fastest as compared to other students because he covered maximum distance in same time.

Long Answer Type Questions

1. Distance between Bholu's and Golu's house is 9 km. Bholu has to attend Golu's birthday party at 7 o' clock. He started his journey from his home at 6 o' clock on his bicycle and covered a distance of 6 km in 40 min. At that point, he met Chintu and he spoke to him for 5 min and reached Golu's birthday party at 7 o' clock. With what speed, did he cover the second part of the journey? Calculate his average speed for the entire journey. **Competency Based Que.**

Ans. From the question, Bholu covers 3 km distance in 15 min.

So, speed of Bholu $= \frac{3}{15} \times 60 \quad \left(1 \text{ min} = \frac{1}{60} \text{ h}\right)$

$= 12$ km/h

Now, average speed is given by

$= \frac{\text{Total distance travelled}}{\text{Total time taken}}$

$= \frac{9}{1} = 9$ km/h

2. The given data regarding the motion of two different objects *C* and *D* is in a tabular form. Check them carefully and state whether the motion of the objects is uniform or non-uniform.

Time	Distance travelled by *C* (in m)	Distance travelled by *D* (in m)
9:30 AM	10	12
9:45 AM	20	19
10:00 AM	30	23
10:15 AM	40	35
10:30 AM	50	37
10:45 AM	60	41
11:00 AM	70	44

Ans. We can check the motion of the objects *C* and *D* by plotting the distance-time graph for the two objects.

Graph for object *C*

Scale On *X*-axis, 1 cm = 15 min and on *Y*-axis, 1 cm = 10 m

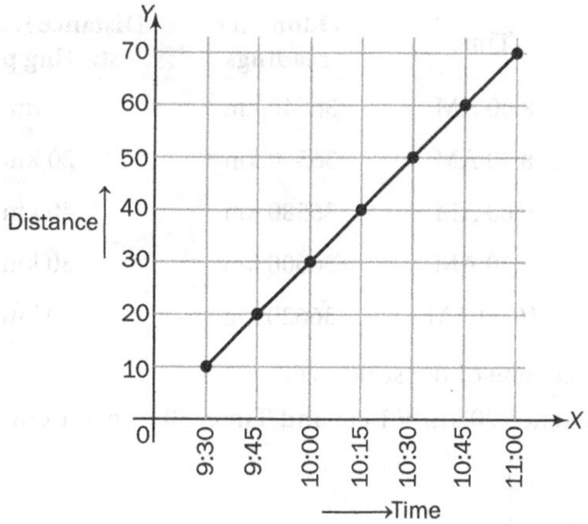

Since, the distance-time graph of the object *C* is a straight line. Therefore, its motion is uniform.

Graph of object *D*

Scale On *X*-axis, 1 cm = 15 min, On *Y*-axis 1 cm = 5 m

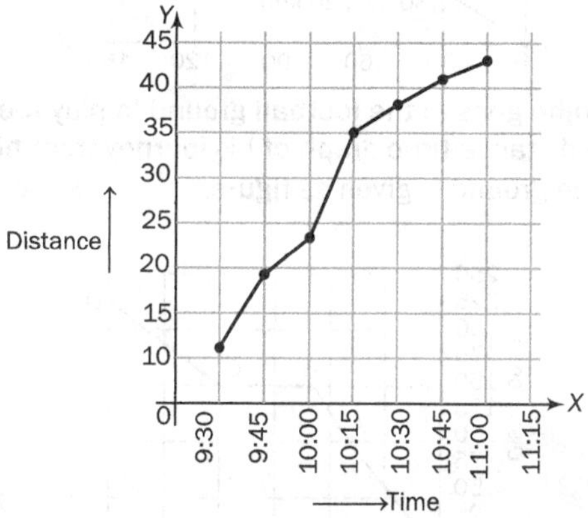

Since, the distance-time graph of the object *D* is not a straight line, therefore its motion is non-uniform.

3. Explain by giving example that how can we choose a suitable scale?

Ans. While choosing the most suitable scale for drawing a graph, we should keep the following points in mind

(i) The difference between the highest and lowest values of each quantity.

(ii) The intermediate values of each quantity, so that with the scale chosen, it is easy to mark the values on the graph.

(iii) To utilise the maximum part of the paper on which the graph is to be drawn, assume that we have a graph paper of size 25 cm × 25 cm and we have to accommodate following data

Time	Odometer readings	Distance from the starting point
8:00 AM	36540 km	0 km
8:30 AM	36560 km	20 km
9:00 AM	36580 km	40 km
9:30 AM	36600 km	60 km
10:00 AM	36620 km	80 km

Since, one of the scales will be

Distance 20 km = 1 cm and Time 30 min = 1 cm

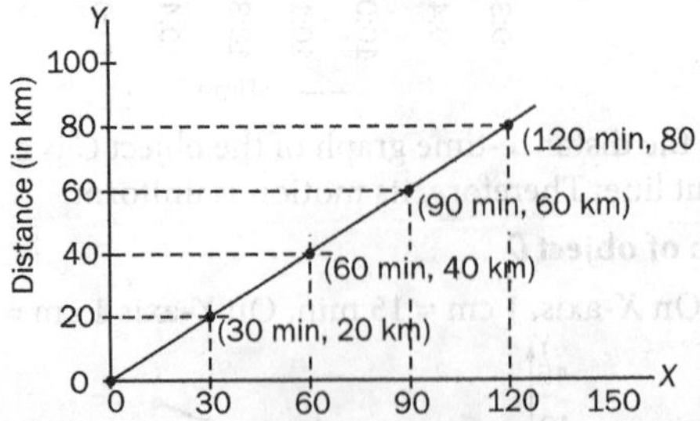

4. Boojho goes to the football ground to play football. The distance-time graph of his journey from his home to the ground is given as figure. **NCERT Exemplar**

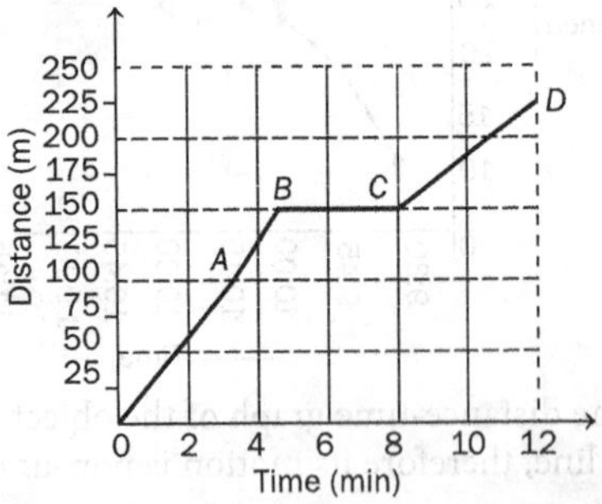

(i) What does the graph between points *B* and *C* indicate about the motion of Boojho?

(ii) Is the motion between 0 to 4 min uniform or non-uniform?

(iii) What is his speed between 8 to 12 min of his journey?

Ans. (i) Since, the graph between *B* and *C* is parallel to time-axis, so it indicates that Boojho is at rest.

(ii) Since, the graph is not straight line, so it is a non-uniform motion.

(iii) As, speed $= \frac{\text{distance}}{\text{time}} = \frac{225-150}{12-8}$

$= \frac{75}{4} = 18.75 \text{ m/min}$

5. Given below in a figure is the distance-time graph of the motion of an object.

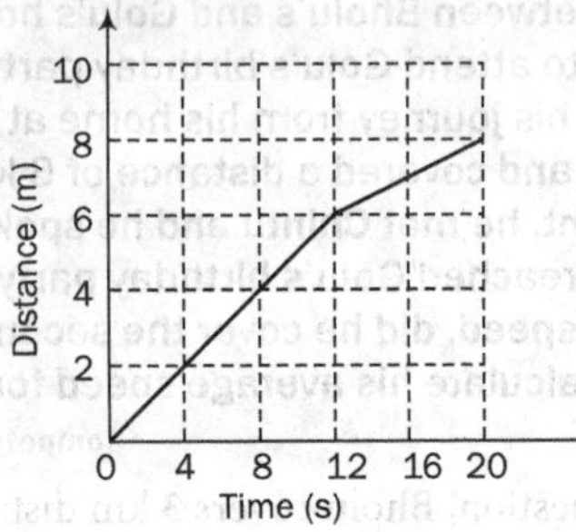

(i) What will be the position of the object at 20 s?

(ii) What will be the distance travelled by the object in 12 s?

(iii) What is the average speed of the object? **NCERT Exemplar**

Ans. (i) From the graph, it is clear that the position at 20 s is 8 m.

(ii) Distance travelled by the body object in 12 s is 6 m.

(iii) As, average speed $= \frac{\text{total distance}}{\text{total time}} = \frac{8}{20} = 0.4 \text{ m/s}$

Case Based Questions

1. The timetable of a train is shown below

Station	Arrival	Departure
New Delhi		06.45 AM
Meerut	08.03AM	08.05 AM
Muzaffarnagar	08.45AM	08.47 AM
Saharanpur	09.50 AM	09.55 AM
Roorkee	10.30 AM	

Competency Based Que., CBSE Diksha

(i) What is the total travel time of the train ?

(a) 3 h 30 min (b) 3 h 45 min

(c) 4 h 15 min (d) 4 h 45 min

(ii) The distance between Meerut and Muzaffarnagar is about 60 km. Calculate the average speed of the train (in km/h) while travelling between the two stations.

2. The table shows the distance travelled by a car in half an hour.

	0-10 min	10-20 min	20-30 min
Distance travelled by the car	6.2 km	5.8 km	6.0 km

Competency Based Que., CBSE Diksha

(i) Draw line in the distance-time graph to show how the car travelled.

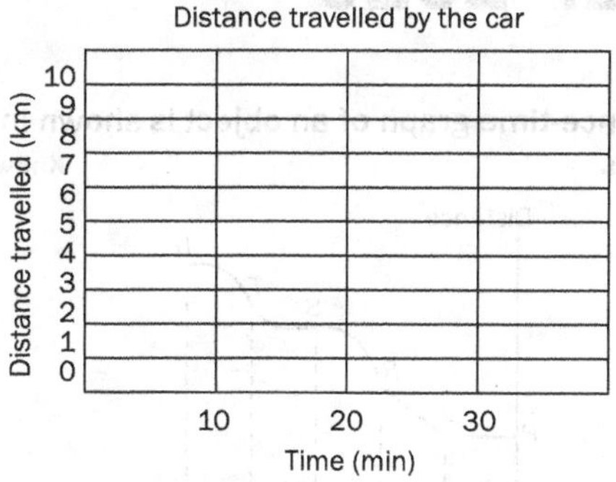

(ii) What can be concluded about the car from the table?

(a) It stopped moving after 30 min

(b) It had a uniform motion throughout the journey

(c) It travelled with increasing speed throughout the journey

(d) It travelled at the highest speed between 10 and 20 min

(iii) What was the average speed of the car during its journey ?

(a) 36 km/h

(b) 5 km/h

(c) 10 km/h

(d) 20 km/h

Ans.

1. (i) (b) 3 h 45 min

(ii) Total distance = 60 km

Total time = 40 min or 2/3 h

$$\text{Speed} = \frac{\text{Total distance}}{\text{Total time}} = \frac{60}{2} \times 3 = 90 \text{ km/h}$$

2. (i)

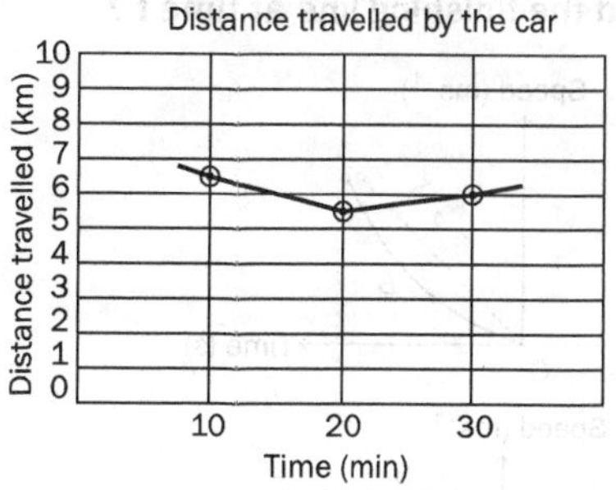

(ii) (a) Because, further distance travelled by car is not given in the table. So, we can conclude that it is stopped after this.

(iii) (a) Total distance covered by car = 18 km.

Total time taken by car = 30 min or $\frac{1}{2}$ h

$$\text{Average speed} = \frac{\text{Total distance}}{\text{Total time}} = \frac{8}{1/2} = 36 \text{ km/h}$$

Skill Based Questions as per NEP 2020

1. In a 400 m race, two athletes *A* and *B* reached the finishing line at the same time. Which of the following graphs shows that both the athletes reached the finishing line at time *t*? **Thinking Skill**

(i)

(a)

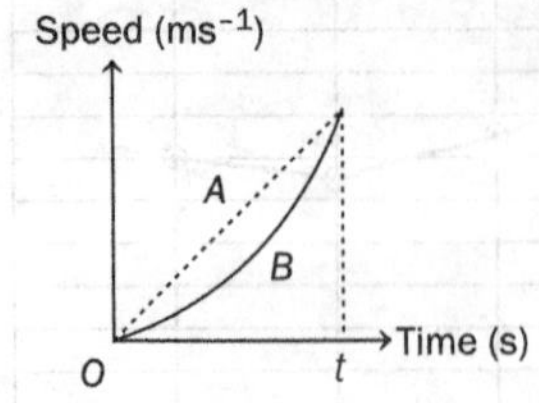

(b)

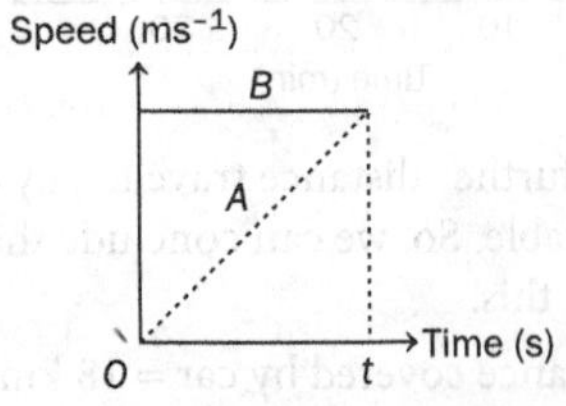

(c)

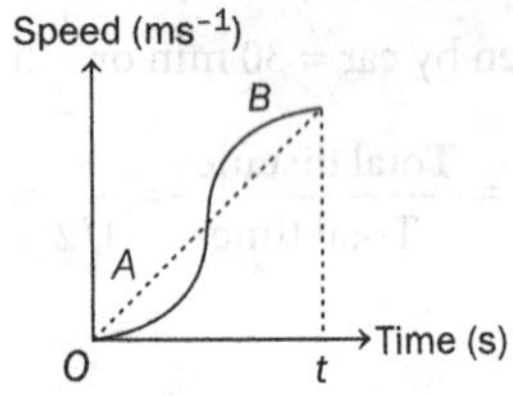

(d)

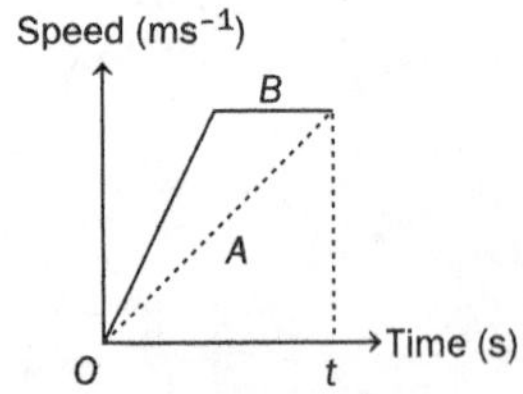

(ii) In the above speed and time graphs, which axis represents the time?

2. Distance-time graph of an object is shown in the figure. **Knowledge Skill**

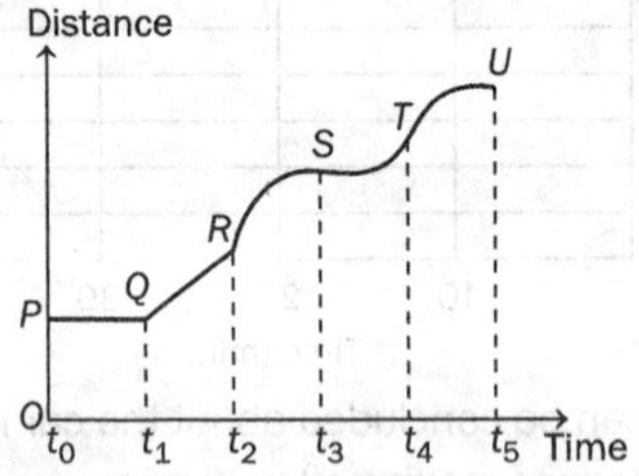

(i) Object is at uniform speed in a time interval from

(a) t_1 to t_2 (b) t_3 to t_4

(c) t_0 to t_1 (d) t_2 to t_3

(ii) How uniform motion is differ from non-uniform motion?

3. A student drops a ball from a slope. He notices the ball rolling down as shown in the diagram.

Which of these statements is true about the motion?

CBSE Question Bank, Experimental Skill

(a) The student is in motion as he is standing

(b) The student is in motion as he drops the ball

(c) The ball is in motion as it rolls down the slope

(d) The ball is in motion as its shape changes over time

ASSESSMENT EXERCISE

Part I

Multiple Choice Questions

1. The standard unit of speed is
(a) km/min (b) km/s
(c) m/s (d) None of these

2. The device which is used to measure speed is
(a) odometer
(b) speedometer
(c) pendulum
(d) Both (a) and (b)

3. The distance moved by an object can be measured by
(a) speedometer (b) odometer
(c) Both (a) and (b) (d) None of these

4. Motion of a satellite around a planet is
(a) circular motion
(b) rectilinear motion
(c) periodic motion
(d) oscillatory motion

5. Time period of a pendulum is expressed in
(a) hour (b) minute
(c) second (d) All of these

Fill in the Blanks

6. When the distance of an object remains constant from a fixed point during its motion, then its motion is ....

7. To and fro motion of pendulum is an example of .... motion.

8. .... is the device used to measure the distance of a vehicle.

True/False

9. The basic unit of speed is km/s.

10. Speedometer is used to measure the distance travelled by an object.

11. A kind of graph which shows the percentage composition of something in the form of slices of a circle is known as pie chart.

Assertion-Reason Questions

The following questions consist of two statements Assertion (A) and Reason (R). Answer these questions by selecting the appropriate option given below

(a) Both A and R are true and R is the correct explanation of A.
(b) Both A and R are true but R is not the correct explanation of A.
(c) A is true but R is false.
(d) A is false but R is true.

12. Assertion (A) The time taken by a pendulum to complete one oscillation is called its time period.

Reason (R) Time period of a simple pendulum does not depend upon the length of pendulum.

13. Assertion (A) The distance covered by an object in unit time is called its speed.

Reason (R) Faster vehicles take less time to cover a certain distance as compare to slower vehicle.

Part II

Very Short Answer Type Questions

14. Mention which of the two is a bigger unit of time, microsecond or nanosecond?

15. Name two types of graphs other than line graphs.

16. Name the instrument which is used
(a) to record the distance covered by a vehicle.
(b) to indicate the speed of a running vehicle.

Short Answer Type Questions

17. A car travelling at a speed of 60 km/h takes 20 min to reach its destination. What distance has the car covered?

18. Write the use of odometer in the vehicle.

19. (a) Name the watch that have an electric circuit with one or more cells.
(b) Name the ancient time measuring device.

Long Answer Type Question

20. The distances travelled by a car at various time intervals are given as follow

Distance (m)	0	5	10	15	20	25
Time (s)	0	2	4	6	8	10

(a) Draw the distance-time graph for the car.
(b) What conclusion do you get from this graph about the nature of motion of the car?

Answers

1. (c) **2.** (b) **3.** (b) **4.** (a) **5.** (d)
6. circular **7.** periodic **8.** Odometer
9. False **10.** False **11.** True **12.** (c) **13.** (b)

CHAPTER 10

Electric Current and its Effects

Electricity is a form of energy which is used to run many electrical appliances like electric bulbs, televisions, stereo systems, refrigerators, washing machines, computers, etc.

Electricity is produced at **power stations** from where it is brought to our homes through wires and electric poles or underground cables (or wires) in the form of electric current. So, **we can define the electric current as the flow of electricity through a conductor (wires, cables).** In our daily life, the word electricity and electric current are used in the same sense.

In this chapter, we will study about electric current and its effects in detail.

10.1 Electric Circuits

Electric circuit is a closed and continuous path of electric current. An electric circuit can be represented with the help of a circuit diagram. A circuit diagram tells us how the various components in an electric circuit have been connected by using the electrical symbols of the component.

Symbols of Electric Components

Some of the commonly used symbols for electric components are shown here

Electric components	Diagrams	Symbols
Electric cell		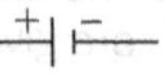
Electric bulb		
Switch in ON position		
Switch in OFF position	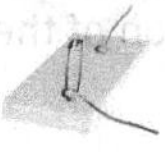	
Battery		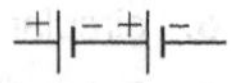
Wire		

- In an electric circuit, the key or switch can be placed anywhere in the circuit.
- When the switch is in the ON position, the circuit is then said to be closed and current will flow throughout the circuit instantly. So, the bulb will glow.
- When the switch is in the OFF position, the circuit is then said to be open and no current will flow through any part of the circuit. So, the bulb does not glow.
- While sometimes, the bulb does not glow even when the switch is in the ON position. This condition can occur only if the bulb gets fused, i.e. its filament breaks.

Electric Cell and Battery

The common source of electricity to run the number of devices (e.g. torches, radio, electric clocks and watches, toys, etc.) is an **electric cell**, but sometimes a single cell is not sufficient to run many devices as they require high voltage to run. So, in such cases, we use the **combination of cells** i.e. called a **battery.**

- When the positive terminal of one cell is joined with the negative terminal of the other cell, then the cells are said to be joined in **series** as shown in the figure given below. So, a battery can be defined as the group of cells joined together in the series, e.g. in a torch, the cells are placed one after the other.

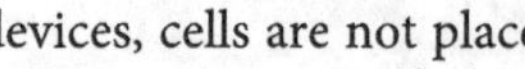

A battery of two cells joined in series

- But in many devices, cells are not placed one after the other, e.g. in a TV remote control, the two cells are placed **side by side** or **parallel** to each other. So, two or more cells connected in side by side manner are said to be joined in parallel. This combination is also known as a battery.

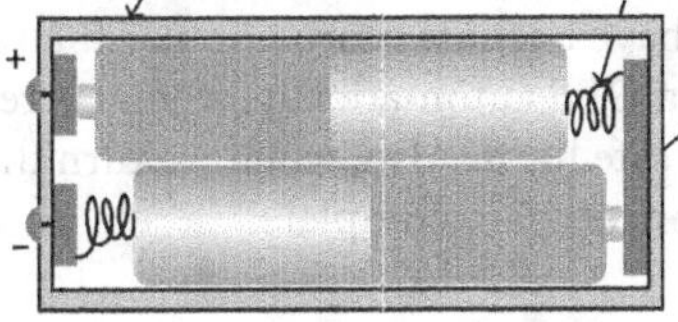

A battery of two cells joined in parallel

Cell Holders

It is a simple device in which more than one cell can be placed properly to form a battery.

To ensure that the cells are placed correctly the cell holder has the symbols (+) and (–) printed on it.

Construction of cell holder/Battery compartment

(i) To prepare a cell holder, we need a wooden block, two iron strips and a rubber band.

(ii) Place the iron strips on wooden board at its two ends.

(iii) Place the cells in series combination between the metal strips.

(iv) Now use a rubber band to hold the metal strips tightly to the cells.

(v) Connect a piece of wire to each metal strips on the cell holder. Your battery is ready for use.

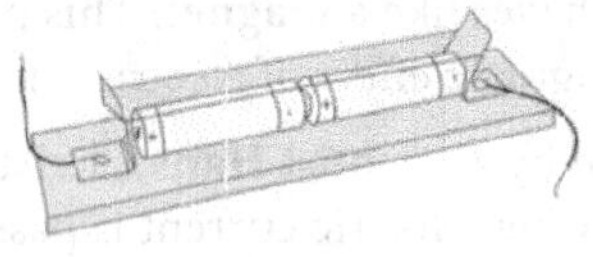
A cell holder

Try These 10.1

1 **Smaller line in the symbol for a cell represents its ....terminal.**

2 **Draw the symbol for a battery which is made of four cells.**

3 **If we connect the positive terminals of two cell with each other, will it work?**

10.2 Heating Effect of Electric Current

The production of heat in an electric device due to flow of electric current is called the heating effect of electric current.

So, when appliances like (electric iron, bulb or room heater) are switched ON after connecting to the electric supply, then a **coil of wire** called **element** present inside the device, becomes red hot and releases the heat.

Nichrome wire is used to make coils or elements because nichrome has a very high melting point and does not melt easily.

Factors on which the heating effect of current depends

(i) Type of material used for wire (ii) Length of wire

(iii) Thickness of wire

Note Never touch a lighted electric bulb connected to the mains electricity supply as it may be very hot and can damage your hands.

Applications of the Heating Effect of Current

This effect is utilised

(i) for the production of light in the electric bulbs.

(ii) to make safety devices like electric fuse.

(iii) for the working of electrical heating appliances such as room heater, water heater, etc.

(a) Bulb glows due to heating effect of current

(b) Red hot coil due to heating effect of current

Compact Fluorescent Lamps (CFLs)

An electric bulb is basically used for producing light but it also releases the heat which is not desirable because a major part of the electricity consumed by the filament of a bulb is converted into heat and results in the wastage of electricity. So, the wastage can be decreased by using fluorescent tubelight or CFLs (as shown in figure) in place of the bulbs.

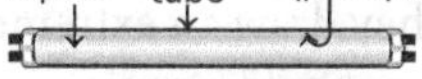

Fluorescent tubelight

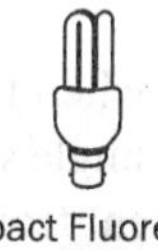
Compact Fluorescent Lamp (CFL)

However, before purchasing bulbs, tubes or CFL's, we should look for the ISI mark (ISI-Bureau of Indian standard). It is because the ISI mark ensures that the appliances are safe and wastage of energy is minimum.

Electric Fuse

A safety device which is used in the electric circuit is called an **electric fuse.** It works on the heating effect of the electric current and prevents electric fires or damage to electrical appliances due to excessive flow of current. It consists of a short length of a thin wire placed inside a glass tube.

The wire used as a fuse should have higher resistance and a low melting point, so an alloy of lead and tin is used which has both of these properties.

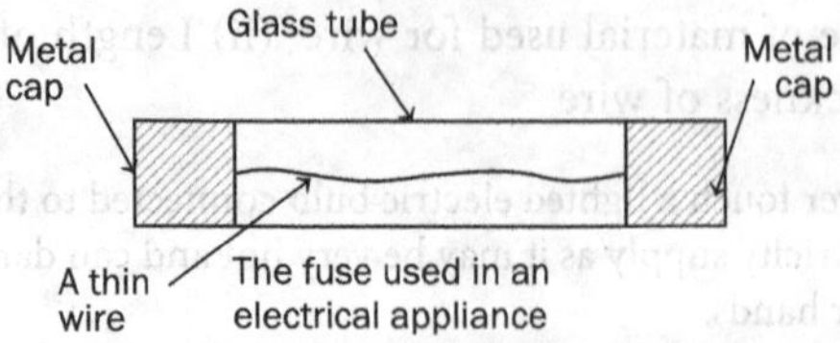

The fuse used in an electrical appliance

SCIENCE INSIGHT Thomas-E-Murray, an american inventor is known as the father of fuse.

Working of an Electric Fuse

The fuse wire has low melting point. If the current in the electric wire suddenly increases too much, then the fuse wire gets heated, it melts and breaks the circuit which means that the current flowing in the household circuit will stop.

This prevents fire in the house and also the damage to various electrical appliances.

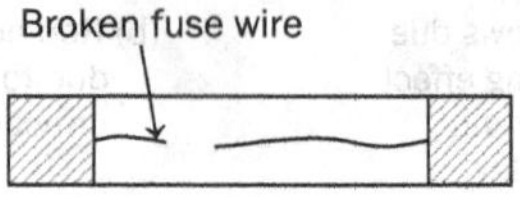

This is a blown up fuse

Cause of Large Current Flow in Household Electric Wiring

An extremely large current can flow in the household electric wiring circuits under two circumstances, **overloading** and **short circuit**.

Overloading

It is a situation when too many electrical appliances are connected to a single socket, they draw an extremely large amount of current from the household circuit.

The flow of large current due to overloading may heat the copper wires of household wiring to a very high temperature and fire may be started.

Short Circuit

Electric current is supplied by household through two insulated wire, i.e. **live wire** and **neutral wire**.

So, if in case, the plastic insulation of the live wire and neutral wire gets torn due to wear and tear, then the two naked wires may touch each other. This touching of live wire and neutral wire directly is known as short circuit.

Miniature Circuit Breakers (MCBs)

These days MCBs have become more popular than fuses. These switches turn OFF automatically, when current in a circuit exceeds the safe limit. Also, when we turn them ON, the circuit is once again complete.

Miniature Circuit Breaker (MCB)

Try These 10.2

1. **Mention any one utilisation of heating effect of electric current in the production of electricity.**
2. **A sudden flow of very large current due to direct contact of a live wire and a neutral wire is known as ....**
3. **Nowadays, which device is commonly used in place of fuses ?**

10.3 Magnetic Effect of Electric Current

If electric current passes through a wire, then the current carrying wire behaves like a **magnet**. This phenomenon is known as the magnetic effect of electric current.

It was discovered by a scientist **Hans Christian Oersted** who found that when electric current is passed in a wire, then the compass needle placed near it gets deflected from its usual north-south position. The magnetic effect is increased, if we use a long coil wire instead of a straight wire.

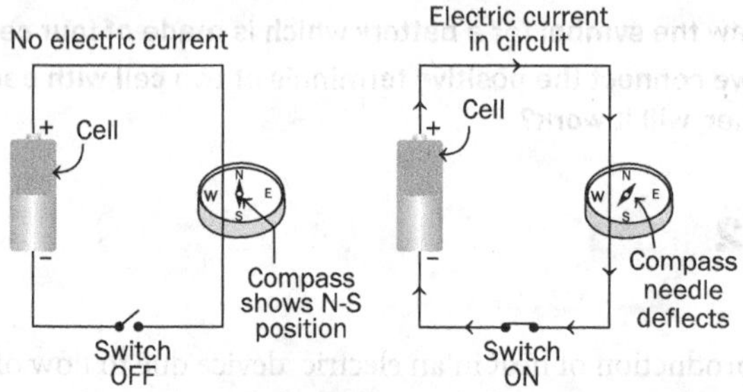

Magnetic compass deflects due to magnetic field produced by electric current

Electromagnet

An electromagnet

When electric current flows through a coil, the coil behaves like a magnet. Such coils are called electromagnets. An electromagnet consists of a coil of insulated wire wrapped around a piece of iron which is magnetised only when electric current is passed through the coil.

There are two factors through which an electromagnet can be made stronger, i.e.

(i) By increasing the amount of current used in the coil.
(ii) By increasing the number of turns forming the coil.

Uses of Electromagnets

- These magnets are used in electrical appliances such as electric bell, electric fan, electric motor.
- These magnets have their utilisation in electric generators where very strong magnetic field is required.
- These magnets deflect electron beam in the picture tube of TV.
- These magnets used to separate iron ores from the earthly substances.
- These are used to prepare strong permanent magnets.

Advantages of Electromagnets over Permanent Magnets

- The magnetism of an electromagnet can be switched ON or switched OFF as desired, while it is not possible with a permanent magnet.
- By increasing the number of turns in the coil and by increasing the current passing through the coil, an electromagnet can be made very strong. On the other hand, a permanent magnet cannot be made so strong.

Electric Bell

An electric bell works on the magnetic effect of current .

Construction of Electric Bell

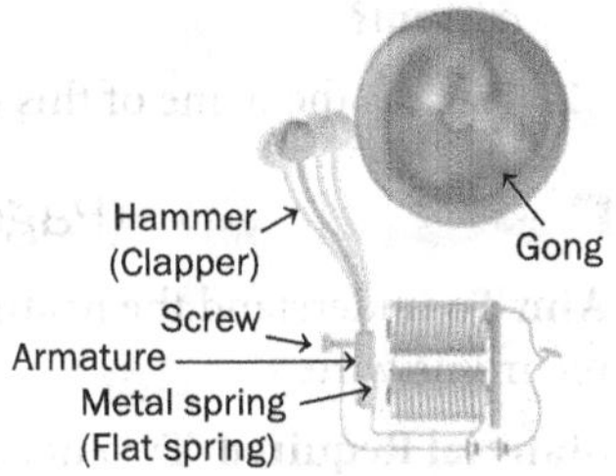

Circuit of an electric bell

The electric bell has a U-shaped electromagnet. There is a small iron bar called **armature** which is held in front of the poles of the electromagnet.
The lower end of iron bar is attached to a flat spring and the flat spring is itself fixed to a metal bracket.

The upper end of iron bar has a clapper attach to it.
A metal gong is fixed near the clapper.

Working of an Electric Bell

- When we pressed the switch of the bell to ring it, an electric current starts flowing in the electromagnet.
- As the electromagnet gets magnetised, it starts attracting the metal spring toward itself.
- As the flat or metal spring moves towards the electromagnet, the clapper which is attached to it strikes the gong and produces a sound.
- When the metal spring is attracted towards the electromagnet, it is no longer in contact with screw and hence circuit breaks.
- When electric circuit breaks, no current flows through the coil, this make the metal spring to go back to its original position and the clapper (hammer) also moves away from the gong.
- This process continues as long as we are pressing the switch.

Try These 10.3

1 **In an electromagnet, which of the two really becomes a magnet : The coil of wire or the pieces of iron?**
2 **Electromagnet can be made stronger by increasing the amount of current used in coil. Is it correct?**
3 **Name the effect on which an electric bell works.**

Science Glossary

Electric current It is defined as the flow of electricity through a conductor.

Electric circuit A closed path through which an electric current flows is called an electric circuit.

Battery A battery is defined as the combination of two or more cells.

Cell Holder It is a simple device in which more than one cell can be placed properly to form a battery.

Electric fuse A safety device used in the electric circuit which prevents electric fires or damage to appliances due to excessive flow of current is called electric fuse.

Electromagnet When electric current flows through a coil, the coil behaves like a magnet. Such coil is known as an electromagnet.

Electric bell It is a device which produces a sound and works on the magnetic effect of electric current.

Let's Investigate

ACTIVITY 1 (Page 111, 112)

Aim To make an electric circuit.

Material Required A bulb, an electric cell, a switch and insulated copper wires.

Procedure

1. Firstly, connect an electric cell to an electric bulb and a switch with wires to form an electric circuit as shown in Fig. (a).
2. When the switch is ON, the bulb starts glowing.
3. Now, turn OFF the switch, you will observe that bulb stops glowing .
4. Represent the circuit in the form of circuit diagram using symbols as shown in Figs. (b) and (c).

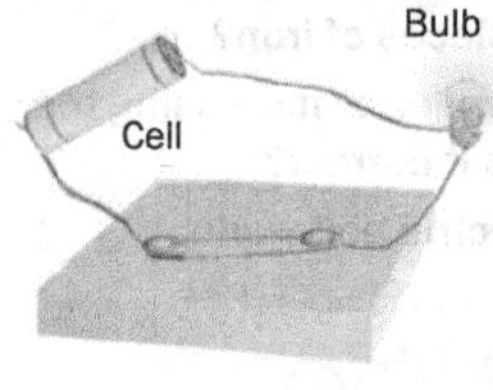

(a) An electric circuit

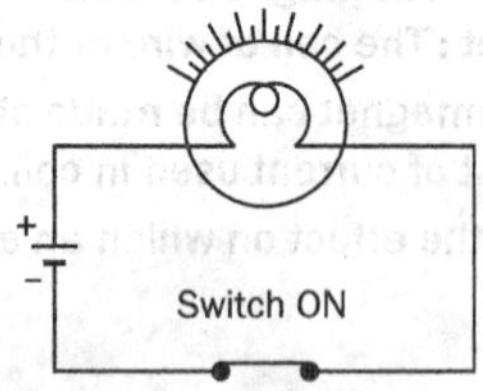

(b) Circuit diagram of electric circuit

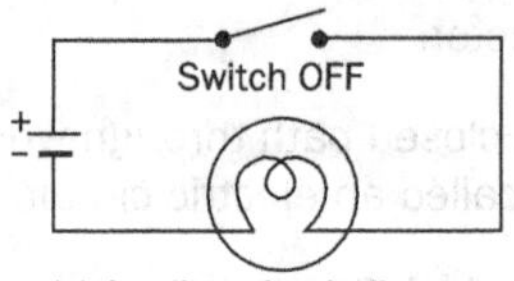

(c) Another circuit diagram

Conclusion We have concluded that when the switch is in ON position, the circuit is said to be closed and current flows throughout the circuit instantly and when the switch is in OFF position, the circuit is said to be open and no current flows throughout the circuit.

Viva Questions

1. If we exchange the placing of a battery and switch with each other, will you observe change in the working of circuit?
2. Draw the symbol for open circuit.

ACTIVITY 2 (Page 112, 113)

Aim To show that electric bulb releases heat.

Material Required A bulb, an electric cell, a switch and connecting wires.

Procedure

1. Firstly, make a simple electric circuit as shown in the figure.
2. Keep the switch in the OFF position, so the bulb does not glow and then touch the bulb.
3. Now, move the switch to ON position, so the bulb glows.
4. Let the bulb glow for 5 - 6 min and touch the bulb glass. You will find that it is warm to touch.

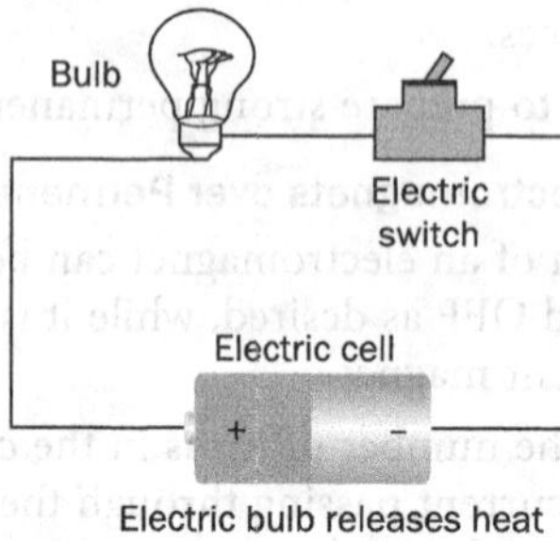

Electric bulb releases heat

Conclusion We have concluded that heat is released by an electric bulb when an electric current passes through it.

Viva Questions

1. Does the heating effect depend on the direction of current?
2. What is the name of this effect?

ACTIVITY 3 (Page 113)

Aim To understand the heating effect of electric current by nichrome wire.

Material Required Two nails, a switch, a cell, a nichrome wire, a copper wire.

Procedure

1. Firstly, take about 10 cm long piece of nichrome wire and tie it between the two nails.
2. Make an electric circuit by connecting the two nails to the terminals of a cell through a switch by using copper wire as shown in the figure.
3. Move the switch to the ON position. After sometime, touch the nichrome wire just for a moment, you will find that the nichrome wire becomes hot.

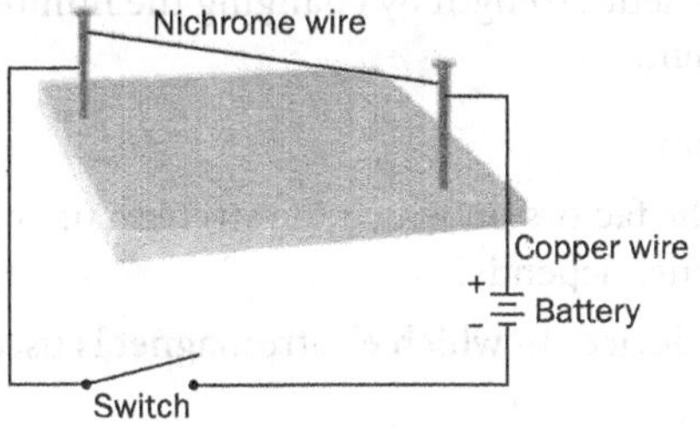

Conclusion We have concluded that when an electric current is passed through a high resistance wire like nichrome wire, the wire becomes hot and produces heat.

Viva Questions

1. Name a wire which we can be used in place of nichrome wire.
2. Name any two devices which work on heating effect of electric current.

ACTIVITY 4 (Page 115)

Aim To show that a thin strand of steel wool acts like an electric fuse .

Material Required Two nails, a thin strand of steel wool, a battery, a bulb, a switch a copper wire.

Procedure

1. Firstly, tie a thin strand of steel wool between two nails.
2. Make an electric circuit by connecting the two nails to the terminals of a battery through a switch by using copper wire as shown in figure.

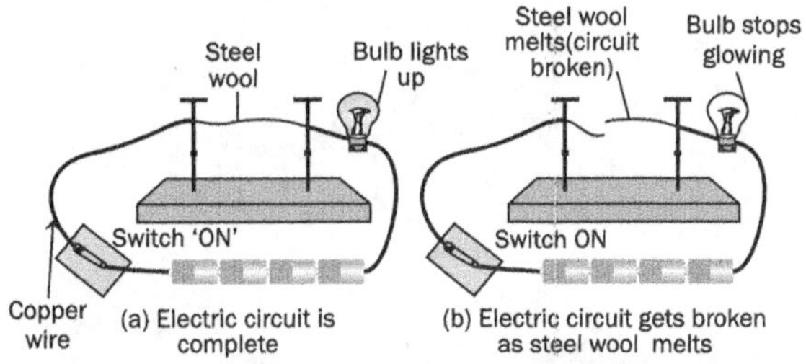

Steel wool used as a fuse wire to break the electric circuit

3. Move the switch to ON position. We will observe that the electric current passes through the circuit and the bulb starts glowing.
4. After few seconds, the thin strand of wool breaks and the bulb stops glowing.

Conclusion We have concluded that steel wool acts like a fuse wire. When large current flows through steel wool, it heat ups and melts, which in result breaks the circuit.

Viva Questions

1. Are fuse wires thick or thin?
2. Name the material used for making a fuse wire.

ACTIVITY 5 (Page 116, 117)

Aim To understand the magnetic effect of current.

Material Required A discarded matchbox, a compass, a bulb, a switch, a cell.

Procedure

1. Take the cardboard tray from inside a matchbox.
2. Now, wrap a copper wire around the cardboard tray as shown in figure.
3. Place a tiny compass inside it and connect the two ends of the wire to a cell through a switch by using connecting wire.
4. When switch is OFF, we will notice that the compass needle is pointing toward north-south direction.
5. When we turn ON that switch, the electric current passes through the wire and we will find that the compass needle gets deflected from its original position.

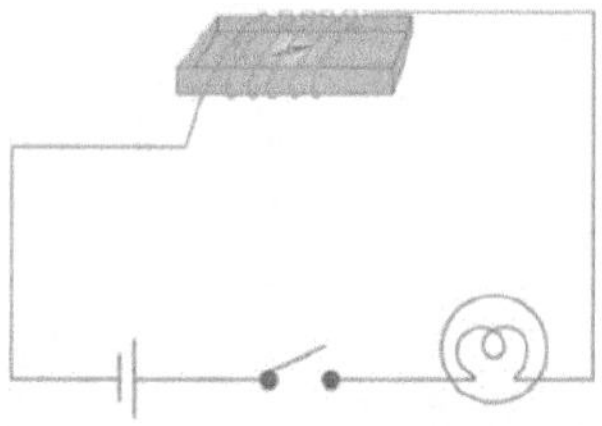

Effect of current on a compass needle

Conclusion The deflection of the compass needle shows that the current carrying wire behaves like a magnet and produces a magnetic field around it.

Viva Questions

1. What is the original direction of a compass needle ?.
2. Does the deflection shown by compass depends upon the amount of electric current?

ACTIVITY 6 (Page 117)

Aim To make an electromagnet.

Material Required An iron nail, an insulated copper wire, a cell, a switch, some iron pins.

Procedure

1. Firstly, wound a insulated copper wire around an iron nail of length 6 -10 cm as shown in figure.
2. Now, connect the free ends of the copper wire to the two terminals of an electric cell through a switch.

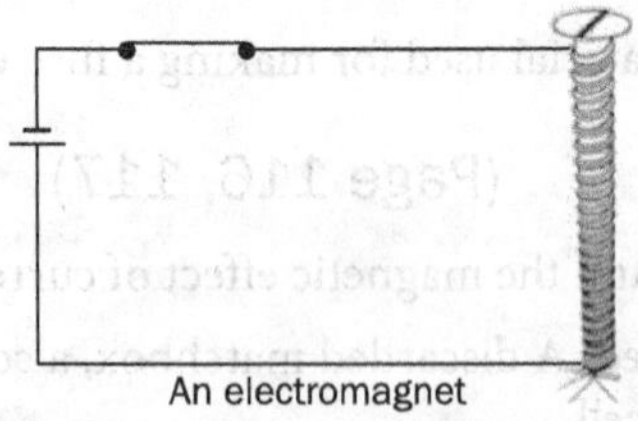

An electromagnet

3. Spread few iron pins near the wounded nail.
4. When we turn ON that switch, we will find that the current starts flowing through iron nail. So, it behaves like a magnet and iron pin starts clinging to the nail.
5. Now, switch OFF the current, we will find that iron nail stops behaving like a magnet and iron pin drops.

Conclusion We have concluded that, when electric current passes through a coil it behaves like a magnet and we can change the magnetic strength by changing the number of coils or electric current.

Viva Questions

1. What are the factors on which the strength of an electromagnet depends?
2. Name two devices in which electromagnet is used.

Mind Map

ELECTRIC CURRENT AND ITS EFFECTS

Electric Current

- It is defined as the flow of electricity through a conductor.

Electric Circuit

- A closed and continuous path of electric current.

Various components of electric circuit

- Electric cell
- Electric bulb
- Switch ON
- Switch OFF
- Battery
- Wire

Cell and Battery

- An **electric cell** is a device which generates the electric current.
- Combination of cells are known as **battery.**
- When +ve terminal of one cell is joined with the –ve terminal of other cell, it is said to be joined in **series.**
- When cells are connected side-by-side, then it is said to be joined in **parallel.**

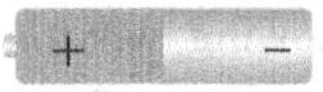

Electric cell

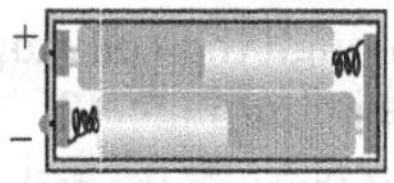

Electric battery

Cell Holder

A device in which more than one cell can be placed properly to form a battery.

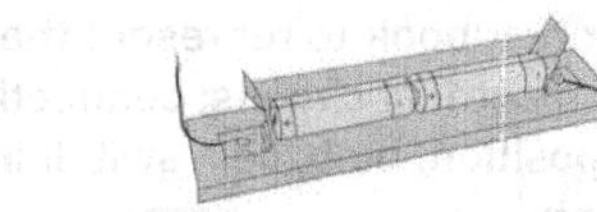

Heating Effect of Electric Current

- Production of heat in an electric device due to flow of electric current.

Factor on which it depends

- Type of material used for wire
- Length of wire
- Thickness of wire

Applications

- Glowing of bulb
- Working of electrical heating devices like iron, oven, etc.

Electric Fuse

- Safety device used in electric circuit.
- Works on heating effect of electric current.
- Wire used as fuse should have higher resistance and a low melting point.
- Fuse wire melts and break the circuit, when large current flow through it.

Electric Fuse

Cause of Excessive Current in a Circuit

Overloading

- Situation when too many electrical appliances are connected to a single socket.

Short-circuit

- Situation when two naked wire touches directly with each other.

Magnetic Effect of Electric Current

- When electric current flows through a wire or coil, it behaves like a magnet.

Applications

Electromagnet

- When current flows through a coil, it behaves like a magnet, such coils are electromagnet.
- It can be stronger if
  - Amount of current increases.
  - Number of turns in coil increases.
- Magnetism of an electromagnet can be switched OFF or ON as desired.
- Used for preparing strong permanent magnet.
- Used in electric motors, fans, etc.

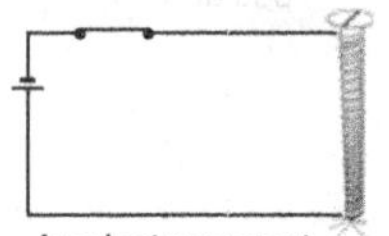

An electromagnet

Electric Bell

- It works on the magnetic effect of electric current.

Parts of electric bell

- Hammer
- Screw
- Armature
- Metal spring
- Gong

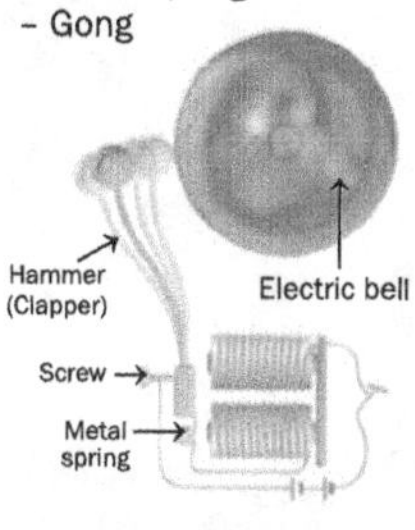

NCERT FOLDER

Complete Explanations of all NCERT's Questions

Intext Questions

Q1. What is a battery? Page 109

Ans. Battery is a combination of two or more cells.

Q2. How are the terminals of the cells connected? Page 110

Ans. In the combination of cells, positive terminal of a cell is connected with the negative terminal of another cell and *vice-versa.*

Q3. If cells are placed side by side, then how are the terminals of the cells connected? Page 110

Ans. If cells are placed side by side, then with the help of some connecting wires, the positive terminal of one cell is connected to the negative terminal of other to produce a combined power of all cells which can be called a battery.

Q4. Paheli and Boojho wondered whether the batteries used in tractors, trucks and inverters are also made from cells. That's why, it is called a battery? Page 111

Ans. The cell is the unit of battery when more than one cell are combined together, it forms a battery. In trucks, tractors and inverters, cells are internally arranged and we need not to connect it externally, so we called it as batteries.

Q5. If the filament of the bulb is broken, would the circuit be complete? Would the bulb still glow? Page 112

Ans. If the filament of the bulb is broken, the circuit will not be complete. So, the bulb will not glow.

Q6. You might have noticed that a glowing electric bulb becomes warm. Do you know, why? Page 112

Ans. The glowing electric bulb becomes warm. It happens due to heating effect of electric current.

Q7. Name some electric appliances where the heating effect of the electric current is used. Page 113

Ans. Some of the electric appliances where the heating effect of the electric current is used are electric heater, geyser, micro-oven, room heater, boiler, etc.

Q8. Is it possible for a wire to melt and break? Page 115

Ans. Yes, if a large current passes through a wire, the wire may become hot and it may even melt and break.

Q9. Does the electric current have other effect except heating? Name it. Page 116

Ans. Yes, electric current have other effects except heating, i.e. magnetic effect of current.

When electric current is passed through a coil, the magnetic field developed around the coil or wire. If magnetic compass is placed near by, it deflects the magnetic needle.

Q10. If the current through the coil stops flowing, will the coil remain an electromagnet? Page 118

Ans. When the current through the coil stops flowing, the coil does not remain an electromagnet.

Exercise

Q1. Draw the symbols in your notebook to represent the following components of electrical circuits: connecting wires, switch in the OFF position, bulb, cell, switch in the ON position and battery. NCERT Exemplar

Ans. Refer to table on page 172.

Q2. Draw the circuit diagram to represent the circuit shown in figure.

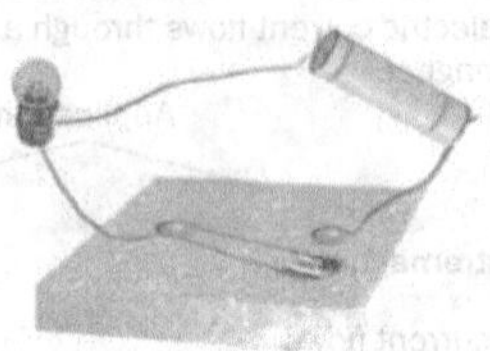

Ans. Complete circuit is shown as below

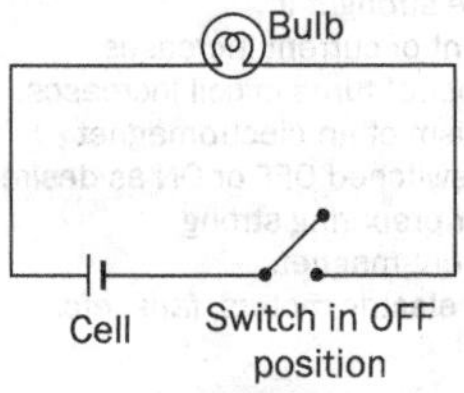

Q 3. Figure shows four cells fixed on a board. Draw lines to indicate how will you connect their terminals with wires to make a battery of four cells.

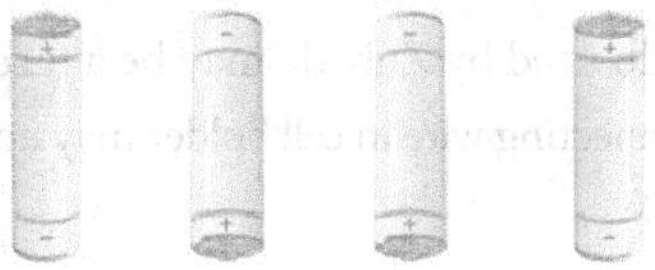

Ans. To connect all the cells, we should join negative terminal of one cell to positive terminal of other *vice-versa*.

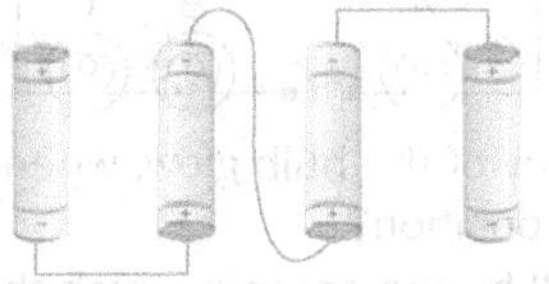

Q 4. The bulb in the circuit shown in figure does not glow. Can you identify the problem? Make necessary changes in the circuit to make the bulb glow.

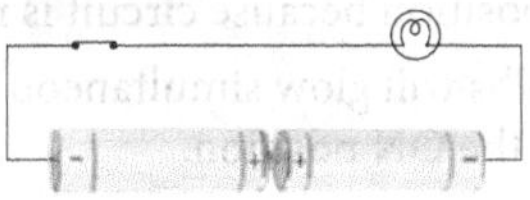

Ans. The two cells are connected with the positive terminal in one side. This can be corrected by joining the negative terminal of one cell to the positive terminal of other cell as shown in figure.

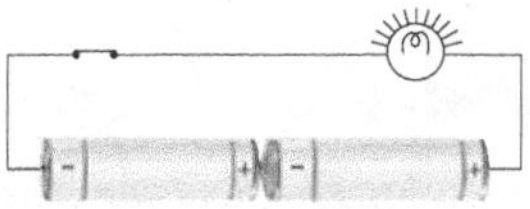

Q 5. Name any two effects of electric current.

Ans. The two effects of electric current are

(i) Heating effect

(ii) Magnetic effect

Q 6. When the current is switched ON through a wire, a compass needle kept nearby gets deflected from its north-south position. Explain.

Ans. When the current is switched ON through a wire or a coil, there is a magnetic field created around the coil or wire and we can say that the wire or coil gets magnetised. Thus, a compass needle kept nearby gets deflected from its north-south position due to other magnet formed by current carrying wire or coil.

Q 7. Will the compass needle show deflection, when the switch in the circuit shown by figure is closed?

Ans. Yes, the compass needle shows the deflection, when switch is closed or circuit is complete. On closing the circuit, current flows through the coil and it gets magnetised. Thus, due to this magnetic effect of current, compass needle shows deflection.

Q 8. Fill in the Blanks

(a) Longer line in the symbol for a cell represents its .... terminal.

(b) The combination of two or more cells is called a ....

(c) When current is switched ON in a room heater, it ....

(d) The safety device based on the heating effect of electric current is called a ....

Ans. (a) positive (b) battery

(c) gets heated (d) fuse

Q 9. Mark T, if the statement is True and F, if it is False.

(a) To make a battery of two cells, the negative terminal of one cell is connected to the negative terminal of the other cell.

(b) When the electric current through the fuse exceeds a certain limit, the fuse wire melts and breaks.

(c) An electromagnet does not attract a piece of iron.

(d) An electric bell has an electromagnet.

Ans. (a) F (b) T

(c) F (d) T

Q 10. Do you think an electromagnet can be used for separating plastic bags from a garbage heap? Explain.

Ans. No, an electromagnet cannot be used for separating plastic bags from a garbage heap because plastic bags are not magnetic materials. Only magnetic materials can be attracted by the magnet, so plastic bags do not get attracted by the magnet.

Q 11. An electrician is carrying out some repairs in your house. He wants to replace a fuse by a piece of wire. Would you agree? Give reasons for your response.

Ans. No, we should not agree for replacing a fuse by a piece of wire.

As we know that fuse wire is made up of special material which can be melt on passing high amount of current or during any short circuit. If it is replaced by some other wire, melting of fuse may not take place on short circuiting or excessive current flow and it may cause fire.

Q 12. Zubeda made an electric circuit using a cell holder shown in figure, a switch and a bulb. When she put the switch in the ON position, the bulb did not glow. Help Zubeda in identifying the possible defects in the circuit.

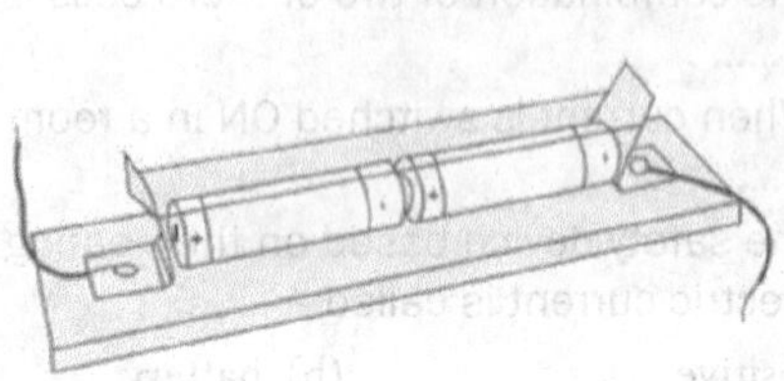

Ans. These may be the reasons by which bulb will not glow

(i) Zubeda may not have arranged the cells in a particular manner, i.e. terminals of cell may not be in alternate form.

(ii) The bulb used by Zubeda may be a fused one.

(iii) The connecting wire in cell holder may not be attached properly.

Q 13. In the circuit shown in figure

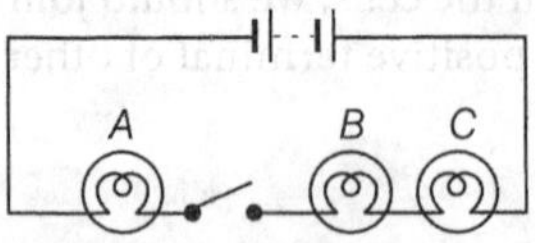

(a) Would any of the bulb glow, when the switch is in the OFF position?

(b) What will be the order in which the bulbs *A*, *B* and *C* will glow, when the switch is moved to the ON position?

Ans. (a) Any of the bulb will not glow when the switch is in the OFF position because circuit is not complete.

(b) All the bulbs will glow simultaneously as the switch is moved to the ON position.

REVIEW EXERCISE

Including Competency Based Questions

Part I

Multiple Choice Questions

1. A battery is a combination of

(a) only single cell (b) only two cells
(c) two or more cells (d) None of these

2. Which of these is the correct arrangement of electric cells in a battery? **Competency Based Que.**

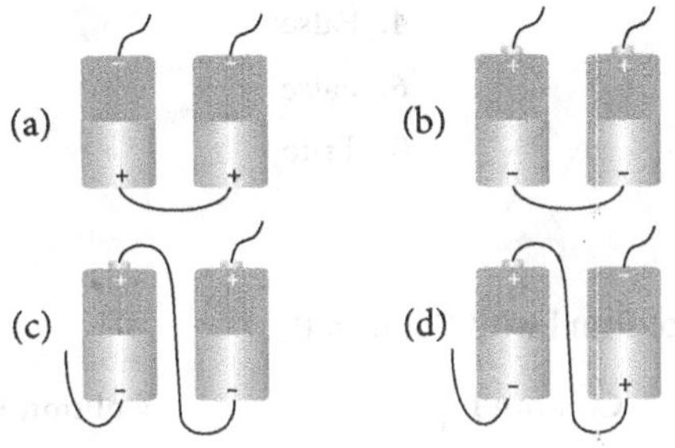

3. Three bulbs *A, B, C* are connected in a circuit as shown in figure. When the switch is 'ON', **NCERT Exemplar**

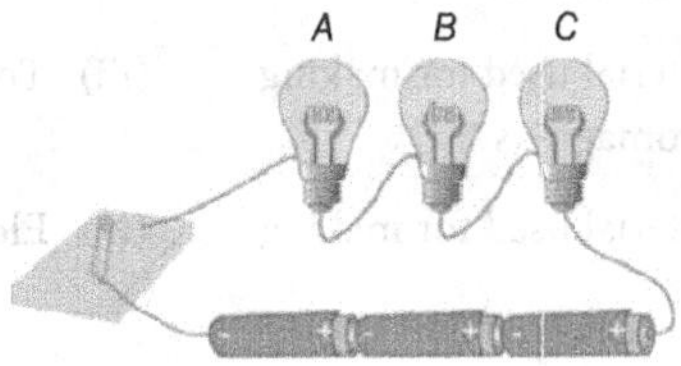

(a) bulb *C* will glow first
(b) bulb *B* and *C* will glow simultaneously and bulb *A* will glow after sometime
(c) all the bulbs *A, B* and *C* will glow at the same time
(d) the bulbs will glow in the order *A, B* and *C*

4. When a switch is in OFF position, **NCERT Exemplar**

(i) circuit starting from the positive terminal of the cell stops at the switch
(ii) circuit is open
(iii) no current flows through it
(iv) current flows after sometime

Choose the combination of correct answer from the following.

(a) All are correct
(b) (ii) and (iii) are correct
(c) Only (iv) is correct
(d) (i) and (ii) are correct

5. Which of the following precautions need not be taken while using electric gadgets/ appliances/circuit?

(a) We should never touch a lighted electric bulb connected to the mains
(b) We should never do experiment with the electric supply from the mains or a generator or an inverter
(c) We should never use just any wire or strip of metal in place of a fuse
(d) We should never turn the switch in ON position

6. Which of these labels on an electric device confirms standard quality? **Competency Based Que.**

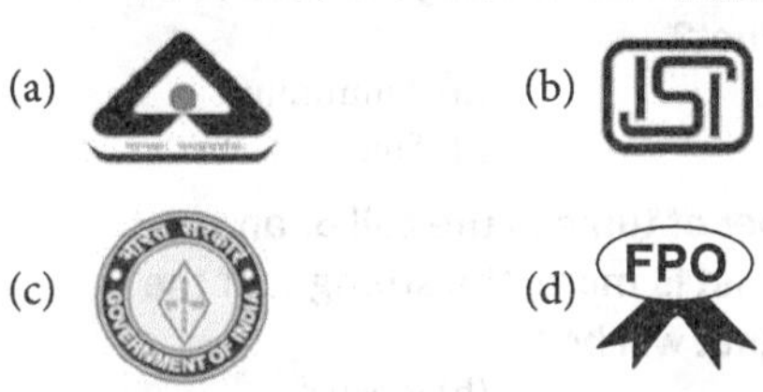

7. Which of these consumes the least electricity for producing the same amount of light ? **Competency Based Que.**

(a) CFL (b) LED
(c) Filament bulb (d) Fluorescent tube

8. Choose the statement which is not correct in the case of an electric fuse. **NCERT Exemplar**

(a) Fuses are inserted in electric circuits of all buildings.
(b) There is a maximum limit on the current which can safely flow through the electric circuits.
(c) There is a minimum limit on the current which can safely flow in the electric circuits.
(d) If a proper fuse is inserted in a circuit, it will blow off if current exceeds the safe limit.

9. Circuit breaker device which can be used in place of fuse in domestic electric wiring is called

(a) DCB (b) MCD
(c) MCB (d) BCM

10. The coil of wire contained in heater is known as

(a) circuit (b) component
(c) spring (d) element

11. Which of these devices work due to the heating effect of electric current ? **Competency Based Que.**

(a) Electric fan (b) Electric bell
(c) Electric kettle (d) Electric torch

12. When an electric current flows through a copper wire *AB* as shown in figure, the wire

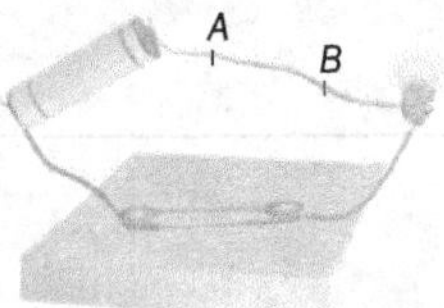

(a) deflects a magnetic needle placed near it
(b) becomes red hot
(c) gives electric shock
(d) behaves like a fuse

13. A common device that uses an electromagnet in its working is **CBSE Question Bank**
(a) a tube light
(b) a room heater
(d) a geyser
(d) an electric bell

14. Which of the following characteristic is most suitable material for making the core of an electromagnet?
(a) Brass (b) Aluminium
(c) Iron (d) Steel

15. If the number of turns in the coil of an electromagnet is more, the strength of the electromagnet will be
(a) lesser (b) greater
(c) double (d) same

Answers

1. (c)	2. (c)	3. (c)	4. (b)	5. (d)
6. (b)	7. (b)	8. (c)	9. (c)	10. (d)
11. (c)	12. (a)	13. (d)	14. (c)	15. (b)

Fill in the Blanks

1. Our body is a .... of electricity. **NCERT Exemplar**
2. An electric cell produces electricity from the .... in it.
3. A combination of two or more cells is called a ....
4. In an electric circuit, a fuse is a .... to prevent possible fire.
5. The core of an electromagnet is made from........... .

Answers

1. good conductor
2. chemicals stored
3. battery
4. safety device
5. iron

True/False

1. The key or switch can be placed anywhere in the circuit.
2. A car battery is just one big cell.
3. The element of an electric iron is made of tungsten.
4. A fuse is used to save energy in the electric circuits.
5. CFLs consume more electricity than an ordinary bulb.
6. Electric fuse is based on the magnetic effect of electric current.
7. MCB works on the magnetic effect of current.
8. When an electric current flows through a wire, it behaves like a magnet.

Answers

1. True	2. False
3. False	4. False
5. False	6. False
7. True	8. True

Match the Columns

1. Match the Column I with Column II.

Column I	Column II
(a) A device used in electric bell	(i) Nichrome wire
(b) A material used for making filament of bulb	(ii) Soft iron
(c) A material used for making electromagnets	(iii) Tungsten
(d) A material used for making heater	(iv) Electromagnet

2. Match the Column I with Column II.

Column I	Column II
(a) Heating effect of electric current	(i) Battery
(b) Magnetic effect of electric current	(ii) Electric bulb
(c) Combination of cells	(iii) Electric bell
(d) Safety device	(iv) Fuse

Answers

1. (a) (iv), (b) (iii), (c) (ii), (d) (i)
2. (a) (ii), (b) (iii), (c) (i), (d) (iv)

Assertion-Reason Questions

The following questions consist of two statements - Assertion (A) and Reason (R). Answer these questions by selecting the appropriate option given below

(a) Both A and R are true and R is the correct explanation of A

(b) Both A and R are true but R is not the correct explanation of A.

(c) A is true but R is false

(d) A is false but R is true.

1. Assertion (A) Electromagnets are permanent magnets.
Reason (R) Magnetic strength of an electromagnet can be changed.

2. Assertion (A) Fuse wires have low melting point and high resistance.
Reason (R) An electric cell produces less amount of electric current.

3. Assertion (A) In a cell, the longer line represents positive terminal and shorter line represent negative terminal.
Reason (R) A battery is a combination of two or more cells.

4. Assertion (A) An electric bulb glass becomes hot after sometime when it is connected to an electric supply.
Reason (R) A bulb becomes hot due to the heating effect of electric current .

Answers

1. (d) Electromagnets are temporary magnets. Magnetic strength can be changed by
   (i) increasing amount of current.
   (ii) increasing number of turns in coil.
2. (b) Fuse wires have low melting point and high resistance, so that they can breaks the circuit in case if high current flow.
3. (b) We can represent a cell in the form given below and the combination of two or more cells are called battery.

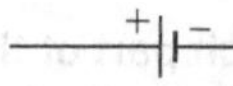

4. (a) When electric current flows, filament wire of bulb becomes red hot due to heating effect of current, which makes electric bulb hot glass after sometime.

Case Based Question

1. Electricity is the most convenient source of energy . It has very important role because it is used to run many electrical appliances. Electricity makes it possible to light our houses, apartment, market and industries. An electric bulb has a thin wire made up of tungsten which gives us light with the help of electricity. The tungsten wire gets heated to such a high temperature that it starts glowing. Now-a-days, CFLs and LEDs bulbs are used for lighting in place of incandescent electric bulbs because they are considered to much better than incandescent electric bulb. It is advisable to use ISI marked electrical appliances and gadgets.

(i) Filament of an electric bulb is made up of
(a) steel (b) tungsten
(c) copper (d) None of these

(ii) What is the full form of CFL?
(a) Compact Fluorescent Lamp
(b) Compressed Fluorescent Lamp
(c) Combined Fluorescent Lamp
(d) Compact Fluorescent Light

(iii) In which of the following places, the electricity can be generated?
(a) Nuclear power plant (b) Hydro power plant
(c) Geothermal power plant (d) All of these

Answer

1. (i) (b) (ii) (a) (iii) (d)

Part II

Very Short Answer Type Questions

1. Briefly mention which part of the symbol of battery shows positive and negative terminals?

Ans. 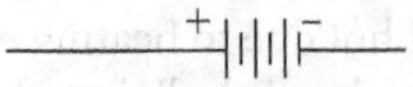

The positive terminal is represented by longer vertical line while negative terminal is represented by shorter vertical line.

2. Unscramble the following words **NCERT Exemplar**

(i) TBTAYER (ii) SFEU
(iii) HTRCO (iv) HICWTS

Ans. (i) BATTERY (ii) FUSE
(iii) TORCH (iv) SWITCH

3. Name the type of mark for which we should look at an electrical appliance before buying.

Ans. ISI mark is the mark for which we should look at an electrical appliance before buying.

4. Paheli does not have a night lamp in her room. She covered the bulb of her room with a towel in the night to get dim light. Has she taken the right step? Give one reason to justify your answer. **Competency Based Que.**

Ans. No, she has not taken the right step. Because due to excessive heat of bulb, the towel may burn and it also results in the wastage of electrical energy.

5. We should not touch the lighted bulb. Explain, why?

Ans. The lighted bulb connected to main supply should not be touched by our hand directly, as a lighted bulb can be very hot and can burn our hand as well.

6. What happens to the current in a circuit at the time of short circuit?

Ans. The flow of the current in a circuit increases heavily at the time of short circuit.

7. Explain why are CFLs (Compact Fluorescent Lamps) preferred over electric bulbs?

Ans. Compact fluorescent lamps are preferred over electric bulbs because electric bulbs use more power of electricity and it also loss electrical energy in the form of heat but it is not so in compact fluorescent lamps.

8. Why is an electric fuse required in all electrical appliances? **NCERT Exemplar**

Ans. Electric fuse is required in all electrical appliances to prevent damage from excessive current flow or during short circuit.

9. State the property of a conducting wire, which is utilised in making electric fuse.

Ans. Electric fuse wire is made up of special material which has low melting point. As if high amount of current is passed, it melts to disconnect the electric circuit and prevent us from causing any damage.

10. Name the device used these days in place of electric fuses in electrical circuits. **NCERT Exemplar**

Ans. The device used in these days in place of electric fuse is MCB (Miniature Circuit Breaker).

11. When does a circuit said to be overloaded?

Ans. When too many devices get connected to a single socket, then a circuit is said to be overloaded.

12. Mention the name of the two devices that work on the basis of magnetic effects of current.

Ans. The devices that work on the basis of magnetic effects of current are loudspeaker and electric bell.

13. A wire bound nail attract the pins. Comment.

Ans. When the current is passed through the wire bound on the nail, it behave as electromagnet. Due to this reason, the nail attracts the pins.

14. Name the scientist who discovered the magnetic effect of electric current.

Ans. The scientist who discovered the magnetic effect of electric current is Hans Christian Oersted.

15. Briefly state the effects of electricity.

Ans. The three effects of electricity are

(i) Chemical effect
(ii) Heating effect
(iii) Magnetic effect

16. Give the name of any two electrical appliances in which electromagnets are used.

Ans. Electric fan and electrical motor are the electrical appliances in which electromagnets are used.

Short Answer Type Questions

1. Why do we cover plug pinholes which are within the reach of children with cellotape or a plastic cover when not in use? **NCERT Exemplar**

Ans. We do cover plug pinholes which are within the reach of children with cellotape or plastic cover to avoid electric shocks. If unconsciously, a child puts his finger in the electric socket, the shock may be fatal.

2. Explain how a battery can be constructed?

Ans. As we know that, a battery is a combination of two or more cells and it can be constructed by placing cells properly in cell holder in such a way that the positive terminal of one cell is connected to the negative terminal of other.

3. Explain the following.

(i) Copper and aluminium wires are usually employed for electricity transmission. Explain the reason.

(ii) Explain how does the resistance of a wire vary with its length?

(iii) The tungsten is used almost exclusively for filament of electric lamp. Comment.

Ans. (i) Due to the low resistance of aluminium and copper both these metals are usually employed for the transmission of electricity.

(ii) The resistance of wire always increases with the increase in its length.

(iii) Since, tungsten has high melting point and high resistance. So, that's why, the tungsten is used exclusively for filament of electric lamp.

4. Can we use the same fuse in a geyser and a television set? Explain. **NCERT Exemplar**

Ans. No, we cannot use same fuse in a geyser and in a television set because the fuse used in every appliances has some limit to withstand the current flows through it. So, different appliances have different fuses.

5. If the current flows through wire, does the wire behave like a magnet?

Ans. Yes, when the current flows through any wire, a magnetic field is developed around that wire or coil and it behaves like a magnet. It can be analysed by placing a magnetic compass around the wire, it will show deflection of the needle.

6. If current is passed through a coil, does the pins cling to the coil?

Ans. When an electric current is passed through a coil, it gets magnetised due to phenomena of magnetic effect of current. When magnetic materials such as pins are placed near to it, it gets attracted by the coil or we can say that pins cling to the coil.

7. Name two electric devices for each where

(i) heating effect of current is used and

(ii) magnetic effect of current is used. **NCERT Exemplar**

Ans. (i) Heating effect of current is used in electric heater and geyser.

(ii) Magnetic effect of current is used in electric bell and cranes to lift heavy magnetic materials from one place to other.

8. Boojho made an electromagnet by winding 50 turns of wire over an iron screw. Paheli also made an electromagnet by winding 100 turns over a similar iron screw. Which electromagnet will attract more pins? Give reason. **Competency Based Que.**

Ans. Since the magnetic effect directly depends on the number of turns of the coil. As, Paheli's coil has more number of turns than Boojho. So, her electromagnet is stronger than Boojho.

So, electromagnet of Paheli attracts more pins as compared to Boojho.

Long Answer Type Questions

1. One day, Pinki was ironing the clothes in her room. After half an hour of ironing, the light went off and Pinki went outside to the lobby of her house to check if there was any problem in the household circuit. At the same time, she listened the voice of her 4 years old daughter from the same room where she was ironing the clothes. Her daughter was about to touch the hot electric iron but at the same moment, Pinki entered in the room and pushed her daughter back from that place.

(i) On which effect of electric current, does the electric iron work?

(ii) Mention the values showed by Pinki here.

Ans. (i) The electric iron works on the basis of heating effect of electric current.

(ii) The values showed by Pinki here is a great concern and love towards her own 4 years old daughter.

2. Paheli took a wire of length 10 cm. Boojho took a wire of 5 cm of the same material and thickness. Both of them connected the wires as shown in the figure. The current flowing in both the circuits is the same.

(i) Will the heat produced in both the cases be equal? Explain.

(ii) Will the heat produced be the same if the wires taken by them are of equal lengths but of different thickness? **NCERT Exemplar**

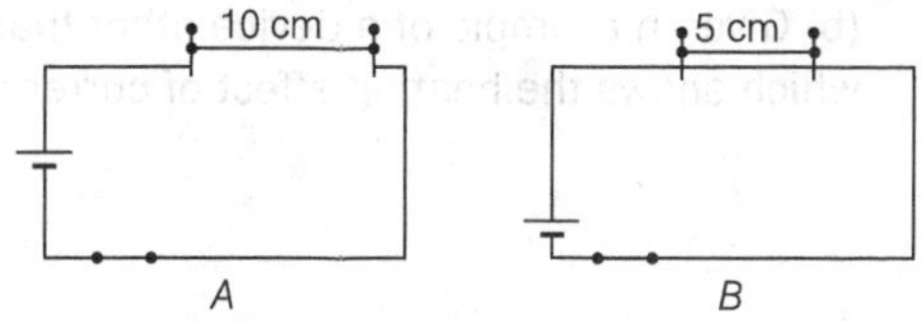

Ans. (i) The amount of heat produced in a wire depends upon the length of wire, so the amount of heat produced in both the cases will not be equal.

(ii) The amount of heat produced in a wire depends upon the thickness of wire, so the amount of heat produced in both the cases will not be equal.

3. Your teacher had shown you the following activity.
Activity : Teacher has wound a long insulated piece of wire around an iron nail in the form of a coil. Free ends of the wire are connected to a cell through a switch as shown in the figure. The current is switched ON and some pins are placed near the ends of the nail.

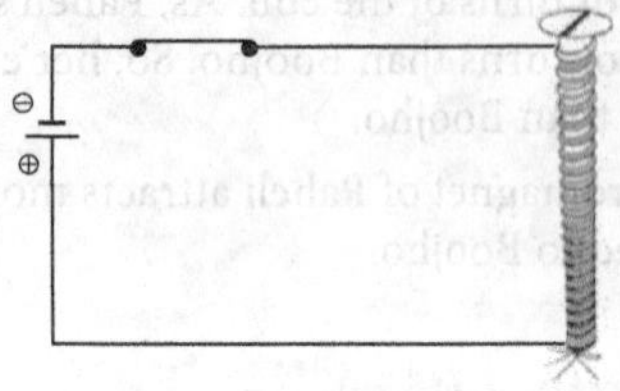

Write down any three questions that come to your mind about this activity. **NCERT Exemplar**

Ans. (i) What will happen, if we increase the number of coil around the iron nail?

(ii) What is the name of this device ?

(iii) Will it behaves like a permanent magnet ?

4. Explain with the help of a diagram, how does the magnetic effect of electric current help in the working of an electric bell.

Ans. Refer to text on page 175.

Case Based Questions

1.

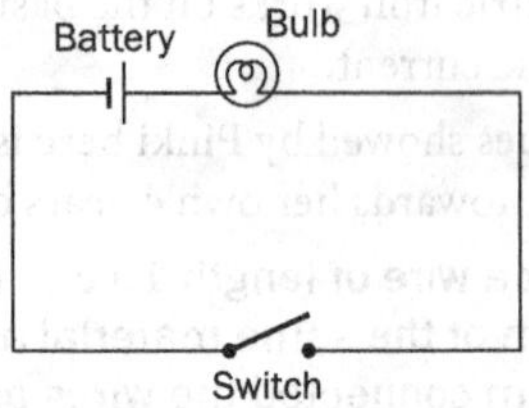

CBSE Question Bank

(i) What is the function of the switch in the circuit ?

(ii) Name the two terminals of a battery.

(iii) Name the alloy used in the filament of bulb. Give its function.

(iv) (a) In the given circuit, name the component that must be hot to work.

(b) Give an example of a device other than a bulb which shows the heating effect of current.

2. An electric fuse consists of a metal wire. The wire breaks the electric circuit when the electricity load is too high. **Competency Based Que.**

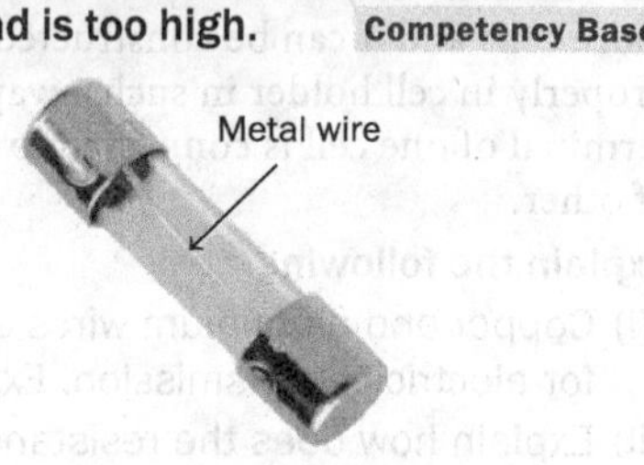

Electric fuse

(i) What makes the wire break when the electricity load is too high ?

(a) It is made of metal.

(b) It has a low melting point.

(c) It is a good conductor of heat

(d) It is a good conductor of electricity.

(ii) Why does the filament of a bulb glow when connected to an electric circuit?

(iii) Which of these can cause a fire in an electric circuit ?

Choose Yes or No for the correct response

	Can this cause a fire in an electric circuit ?	Yes or No
(a)	Use of multiple electric fuses	Yes / No
(b)	Flow of a very high electric current	Yes/ No
(c)	Direct touching of two uncovered wires	Yes/No

Answers

1. (i) It is used to turn ON and turn OFF the equipments of daily uses.

(ii) (a) Positive terminal (b) Negative terminal

(iii) Tungsten, it helps in glowing the bulb.

(iv) (a) Filament of the bulb

(b) Iron, Geyser, Heater

2. (i) (b)

(ii) Due to heating effect of electric current.

(iii) (a) No, (b) Yes, (c) Yes

Skill Based Questions as per NEP 2020

1. 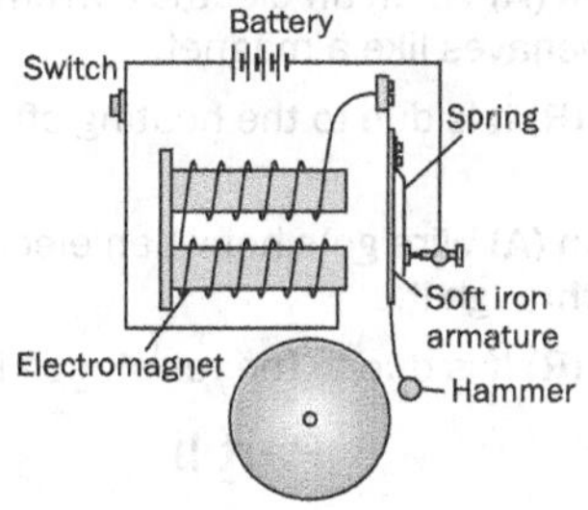

Knowledge Skill

(i) As shown in the above picture, why does the circuit acquire magnetism?

(ii) How can the magnetic strength of an electromagnet can be increased?

(iii) Name two commercially used devices that work on electromagnetism.

2. **Geeta had setup the experiment as shown in figure.**

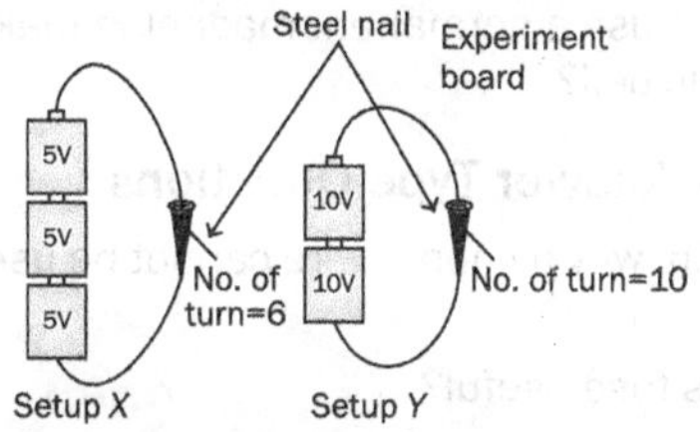

She found out that the steel nail in setup *X* had attracted less iron pins than the steel nail in setup *Y*. What could be the reason for this? **Experimental Skill**

3. **In the set up shown here, the bulb has lighted up.**

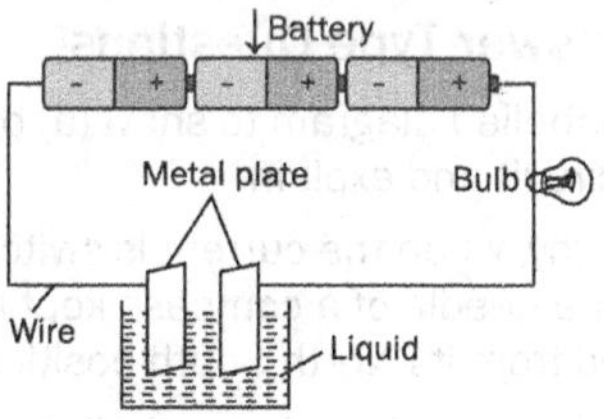

Which of the following statement about liquid is/are correct? **Thinking Skill**

I. Liquid is a distilled water.
II. Liquid is a tap water.
III. Liquid is a good conductor of electricity.

(a) III only
(b) II only
(c) I and III only
(d) II and III only

4. **A student performs an experiment where he uses a heating coil to heat the water as shown in the figure. The initial temperature of the water is measured as 10 °C. After switching it ON for 5 min, the student records the temperature of the water as 18 °C.** **Experimental Skill**

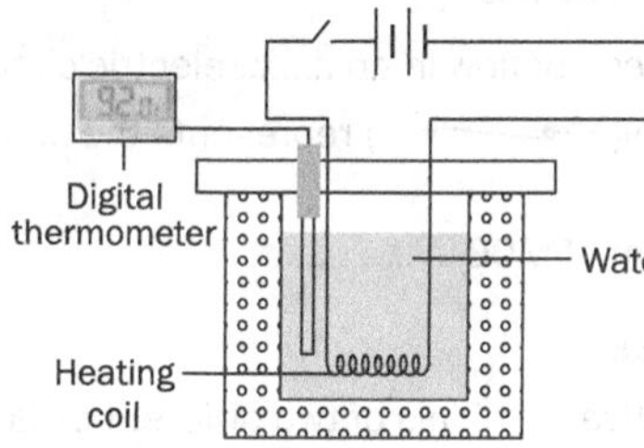

The water is allowed to return back to its initial temperature. The activity is then repeated with another heating coil having half the length of the original heating coil. He notices that after 5 min, the temperature of the water reads 14 °C. Which statement can be concluded based on the activity?

(a) Reading on thermometer reduces with time.
(b) Temperature of water drops with every repetition.
(c) Length of the material affects the amount of heating.
(d) Temperature of the water increases after a certain period of time.

ASSESSMENT EXERCISE

Part I

Multiple Choice Questions

1. The most suitable material for making the core of an electromagnet is
(a) copper (b) zinc (c) iron (d) brass

2. Electromagnets are used in
(a) electric bell (b) electric bulb
(c) Both (a) and (b) (d) None of these

3. The filament of the bulb is made up of
(a) tungsten (b) iron (c) steel (d) silver

4. A battery is a combination of
(a) two cells only (b) one cell only
(c) two or more cells (d) None of these

Fill in the Blanks

5. Current does not flow in an .... electric circuit.

6. This symbol(—•——•—) represents the .... position.

7. The full form of MCB is ....

True/False

8. When positive terminals of two different cells are connected with each other, it becomes a battery.

9. When two or more appliances or devices are connected to a single socket. This is the condition of short circuiting.

10. A fuse works on the principle of heating effect of electric current.

Assertion-Reason Questions

The following questions consist of two statements Assertion (A) and Reason (R). Answer these questions by selecting the appropriate option given below

(a) Both A and R are true and R is the correct explanation of A
(b) Both A and R are true but R is the not the correct explanation of A
(c) A is true but R is false
(d) A is false but R is true

11. **Assertion (A)** When an electric current flows through a wire, it behaves like a magnet.
Reason (R) It is due to the heating effect of electric current.

12. **Assertion (A)** Wire gets hot when electric current passes through it.
Reason (R) It is due to the resistance in the wire.

Part II

Very Short Answer Type Questions

13. Write the symbol of electric bulb.

14. Write a name of a device which is used to open and close electric circuit.

15. State the role that a switch plays in an electric circuit.

16. On what factors does the heat produced in a wire depend?

17. Can we use a permanent magnet in making an electric bell?

Short Answer Type Questions

18. Explain why a copper wire cannot be used as a fuse wire?

19. How is fuse useful?

20. Why MCBs are being used in place of fuses?

21. Explain how does an electric iron work?

22. Write one advantage and one disadvantage of an electromagnet relative to a bar magnet.

Long Answer Type Questions

23. Draw a labelled diagram to show (a) open circuit (b) closed circuit and explain.

24. Explain why, when the current is switched ON through a wire, the needle of a compass kept nearby gets deflected from its North-South position?

25. Draw a diagram of an electric bell. On what principle, does an electric bell work?

Answers

1. (c) **2.** (a) **3.** (a) **4.** (c)
5. open **6.** switch ON **7.** Miniature Circuit Breaker
8. False **9.** False **10.** True **11.** (c)
12. (a)

CHAPTER 11

Light

Light is a form of energy. We are able to see things around us because of light. Light coming from a source can be seen as a beam of light.

Beam of light is defined as a group of light rays coming out from a source. In our daily life, we can easily observe a group of light rays enters a dark room through a narrow hole or coming out from the head lamps of scooters, cars and engines of trains, these all are the examples of beam of light.

(a) Train engine (a) Light house

Beam of light

11.1 Light Travels Along a Straight Line

We can easily prove that light travels in a straight line from an example. If we try to see a lighted candle through a straight pipe with one eye (keeping the other eye closed), then we can see the light of candle flame and if we look at the lighted candle through a bent pipe in a similar way, then we will not be able to see the light of candle flame.

(a) Able to see (b) Unable to see

Looking at a candle through a straight and a bent pipe

It means that the light of candle flame can travel through the straight hole of a straight pipe but not through the bent hole of a bent pipe. It proves that light travels in a straight line.

11.2 Reflection of Light

The phenomenon of change in the direction of light or the bouncing back of light when it falls on a shiny, polished surface or mirror is called **reflection of light**.

e.g. When light falls on shiny surfaces like stainless steel or shining spoon, it change its direction.

In these certain situations, the shiny surface acts as **mirror.**

Similarly, the surface of water can also act like a mirror and change the path of light and that is why we see the reflection of trees or building in water.

Reflection of tree in water

Image of an object

When we see an identical object inside a shiny object like a mirror, it is called an image of that object.

Two types of images are formed

(i) **Real image** It is an image which can be obtained on a screen, e.g. the image formed on a cinema screen.

(ii) **Virtual image** It is an image which cannot be obtained on a screen, e.g. image formed by a plane mirror.

It is not possible to form a virtual image on the screen because light rays actually **do not pass the screen** or cannot be received on a screen.

Plane Mirror

A mirror with a flat reflective surface is called a plane mirror. Reflection of an object in a plane mirror is known as the image of the object.

Characteristics of Image Formed by a Plane Mirror

(i) Image formed by a plane mirror is always behind the mirror, i.e. **virtual image**.

(ii) Image formed by a plane mirror is always upright, i.e. **erect**.

(iii) Image formed by a plane mirror is of the s**ame size as the object**.

(iv) Image formed by a plane mirror is **laterally inverted**, i.e left appears to be on the right and *vice-versa*.

(v) Image formed by a plane mirror is **as far behind the mirror as the object is in front of it.**

Side Inversion (Right ⇌ Left)

The phenomena of reversing the sides of an image w.r.t. object is called **lateral inversion**. This means that the right side of a body becomes the left side of the image while the left side of a body becomes the right side of the image.

For example, the word AMBULANCE is written as ƎƆИA⅃UBMA. When a driver of a vehicle, ahead of an ambulance looks in his/her rear view mirror, then he/she can read AMBULANCE written on it and give way to it.

Try These 11.1

1. **An image formed by a mirror is virtual and of same size. Which mirror is it?**
2. **A image is formed behind the mirror. Which type of image is it ?**
3. **A boy is observing his image in a plane mirror. The distance between the mirror and his image is 4 m, then what will be the distance between the boy and his image ?**

11.3 Spherical Mirrors

The mirrors which have a curved reflecting surface are known as **spherical mirrors**. e.g. A shining surface of spoon, cosmetic mirror, shaving mirror, side-view mirror in a car, etc.

Spherical mirrors are of two types:

1. Concave Mirror

A spherical mirror where the reflecting surface is on the inner side of the curved shape is called **concave mirror**. e.g. Shaving mirror.

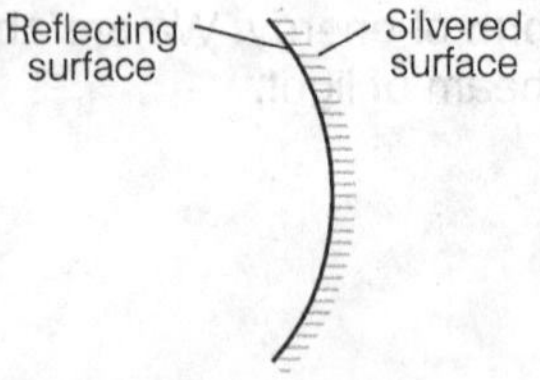

Concave mirror

Image Formed by a Concave Mirror

- **If the object is far away from the mirror**, the image formed is **real, inverted** (opposite side up as the object) and **diminished** (smaller than the object).
- **If the object is very close from the mirror,** the image formed is **virtual, erect** (same side up as the object) and **enlarged** (larger than the object).

Uses of Concave Mirrors

- Concave mirrors are used by dentist to see the large image of teeth.
- Concave mirrors are used as reflectors in torches, headlights of vehicles and searchlights, etc., to get a strong and straight beam of light.
- Concave mirrors are used as shaving mirrors to see a large image of face.

(a) A dentist examining a patient

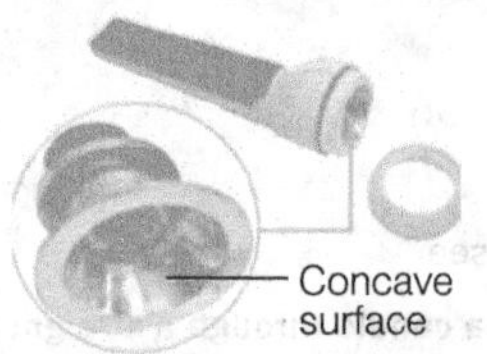

(b) Reflector of a torch

2. Convex Mirror

A spherical mirror where the reflecting surface is on the outer side of the curved shape is called **convex mirror**. e.g. Rear-mirror of a car.

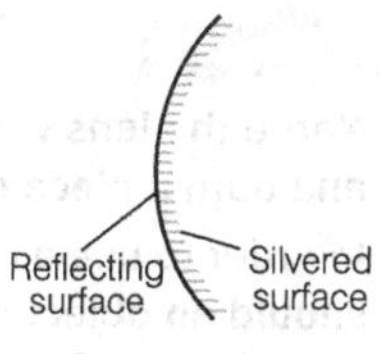

Convex mirror

A shining steel spoon represents both a convex mirror as well as concave mirror

As the front side (or inner side) of a spoon is bent inward, so the front side of a shining spoon represents a concave mirror, while the back side (or outer side) of a spoon is bulging outward, so the back side of a shining spoon represents a convex mirror as shown in figure.

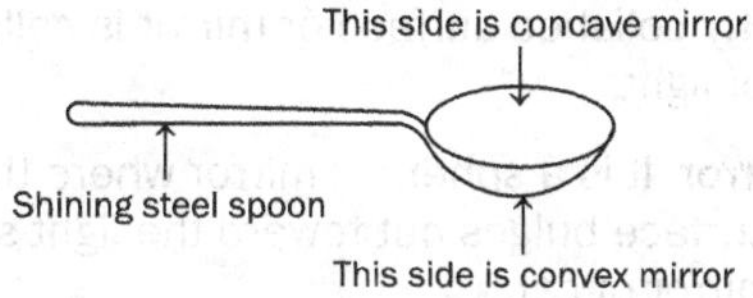

Image Formed by Convex Mirror

A convex mirror forms an image which is always **virtual , erect, diminished than the object.**

Uses of Convex Mirrors

- To see the wide area of traffic at the rear side or backside on the road, convex mirrors are used as rear view mirrors or side view mirrors in vehicles such as cars, scooters, buses, etc.

Convex mirror as side view mirror

- Big convex mirrors are used as shop security mirrors.

Try These 11.2

1. **Which type of mirror has its reflecting surface on the inner side of the curved shape?**
2. **For which position of the object, does a concave mirror produce a virtual, erect and magnified image?**
3. **What type of mirror is the bulged out and inner surface of a shining steel spoon?**

11.4 Spherical Lens

A transparent glass, which has two curved surfaces is called a spherical lens. There are two types of lens

1. Convex Lens

A spherical lens which is thicker at the centre and thinner at the edges is known as **convex lens**. e.g. Magnifying glass, microscopes.

Convex lens

Image Formed by a Convex Lens

- **When an object is placed far away from the lens**, the image will be **real, inverted** and **diminished** than the object.
- **When an object is placed very close to the lens**, the image will be **virtual, erect** and **enlarged** than the object.

Uses of Convex Lens

It is used to make magnifying glass, spectacles, cameras, microscopes, telescopes and binoculars.

Magnifying glass

Microscope

2. Concave Lens

A spherical lens which is thinner at the centre than at the edges is called **concave lens**. e.g. peep-holes in the door, spectacles etc.

Concave lens

Image Formed by a Concave Lens

A concave lens always forms virtual, erect and diminished image of the object.

SCIENCE INSIGHT Convex lens is also known as **converging lens** because when parallel light rays passes through it, then all the rays converge to a single point. Whereas, concave lens diverges the rays of light, when it passes through the lens. So, concave lens is also known as **diverging lens.**

Uses of Concave Lens

Concave lens is used to prepare certain kind of spectacles, eye hole in the door to see the person standing outside.

Spy hole in doors

Flashlights

11.5 Sunlight : White or Coloured

We might have noticed that a rainbow which is usually appears after the rain when the sun is low in the sky. All the colours of a rainbow come from sunlight. This shows that **sunlight consists of seven different colours. i.e. Red, Orange, Yellow, Green, Blue, Indigo and Violet.**

When sunlight falls on the raindrops, then it splits into seven different colours which is also known as VIBGYOR.

We might also have seen that when we blow soap bubbles, they appear colourful. Similarly when we allow the white light to pass through a glass prism, then it splits to form a band of seven different colours as similar to rainbow.

On the basis of these observations, we can say that sunlight or white light is a mixture of different colours.

A rainbow

A CD placed in sun

Note The phenomenon of splitting of white light into seven colours is known as **dispersion of light.**

Try These 11.3

1. **Name the lens which can converge sun's rays to a point and burn a piece of paper.**
2. **In order to use a convex lens as a magnifying glass, where should an object be placed ?**
3. **Name the type of lens that can form real and inverted images as well as virtual and erect images of an object.**
4. **In which direction, rainbow is formed with respect to the sun?**

Science Glossary

Reflection of light The phenomenon of change in the direction of light or the bouncing back of light when it falls on shiny polished surface or mirror is called reflection of light.

Convex mirror It is a spherical mirror where the reflective surface bulges out toward the light source. e.g. Rear-mirror of car.

Concave mirror It is a spherical mirror where the reflecting surface is on the inner side of curved shape. e.g. Shaving mirror.

Real image A real image is one that can be formed on a screen.

Virtual image A virtual image is one that cannot formed on the screen.

Convex lens A spherical lens which is thicker at the centre and thinner at the edges is called convex lens.

Concave lens A spherical lens which is thinner at the centre and thicker at the edge is called concave lens.

Rainbow An arc of seven colours that sometimes appears in the sky when the sun shines through rain is called rainbow.

Let's Investigate

ACTIVITY 1 (Page 124, 125)

Aim To show the reflection of light by a plane mirror.

Material Required A torch, a plane mirror, black chart papers.

Procedure

1. Take a black chart paper, make three long and narrow slits in it.
2. Try to cover the glass of the torch with this black chart paper having long and narrow slits.
3. Spread another black chart paper on a drawing board and fix a rectangular plane mirror strip vertically on this chart papers as shown in figure.
4. Switch ON the torch and place it in such a way that all the three rays of light coming from the three slits fall on the plane mirror at an angle to its surface.

Reflection of light from a mirror

Conclusion We can see that the plane mirror changes the direction of the three rays of light falling on it.

Viva Questions

1. Can the mirror change the direction of light falling on it ?
2. Is reflection possible, if light rays fall on unpolished surface?

ACTIVITY 2 (Page 125)

Aim To observe the characteristics of image formed by a plane mirror.

Material Required A candle, a plane mirror, a screen.

Procedure

1. Put a lighted candle in front of plane mirror. We can observe that the flame of the candle appears as if an identical candle is placed behind the mirror.
2. Now, move the candle to a different position in front of mirror. We will observe that image formed is always erect and of the same size as the object.
3. Now, place a screen in front or behind the mirror, we will observe that image of the candle cannot be obtained on the screen. Image formed is virtual.

Image of a candle in a plane mirror

Conclusion We have concluded that image formed by a plane mirror is always virtual, erect and of the same size as the object.

Viva Questions

1. What do you mean, when we say that an image is formed behind the mirror?
2. Is it possible to form a diminished image by plane mirror?

ACTIVITY 3 (Page 126)

Aim To verify that the image formed by a plane mirror is at the same distance behind the mirror as the object is in front of it.

Material Required A chess board, a plane mirror, a sharpner.

Procedure

1. Take a chess board and fix a plane mirror vertically on line.
2. Place a sharpner at the boundary of the third square counting from the mirror and note the position of the image.
3. Now, shift the sharpner to the boundary of the fourth square and again note the position of the image.

Locating image in a plane mirror

4. Try to find the relation between the distance of the image from the mirror and that of the object in front of it.

Conclusion We have concluded that the image is at the same distance behind the mirror as the object is in front of it.

Viva Questions

1. Which thing can be used in place of chess ?
2. Can we form real image with the help of plane mirror?

ACTIVITY 4 (Page 127)

Aim To show that image formed by plane mirror is laterally inverted.

Material Required A plane mirror

Procedure

1. Firstly, stand in front of a plane mirror and look at your image in mirror.
2. Now, raise your left hand and observe carefully.
3. Now, touch your right ear. You will observe that the right appears left and *vice-versa*.
4. Now, write down your name on a paper and hold it in front of paper. You will find that image is laterally inverted.

Left hand appears on the right side in the image

Conclusion We have concluded that only sides of an image are interchanged while the image does not appear upside down.

Viva Questions

1. What does it mean, when you say that a mirror interchanges the side of an image ?
2. Which hand does your image raise, if you raise your right hand in front of mirror?

ACTIVITY 5 (Page 128)

Aim To show the formation of an image by the inner side or outer side of a spoon.

Material Required A steel spoon

Procedure

1. Firstly, take a stainless steel spoon.
2. Bring the outer side of the spoon near your face. You will find that image is erect and diminished than our face.
3. Now, bring the inner side of the spoon very close to your face. You will find that our image is erect and enlarged in size. If you increase the distance of the spoon from your face, you will notice that your image is inverted.

Image from the inner side of a spoon

Image from the outer side of a spoon

Conclusion We have concluded that the outer side of a spoon behaves like a convex mirror and inner side of a spoon behave like a concave mirror.

Viva Questions

1. Which part of spoon behaves as a convex mirror?
2. What is the nature of image, if object is very close to concave mirror ?

ACTIVITY 6 (Page 129)

Aim To show that a concave mirror converges the light rays of the sun.

Material Required A paper sheet, a concave mirror.

Procedure

1. Take a concave mirror and hold it facing the sun, so that sun's rays fall on it.
2. Hold a sheet of paper in the other hand and try to get the light rays reflected by concave mirror on the sheet of paper.
3. Now, adjust the distance of paper from concave mirror until we get a sharp and bright spot of light on paper.
4. Hold the concave mirror and paper sheet in this position for few minutes. You will notice that after sometimes, the paper starts burning at that spot.

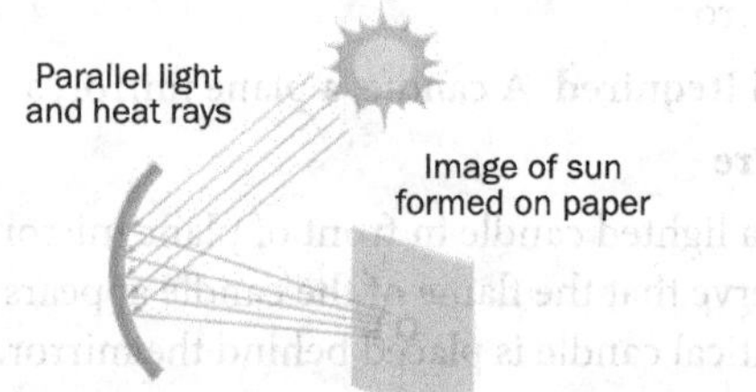

A concave mirror forms a real image of the sun

Conclusion We have concluded that a concave mirror converges the light rays and when an object is placed at a far off distance from it, then the image formed by concave mirror is real, inverted and highly diminished.

Viva Questions

1. Can we burn a paper sheet with the light of a bulb ?
2. What is the another name of a concave mirror ?

ACTIVITY 7 (Page 129, 130)

Aim To observe the image formed by a concave mirror in different conditions.

Material Required A candle, a screen, a concave mirror.

Procedure

1. Place a concave mirror in line with candle at a large distance away in a dark room.
2. Now, place a screen between candle and a mirror in such a way that it does not block the path of light rays coming out from candle.
3. Move the screen till a sharp image of flame is obtained, we will find that image is real and of same size.
4. Now, move the screen away from the mirror. You will observe that at a certain distance, the image of candle will be real, inverted and diminished on the screen.
5. Now, move the mirror closer to the candle. You will observe that the image of the candle disappears from the screen. This shows that when an object is placed close to the concave mirror, the image formed is virtual, erect and enlarged than the object.

Real image

Virtual image

Conclusion We have concluded that concave mirror can show both real and virtual images.

Viva Questions

1. What are the uses of concave mirror ?
2. Can we obtain the same size of image as that of object size from a concave mirror?

ACTIVITY 8 (Page 131)

Aim To observe that the image formed by a convex mirror is always virtual, erect and diminished than the object.

Material Required A candle, a screen, a convex mirror.

Procedure

1. Take a convex mirror, fix it on a stand and keep it on a table.
2. Now, put a screen in front of the convex mirror in such a way that it should not obstruct the path of light rays coming from the candle flame and falling on the convex mirror.
3. Move the screen towards or away from the mirror and try to obtain the image of candle flame on the screen.

   We will find that, we cannot form the image of candle flame on the screen.

Image formed by a convex mirror

Conclusion We have concluded that we cannot obtain a real image by convex mirror, it forms an image which is always virtual, erect and diminished than the object.

Viva Questions

1. What is the another name of a convex mirror ?
2. Can we obtain the image of an object on the screen by convex mirror?

ACTIVITY 9 (Page 133)

Aim To show that a convex lens converges the light rays of the sun.

Material Required A convex lens, A paper sheet.

Procedure

1. Hold a convex lens above a piece of paper such that sun rays passes through it.
2. Now, focus the sun rays at one point on the paper sheet through the lens. You will find a bright spot on the paper.
3. Hold the convex lens and paper sheet in this position for few minutes. You will notice that after sometimes, the paper starts burning at that spot.

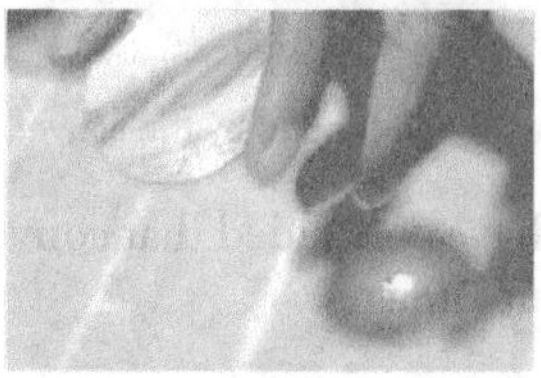

Real image of the sun by a convex lens

Conclusion We have concluded that a convex lens converges the light rays of the sun on the paper that's why paper starts burning.

Viva Questions

1. Is it true that convex lens is also known as converging lens?
2. Write any two examples where we use convex lens.

ACTIVITY 10 (Page 133)

Aim To observe the image formed by a convex lens in different conditions.

Material Required A candle, a screen, a convex lens.

Procedure

1. Place a convex lens in line with candle at a large distance away in a dark room.
2. Now, place a screen between candle and a lens in such a way that it does not block the path of light ray comes out from candle.
3. Now, move the screen away from the lens. You will observe that at a certain distance, the image of candle will be inverted and diminished on the screen.
4. Now, move the lens closer to the candle. You will observe that the image of the candle disappears from the screen. This shows that when an object is placed close to the convex lens, the image formed is virtual, erect and enlarged than the object.

(a) (b)

Image by a convex lens of object placed at different distance from it

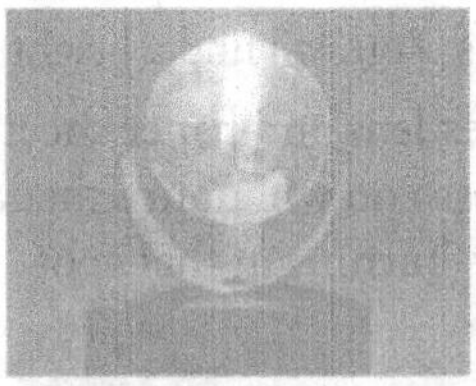

Virtual image formed by the convex lens

Conclusion We have concluded that convex lens can show both real and virtual images.

Viva Questions

1. Can we obtain the same size of image as that of object size by a convex lens ?
2. What is the main difference between real and virtual image?

ACTIVITY 11 (Page 135)

Aim To show that sunlight consists of seven colours.

Material Required A glass prism, white sheet of paper.

Procedure

1. Firstly, take a glass prism and place it in a dark room.
2. Now, allow a narrow beam of sunlight to fall on face of the prism.
3. Now, let the light coming out from the other face of the prism fall on a white sheet of paper. You will find that the sunlight splits into seven different colours.

A prism splits a beam of sunlight into seven colours

Conclusion We have concluded that sunlight or white light consists of seven different colours.

Viva Questions

1. What are the seven colours in a white light ?
2. Do you see colours similar to those in a rainbow ?

ACTIVITY 12 (Page 136)

Aim To show that mixing of the seven colours gives us white light.

Material Required A pencil, a circular disc with seven rainbow colours.

Procedure

1. Take a circular disc with seven rainbow colours divided into equal segments.
2. Make a small hole at the centre of disc and fix the pencil in it, so disc can rotate freely.
3. When you rotate the disc speedly, you will observe that the disc appears to be white.

A disc with seven colours It appears white on rotating

Conclusion We have concluded that all the seven colours of the disc, mix together due to the rotation and give us white light.

Viva Questions

1. What are the seven colours in a rainbow ?
2. Can you observe mixing of colours in dark room ?

Mind Map

LIGHT

Mirror

Plane Mirror

- Mirror with flat reflective surface

Characteristics of image formed by it

→ Virtual image
→ Erect
→ Same size as the object
→ Laterally inverted (left appears to be on the right and *vice-versa*)
→ Image is formed behind the mirror as the object is in front of it

Spherical Mirror

- Mirror which have a curved reflecting surface.

Types of Mirror

Concave Mirror

- Reflecting surface is on the inner side of the curved shape.

Image formed by it

→ Image is real, inverted and diminished, when object is far away from mirror.
→ Image is virtual, erect and enlarged, when object is very close from mirror.

Uses

→ Used by dentist
→ Used as a shaving mirror
→ Used as reflectors in torches, search light, etc.

Convex Mirror

- Reflecting surface is on the outer side of the curved shape.

Image formed by it

→ Always virtual
→ Erect
→ Diminished than the object

Uses

→ Used as a rear view mirror
→ Used in sunglasses

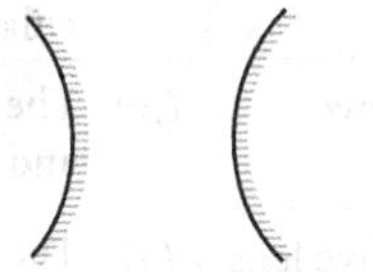

Image

When we see an identical object inside a shiny object like a mirror, it is called image of that object.

Types of image

Real Image

Image which can be obtained on screen

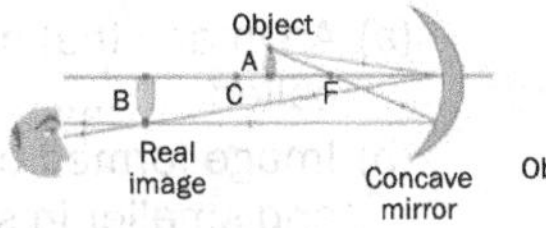

Virtual Image

Image which cannot be obtained on screen

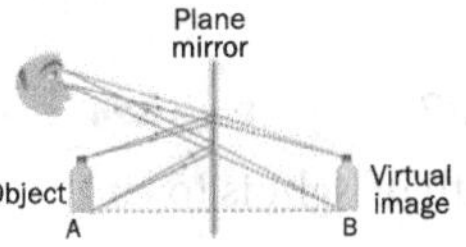

Reflection of Light

Bouncing back of light when it falls on a shiny and polished surface.

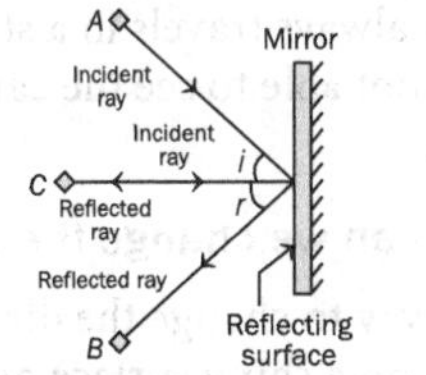

Light Beam

Beam of light is defined as a group of light rays coming out from a source.

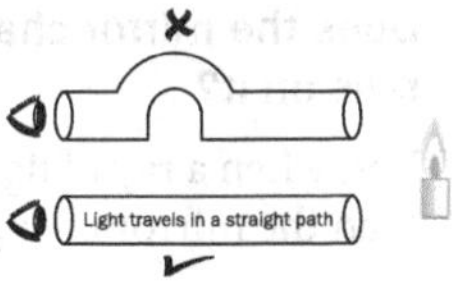

Sunlight

- Sunlight or white light is the mixture of seven different colours.
- Seven colours are

V Violet	I Indigo
B Blue	G Green
Y Yellow	O Orange
R Red	

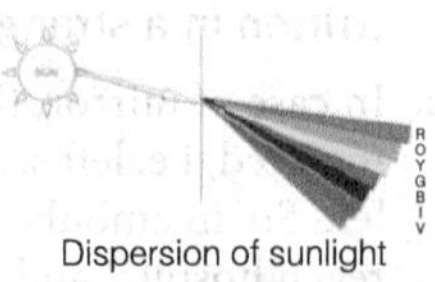

Dispersion of sunlight

Spherical Lens

- Lens with two curved surface that causes light rays to converge or diverge.

Types of Lens

Concave lens

- Spherical lens which is thinner at the centre than at the edges.

Image formed by it

→ Always forms virtual, erect and diminished than the object.

Uses

→ Used in spectacles.
→ Used in eye hole in doors.

Convex lens

- Spherical lens which is thicker at the centre and thinner at the edges.

Image formed by it

→ Image is real, inverted diminished, when object placed far away from it.
→ Image is virtual, erect and magnified, when object placed closed to it.

Uses

→ Used to make magnifying glass
→ Used in microscopes, cameras.

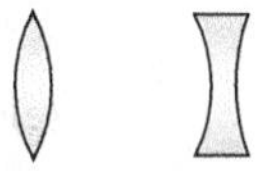

NCERT FOLDER

Complete Explanations of all NCERT's Questions

Intext Questions

Q.1 Why was Boojho not able to see the candle flame through a bent pipe? Page 124

Ans. Light always travels in a straight path. That's why, he does not able to see the candle flame through a bent pipe.

Q.2 How can we change the path of light? Page 124

Ans. The way to change the direction or path of light is to let it fall on a shiny surface or mirror.

Q.3 What happens when light falls on a polished or shiny surface ? Page 124

Ans. When light falls on a polished or shiny surface like mirror, then it reflects and change the path of light.

Q.4 Does the mirror change the direction of light that falls on it? Page 125

Ans. Yes, when a ray of light is incident on the mirror surface, then the mirror changes the direction of light.

Q.5 The image is of the same size as object whether the mirror is small or large. Why? Page 126

Ans. The plane mirror always forms an erect and same size image as of object size. The properties and characteristics of the mirror does not depend on the size of mirror.

Q.6 Boojho saw an ambulance on the road. He was surprised to see the word 'AMBULANCE' in front was written in a strange manner. Why ? Page 127

Ans. In case of mirror, the image formed by it is laterally inverted, i.e. left seems to be right and right seems to be left. So, in ambulance there is emergency for patients to reach hospital and by viewing in rear mirror, it can be easily identified and everyone can give him a way.

Q.7 A shiny and polished bell forms an image which is erect and diminished. Can you recognise the type of the mirror? Page 131

Ans. Convex mirror always forms an erect and diminished image of an object.

Q.8 How many colours are present in a rainbow? Page 135

Ans. Seven

Q.9 Does the white light consist of seven colours? Page 135

Ans. Yes, white light splits into seven colours when it passes through a prism. So, we can say that white light consist of seven colours.

Exercise

1. Fill in the Blanks

(a) An image that cannot be obtained on a screen is called ....

(b) Image formed by a convex .... is always virtual and smaller in size.

(c) An image formed by a .... mirror is always of the same size as that of the object.

(d) An image which can be obtained on a screen is called a .... image.

(e) An image formed by a concave .... cannot be obtained on a screen.

Ans. (a) virtual image (b) mirror (c) plane (d) real (e) lens

2. Mark T if the statement is true and F if it is false.

(a) We can obtain an enlarged and erect image by a convex mirror.

(b) A concave lens always form a virtual image.

(c) We can obtain a real, enlarged and inverted image by a concave mirror.

(d) A real image cannot be obtained on a screen.

(e) A concave mirror always form a real image.

Ans. (a) F (b) T (c) T (d) F (e) F

3. Match the items given in Column I with one or more items of Column II.

Column I	Column II
(a) A plane mirror	(i) Used as a magnifying glass.
(b) A convex mirror	(ii) Can form image of objects spread over a large area.
(c) A convex lens	(iii) Used by dentists to see enlarged image of teeth.
(d) A concave mirror	(iv) The image is always inverted and magnified.
(e) A concave lens	(v) The image is erect and of the same size as the object.
	(vi) The image is erect and smaller in size than the object.

Ans. (a)–(v), (b)–(ii), (vi), (c)–(i), (d)–(iii), (e)–(iv)

4. State the characteristics of the image formed by a plane mirror.

Ans. Characteristics of the image formed by the plane mirror are

(i) It is virtual. (ii) It is erect.

(iii) It is same in size.

(iv) It is at same distance from the mirror as the distance of an object from the mirror.

5. Find out the letters of English alphabet or any other language known to you in which the image formed in a plane mirror appears exactly like the letter itself. Discuss your findings.

Ans. Image formed by the plane mirror shows lateral inversion, i.e. left seems to be right and *vice-versa*. In case of alphabetic letters A, H, I, M, O, T, U, V, W, X, Y show same image in the plane mirror.

6. What is a virtual image? Give one situation, where a virtual image is formed.

Ans. An image that cannot be obtained on a screen is called virtual image.
In case of plane mirror, virtual image is formed.

7. State two differences between a convex and a concave lens.

Ans. Difference between convex and concave lenses

Convex lens	Concave lens
It can form real and virtual images both.	It always form virtual image.
Image formed by convex lens can be enlarged or diminished depend upon the position of object.	Image formed by concave lens is always diminished.

8. Give two uses each of a convex and a concave mirror.

Ans. Uses of convex mirror

(i) It is used in side mirrors of vehicles.

(ii) It is used as shop security mirror.

Uses of concave mirror

(i) It is used in reflector of torch.

(ii) It is also used by dentists to see an enlarged image of the teeth.

9. Which type of mirror can form a real image?

Ans. A concave mirror can form a real image of an object.

10. Which type of lens forms always a virtual image?

Ans. A concave lens always forms a virtual image.

11. A virtual image larger than the object can be produced by a

(a) concave lens

(b) concave mirror

(c) convex mirror

(d) plane mirror

Ans. (b) Concave mirror can form real image and virtual image of larger size than the object.

12. David is observing his image in a plane mirror. The distance between the mirror and his image is 4 m. If he moves 1m towards the mirror, then the distance between David and his image will be

(a) 3 m (b) 5 m

(c) 6 m (d) 8 m

Ans. (c) As we know that in case of plane mirror, an image distance is equal to the object distance from the mirror. So, his image will be at $4-1=3$ m from mirror and distance between David and his image is 6m.

13. The rear view mirror of a car is a plane mirror. A driver is reversing his car at a speed of 2 m/s. The driver sees in his rear view mirror, the image of a truck parked behind his car. The speed at which the image of the truck appears to approach the driver will be

(a) 1 m/s (b) 2 m/s

(c) 4 m/s (d) 8 m/s

Ans. (b) The speed at which the image of the truck appears to approach the driver will be same as that the reverse speed of the car, i.e. 2 m/s.

REVIEW EXERCISE

Including Competency Based Questions

Part I

1. Which letter's image on a plane mirror will not be inverted sideways? CBSE Diksha, Competency Based Que.

(a) L (b) P

(c) M (d) B

2. A virtual image

(a) can be formed on the screen

(b) cannot be formed on the screen

(c) is formed only by a plane mirror

(d) is formed only by the convex mirror

3. An erect and enlarged image can be formed by

(a) only a convex mirror

(b) only a concave mirror

(c) only a plane mirror

(d) Both convex and concave mirrors

4. Which of the following can be used to form a real image? NCERT Exemplar

(a) Only concave mirror

(b) Only plane mirror

(c) Only convex mirror

(d) Both concave and convex mirrors

5. Boojho and Paheli were given one mirror each by their teacher. Boojho found his image to be erect and of the same size, whereas Paheli found her image erect and smaller in size. This means that the mirrors of Boojho and Paheli respectively are

(a) plane mirror and concave mirror

(b) concave mirror and convex mirror

(c) plane mirror and convex mirror

(d) convex mirror and plane mirror

6. If an object is placed at a distance of 0.5 m in front of a plane mirror, the distance between the object and the image formed by the mirror will be NCERT Exemplar

(a) 2 m (b) 1 m

(c) 0.5 m (d) 0.25 m

7. Which of the following always diverge light rays?

(a) Convex mirror and plane mirror

(b) Concave lens and convex mirror

(c) Concave mirror and convex lens

(d) Concave lens and convex mirror

8. Which of the following would you prefer to use while reading small letters found in a dictionary?

(a) A convex lens (b) A convex mirror

(c) A concave lens (d) Either (a) or (b)

9. You are provided with a concave mirror, a convex mirror, a concave lens and a convex lens. To obtain an enlarged image of an object, you can use either NCERT Exemplar

(a) concave mirror or convex mirror

(b) concave mirror or convex lens

(c) concave mirror or concave lens

(d) concave lens or convex lens

10. You are provided with a convex mirror, a concave mirror, a convex lens and a concave lens. You can get an inverted image from Competency Based Que.

(a) both concave lens and convex lens

(b) both concave mirror and convex mirror

(c) both concave mirror and convex lens

(d) both convex mirror and concave lens

11. An image formed by a lens is erect, such an image could be formed by

(a) convex lens provided the image is smaller than object

(b) concave lens provided the image is smaller than object

(c) concave lens provided the image is larger than object

(d) concave lens provided the image is of the same size

12. The colour of light which is deviated the least by prism in the spectrum of white light is

(a) violet (b) green

(c) yellow (d) red

13. A rainbow can be seen in the sky

(a) when the sun is in front of you

(b) when the sun is behind you

(c) when the sun is overhead

(d) only at the time of sunrise

14. Alice looks inside a round steel bowl very closely. She sees her image on the inside of the bowl. Competency Based Que.

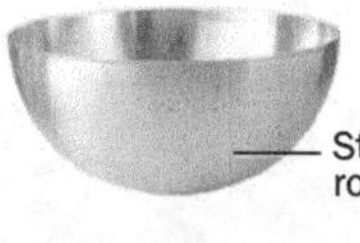

What type of image is formed inside the bowl ?

(a) Real and small (b) Virtual and small

(c) Real and enlarged (d) Virtual and enlarged

Answers

1. (c)	2. (b)	3. (b)	4. (a)
5. (c)	6. (b)	7. (b)	8. (a)
9. (b)	10. (c)	11. (b)	12. (d)
13. (b)	14. (d)		

Fill in the Blanks

1. Changing of left side of an object to right side of image is called ....
2. The inner surface of a steel spoon acts as a .... mirror. **NCERT Exemplar**
3. The outer surface of a flat steel plate acts as a .... mirror.
4. The outer shining surface of a round bottom steel bowl acts as a .... mirror.
5. The inner surface of the reflector of a torch acts as a .... mirror.
6. Convex lenses are .... in the middle than at the edges whereas concave lenses are .... in the middle than at the edges.
7. The image formed by a .... lens is always virtual. **CBSE Question Bank**

Answers

1. lateral inversion
2. concave
3. plane
4. convex
5. concave
6. thicker, thinner
7. concave

True/False

1. An object can be seen only if it emits light. **NCERT Exemplar**
2. The sides of an object and its image formed by a concave mirror are always interchanged. **NCERT Exemplar**
3. The mirror which can form a magnified image of an object is both convex and concave mirrors.
4. In a convex spherical mirror, reflection of light takes place at a bent in surface.
5. A convex lens always produces a real image.
6. A concave lens can be used to produce an enlarged and erect image.

Answer

1. False
2. True
3. False
4. False
5. False
6. False

Match the Columns

1. Match the Column I with Column II.

Column I	Column II
(a) Erect image	(i) Cannot be formed on the screen
(b) Diminished image	(ii) Upside down image
(c) Virtual image	(iii) Smaller than the object
(d) Inverted image	(iv) Upright image
(e) Real image	(v) Formed on the screen

Answer

1. (a)-(iv), (b)-(iii), (c)-(i), (d)-(ii), (e)-(v)

Assertion-Reason Questions

The following questions consist of two statements Assertion (A) and Reason (R). Answer these questions by selecting the appropriate option given below

(a) Both A and R are true and R is the correct explanation of A.
(b) Both A and R are true but R is not the correct explanation of A.
(c) A is true but R is false.
(d) A is false but R is true.

1. **Assertion** (A) Light cannot visible through a bent rubber pipe.
   Reason (R) Light travels in a straight path.
2. **Assertion** (A) A plane mirror forms a virtual and erect image.
   Reason (R) The size of image is diminished than the size of object in plane mirror.
3. **Assertion** (A) Concave mirrors are used as a shaving mirror in barber shop.
   Reason (R) Concave mirror forms enlarged image of the object when it is placed very close to the object.
4. **Assertion** (A) A white light consists of seven different colours.
   Reason (R) When a white light passes through a prism, it splits into seven colours.

Answers

1. (b) Light travels in a straight line, so it cannot be visible through a bent pipe.
2. (c) A plane mirror forms a virtual, erect and same size image as that of object.
3. (a) Concave mirror forms enlarged image of the object when it is placed very close to the object that's why it is used as a shaving mirror or by dentist.
4. (a) A white light consists of seven different colours. That's why, it splits into seven colours when it passes through a prism.

Case Based Question

1. Ayesha keeps a toy in front of a plane mirror, then she looks at the mirror to see the image of the toy. Competency Based Que., CBSE Diksha

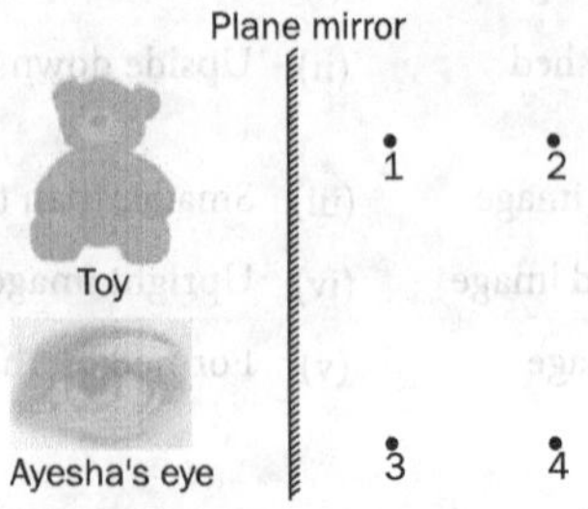

(i) At which point will the image of the toy be formed in the mirror ?
(a) Point 1
(b) Point 2
(c) Point 3
(d) Point 4

(ii) What type of image is formed in the mirror ?
(a) Real and upright
(b) Virtual and upright
(c) Real and upside down
(d) Virtual and upside down

Answer

1. (i) (a), (ii) (b)

Part II

Very Short Answer Type Questions

1. Give the form of energy that produces the sensation of vision.

Ans. Light energy is the form of energy which produces the sensation of vision.

2. Briefly mention what makes things visible to us.

Ans. When a light ray after getting reflected by an object falls on our eyes, it allows us to see things around us.

3. Briefly tell that how many reflected rays can be obtained from a single incident ray in respect of a plane mirror?

Ans. For a single incident ray, there will be only one reflected ray that can be obtained in respect of a plane mirror.

4. Can you get a real image at any distance of the object from the convex mirror?

Ans. No, we cannot get a real image for any position of an object from the convex mirror because convex mirror always forms virtual, erect and diminished image in spite of the position of object.

5. Name the phenomenon that is involved in the formation of image of an object by a concave mirror.

Ans. Reflection of light is the phenomenon which is involved in the formation of image of an object by a concave mirror.

6. As we know that an image is formed by the actual intersection of rays and can be obtained on the screen. So, state whether it is real or virtual image.

Ans. After the actual intersection of rays, the image obtained on the screen is always real image.

7. What type of mirror is used as a side mirror in a scooter? Why is this type of mirror chosen? NCERT Exemplar

Ans. Convex mirror is used as a side mirror in a scooter because it can form images of objects spread over a larger area.

So, this helps the driver to view the traffic over a large area behind them.

8. Mention the name of lens which can converge the sun's rays to a point and burn a hole in the piece of paper.

Ans. Convex lens is a lens which can converge the sun's rays to a point and burn a hole in the piece of paper.

9. An erect and enlarged image of an object is formed on a screen. Explain how this could be possible? NCERT Exemplar

Ans. An erect and enlarged image of an object is formed only by the concave mirror or convex lens when it is placed very close to the object.

10. Consider if one half of a convex lens is covered with a black paper, then state whether this lens produces a complete image of the object.

Ans. If one half of a convex lens is covered with a black paper, then also, the convex lens will produce the complete image of the object.

11. The given figures show the path of light through lenses of two different types represented by rectangular boxes *A* and *B*. What is the nature of lenses *A* and *B* ? Competency Based Que.

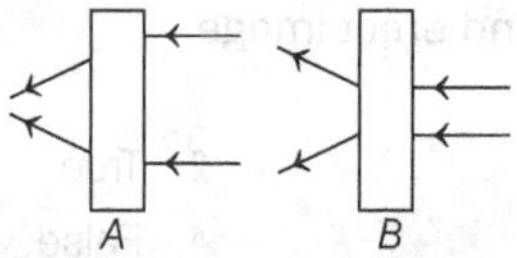

Ans. In first case light rays are converging towards a point, so the lens *A* will be convex and in case of lens *B*, light rays diverge or spread out. So, the lens will be concave lens.

12. The image formed by a lens is always virtual, erect and smaller in size for an object kept at different positions in front of it. Identify the nature of the lens. **NCERT Exemplar**

Ans. Such types of lenses which always form virtual, erect and smaller image in spite of the different positions of an object are called concave lens.

13. State in brief what we can demonstrate by rotating Newton's colour disc very fastly.

Ans. By rotating Newton's colour disc, we can demonstrate that when seven colours are mixed together, then a white colour is formed.

Short Answer Type Questions

1. We need a shiny surface for reflection. Explain why?

Ans. The extent of reflection depends upon the shine and smoothness of the surface. Greater the shining and smoothness of the surface, greater will be the reflection. So, this is the reason why we require a shiny surface for reflection.

2. Mention the type of image
(i) which can be formed on the screen.
(i) which cannot be formed on the screen.

Ans. (i) The image which can be formed on the screen is real image.
(ii) The image which cannot be formed on the screen is virtual image.

3. Mention any two letters of English alphabet whose image formed in a plane mirror appears exactly similar to the letters.

Ans. Image formed by the plane mirror shows lateral inversion, i.e. left seems to right or *vice-versa.* But in the case of alphabets A and H, these letters show the same image in the plane mirror.

4. Explain the term lateral inversion.

Ans. An image is formed by the mirror, then the left side of image is object's right side and right side of image is object's left side. This process of change in the sides of the image w.r.t. the object is known as lateral inversion.

5. Assume, a person is standing in front of a plane mirror. The distance between the mirror and his image is 6 m. If the person moves 2 m towards the plane mirror, what would be the distance between the person and his image?

Ans. The image is 6 m away from the plane mirror. It means that the object is also 6 m away from the mirror.

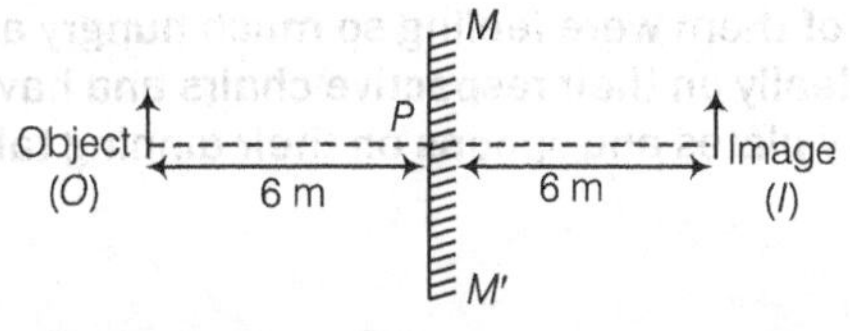

[Because $OP = PI$]

When the person moves 2 m towards the plane mirror, then the distance between the person and the plane mirror will be equal to (6 m – 2 m) = 4 m, this means that distance between the image and the mirror will be 4 m.

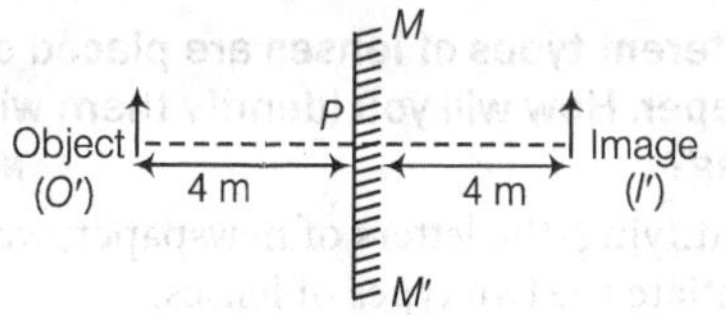

The distance between the person and his image
$= PO' + PI' = 4 + 4 = 8\text{m}$

6. The side mirror of a scooter got broken. The mechanic replaced it with a plane mirror. Mention any inconvenience that the driver of the scooter will face while using it. **NCERT Exemplar**

Ans. As we know that the side mirror of a scooter must be of convex mirror, so that we can view a wide range of traffic spread over a large area. But if plane mirror is used, we are not able to see large area of traffic which may be difficult for driving vehicle and can cause accident.

7. Differentiate between a plane mirror, concave mirror and a convex mirror without touching them.

Ans. These mirrors can be differentiated by bringing our face close to each mirror turn-by-turn.

A plane mirror will produce an image of the same size as our face, a concave mirror will produce a magnified image and a convex mirror will produce a diminished image and our face will look much smaller than real face.

8. The concave reflecting surface of a torch got rusted. What effect would this have on the beam of light from the torch? **NCERT Exemplar**

Ans. If the reflecting surface of a torch got rusted, it will produce diffused light with lower intensity and the objects are not clearly visible in this diffused and lower intensity of light.

9. A shopkeeper wanted to fix a mirror which will give a maximum view of his shop. What type of mirror should he use? Give reason. **Competency Based Que.**

Ans. If a shopkeeper wanted to fix a mirror which will give him maximum view of his shop, he should use convex mirror.

In case of convex mirror, it will give a wider field of view, i.e. it can collect light from a large area spread over them.

10. Suppose we wish to obtain the real image of a distant tree. Explain two possible ways in which we can do it.

Ans. (i) In first case, we will use a concave mirror, as we know that concave mirror can form real image, i.e. image on screen. The image of distant tree will be at focus in case of concave mirror.

(ii) In second case, we can use a convex lens as it forms real image of a distant object at focus, i.e. Image of distant tree in case of convex lens will be formed at focus.

11. Two different types of lenses are placed on a sheet of newspaper. How will you identify them without touching? **NCERT Exemplar**

Ans. On identifying the letters of newspaper, we can differentiate the two types of lenses.

If image is large or magnified, then the lens is a convex lens and if the image is smaller or diminished in size for all the positions of object, then the lens is a concave lens.

12. The distance between an object and a convex lens is changing. It is noticed that the size of the image formed on a screen is decreasing. Is the object moving in a direction towards the lens or away from it?

Ans. In case of convex lens, when we move the object far away from the lens, the size of image decreases and ultimately, when object is at infinity, it will form a point image at focus.

13. State the correct sequence (1-7) of colours in the spectrum formed by the prisms *A* and *B* shown in the figure. **NCERT Exemplar**

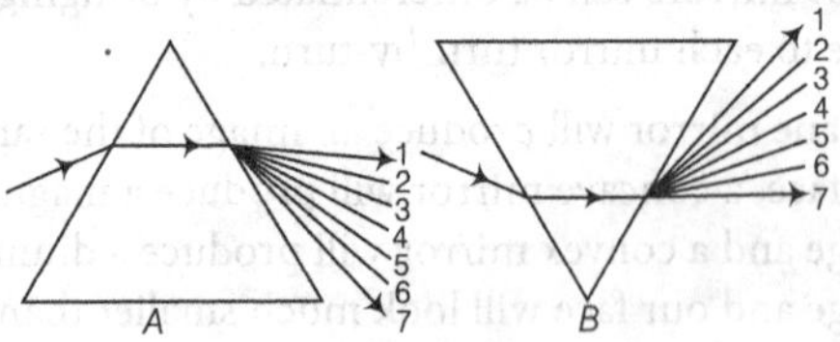

Ans. When white light is passed through a prism, it disperses into its seven constituent colours.

For *A*	For *B*
1. ⟶ Red	1. ⟶ Violet
2. ⟶ Orange	2. ⟶ Indigo
3. ⟶ Yellow	3. ⟶ Blue
4. ⟶ Green	4. ⟶ Green
5. ⟶ Blue	5. ⟶ Yellow
6. ⟶ Indigo	6. ⟶ Orange
7. ⟶ Violet	7. ⟶ Red

14. Boojho made light from a laser torch to fall on a prism. Will he be able to observe a band of seven colours? Explain with a reason. **NCERT Exemplar**

Ans. No, he will not observe band of seven colours because laser light consists of monochromatic light of single colour. But seven colours of bands are only observed, when a white light is passed through a prism and dispersion takes place.

15. Shreya spins a multicoloured wheel rapidly. **Competency Based Que.**

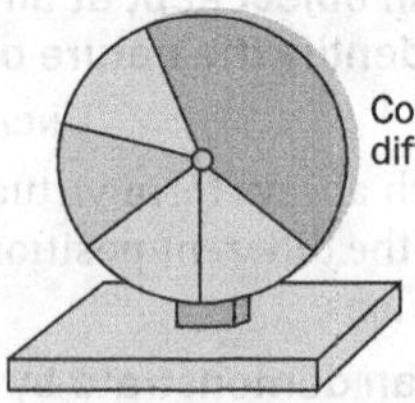

What colour will the rapidly spinning wheel appear to be?

Ans. A rapidly spinning multicolour wheel appears as white. This is because white colour is mixture of all the colour and when wheel spins with high speed, all colours get mixed and appear to be white.

Long Answer Type Questions

1. You are given three mirrors of different types. How will you identify each one of them?

Ans. We can identify the mirrors by forming image of an object.

(i) **Plane mirror** In case of plane mirror, image will be virtual, erect and of the same size as that of object.

(ii) **Concave mirror** In case of concave mirror, image may be real, virtual and magnified or diminished.

(iii) **Convex mirror** In case of convex mirror, image formed will always be virtual, erect and diminished.

2. Namit was driving a car and suddenly became aware of a loud sound coming from behind. He looked through his rear view mirror and saw an ambulance. He recalled reading that such emergency vehicles often have their name written in the mirror AMBULANCE or writing, i.e.ƎƆNA⅃UBMA
He quickly made way for the ambulance, murmuring a quick prayer for the speedy recovery of the patient inside the ambulance.

(i) Name the type of mirror which is used as a rear view mirror and why?

(ii) What values did Namit exhibit.

Ans. (i) Convex mirror is a mirror which are used as a rear view mirror. It is used to get a wide view of traffic behind.

(ii) The values exhibit by Namit here are courtesy concern for other, sympathy and knowledgeable person.

3. Last Sunday Girish's mother, Priyanka was preparing the dinner in her kitchen for Girish and his father. Both of them were feeling so much hungry and they sat ideally on their respective chairs and having empty plates and spoons on their dinning table. They

were shouting like a 5 years old child that they wanted the dinner so eagerly to fulfil their stomach. After sometime, Girish's mother served the cooked food to both of them and when Girish was just about to eat the rice with the help of spoon, he noticed that the spoon has such a shining surface that it reflected the light rays incident on it.

(i) Explain the importance of shining surface in the reflection of light.
(ii) Name the type of spherical mirror represented by the shining steel spoon.
(iii) Mention the values shown by Priyanka here towards her family. **Competency Based Que.**

Ans. (i) As we know that, the extent of reflection depends upon the shining of surface. So, greater the shining of the surface, more will be the reflection.
(ii) Both convex and concave mirrors are represented by the shining steel spoon.
(iii) The value shown by Priyanka here is concern and satisfaction that she gets after serving the cooked food for her son and her husband.

4. It was observed that when the distance between an object and a lens decreases, the size of the image increases. What is the nature of this lens? If you keep on decreasing the distance between the object and the lens, will you still able to obtain the image on the screen? Explain. **NCERT Exemplar**

Ans. On decreasing the distance between the object and lens, the size of the image increases hence the lens will be of convex type.

If the distance between object and lens is less than the focus of the lens, then it forms a virtual image and this image cannot be obtained on a screen but formed on the same side of the object.

5. One day, Ramesh's friends were performing their respective experiments given by their teacher. While sitting in the practical lab instead of performing experiment, Ramesh was playing with his meter scale. All of the sudden, he held the scale in his hand and started moving in front of tubelight, then he observed the seven colours of white light. After sometimes, he got scolded by his lab teacher for not performing the experiment.

(i) Give the name of phenomenon that leads to the formation of band of seven colours.
(ii) Name the constituent colours of white light.
(iii) Mention the values shown by Ramesh here.

Ans. (i) Dispersion of white light is the name of phenomenon which leads to the formation of band of seven colours.
(ii) There are seven constituent colours of white light. They are Violet, Indigo, Blue, Green, Yellow, Orange, Red, i.e. VIBGYOR.
(iii) Ramesh seems to be quite innovative with respect to the scientific methods and also very eager to learn science regarding phenomena.

Case Based Questions

1. The picture shows a glass bowl.

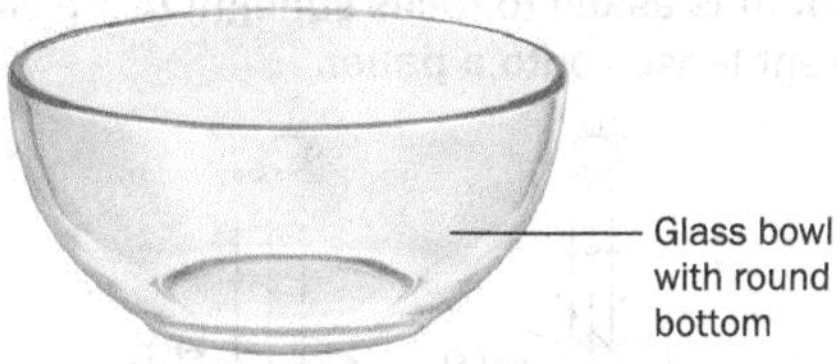

(i) What should be done to make the glass bowl act as a mirror?
(a) Fill the bowl completely with water
(b) Break the bowl into smaller pieces
(c) Wrap the bowl fully with a plastic sheet
(d) Cover the bowl's outer side with aluminium foil
(ii) Microscopes are used to view microorganisms. What type of lens is used in a microscope ?

2. Seema dropped a water droplet on a newspaper. She found that the letters are appearing larger through the droplet.

(i) Why are the letters appearing larger through the droplet ?
(ii) Which of these is true about the image formed by a concave lens ?

	Is this true about the image formed ?	Yes or No
(a)	It is real.	Yes/ No
(b)	It is erect.	Yes/ No
(c)	It is larger than the object	Yes/ No

Answers

1. (i) (a)
(ii) Convex lens
2. (i) This is because water droplets behave like a convex lens.
(ii) (a) No (b) Yes (c) No

Skill Based Questions as per NEP 2020

1. A student is asked to focus sunlight using two different lenses onto a paper.

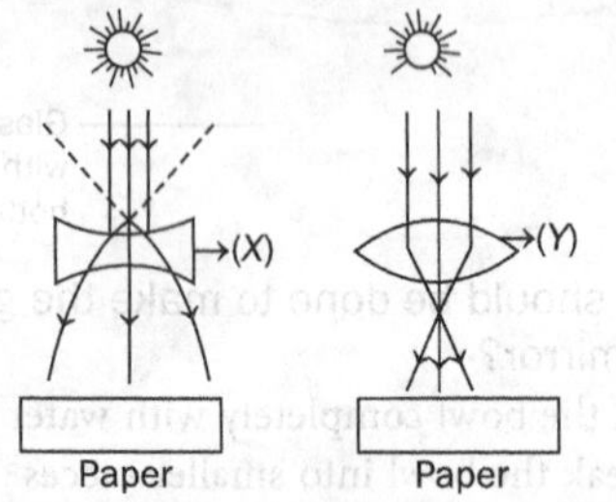

Observe the image carefully and answer the following questions. **Experimental Skill**

(i) State the name for the shape of lenses *X* and *Y*.

(ii) Which of these two lenses can be used to magnify images ?

(iii) Explain the changes that happen to the paper kept under both the lenses.

(iv) Differentiate between convex and concave lenses.

2. Label *A* denotes the lens used in microscope to see objects. Which type of lenses are used in the microscope which helps to see the microbes? **Knowledge Skill**

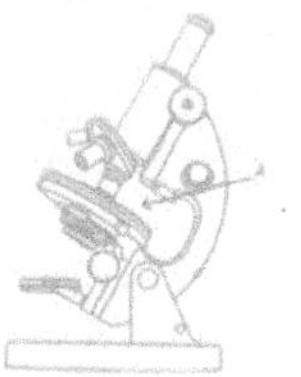

3. When white light is reflected from the surface of a Compact Disc (CD), many colours are seen. When we blow soap bubbles, they appear colourful. The disc painted with seven colours of the spectrum is called Newton's disc. **Thinking Skill**

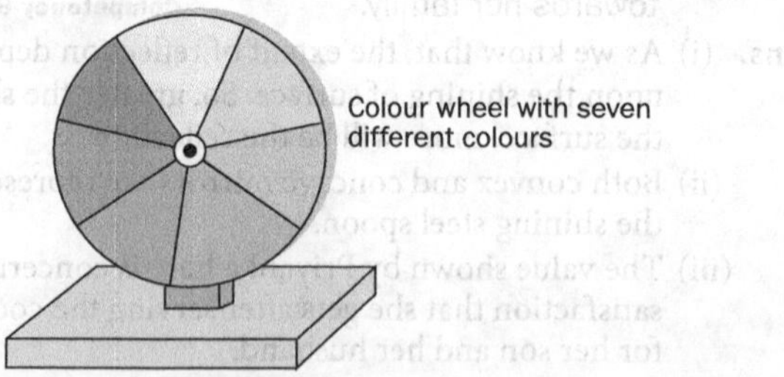

David spins a multicoloured wheel rapidly.

(i) What colour will the rapidly spinning wheel appear to be?

(ii) What acts like a prism in the formation of a rainbow in nature?

(iii) What happen when we pass a red laser light through the prism?

(iv) Explain how to construct a Newton's disc and describe how it can be used to show that white light is made up of all colours?

ASSESSMENT EXERCISE

Part I

Multiple Choice Questions

1. Image formed by a plane mirror is
   (a) real and enlarged (b) virtual and same size
   (c) real and erect (d) virtual and diminished
2. An erect and enlarged image can be obtained from
   (a) convex mirror (b) concave mirror
   (c) plane mirror (d) None of these
3. Which of the following lens is used in microscopes?
   (a) Convex lens (b) Concave lens
   (c) Both (a) and (b) (d) None of these
4. When a white light passes through a prism, it splits into
   (a) eight colours (b) seven colours
   (c) five colours (d) No colour

Fill in the blanks

5. The image formed by .... mirror is always virtual and of same size .
6. .... mirror is used in hair cutting salon.
7. A white light splits into ...... colours when passes through the prism.

True /False

8. The outer part of the shining spoon acts as a concave mirror.
9. Convex mirror is used to see the wide area.
10. The rainbow formation is due to the reflection of light.

Assertion-Reason Questions

The following questions consist of two statements Assertion (A) and Reason (R). Answer these questions by selecting the appropriate option given below

(a) Both A and R are true and R is the correct explanation of A.
(b) Both A and R are true but R is not the correct explanation of A.
(c) A is true but R is false.
(d) A is false but R is true.

11. **Assertion (A)** During the formation of rainbow, the light splits into its seven constituent colours.
    Reason (R) Air has lots of suspended dust particles in it.
12. **Assertion (A)** The image which is formed behind the mirror is called virtual image
    Reason (R) When the light rays meet virtually, then it forms virtual image.

Part II

Very Short Answer Type Questions

13. What type of image is formed by a plane mirror?
14. A shopkeeper wanted to fix a mirror which will give a maximum view of his shop. What type of mirror should he use? Give reason.
15. Explain that a convex lens converges the sun rays to a single point.
16. Concave lens is called a diverging lens. Is it correct?
17. What is the cause of rainbow formation?

Short Answer Type Questions

18. State any two observations from everyday life which show that light travels in straight lines.
19. Write the differences between virtual image and real image.
20. State the nature of the image formed in different mirrors when held close to the face.
21. Write the characteristics of the image formed by a concave lens.

Long Answer Type Questions

22. State any two uses of each (i) plane mirror (ii) convex mirror (iii) concave mirror (iv) concave lens and (v) convex lens.
23. What do you mean by converging and diverging natures?
24. Briefly explain that white light is composed of seven colours.

Answer

1. (b) 2. (b) 3. (a) 4. (b) 5. plane 6. Concave 7. seven 8. False 9. True 10. False 11. (b) 12. (a)

CHAPTER 12

Forests: Our Lifeline

In ancient times, we used to live in forests. It met all our requirements for leading a normal life at that time. Now-a-days, we live in cities and towns far off from forests, so we really do not know the importance of forests in our life. Forests cover approximately 30% of the total area of the world. They are a precious natural resource and a habitat (home) for many forms of wildlife like boar, bison, jackal, deer, porcupine, elephant, etc. The forest also contains insects, butterflies, honeybees and birds which help in pollination in the flowering plants of the forest.

12.1 Structure of a Forest

A well-developed forest has different types of trees, climbers, creepers, herbs and shrubs. These make different layers in the forest, which are described below.

1. Canopy

The uppermost branches and leaves of tall trees which act like a roof over the other plants in the forest is called canopy. It is the highest layer of vegetation in the forest. The branchy part of a tree above the stem is known as the **crown** of the tree.

Some crown shapes

2. Understorey

The different horizontal layers formed due to the different types of crowns in the forest are called understoreys. The constituents of understorey can be described as follows

(i) **Top Layer** It constitutes the giant and tall trees followed by shrubs and tall grasses.

(ii) **Shrub Layer** It has many shrubs and bushes of approximately 1-2 metres of height from the forest floor. It makes dense layer at some places of forest where enough sunlight is not present.

(iii) **Herb Layer** It occurs just below the shrub layer of plants. It is the lowest layer of vegetation in the forest having leafy plants. Most of the plants in herb layer have short lifespan.

3. Forest Floor

It is covered with different types of creepers. It has many kinds of insects, worms, toad stool, etc. Most of the forest floor is covered with dead and decaying leaves, fruits, seeds, twigs and small herbs.

Walking over the dead leaf layer on the forest floor feels like walking over a spongy carpet. It is generally dark as not much sunlight reaches here. Forest floor is warm and humid.

Thus, providing favourable conditions for seeds to germinate and develop into seedlings and saplings.

Different layers of plants in forest

12.2 Components of the Forest

The **living organisms** found in the forest are plants, animals, decomposers and scavengers. The non-living component of the forest consists of soil, water and air which provide nutrients, water and carbon dioxide for the growth of the living organisms.

These are described as follows

1. Plants

Green plants are living organisms that are also called **autotrophs** as they produce food by photosynthesis (by absorbing nutrients and water from soil, CO_2 from air and using sunlight as energy source).

They provide food to all living organisms. Hence, they are called producers (of food), e.g. sal, teak, fig, khair, amla, bamboo, sheesham, etc .

2. Animals

They are **heterotrophs** (consumers) as they are dependent on green plants directly or indirectly for their food. In the forest, some animals are **herbivores** (which eat only plants and their parts) while some are **carnivores** (flesh eating animals). e.g. boar, bison, jackals, porcupine, etc.

3. Decomposers

The organisms like bacteria and fungi, e.g. mushrooms, that feed on dead plants and animals are called **saprotrophs**. These microorganisms are also called **decomposers** as they breakdown dead parts of plants and dead bodies of animals into simple substances.

The dead leaves, flowers, fruits , etc. are converted into a dark coloured substance called **humus** by decomposers on coming into contact with water. Humus release nutrients into the soil. These nutrients make the soil fertile. They play a very important role in sustaining the forests.

4. Scavengers

Those animals which eat dead animals are called scavengers, e.g. vultures, crows, jackals, hyena, some insects (ants, beetles, termites, wood lice, maggots, millipedes and earthworms), etc. Scavengers are the cleaning agents of our environment.

But these are not decomposers as they do not breakdown complex dead organic matter into simple ones.

Food Chain

Food chain can be defined as a sequence of living organisms in which one organism feeds on another.

A typical example of food chain in the forest is

Grass → Insect → Frog → Snake → Eagle.

There are many food chains present in the forest. All food chains are linked . If any one food chain is disturbed, it affects other food chains. If we remove one component, say trees, all other components would be affected.

Try These 12.1

1. **Who provides food to all living organisms that live in the forests?**
2. **Name the organisms responsible for the formation of humus.**
3. **Name a scavenger which can be found in forests as well cities and towns.**

12.3 Importance of the Forests

The forests provide us with a large number of products. They purify air and improve water quality. They also maintain soil moisture and climate. So, they are called our **lifeline**.

1. Forests Maintain Balance between Oxygen and Carbon Dioxide

Plants in the forest release oxygen during the process of **photosynthesis**. This provides all animals including us with oxygen to breathe. They also help to maintain the balance of oxygen and carbon dioxide in the atmosphere. That's why, forests are known as **green lungs**.

If amount of carbon dioxide increases in the atmosphere, it would result in increase in Earth's temperature. Plants in the forest take carbon dioxide from the atmosphere during photosynthesis. Hence, they help to maintain the right amount of carbon dioxide in the atmosphere and also keep the atmosphere cool.

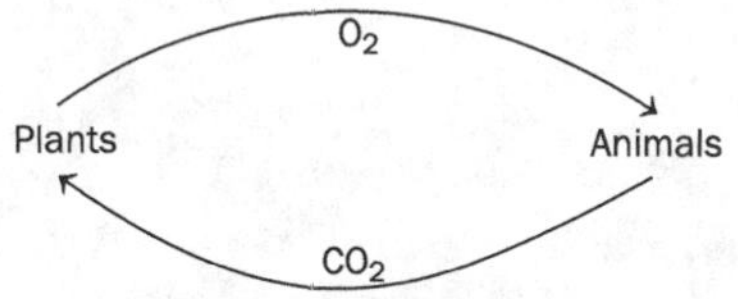

Balance of oxygen and carbon doixide

2. Forests Provide Many Useful Products

The various things which are obtained from the forests are called **forest products**. Forests give us a large number of useful products. Many trees in the forests have medicinal value and chemicals extracted from them are used in pharmaceutical or cosmetic industries.

Some of the important products which we get from the forests are wood, honey, gum, sealing wax (or lac), catechu (kattha), fruits, oils, spices, natural rubber, cork, dyes, medicinal plants and fodder for cattle.

Perhaps the most important product obtained from forests is the wood (which is obtained by cutting down the forest trees). The wood obtained from forests is used for a large number of purposes in our day-to-day life.

SCIENCE INSIGHT Sheesham wood is an excellent choice for furniture and is used for making doors and windows. Its root wood is often used for making tobacco pipes.

3. Forests Maintain Water Cycle

The trees in forest absorb water from the soil through their roots and release water vapour into the air through evaporation. This water vapour helps in the formation of clouds and brings rain on the Earth. Thus, forests bring sufficient rainfall on the Earth. In this way, forests help in maintaining a perfect water cycle in nature and meet our freshwater requirements.

4. Forests Prevent Occurrence of Flood and Soil Erosion

Rainwater does not stagnate in the forest as the upper most layer of the forest canopy intercepts the flows of raindrops. This results in most of the water coming down through the branches and the stems of the tree. The forest acts as a natural absorber of rainwater and allows it to seep.

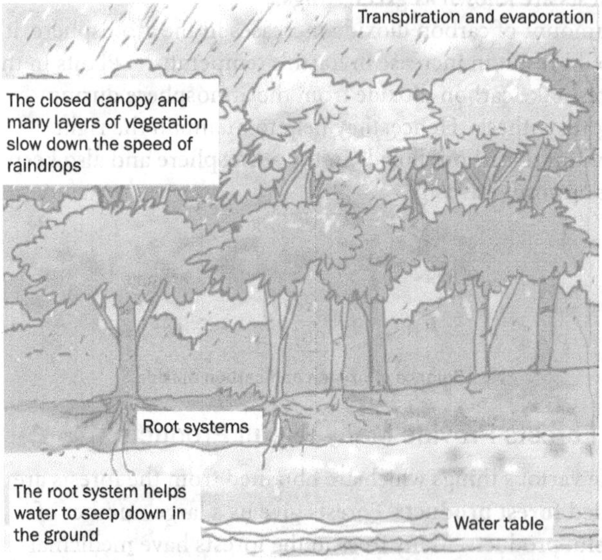

Rainwater drips from the trees and seeps into the ground

It helps to maintain the water table throughout the year. Forests not only help in controlling floods, but also help to maintain the flow of water in the streams, so that we get a steady supply of water.

On the other hand, if trees are not present, rain hits the ground directly and may flood the area around it. Heavy rain may also damage the soil. Roots of trees normally bind the soil together, but in their absence, the soil is washed away or eroded.

In the absence of plants/trees, the soil will not hold water which will cause flood and soil erosion.

5. Forests Provide Habitat for Wildlife

The different types of vegetation present in a forest provide food and shelter to animals, birds and insects which live in the forest.

The dense bushes and the tall grass provide animals with the food and shelter. They also protect the herbivores from the carnivores that live in the forest.

The forest is not just home to plants and animals. Many people also live in the forest that may belong to different tribes. These people depend mostly on the forests for food, shelter, water and medicines. They also have traditional knowledge about many medicinal plants in the forest.

6. Forests can Regenerate on their Own

The dead parts of trees and plants, dead animals and animal wastes (like animal dung or droppings) keep on collecting on the forest floor. Decomposers (fungi and bacteria) degrade them into dark substances called humus.

The humus makes the forest soil fertile by returning back the nutrients to the soil. Several beetles and grubs also feed on decaying heaps of animal droppings and bunch of seedlings sprout on them.

The animals, birds, wind and water disperse the seeds of trees and plants on the forest soil. These seeds obtain nutrients from the soil and germinate to form seedlings. These seedlings ultimately grow to form the forest vegetation.

Note Forests also reduce the noise pollution as they absorb the noises.

Dynamic Living Entity

By harbouring greater variety of plants, the forest provides great opportunities of food and habitat for the herbivores. Larger number of herbivores means increased availability of food for a variety of carnivores.

The wide variety of animals helps the forest to regenerate and grow. Decomposers help in maintaining the supply of nutrients to the growing plants in the forest. Therefore, the forest is a **dynamic living entity**, i.e. full of life and vitality. There is a continuous interaction between soil, water, air, plants and animals in a forest.

12.4 Deforestation

The removal of forest to meet the various demands of the increasing population, is called deforestation.

Factors Responsible for Deforestation

The factors which are responsible for the deforestation are as follows

(i) Expansion of agriculture
(ii) Construction of road
(iii) Industrial development
(iv) Increasing demand of wood
(v) Overgrazing by animals

Consequences of Deforestation

Following are the consequences if forest disappear

(i) **Increase of the Earth's temperature** If there are no trees and plants, there will be no photosynthesis. So, no CO_2 of the atmosphere will be used. This will increase the level of CO_2, resulting in the increase of the Earth's temperature.

(ii) **No food and shelter to wildlife** In the absence of trees and plants, animals will not get food and shelter. So, this will disrupt the whole cycle of life and gradually life might disappear from the land area of the Earth.

(iii) **There will be more floods** The tree roots help in holding the soil during rains and also soil is able to hold water. In the absence of trees, the soil will not hold water which will cause floods.

(iv) **Deforestation endanger the environment** Continuous deforestation is threatening the different forms of life including human beings. So, there is necessity to think and set ways to conserve forests.

Natural calamities like floods, cyclones, hail storms are more in the absence of trees and forest. People become homeless when such disasters occur.

12.5 Forest Conservation

Paper is made from wood pulp that is produced from the wood of forest trees. So, to make paper, many trees have to be cut down from the forests. If all of us keep on collecting old newspapers, magazines, books, notebooks, etc., and send them to paper mills for recycling through a junk dealer (kabadi wala), we will be able to save many forest trees from being cut down.

Some of the other ways to conserve forests are also given below

(i) Excessive cutting down of forest trees should not be allowed by the government to conserve forests.

(ii) More trees should be planted in the forest in place of cutting down trees to conserve forests.

(iii) Paper products such as old newspapers, magazines, books, notebooks, etc. should be recycled to conserve forests.

Try These 12.2

1. **Which part of the tree prevents soil erosion?**
2. **Does the planting of trees on the roadside help to reduce noise pollution?**
3. **Does the expansion of agriculture lead to the cutting of trees or not?**
4. **What will be the consequence of deforestation on the occurrence of floods?**

Science Glossary

Canopy Roof formed by the tree branches in the upper regions.

Crown Branchy part of a tree above the stem.

Decomposers Organisms which decompose the dead and decaying matter.

Deforestation Destruction of forests or felling of trees on a large scale.

Humus Dark colour substance produced by decomposers.

Regeneration Process of renewal and restoration.

Seed dispersal Scattering of seeds over a large area.

Soil erosion Removal of the fertile top soil by wind, rain or river water.

Let's Investigate

ACTIVITY 1 (Page 144)

Aim To make a list of materials in your home which have been obtained from plants.

Procedure Look around your house and observe the materials derived directly or indirectly from plants.

Observation The table given below list the plants based products that we get from them.

Gums	Timbers	Medicinal	Oils
Babool	Sheesham	Neem	Sandalwood
Catechu	Pine	Tulsi	Soybean
Datura	Fir	Aloe vera	Sunflower
Neem	Cedar	Basil	Canola
Khair	Spruce	Thyme	Coconut

Conclusion From this activity we can conclude that the plants provide us with many useful products.

Viva Questions

1. Name any two products obtained from plants.
2. Write one importance of plants.

ACTIVITY 2 (Page 147)

Aim To show that heat is released during decomposition of plant waste.

Materials Required Leaves , vegetable waste, soil.

Procedure

1. Dig a small pit in the garden of your school under the supervision of your teacher.
2. Put leaves and vegetable waste in it.
3. Cover the pit with soil and add some water.
4. Remove the covering of soil after 3 - 4 days.

Observation After 3 - 4 days, the pit filled with leaves and vegetable waste feels warm.

Conclusion From this activity, we can conclude that heat is released during the process of decomposition.

Viva Questions

1. Define decomposition.
2. Name any two decomposers.

Mind Map

FORESTS: OUR LIFELINE

Structure of a Forest

Canopy
Uppermost branches and leaves of tall trees makes roof over other plants.

Understorey
Different horizontal layers formed due to the different types of crowns.

Forest floor
It has many insects worms, toadstool, etc. Covered with dead and decaying leaves, fruits and seeds, etc.

Forest Conservation

It can be done by
- Not allowing excessive cutting of forest trees.
- More trees should be planted in the forest.
- Paper products such as old newspapers, magazines, book, notebooks, etc. should be recycled.

Deforestation

Removal of forest to meet various demands.

Factors Responsible for Deforestation

- Expansion of agriculture.
- Construction of road.
- Industrial development.
- Increasing demand of wood.
- Overgrazing by animals.

Consequences of Deforestation

- Amount of CO_2 would increase resulting in increase in Earth's temperature.
- Animals will not get food and shelter.
- Soil will not hold water causing flood.
- Endanger our life and environment.

Components of the Forest

Plants
- Produce food through photosynthesis.
- Provides food to all living organisms.

Animals
Dependent on green plants directly or indirectly for food, e.g. herbivores, carnivores, etc.

Scavengers
- Eat dead animals.
- Cleaning agents of our environment, e.g. crows, jackals, hyena, maggots, etc.

Decomposers
- Feed on dead plants and animals.
- Breaks complex substances of dead parts into simple substances.
- It forms dark coloured substance i.e. humus.
- Humus makes soil fertile by releasing nutrients . e.g. fungi and bacteria

Importance of Forests

- Maintain balance between oxygen and carbon dioxide.
- Provide many useful products.
- Maintain water cycle.
- Prevent flood and soil erosion.
- Provides habitat for wildlife.
- Forest can regenerate on their own.
- Reduces noise pollution.

NCERT FOLDER

Complete Explanations of all NCERT's Questions

Intext Questions

Q.1 'Would we see similar kind of trees in every forest? Asked Boojho'. **Page 146**

Ans. No, we would not see similar kind of trees in every forest. Due to different climatic conditions there are variations in the types of trees and other plants. The types of animals also differ from forest to forest.

Q.2 Is the decaying matter always warm? **Page 146**

Ans. Yes, the decaying matter is always warm.

Q.3 Paheli asked. "There are so many trees here. Also, there are many forests like this. What difference will it make if we cut some trees for a factory"? **Page 147**

Ans. Green plants produce food. All animals whether herbivores or carnivores, depend ultimately on plants for food. Organisms which feed on plant often get eaten by other organisms. Every part of the forest is dependent on the other parts. If we remove one component, e.g. trees, all the other components would be affected.

Q.4 In which layer of the soil would you find humus? What is its importance to the soil? **Page 148**

Ans. A layer of humus is found on forest floor or topsoil layer. It ensures that the nutrients of the dead plants and animals are released into the soil.

Q.5 What happens if an animal dies in the forest?

Ans. The dead animals become food for vultures, crows, jackals and insects. **Page 148**

Q.6 If there were fewer trees, how will the water cycle be affected? **Page 148**

Ans. If there are less number of trees then there would be less evaporation from plants and consequently less water vapour in the air. This would lead to fewer clouds. Hence, there would not be much rain. So the presence of fewer trees affects the water cycle.

Q.7 Paheli remembered that she saw a pipal sapling on the sidewall in her school. Can you help her to understand how this would have happened? **Page 149**

Ans. Due to the process of seed dispersal, some seeds of pipal may have dispersed on side of wall through winds, animals, birds, etc. and have grown into pipal plant.

Q.8 What would happen if it rains heavily in your town? **Page 151**

Ans. If it rains heavily in the town, it would have flooded the drains and roads.

Q.9 What would happen if forests disappear? **Page 151**

Ans. If forest disappear following consequences can occur

(a) If the forest disappear, the amount of carbon dioxide in air will increase, resulting in the increase of Earth's temperature.

(b) In the absence of trees and plants, the animals will not get food and shelter.

(c) In the absence of trees, the soil will not hold water, which will cause floods.

(d) Deforestation will endanger our life and environment.

Exercise

Q.1 Explain how animals dwelling in the forest help it to grow and regenerate?

Ans. (i) The animals in forests are of various types. These could be herbivores, carnivores, microorganisms, etc. These plays an important role in maintaining the food chains.

(ii) Microorganisms convert the dead plants and animals into humus. This humus helps in returning the nutrients back to the soil. These are then absorbed by plants.

(iii) The animals also help in dispersing the seeds of certain plants.

(iv) The decaying animal dung provides nutrients.

All these activities of animals dwelling in the forest help it to grow and regenerate.

Q.2 Explain how forests prevent floods?

Ans. Refer to text on page no. 212.

Q.3 What are decomposers? Name any two of them. What do they do in the forest?

Ans. Decomposers are the microorganisms that convert the dead plants and animals into humus. Bacteria and mushroom are the examples of decomposers.
They help in the process of recycling of nutrients by decomposing various dead organisms such as plants and animals to form humus. Therefore, decomposers are helpful for the environment.

Q.4 Explain the role of forests in maintaining the balance between oxygen and carbon dioxide in the atmosphere.

Ans. Forests are called the green lungs. This is because plants in forests release oxygen through the process of photosynthesis and help in providing oxygen to animals for respiration.

They consume carbon dioxide released by the animals. In this way, plants help in maintaining a balance of oxygen and carbon dioxide in atmosphere.

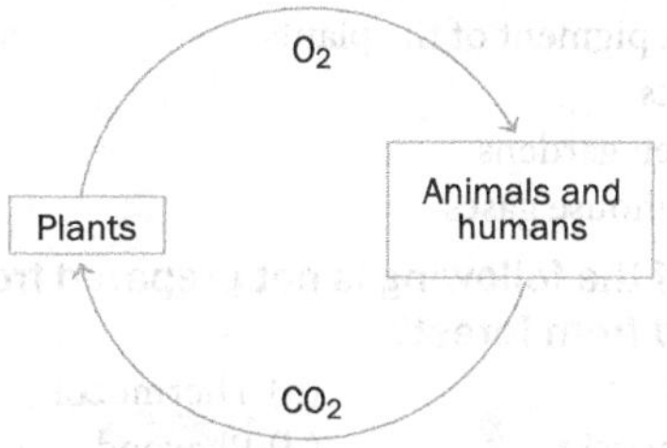

Q.5 Explain why there is no waste in a forest?

Ans. There is no waste in a forest because microorganisms act on the waste and convert into humus. The humus ensures that the nutrients are returned back to the soil.

Q.6 List five products we get from forests.

Ans. The five products we get from forests are

(i) Fruits (ii) Honey

(iii) Medicines (iv) Oxygen

(v) Gum

Q.7 Fill in the blanks.

(a) The insects, butterflies, honeybees and birds help flowering plants in ....

(b) A forest is a purifier of .... and ....

(c) Herbs form the .... layer in the forest.

(d) The decaying leaves and animal droppings in a forest enrich the ....

Ans. (a) pollination (b) air, water

(c) lowest (d) soil

Q.8 Why should we worry about the conditions and issues related to forest far from us?

Ans. There are various reasons for which we should be vigilant about matters related to forests

Refer to text on page no. 211-212.

Q.9 Explain why there is a need of variety of animals and plants in a forests.

Ans. Refer to text on page no. 212 and 213.

Q.10 In figure, the artist has forgotten to put the labels and directions on the arrows. Mark the directions on the arrows and label the diagram using the labels clouds, rain, atmosphere, carbon dioxide, oxygen, plant, animal, soil, roots, water table.

Ans.

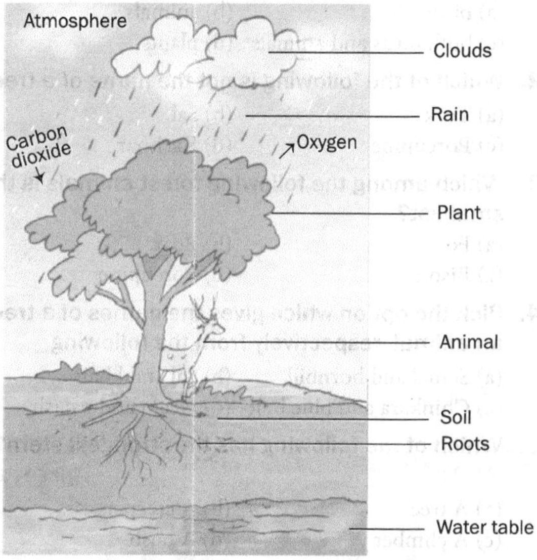

Q.11 Which of the following is not a forest product?

(a) Gum (b) Plywood

(c) Sealing wax (d) Kerosene

Ans. (d) Kerosene is a fossil fuel, it is not a forest product.

Q.12 Which of the following statements is not correct?

(a) Forests protect the soil from erosion

(b) Plants and animals in a forest are not dependent on one another

(c) Forests influence the climate and water cycle

(d) Soil helps forest to grow and regenerate

Ans. (b) Plants and animals in a forest are not dependent on one another.

Q.13 Microorganisms act upon the dead plants to produce

(a) sand (b) mushroom (c) humus (d) wood

Ans. (c) Microorganisms act upon the dead plants to produce humus. It forms the fertile layer of the soil.

REVIEW EXERCISE

Including Competency Based Questions

Part I

Multiple Choice Questions

1. Boojho visited a forest near his town with his classmates and his teacher. As they were entering the forest, their class teacher told them not to make a noise in the forest as noise could disturb the NCERT Exemplar

(a) birds (b) animals
(c) both birds and animals (d) plants

2. Which of the following is not the name of a tree?

(a) Teak (b) Sal
(c) Porcupine (d) Kachnar

3. Which among the following forest animals is the smallest?

(a) Fox (b) Boar
(c) Bison (d) Porcupine

4. Pick the option which gives the names of a tree and an animal, respectively from the following

(a) Semal and hornbill (b) Sal and khair
(c) Chinkara and blue bull (d) Neem and palash

5. Which of the following has the strongest stem? NCERT Exemplar

(a) A tree (b) A creeper
(c) A climber (d) A bush

6. The lowest layer in the understorey is formed by

(a) shrubs (b) herbs (c) trees (d) tall grasses

7. Plants do not depend on animals for

(a) pollination (b) food
(c) seed dispersal (d) nutrients

8. Flow of energy in nature takes the following path

(a) Carnivores → Herbivores → Green plants
(b) Green plants → Herbivores → Carnivores
(c) Sun → Green plants → Herbivores → Carnivores
(d) Sun → Carnivores → Herbivores → Green plants

9. Mushrooms are an example of ...... Competency Based Que.

(a) autotrophs (b) heterotrophs
(c) parasites (d) saprophyte

10. Microorganisms act upon the dead plants to produce

(a) sand (b) mushroom
(c) humus (d) wood

11. Which of the following serve as green lungs? NCERT Exemplar

(a) Green pigment of the plants
(b) Forests
(c) Kitchen gardens
(d) Greenhouse gases

12. Which of the following is not prepared from the wood obtained from forest?

(a) Paper (b) Thermocol
(c) Matchsticks (d) Plywood

13. Which of the products is not obtained from a forest? NCERT Exemplar

(a) Honey (b) Catechu
(c) Gum (d) Ginger

14. Which one of the following is an animal product? Competency Based Que.

(a) Gum (b) Catechu
(c) Honey (d) Rubber

15. Forests are not responsible for

(a) providing medicinal plants
(b) maintaining the flow of water into the streams
(c) creating flood conditions
(d) absorbing rainwater and maintaining water table

Answers

1. (c)	2. (c)	3. (d)	4. (a)	5. (a)
6. (b)	7. (b)	8. (c)	9. (d)	10. (c)
11. (b)	12. (b)	13. (d)	14. (c)	15. (c)

Fill in the Blanks

1. Animals often give .... to alert other animals.

2. The part of a tree above the stem is called .... of the tree.

3. The microorganisms which convert dead plants and animals to humus are called ....

4. The decaying leaves and animal droppings in a forest enrich the ....

5. In the absence of trees, the soil will not hold ....

Answers

1. warning call 2. crown 3. decomposers
4. soil 5. water

True/False

1. **Roots of the tree are called crown of the tree.**
2. **Plants release CO_2 in the process of photosynthesis.**
3. **Forests are lifeline for forest dwelling communities.**
4. **Forest influence climate, water cycle and air quality.**
5. **We get various products from forests.**

Answers

1. False, the branchy part of tree above the stem is known as crown of the tree.
2. False, plants take carbon dioxide from the atmosphere during photosynthesis.
3. True 4. True 5. True

Match the Columns

1. **Match the Column I with Column II.** **NCERT Exemplar**

	Column I		Column II
A.	Decomposers	1.	Dead plant and animal tissues
B.	Canopy	2.	Habitat for wildlife
C.	Porcupine	3.	Microorganisms
D.	Humus	4.	Wild animal
E.	Forest	5.	Uppermost branches of tall trees

Answer

A–3, B–5, C–4, D–1, E–2

Assertion-Reason Questions

The following questions consist of two statements-Assertion (A) and Reason (R). Answer these questions by selecting the appropriate option given below.

(a) Both A and R are true and R is correct explanation of A
(b) Both A and R are true, but R is not the correct explanation of A
(c) A is true, but R is false
(d) A is false, but R is true

1. **Assertion** (A) Fungi are decomposers.
Reason (R) They maintain the balance of oxygen and carbon dioxide in the atmosphere.
2. **Assertion** (A) Forest helps to purify the air .
Reason (R) They prevent the soil erosion.
3. **Assertion** (A) Forests encourages soil erosion.
Reason (R) The trees in forest hold up the soil together in their roots.

Answers

1. (c) A is true, R is false. R can be corrected as Plants maintain the balance of O_2 and CO_2 in the atmospheric .
2. (b) Both A and R are true, but R is not the correct explanation of A. It can be corrected as Forest helps to purify the air by taking in carbon dioxide from the atmosphere and releasing oxygen into it.
3. (d) A is false, but R is true. A can be corrected as Forest prevents soil erosion by holding the soil together in their roots thus, preventing washing away of the soil.

Case Based Questions

1. **The picture shows the different layers of a forest.** **Competency Based Que.**

(i) **Which is the canopy layer of the forest?**
(a) Layer 1 (b) Layer 2 (c) Layer 3 (d) Layer 4

(ii) **In which layer of the forest are decomposers present?**
(a) Layer 1 (b) Layer 2 (c) Layer 3 (d) Layer 4

(iii) **Which type of plant is found in layer 4 of the forest?**
(a) Herbs (b) Shrubs
(c) Tall grass (d) Big trees

2. **Which of these are the effects of deforestation? Circle 'Yes' or 'No' for the correct response.** **Competency Based Que.**

	Is this an effect of deforestation?	Yes/No
(a)	Increase in the Earth's temperature	Yes/No
(b)	Decrease in the occurrence of floods	Yes/No
(c)	Increase in the oxygen level in atmosphere	Yes/No

Answers

1. (i) (b), (ii) (d), (iii) (a)
2. (a) Yes (b) No (c) No

Part II

Very Short Answer Type Questions

1. List some animals which live in deeper areas of the forest.

Ans. Animals like boar, bison, jackal, porcupine, elephant, etc. live in the deeper areas of the forest.

2. Give names of any four birds which you expect to see in a forest. NCERT Exemplar

Ans. The four birds which we expect to see in a forest are jungle crow, hornbill, mynas and koel.

3. While going inside a forest, it becomes darker. Why?

Ans. The canopy of forest blocks a significant amount of sunlight from reaching the forest floor.
As a result less than 50% of the sunlight that hits the top of the forest makes it through canopy to the plants below. This makes the darkness of the forest floor.

4. What is a canopy?

Ans. The uppermost branches and leaves of tall trees act like a roof over the forest ground, this is called canopy.

5. Name any four useful products other than wood, which we get from forests. NCERT Exemplar

Ans. Four useful products other than wood which we get from forests are gum, spices, fodder for animals and medicinal plants.

6. Give the reason behind variations found in the forests of different regions.

Ans. The variations in the type of plants and animals are found in forests of different regions because of the different climatic conditions.

7. Consider the following organisms
Grass, birds, frog, crow, tiger, vulture, toadstool, deer. Which of these
(i) can eat the dead animals?
(ii) can form a three step food chain?

Ans. (i) Crow, vulture

(ii) Grass $\longrightarrow$ Deer $\longrightarrow$ Tiger

8. Paheli wrote a food chain in the following way
Frog → Eagle → Insects → Grass → Snake
The chain is not in the correct order. Help her to write the food chain correctly. NCERT Exemplar

Ans. The correct food chain is
Grass → Insects → Frog → Snake → Eagle

9. State the consequence when one food chain is disturbed in an ecosystem.

Ans. Since, all food chains are interlinked, disturbance in one food chain will affect the other food chain in a forest.

10. A bunch of seedlings were seen sprouting on a heap of animal dropping in a forest. How do you think is the seedling benefited from the animal dung? NCERT Exemplar

Ans. The seedling was being benefited from the animal dung as the decaying animal dung provided nutrients to the growing seedlings.

11. All the needs of animals living in a forest are fulfilled. Justify this statement in a few sentences.

Ans. Forest provides home (shelter), food and water to the animals living there. Thus, all the needs of animals living in a forest are fulfilled.

12. Deforestation may lead to floods. Why?

Ans. Deforestation leads to floods as lesser number of trees will be available due to deforestation. In the absence of trees, the soil will not hold water leading to floods.

13. Paheli while moving in a forest observed that there was no noise pollution, though lots of heavy vehicles were passing from the nearby highway. Explain why? NCERT Exemplar

Ans. Paheli observed that there is no noise pollution in a forest even though there are lots of heavy vehicles passing from the nearby highway. It is because trees present in the forest absorb the noise.

Short Answer Type Questions

1. Crown is different from canopy. Explain how?

Ans. The part of the tree with branches is known as the crown. When the crown of tall trees in the forests forms a roof-like covering over the others plants, it is known as a canopy.

2. Two friends shared their experiences of their vacation trip to two different forests. Do you think they would have seen the same type of plants and animals during their respective trips? Give reason. NCERT Exemplar

Ans. No, they would not have seen the same type of plants and animals. This is so because climatic conditions in the two forests would vary leading to variations in the types of plants and animals.

3. Plants are known as the producers of a food chain. Give reason.

Ans. Plants are known as the producers of a food chain. It is because green plants (autotrophs) make their own food from carbon dioxide and water in the presence of sunlight and chlorophyll by the process called photosynthesis and provide food to all living organisms which live in the forest.

4. If one component of the forest is removed, what would be its affect on the ecosystem?

Ans. Every component of forest depend on each other. If we remove one component the other will be affected, e.g. if we remove top carnivores (lion/tiger) in a forest, herbivores will increase and if they increase they will end up eating all plants, so ecosystem will get disturbed.

5. Write differences between decomposers and scavengers.

Ans. Differences between decomposers and scavengers is as follows

Decomposers	Scavengers
These are the microbes which break dead organic matter into simple molecules which are used by plants again, e.g. fungi, millipedes are decomposers, etc.	These animals eat the body of dead animals and are called cleaning agent of forests, e.g. jackal, fox, vulture, etc.

6. Y and Z are two types of organisms which are found in the forests. Y eats up dead animals, while Z breakdown the body of the dead animals into simpler substances. **Competency Based Que.**

(a) What is the general name of organism Y?
(b) Write one example of Y type organism.
(c) What is general name of organism Z?
(d) Write one example of Z type organism.

Ans. (a) Scavenger (b) Vulture
(c) Decomposers (d) Fungi (mushroom)

7. Sketch a diagram to show how plants maintain the balance between carbon dioxide and oxygen in the atmosphere?

Ans.

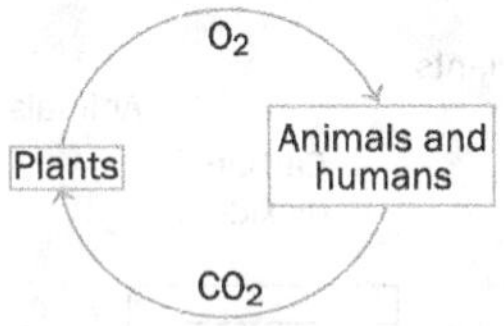

8. Forests are called green lungs. Why?

Ans. Forests are called green lungs because they play a crucial role in maintaining the balance of the environment by providing oxygen and removing carbon dioxide.

9. Explain how root system of plants help in the prevention of flood?

Ans. The roots of the trees hold the topsoil and make it porous which allows rainwater to seep through it. Thus, forests help to reduce flood by absorbing excess rainwater and slowing down water flow.

10. "You conserve forest, you conserve soil". Do you agree? Justify.

Ans. Yes, forests bind soil with roots and prevent soil erosion. They also maintain fertility of soil and check flood. So, it can be said that conserving forest results in conservation of soil.

11. Give any four factors which are responsible for the destruction of forests. **NCERT Exemplar**

Ans. The four factors which are responsible for the destruction of forests are

(i) Construction of roads.
(ii) Construction of buildings.
(iii) Industrial development.
(iv) Increasing demand of wood.

12. Forests are considered as the most valuable resources. Explain.

Ans. Forest products play vital role in socio-economic development. We get food (cereals, pulses, fruits), fire wood, fibre, construction material, industrial products (tannins, lubricants, dyes, resins, perfumes) and products of medicinal importance. It is also the home of diverse wildlife. Thus, forests are the most valuable resources.

13. Deforestation can increase the Earth's temperature. Is it true? Give reason.

Ans. Yes, if there are no trees and plants, there will be no photosynthesis. Thus, no CO_2 of the atmosphere will be used. This will increase the level of CO_2 in the atmosphere, resulting in the increase of Earth's temperature.

Long Answer Type Questions

1. Describe the different layers of plants in the forest.

Ans. Refer to text on page no. 210.

2. Figure shows a part of a forest.

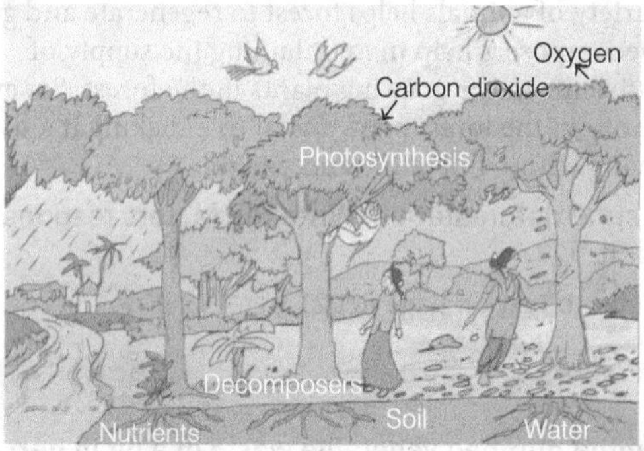

Write any three activities going on in the forest on the basis of this figure. **NCERT Exemplar**

Ans. The three activities going on in the forest on the basis of the given figure are

(i) Oxygen is given out by plant leaves.
(ii) Carbon dioxide is consumed by the plants to prepare their food by the process of photosynthesis.
(iii) Nutrients are being added to the soil by the action of decomposers.

3. People say that nothing goes waste in a forest. Can you explain how? **NCERT Exemplar**

Ans. Nothing goes waste in a forest because of the following reasons

(i) Dry leaves and remains of dead animals are converted to a dark coloured substance called humus. This provides nutrients to the plants.

(ii) Dead animals become food for vultures, crows, jackals and insects.

(iii) Broken branches of trees are used as fuel by the people living in the vicinity of the forest.

4. "Forest are our lifeline". Write five sentences on this topic. **NCERT Exemplar**

Ans. Refer to text on page no. 211-212.

5. All the needs of animals living in a forest are fulfilled. Justify this statement in a few sentences.

Ans. Plants present in the forest fulfill all the needs of animals present there is following ways

(i) Plant provide oxygen to the animals to respire.

(ii) They also provide food to all the animals directly or indirectly. Herbivores obtain food directly from plants, carnivores depend on herbivores for food.

(iii) Trees in forest provide shelter to animals.

(iv) Decomposers help in maintaining the supply of nutrients to the growing plants in the forest.

6. "Forest is a dynamic entity, full of life and vitality". Explain briefly.

Ans. Forests harbour great variety of plants and animals. Larger number of herbivores means increased availability of food for a variety of carnivores. Wide variety of animals helps forest to regenerate and grow. Decomposers help in maintaining the supply of nutrients to the growing plants in the forest. So, every entity in the forest plays a vital role making it a dynamic living entity, full of life and vitality.

7. Define deforestation. Write the factors responsible for it.

Ans. Refer to text on page no. 213.

Case Based Questions

1. Sudha dumped vegetable waste in a pit in her garden. She then added a layer of soil and covered the pit tightly. The picture shows what Sudha found after a year. **Competency Based Que.**

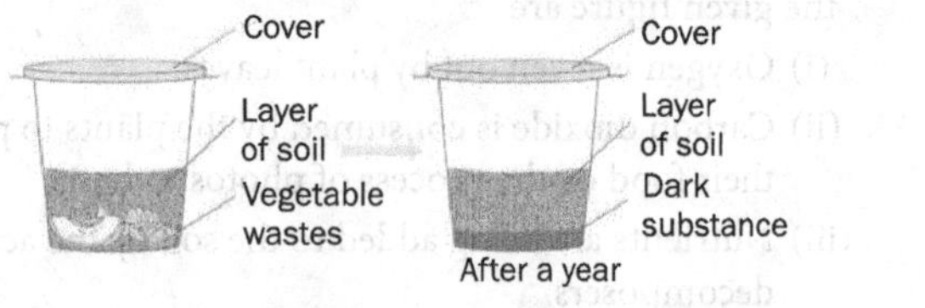

(i) What is the name of the dark substance formed at the bottom of the pit?

(ii) How can she use the dark substance most effectively?

(a) Use it as fuel for cooking food

(b) Mix it in water and use as ink

(c) Use it to seal leakages in water pipes

(d) Mix it with garden soil to make it fertile.

2. The table lists some animals of a forest and what they eat.

Animals	What does it eat?
Frog	Grasshopper
Snake	Frog
Grasshopper	Grass

(i) Complete the food chain with the animals listed in the table.

Grass → ☐ → ☐ → ☐

(ii) How many carnivores are listed in the table?

(a) One (b) Two

(c) Three (d) Four

3. The picture shows how oxygen and carbon dioxide are balanced in a forest? Fill in the empty boxes correctly using the following labels **Competency Based Que.**

- **Photosynthesis**
- **Respiration**

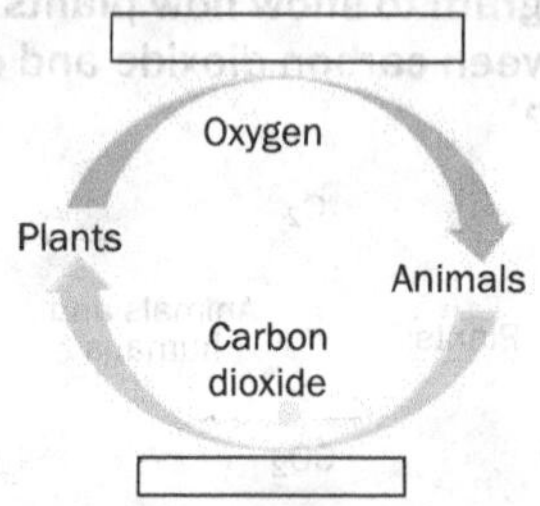

Ans. 1. (i) The dark substance formed at the bottom of the pit is known as humus.

(ii) (d) Mix it with garden soil to make it fertile.

2. (i) Grass → Grasshopper → Frog → Snake

(ii) (b) Two

3.

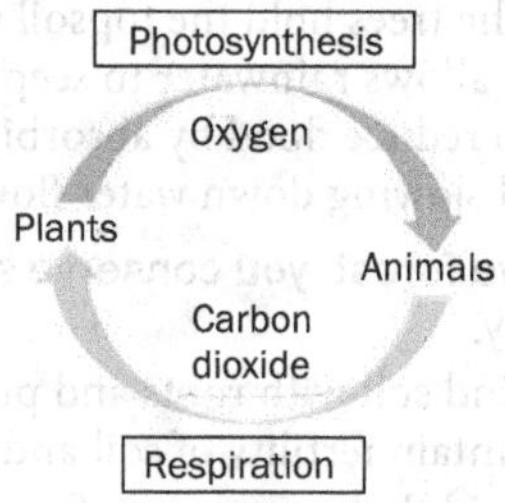

Skill Based Questions as per NEP 2020

1. **Given below are the figures representing various components of a food chain. Make 3 food chains using these figures. Make some to use each figure atleast once. Also, some figure can be used more than once.** **Research skill**

2. **Visit a forest with your parents by taking permission from the respective authority (forest officials).** **Research skill**

(i) **Make a list of the things you see in the forest.**

(ii) **Try to recognise various types of trees and different layers formed by them.**

3. **A snake charmer came to the society and smelled the presence of a cobra near the guardroom. The head of the society agreed to allow the man to search, catch and take away the snake with him. Little Krishi who was seeing all this, disagreed. She explained the people that it might disturb the food chain in the environment. Now, answer the following questions.** **Observation skill**

(i) **Describe food chain.**

(ii) **Construct a food chain involving snake at one of its level.**

4. **Sachin lives in a village, this village is surrounded by a forest. One day he noticed that in nearby pond sedimentation is increased so much that water has become muddy, streams are drying up. There is scarcity of fuel wood. He soon realised that he has to raise the issue of forest protection from cutting down trees, etc. Soon he gathered the nearby village people and made an organisation to take an initiative.**
Now, answer the following questions

(i) **What changes might have Sachin noticed in his area?**

(ii) **Give the probable reason for such changes mentioned above.** **Thinking skill**

ASSESSMENT EXERCISE

Part I

Multiple Choice Questions

1. Which of the following is influenced by forest?
(a) Temperature (b) Climate
(c) Animals (d) All of these

2. Which of the following statements is not correct ?
(a) Plants release carbon dioxide during the process of photosynthesis
(b) Forest are lifeline for all forest dwelling animals
(c) Forest help to reduce noise
(d) Forest protect the soil from erosion

3. Find the missing link from the following food chain
Grass → Insects → Frog → .... → Eagle
(a) Crow (b) Peacock
(c) Koel (d) Snake

4. The table shows the area under forest in four different regions

Regions	Forest Area (in acres)
P	3,000
Q	42,30,000
R	45,000
S	5,00,000

Which of the following area is most resistant to flood ?
(a) P (b) Q (c) R (d) S

5. Forest can be conserved by
(a) overgrazing
(b) expansion of agriculture
(c) protecting wildlife and reforestation
(d) deforestation

Fill in the Blanks

6. Components of forest are .... on each other.

7. Cutting of trees in the forest is called ....

True/False

8. Forests are called green lungs.

9. The forests keep on growing and can regenerate.

Match the Columns

10. Match the Column I with Column II.

	Column I		Column II
A.	Humus	1.	Depend on plants for food
B.	Forests	2.	Branchy part of the tree
C.	Herbivores	3.	Helps forests to grow
D.	Crown	4.	Dark coloured matter
E.	Soil	5.	Protect soil from erosion

Assertion-Reason Questions

The following questions consist of two statements **Assertion** (A) and **Reason** (R). Answer these questions by selecting the appropriate option given below.
(a) Both A and R are true and R is the correct explanation of A
(b) Both A and R are true, but R is not the correct explanation of A
(c) A is true, but R is false
(d) A is false, but R is true

11. Assertion (A) Plants are called as consumers.
Reason (R) They prepare their own food by the process of photosynthesis.

12. Assertion (A) Forests are the dynamic living entities.
Reason (R) Forests provide habitat for wildlife.

Part II

Very Short Answer Type Questions

13. Give one example of a food chain.

14. Explain why forest should be conserved?

Short Answer Type Questions

15. The decaying matter is always moist and warm. Explain why?

16. Write the importance of bacteria in the forest ecosystem.

Long Answer Type Question

17. Forests help in maintaining a perfect water cycle in nature. Explain two other ways in which forests benefit us.

Answers

1. (d) 2. (a) 3. (d) 4. (b) 5. (c) 6. dependent 7. deforestation 8. True 9. True 10. A-4, B-5, C-1, D-2, E-3 11. (d) 12. (b)

CHAPTER 13

Wastewater Story

Water is the elixir of life. We use water everyday in our day-to-day activities. For example, drinking, bathing, washing clothes, cooking food, washing utensils, flushing toilets, mopping the floors, etc. Thus, we cannot think of our life without water. We all use water and in that process make it dirty. The water rich in lather, mixed with oil and other pollutants that goes down the drains from sinks, showers, toilets, laundries, etc., is dirty. It is called **wastewater**. This used water should not be wasted. We must clean it by removing pollutants.

13.1 Water: Our Lifeline

Water is needed by all forms of life. Clean water is a basic need of human beings. Unfortunately, it is not available to a large segment of human population.

The water which is unfit for human consumption, becomes the source of many water-related diseases and even deaths. It is estimated that more than one billion people have no access to safe drinking water.

There is an increase in the scarcity of freshwater due to population growth, pollution, industrial development, mismanagement and other factors.

So, realising the importance of water, we celebrate March 22 as **World Water Day** to raise awareness amongst people about safe water that is fit for human consumption.

The clearning of water is a process of removing pollutants from wastewater before it enters a waterbody or is reused. This process of wastewater treatment is commonly known as **sewage treatment**. It takes place in several steps that are discussed later in this chapter.

> **Water for Life**
>
> On World Water Day, i.e. 22 March, 2005, the General Assembly of the United Nations proclaimed the period 2005-2015 as the International Decade for Action on **Water for Life.** All efforts made during this decade aim to reduce by half the number of people who do not have access to safe drinking water.
>
> **WATER FOR LIFE 2005–2015**

13.2 Sewage

It is wastewater released by homes, industries, hospitals, agricultural fields and other places of human activities. It also includes rainwater that has run down the street during a storm or heavy rain. Sewage is a liquid waste. Most of its water has dissolved and suspended impurities.

Composition of Sewage

The sewage constitutes the following components

(i) **Organic impurities**, e.g. human faeces, animal wastes (animal dung), urea (as urine), oil, fruits and vegetable wastes, pesticides, herbicides, etc.

(ii) **Inorganic impurities**, e.g. nitrates, phosphates and metals.

(iii) **Nutrients**, e.g. nitrogen and phosphorus.

(iv) **Bacteria**, e.g. *Vibrio cholerae* and *Salmonella paratyphi* that cause water-borne diseases namely cholera and typhoid, respectively.

(v) **Other microbes**, e.g. Protozoa that causes a water-borne disease called dysentery.

13.3 Water Freshens Up: An Eventful Journey

In a house or public building, there are generally two sets of pipes. One set of pipes brings clean drinking water into the house and the other set of pipes takes away wastewater (sewage) from the house. For proper sanitation, a well maintained sewerage system is required.

Sewerage System

An underground network of pipes that carries away dirty drainage water and waste matter or sewage from houses and other buildings is called **sewer.**

The provision of drainage at a place by laying sewers under the ground is called **sewerage**. It is like a transport system that carries the sewage from the point of origin to the point of disposal, i.e. sewage treatment plant.

Manholes

These are covered vertical holes in the ground, pavement or road positioned above the underground sewer pipeline. Through these holes, workers can go down to inspect and clean the sewer pipes.

Manholes are located every 50-60 m distance in the sewer pipeline. These are present at the junction of two or more sewers and at points where there is a change in the direction of sewer line.

Try These 13.1

1. **Name the process that involves the removal of pollutants from wastewater before it enters a waterbody or is reused.**
2. **Name one microorganism found in liquid waste other than bacteria.**
3. **Name the vertically covered holes in the ground that are located every 50-60 m distance in the sewer pipelines.**

13.4 Wastewater Treatment Plant (WWTP)

A place where wastewater or sewage from houses and other buildings is brought for processing is called wastewater treatment plant. Treatment of wastewater involves physical, biological and chemical processes depending on the nature of contaminants.

1. Physical Process (Screening)

Wastewater is passed through bar screens. These screens remove large objects like rags, sticks, cans, polybags, napkins, etc., from the wastewater.

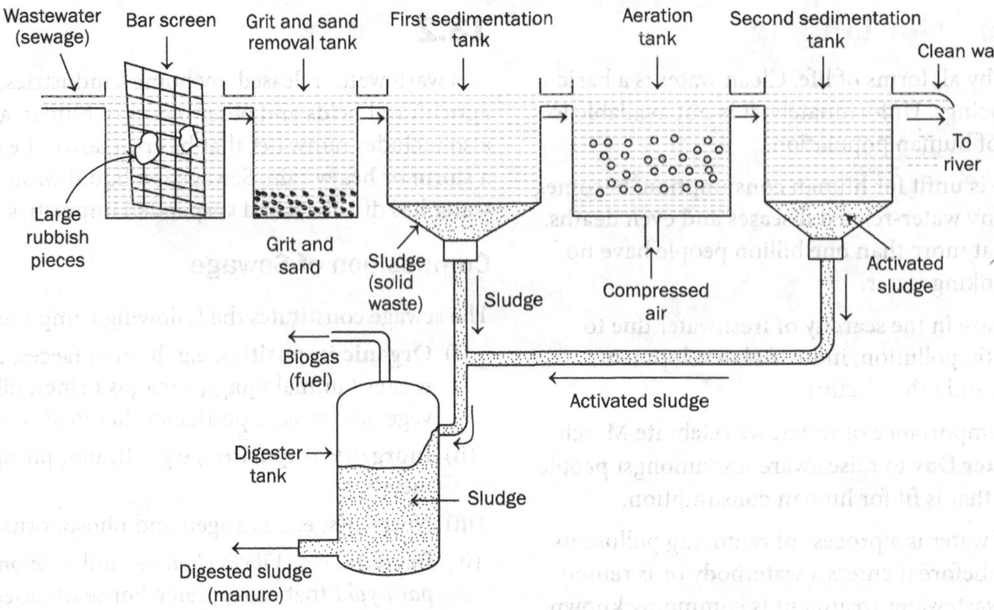

Wastewater treatment plant

After passing through the bar screen, wastewater is taken to a tank called **grit** and **sand removal tank**. In this tank, the speed of the incoming wastewater is decreased that allows sand, pebbles and grit to settle down at the bottom of the tank.The settled sand and impurities are removed from the tanks from time to time.

2. Biological Process

The biological treatment of wastewater involves the following ways

- The wastewater is allowed to settle in a large tank called the **first sedimentation tank** which is sloped towards the centre. Solid waste like faeces settle at the bottom and is called **sludge**. It is removed from the tank by a **scraper**. Oils and grease that float at the surface of water are removed by skimmer. The cleared water is called **clarified water**.
- The sludge is then transferred to a separate tank called the **digester tank**. Here, it is decomposed by the **anaerobic bacteria**. The biogas produced in the process can be used as fuel or to produce electricity.
- The clarified water is sent to **aeration tank**. Air is pumped into the clarified water that help in the growth of aerobic bacteria. These bacteria ultimately consume human waste, food waste, soaps and other unwanted matter still remaining in clarified water.

3. Chemical Process

The chemical treatment of wastewater is carried out in the following ways

- The water from the aeration tank is allowed to stand for several hours in a tank called **second sedimentation tank**. The suspended microbes settle at the bottom of the tank in the form of **activated sludge**. The water is then removed from the top.
- The activated sludge is about 97% water. This water is removed by sand drying beds or machines. The dried sludge is used as **manure**, that helps in returning organic matter and nutrients to the soil.
- The treated water has a very low level of organic material and suspended matter. It is discharged into a river, sea or ground.
- The water in a river is cleaned naturally by the processes that are similar to wastewater treatment plant.
- Sometimes, it is necessary to clean or disinfect water with chemicals like chlorine and ozone before releasing it into the distribution system.

SCIENCE INSIGHT Public treatment facilities are required to treat over 8 million tons of dry weight sludge per year. It accounts for one-third of their total electricity consumption.

Become an Active Citizen

Waste generation is a natural part of human activities. But we can limit the type and quantity of waste produced by us. Often, we have been repelled by offensive smells. The sight of open drains is disgusting. The situation worsens in the rainy season when the drains start overflowing. We have to wade through the mud pools on the roads. Unhygienic and unsanitary conditions fasten the breeding of flies, mosquitoes and other insects. As enlightened citizens we should approach the Municipality or Gram Panchayat. We should insist that open drains should be covered. If the sewage of any particular house makes the neighbourhood dirty, we should request them to be more considerate about other's health.

Note Planting *Eucalyptus* trees all along sewage ponds should be encouraged. These trees absorb surplus wastewater rapidly and release pure water vapour into the atmosphere.

13.5 Better Housekeeping Practices

We must minimise and manage waste at our houses before its disposal in the following manner :

(i) Cooking oil and fats should not be thrown down the drain. They can harden and block the pipes. In an open drain, the fats clog the soil pores and reduce its effectiveness in filtering water. Throw oil and fats in the dustbin.

(ii) Used tea leaves, solid food remains, soft toys, cotton, sanitary towels, etc. should also be thrown in the dustbin. These wastes choke the drains. They do not allow free flow of oxygen and hamper the degradation process.

(iii) Chemicals like paints, solvents, insecticides, medicines and motor oils should not be thrown in drains as they may kill microbes that help to purify water.

Do not throw everything in the sink

Swachh Bharat

In the year 2016, the Government of India initiated a new mission called 'Swachh Bharat'. Under this mission a lot of drives, such as proper sewage disposal and providing toilets for everyone have been started.

Try These 13.2

1. **Scrapers and skimmers are used in wastewater treatment plants. Which of these is used to remove oil and grease that float on the surface of water?**
2. **Name the tree that absorbs wastewater and release pure water vapours into the atmosphere.**
3. **Fats and oils are the important energy sources in the human diet. Does their direct disposal in drains cause any harm in the treatment of wastewater?**

13.6 Sanitation and Disease

Contaminated drinking water and poor sanitation practices are the major causes of a large number of infectious diseases in our country.

Safe sewage disposal facilities are still not available in many cities and villages in India. So, people go to open places to defecate. For example, on dry riverbeds, on railway tracks, near fields and many times directly in water.

Untreated human excreta is a health hazard which causes both soil pollution and water pollution. It pollutes both the surface water and groundwater.

Groundwater is a source of water for wells, tubewells, springs and many rivers. The contaminated groundwater can spread many water borne diseases like cholera, typhoid, polio, meningitis, hepatitis and dysentery.

Vermi-processing Toilets

In the vermi-processing toilets, human excreta is treated by earthworms in a pit. The earthworms usually eat all the organic matter present in human excreta and turn it into compost. These toilets use very less water for the safe processing of human waste.

13.7 Alternative Arrangement for Sewage Disposal

In places (such as Rural areas and isolated buildings) that do not have proper sewage disposal system, low cost on-site sewage systems are installed. For example, septic tanks, chemical toilets, compositing pits.

(i) **Septic tanks** These are suitable for places where there is no sewerage system, hospitals, isolated buildings or cluster of 4 to 5 houses. These tanks need cleaning every four to six months.

(ii) **Composting pits** These are self sustained human waste disposal units that are not connected to a sewer line or a septic tank. A composting toilet breaks down and dehydrate human waste to compost.

(iii) **Chemical toilets** These toilets have limited storage capacity for human waste and need to be emptied periodically. These toilets use chemically treated reservoir located just below the toilet seats. The chemicals reduce the foul smell emitting from human excreta and carry out partial disinfection of human waste.

Some organisations offer hygienic on-site waste disposal technology. These toilets do not require scavenging. The waste from these toilets flow through covered drains into a biogas plant for the generation of biogas. The produced biogas is used as a source of energy.

13.8 Sanitation at Public Places

In our country, fairs are organised periodically. A large number of people participate in them. In the same way, railway stations, bus depots, airports and hospitals are very busy places. Thousands of people visit these place daily which generate a large amount of waste. It must be disposed off properly otherwise epidemics could break out. The government has laid down certain standards of sanitation, but unfortunately, they are not strictly enforced. We should not scatter litter anywhere. If there is no dustbin in sight, we should carry the litter home and throw it in the dustbin.

Conclusion

We all must contribute in keeping our environment clean and healthy. We must realise our responsibility to maintain the water sources in a healthy state. Adopting good sanitation practices should be our way of life. As agents of change, our individual initiative will make a great difference. We should be able to influence others with our energy ideas and optimism. A lot can be done if people work together. There is great power in collective action.

As active citizens, we have many responsibilities regarding sanitation. These can be listed as follows

(i) To ensure that our surroundings are clean.

(ii) To ensure that the sewerage system in our house is properly managed.

(iii) If any leakage or any open drain in the sewerage system is present, then it should be reported to the Municipality or the Gram Panchayats to insist that the open drain must be covered properly so that several air and water-borne diseases can be prevented.

Try These 13.3

1. **Name the type of pollution other than water pollution which is caused by untreated human excreta.**
2. **Are meningitis and hepatitis water-borne diseases?**
3. **Which alternate sewage disposal system is best suited for hospitals and isolated buildings?**
4. **What is the use of biogas produced in biogas plants?**

Science Glossary

Aeration Introduction of air into a material.

Aerobic bacteria Organism / bacteria that require oxygen for its growth.

Anaerobic bacteria Organism that does not require oxygen for its growth.

Biogas A fuel that is produced when organic matter such as food or animal waste is broken down by microorganism in the absence of oxygen.

Contaminant Dissolved and suspended impurities in the sewage or wastewater.

Sanitation Process of settling solid particles at the bottom of a liquid.

Sewage Wastewater released by homes, industries, agricultural fields, etc.

Sewer An underground pipe that carries away dirty drainage water.

Sewerage The provision of drainage at a place by laying sewers under the ground.

Sludge Solid waste that settles at the bottom of the first sedimentation tank during wastewater treatment.

Wastewater The dirty water that goes down the drains from sinks, showers, toilets, laundaries.

Let's Investigate

ACTIVITY 1 (Page 157)

Aim To do a survey of open drains near your home.

Procedure Locate an open drain near your home, school or on the roadside and inspect the water flowing through it.

Observation The observations made from the survey of open drains are tabulated below.

S. No	Types of sewage	Point of origin	Substances which contaminate	Any other remark
1.	Sullage water	Kitchen	Cooking oils, fats, etc.	Choke drains
2.	Foul waste	Toilets	Faeces and urine	Cause diseases like dysentery cholera, etc.
3.	Trade waste	Industrial and commercial organisations	Chemicals like paints, solvents, motor oil, etc.	Causes water and soil pollution

Viva Questions

1. Write down any three types of sewage.
2. What is the point of origin of trade waste ?

ACTIVITY 2 (Page 158)

Aim To treat polluted water and make it clean.

Materials Required Funnel, glass jar, filter paper, funnel stand, soil, grass piece, orange peels, detergent, ink, strainer, beaker, water, aerator, test tube, sand, gravel, chlorine tablet.

Procedure

1. Fill a large glass jar 3/4 full of water. Add some dirty organic matter such as grass pieces or orange peels, a small amount of detergent and a few drops of any ink or any colour.
2. Cap the jar, shake it well and let the mixture stand in the Sunlight for two days.
3. After two day, shake the mixture and pour the sample into a test tube. Label this test tube as 'Sample A'.
4. Now , use an aerator to bubble air through the sample in glass jar. Allow several hours for aeration by leaving the aerator attached overnight.
5. The next day when aeration is complete, pour another sample into a second test tube. Label it as 'Sample B'
6. Fold a piece of filter paper to form a cone. Wet the paper with tap water and then insert the cone into a funnel. Mount the funnel on a funnel stand.
7. Place layers of sand, fine gravel and finally medium gravel in the funnel.
8. Pour the remaining aerated liquid through the filter into the beakers.
9. Do not allow the liquid to spill over the filter. If the filtered liquid is not clear, filter it a few times until you get clear water.
10. Pour a sample of filtered water into a third test tube and label it as 'Sample C'.
11. Pour another sample of the filtered water into a fourth test tube. Add a small piece of chlorine tablet in this test tube.
12. Mix it well, until the water is clean and label it as 'Sample D'.

Observation The observations made on different samples of water are tabulated below.

Samples	State	Colour	Transparency	Smell
A.	Raw sample (before treatment)	Greyish	Almost opaque	Foul smell
B.	After aeration	Greyish	Almost opaque	Unpleasa-nt smell
C.	After filtration	Almost colourless	Almost transparent	No smell
D.	After chlorination	Colourless	Transparent	Odourless

Conclusion From this activity, we can understand the processes that take place at the wastewater treatment plant.

Viva Questions

1. After aeration, does the smell disappear?
2. After which process does the water become colourless?

Mind Map

Wastewater Story

Water
Water is needed by all forms of life. Clean water is a basic need of human beings.

Wastewater
The water rich in lather, mixed with oil and other pollutants that goes down the drains from sinks, showers, toilets, laundries, etc., is dirty.

Sewage
Wastewater released by homes, industries, hospitals, agriculture, etc.

Composition
Organic and inorganic impurities, nutrients, microbes, etc.

Alternate Arrangement for Sewage Disposal
- **Septic tanks** In area where sewerage system is lacking.
- **Composting pits** Breakdown and dehydrate waste to compost.
- **Chemical toilets** Use chemically treated reservoir below toilet seats.
- **Vermi-composting toilets** Earthworms decompose excreta to form compost.

Wastewater Treatment Plant
- Place where wastewater from houses and other places is brought for processing.
- Involves three stages of processing.

Physical Processing
- Bar screens remove large materials from wastewater.
- In grit and sand removal tank, sand, pebbles and grit settle down.

Biological Processing
- Solid waste settles in first sedimentation tank to form sludge.
- In digester tank, sludge is decomposed by anaerobic bacteria.
- Clarified water is pumped with air in aeration tank.

Chemical Processing
- In second sedimentation tank, activated sludge is formed.
- Sometimes, chlorine and ozone are added in water as disinfectants.

Better Housekeeping Practices to Manage Waste
- Cooking oil and fats should not be thrown down the drain. They can harden and block the pipes.
- Used tea leaves, solid food remains, soft toys, cotton, sanitary towels, etc. should also be thrown in the dustbin. These wastes choke the drains.
- Chemicals like paints, solvents, insecticides, medicines and motor oils should not be thrown in drains as they may kill microbes that help to purify water.

NCERT FOLDER

Complete Explanations of all NCERT's Questions

Intext Questions

Q.1 Have you ever thought where the wastewater goes and what happens to it? **Page 156**

Ans. The wastewater goes into the sewers and then it gets treated in a wastewater treatment plant.

Q.2 In case you do not have a sewerage system in your locality, find out how sewage is being disposed off? **Page 158**

Ans. Refer to text on page no. 228.

Q.3 What changes did you observe in the appearance of the liquid after aeration? **Page 159**

Ans. The colour changed slightly after aeration.

Q.4 Did aeration change the odour? **Page 159**

Ans. Yes, aeration changes the odour slightly.

Q.5 What was removed by the sand filter? **Page 159**

Ans. Sand filter is used to remove the suspended matter from wastewater.

Q.6 Did chlorine remove the colour? **Page 159**

Ans. Yes, chlorine removed the colour of contaminated water.

Q.7 Did chlorine have an odour? Was it worse than that of the wastewater? **Page 159**

Ans. Chlorine has an odour. But it is not worse than that of the wastewater.

Q.8 Do not add to the load of WWTP. Paheli wonders how? **Page 161**

Ans. We can reduce the load of WWTP by adopting proper sanitation and house-keeping practices and by generating less waste at an individual level.

Q.9 A vast number of our people are still without sewerage facilities. Where do they relieve themselves? **Page 162**

Ans. A large fraction of our people defecates in the open on dry riverbeds, on railway tracks, near fields and many times directly in water.

Q.10 Bhoojo wants to know how sewage is disposed off in an aeroplane? **Page 162**

Ans. Wastewater generated in flights is stored in a holding tank on the aircraft until the plane sets down. When its on the ground, a service truck rolls up and pumps the contents of the plane's holding tank abroad. A work station at the airport serves to empty the truck's tank into community wastewater processing system.

Exercise

Q.1 Fill in the blanks.

(a) **Cleaning of water is a process of removing ....**

(b) **Wastewater released by houses is called ....**

(c) **Dried .... is used as manure.**

(d) **Drains get blocked by .... and ....**

Ans. (a) pollutants

(b) sewage

(c) sludge

(d) solid food remains, oil

Q.2 What is sewage? Explain, why it is harmful to discharge untreated sewage into rivers or sea?

Ans. Sewage is the wastewater containing both liquid and solid wastes (suspended solids) produced by human activities in homes, industries, hospitals, offices, etc.

Sewage contains various contaminants including disease causing bacteria and other microbes. If untreated sewage is discharged into rivers or sea, then the water in the rivers or sea would get contaminated.

If this contaminated water is used for drinking, it can cause diseases such as cholera, typhoid, dysentery, etc. which may lead to death. That is why, it is harmful to discharge untreated sewage into rivers or the sea.

Q.3 Why should oils and fats not be released in the drain? Explain.

Ans. Refer to text on page no. 227.

Q.4 Describe the steps involved in getting clarified water from wastewater.

Ans. Refer to text on page no. 227.

Q.5 What is sludge? Explain, how it is treated?

Ans. Collected semi-solid wastes such as faeces that settle down during wastewater treatment are called sludge.

The sludge is removed by using a scraper and then transferred to a tank where it is decomposed by anaerobic bacteria to produce biogas. This biogas is used as a low cost fuel for heating, cooking, etc. Activated sludge produced by the decomposition of bacteria is used as manure.

Q.6 Untreated human excreta is a health hazard. Explain.

Ans. Human excreta may cause water pollution and soil pollution which can lead to a lot of health related problems. Water polluted with it contains disease causing bacteria which can spread epidemics and become the most common route for water-borne diseases like cholera, dysentery, typhoid, etc.

Q.7 Name two chemicals used to disinfect water.

Ans. Two chemicals used to disinfect water are chlorine and ozone.

Q.8 Explain the function of bar screens in a wastewater treatment plant.

Ans. The wastewater is allowed to pass through bar screens so that large solid objects such as rags, napkins, cans, plastic bags, polythene, etc. present in the wastewater can be removed during the filtration process.

Q.9 Explain the relationship between sanitation and disease.

Ans. Sanitation and disease are related to each other. A lack of sanitation can cause diseases. In our country, a large number of people, even today, do not have sewerage facilities and thus, they defecate in open fields, railway tracks, etc. The untreated human excreta, pollutes soil and water resources (including underground water). When this contaminated water is used for drinking, it can cause diseases such as cholera, typhoid, hepatitis, dysentery, etc., which may even lead to death.

Q.10 Outline your role as an active citizen in relation to sanitation.

Ans. Refer to text on page no. 228-229.

Q.11 Study the following statements about ozone.

I. It is essential for breathing of living organisms.

II. It is used to disinfect water.

III. It absorbs ultraviolet rays.

IV. Its proportion in air is about 3%.

Which of these statements are correct?

(a) I, II and III
(b) II and III
(c) I and IV
(d) All of the above

Ans. (b) Ozone is used as a water disinfectant. It absorbs harmful ultraviolet rays from the Sun.

REVIEW EXERCISE

Including Competency Based Questions

Part I

Multiple Choice Questions

1. Which of the following is wastewater? NCERT Exemplar
(a) Water trickling from a damaged tap
(b) Water coming out of a shower
(c) Water flowing in a river
(d) Water coming out of a laundry

2. Which of the following is not a source of wastewater? NCERT Exemplar
(a) Sewers (b) Homes
(c) Industries (d) Hospitals

3. Sewage is mainly a NCERT Exemplar
(a) liquid waste (b) solid waste
(c) gaseous waste (d) mixture of solid and gas

4. Which of the following is not an inorganic impurity present in sewage?
(a) Nitrate (b) Phosphorus
(c) Urea (d) Metal salt

5. Which of the following is a part of inorganic impurities of the sewage?
(a) Pesticides (b) Urea
(c) Phosphates (d) Vegetable waste

6. Why should we not use detergents while washing clothes in ponds and rivers?
(a) Detergents contain chlorine
(b) Detergents have an odour
(c) Detergents contain phosphates
(d) Detergents absorb dissolved oxygen

7. The system of a network of pipes used for taking away wastewater from homes or public buildings to the treatment plant is known as NCERT Exemplar
(a) sewers (b) sewerage
(c) transport system (d) treatment plant

8. In a filtration plant, water is filtered using layers of
(a) sand and clay
(b) clay and fine gravel
(c) sand and fine gravel
(d) sand, fine gravel and medium gravel

9. Pick from the following one chemical used to disinfect water.
(a) Chlorine (b) Washing
(c) Silica (d) Coal

10. Chlorine is used in municipal water treatment plants to
(a) change the taste of water
(b) prevent evaporation
(c) kill the harmful microorganisms
(d) prevent sedimentation

11. Which of the following organisms produce biogas from sludge in the digester tank of a wastewater treatment plant?
(a) Anaerobic bacteria (b) Fungi
(c) Aerobic bacteria (d) Protozoa

12. The aerobic bacteria can be grown in clarified water by
(a) filtration (b) sewage
(c) aeration (d) sedimentation

13. Which of the following is/are products of wastewater treatment? NCERT Exemplar
(a) Biogas (b) Sludge
(c) Both (a) and (b) (d) Aerator

14. One of the following types of trees is helpful in purifying wastewater quite rapidly when planted all along the sewage ponds. These are
(a) *Eucalyptus* trees (b) *Ficus* trees
(c) neem trees (d) peepal trees

15. Which one of the following is a quality of wastewater?
(a) Fowl smell (b) Bad taste
(c) Dirty look (d) All of these

16. Open drain system is a breeding place for which of the following? NCERT Exemplar
(a) Flies
(b) Mosquitoes
(c) Organisms which cause diseases
(d) All of the above

17. Which of these diseases can be caused by polluted water? Competency Based Que.
(a) AIDS (b) Cancer (c) Cholera (d) Influenza

18. Water polluted by various human activities causes a number of water borne disease. Which of the following is not a water borne disease? NCERT Exemplar
(a) Cholera (b) Typhoid
(c) Asthma (d) Dysentry

19. **Choose the most appropriate option regarding the measure that can be taken in households to ensure protection from water borne diseases.**
(a) Boil the tap water before cooking or drinking
(b) Test the tap water for bacterial culture growth
(c) Disinfect the village water supply using UV light
(d) Filter the water before irrigation fields of food crops

Answers

1. (d)	2. (a)	3. (a)	4. (c)	5. (c)
6. (c)	7. (b)	8. (d)	9. (a)	10. (c)
11. (a)	12. (c)	13. (c)	14. (a)	15. (d)
16. (d)	17. (c)	18. (c)	19. (a)	

Fill in the Blanks

1. **Wastewater released by houses is called ....**
2. **Wastewater is treated in ....**
3. **Dried sludge is used as ....**
4. **Untreated human excreta is a .... hazard.**
5. **Fill in the blanks in the following statements using words given in the box.**

air, handpumps, cholera, water, large, ground

A very .... number of people defecate in the open. It may cause .... pollution and soil pollution. Both the surface water and .... water gets polluted, ... water is the source for wells, tubewells and .... Thus, it becomes the most common route for .... borne disease like ...., dysentery, etc. **NCERT Exemplar**

Answers

1. sewage
2. wastewater treatment plant
3. manure
4. health
5. large, water, ground, ground, handpumps, water, cholera.

True/False

1. **Used water is wastewater.**
2. **Wastewater could be reused.**
3. **Sewage is a solid waste which causes water pollution and soil pollution.** **NCERT Exemplar**
4. **Microorganisms are present in the domestic waste also.**
5. **Sewage should not be treated before being disposed off into the water bodies.**

Answers

1. True
2. True
3. False, sewage is a liquid waste which causes water pollution and soil pollution.
4. True
5. False, sewage should be treated before being disposed off into the water bodies.

Match the Columns

1. **Match the Column I with Column II.** **NCERT Exemplar**

	Column I		Column II
A.	Inorganic impurities	1.	Phosphorus and nitrogen
B.	Organic impurities	2.	Nitrates and phosphates
C.	Nutrients	3.	Cholera and typhoid
D.	Bacteria	4.	Pesticides and herbicides

2. **Match the Column I with Column II.**

	Column I		Column II
A.	Chlorine	1.	Second sedimentation tank
B.	Activated sludge	2.	Disinfectant
C.	Biogas	3.	Scraper
D.	Sludge	4.	Anaerobic bacteria

Answers

1. A–2, B–4, C–1, D–3
2. A–2, B–1, C–4, D–3

Assertion-Reason Questions

The following questions consist of two statements, Assertion (A) and Reason (R). Answer the following questions by selecting the appropriate option given below.

(a) Both A and R are true and R is the correct explanation of A
(b) Both A and R are true, but R is not the correct explanation of A
(c) A is true, but R is false
(d) A is false, but R is true

1. **Assertion** (A) Nitrates, phosphates and metals are inorganic impurities in sewage.
   Reason (R) Aeration is the first step to treat polluted water.
2. **Assertion** (A) *Eucalyptus* trees should be planted along the sewage ponds.
   Reason (R) *Eucalyptus* trees absorb surplus wastewater rapidly.
3. **Assertion** (A) Cooking oil and fats should be thrown down the drain.
   Reason (R) They can harden and block the pipes.

Answers

1. (c) A is true, but R is false. R can be corrected as Aeration is a part of secondary treatment process.
2. (a) Both A and R are true and R is the correct explanation of A.
3. (d) A is false, but R is true. Acan be corrected as Cooking oil and fats should not be thrown down the drain.

Case Based Questions

1. Which of these actions can cause water pollution? Circle 'Yes or No' for the correct response.

	Will this cause water pollution?	Yes or No
(i)	Dumping of car battery in drains	Yes/No
(ii)	Catching fish from rivers	Yes/No
(iii)	Swimming in ponds and lakes	Yes/No

Competency Based Que.

2. Which of these is a safe practice to find out if a water sample is polluted? Circle 'Yes or No' for the correct response.

	Is this a safe practice?	Yes or No
(i)	Check for odour in the water sample	Yes/No
(ii)	Check the taste of the water sample	Yes/No
(iii)	Check the colour of the water sample	Yes/No

Competency Based Que.

Answers

1. (i) Yes
   (ii) No
   (iii) No
2. (i) Yes
   (ii) No
   (iii) Yes

Part II

Very Short Answer Type Questions

1. The used water should not be wasted. Do you agree? Justify.

Ans. The used water should not be wasted, infact it should be cleaned and reused.

2. What is wastewater released from homes commonly known as?

Ans. The wastewater released from homes is commonly known as sewage.

3. World Water Day is celebrated on ....

Ans. 22 March.

4. Mention the period proclaimed as the international decade for action on water for life.

Ans. The period between 2005 -2015 is proclaimed as the international decade for action on water for life..

5. Mention the common process of cleaning of wastewater.

Ans. Sewage treatment.

6. Name two inorganic impurities present in sewage.

Ans. Inorganic impurities present in sewage are nitrates and phosphates. **NCERT Exemplar**

7. Animal waste, oil and urea are some of the organic impurities present in sewage. Name two more organic impurities present in sewage. **NCERT Exemplar**

Ans. Fruits and vegetable wastes, pesticides and herbicides are organic impurities present in sewage other than animal wastes, oil and urea.

8. Protozoa is causative organism of which waterborne disease?

Ans. Dysentry.

9. Sewage contains some organic impurities in it. Name them.

Ans. Human faeces, animal wastes, oil, urea, pesticides, herbicides, fruits and vegetables are the organic impurities present in sewage

10. Explain sewers and sewage.

Ans. Sewers are the pipes that act as a transport system to carry sewage from point of origin to the point of disposal. The wastewater released from homes, industries, hospitals, offices and other uses is called sewage.

11. Name the three processes involved in the treatment of wastewater.

Ans. Treatment of wastewater involves physical, chemical and biological processes for removing different types of contaminants.

12. Mention the use of dried sludge.

Ans. It is used as manure, that help in returning organic matter and nutrients to the soil.

13. Name two things that are formed from sludge and are extracted during the treatment of sewage.

Ans. Biogas and manure.

14. *Eucalyptus* trees are planted along sewage ponds. Give reason.

Ans. The *Eucalyptus* trees are planted along sewage ponds because these trees absorb surplus wastewater rapidly and release pure water vapour into the atmosphere.

15. Sanitation can be improved. Explain, what steps should be taken to improve it?

Ans. Low cost onsite sewage disposal system must be encouraged to improve sanitation.

Short Answer Type Questions

1. Sewage also contains some nutrients. Comment.

Ans. Sewage is a complex mixture which contains suspended solids, organic and inorganic impurities, nutrients, saprotrophic and disease causing bacteria and other microbes.

The nutrients present in sewage are phosphorus and nitrogen.

2. The terms sewage, sewers and sewerage are interlinked with each other. Can you explain, how? **NCERT Exemplar**

Ans. The terms sewage, sewers and sewerage are interlinked with each other because sewage is a mixture of wastewater coming out of homes and other places. Sewers are pipes that carry sewage and sewerage is a network of sewage carrying pipes.

3. A sewage treatment plant involves a few steps.

Aeration tank, grit and sand removal tank, second sedimentation tank, bar screen, first sedimentation tank.

(i) Arrange all the above steps in the correct order in which they occur in the sewage treatment plant.

(ii) Which step gives most of the sludge?

Ans. (i) Bar screen, grit and sand removal tank, first sedimentation tank, aeration tank, second sedimentation tank.

(ii) First sedimentation tank.

4. Given below is a jumbled sequence of the processes involved in a wastewater treatment plant. Arrange them in their correct sequence.

(i) Sludge is scraped out and skimmer removes floating grease.

(ii) Water is made to settle in a large tank with a slope in the middle.

(iii) Large objects like plastic bags are removed by passing wastewater through bar screens.

(iv) Sand, grit and pebbles are made to settle by decreasing the speed of incoming wastewater.

(v) Wastewater enters a grit and sand removal tank. **Competency Based Que.**

Ans. The correct sequence of wastewater treatment in treatment plant is

(iii) Large objects like plastic bags are removed by passing wastewater through bar screens.

(v) Wastewater enters a grit and sand removal tank.

(iv) Sand, grit and pebbles are made to settle by decreasing the speed of incoming wastewater.

(ii) Water is made to settle in a large tank with a slope in the middle.

(i) Sludge is scraped out and skimmer removes the floating grease.

5. Observe the given figure and answer the following

(a) What does this figure show?

(b) State the functions of each part of the figure.

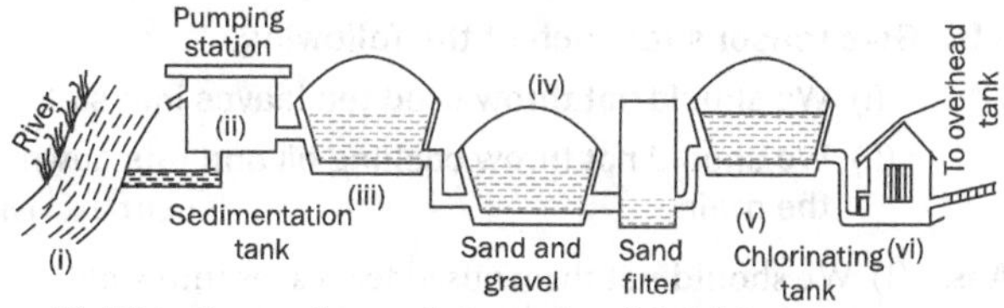

Ans. (i) This figure shows the supply of drinking water, its processing and the source of water. Functions of each part of the figure.

(ii)
- **River** It is the source of water.
- **Pumping station** Pump the water to collect it in reservoir.
- **Sedimentation tank** Impurities settle in the bottom of tank.
- **Sand and gravel and sand filter** Remove the dirt from the water.
- **Chlorinating tank** Chlorine is mixed in water to disinfect the water and kill the germs.
- **To overhead tank** Purified water is stored in this tank for supply to households for drinking.

6. Three statements are provided here which define the terms, i.e. sludge, sewage and wastewater.

Pick out the correct definition for each of these terms.

(i) The settled solids that are removed in wastewater treatment with a scraper.

(ii) Water from kitchen used for washing dishes.

(iii) Wastewater released from homes, industries, hospitals and other public buildings. **NCERT Exemplar**

Ans. (i) The settled solids that are removed in wastewater treatment with a scraper is sludge.

(ii) Water from kitchen which is used for washing dishes is wastewater.

(iii) Wastewater released from homes, industries, hospitals and other public buildings is sewage.

7. Water in a river is cleaned naturally. Do you agree? Think and explain.

Ans. Yes, river water is cleaned naturally by a process that is similar to wastewater treatment plant.

When muddy water, flows through grass or weeds on its way to a stream, mud and solid particles get filtered out. At the bottom of a lake or stream, microorganism brings chemical changes in the water.

The natural filtration process removes pollutants from the groundwater thus, making it clean and fit for drinking.

8. Open drain is a big concern now-a-days. Justify.

Ans. Open drain is a big concern for the society now-a-days because it creates unhygienic conditions. It provides favourable conditions to flies, mosquitoes and other insects to breed and spread a number of diseases.

9. Give reasons for each of the following.

(i) We should not throw used tea leaves into sink.

(ii) We should not throw cooking oil and fats down the drain. **NCERT Exemplar**

Ans. (i) We should not throw used tea leaves into sink because these may choke the drain-pipe of the sink.

(ii) We should not throw cooking oil and fats down the drain as these can harden and block the drain-pipes.

10. Recall and enlist some better housekeeping practices.

Ans. Refer to text on page no. 227.

11. Describe on-site disposal systems.

Ans. Some organisations offer hygienic on-site human waste disposal technology. These toilets do not require scavenging.

Excreta from the toilets flow through covered drains into a biogas plant. The biogas thus, produced is used as a source of energy.

12. Suggest two alternative arrangements for sewage disposal where there is no sewerage system.

Ans. The two alternative arrangements for sewage disposal, where there is no sewerage system are as below

(i) Septic tanks

(ii) Composting pits.

13. Can we contribute in sanitation at public places? Explain.

Ans. Yes, we all have a role to play in keeping our environment clean and healthy. All of us can contribute in maintaining sanitation at public places. We should not scatter litter anywhere. If there is no dustbin in sight, we should carry the litter home and throw it in the dustbin.

14. A man travelling in a train threw an empty packet of food on the platform. Do you think this is a proper waste disposal method? Elaborate. **NCERT Exemplar**

Ans. No, one must always put the waste in a nearby dustbin or carry it home and dispose it in dustbins there.

If the waste is not properly disposed, it may enter into the drains and choke them. It also makes public places dirty and unhygienic.

Long Answer Type Questions

1. Explain the different types of inorganic and organic impurities generally present in sewage.

Ans. Refer to text on page no. 225.

2. Think and suggest some ways to minimise waste and pollutants at their source, taking your home as an example. **NCERT Exemplar**

Ans. We can minimise waste and pollutants entering the water and create less wastewater by taking following few steps at home.

(i) By not throwing used tea leaves, solid food remains, etc. in the drain. We should throw them in the dustbin.

(ii) By not throwing chemicals like medicines, paints, insecticides, etc., in the drain as they increase the pollution load of the sewage.

3. Discuss vermi-processing toilets. Name the useful product obtained from such toilets.

Ans. In the vermi-processing toilets, human excreta is treated by earthworms in a pit. The earthworms gradually eat all the organic matter present in human excreta, decompose it and pass out from their body in the form of warm castings (also called vermi cakes).

The useful products obtained from vermi-processing toilets include vermi cakes which are a kind of high quality manure.

4. Discuss various steps of cleaning waste water in a wastewater treatment plant. **NCERT Exemplar**

Ans. Refer to text on page no. 226 and 227.

Case Based Questions

1. The diagram shows a typical wastewater treatment process **Competency Based Que.**

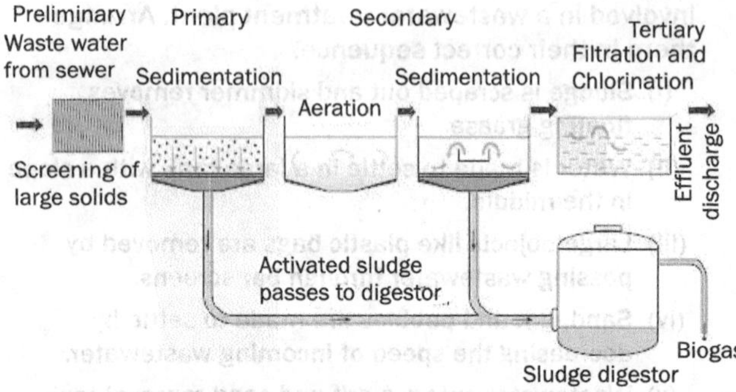

(i) What can be concluded about wastewater treatment process from the diagram?

(a) Sedimentation occurs at the preliminary stage

(b) Aeration of wastes occurs at the primary stage

(c) Removal of solid substances occurs at the tertiary stage

(d) Sedimentation occurs in both primary and secondary stages

(ii) **What is the purpose of chlorination in the wastewater treatment process?**

(a) Removal of large solids

(b) Killing of microorganisms

(c) Addition of dissolved oxygen

(d) Removal of suspended particles

(iii) **What makes the residue from the sludge digestor suitable as organic manure?**

2. The picture shows how human activities can pollute groundwater. An aquifer is a huge reservoir of groundwater.

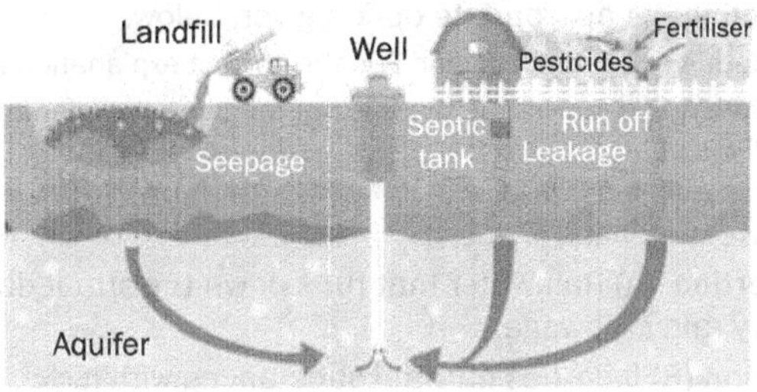

Groundwater pollution

(i) **Which of these measures can reduce groundwater pollution?**

(a) Keep all wells covered

(b) Construct large septic tanks

(c) Grow crops in farms away from water bodies

(d) Make sure that landfill wastes do not contain toxic substances

(ii) **How does defecating in the open cause groundwater pollution?**

Answers

1. (i) (d) Sedimentation occur in both primary and secondary stages.

(ii) (b) Killing of microorganisms.

(iii) Sludge residue is rich in nutrients which makes it suitable as organic manure.

2. (i) (d) Make sure that landfill wastes do not contain toxic substances.

(ii) Defecating in the open causes groundwater pollution because harmful microorganisms from faeces can percolate through the soil and reach the groundwater.

Skill Based Questions as per NEP 2020

1. Visit a village with your parents. Find out the sewage disposal system available there. Compare it with sewage disposal system available in the cities. Observation skill

2. Typhoid and cholera are water-borne disease and caused by *Salmonella paratyphi* and *Vibrio cholerae*, respectively. Find out causative agent for meningitis and hepatitis, which are also water- borne diseases. Experimental skill

3. Trisha has seen huge garbage dumps outside the school campus which are not being regularly disposed off by municipality of the area. She discussed the problem with her biology teacher and decided to organise a rally to spread awareness among local people. Next day she delivered this information in the assembly and convinced the school mates to join her. She also explained them about the importance of sanitation at public places which she had recently studied in biology. Thinking skill

(i) **In your views, who is responsible to maintain sanitation at public places?**

(ii) **What would happen, if all the wastes produced at public places are not disposed off regularly?**

4. One day Sachin had gone to his uncle who lives in a village. He saw there a large number of people defecate in an open area because proper toilet facilities are not there. He wondered about the groundwater contamination, as he studied in his class that this act may cause water-borne diseases. He convinced village people to make toilets in order to avoid such an out break of water-borne diseases. Observation skill

(i) **Name two water-borne diseases.**

(ii) **What values are shown by Sachin?**

ASSESSMENT EXERCISE

Part I

Multiple Choice Questions

1. The period 2005-2015 is being celebrated as the international decade for action on
(a) water for life
(b) education for all
(c) global warming
(d) terrorism

2. In sewerage, manholes are located at every
(a) 20-25 m (b) 50-60 m
(c) 90-100 m (d) 100-110 m

3. Which of these is a part of the wastewater treatment plant?
(a) Septic tank (b) Compost pit
(c) Aeration tank (d) All of these

4. Which of these methods should not be used for the disposal of urine and faeces if no sewage system is available?
(a) Allowing untreated sewage to flow into rivers
(b) Making septic tanks for sewage to flow into
(c) Allowing sewage to flow into a biogas plant
(d) Using a vermi-composting toilet

5. Among the following options which one is a source of wastewater?
(a) Homes (b) Sewerage
(c) Manholes (d) Sewage

Fill in the Blanks

6. Bacteria play an important role in .... tank.
7. The full form of WWTP is ....
8. In hospitals .... toilets are found.

Match the Columns

9. Match the Column I with Column II.

Column I	Column II
A. Oils and grease	1. Low cost onsite sewage
B. Chemical toilets	2. Skimmer
C. Vermicomposting toilets	3. Remove large object
D. Bar screens	4. Earthworms

True/False

10. Urea is an inorganic impurity present in sewage.
11. Aerobic bacteria produces biogas sludge in the digester tank.
12. Typhoid is a water-borne disease.

Assertion-Reason Questions

The following questions consist of two statements Assertion (A) and Reason (R). Answer these questions by selecting the appropriate option given below.
(a) Both A and R are true and R is the correct explanation of A
(b) Both A and R are true, but R is not the correct explanation of A
(c) A is true, but R is false
(d) A is false, but R is true

13. **Assertion** (A) Rainwater that runs down the street during heavy rain is sewage.
Reason (R) It carries harmful substances with it.

14. **Assertion** (A) Ozone is used as a disinfectant.
Reason (R) It kills microorganism present in water.

Part II

Very Short Answer Type Questions

15. Mention two things that we can do to reduce the burden on the wastewater disposal system.
16. Explain how organic matter is separated from sewage?

Short Answer Type Questions

17. Mention one way of overcoming the problem of the lack of sewage systems in villages.
18. Discuss the primary stage of sewage treatment.
19. List the ways in which wastewater present in sewage is generated and the kind of contaminants present in each.

Long Answer Type Question

20. In a city, there are separate pipes for disposing sewage and storing water. Why is this necessary?

Answers

1. (a) 2. (b) 3. (c) 4. (a) 5. (a)
6. digester 7. Wastewater treatment plant
8. Septic tank 9. A–2, B–1, C–4, D–3 10. False
11. True 12. True 13. (b) 14. (a)

Explanations of Skill Based Questions

Chapter 01 Nutrition in Plants

1. Plant identified as pitcher plant grows in nitrogen-deficient soil and feeds on insects to obtain nutrients such as nitrogen.

2. The leaves of pot '*A*' initially give positive iodine test as in the sunlight the plant perform photosynthesis and produce starch. After 3 to 4 days, it might gives negative iodine result due to water deficiency, because both water and sunlight are essential for photosynthesis.

   Plant '*B*' and '*C*' will not give positive iodine test as in the case of plant '*B*' there is no sunlight and plant '*C*' would also not receive any sunlight due to black polythene bag.

3. (i) Decreased level of minerals in soil leads to decrease in crop productivity.

   (ii) After growing leguminous plants, the mineral content of soil is restored and enriched to new level. Yes, the benefit of leguminous plant is the re-enrichment of soil minerals.

4. A greenhouse is generally a glass house that is often used for growing plants in controlled conditions. It helps to grow plants in cold weather by providing regulated conditions.

   (i) Light- It traps maximum sunlight.

   (ii) Water - Capillary mats are used for water. It ensure that plants receive adequate water supply.

   (iii) Carbon dioxide - Fans are placed horizontally that ensures plants get enough CO_2.

5. **Aim** Growing a sweet potato in water.

   Materials Required Sweet potato tuber, glass jar, toothpicks, water.

   Procedure

   1. Select a healthy sweet potato tuber with several buds on its surface.
   2. Fill a glass jar with enough water to submerge the bottom half of the sweet potato.
   3. Insert toothpicks into the sides of the sweet potato, near the top, to hold it in place on the rim of the jar. The toothpicks should rest on the rim, suspending the sweet potato in the water.
   4. Place the jar under direct sunlight.

   Observation We observe some branches of vines sprouting out from the potato within two or three weeks.

Chapter 02 Nutrition in Animals

1. (i) Before having an operation, general anesthetic (drugs that cause anesthesia, which is the loss of sensation) will be given to patient. It will temporarily stop the body's reflexes. In that case if patient eats food just after being operated there is a risk of vomiting or bringing up food into the throat.

   (ii) Glucose is the simplest form of carbohydrate that is directly poured into the blood and absorbed by the body cells. It provides instant energy to all the organs of the body to perform their functions. Thus, it helps the patient to recover fast.

2.

Digestion in human	Digestion in cow
Oral cavity or Mouth (breaks down food, partial digestion of carbohydrate in the presence of salivary enzymes) ↓	Food taken through mouth ↓
Oesophagus (receives food from mouth and passes it to the stomach) ↓	**Rumen** (food partially digested and is called cud) ↓
Stomach (digestion of food, protein digestion in the presence of enzyme) ↓	Cud return to the mouth and animal chews it process called rumination. ↓
Small intestine (intestinal juice completes the digestion of all components of the food, absorption of digested food) ↓	**Reticulum** (filtration of food material) ↓

Digestion in human	**Digestion in cow**
Large intestine (absorb water and some salts from the undigested food material remaining waste passes into the rectum) ↓	**Omasum** (grinding of food) ↓
Rectum (storage of waste) ↓	**Abomasum** (action of digestive juices) ↓
Anus (egestion of faecal matter) ↓	**Small intestine** (absorption of food) ↓
	Large intestine ↓
	Rectum ↓
	Anus (egestion) ↓

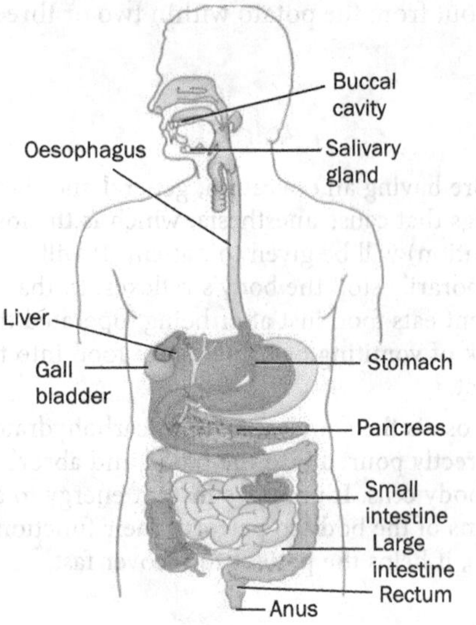

Human digestive system

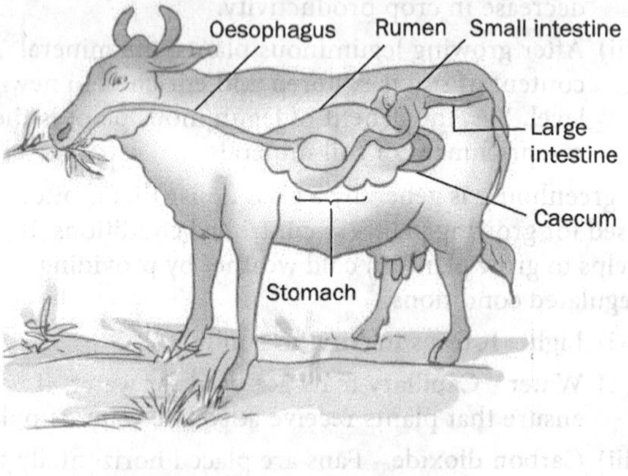

Digestive system of ruminant (cow)

Differences between digestion in human and cow are as follows

Digestion in human	Digestion in cow
Humans primarily use enzymatic digestion.	Cows use fermentation to breakdown cellulose.
They have a single undivided stomach.	They have four-chambered stomach.
They do not have rumination capability.	Cows regurgitate their food and chew it again.
They do not have cellulose digesting bacteria.	They have cellulose digesting bacteria.

3. (i) Hiccups are involuntary contractions of the diaphragm muscle that separates the chest and abdominal cavities. These contractions cause the vocal cords to close, producing the characteristic 'hic' sound.

(ii) When we eat in a hurry talk or laugh, while eating we may get hiccups. This happens when food particles enter the windpipe. Hiccups clears the passage of wind pipe and bring back the food into food pipe.

4. (i) This condition is known as diarrhoea.

(ii) A solution of sugar and salt in water is called Oral Rehydration Solution (ORS).
It contains sodium and potassium salts with glucose. The glucose enables the intestine to absorb the fluid and salts more efficiently. This solution rehydrates the body more effectively than water alone can.

Chapter 03 Heat

1. (i) Radiation

(ii) (b)

(iii) This is because the breeze is flowing towards the land from the sea during the day-time. This helps in keeping the house cool.

(iv) **Spray foam insulation** This method creates an air tight barrier of foam that prevents heat transfer.
Reflective roof coatings Costal areas receive a lot of heat. Applying reflective roof can reduce the absorption of solar heat.

2.(d)

3. Last to first

$A > Z > B > Y > C > X$

Chapter 04 Acids, Bases and Salts

1.Among the three test tubes *A*, *B* and *C*, '*A*' will change the red litmus to blue as baking soda '*A*' is a basic in nature.

2. (i) The reaction takes place is neutralisation reaction in which dil. hydrochloric acid is reacted with sodium hydroxide.

(ii) The complete reaction is as follows

$$\text{Sodium hydroxide} + \text{Hydrochloric acid} \longrightarrow \underset{\text{(salt)}}{\text{Sodium chloride}} + \text{Water}$$

(iii) Sodium hydroxide is a base when it was added to the colourless solution of dil. hydrochloric acid and phenolphthalein indicator, it produced pink colour in the flask.

3. When we write the secret message with the help of lemon juice, it cannot be seen. But when the message is rubbed by the China rose solution it starts appear this is because, lemon juice is acidic in nature and when China rose solution is rubbed it turns to dark pink colour by reacting with an acid and message can be seen.

4. (i) Pain and irritation in the stomach can be due to excess of acids present in stomach. It can be neutralised by taking base such as baking soda, etc.

(ii) Baking soda is basic in nature which can neutralise the excess of acid present in the stomach and provide relief from the pain.

(iii) The values shown by Rahul are intelligent and caring.

Chapter 05 Physical and Chemical Changes

1. (i) The change observed by the Amit is reversible as dissolved sugar in water can be taken back by the process of evaporation.

(ii) Changes observed by Amit is reversible thus, it is a physical change while heating of sugar on a high flame leads to formation of carbon dioxide and water hence, it is a chemical change
Note Melting of sugar is a physical change.

2. (i) Substance '*X*' is magnesium.

(ii) Magnesium oxide.

(iii) The solution of white ash, i.e. magnesium oxide and water, i.e. magnesium hydroxide is basic in nature as it turns red litmus blue.

3. (i) Rahul's cycle gets rusted because it is made up of iron. If iron comes in contact with air and moistures, a brown layer is deposited on it called rust.

(ii) Rusting of iron is the process in which iron is coated with a brownish layer after coming in contact with air and moistures.

4. (i) Sea water, when enclosed in shallow pits, evaporates naturally under the sunlight into vapour, leaving behind a residue containing salt. The residue, i.e. then purified by crystallisation.

(ii) Salt is obtained from sea water by the process of evaporation.

Chapter 06 Respiration in Organisms

1. (i) The breathing rate of males and females are different.

(ii) Breathing rate does not change with age, however the lung functioning decreases.

2. Plants in marshy areas have special type of roots called pneumatophores. These roots help such plants to survive in marshy areas.

3. (i) As a precautionary step, we should cover the nose while sneezing.

(ii) Sneezing is a reflex to expel irritants from nasal passage.

4. (i) Palak had cramps due to muscle fatigue from extended cycling.
   (ii) Yes, breathing rate is affected after prolonged exercising due to increased oxygen demand by the body.
5. (i) Smoking hazards include: 1. lung cancer, 2. cardiovascular diseases, 3. hampered breathing, etc.
   (ii) Yes, passive smoking can affect non-smokers.

Chapter 07 Transportation in Animals and Plants

1. Patients with kidney diseases are advised to take less salt because excess salts can increase blood pressure and worsen kidney problems.
2. In summers, there is increased water loss through sweating. Therefore, the urine gets concentrated and it appears yellow.
3. Birds excrete uric acid that appears white. On the other hand humans excrete out urea.
4. In dry regions, leaves are modified to conserve water and survive in hot conditions.
5. Animals like frogs, earthworms, etc. excrete waste through their skin.

Chapter 08 Reproduction in Plants

1. The organisms covering the pond are algae. The massive growth of these algae form a dense layer on the surface of lake and water bodies. It makes water toxic to humans and organisms living inside the pond. It also reduces oxygen concentration in the water bodies.
2. List of wind pollinated flowers include
   - Wheat
   - Corn
   - Barley
   - Rice
   - Rye
3. (i) Vegetative propagation is the formation of new plants from vegetative parts of the plant such as roots, stems and leaves.
   (ii) The stems of plants normally bear buds in the axils which can be used in a vegetative propagation to produce new plants. New plants can be obtained from the stem of an existing plant by cuttings. A small part of stem having nodes and buds is removed by making a cut with a sharp knife. The lower end of stem cutting is buried in the moist soil. After a few days the cutting develops roots. The buds grows and produces a shoot.
4. (i) Flowers are the reproductive parts of a plant. Functions of a flower are as follows.
   1. It carry out sexual reproduction.
   2. It forms male and female gametes.
   3. It forms seeds and fruits.
   (ii) Yes, flowers help in pollination and fertilisation. Flowers are essential for pollination and fertilisation because they attract pollinators have a structure that is specifically designed for pollination. These factors all work together to ensure that pollen is transferred from one flower to another which is necessary for fertilisation to occur.

Chapter 09 Motion and Time

1. (i) (a) (ii) *X*-axis
2. (i) (a)
   (ii) When an object moves with constant speed along a straight line, it is said to be in uniform motion. While an object which changes its speed during its motion, it is said to be in non-uniform motion.
3. (c)

Chapter 10 Electric Current and its Effects

1. (i) The circuit acquires magnetism due to the magnetic effect of electric current, which states that a current carrying wire behaves as a magnet.
   (ii) The magnetic strength of the electromagnet can be increased by
   (a) increasing number of turns in the coil.
   (b) increasing the current passing through the coil.
   (iii) Electric bell and loudspeaker.
2. As clearly shown in the figure, the strength of battery used in setup *Y* (20 V) is more than that used in setup *X* (15 V). So, more current flows in setup *Y*, that is why setup *Y* attracts more nails.
3. (d)
4. (c)

Chapter 11 Light

1. (i) Lens $X \rightarrow$ Concave
   Lens $Y \rightarrow$ Convex
   (ii) Lens *Y* is convex in nature. Hence, it can be used to magnify images.
   (iii) The paper under lens *X* will remain as it is. But in case of lens *Y*, due to its converging nature, the sun rays will be focussed at a point. Ultimately, the paper will start burning.
   (iv) Refer to Ans-7, NCERT Mate on page 201.
2. Microscope uses convex lens in order to focus light. A convex lens of short focal length is used to see magnified images of microbes.
3. (i) It will appear to white as all colours mix due to rotation and give white light.
   (ii) Raindrops act like prisms when sunlight passes through them to form a rainbow.
   (iii) When a red laser light passes through a prism, it stays together and appears as one colour, i.e. red.
   (iv) Refer to Activity 12 on page 198.

Chapter 12 Forests : Our Lifeline

1.Different types of food chain are as follows

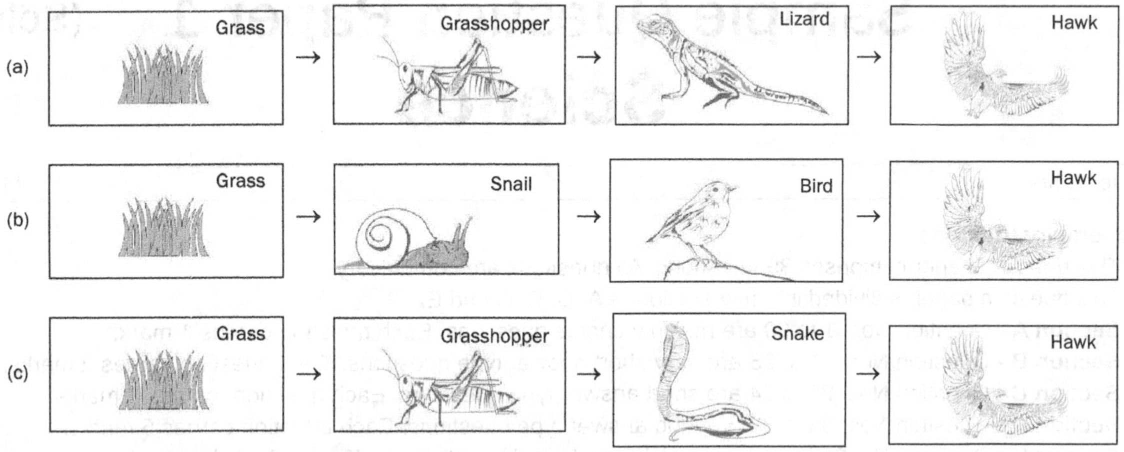

2. (i) The list of things we see in the forest are as follows
   - **Wild animals** – Boar, bison, jackal, elephant, monkey, etc.
   - **Birds** – Woodpecker, jungle crow, hornbill, etc.
   - **Plants** – Sal, teak, semal, bamboo, mosses, ferns.
   - **Insects** – Beetles, ants, butterflies, moth, bees, etc.
   - **Fungi** – Mushroom

   (ii) Various types of trees and layers formed by them include
   1. **Canopy** It is the uppermost layer of the forest, consisting of the tallest trees that form a dense covering. Mostly trees of sal, teak, semal, etc. form the canopy.
   2. **Understorey** It is located beneath the canopy and consisting of smaller trees, sapling and shrubs. The constituents of understorey are as follows
      - **Herb layer** It is located on the forest floor and consists of herbaceous plants such as wild flowers, ferns and mosses.
      - **Forest floor** It is the lowest layer of the forest and is covered with fallen leaves, decaying organic matter and soil.
   3. (i) A food chain is the sequence of events in an ecosystem where one organism consumes another and then that organism is consumed by another larger organism.

      (ii) Plant → Grasshopper → Frog → Snake → Hawk

4. (i) Sachin noticed that pond sedimentation is increased and water became muddy.

   (ii) The probable reasons for such change are as follows

   (a) Deforestation

   (b) Soil erosion

Chapter 13 Wastewater Story

1. In villages, sewage disposal system may involve septic tanks, whereas cities have well established and extensive sewer networks.
2. The causative agent of meningitis is a bacteria, either under lined separately or written in it alies *Neisseria meningititis*. Hepatitis is caused by the virus Hepatitis A and B.
3. (i) Local municipality and citizens.

   (ii) If wastes at public places are not disposed off regularly, it can lead to the spread of diseases, environmental pollution, decreased hygiene, etc.
4. (i) Cholera and typhoid.

   (ii) Sachin demonstrated a sense of social responsiblity, hygiene awareness and **compassion** for the well-being of villagers.

Sample Question Paper 1 (Solved)
Science

Time : 3 hrs	M.M. : 80

General Instructions

1 This question paper comprises 39 questions. All questions are compulsory.
2 This question paper is divided into five sections - A, B, C, D and E.
3 **Section A** - Question Nos. 1 to 20 are multiple choice questions. Each question carries 1 mark.
4 **Section B** - Question Nos. 21 to 25 are very short answer type questions. Each question carries 2 marks.
5 **Section C** - Question Nos. 26 to 34 are short answer type questions. Each question carries 3 marks.
6 **Section D** - Question Nos. 35 to 38 are long answer type questions. Each question carries 5 marks.
7 **Section E** - Question No. 39 is source-based/case-based question which carry 3 marks.

Section A

1. Which of the following is not a forest product ?
(a) Gum (b) Plywood
(c) Sealing wax (d) Kerosene

2. Which of the following describes the process of depositing a zinc layer on iron ?
(a) Galvanisation (b) Crystallisation
(c) Rusting (d) Sublimation

3. Image formed by a plane mirror is
(a) virtual, behind the mirror and enlarged
(b) real, behind the mirror and of same size as the object
(c) virtual, behind the mirror and of the same size as the object
(d) real at the surface of the mirror and enlarged

4. When we suffer from acidity, we should take
(a) iron tonic (b) vitamins
(c) antacid (d) lactocalamine

5. The period celebrated as the International Decade for Action on 'Water for Life' is
(a) 2000-2005 (b) 2005-2010
(c) 2005-2013 (d) 2005-2015

6. An iron ball at 40°C is dropped in a mug containing water at 40°C. The heat will
(a) flow from iron ball to water
(b) not flow from iron ball to water or water to iron ball
(c) flow from water to iron ball
(d) increase the temperature of both

7. The process of formation of substances in their pure state from their solutions is known as
(a) galvanisation
(b) crystallisation
(c) neutralisation
(d) evaporation

8. The end products of photosynthesis are
(a) carbohydrates and oxygen
(b) carbohydrates and hydrogen
(c) carbohydrates and water vapours
(d) carbohydrates, oxygen and water vapours

9. A car covers 35 km in first hour, 80 km in next two hours and 45 km in next one hour. Find out its average speed.
(a) 100 km/h (b) 66.6 km/h
(c) 50 km/h (d) 40 km/h

10. The acid that our stomach releases is
(a) sulphuric acid
(b) nitric acid
(c) hydrochloric acid
(d) formic acid

11. Which thermometer records the highest and lowest temperature during a period of time ?
(a) Laboratory thermometer
(b) Clinical thermometer
(c) Minimum and maximum thermometer
(d) None of the above

12. In cockroaches, air enters the body through
(a) lungs (b) gills (c) spiracles (d) skin

13. When a man with stomach pain went to the doctor, the physician diagnosed that he was suffering from acidity. Which of the following remedy would the doctor suggest for him ?
(a) Lemonade drink (b) Baking soda
(c) Aerated drink (d) Vinegar

14. Which of these appliances does not use on electromagnet ?
(a) Washing machine (b) Refrigerator
(c) Room heater (d) Electric bell

15. Which blood vessel does not carry any carbon dioxide ?
(a) Pulmonary artery
(b) Vena cava
(c) Hepatic vein
(d) Pulmonary vein

Direction (Q. Nos. 16-20) *The following questions consist of two statements* ***Assertion*** *(A) and* ***Reason*** *(R). Answer these questions by selecting the appropriate option given below.*
(a) Both A and R are true and R is the correct explanation of A
(b) Both A and R are true, but R is not the correct explanation of A
(c) A is true, but R is false
(d) A is false, but R is true

16. Assertion (A) Gas bubbles are observed when sodium carbonate is added to dilute hydrochloric acid.
Reason (R) Carbon dioxide is given off in the reaction.

17. Assertion (A) A body in motion always covers equal distances in equal intervals of time.
Reason (R) The speed of a body is constant.

18. Assertion (A) The presence of haemoglobin makes blood appear red.
Reason (R) Haemoglobin binds with oxygen and transports it to all parts of the body.

19. Assertion (A) Concave mirrors are used as make-up mirrors.
Reason (R) When the face is held within the focus of a concave mirror, then a diminished image of the face is seen in the concave mirror.

20. Assetion (A) Solar energy is absorbed by the chlorophyll present in leaves.
Reason (R) Chlorophyll is a red pigment present in algae.

Section B

21. Which material used for making the armature of electric bell ?

Or

Who was the first person to observe that the compass needle deflected each time electric current was passed through the wire.

22. Which acid is injected into our body by an ant sting that causes pain ?

23. Name a plant which has both autotrophic as well as heterotrophic modes of nutrition.

Or

State the role of chlorophyll in the process of photosynthesis.

24. What is the chemical name of the milk of magnesia?

25. Explain the condition or disease which can lead to the dehydration of our body.

Section C

26. What are the causes of indigestion ?

Or

What does organic matter do in soil?

27. What are decomposers ? Name any two decomposers. What decomposers do in a forest?

28. Define average speed. Write down formula to calculate it.

Or

If a pendulum completes 40 oscillations in 10 s. Calculate its time period.

29. Sketch the reproductive parts of a flower.

30. Why cloud formation is a physical change ?

31. Explain why concave mirror is known as a converging mirror?

Or

Why does obtaining the image of the sun on a paper with the help of a concave mirror burn the paper ?

32. How does nasal cavity help in respiration ?

33. What is the use of litmus paper ?

34. Why conduction is only possible in solid ?

Or Is the distilled water acidic/basic/neutral? How would you verify it?

Section D

35. When a candle burns, both physical and chemical changes take place. Identify these changes. Give another example of a familiar process in which both the physical and chemical changes take place.

36. (i) What is meant by the term rumination ?

(ii) Explain why a cow can digest grass, but we cannot?

Or How oral Rehydration solution

(i) ORS can be prepared at home? When a person is given ORS?

(ii) What is the function of large intestine?

37. State differences between clinical thermometer and laboratory thermometer.

Or How does wearing woolen clothes keep us warm in winters?

38. Respiration can occur in two different manners. Briefly explain the process of aerobic respiration. How does it differ from anaerobic respiration ?

Section E

39. During an activity, Mr. Abhi took some sugar in a spatula and heated it on bunsen burner. A black mass was obtained.

Then, he dissolved some sugar in water in a beaker using a water bath till a white powder was left at the bottom of the beaker.

(i) Identify the physical change took place in above activity.

(ii) How can Mr. Abhi get the sugar back in its original form ?

(iii) Write a difference between the physical change and chemical change with the help of the activity done by Mr. Abhi.

Answers

1. (*d*) Kerosene is not a forest product. It is a fossil fuel that is refined from crude oil or petroleum, which is found deep under the Earth's surface.

2. (*a*) Galvanisation is the process of depositing layer of zinc on iron materials to protect it from rust.

3. (*c*) Image formed by a plane mirror is virtual, behind the mirror and of the same size as the object.

4. (*c*) When we suffer from acidity, we should take antacid as it is a base and neutralises the effect of excess acid present in the stomach.

5. (*d*) The United Nations general assembly proclaimed the years 2005-2015 as the International Decade for Action on "Water for Life". The decade officially began on March 22, 2005, which is World Water Day.

6. (*b*) The heat will not flow from iron ball to water or from water to iron ball.

7. (*b*) The process of formation of substance in their pure state from their solution is called crystallisation.

8. (*a*) The end products of photosynthesis are carbohydrates and oxygen. It is the process by which plants produce their own food from raw material such as sunlight, chlorophyll, water and carbon dioxide.

9. (*d*) Total distance covered $= 35 + 80 + 45 = 160$ km

Total time taken $= 1 + 2 + 1 = 4$ h

Average speed $= \frac{160}{4} = 40$ km/h

10. (*c*) Our stomach releases little amount of hydrochloric acid that helps in digestion of food in our body.

11. (*c*) Minimum and maximum thermometer records the highest and lowest temperatures during a period of time.

12. (*c*) In cockroaches, air enters the body through spiracles. Spiracles are external openings that are part of the cockroach's respiratory system.

13. (*b*) Baking soda is a base and neutralises the effect of acidity which cause stomach pain.

14. (*c*) Room heater does not use on electromagnet.

15. (*d*) The pulmonary vein is the blood vessel that does not carry carbon dioxide. It carries oxygenated blood from the lungs to the left atrium of the heart.

16. (*a*) Both A and R are true and R is the correct explanation of A.

17. (*d*) A is false, but R is true. A can be corrected as

A body in motion does not always cover equal distance in equal intervals of time. It only happens when the body is moving at a constant speed.

18. (*b*) Both A and R are true, but R is not the correct explanation of A.

Blood contain a red pigment called haemoglobin. It binds with oxygen and transports it to all the parts of the body and ultimately to all the cells.

19. (*c*) A is true, but R is false. R can be corrected as When face is placed between the concave mirror and its focus, it produce a magnified image. This enlarged image of face is helpful in makeup as even pores of skin are clearly visible.

20. (*c*) A is true, but R is false. R can be corrected as

Chlorophyll is a green pigment present in plants and algae.

21. The material used for making the armature of electric bell is iron.

Or

The first person to notice compass needle deflection was Hans Christian Oersted.

22. Formic acid is injected into the skin of a person when an ant bites.

23. Pitcher plant has both autotrophic and heterotrophic modes of nutrition. It is green and performs photosynthesis, but it grows in soil which is nitrogen deficient. So it eats insects to fulfill its nitrogen requirements.

Or

Chlorophyll is the green colour pigment which help leaves to capture energy from sunlight to carry out the food making the process of plants by the leaves. It is the green photosynthesis pigment which provides energy necessary to photosynthesis.

24. The chemical name of the milk of magnesia is magnesium hydroxide.

25. Diarrhoea is a condition where a person has three or more loose or watery bowel movements in a day. This infection can be caused by bacteria, viruses or parasites. This leads to dehydration of our body.

26. Indigestion is caused by acidity, which in turn is caused due to the excess secretion of hydrochloric acid in the human stomach.

Or

If the soil is too acidic or too basic, crops do not grow well. If the soil is too basic, organic matter is added to it. Organic matters releases acids which neutralises the basic nature of the soil.

27. The microorganisms which breakdown the dead parts of plants and dead bodies of animals into simpler substances such as minerals, salts, carbon dioxide and water, which can be reused by the plants called decomposers.

The two decomposers are bacteria and fungi. The decomposers help in recycling the nutrients. They return the nutrients back in the soil, which are used by plants for their growth.

28. Average speed is the total distance covered divided by total time taken.

$$\text{Average speed} = \frac{\text{Total distance covered}}{\text{Total time taken}}$$

Or

Given, total time period $=10$ s

Number of oscillations $=40$

As it is known as time period of a simple pendulum

$$\text{Thus, time period} = \frac{\text{Total time taken}}{\text{Total number of oscillation}}$$

$$= \frac{10}{40} = 0.25 \text{ s}$$

29. Labelled diagram of the reproductive parts of a flowers.

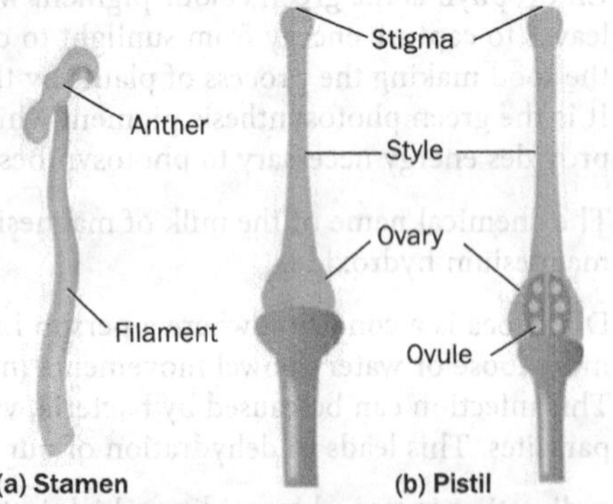

(a) Stamen (Male reproductive parts) (b) Pistil (Female reproductive parts)

30. Clouds are formed by the condensation of water vapour present in the atmosphere. When rainwater goes back on the Earth, no new product is formed, therefore it is a physical change.

31. Concave mirror is known as a converging mirror because it converges a beam of parallel rays of light (reflecting from it) at one point.

Or

Obtaining the image of the sun on a paper with the help of a concave mirror burn the paper because concave mirror converge the sunrays to one point.

32. Nasal cavity has external nostrils through which air is drawn into nasal cavity. The nasal cavity is separated from oral cavity by a bony plate, so that air can be breathe in even while we eat. At body temperature, the nasal cavity is warmed, moistened to avoid friction and dust particles are removed by mucus secreted by mucous glands. It provides passage to air from external nostrils to pharynx through internal nostrils.

33. Litmus paper is used as one of the chemical indicators. The natural colour of litmus is purple. It is used to determine whether a solution is acidic or basic.

If the blue litmus paper is put in an acidic solution, it turns red and when red litmus paper is put in basic solution, it turns blue.

34. In solids, generally, the heat is transferred by the process of conduction because particles of solids are closely placed and heat is transferred from the hotter end to the colder end of an object.

Or

Distilled water is neither acidic nor basic. When we test its nature through litmus paper strips, we have found neither red nor blue changes in colour which verifies its neutral nature.

35. Due to heat produced during the burning of a candle, the wax melts which is a physical change because the state of wax is changing from solid to liquid.

The burning of the wax is a chemical change as various chemicals such as fatty acids, etc. burn and new compounds are formed.

Therefore, both chemical and physical changes can be observed, while the candle is burning. Another such example is digestion of food in which the larger food particles are broken into smaller ones which is a physical change.

The chemical action of enzymes and hydrochloric acid on the food is a chemical change.

36. (i) Rumination is the process where animals rechew cud to breakdown plant matter further and to stimulate digestion. Such animals are called ruminants and they have rumen (a specialised digestive organ) to help them breakdown cellulose. Examples of ruminants include goat, cow, deer, etc.

(ii) Humans cannot digest grass because they lack enzymes needed to breakdown cellulose. Herbivorous animals like cows, goats have bacteria in their rumen that can digest cellulose.

Or

(i) Oral Rehydration solution (ORS) can be made by dissolving a pinch of salt and sugar in a boiled and cooled water.

ORS is given to a person who suffers from diarrhoea, i.e. passes watery stool frequently.

(ii) Large intestine function is to absorb water and salts from the undigested food material.

37. Clinical Thermometer

(i) It is used to measure the temperature of human body only.

(ii) It has temperature range from 35℃ to 42° C.

(iii) It has a small constriction heat the mercury bulb.

(iv) It can be tilted while taking reading.

Laboratory Thermometer

(i) It is used to measure the temperature of different objects in laboratory and factories.

(ii) It has temperature range from 10° C to 110℃.

(iii) Usually, it does not have any constriction.

(iv) It has to be kept upright, while taking the reading.

Or

Wollen clothing is good for the winter since it keeps us warm, this is because

- Wool conducts heat poorly, it does not conduct body heat.
- Air trapped between the pores of woolen fibres is a poor heat conductor.
- This also reduces the transfer of the heat from the body to the environment.

38. On the basis of the presence or absence of oxygen, respiration is classified into two types

(i) **Aerobic respiration** When breakdown of glucose occurs with the use of oxygen, it is called aerobic respiration.

Glucose is completely breakdown into carbon dioxide, and water and energy is released. It takes place in mitochondria. It can be shown by the following equation

$$\text{Glucose} \xrightarrow{\text{Oxygen}} \text{Carbon dioxide} + \text{Water} + \text{Energy}$$

(ii) **Anaerobic respiration** When breakdown of glucose takes place without using oxygen, it is called anaerobic respiration. The glucose is not completely broken down into carbon dioxide and water. It can be shown as follows

$$\text{Glucose} \xrightarrow[\text{oxygen}]{\text{No}} \text{Alcohol} + \text{Carbon dioxide} + \text{Energy}$$

Yeasts and certain bacteria carry out anaerobic respiration. Our muscle cells can also respire anaerobically.

39. (i) When sugar solution is heated in a water bath, water evaporates and sugar is left behind as a white powder. This is a physical change.

(ii) Sugar can be taken back by the process of evaporation, i.e. by heating the beaker containing sugar water solution.

(iii) Physical change is easily reversible. For example, we can get back sugar after dissolving it in water, while chemical change is irreversible. For example, when sugar is heated.

Sample Question Paper 2 (Solved)
Science

Time : 3 hrs	M.M. : 80

General Instructions

1 This question paper comprises 39 questions. All questions are compulsory.
2 This question paper is divided into five sections - A, B, C, D and E.
3 **Section A** - Question Nos. 1 to 20 are multiple choice questions. Each question carries 1 mark.
4 **Section B** - Question Nos. 21 to 25 are very short answer type questions. Each question carries 2 marks.
5 **Section C** - Question Nos. 26 to 34 are short answer type questions. Each question carries 3 marks.
6 **Section D** - Question Nos. 35 to 38 are long answer type questions. Each question carries 5 marks.
7 **Section E** - Question No. 39 is source-based/case-based question which carry 3 marks.

Section A

1. The reaction between an acid and a base to form salt and water is called
(a) carbocation (b) hydrogenation
(c) neutralisation (d) titration

2. The person who first noticed the magnetic effect of an electric current is
(a) Newton
(b) Maxwell
(c) Faraday
(d) Hans Christian Oersted

3. *Cuscuta* is an example of
(a) autotroph (b) parasite
(c) saprotroph (d) host

4. What kind of change occurs when the tip of the blade is placed on a gas stove ?
(a) Chemical change (b) Physical change
(c) No change (d) Irreversible change

5. A simple pendulum take 40 s to complete 20 oscillations. So, the time period of the pendulum is
(a) 2 s (b) 4 s
(c) 6 s (d) 1 s

6. Normal range of breathing rate per minute in an average adult person at rest is
(a) 9-12 (b) 15-18
(c) 21-24 (d) 30-33

7. Which of the following is a physical change ?
(a) Cutting a log of wood into pieces
(b) Ripening of a fruit
(c) Formation of manure from leaves
(d) Formation of salt from acid and base

8. The magnifying glass is actually a type of
(a) convex lens
(b) concave lens
(c) plane mirror
(d) concave mirror

9. The phloem tissue in plants is responsible for the transport of
(a) water (b) water and minerals
(c) glucose (d) chlorophyll

10. Which of the following is acidic in nature ?
(a) Human blood (b) Lime juice
(c) Lime water (d) Antacid

11. Thermometer should be washed before and after use with
(a) tap water (b) antiseptic solution
(c) distilled water (d) cold water

12. Which of the following is/are role of forests ?
(a) Prevent flood
(b) Prevent soil erosion
(c) Provide food, shelter, water and medicines
(d) All of the above

13. The substance which can turn blue litmus to red is

(a) baking soda (b) milk of magnesia
(c) lemon juice (d) antacid

14. Which of the following can be used to form a real image ?

(a) Only concave mirror
(b) Only plane mirror
(c) Only convex mirror
(d) Both concave and convex mirrors

15. Sewage is mainly a

(a) liquid waste
(b) solid waste
(c) gaseous waste
(d) mixture of solid and gaseous wastes

Direction (Q. Nos. 16-20) *The following questions consist of two statements* ***Assertion*** *(A) and* ***Reason*** *(R). Answer these questions by selecting the appropriate option given below.*

(a) Both A and R are true and R is the correct explanation of A
(b) Both A and R are true, but R is not the correct explanation of A
(c) A is true, but R is false
(d) A is false, but R is true

16. Assertion (A) The body temperature of every person is not 37°C.

Reason (R) It is an average temperature of human body.

17. Assertion (A) Formation of rust is a chemical change.

Reason (R) For formation of rust, iron must be exposed to air and water.

18. Assertion (A) In asexual reproduction new plants are obtained from seeds.

Reason (R) Vegetative propagation is a type of asexual reproduction in which new plants are produced from roots, stems, leaves and buds.

19. Assertion (A) Burning of wood is a physical change.

Reason (R) The products such as ash and smoke formed on burning of wood cannot be converted to wood.

20. Assertion (A) If distance is 500 m and time is 100 s, then speed will be 5 m/s.

Reason (R) Speed is equal to the time taken over the distance travelled.

Section B

21. Why do we get instant energy from glucose ?

22. Write some uses of battery.

Or

If the filament of the bulb is broken, would the circuit be complete. ? Would the bulb still glow ?

23. Where is the bile produced ? Which component of the food does it help to digest ?

24. What are the two basic substances which we use in our daily life ?

Or

Name the substances that are used to cure indigestion in our body.

25. What is an odometer ?

Section C

26. What happens when a drop of dilute sulphuric acid is added to the China rose indicator ?

27. What are the uses of heating effect of electric current ?

Or

While measuring the temperature, a few sharp jerks are given to the clinical thermometer before using it. Why is it done so ?

28. In the figure, the artist has forgotten to put the labels and directions on the arrows. Mark the direction on arrows and label the diagram using the following labels ?

Clouds, Rain, Atmosphere, Carbon dioxide, Oxygen, Plants, Animals, Soil, Roots, Water table

29. Why are acids not stored in metal containers ?

Or Blue litmus paper is dipped in a solution it remains blue . What is the nature of the solution? Explain.

30. How can you show the image of a sun on a paper?

Or Write down four uses of a concave mirror.

31. (i) Why should oils and fats not be released in the drain ? Explain.

(ii) What are the different constituents of sewage water ?

Or Suggest some ways to minimise or eliminate waste and pollutants at their source.

32. What are salts ? Explain with the help of an example.

33. Why one thick blanket is less warm than two thin blankets joined together ?

34. What are the main reasons for forest destruction?

Section D

35. Show the shape of the distance-time graph for motion in the following cases

(i) A car moving with a constant speed.

(ii) A car parked on a side road.

Or

Define

(a) Non - uniform speed

(b) Instantaneous speed

36. Why we take an antacid tablet when we suffer from acidity ?

37. Describe the structure of the human heart with the help of labelled diagram and state their functions.

Or

(i) Write different types of cells suspended in the plasma of blood. Explain their function.

(ii) Differentiate between arteries and veins.

38. Explain the working of an electric bell with diagram.

Section E

39. The picture below shows the lichen. It is the association between chlorophyll- containing algae and a fungus. The fungus provides shelter, water and minerals to the algae and in return, the algae prepares and provides food to the fungus.

(i) The association between algae and a fungus in lichen shows

(a) symbiosis

(b) parasitism

(c) saprophytic nutrition

(d) heterotrophic nutrition

(ii) Why fungus cannot make their own food and depend on algae for the food ?

Answers

1. (*c*) The reaction between an acid and a base to form salt and water is called neutralisation reaction.
2. (*d*) Hans Christian Oersted first observed the magnetic effect of an electric current. He noticed the deflection of compass needle every time the current was passed through the wire.
3. (*b*) *Cuscuta* also known as dodder or amarbel is an example of a parasitic plant. It can be seen around in the form of yellow tubular structures growing on the stems of other plants.
4. (*b*) When tip of the blade is kept on a gas stove, it becomes red due to heating, which is a physical change as it is reversible in nature.
5. (*a*) Total time taken simple pendulum = 40 s

   Number of oscillations = 20

   $$\text{Time period} = \frac{\text{Total time taken}}{\text{Number of oscillations}}$$

   $$\Rightarrow \text{Time period} = \frac{40}{20} = 2\text{ s}$$
6. (*b*) The normal range of breathing rate per minute in an average adult at rest is 15 – 18 breaths per minute. Any person having a breathing rate under 12 or over 25 is considered to be breathing abnormally.
7. (*a*) Among the given options, cutting of a log of wood into pieces is a physical change as no new substance is formed in this case.
8. (*a*) The magnifying glass is actually a type of convex lens as it forms a magnified image.
9. (*c*) The phloem tissue in plants is responsible for the transporting glucose (food) from the leaves to the rest of the plant.
10. (*c*) Among the given options, lime water is acidic in nature.
11. (*b*) In order to avoid the transfer of germs from one person to another, thermometer should be washed before and after use with an antiseptic solution.
12. (*d*) Forests have many roles, including
    (i) Preventing floods.
    (ii) Preventing soil erosion.
    (iii) Forests provide food, fuel, shelter and water.
    (iv) Medicinal plants provide many medicines.
13. (*c*) Acid turns blue litmus to red. Among the given options, lemon juice is acidic in nature and hence can turn blue litmus to red.
14. (*a*) As only a concave mirror can form a real image. Plane mirror and convex mirror always form a virtual image of an object.
15. (*a*) Sewage is mainly liquid waste. It is a type of wastewater that contains both liquid and solid wastes from human activities.
16. (*a*) Both A and R are true and R is the correct explanation of A. 37°C is considered as the normal human body temperature.

    It is the average body temperature of a large number of healthy persons, however it could be slightly higher or slightly lower.
17. (*b*) Both A and R are true, but R is not the correct explanation of A. Formation of rust is chemical change as there is the formation of new substance on the surface of iron when it is kept in air and moisture.
18. (*d*) A is false, but R is true. A can be corrected as In asexual reproduction new plants are obtained without production of seeds.
19. (*a*) Both A and R are true and R is the correct explanation of A.
20. (*c*) A is true, but R is false. R can be corrected as

    Speed is equal to the distance travelled over the time taken.

    $$\text{Speed} = \frac{\text{Distance}}{\text{Time}} = \frac{500}{100} = 5\text{ m/s.}$$
21. We get instant energy from glucose because glucose can be easily breakdown in the cell with the help of oxygen and gives carbon dioxide, water and energy.
22. Many devices such as torches, transistors, toys, TV, remote controls use batteries.

    Or

    If the filament of the bulb is broken, the circuit is not be complete. So, the bulb will not glow.

23. The bile is produced in the liver. The bile plays an important role in the digestion of fats.

24. Two basic substances which we use in our daily life are

1. Baking soda
2. Soap or detergent

Or Substance that are used in indigestion are magnesium hydroxide, calcium carbonate etc.

These substances neutralise the effect of excess release of acid or base in our stomach.

25. Odometer is an instrument that indicates the distance travelled by a vehicle.

26. When a drop of dilute sulphuric acid is added to the China rose indicator the colour of the China rose indicator turns from light pink colour to dark pink.

27. Electrical appliances such as immersion heaters, hotplates, irons, geysers, electric kettles, hair dryers uses of heating effect of electric current.

Or The jerks given to the thermometer before using it in order to get an accurate reading, the jerks allow the mercury level to flow into the bulb, below from the normal temperature.

28.

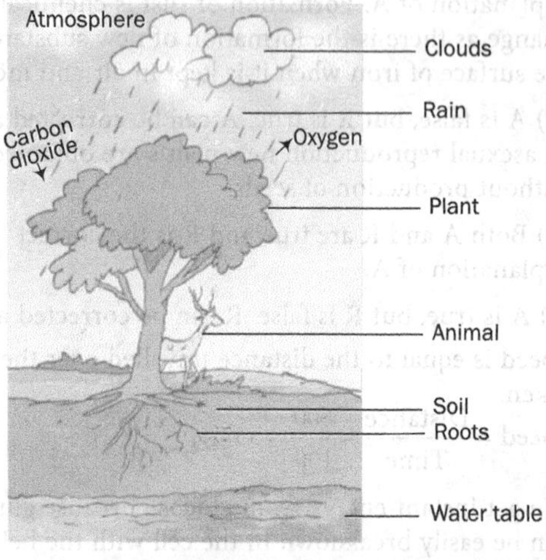

29. Acids are corrosive in nature. They can react with metals and corrode them. That is why acids are not stored in metal containers.

Or Solution can be identified on the basis of the following observation. Bases change the colour of litmus paper to blue. As the colour of blue litmus paper is not affected, the solution must be basic.

If the solution is neutral, if the colour of litmus will not change.

30. Take a concave mirror. Hold it facing the sun. Try to get the light reflected by the mirror on a sheet of paper. Adjust the distance of the paper until you get a sharp bright spot on it. This bright spot is in fact the image of the sun.

Or

1. Use by ENT specialists and dentists to see mouth parts.
2. Used as a shaving mirror.
3. Makeup artists use a concave mirror.
4. Used in torches and car headlight to get a parallel light beam.

31. (i) Oils and fats should not be released in the drains because they harden in the pipes and block them.

Fats get clogged in the holes of the soil in the open drain and block it. It does not allow the wastewater to flow and thus the whole sewer system is blocked.

(ii) Sewage is a complex mixture containing suspended solids, organic and inorganic impurities, nutrients, saprophyte and disease causing bacteria.

Or

Some ways to minimise or eliminate waste and pollutants at their source are as follows

- Cooking oils and fats should not be thrown down the drain as they can harden and block the pipes.
- Chemicals like paints, solvents, insecticides, etc. may kill microbes that help to purify water, should not be thrown in the drain.
- Used tea leaves, solid food remains, soft toys, etc should also be thrown in the dustbin.

32. As the results of reaction between acid and base, salt and water are formed, which is called neutralisation reaction.

Salt may be acidic, basic or neutral.

For example,

Hydrochloric acid (HCl) + Sodium hydroxide (NaOH) $\rightarrow$ Sodium chloride (NaCl) + Water (H_2O)

In the given reaction, sodium chloride is produced in the form of salt.

33. There is a layer of air in between the two blankets. Since, air is bad conductor of heat, prevent body heat to escape out, two thin blankets provide more heat than one thick blanket.

34. The main reasons for forest destruction are as follows

(i) To create land for housing because of increase in human population.

(ii) For producing more food for large human population.

(iii) For creating transport facilities.

(iv) For industrialisation.

(v) Converting forests into agricultural plantation.

(vi) Mining is another important factor for the increased cutting down of forest.

35. (i) A car moving with a constant speed.

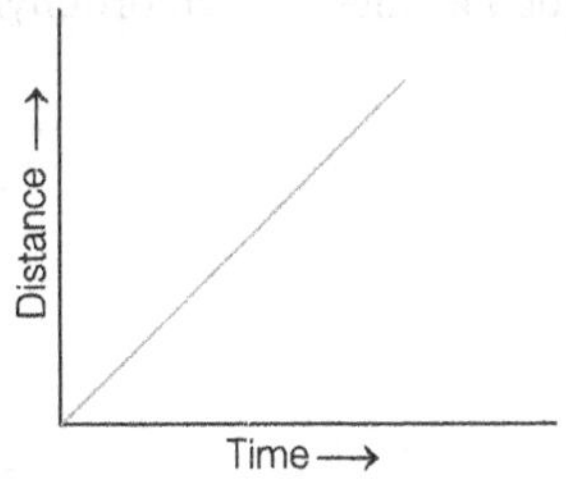

(ii) A car parked on a side road.

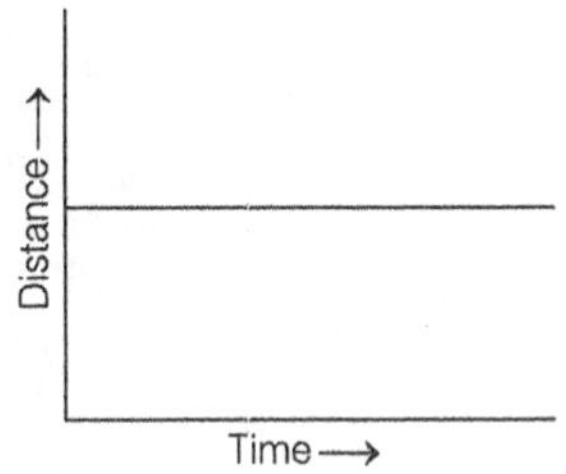

Or (a) **Non-uniform speed** An object is said to be travelling with non-uniform speed, if it covers equal distance in unequal interval of time or unequal distance in equal interval of time.

(b) **Instantaneous speed** The speed of a moving object at any particular instant of time is called instantaneous speed.

36. Our stomach contains hydrochloric acid, it helps us to digest food. But too much of acid in the stomach causes indigestion. Sometimes indigestion is painful.

To relieve indigestion, we take an antacid such as milk of magnesia, which contains magnesium hydroxide. It neutralises the effect of excessive acid.

37. Heart is located in the chest cavity with its lower tip slightly tilted towards the left. It has four chambers. The two upper chambers are called the atria and the two lower chambers are called ventricles. The partition between the chambers helps to avoid mixing up of blood rich in oxygen with the blood rich is carbon dioxide.

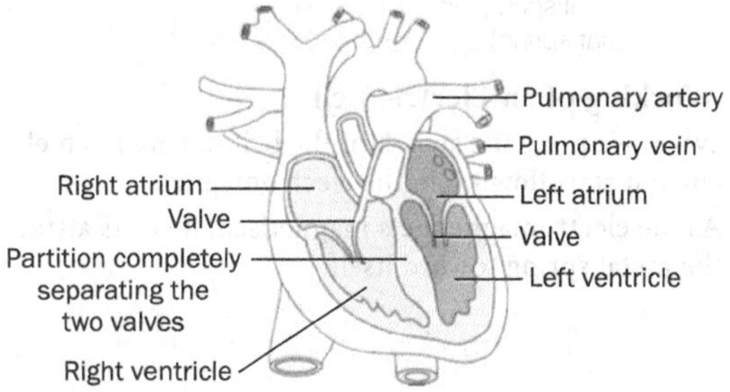

Functions The heart acts as a pumping organ for the transport of blood. The rhythmic contraction and relaxation of the various chambers of the heart maintain circulation of blood and transport of substances to the different parts of the body.

Or (i) The different types of cells suspended in the plasma of blood are red blood cells, white blood cells and platelets. Their functions are as follow

Red blood cell (RBC) It contain a red pigment called haemoglobin, which binds with oxygen and transports it to all the parts of the body.

White blood cells (WBC) It fight against germs that may enter our body.

Platelets They helps in clotting of blood.

(ii) The differences between arteries and veins are as follows

Arteries	Veins
Arteries are the vessels that carry oxygen rich blood from the heart to all the parts of the body.	Veins are the vessels which carry carbon dioxide rich blood from all parts of the body back to the heart.
They have thick elastic walls .	They have thin walls

38.

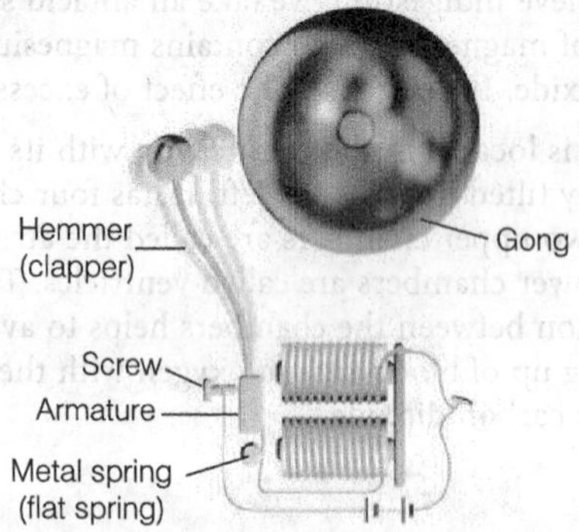

Working of an Electric Bell

- When we press the switch of the bell to ring it, an electric current start flowing in the electromagnet.
- As the electromagnet gets magnetised, it starts attracting the metal spring toward itself.
- As the flat or metal spring moves towards the electromagnet, the hammer which is attached to it strikes the gong and produces a sound.
- When the metal spring is attracted towards the electromagnet it is no longer in contact with screw and hence circuit breaks.
- When electric circuit breaks, no current flows through the coil, this make the metal spring to go back to its original position and the clapper (hammer) also moves away from the gong.
- This process continues as long as we are pressing the switch.

39. (i) In lichen, algae and fungus live together and share both shelter and nutrients. This type of association known as symbiosis.

(ii) Fungus is a saprophytic organism which feed on dead and decaying matter. They cannot make their food as they lack chlorophyll.

Sample Question Paper 3 (Unsolved)
Science

Time : 3 hrs	M.M. : 80

General Instructions

1 This question paper comprises 39 questions. All questions are compulsory.
2 This question paper is divided into five sections - A, B, C, D and E.
3 **Section A** - Question Nos. 1 to 20 are multiple choice questions. Each question carries 1 mark.
4 **Section B** - Question Nos. 21 to 25 are very short answer type questions. Each question carries 2 marks.
5 **Section C** - Question Nos. 26 to 34 are short answer type questions. Each question carries 3 marks.
6 **Section D** - Question Nos. 35 to 38 are long answer type questions. Each question carries 5 marks.
7 **Section E** - Question No. 39 is source-based/case-based question which carry 3 marks.

Section A

1. A car is at a distance of 8 m from the mirror. If it moves 2 m towards the mirror, the image will be formed at

(a) the same distance
(b) 2 m away from the mirror
(c) 8 m
(d) 6 m

2. What is the another name of milk of magnesia?

(a) Calcium hydroxide
(b) Ammonium hydroxide
(c) Magnesium hydroxide
(d) Potassium hydroxide

3. During the process of exhalation, the ribs move

(a) down and outwards
(b) up and inwards
(c) down and inwards
(d) up and outwards

4. The pattern obtained on passing Sunlight through a glass prism is known as

(a) rainbow (b) spectrum
(c) sequence (d) spectra

5. When magnesium is burned in the air, it produces powdery ash, when this ash is dissolved in water, yields an aqueous solution. What is the nature of this aqueous solution?

(a) Acidic (b) Neutral
(c) Basic (d) Cannot be predicted

6. In which of the following parts of human body, sweat glands are absent?

(a) Scalp (b) Armpits
(c) Lips (d) Palms

7. Which of the following is being used in place of fuses?

(a) MCB (b) Nichrome
(c) Filament (d) Switch

8. What kind of change is the explosion of fireworks?

(a) Physical change
(b) Chemical change
(c) Not a change
(d) Reversible change

9. The plant which traps and feeds on insect is

(a) *Cuscuta* plant
(b) China rose
(c) pitcher plant
(d) rose plant

10. Speedometer records the reading in

(a) m/h (b) km/s
(c) m/s (d) km/h

11. Which of the following chemical compounds is responsible for making lime water milky?

(a) Calcium carbonate
(b) Calcium hydroxide
(c) Calcium chloride
(d) Calcium oxide

12. Which of the following is not a correct statement?

(a) Forest trees are cut down to obtain timber
(b) Forest trees are cut down to obtain paper
(c) Forest trees are cut down to obtain fine wood
(d) Forest trees are cut down to obtain natural rubber

13. In a tropical country, during summers, which of the following materials is likely to absorb the least heat?

(a) Yellow rayon cloth
(b) White cotton cloth
(c) Blue denim cloth
(d) Maroon silk cloth

14. What name is given to the solutions that do not change the colour of either red or blue litmus paper?

(a) Acidic solutions
(b) Salt solutions
(c) Basic solutions
(d) Neutral solutions

15. A section of root is given below. Some of their parts are labelled as *X, Y* and *Z*. Which of the following labelled part of root increases the surface area for the absorption of water and mineral.

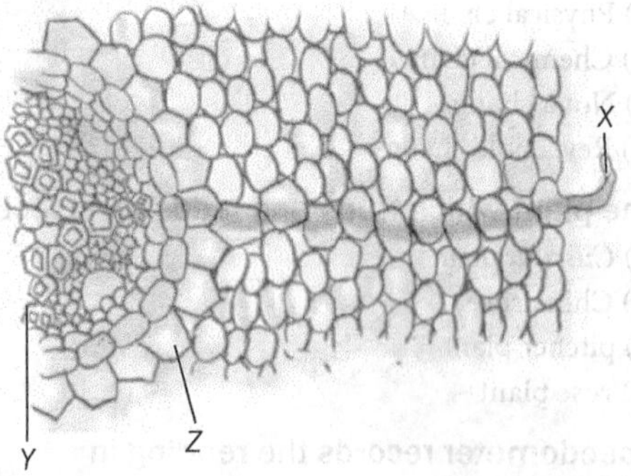

(a) *X* (b) *Y*
(c) *Z* (d) *X* and *Z*

Direction (Q. Nos. 16-20) *The following questions consist of two statements **Assertion** (A) and **Reason** (R). Answer these questions by selecting the appropriate option given below.*

(a) Both A and R are true and R is the correct explanation of A
(b) Both A and R are true, but R is not the correct explanation of A
(c) A is true, but R is false
(d) A is false, but R is true

16. Assertion (A) A speed is distance time, the basic unit of speed is m/s.

Reason (R) We can write 50 km and not 50 kms or 8 cm and not 8 cms.

17. Assertion (A) Xylem is the vascular tissue of the plant.

Reason (R) It forms a continuous network of channels that connect roots to the leaves through stem and transport water to the entire plant.

18. Assertion (A) Phenolphthalein gives pink colour in basic solution.

Reason (R) Phenolphthalein is a natural indicator.

19. Assertion (A) Plants produced by vegetative propagation take less time to grow and bears flowers and fruits earlier than those produced from seeds.

Reason (R) The new plants produced through vegetative propagation are exact copies of the parent plant.

20. Assertion (A) Baking soda creates acidity in the stomach.

Reason (R) Baking soda is basic in nature.

Section B

21. What do you mean by one oscillation?

22. Why are antacids used to cure acidity?

23. Give the form of energy that produces the sensation of vision.

Or

What is a virtual image? Give one situation where a virtual image is formed.

24. How does nutrition occur in *Amoeba*?

Or

What is the difference between milk teeth and permanent teeth?

25. What do you mean by neutral solution? Give examples.

Section C

26. Explain how water heated convection?

Or

State the similarities and differences between the laboratory thermometer and the clinical thermometer.

27. What is rusting of iron? How can we prevent it?

28. What is meant by fragmentation? Name one plant which reproduces by fragmentation.

Or

What are different modes of asexual reproduction? How *Bryophyllum* reproduce vegetatively?

29. Write the characteristics of the image formed by a plane mirror.

30. Photosynthesis is a chemical change or physical change. Give reason in support of your answer.

Or

Describe any two chemical changes that you consider harmful. How you can prevent them?

31. Consider the following food chain :

Grass $\rightarrow$ Deer $\rightarrow$ Lion

What will happen if the lions are removed from the above food chain?

Or

There is minimal risk of soil getting eroded in forests due to raaindrops?

32. What is the relation between Celsius, Fahrenheit and Kelvin scales?

33. How does rainwater become acidic?

34. What is sewage? Explain why is it harmful to discharge untreated sewage into rivers or seas.

Section D

35. Differentiate between uniform and non-uniform motion.

Or

(i) The distance between two stations is 240 km. The distance is covered in 4 h by train. Calculate the trains speed.

(ii) It takes 32 s for a simple pendulum to complete 20 oscillations. What is the pendulum's time period?

36. State the condition necessary for rusting of iron. How galvanisation process is used to prevent it?

37. Describe the various ways by which the seeds are dispersed with the help of suitable diagram.

38. Explain why burning of wood and cutting it into small pieces are considered as two different types of changes.

Or

Ripening of fruits is a chemical change. Justify this statement.

Section E

39. Lenses are transparent and light can pass through them. Lenses are classified as convex lens and concave lens and we can distinguish between these two types of lenses by just touching them. Lenses are widely used in various appliances that we come across in our daily life.

(i) How we can identify the type of lens?

(ii) What is the nature of image formed by convex lens?

(iii) Which lens is suitable for side mirror in cars?

(iv) Which lens form only virtual image?

(v) What is the use of concave lens in daily life?

Answers

1	(d)	2	(c)	3	(c)	4	(b)	5	(c)	6	(c)	7	(a)	8	(b)	9	(c)	10	(d)
11	(a)	12	(d)	13	(b)	14	(d)	15	(a)	16	(a)	17	(a)	18	(d)	19	(b)	20	(d)